DEMONSTRATION EXPERIMENTS
IN PHYSICS

DEMONSTRATION EXPERIMENTS IN PHYSICS

EDITED BY

RICHARD MANLIFFE SUTTON, PH. D.

Professor of Physics at California Institute of Technology

Prepared under the Auspices of

THE AMERICAN ASSOCIATION OF PHYSICS TEACHERS

McGRAW-HILL BOOK COMPANY

NEW YORK AND LONDON

1938

PREFACE

The collection of these demonstration experiments has been from the first a cooperative undertaking.   The idea originated nearly five years ago as a pipe dream during a meeting of the Committee on Cooperative Tests of the American Association of Physics Teachers, in a suggestion by Professor C. J. Lapp.   In 1934 a small committee, consisting of Professors John Zeleny, C. T. Knipp, and H. W. Farwell, reported favorably upon the "desirability and feasibility" of preparing such a collection and the editor was appointed early in 1935.   He was assisted in the formulation of a suitable policy by a committee whom he asked to advise him, namely, Professors D. W. Cornelius and H. W. Farwell and Dr. P. E. Klopsteg, and the first four presidents of the Association, Professors H. L. Dodge, F. Palmer, D. L. Webster, and F. K. Richtmyer.   A group of collaborating editors, whose names appear facing the title page, have given tremendous assistance in the critical examination of experiments. These men drew upon their own experience, assisted in the search for suitable demonstrations, tested many of the experiments which were contributed, and have been a constant help to the editor in the preparation of the manuscript.

Throughout the program of preparation the editor has been sustained by the helpful suggestions and the interest shown by many members of the American Association of Physics Teachers. Contributed experiments began to arrive soon after the first appeal was made in May, 1935, and ever since that time the editorial office has been kept busy.   More than 200 members of the Association have shared their experience with other teachers of physics in this way.   A number of industrial organizations have responded as well.   Each experiment was allotted to the appropriate collaborating editors for trial and criticism.   These men returned their findings to the editorial office where they were finally organized.

It would be phenomenal if this book were to fulfill the expectations of all those who have shown so much interest in it.   We

v

beg our readers to realize that one such volume cannot possibly be "all things to all men," and that the editors have had to reject many interesting but conflicting suggestions. Otherwise the book would have been a cross between a loose-leaf household formulary and the International Critical Tables. It has not been possible to include in a single volume all the contributions submitted, but these have been preserved against the time when the Association may promote an extension of the program.

Demonstration is an art and, like every art, it develops from year to year. It is probable that many good experiments have not been submitted at all, and we hope that this book itself will stimulate those teachers of physics who have not contributed in the past to share their experience with other teachers in the future, either by suggesting to the editor (who assumes only the function of custodian) good experiments which have been overlooked or improvements on those here described, or by publishing accounts of such experiments in a journal like *The American Physics Teacher*.

It is a pleasure to acknowledge the help of Professors R. B. Abbott, R. S. Minor, and W. Schriever, who served as collaborating editors in the early stages of our work; to thank each of the thirty or forty persons who assisted by reading and criticizing portions of the manuscript; and to thank Mr. R. C. Hitchcock, who checked all the page proof.

The editor wishes to give special acknowledgment to Mr. Joseph D. Elder, who has had intimate contact with the book almost from the first. His ability to combine the functions of physicist and of typist has made him invaluable and he has helped with the critical examination of every word of the text. The editor is indebted to his colleague and beloved teacher, Professor Frederic Palmer, for his constant encouragement. Only those who have followed the development of this undertaking know the extent to which the Association is indebted to Professor Palmer.

If this book proves to be useful to teachers of physics, if it helps to make the science more vivid to students and lead them to a better understanding of the world, then it will justify the labors of all those who have assisted in its preparation.

HAVERFORD COLLEGE,   RICHARD M. SUTTON.
June, 1938.

CONTENTS

PART V

PART VI

DEMONSTRATION EXPERIMENTS IN PHYSICS

INTRODUCTION

This is a "cookbook" for teachers of physics, a book of recipes for the preparation of demonstration experiments to illustrate the principles that make the subject of physics so fascinating and so important to our understanding of the world about us. The skillful cook takes cognizance of the equipment of her kitchen, of the number of persons she is to feed, and even recalls their individual capabilities of digestion; she adapts her recipes accordingly. Likewise, the teacher of physics must adapt his experiments to the needs of his class and to the equipment of his lecture room and laboratory.

The cookbook seldom tells how good a particular dish tastes, and it never insists that any dish must be served at least once a week. Fortunately, some latitude is left to the discretion of the cook. Likewise, in the preparation of demonstration experiments much is left to the individual teacher. This book aims to furnish him with numerous suggestions so that his menu of experiments can be satisfying even if his larder of apparatus is meager. Many recipes in a cookbook end with the admonition, "Season to taste." The same remark would be appropriate after each of the experiments described herein. The teacher himself must decide what seasoning of language he will use to accompany his demonstrations, so that his students will take to them with relish.

Physics, more than any other science, can be demonstrated principle after principle by direct and simple experiments. The implements of the present attack upon the unknown are great cyclotrons, stratosphere balloons, 200-in. telescopes, and 10-million-volt generators, but the basic principles of our physical knowledge are demonstrable with inclined planes, pendulum bobs, electroscopes, and other pieces of homely apparatus to be found

1

in any laboratory. Logic and insight transform the common-place rolling of a ball down an incline into a profound experiment. Both students and teachers need to realize that great discoveries may still be made with the common appliances found in the humblest laboratory, where there are far better facilities than were available to those who laid the foundations of our science. Faraday made a great advance in his understanding of electricity when he performed what is now known as the "ice-pail experiment" with the most elementary equipment.

In the study of physics, there is no substitute for experimental observation. In the laboratory students receive training in precise observation and acquire respect for the experimental verification of principles. However, neither time nor equipment permits a student to perform more than a score or two of the countless experiments that contribute to a thorough understanding of the subject. There are a great many important physical phenomena that he may miss altogether unless he is introduced to them. Hence we turn to demonstration experiments, which by their very number and variety fill a real need in the physics course and at the same time provide the instructor with one of the most helpful methods of "selling" physics to a class of students. When demonstration experiments are used in proper proportion, particularly in the introductory stages of the course, there is no more potent way to maintain interest, to make principles concrete and vivid, and to stimulate discussion and active thinking. Since most of this book is concerned with describing *what* to demonstrate, a little space is devoted here to suggestions from a number of sources on *how* to demonstrate.

PRINCIPLES OF DEMONSTRATION

Demonstrations are for the student and not for the instructor. If this simple truth were kept constantly in mind, many of the major crimes of the physics lecture room would be eliminated. The student in the back row, as well as the student in the front row, should see and hear what is going on. The instructor must examine critically every experiment to be demonstrated with this thought in mind; he should consider the value of an experiment by judging what the student sees and understands rather than by his own personal enjoyment and satisfaction in performing an operation that may be perfectly clear from his vantage point but perfectly invisible to most of the students in his class. After an experiment is set up, the instructor may be astonished to see what it looks like from the back of the room.

"The impact of an experiment upon the student's mind is proportional to the solid angle which the apparatus subtends." With this thought in mind, the instructor must adapt his methods to the size of the group before him. Large-scale apparatus, adequate facilities for projection, clearly visible indicators, and readable charts and drawings are essential. Projection of small-scale apparatus by optical methods is necessary in some cases, but at best it is a makeshift.

Simplicity (but not crudity) of arrangement and manipulation is paramount. Teachers often avoid simple experiments, favoring those which require elegant and elaborate facilities. By such displays, the student may be impressed and even overawed, but it would be a mistake to consider that he is better instructed. He deserves to see as much of the working arrangement of every experiment as he can understand without being confused by unnecessary detail. It might be stated as a corollary that the experimental arrangement should be more easily understood than the concept that it is designed to illuminate.

The foremost purpose of any demonstration experiment is to *clarify* a physical principle or to show some interesting application of a principle. If, at the same time, it can amaze and intrigue the student and cause him to do some independent thinking, it more than fulfills its mission. But its primary purpose is not to mystify. Whenever a physics instructor presents a demonstration, he becomes a showman; some of his experiments are as clever as any magician's tricks, and he should make the most of their "show" qualities. His purpose, however, is very different from the magician's: the latter makes every effort to conceal and to mystify; the former makes every effort to expose and to clarify the underlying physical principles.

Of the many principles taught in elementary physics courses, almost every one is reducible to a mathematical statement that involves three or four symbols only. Yet students constantly stumble over these mathematical expressions which might be made vivid and meaningful if illustrated concretely by simple experiments. Every statement of a physical principle embodies (at least implicitly) a set of operational procedures by which it can be verified. Every mathematical formulation of a principle can be translated into an experiment, and the skillful teacher will constantly resort to simple demonstrations to emphasize the relationships involved. $F = ma, pv = RT, Q/V = C, E/I = R,$ and numerous other forbidding expressions are *alive* with possibilities for demonstration. These are not algebraic equations alone but shorthand statements of physical relationships, and the symbols take on new meaning when they are translated, one by one, into their equivalents as parts of a working experiment.

METHODS OF DEMONSTRATION

There are as many ways of presenting demonstrations as there are instructors of physics. Each instructor develops special methods of his own that have merit for his own situation. The following are some suggested methods; no single one is sufficient.

Each experiment should be accompanied by a large-scale drawing of the apparatus employed. The drawing may be made while the instructor explains the function of each part. Chalk of different colors adds clarity and life to such a diagram.

Student assistance in the performance of an experiment may be called for from time to time, *e.g.*, in the reading of thermometers and small scales. In experiments such as M-110 and E-228, the class as a whole may be asked to share in taking data. Observation of phenomena is more important than accuracy of result, unless the experiment is used as a substitute for a laboratory experiment where greater precision of measurement is required. Such a substitution is necessary in some institutions where the lack of time or facilities prevents individual experimentation.

Demonstration experiments frequently lead to interesting problems, and conversely, many problems may be translated into experiments. There is danger, however, of killing interest in the experiments themselves if they are turned into problems too frequently.

In many experiments, the expected result is by no means obvious to the class, even after the proposed procedure has been described exactly. Class interest may be whetted by calling for a vote on the various possible outcomes of the experiment. M-112 is a good experiment of this type.

The element of surprise should not be neglected; something may be left untold before the experiment is performed. As the class observes the demonstration, new aspects not yet considered will appear, and class discussion can center on the interpretation of unexpected results. As a very simple example, suppose the instructor has shown step by step how to charge an electroscope by induction (E-23). If after the electroscope is so charged the charging rod is brought toward it, the leaves collapse; but if the rod is brought still closer, the leaves diverge. The interpretation of this apparent duplicity of effects from a single cause calls for original thought and interesting class discussion.

An occasional hoax, such as those described in M-104 and M-161, deliberately introduced without complete explanation in advance, arouses both mirth and thought. In this connection, it is useful to keep a class in suspense now and then while leading them forward to a satisfactory physical interpretation of what they have just witnessed.

Demonstrations may be employed effectively in presenting material by the "method of contrast," since different final results may be shown to come from initial conditions that are similar though not identical. M-100 and M-209 are examples of experiments of this type. Freezing mercury and then burning iron with liquid air, lighting a fire with an ice lens, etc., are processes that offer strong contrasts.

Paradoxical results are often of great value in emphasizing principles. After a class has reached the point where its members feel complacent about their mastery of a principle, it is well to show some striking experiment that leads to a result unlooked for on the basis of their knowledge. Such a method necessitates renewed thinking about the principle from another viewpoint. M-24, M-186, S-134, E-97, and E-98 are examples of this method.

Now and then the apparatus for an experiment can be assembled and set up as the class watches. After discussing the problem or principle to be examined, the instructor may arrange a suitable experiment *under class direction*, asking frequently for suggestions as to the next step or the next piece of apparatus required. Thus the experimental arrangement takes form under student observation and, in part, under student guidance. Evidently, the instructor must have all of the necessary facilities close at hand so as to avoid undue confusion during the progress of such an "assembly technique." Those who know what painstaking preparation and adjustment are required for many experiments will rely upon this device only as an occasional variant of the usual method, in which experiments are completely arranged ahead of time.

One instructor suggests that a good experiment involves a maximum of manipulation and a minimum of explanation. He goes so far as to suggest giving a demonstration lecture of selected experiments without saying a word!

The inspirational value of experiments depends so much upon the manner in which they are presented that the instructor cannot give too much attention to planning his experiments so that they will be given in the proper setting. There is an appropriate time at which to perform an experiment: to show it too soon is to find a class unprepared to appreciate its importance; to delay it by prolonged explanation is to diminish its effectiveness. Thought should be given to exposition, and the lecture should move steadily forward toward some climax. The physics instructor needs to develop a sense of what on the stage is called "timing."

Each class hour or lecture period may be regarded as a unit, complete in itself, which fits into the larger pattern of a carefully planned course. Having settled upon some significant principle or group of principles to be treated during the hour, the instructor can plan his experiments so that they help to develop the subject by logical steps. The hour may close with the showing of some final experiment that gives beautiful and striking confirmation of the principles under discussion.

It is generally more profitable to show a few experiments carefully during a class hour than it is to run hastily through a great number of those bearing upon the topic under discussion. Nevertheless, an occasional "show" raises the class morale. For example, an annual liquid-air display with 20 or 30 experiments presented in rapid succession is worth while. (In many cases, of course, it is obligatory to show liquid air in a single hour because of the cost and inconvenience of securing the air.)

At the beginning of any general subject, an introductory lecture with numerous experiments may serve to arouse interest and to create a predisposition toward the new study. This preliminary lecture should be designed to raise questions but not to answer them. Many of the experiments may then be repeated when the class is better informed. There is a danger that this practice will take the edge off student interest, and it must be used sparingly, reserving some of the best experiments for a later showing so that the instructor's repertoire is not exhausted before the study is well begun.

The lecture table should present a well-ordered aspect; it is not meant to look like an African jungle scene. The instructor who gives a little thought to his experimental arrangements can convey by the pleasing appearance of his lecture table something of the quality of orderly thinking that he expects of his students.

In many cases, it is a good plan to keep the center of the table clear and to move pieces of apparatus to this space as they are needed. The attention of the class is thereby directed to a single point, and the confusion is thus avoided that arises in the student's mind when he tries to isolate the parts of a demonstration apparatus from a maze of surrounding pieces, which have, at the moment. no relation to the experiment being performed.

TOOLS OF DEMONSTRATION

It is well to acquaint the student with the "tools of demonstration" so that he may acquire confidence in interpreting what he sees. It is not necessary that a student know all about the physical principles of an instrument in order to appreciate the effects shown by it in experiments in which its use is an incidental means to an end and not an end in itself.

The lecture thermometer (H-6) may be introduced and used freely for the measurement of temperature, even though the student may be quite ignorant of the underlying principles of thermoelectricity.

The cathode-ray oscilloscope may be used as an indicator of numerous phenomena, even though the student may know little about its operation as a whole.

The stroboscope offers a means of apparently "stopping" rapid periodic motions and of studying them under "slow motion" conditions (*e.g.*, see M-149, S-36, and S-49). Its principles are simple, and its effectiveness as a tool of demonstration is great.

Shadow projection is useful for enlarging small pieces of apparatus. It is accomplished by illuminating the object with light from an intense source (carbon arc or concentrated filament lamp without lenses) and casting its shadow upon the screen where the size of silhouette obtained may be varied by changing the distance from source to object.

In many cases, the instructor may prefer to project an image of a piece of apparatus, by either the vertical or the horizontal arrangement described in L-1. The student may become acquainted with the inversion of image in this type of projection and may thereafter take proper account of it in the interpretation of what he sees. However, an inverting prism may be used to show an erect image of the object.

Projection equipment for showing slides and for shadowing or for projecting apparatus should be available at all times. In one laboratory, the arc lamp housing is in an adjoining room, with its condensing lens set in the lecture-room wall, in such a manner that the light beam runs longitudinally above the lecture table at a convenient height. This arrangement is especially helpful for showing experiments in which even small amounts of stray light may be confusing.

In addition to the usual screens for projection, flashed opal glass (milk glass) is very desirable. It works equally well for projection by transmission or by reflection; images may be seen clearly even though the screen is viewed obliquely. A piece of this glass in a frame may be set vertically upon the lecture table as a screen on which to project, for example, the leaves of an electroscope. Both student and instructor can see the image, although they are on opposite sides of the glass screen. This arrangement has the further advantage that the student looks in the same direction to see both the apparatus and its image. Thus he is saved from the bothersome shift of attention that is one of the greatest objections to the use of projection in lecture demonstrations.

Electric meters may be arranged for projection by cutting away the backs of their cases and equipping them with glass scales either drawn by hand or photographed. Such meters are in many ways preferable to the more expensive large-scale wall meters. The mechanism of the meter should be carefully protected from dust at all times.

Electrical arrangements should be made as simple as possible and should be set, in most cases, on vertical panels with large, plainly visible connecting wires.

The lecture room should contain a wall galvanometer with lamp and scale permanently mounted and ready for immediate use.

It is better to err on the side of making things too large than too small. Large models, large pointers, strong contrasts of color (preferably black and white), and *strong* illumination are important. Floodlights over the lecture table or desk lamps properly placed to illuminate apparatus without obscuring it are helpful.

A large box with opal-glass front, within which several 60-w lamps are housed, makes a good background of diffused light against which pieces of apparatus may be shown. In other cases, especially with apparatus painted white, contrast is enhanced by exhibiting experiments under strong illumination before a dark background such as a piece of black velvet.

It is beyond the scope of this book to describe the architectural features of a physics lecture room. A well-designed room has adequate lighting and ventilation, elevated seats, blackboards, screens for projection, a convenient lecture table with water, gas, and electric connections, and electric outlets for alternating current and direct current from generator or storage batteries. It should be possible to darken the room completely. Numerous window-shade controls are in use, some electrical,[1] some mechanical, some hydraulic. These controls and those of the lights should be arranged so that the lecturer has easy access to them. A simple convenience is a push button on the end of a cord by which the lecturer can control the room lights from any part of the lecture table. An electric clock set face upward in the lecture table and covered by a piece of plate glass flush with the table top is an inconspicuous reminder of the passage of time.

In a lecture room with high ceiling, a trap door or a balcony above the lecture table may be of use in numerous experiments. Such an arrangement makes it possible to suspend objects from the ceiling of the room, which is a convenience in certain experiments with falling bodies and pendulums (M-80, M-98, M-124, etc.).

Adjacent to the lecture room should be a room in which apparatus may be stored in glass cases. Orderliness of storage is a virtue to which the instructor may well give thought and in which he should train his assistants. The habit of returning

[1] One laboratory reports a simple method in which the springs are removed from the shade rollers, and each shade is controlled by a separate d.c. reversible motor.

apparatus to its proper place is a rewarding one, for it saves much time in lecture preparation, besides the obvious contribution that it makes to the order of the laboratory. Movable tables on casters or rollers are a great aid, especially in institutions where several instructors must use the same room. Experiments may be arranged and adjusted on such tables, which are rolled into the lecture room when needed. There is no quicker way to "change scenes." The rolling tables may be locked in position by ordinary doorstops fastened to one or more of the legs and used as lecture tables.

GENERAL CONSIDERATIONS

A book such as this cannot specify the exact piece of apparatus required for a given experiment; its purpose is to outline a variety of useful experiments that may be adapted, both in number and in difficulty, to the needs of a particular institution. Since so much time is consumed in setting up apparatus, it is desirable to keep a card catalogue or a notebook of experiments giving details of apparatus and its arrangement. Such a catalogue or notebook that records successful arrangements will, in the course of a few years, become invaluable.

Apparatus for showing many of the demonstrations described in this book is procurable from scientific supply houses. Most instructors will doubtless secure ready-made apparatus, but those who desire to construct their own will find the details given here of material assistance. Good apparatus can rarely be made without the facilities of a well-equipped shop. Apparatus for a number of the experiments described herein is not commercially available and must be specially constructed; in a few cases, considerable skill is required, but in most cases the apparatus may be assembled from the common appliances ordinarily at hand. A trip through any 5-and-10-cent store will discover dozens of humble and inexpensive articles that can be turned to good advantage in the physics lecture room. If a few new experiments are assembled each year, the departmental facilities will steadily increase.

Above all, the instructor should investigate the possibilities of new commercial products as they appear on the market. Many new materials and new devices have remarkable properties that make them useful in lecture demonstrations. Low-voltage neon lamps, amplifier tubes and photoelectric cells, cathode-ray oscilloscopes, polaroid sheets for polarizing light, plastics for showing photoelasticity, cellophane, cobalt-steel magnets, and numerous other products have appeared in recent years and have found great usefulness in the lecture room and the laboratory. It would be impossible to enumerate them all or to point out all the possible uses of any one of them.

In large institutions where the physics class is divided into sections and different instructors must use the same apparatus, orderly storage of the equipment is imperative. In this regard, the system in operation at one large state university is worthy of comment. Demonstration is a departmental undertaking. Each lecture demonstration is thoroughly discussed by the staff and perfected to the point where it shows just what is desired. A set of apparatus is assembled in a box or built up on a panel or framework, and each set is accompanied by a list of parts and a summary of directions for the conduct of that experiment. Much time is spent in organizing the work so that the time required of any one instructor in arranging a particular lecture is greatly reduced. Each instructor is obliged to see that the apparatus is returned to its proper place in readiness for the next instructor. The advantages of this system are to some extent offset by the cost of duplication of apparatus and the increase in storage space demanded.

If each one of the experiments described in this book were accompanied by a full discussion of the physics involved and by a detailed account of what to say, it is evident that *six* volumes would scarcely suffice. The instructor is assumed to have sufficient knowledge of physics to interpret the observed results of experiments and to know which ones he cares to use. Any good college text will supply the background against which nine-tenths of these experiments may be shown. There is an accompaniment of fact and theory that is logically associated with each experiment, but bare fact and theory are not sufficient to carry a class along. There must be life and action, and to attain them, the instructor himself must be alive and alert, enthusiastic and imaginative. His manner of presentation is important, but this is a quality that cannot be acquired solely from books. It comes best from a keen awareness of his class and their capabilities and from a well-developed ability to express his thoughts in clear and forceful language. Observing successful lecturers helps to suggest ways of improvement, but no two men use just the same technique.[1] Expertness of manipulation and agility on the part of the lecturer are never-failing sources of satisfaction to a class.

In a sense, the instructor should start fresh each year and not rely too much upon what he has done before. This applies especially to his mental approach to an experiment, although the physical setup may be very similar from year to year. He must keep in mind that an experiment that may seem old and hackneyed to him may be new to his students.

Every experienced lecturer has had experiments fail at the crucial moment. Some experiments are, by their very nature, reproducible only by starting afresh, but one should make as certain as possible that everything is working properly before the class arrives. Such preparation acquaints the demonstrator with the vagaries of apparatus and the pitfalls to be avoided. When Ernest Fox Nichols, while preparing a lecture in England, remarked that he was trying out his experiments, Sir William Dampier-Whetham replied, "Do you think that is quite sporting?" The sporting element is large enough in any case without augmenting it by inadequate preparation! Unexpected events, when they occur, can help to make or mar a lecture, depending upon the lecturer's skill in turning failures to good account. In any physics experiment, what actually happens is what *ought* to happen under the existing conditions; it may not be what the lecturer *expects* to happen, but if he is on his toes, he can make excellent use of apparent upsets.

Any experiment is commonplace if it is presented in a dull and commonplace manner. As a single example of the kind of treatment that can be given to an average experiment to make it outstanding, consider M-18. The lecturer draws the attention of the class to the forces acting upon a car resting on an inclined plane and kept from rolling down the plane by a block in front of its wheels. First he adds weights to the end of a string attached to the car and passing over a pulley at the top of the plane, until

[1] The instructor may find inspiration in the writings of great experimenters and lecturers like Faraday and Tyndall. A number of the Christmas Lectures of the Royal Institution (Great Britain) are in print (see bibliography in Appendix A).

the car ceases to press against the block. "Now we no longer need the block." Then he adds weights to a second string, which passes over another pulley in such a manner as to exert a force on the car perpendicular to the plane (Fig. 6) until the pressure of the car upon the plane is reduced to zero. "Now we no longer need the plane." There the car hangs in midair as if still ready to run along an imaginary inclined plane of the same slope. Simple? Yes, but not easily forgotten. Such picturesque presentations are possible with great numbers of these experiments if the instructor will but use his imagination.

MUSEUMS

In recent years, a number of large scientific museums have been established. They serve a useful purpose in acquainting the public with the place of science in modern technical, industrial, and social life. An excursion to any one of these great institutions is a rewarding experience for either student or instructor. In many of them, apparatus for showing fundamental physical or chemical phenomena is so arranged that the individual observer can operate it by pushing a button.

The essential features of such a museum are not beyond the reach of any physics department in high school or college, where a small museum can fill a very important place in the teaching of science. Exhibits that work are so arranged that the student may operate them at his leisure, thus allowing him to observe effects at close hand, to vary conditions of performance within limits, and to ponder deliberately over what he observes. Several institutions have devoted rooms to such exhibits in which numerous experiments, arranged in an orderly and attractive manner, are set up permanently, each accompanied by a brief description of its purpose and operation.

The museum method is particularly desirable for those experiments of the "peep-show" type (diffraction, interference, Brownian movements, etc.) which are best seen by individual observation. Others (*e.g.*, Cavendish balance, M-128) require so long to perform that it is better to allow the interested student an opportunity to carry out such experiments by himself. Students should be directed to particular exhibits from time to time, and they may even be asked to make use of the apparatus in the exhibits for quantitative measurements or for the solution of problems.

A slight variant of the physics museum that has several advantages is to be found in some departments, where a display case or a table is arranged to make one or two experiments available at a time. The success of this method depends upon frequent change of exhibits. Some experiment that relates to the current work of the class may be on display, perhaps one designed expressly to mystify the student and arouse his curiosity.

Such an exhibit table is well worth the effort expended upon it. There are many experiments that should be set up for student operation, the purpose of which is qualitative observation rather than precise or quantitative measurement. Sturdy apparatus is required, and the experiment should be as foolproof as possible. This restriction eliminates experiments in which there is any element of danger or those requiring critical adjustment, unless the adjustable parts are out of reach of the observer. If electrical circuits are used, each circuit should be protected in such a way that no damage can be done by any possible combination of switch connections. Some student, perhaps more curious than others, is sure to try unconventional combinations of switches. At best, there is considerable wear and tear on apparatus in such exhibits; for if there are n usual ways of using a piece of apparatus, some student will discover the $(n + 1)$th way!

Descriptions of physics museums at two large universities[1] are to be found in *The American Physics Teacher*. These institutions consider them a great asset in their teaching program, because of the valuable collateral experience that they give to individual students.

[1] INGERSOLL, L. R., *Am. Phys. Teacher*, **4**, 112, 1936; LEMON, H. B., *Am. Phys. Teacher*, **2**, 10, 1934.

PART I

MECHANICS

STATICS OF RIGID BODIES

M-1. Magnitude of Forces. The first lecture on statics may well begin with a display of forces of varying magnitudes, best shown by weights of familiar objects. A 35-lb weight or a 16-lb hammer from the track department may be shown. Illustrate "a pint's a pound the world around" with milk, eggs, and vegetables. Mention the English and Canadian 10-lb gallon and the correspondence between the German *pfund* and the demikilo. Compare side by side the metric system of weights and the pound-ounce-grain system. Arrange a series of springs of varying stiffness to which may be attached the weights previously discussed so that the relation between stretch and magnitude of force will be clearly appreciated. Finally, show a slide, or display a diagram of typical masses:

Typical mass	Weight, g	Typical mass	Weight, g
Universe...............	10^{50}	Man...................	10^5
Star cluster............	10^{40}	Common pin...........	10^{-1}
Sun....................	10^{33}	Pencil mark...........	10^{-6}
Earth..................	10^{28}	Speck of dust..........	10^{-12}
Moon..................	10^{26}	Heavy molecule........	10^{-21}
Mount Everest..........	10^{18}	Hydrogen atom........	10^{-24}
Pyramid of Cheops......	10^{11}	Electron..............	10^{-27}

M-2. Error in Judgment of Weight. Several pairs of specimens, consisting of a pine block 2 by 2 by 10 in. and a brass tube 1.3 in. in diameter and 1.5 in. long, filled with lead, are passed about the class. The wood should be adjusted in length so that it is about 2 or 3 g lighter than the metal. The class will, however, almost unanimously pronounce the wood heavier. The error may be shown readily with an ordinary balance. The effect is heightened if a large piece of balsa wood, whose density is about one-third that of pine, is compared with an iron weight slightly heavier than the balsa.

M-3. Components of a Vector. Two screens are set at an angle of 90° to each other and facing the class. Between them is placed a horizontal wooden arrow 5 or 6 in. long, to represent a vector. Two projection lanterns are used to cast shadows of the arrow normally on the two screens. As the arrow is rotated by a vertical wire spindle, the class can watch one component grow as the other decreases; when one component is zero, the other is equal to the true magnitude of the vector and is parallel thereto. For generality, a third light may be added, if desired, to give the third component of a vector in a plane perpendicular to the other two.

M-4. Resolution of Forces. A spring balance S_1 with a large

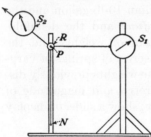

dial is supported from a rigid vertical rod so that it may be pulled horizontally (Fig. 1). A string from it passes to a ring R that is kept from falling by a peg P in a vertical support. A second string leads from the ring to a nail N at the bottom of the upright. The third force is provided by another spring balance S_2. The direction and magnitude of this force are varied

Fig. 1.—Resolution of forces.

until equilibrium is established, whereupon the peg can be removed without causing a change in the position of the ring. By changing the position of the first balance, various combinations of forces may be produced.

M-5. A heavy weight (20 to 30 lb) is suspended by a rope from the ceiling or from a sturdy wall hook so as to form a pendulum 10 to 20 ft long. The weight is displaced from its equilibrium position by a horizontal force whose magnitude (1 to 2 lb per ft of displacement) is shown by a spring balance.

M-6. Sailboat. A large photographic tray or similar shallow container not less than 2 ft square is filled to the brim with water. An electric fan is set up 6 or 8 ft distant so as to blow a uniform breeze across the water surface. A boat (Fig. 2) is made of a 3-in. cork stopper; a thin strip of metal is inserted in a diametral saw cut to serve as a keel. The simple resolution of the force due to wind pressure on the cork alone is illustrated by watching the motion when the keel is pointed in various directions with respect to the wind.   The double resolution of force is shown by erecting a sail (a calling card supported with a pin) on the hull.   By proper adjustment of the angle between the plane of the keel and the plane of the sail, the boat can be made to sail close to the wind.   An enlarged black-board diagram or a projected slide show-ing the forces involved should accompany the demonstration.

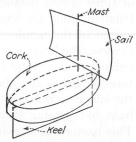

Fig. 2.—Simple sailboat as an example of the resolution of forces.

M-7. Resolution of Forces. This experiment demonstrates the resolution of a vertical force into many oblique forces, each having a vertical and a horizontal component.   A collar is sol-dered to a 1-ft length of $\frac{1}{2}$-in. brass tubing, and the tube is supported vertically from a strong stand (Fig. 3).   A $\frac{3}{8}$-in. wooden dowel is adjusted to slide loosely in the tube.   Two or

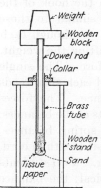

Fig. 3.—Resolu-tion of forces. A heavy weight is sup-ported by the sand, although only a thin tissue keeps the sand in the tube.

three thicknesses of soft tissue paper are fas-tened over the lower end of the tube with a rubber band, and fine dry sand is poured into the tube to a depth of 2 or 3 in.   The dowel rod is then introduced, and a wooden block with a $\frac{3}{8}$-in. hole bored part way through it is placed on top of the rod.   Weights are applied to the block until the tissue breaks.   Fifty pounds will be supported indefinitely, and a much greater weight may be used before the paper breaks.   Most of the weight is of course supported by the vertical components of the forces between the tube and the particles of sand next it.   It may be shown that without the sand the paper alone will support only a very small weight.

M-8. Addition of Forces.   A cord is attached to each end of a series of three or four spring balances connected hook to ring and laid on the table.   The cords run over pulleys at opposite ends of the table, and a 10-lb weight is hung on each cord.   The students are asked to decide what the readings of the balances should be.   In most cases, they are surprised to discover that all the balances read the same and that this reading is 10 lb and not 20 lb.

M-9. A heavy plank (say 25 lb) is hung horizontally by means of three spring balances hooked into screw eyes uniformly distributed along the top edge. Each balance reads one-third the weight of the plank. The three balances are then arranged in tandem, the lower one hooking into the center screw eye. Each balance reads, except for the weight of the balances below it, the total weight of the plank. Finally, two balances are hooked to the outside screw eyes, and the third to an eye in the center of a light bar passing through the rings of the first two balances. This balance then reads the full weight, the other two one-half each. If a heavy plank is used, the weights of the balances are more nearly negligible, and the distribution of forces throughout the array is more obvious.

M-10. Equilibrium of Two Forces. A student is asked to lift a heavy weight (50 to 100 lb) with a spring balance. The weight is given by the reading of the balance. The weight is removed, and another student then pulls horizontally on the hook of the balance while the first holds the ring. Grips similar to those used for a 16-lb track hammer are convenient. Although each student pulls with the same exertion as when lifting the weight, the reading of the balance is the same as before. The single balance is then replaced by two in tandem, and each then reads the force previously given by the single balance. The forces involved must be large compared with the weights of the balances.

M-11. Equilibrium of Three Forces. Two spring balances, with large dials for visibility, are attached to a 4-ft length of cord, from the middle of which a 20-lb weight is hung. Two students hold the balances so that the strings are vertical; the balance readings are each 10 lb. If the students then move apart, so that the angle between the strings increases, the readings of the balances increase but remain equal to one another. With the aid of a large protractor the angles may be determined, and from them and the known value of the weight the tensions in the cords may be calculated and compared with the balance readings, and their horizontal and vertical components may be computed.

M-12. A circular board, mounted with its plane vertical, carries a peg at its center and three or more pulleys around its rim. Strings passing over the pulleys are attached to a ring

fitting loosely over the central peg.   Weights are hung from each
string, and their magnitudes and the positions of the pulleys are
adjusted until the ring is free of the peg, which may then be
removed.   The forces are now in equilibrium.   They may be
represented to scale by lines drawn on the blackboard parallel to
the strings.   Application of the parallelogram method to this
diagram shows that the resultant force is zero; or the three
vectors representing the forces form a closed triangle.

M-13. Two spring balances are hung from nails at opposite
ends of the blackboard and are connected by a string, from the
middle of which weights are hung.   Lines are drawn on the blackboard under the strings, and lengths are laid off on them proportional to the forces.   The resulting lines may then be moved
parallel to themselves so as to form a closed triangle (zero
resultant force); or if two of the lines are made the sides of a
parallelogram, its diagonal, which represents the resultant of the
two forces, will be found equal in length and opposite in sense to
the third force, the equilibrant.   If the string supporting the
weights is *knotted* to the string connected to the hooks of the two
spring balances at some point other than the center of this string,
then in general no two of the forces involved will be equal.

The experiment is capable of many variations.   A third spring
balance may be used to apply a force near the middle of the string,
and this force need not then be vertical.   All the forces may be
produced by weights if pulleys are fastened to the top or to the
sides of the blackboard, and the spring balances are then
eliminated.

M-14. Another method is to use a square wooden frame
equipped with a number of screw hooks projecting inward.   The
frame is hung against the lecture-room blackboard, and a system
consisting of several light spring balances attached by cords to a
ring is stretched out within the framework so that the directions
and magnitudes of the several forces applied to the common
point have any desired value.   The directions of the cords are
then recorded by ruling along them on the blackboard with chalk.
The frame is removed from the board and a force diagram completed upon the basis of the recorded chalk lines.

M-15. Inexpensive Force Apparatus.   The spring balances of
M-14 may be replaced with long closely wound screen-door
springs, four or more of which are fastened to a common ring.

The springs may be simply calibrated with known weights so that by the aid of the straight-line graph of Hooke's law the tension in any spring may be found in terms of its length. The frame may be provided with a number of holes into which violin pegs are fitted. In this way, the length of a given cord attached to a spring and hence the directions of other forces may be varied. Vector diagrams may be quickly drawn upon the blackboard by indicating the position of the ring, the direction of each spring, and its length. If springs of equal length and stiffness are used, then each force vector will be proportional to the *extension* of its corresponding spring (but not proportional to the total length).

M-16. Components of Force. Two pieces of wood, each 1 by 3 in. and 1 ft long, are hinged together (Fig. 4). An 18-in. length of stout rope is fastened to two heavy screw eyes in two blocks of wood provided with notches. When the ends of the hinged pieces are placed in the notches and the hinged joint is loaded, the rope may be broken by the application of a much smaller force than would be required in the case of a direct pull.

Fig. 4.—Components of force. A small force applied vertically downward at the hinged joint will break the rope.

M-17. The method of swinging on the halyards employed in hoisting a sail may be demonstrated. A rope passes over a pulley in the ceiling to a weight sufficiently heavy so that no one can lift it directly (Fig. 5). The rope passes under a second pulley attached to the floor beneath the first and thence to a cleat. One student pulls horizontally on the vertical rope between the pulleys and after he has drawn it aside 6 in. or 1 ft suddenly releases it. A second student takes a turn around the cleat when the first pulls and takes up the slack quickly when the strain is released. Two light students can lift a weight in this way that the heaviest man in the class cannot move by direct pull. Rope at least $\frac{1}{2}$ in. in diameter should be used.

M-18. Car on Inclined Plane. A small car is held on an inclined plane by a wooden block under its wheels. A string parallel to the plane passes from the car over an independently supported pulley at the top of the incline to a weight holder, where by the addition of weights the component of gravity parallel to the plane is balanced (Fig. 6). The block may then be removed. A second string attached to the car at its center of gravity passes perpendicular to the plane over another pulley to another weight holder, to which weights are added until the pressure of the car on the plane is reduced to zero. The plane may then be removed.

M-19. Rolling Wedge. Three $\frac{3}{4}$-in. rollers about 6 in. long are

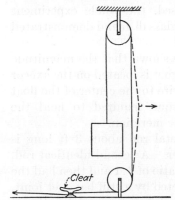

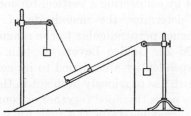

FIG. 5.—Swinging on the halyards. The heavy weight may be lifted by the application of successive small horizontal forces to the vertical rope.

FIG. 6.—Forces parallel and perpendicular to the plane will support the car when the plane is removed.

mounted between pivot points near the corners of two triangular endpieces about 2 in. on a side held together by a long bolt (Fig. 7a). The wedge so made rolls down an inclined board; above this at a distance slightly less than the height of the wedge is hinged a second board, upon which a weight may be placed

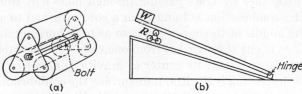

(a)   (b)

FIG. 7.—The rolling wedge (a) lifts the weight as it descends the plane (b).

(Fig. 7b). The comparatively light wedge R will raise the hinged board and a heavy weight W as it rolls down the incline.

PARALLEL FORCES AND MOMENTS

M-20. Couple, a Free Vector. A strong permanent magnet is centered on a circular wooden or cork float. The magnet is set in the east-west direction, and upon release the float rotates about its center of gravity. The magnet is next placed on one end of a wooden strip laid across the float and counterbalanced by a brass bar at the other end. Upon release, the float again rotates about its center, in spite of the fact that the axis of the couple has been displaced. If small magnets are used, the whole experiment may be performed in a flat-bottomed glass dish and demonstrated by vertical projection.

With greater refinement, it may be shown that the magnitude of torque is the same whether the magnet is located on the axis or not by connecting a vertical torsion wire to the center of the float to determine the magnitude of torque required to hold the magnet perpendicular to the magnetic meridian.

M-21. Galileo Lever. A $\frac{1}{4}$-in. metal rod about 3 ft long is suspended by a cord tied to its center. A second identical rod, which has previously been cut in the ratio of 3:1 and then had the two parts threaded together or connected by a stiff bayonet joint, is suspended from the first by means of two equal lengths of string ending in rings, which can slip along the rods. First, the supporting strings are at the ends of each rod. Equilibrium obtains. Next the strings are slipped inward until each is vertical and at the center of one part of the lower rod. This rod is then separated into its parts, and equilibrium again obtains. The law of moments is demonstrated, as the forces applied to the upper rod are inversely proportional to their distances from the center.

M-22. Two pieces of 2-by-4, each 4 ft long (Fig. 8a), are fastened together by bolts passing through holes 6 in. from each end. The combination is hung from a cord attached to a screw eye in the middle of the upper piece, so as to be horizontal. The lower piece is cut through 1 ft from one end. The shorter piece is now supported from its center of gravity and can be turned about its supporting bolt without disturbing the equilibrium of the system; but if the longer part is turned, the equilibrium is upset.

M-23. Bridge and Truck Problem. Two kitchen platform scales with large dials reading to 10 or 20 lb are placed 5 or 6 ft apart. Across them is laid a light board, which rests on two triangular wooden fulcrums placed on the flat tops of the scales. The board may be stiffened by screwing to the under side a lengthwise strip, edge on. Heavy black lines 6 in. or 1 ft apart mark distances along the board. With the board in position, the pointers of the scales are adjusted to zero. A toy truck loaded with weights is placed directly over one scale. The class observes its weight.   Then the dials of both scales are concealed, and the truck is drawn a quarter or a third of the distance along the bridge.   The class is asked to compute the readings of the scales before the experimental values are revealed.

M-24. Action of a Torque.   A large spool such as is used for wire has a string wrapped around it several times so that it will come off the bottom of the shank as the spool rolls along the table. Few students will guess correctly which way the spool will roll if the string is pulled parallel to the table.   The spool may be made to roll in either direction by making the line of pull on the string cut the table to one side or the other of the line of contact of the spool with the table.   If the two lines intersect, the spool

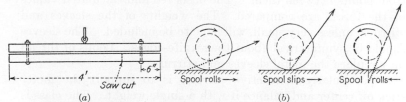

(a)   (b)

Fig. 8a.—Galileo lever.   Turning the short piece of the lower board leaves the equilibrium undisturbed; turning the long piece destroys equilibrium.
Fig. 8b.—Angle of pull determines direction of motion.

slides.   If a string is wound around each end of the shank, the tendency of the spool to turn about a vertical axis may be reduced (Fig. 8b).

This experiment may be made more effective if the spool rolls along a light horizontal plank suspended by four long cords. Then, if the radius of the shank is one-half that of the rim, a horizontal pull on the cord will not move the plank.   If the radius of the shank is less than this, the plank will be moved in the direction of the pull; if it is more, the plank will move in a direction opposite to the pull.   This experiment illustrates the apparently paradoxical case of a frictional force acting either in the direction opposite to the pull or in the *same* direction.

M-25.   A bicycle is held upright with one pedal at its lowest point.   The demonstrator pulls backward on a horizontal rope attached to this pedal.   The bicycle moves *backward!*

M-26. Addition of Parallel Forces and Torques.   A 4-ft board, 12 in. wide, is suspended horizontally from two spring balances hung from the ceiling or a supporting frame.   Weights are laid on the board at various points, and the calculated and observed extensions of the balances are compared.

M-27. A meter stick is equipped with several light metal sleeves, which may be clamped in any position along its length and which are extended on either side by short strips of metal that serve as knife-edges. Wire stirrups ending in rings that slip over these knife-edges enable the meter stick to be supported at any point and also serve for attaching weights at various positions. The meter stick is supported from a spring balance hooked into the center stirrup, and weights are hung from the others until the stick balances; or the stick may be hung from two balances near its ends, and one or more weights may be hung from points between them. The observed and calculated values of the forces are compared. The weights of the sleeves and stirrups, unless very small, will have to be included. The sleeves should be symmetrical about their knife-edges. Loops of thread may replace the metal sleeves and stirrups.

A particularly instructive exercise is to support the meter stick off center and balance it with a single weight. The class is then asked to compute the weight of the meter stick from the positions of the known weight and the center of gravity of the stick.

M-28. Equilibrium of Moments. A drawing board is supported on a horizontal axis through its center, so that it can turn freely in a vertical plane. Weights are hung from threads looped over thumbtacks stuck into the board at various points and are adjusted until equilibrium is attained. The algebraic sum of the moments of all the forces is then shown to be zero. If the axis about which the board turns is hung in a wire stirrup from a spring balance, it can also be shown that the algebraic sum of all the forces (which in this case are all vertical) is also zero.

The experiment can be extended to include the case of non-parallel forces by running some of the strings over pulleys, but the adjustments and calculations are not so simple in this case.

M-29. Ladder Problem. A stick 12 to 15 in. long is hung by a thread from its upper end, and the lower end of the stick rests on a wooden float in a pan of water (Fig. 9). The stick may be inclined at any angle; but when equilibrium is attained, the thread is always vertical, since there can be no horizontal component of force at the float.

M-30. A short ladder, 6 or 7 ft long, is equipped with wheels or casters at its upper end so that as it leans against the wall, the reaction of the wall may be considered horizontal, tangential friction being negligible. The ladder is leaned against the wall at such an angle that it just does not slip. A cleat is firmly fastened to the floor about 6 in. from the foot of the ladder. A sheet of heavy galvanized iron will make the friction between the floor and the base of the ladder more dependable. The forces holding the ladder in equilibrium are discussed: (1) the ladder alone, (2) the ladder with the instructor standing on the first rung, (3) the ladder with the instructor standing on a higher rung so that the ladder will begin to slip. The demonstration consists in cautiously climbing the ladder until it slips. The cleat prevents a serious fall.

M-31. Center of Gravity. A flat irregularly shaped board is suspended from a point near one edge. The vertical direction through the point of support is indicated by a plumb line, and a line is drawn on the board to coincide with the vertical. This process is repeated with another point of support.

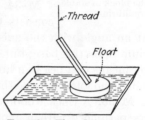

Fig. 9.—The float moves until the thread is vertical.

The point of intersection of the two lines locates the center of gravity of the board. Lines similarly drawn from other points of support will pass through this intersection. If a nail is driven through the board at the intersection of these lines, it passes through the center of gravity; and if the ends of the nail are supported by two loops of string or by two horizontal rods, the board is in equilibrium in any position in a vertical plane.

M-32. Equilibrium. Large models, a foot or more across, cut from plywood in various geometrical shapes, such as a triangle, semicircle, cycloid, or parabola, are suspended by means of a steel knitting needle thrust in turn through each of two or more holes several inches away from the center of gravity, which may be located as described in M-31. Another hole may be drilled at the experimentally determined center of gravity to show that each model is in neutral equilibrium when supported at that point. If desired, the experimentally located points may be compared with those determined by calculus.

M-33. A body is in stable equilibrium if its center of gravity is below the point of support, if a vertical line through the center of gravity passes within the area of support, or if any slight disturbance tends to raise the center of gravity. A familiar child's toy is a horse from the body of which extends a long bent rod carrying a lead weight at its end. The horse may be supported by resting its hind legs on a horizontal rod, a feat that would obviously be impossible without the bent rod and weight. The principle may easily be demonstrated with a block of wood and lead weight (Fig. 10) or with a wooden pencil and a jackknife.

FIG. 10.—The heavy ball keeps the block in stable equilibrium.

M-34. Another demonstration of equilibrium consists of a truncated cone whose base is cut at an angle with the axis. The cone will rest in stable equilibrium upon this base; but if a short cylinder is fastened to the top by means of a peg in a hole, the center of gravity of the combination is no longer above the area of support, and the "tower" falls.

M-35. A thick wooden disk, 12 in. in diameter, is loaded near its periphery with a plug of lead. If it is placed on a gentle incline with the lead plug near the top, it may be made to roll uphill and will then come to rest with its center of gravity above the line of support in such a position that a slight displacement of the disk in either direction will raise its center of gravity, so that its equilibrium is stable.

The class may be alarmed to see the disk roll toward the edge of the lecture table, stop just short of the edge, and return. The starting point on the table and the corresponding point on the disk are of course found by trial and carefully marked in advance.

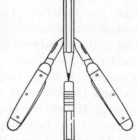

FIG. 11.—The center of gravity of the system is below the point of support.

M-36. A pencil, into which two jackknives have been stuck, may be balanced with its point resting on the end of another pencil (Fig. 11).

M-37. A double cone will appear to roll up an incline made of two gradually separating rails if the slope is such that the center of gravity of the body is slowly lowered as it rolls.

M-38. Two equal weights A and B (Fig. 12) are supported by vertical rods that slide in holes through the ends of a horizontal rod R and are held by setscrews. A third vertical rod passes through a hole in the center of the horizontal rod and can also be held by a setscrew. It carries a needle at its lower end, which rests on the head of a common pin driven into a vertical wooden support. The effects of raising or lowering the two weights and the point of support C on the equilibrium of the system are demonstrated. In the upper end of each rod is cut a notch, into which fits a tongue on a short section of the same rod. A pin is passed through the joint so that a hinge is formed. When the rods are slipped down until they hang from the short hinged section, the system is changed from stable to unstable equilibrium, although the center of gravity is far below the point of support.

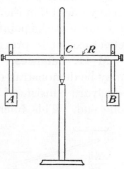

Fig. 12.—The center of gravity may be raised or lowered.

M-39. A cone turned from wood or metal serves well to illustrate stable, neutral, and unstable equilibrium.

M-40. Neutral Equilibrium. From a piece of 2- by 12-in. plank is cut an arc of the catenary $y = c \cosh x/c$, where c is 6 to 10 in. and the y-axis is perpendicular to the side of the board opposite the arc (Fig. 13). A similar plank is cut to form a polygon (*e.g.*, a rectangle) such that its center of gravity is at a distance c from one edge. The first board is set upright on the table and leveled if necessary so that the y-axis is vertical. The second board stands on the first so that its base is horizontal and its center of gravity lies in the y-axis (produced). Then if the polygon is rolled along the arc of the catenary it will remain in neutral equilibrium, since its center of gravity will move along a horizontal line. This can be shown by measurement with a meter stick, or by clearly marking the center of gravity and

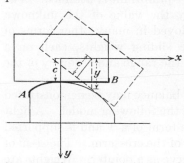

Fig. 13.—The rectangle is in neutral equilibrium on the catenary.

stretching a horizontal string at its height above the table, so that
the mark will move along behind the string. As the curve
becomes steeper, friction will no longer be sufficient to keep the
board in place. To remove this difficulty, a piece of cotton tape
may be tacked to the two boards in the position shown by the
heavy line AB in the figure. Since its pull can only be tangent to
the curve at the point of contact of the two boards, it can have no
effect except to prevent slipping.

M-41. Balances. The principle and operation of balances
may be demonstrated with as many types as are available. The
steelyard consists of a graduated metal bar with a fulcrum near
one end. This fulcrum is usually supported in the hand, the

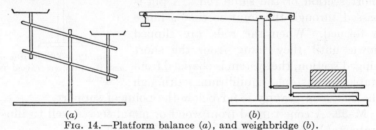

(a)   (b)
Fig. 14.—Platform balance (a), and weighbridge (b).

unknown weight is hung on the short arm, and a sliding weight is
moved along the longer arm until equilibrium is attained. The
arm is graduated to read directly the value of the unknown
weight. The same design is employed in many other forms of
balance, often with two or three sliding weights, each on a
graduated arm, by means of which the range and accuracy of the
balance may be increased.

M-42. The equal-arm analytical balance may be demonstrated
with the actual instrument or with the following model. A light
wooden frame is constructed in the form of a T and is supported
by a nail driven through the center of the crossarm. The stem of
the T is tapered at the bottom to serve as a pointer. Weights are
hung from the arm at equal distances from the support. A
threaded rod carrying a heavy nut projects upward from the
center of the crossarm. By varying the position of the nut, the
height of the center of gravity of the system can be changed.
Thus one may demonstrate both stable and unstable equilibrium
as well as the effect on period and sensitivity of the relative position of center of gravity and point of support. The same effect

may be demonstrated with an actual balance by replacing the weight attached to the pointer for adjusting the center of gravity by a much heavier weight so as to accentuate the effect.

Simple models made of wooden strips and brass pivots may be constructed to demonstrate the principles of various other types of balance, such as the drugstore or platform balance (Fig. 14*a*) and the so-called weighbridge (Fig. 14*b*), commonly used for weighing heavy loads.

MACHINES

M-43. Lever. The simplest machine is the lever. It may be demonstrated in simple form by a meter stick equipped with three movable knife-edges (M-27), one to serve as fulcrum, the other two to support weights. The three classes of lever can be demonstrated by the arrangements shown in Fig. 15. In each case, when equilibrium is established, the sum of the moments about any point is shown to be zero.

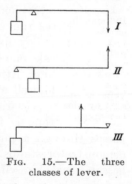

Fig. 15.—The three classes of lever.

Such practical applications of the lever as a crowbar, wrecking bar, claw hammer, scissors, nutcracker, pointers on instrument dials (where the emphasis is on multiplication of motion or speed rather than force) may be exhibited.

The foot forms an interesting lever. How can the body be lifted by a muscle of which the upper end is attached to the body? If the foot rests on the floor, at a place three times as far from the ankle joint as the place of attachment of the tendon of Achilles, what is the force in that tendon if a man of weight 150 lb raises himself on the ball of one foot?

M-44. Windlass. A windlass is simply a lever arranged for continuous action. The fulcrum is the axis of rotation, and the lever arms are the radii of the crank and axle respectively. A model windlass may be demonstrated. The crank may be replaced by a pulley having a radius equal to that of the crank, in which case the machine is called a wheel and axle. Cords are wrapped around the wheel and the axle, and weights are hung on the cords to demonstrate the equality of moments. Mechanical advantage may be determined by finding the ratio of distances traversed by the two weights during a given motion of the wheel and axle.

M-45. Pulleys.　As many types of pulley as are available may be demonstrated. Small models can be enlarged by shadow projection, but if possible full-sized blocks and tackles should be shown and heavy weights lifted by their aid (see M-17).

The differential pulley or chain hoist may be demonstrated, preferably with an actual machine.

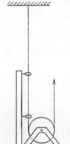

M-46.　The way in which the mechanical advantage of a pulley system depends upon the number of ropes supporting the weight may be shown by means of a boatswain's chair. This is simply a 2-ft board, on which the demonstrator sits, held in a large loop on the end of a rope. The rope passes over a pulley fixed to the ceiling, and the demonstrator asks one of the lighter members of the class to raise him. After he has failed, the demonstrator raises himself with one hand.

FIG. 16.— By standing on the platform and pulling upward on the rope, the operator "lifts himself by his bootstraps."

A variation is shown in Fig. 16. One end of the rope is fixed to the ceiling, while the other end passes through a pulley attached to a platform on which the demonstrator stands. By pulling on the free end of the rope, he can "raise himself by his bootstraps." It is well to have the rope pass through a sleeve on a post several feet high rigidly fastened to the platform, to prevent the platform from tipping.

M-47.　Let the student who has had experience in calculating mechanical advantages of ordinary tackles try his ingenuity on the arrangement shown in Fig. 17, sometimes called "fool's tackle." If necessary, set the arrangement up with pulleys and weights.

FRICTION

M-48. Tribometer.　An inclined plane of wood, covered with metal on one face, is hinged at the bottom so that its angle can be varied and so that either face can be made the upper one. Smooth blocks of wood or metal can be laid on the plane, and the angle

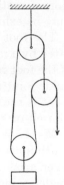

FIG. 17.— "F o o l ' s tackle."

varied until they will just slip down without acceleration
after they have been started.   The coefficient of sliding friction is
then equal to the tangent of the angle of slope.   In the same way,
the coefficient of starting friction can be determined and shown
to be larger than that of sliding friction.

The difference between starting and sliding friction may be
shown with a piece of soft cloth (*e.g.*, a bath towel) laid over a
long smooth rod or a piece of straight glass tubing 2 in. in diameter and 5 or 6 ft long.   One end of the towel may be perhaps 6 in.
lower than the other, without the towel slipping off the glass.
However, if the tube is inclined enough so the towel slides along,
then it will also run across the tube and fall off on one side.
While moving lengthwise of the tube, it easily moves crosswise.

M-49. To show that sliding friction is independent of the area
of contact between the two materials, a wooden block a foot long
is cut in the form of a prism whose cross section is an irregular
polygon.   The angle of slope of the inclined plane at which the
block will slide uniformly is the same whatever face it may be
resting on.   The same fact may be shown by pulling the block
across the top of the lecture table with a spring balance.   As long
as the speed is constant, the reading of the balance is the same
regardless of the area of contact.

M-50. Dependence of Friction on Pressure.   Hold a meter
stick horizontally on the index fingers of the two hands, one finger
at 10 cm, the other at, say, 70 cm.   Ask the class on which side
the stick will fall as the two fingers are brought slowly together.
The two fingers always meet at the middle of the bar, with the
bar still poised above them.   The same thing is true even though
the stick is supported on substances as dissimilar as rubber and
steel.

M-51. Angle of Friction.   A pencil is held by the point with
the rubber eraser resting against the table; starting in the vertical
position, the pencil is pushed longitudinally and is inclined until
it slips.   The angle between pencil and vertical at which slipping
occurs is the angle of friction (M-48), and its tangent is equal to
the coefficient of friction of rubber against the material of the
table.   A slight twisting motion is sufficient to overcome starting
friction.

M-52. Snubbing.   The application of friction to the method of
snubbing may be demonstrated.   More reproducible results are

secured if instead of a wooden post and ordinary rope one uses a polished laboratory support rod about an inch in diameter with tightly twisted cord like fishline. The rod is mounted horizontally, and a light spring balance is attached to one end of the cord. Weights are hung on the other end, and the weight required to produce a given reading on the balance is plotted against the number of turns around the snubbing post. The frictional force rises rapidly with the number of turns around the rod.

M-53. Automobile Skidding. The effect on the course of a skidding automobile of locking front or back wheels is demonstrated with a small model. Either pair of wheels may be locked by thrusting a pin through them into holes in the body. The car is released upon a steep incline made of wallboard. It either straightens out or skids further according as front or back wheels are locked.[1]

M-54. Friction Pendulum. Suspend a ball on a thread from a loop of thread 4 to 6 in. long, hung over a round horizontal wooden bar that can turn in bearings. As the bar turns slowly, the pendulum starts oscillating and builds up a large amplitude. The alternate drag and release of the thread by the turning bar may be compared with the intermittent friction between a violin bow and string.

M-55. Fluid Friction—Viscosity. A cylindrical vessel containing a liquid (water or oil) is mounted on a vertical axis so that it can be rotated. Inside the vessel and coaxial with it is a second cylinder supported by a torsion fiber carrying a small mirror. When the vessel is rotated, friction in the liquid causes a drag on the inner cylinder, which is indicated by the motion of a spot of light reflected from the mirror. This principle is used in one type of viscosimeter.

M-56. A flat sheet of metal supported by two long threads is hung in a vertical position in a glass projection cell containing water or glycerin. A metal disk is mounted so that it is parallel with the sheet and partly dips into the liquid in the cell. When the disk is rotated, the sheet is displaced in the direction of motion of the disk in the liquid, as may be shown by projection.

M-57. Effect of Temperature on Viscosity. If a cylinder containing castor oil (M-55) is placed within a water bath on a

[1] JONES, A. T., *Am. Phys. Teacher*, **5**, 187, 1937.

horizontal turntable rotated by a friction-drive motor, the effect of temperature on viscosity may be shown. As the water bath is heated from 5 to 40°C, the viscosity of the castor oil falls off in a ratio of 15:1.

M-58. Fall of Pressure in Pipe. A number of equal small holes are bored in a long horizontal $\frac{3}{4}$-in. pipe, and the pressure drop in the pipe due to friction as water runs through it is indicated by the decreasing heights to which the water rises from the holes toward the exit end of the pipe. A piece of shallow gutter pipe running to the sink will serve to catch both the water flowing through the pipe and that coming from the holes. Illuminating gas flowing through a $\frac{3}{8}$-in. pipe will show the same effect by the heights of flames at a series of holes along its length (L-31).

M-59. A more ambitious scheme is to have a pipe connected to the water mains running up one side of the lecture room, across the top, and down the other side, and finally emptying into a sink. Four pressure gauges, one at the top and one at the bottom of each side, indicate the pressure. The difference between static and kinetic pressure is clear at once when the water faucet at the sink is turned on.

M-60. Egg Torsion Pendulum. Two eggs, one raw and the other hard-boiled, are supported in wire baskets by similar torsion wires. Each is set oscillating as a torsion pendulum; the hard-boiled egg continues for some time, but the motion of the raw egg is quickly damped by internal friction. Similarly a hard-boiled egg may be spun on a plate much more readily than a raw egg. Once spinning, however, if the raw egg is stopped by touching it momentarily with the finger, it may resume rotation when released.

M-61. Viscosity in Gases. Frictional drag in gases may be shown by fastening two vertical parallel sheets of metal to one arm of a balance, with a disk arranged to rotate between them. The displacement of the parallel sheets in the direction of motion of the part of the disk between them is made evident by a disturbance of the equilibrium of the balance. This and the earlier experiment (M-56) may be interpreted in terms of the transfer of momentum from layer to layer of the fluid.

M-62. A metal disk is hung horizontally by a three-point support from a single vertical thread. A short distance below it is located a parallel disk driven by a motor. The upper disk, which carries a prominent index, may be displaced or even set into rotation by the frictional drag of the air.

ELASTICITY

M-63. Hooke's Law and Young's Modulus. A length of wire is hung from the ceiling (avoiding kinks), and a weight pan is attached to the bottom. Near the bottom of the wire is clamped a small collar with a wedge-shaped top, on which rests one end of a horizontal brass bar 10 cm long (Fig. 18a). The other end of the bar is supported by a knife-edge or by two pointed legs and

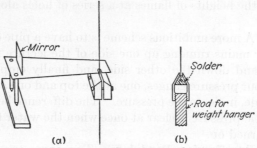

(a)   (b)

Fɪɢ. 18.—Young's modulus. Optical lever for showing elongation (a) and method of holding end of wire (b).

carries a small vertical mirror from which a spot of light is reflected to a screen, thus forming an optical lever by means of which the motion of the end of the wire is made visible. Weights are hung on the weight pan, and the elongation of the wire is shown to be proportional to the force applied. That the elongation is also proportional to the length of the wire may be shown by using wires of different lengths. From the constants of the optical lever, it is possible to compute the actual elongation under a given load and thus to compute Young's modulus for any wire. The optical lever and its support may be easily transferred from one wire to another if their lower ends are all near together. For shorter wires, this necessitates hanging them from some support lower than the ceiling.

The chief difficulty in this experiment is to hold the ends of the wires satisfactorily. Clamps will either slip or pinch the wire so that it breaks easily. A satisfactory support is shown in Fig. 18b.

A piece of brass rod has a cone turned on one end. The other end is drilled and tapped, and the cone is drilled out, with a hole through the apex somewhat larger than the wire to be used. The end of the wire is pushed through the hole, and a knot is tied in it. The knot is drawn part way into the cone, and the latter is filled with solder. A threaded rod is screwed into the tapped end to serve at the top for holding the wire or at the bottom for holding the weight pan.

If desired, the weight may be increased until the yield point of the material is reached. With one sample of copper wire (No. 20 d.c.c.) this was about 7000 g, but it varies considerably. The wire suddenly stretches very much more than before. As weights are added, the great increase of length continues; but the modulus of elasticity changes as well, so that the force needed to stretch the wire continually increases. A piece of copper wire may be stretched as much as 20 per cent or more of its original length before it breaks. It is of interest to show with a micrometer caliper that the diameter of the stretched wire is markedly less than that of the unstretched wire.

Experiments like the preceding for the verification of Hooke's law can also be performed with spiral springs of various materials and stiffnesses and with rubber bands or tubes.

M-64. Bending, Shearing, Torsion. A rectangular block of rubber is very convenient for demonstrating various kinds of strain and the stresses that produce them. If a sufficiently large block is not available, rubber erasers with the ends cut off square may be passed around the class or demonstrated by opaque projection. It is particularly interesting to show the change in the shape of cross section under bending and torsional stresses.

M-65. A pile of paper, cards or glass plates, or a thick book with flexible binding may be used to demonstrate the sliding of elementary planes over one another (due to shearing stress). A similar model to show torsion may be made of a number of slotted weights set on top of one another with a rod passing through their central holes. Another rod is placed in the slots, where it must fit loosely. When the top weight is twisted, all the others will also be turned through progressively smaller angles.

A very effective way of showing bending and other strains is by means of models made of transparent plastic and projected with polarized light (L-133).

M-66. The bending of rods and bars of various materials and cross sections may be demonstrated. The specimen may be supported from knife-edges at various separations, or it may be clamped at one or both ends. Various loads may be hung from the free end or the middle, and the amount of bending indicated by some form of optical lever or measured directly with a micrometer screw mounted vertically above the point of loading. Another method is to use shadow projection. At the point of loading, a small vertical piece of card or metal is attached to the beam or rod. A second similar piece is held just above the first and in the same plane by means of an independent support. The shadow of the two is cast on the screen, and the height of the second is adjusted until only a fine line of light appears. From the widening of this line when the specimen is loaded, the bending will be apparent.

M-67. Deformation under Stress. A pattern (*e.g.*, a circle, an inscribed square, and a set of radial lines) is painted on a sheet of rubber cut from an old inner tube. Opposite edges of the sheet are shellacked and held between two strips of wood tightly bolted together. Changes of shape of the pattern when the two sticks are pulled apart show the effect of deformation under stress. Nonuniform changes may be demonstrated with a similar sheet in which only one edge is held clamped while forces are applied to the corners or elsewhere.

M-68. Impact. Elastic and inelastic impact may be demonstrated with two heavy steel balls supported by bifilar suspensions so that they just touch one another. If the balls are of the same mass, when one is drawn aside through a measured arc and allowed to swing and hit the second, the latter will be driven out through nearly the same arc while the first will be brought to rest. If the balls are of different masses, bearing a simple ratio to one another, the laws of momentum transfer (M-124 and M-127) may still be verified approximately. Inelastic impact may be illustrated by sticking a small bit of modeling clay or soft wax to one of the balls at the point of contact so that the two balls stick together after impact.

M-69. The coefficient of restitution may be determined approximately by dropping balls on a horizontal plate. Glass marbles may be dropped on a piece of glass, or steel balls on a heavy smooth steel plate. The plates should be rigidly mounted on an unbending support.   Indexes attached to a vertical meter stick are used to indicate the initial height and the height of rebound.   The square root of the ratio of height of rebound to height of fall is the coefficient of restitution.   The apparatus should be brilliantly illuminated to increase visibility, or shadow projection should be used.

VELOCITY

M-70. Measurement of High Velocity. The shaft of a synchronous motor is extended at each end, and to each of these extensions is attached a disk of polar coordinate paper about a foot in diameter.   The axial distance between the disks may be made 1 ft.   Bullets are fired through the disks parallel to the axis, both when the motor is at rest and when it is rotating at a known speed.   The change in angular position of the bullet hole in the second disk is made obvious to the class by passing straight rods through the two pairs of holes.   By laying one disk upon the other in such a position that a nail may pass through the holes made when the motor was at rest, the angle through which the disks turned while the bullet was in flight between them may be measured, and hence the time of flight through a measured distance.   If a synchronous motor is not available, any type of motor may be used and its speed of rotation measured with a tachometer.

M-71. Observation of Low Velocities.   Project as for microscopic objects (A-50) the movement of the end of the minute hand of a clock.   It will probably be necessary to extend the minute hand with a bit of wire for convenience in projection.

M-72. Velocity Magnitudes.   Make a diagram showing typical velocities expressed in centimeters per second:

	Cm per sec
Geologic movement	3×10^{-7}
Glaciers	2×10^{-5}
Growth in plants	10^{-4}
Point of hour hand of watch	3×10^{-4}
Point of minute hand of watch	5×10^{-3}
Snail	15×10^{-2}
Point of second hand of watch	3×10^{-1}
Blood	7
Snowflake	20
Light wind	5×10^{2}

	Cm per sec
Sprinter...	10^3
Hurricane......................................	5×10^3
Earthquake wave.............................	3×10^4
Moon around earth............................	10^5
Earth around sun.............................	3×10^6
Halley's comet near sun......................	4×10^7
Cathode rays.................................	3×10^9
Light...	3×10^{10}

M ·73. Vector Addition of Displacements. A bead is pulled vertically along a wire rod fixed in a frame that may move horizontally. The string lifting the bead passes over a pulley on the frame and is made fast to the fixed coordinate system (Fig. 19). The vertical lift of the bead, therefore, equals the hori-· zontal movement of the frame, and the line $y = x$ is plotted.

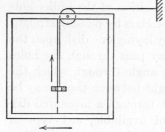

If now the bead is made a movable pulley by passing the string around the bead and tying it to the frame, the vertical movement is halved, and the bead traces the line $y = x/2$. A small frame approximately 6 in. square is suitable for shadow projection.

FIG. 19.—Vector addition of displacements.

M-74. A ball is tied at the center of a piece of twine 6 ft long, by means of which it may be pulled in either direction through a horizontal glass tube 2 ft long. By holding one end of the string against the table and raising the tube, the ball may be made to follow the resultant of a horizontal and a vertical motion.

M-75. Vector Addition of Velocities. A small rug or piece of canvas, across which runs a slow-moving mechanical toy, is drawn at uniform speed along the lecture table. The resultant motion of the toy relative to the table may be indicated by a chalk line connecting the start with the finish.

UNIFORM ACCELERATION

M-76. Self-timing Inclined Plane. A wide shallow rounded groove is cut lengthwise in the face of a 2-in. plank, 6 ft long and 8 in. wide. The groove is painted black. A heavy iron ball 3 or 4 in. in diameter, rubbed well with chalk, is rolled down the plane so as to oscillate from side to side of the groove. The ball leaves a wavy trace. The increasing length of the waves shows the increasing distance passed over in the constant time of oscillation, from which the constant linear acceleration may be determined. The *difference* between successive half wave lengths is constant.

M-77. Timed-interval Inclined Plane. Two so-called "highly polished rounds" of steel, $\frac{1}{2}$ in. by 12 ft, clamped closely together on a plank, form an excellent groove for rolling a 1-in. steel ball. Small lights flashed at regular intervals are attached to the plank at such points that a flash occurs each time the ball passes one of the lights. Neon or flashlight lamps are suitable, and the timing may be done by a pendulum with a mercury contact at the lowest point of its swing. The acceleration may be calculated from the increased distance passed over in successive equal time intervals.

M-78. Inclined Wire. A small car suspended from overhead wheels slides down an inclined steel piano wire stretched very taut by turnbuckles. The wire should be about a millimeter in diameter, and the car as light as possible. This setup may be permanently attached close to one wall of the lecture room, with large numbers painted thereon to show the time-distance relation. A metronome designates the proper equal time intervals.

M-79. Guinea-and-feather Tube. That the acceleration of free fall is independent of mass is readily shown by quickly inverting a long evacuated glass tube of large diameter containing a bit of lead and a feather. It is best to demonstrate the fall of the two bodies both before and after exhausting the tube, to show the contrast.

M-80. Rate of Fall Independent of Mass. An iron ball and a wooden ball of the same size into which is driven an iron plug are suspended at the top of the lecture room from the poles of an electromagnet. A bit of paper between each pole and ball insures quick release when the magnet circuit is broken. The balls fall together and simultaneously strike a tin pan placed on the floor beneath the magnet.

M-81. Suspend from the lecture-room ceiling two simple pendulums of equal length, one with a large cork bob, the other with a bob of lead. Pull them to one side 5 ft or more, and release simultaneously. The bobs fall back to their equilibrium position together.

M-82. Velocity Acquired by Ball on Inclined Plane. The velocity acquired by a ball rolling down an incline may be found, as Galileo determined it, by measuring the distance traversed by the ball in one unit of time along a horizontal extension of the track. This extension is slightly inclined so that a ball rolls along it without acceleration. The ball is released on the incline at such a height that its passage to the horizontal track coincides with a click of the metronome. A movable block placed on the track is then adjusted until the next click of the metronome coincides with the impact of the ball on the block.

M-83. A more spectacular experiment (similar in purpose to M-82) consists in arranging a seconds pendulum (approximately 1 m long) so that it is held aside by an electromagnet and released by the passage of the rolling ball from the incline to the horizontal track. The position of the pendulum is adjusted so that as it swings across the track it strikes the rolling ball laterally.

M-84. Freely Falling Bodies. A series of lead or iron balls, $\frac{1}{2}$ to 1 in. in diameter, is threaded on a fishline with their positions fixed by knots so that the intervals between them increase in arithmetical progression; 6, 10, 14, 18, . . . , in. are suitable intervals. The string is attached to the ceiling so that the lowest ball is 2 in. above a tin pan placed on the floor. The balls start falling simultaneously when the upper end of the string is released. They strike the pan with a constant frequency of impact (in this case, approximately 10 per sec). The more balls the more effective the experiment. By passing the string through a hole in the ceiling or by hanging it in a stair well, the advantage of additional height is gained.

M-85. Freely Falling Slab. A synchronous or properly timed motor is mounted with its axis vertical. On the upper end of its shaft is mounted a small ink bottle with a side tube (a bit of $\frac{3}{4}$-in. brass rod with a $\frac{5}{8}$-in. hole drilled in it serves for the bottle, and an 8-32 screw pierced with as small a hole as possible serves for the side tube). A cylindrical guard in the plane of the rotating nozzle protects the clothing of the experimenter. A slab of wood, $\frac{1}{2}$ by 2 by 18 in., has a strip of paper tacked to it and is dropped between the guard and the rotating nozzle. The ink squirted from the bottle cuts the falling slab in a series of nearly horizontal parallel lines separated by ever increasing vertical distances. If the speed of the motor is known, the acceleration of free fall may be determined from measurement on these lines.[1]

M-86. Pendulum-timed Free Fall. A rectangular iron block (2 by 5 by 10 cm) is hung by two steel wires so as to swing like a pendulum (Fig. 20). A thread attached to the back of the block by a screw eye passes around horizontal rods A and B and over a hook at C to a 1-in. metal ball. The position of the hook C is such that the ball is tangent to the vertical plane through the front face of the block in its rest position.

The pendulum is drawn aside, and the length of the thread adjusted until the ball hangs at a point whose height above the rest position of the center of the block is $\pi^2 l/8$, where l is the length of the pendulum. The weight of the ball and friction on the rods A and B are sufficient to hold the pendulum aside. The face of the block is covered with slips of paper and carbon paper held by rubber bands. The thread is burned near C so as to release ball and pendulum simultaneously. The pendulum strikes the ball laterally, and the point of

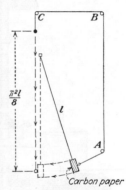

Fig. 20.—Pendulum-timed free fall.

impact is clearly marked by the carbon paper. Thus h, the distance the ball falls, is determined, and t, the time of fall, is equal to a quarter period of the pendulum. The acceleration of gravity is readily calculated from the equation $h = \frac{1}{2}gt^2$.

M-87. Free-fall Apparatus. Another arrangement for finding the acceleration of gravity is shown in Fig. 21. Two magnets are connected in series; the upper retains a steel ball, while the lower retains an arm that carries a stylus in contact with a revolving drum. When current is interrupted, the ball starts to fall, and the stylus arm is released simultaneously, thereby making a mark on the revolving drum. The ball falls upon the platform and causes the stylus to make a second mark on the drum. The time of fall may be directly determined from the positions of these two marks and the speed of rotation of the drum.

---

[1] For reduction of data, see Millikan, Roller, and Watson, "Mechanics, Molecular Physics, Heat and Sound," p. 25, Ginn and Company, Boston. 1937.

M-88. Galileo's Inclined Plane. A stiff circle, 4 or 5 ft in diameter, is constructed from metal rod or strap. Upon tightly drawn wire chords, radiating every 15° from the top of the circle, a set of glass or metal beads (Fig. 22) slides freely. If the beads are released simultaneously, their locus is a circle of increasing diameter that finally coincides with the stiff frame. Thus it is shown that the time of fall along any chord is independent of its slope.

M-89. In another method, the circle and chords are laid out upon a large piece of plywood, stiffened by backing strips to insure that

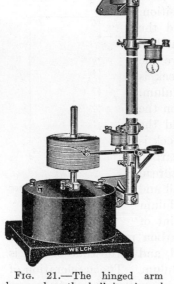

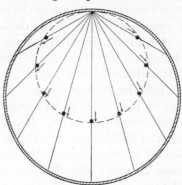

FIG. 21.—The hinged arm drops when the ball is released and rises again when the ball strikes it. Its motion is recorded by the stylus on the revolving drum.

FIG. 22.—Balls are released simultaneously on all the chords. As they fall their locus is always a circle.

the sheet remains plane. A series of circles tangent at the top is drawn upon the board, and the chords are delineated by means of No. 14 copper wire drawn tightly between holes. The plane is inclined with a slope of 1 in 10 or 20, so that $\frac{1}{4}$-in. balls will roll down the wire guides. Initially, the balls are retained within a small ring, coincident with the first circle, which is quickly but cautiously raised so as to set all the balls in motion at once. Stops at the ends of the various chords should give off sufficient sound so that the simultaneous arrival of the balls is made audible by a single click. The board may be reversed so that the common point of the chords is at the bottom. If the balls are all started from any one of the circles, they reach the common point simultaneously.

MOTION IN TWO DIMENSIONS

M-90. Water-stream Parabola. A glass or metal nozzle, connected by rubber tubing to a supply of water (either a tank of variable height or the water mains from which the flow can be controlled by a valve), is attached to a stick so that initially the jet of water is parallel to the length of the stick. Suspended by threads along the stick at equal intervals, measured from the orifice, are balls or rings hanging at lengths respectively proportional to the numbers 1, 4, 9, 16, . . . n^2. The stream may be adjusted by a pinchcock so that it passes through the rings or just beneath the balls however the angle of elevation of the jet may be changed, since the balls always lie on a parabola. For large classes, shadow projection may be used to show the parabolic path of the stream.

M-91. Rate of Fall Independent of Horizontal Motion. Two simple types of apparatus are available for dropping one ball vertically at the moment when another is projected horizontally. The first consists of a horizontal shaft, which when released by a trigger is forced by a compression spring into an endwise movement. From one end of the shaft, a ball is pushed off as the shaft moves into one bearing. The other end of the shaft strikes another ball as it comes out from the other bearing.

The second type consists of a board at one corner of which are placed the two balls. One is held over a hole by a retaining spring strip; the other is ready for projection. A flexible metallic strip with a projecting screw is drawn back and released. As it strikes the ball to be projected, the projecting screw strikes the strip retaining the other ball and releases it. Both balls may be heard to strike the floor simultaneously.

M-92. Falling Target. A $\frac{1}{2}$-in. brass tube 2 ft long supported in a laboratory stand serves for the gun (Fig. 23). The target, not more than 3 in. square, is a sheet of iron suspended from a doorbell magnet. A bit of paper inserted between target and pole pieces insures prompt release of the target when the current is interrupted. The gun is bore-sighted at the target, and the aim is demonstrated to the class by passing a beam of light from a pocket flashlight through the tube to the target. The bullet consists of a cylindrical brass plug or a steel ball that fits the tube smoothly. A No. 40 copper wire in series with the electromagnet is stretched on an insulating frame across the center of the muzzle of the gun. The projectile is inserted in the gun and blown toward the target, either by the lungs or by compressed air. On emerging from the tube, it cuts the wire and breaks the magnet circuit, releasing the target. The bullet hits the falling target. The experiment is equally successful with different angles of elevation of the gun and different muzzle velocities. A labora-tory apron makes a good backstop.

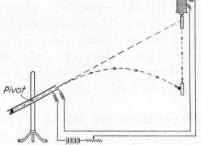

Pivot

FIG. 23.—The target is released when the bullet leaves the gun. The bullet always hits the target.

There are numerous varia-tions and refinements of this popular experiment. In one the projectile is a ball that acquires its initial velocity by rolling down a steep incline; it leaves the incline on a line directed at the target, which is a second ball.[1] In another, the gun is simply an inclined groove along which a steel ball is propelled by a ruler; the target is a golf ball. In a third, the projectile is a pointed dart, blown from a tube or shot from a crossbow, and the target is a cat's fur held to the magnet by a piece of iron. In a fourth, the magnet circuit is opened by a carefully adjusted switch or by a pressure-controlled contact that operates at the instant when the projectile passes a small hole near the end of the gun tube. In a fifth, the air gun and the magnet are attached to a long 2-by-4 so that, regardless of its angle of elevation, the gun is always aimed at the target.

M-93. Brachistochrone. Two $\frac{1}{4}$-in. polished-steel rounds, bent to form a cycloidal track and laid side by side in contact, may be attached to the wall or a wooden frame. An excellent groove is thus formed in which to roll $\frac{1}{2}$-in. steel balls. The cycloid should be of such an extent that even near its ends the balls roll without slipping. Two balls started simultaneously at points on opposite sides of the cycloid always strike in the center,

---

[1] SCHILLING and EICKHOFF, *School Science and Math.*, January, 1934.

a "dead heat" no matter what the handicap. The motion of a single ball rolling to and fro is isochronous, as in the cycloidal pendulum (M-94).

Two straight rounds, clamped together, may be pivoted at the lowest point on the cycloid so as to form an incline of variable pitch. Steel balls may thus be raced from any point on the cycloid by the two paths. The ball rolling on the cycloidal path always wins.

M-94. Cycloidal Pendulum. A circular piece of plywood 2 ft in diameter is rolled without slipping along the frame above the chalk rail at the lower edge of the blackboard. It is pushed along by a peg through its center, and the cycloid is described by a piece of chalk placed in a hole near the periphery. Two other

pieces of plywood shaped in the form of a cycloid may be shown to fit this curve and then inverted to form a cusp, between the sides of which a simple pendulum may be made to oscillate with large amplitude (Fig. 24). Direct comparison with the small-angle swings of a simple pendulum of the same length but without the cycloid attachment shows that the

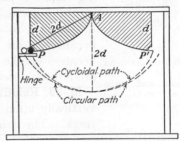

Fig. 24.—Comparison between simple and cycloidal pendulums.

cycloidal pendulum is isochronous, regardless of amplitude. If both pendulums are swung through large arcs, the cycloidal pendulum gains on the simple.

M-95. Range of a Projectile. A toy popgun, spring pistol, or simple crossbow is adjusted to shoot a projectile at an elevation of 45° as far as conveniently possible within the confines of the lecture room. The elevation is then shifted to 30° and 60° and the new range compared with the calculated value. A chalk box placed at the computed range will catch the projectile.

M-96. Parabolic Path of Projectile. A spring gun mounted at one corner of an inclined sheet of plywood is used to fire a steel ball, which may be caught in a box placed at the correct distance. The ball will trace its parabolic path if it rolls over a fresh piece of carbon paper covering a sheet of white paper tacked to the board. The ball should be heavy and the angle of the plane not too large.

RELATIVE MOTION

M-97. Acceleration Relative. A 1.5-in. glass tube 1 ft long with its lower end plugged with a metal disk is suspended close to the ceiling by a thread. A metal ball is also suspended by the thread so as to hang within the tube. The thread is cut above the point A (Fig. 25), and both tube and ball fall freely. The tube is caught in a well-padded box or in the hand, and the ball will be seen and heard to strike the metal end *after* the tube is caught.

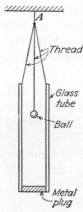

Fig. 25.— When the thread is cut above A, ball and tube fall with the same acceleration.

M-98. Freely Falling Candle. A steadily burning candle is placed inside a lamp chimney closed at the bottom. If the candle and chimney are dropped 2 to 3 m, the candle goes out, not because of air currents blowing the flame but because of the absence of convection currents around the accelerated candle.

M-99. Relativity Car. A spring gun is mounted vertically upon a car that rolls along a horizontal track. The trigger of the gun is tripped by a projection between the rails of the track as the car reaches a certain point (Fig. 26). The gun projects a steel ball some 3 ft upward between two rings vertically in line with the gun and attached to a mast fixed to the car. The muzzle of the gun is enlarged with a funnel to insure catching the ball on its return. If the motion of the car is uniform, the gun catches the ball regardless of the speed of the car. The distinction between the fixed and moving axes is emphasized if the car with mast removed is obscured by a screen during the flight of the ball.

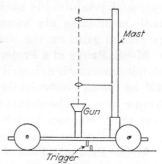

Fig. 26.—When the car is at rest or in uniform motion, a ball shot vertically from the gun falls back into the muzzle.

MASS OR INERTIA

M-100. Inertial Reaction. Short pieces of the same stout string are attached to screw eyes on opposite sides of a large mass, *e.g.*, a 16-lb shot. The ends of these strings are tied in loops with a bowline knot[1] so that a $\frac{3}{4}$-in. laboratory rod may pass through them.   The weight is suspended by one loop from a hook on the wall.   A rod is inserted through the lower loop, and the class is asked whether it wishes the string broken above or below the ball.   A steady downward pressure on the rod plus the weight of the ball will snap the string above.   Raising the rod a few inches and then giving it a quick downward flip will break the lower string.   By a sufficiently quick jerk it is possible to break two strings below the weight while it is supported by only a single string.   A padded box is used to catch the weight, or the weight itself may be wrapped with rags.

M-101. Breaking a Rope by Inertia.   A heavy iron ball is hung from a hook by a light cord.   One end of a piece of ordinary clothesline is tied to a screw eye in the ball; the other end is attached to the head of a hammer.   A full-arm swing of the hammer away from the ball takes up the slack in the rope at the moment when the hammer acquires its highest speed.   The clothesline may thus be snapped in two without disturbing the heavy ball appreciably.

M-102. Vibrograph.   A mass of several kilograms rests upon a glass plate that is supported by two steel needles (diameter about 0.5 mm).   These needles are free to roll on a second glass plate placed on the table top.   The upper part of the system remains at rest relative to the floor when the table is set in vibration by a hammer blow.   The resulting motion of the needles is made evident by reflecting light from a mirror cemented to one of them. Fundamentally, the system is a vibrograph, accelerometer, or seismograph.   A rotating mirror (S-76) may be used to show a time trace of the motion.

M-103. Weight vs. Inertial Reaction.   A heavy weight is lifted slowly from the floor with a light cord.   If, however, the cord is suddenly pulled, it breaks without lifting the weight. Similarly, a 10-lb weight is suspended from a spring balance; by suddenly raising or lowering it, the balance reading may be doubled or halved.   The experiment demonstrates in simple fashion the reason for one's sensations in an accelerated elevator.

M-104. Inertia Tricks.   A tumbler of water stands on a sheet of paper resting near the edge of the lecture table.   The free end

[1] See "Boy Scout Manual," Boy Scouts of America, New York.

of the paper is held in the right hand at about the level of the table top. The paper between the right hand and the tumbler is struck a sharp downward blow with the left hand. The paper comes out from under the tumbler, and the latter is hardly moved.

Snap a card out from under a coin. If the card rests on a tumbler, the coin falls therein; or the card and coin may be balanced on the finger tip. The coin remains after the card departs. A white silk "tablecloth" may be suddenly jerked from under tools, beakers of colored water, etc., set on the table.

Even the initiated who know the coin-and-card trick may fail in an attempt to remove a slip of paper from beneath a *tall* metal cylinder without upsetting it. The essential element of success is a *sudden* impulse of short duration, more sudden than ordinary hand jerks can give. Place a tall cylinder (4 by $\frac{1}{4}$ in.) on top of a long slip of paper, allowing the end of the slip to project beyond the table edge. Strike the projecting paper a sharp downward blow with the wetted finger tips as the hand descends from a full-arm swing.

Two similar mercury jugs are placed side by side on the table. One contains mercury or lead shot; the other is empty. A student is asked to seize and lift one jug with each hand quickly at the instant a signal is given. The result is surprising to all. Naturally, the student must not know beforehand which jug is heavier.

An apparent departure from Newton's laws of motion may emphasize to students how intuitively they accept those laws from their everyday experience. If a ball is at rest, they expect it to remain at rest; if it is rolling across the table, they expect it to continue in a straight line with only slight retardation by friction. It therefore astonishes an unsuspecting class to see a ball suddenly start rolling or another swerve aside as it rolls across the table. A strong electromagnet planted beneath the lecture table at a spot inconspicuously marked so that the instructor alone knows its position may be controlled with a foot switch so that a steel ball will perform unexpected motions in its field. A piece of plate glass carefully leveled on the table reduces frictional and gravitational influences on the ball.

M-105. Inertia Cart. A horizontal bar is arranged to rotate freely about P, the vertical axis of a post mounted on a cart or car

(Fig. 27).   At the extremities of this bar are pins over which may be slipped cylinders C_1 and C_2 of equal volume but different mass. As the car is accelerated, the greater mass lags behind, but the reverse happens on stopping.

M-106. Inertia Balance. The concept of inertia, as distinct from that of weight, may be clarified by means of an inertia balance[1] in which the force due to gravity plays no part. The balance consists of a horizontal metal bar 20 cm long supported from a heavy stand by two 25-cm spring-steel strips (Fig. 28).

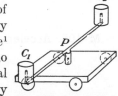

Fig. 27.—Inertia cart.

The body whose inertia is to be determined is set on the horizontal carriage, and the balance is made to vibrate in a horizontal plane. The period of the balance is measured with a stop watch.   The inertia M is then given in terms of the period T by the equation $M = aT^2 - b$, where a and b are positive constants.   Thus the inertias of several bodies, *e.g.*, those comprising a set of weights, may be compared without recourse to the forces of gravity upon

Fig. 28.—Inertia balance.

them.   The constants of the balance may be determined by assigning a value of inertia to some body that is to be taken as a standard.

M-107. Static vs. Dynamic Forces. Drop a 50- to 100-g cylinder on a flat surface of modeling clay, well-worked putty, or soft wax.   Move the cylinder to another spot, and cautiously lay

[1] Schriever, W., *Am. Phys. Teacher*, **5**, 202, 1937.

weights on top of it until a depression of the same depth results. This may necessitate adding many times the weight of the cylinder itself, thus showing the large force brought into play by sudden stopping of the falling cylinder.

NEWTON'S SECOND LAW

M-108. Acceleration on a Horizontal Plane. A car is accelerated along a horizontal track by a string passing over a pulley and tied to a weight. The accelerating weight and the mass of the car may be varied. The acting force may be made of longer duration if the cord passes over a pulley high above the lecture table (Fig. 29). The acceleration may be measured by marking the table with chalk to indicate the position of the car at several successive clicks of a metronome; or the acceleration may be made immediately visible by means

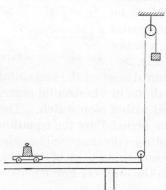

Fig. 29.—The car is accelerated by the descending weight.

of a liquid accelerometer (M-288) carried on the car.

M-109. Negative Acceleration Due to Friction. A block of wood is drawn over the table top by a spring balance and the force of friction observed. Then it is placed on the board of a rigid swing that comes to rest just at the level of the table top (Fig. 30). The swing is drawn aside a known distance, released, and allowed to collide with the table. The block is thus shot from the swing with a known initial velocity and comes to rest after skidding across the table. The acceleration is computed and the force equation checked. If desired, the energy aspect of this experiment may be emphasized, since a measurable amount of potential energy is wasted in frictional work.

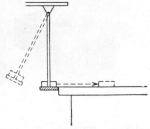

Fig. 30.—Negative acceleration due to friction.

M-110. Atwood's Machine. At the top of a large scale (divisions about 10 cm apart), which reaches from floor to ceiling,

is mounted a light, carefully balanced pulley. Two equal combinations of weights are suspended from the ends of a string
passing over the pulley. About one twenty-fifth of the weight on
one side is removed and placed on the other side. The heavier
weight is raised to the ceiling. A metronome is set beating
seconds. After instructing successive rows of the class to observe
the position of the rising weight at the end of successive seconds,
the instructor counts "zero" as he releases the weight. The first
row observes the position of the weight when the instructor
counts "one," the second row when he counts "two," etc. The
observations of each row are quickly averaged, and the acceleration $(g/25)$ is computed from the observations and compared
with the value obtained from $F = ma$. Allowance for friction
may be made by adding a small weight to the descending side so
that the system moves in the desired direction without acceleration prior to shifting weight from one side to the
other.

M-111. Tension in Atwood's Machine. When
the weights are at rest, each cord is under a tension
equal to the weight it sustains; but when the
weights are released, the tensions in the two sides
become equal, since $m_1(g + a) = m_2(g - a)$ for the
rising and falling weights respectively. This fact
may be shown by hanging the weights from large-
dial spring balances on the two sides.

M-112. Double Atwood's-machine Problem.
Over a light balanced pulley hangs a cord, with
masses of 1 and 2 kg, respectively, at its ends.
This pulley is supported from one end of another
cord, which passes in turn over a fixed pulley with
a 3-kg mass tied to its other end (Fig. 31). The
first pulley is prevented from turning by a pin
between wheel and yoke. Enough mass is added to the 3-kg
mass to balance the suspended pulley, and the class is asked to
predict the motion of the 3-kg mass when the pin is removed
and the two smaller masses are free to accelerate. The arrangement may be hung in front of the blackboard, and the original
positions of the masses marked thereon.[1]

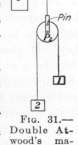

Fig. 31.—
Double At-
wood's ma-
chine.

[1] For the analysis of a similar problem, see W. E. Byerly, "Generalized
Coordinates," p. 19, Ginn and Company, Boston, 1916.

M-113. Climbing-monkey Problem.

"A monkey hangs on a rope that passes over a frictionless pulley to a coconut that weighs just as much as the monkey. How can he get the coconut?" This provocative experiment can be shown with varying degrees of elaborateness. The system consists of two equal masses balanced from the ends of a cord hung over a light fixed pulley. One of the masses is equipped with a mechanism for winding up the cord. As the cord is wound up, *both* masses rise at the same rate.

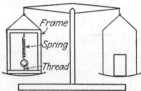

Fig. 32.—Disturbance of equilibrium by acceleration.

In the simplest arrangement, a spring tape measure, or a spring chain such as is used for holding eyeglasses, plays the role of the monkey. In another form, a brass rod, 50 to 75 cm long and weighted at its lower end, is drawn up into a brass tube, into which it fits loosely, by means of an old shade-roller spring. The spring is previously stretched by pushing the rod down and locking it with a trigger. Upon release of the rod, the weight is accelerated upward. A yet more complicated arrangement uses a small electric motor with shaft geared down to a spindle upon which the string may be wound up. This should preferably be a toy motor run with flashlight batteries, in which case the "monkey" is completely isolated, or it may be a more powerful type with the current leads as light as possible and so hung as to impede the "monkey's" progress as little as possible. If an electric motor is used, the direction of motion may be reversed.

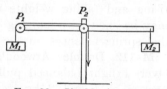

Fig. 33.—If M_1 is at rest or in uniform motion, the balance is in equilibrium.

M-114. Acceleration on a Balance.

A wooden frame is placed upon one table of a platform balance or in one pan of a large beam balance and brought to equilibrium (Fig. 32). Within the frame, a large ball, 3 to 5 kg, is suspended on a spring and pulled, stretching the spring farther, by a string that is tied to the bottom of the frame. The string is burned and the motion of the balance observed.

M-115. Reaction Balance.

A pulley P_1 is fastened to one end of a stiff bar, which is supported as the beam of an equal-arm balance, with a second pulley P_2 centered at the fulcrum (Fig. 33). A mass M_1 is hung from a string passing over the two pulleys, and an equal mass M_2 is hung from the other end of the balance beam. When the end of the string is held fast or is moved with uniform velocity, the balance is in equilibrium. But when the end of the string is pulled so that M_1 moves with acceleration either up or down, the equilibrium is destroyed.

M-116. Galileo's Water Balance.
Galileo suspended from one arm of a beam balance two buckets, one above the other (Fig. 34). The upper contained water, the lower was empty. When the water was allowed to run out of the upper bucket into the lower, Galileo expected to see that arm of the

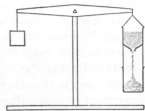

Fig. 34.—Galileo's balance.

balance drop on account of the impact. Actually it rose slightly when the water began to flow, but as soon as the water reached the lower bucket, equilibrium was reestablished. The experiment may also be done with sand.

M-117. Gas-pressure Analogy. Pressure caused by change of momentum of numerous bombarding particles may be shown by

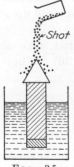

pouring lead shot steadily upon the apex of a cone mounted on a float in a vessel of water (Fig. 35). The resulting transfer of momentum causes a depression of the float. There is a close analogy between this experiment and the kinetic theory of gas pressure, as both the number of the particles striking the cone per second and their velocity may be varied. A similar (gaseous) reaction may be shown by causing an idle electric fan to rotate in the wind stream of another fan.

Fig. 35.—
Gas-pressure
analogy.

ACTION AND REACTION

M-118. Reaction Carts. Two light planks, 6 to 8 ft long, reinforced with cantilevers to prevent excessive bending, are equipped with rubber-tired wheels. Two students stand on the carts holding a rope between them. If the students weigh the same, then as both pull the rope, the carts meet midway between their original positions. The carts are again separated, and the rope is made fast to one cart while the student on the other pulls the rope.　The carts meet at the same spot as before.

A man standing on a cart at rest may start to run along it. The cart moves in the opposite direction.　Conversely a man running along the floor may stop on the cart.　The cart moves, of course, in the direction of his original motion.　With the two carts tied together, two men may start from the ends toward the center. Finally, a man running at *constant* speed may, in the course of crossing the room, run along a cart without moving it, since there is no transfer of momentum if his speed is constant.

M-119. Rocket Car. A heavy medicine ball may be tossed from one man to the other as they stand on two carts, with resulting transfer of momentum.　The two men may throw a baseball back and forth.　One man supplied with a dozen baseballs may throw them at some protected spot on the wall.

M-120. Reaction Swings. Experiments similar to those performed with the reaction carts may be done with swings, consisting of two planks each suspended from the ceiling by means of four equal ropes so that they hang about 6 in. above the floor.　Or a seat may be placed on one swing upon which the demonstrator sits.　He pushes on a heavy iron weight suspended from the ceiling.　In case the demonstrator throws baseballs from one swing, it may be possible by proper timing to build up a considerable amplitude.

M-121. Reaction Cars. Two small cars connected with a rubber band are placed on a track a meter apart (Fig. 36).　They

Fig. 36.—Reaction cars.

are released simultaneously, and the stretched band pulls them together with accelerations inversely proportional to their masses. The masses are adjusted to simple ratios.　The point at which the cars will meet may be predicted; for since the same force acts on each at every instant, the distances traversed are inversely proportional to their masses.

In place of a stretched elastic band, a string may join the two cars.　It passes over two fixed pulleys in the middle of the track and then to a movable pulley attached to a descending weight.

M-122. Cannon Car. A small brass cannon mounted on one
car fires a lead bullet into a block of wood mounted on another
(Fig. 37). The powder is set off by a gas flame on the end of a
long tube. The class should be protected by a sheet of heavy
plate or safety glass. If the masses of
the cars are equal, they will recede from
one another at equal speeds. If the two
cars are tied together with wire, they
will not depart from their original posi-
tions despite the firing of the cannon, showing the equality of
action and reaction.

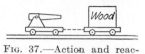

Fig. 37.—Action and reaction.

M-123. Reaction Track. About 4 ft of straight toy track is
mounted on a light board, which in turn is placed on steel rollers.
A toy locomotive of either the spring or electric type and a car or
two, properly weighted, run along the track. The track moves
in the opposite direction, thus showing the resultant reaction.
Extra rollers should be in line to take care of the movement of the
board, which may be beveled on the end to insure its taking the
rollers smoothly.

Conservation of angular momentum (M-184) may be shown in
similar fashion by mounting a circular track on a bicycle wheel
free to revolve about a vertical axis. By changing the loading of
the train, it is possible to control the velocities imparted to both
train and track relative to a fixed point.

IMPACT AND MOMENTUM

M-124. Velocity of Bullet by Ballistic Pendulum. A gun or
revolver carefully mounted fires a bullet into a ballistic pendulum
consisting of a block of wood about a foot long turned to fit
tightly into a length of iron pipe 4 or 5 in. in diameter (Fig. 38).
This pipe is suspended horizontally from the ceiling by four
parallel wires, whose lengths may be adjusted by violin pegs.
The horizontal deflection of the block is recorded by the position
of a light rod, which is pushed by the pendulum into a tube
supported on a stand. It is advisable to push the rod almost to
its final position before firing the gun, in order to avoid spurious
results due to friction or to momentum imparted to the rod. The
equation for the velocity v of the bullet is $v = \dfrac{M + m}{m}\sqrt{\dfrac{g}{l}}d,$

where M is the mass of the pendulum, m the mass of the bullet, l

the length of the supporting wires, and d the displacement of the pendulum.

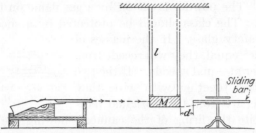

FIG. 38.—Ballistic pendulum.

M-125. Momentum Pendulum. A heavy pendulum bob is suspended from a light wooden framework mounted on a flat board (Fig. 39). On the bottom of the board are two metal strips that rest on steel rollers; these in turn rest across steel rails. When the pendulum oscillates, changing the direction of its momentum, the periodic movement of the frame shows the reaction upon the support.

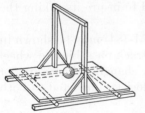

FIG. 39.—Momentum pendulum.

M-126. Momentum Cars. The same effect as with the momentum pendulum (M-125) may be shown by two cars resting on a level track. They are joined by a light elastic band stretched between uprights. A motor mounted on one is geared to a wheel that carries an eccentric arm reaching to the other. With the motor running, the cars alternately separate and approach. The system as a whole is at rest, as is shown by a light rider hung on the elastic band to indicate the point of no motion. The relative masses of the cars may be changed by moving a weight from one to the other, thereby changing the position of the point at rest (center of gravity of the system).

M-127. Impact Pendulums. Two steel or ivory balls are hung by bifilar suspensions. The suspending threads should make a considerable angle with one another, so that the balls swing accurately in a plane. The balls should just be in contact at their equilibrium positions. Velocities at the time of contact are, to a first approximation, proportional to horizontal displacements from rest positions.   Cardboard uprights set on the table help to make these distances evident.   Several different cases of impact may be shown.   In elastic impact with equal masses, one being at rest and the other in motion or both being in motion, the velocities are interchanged.   A bit of wax on the balls makes the collision inelastic with a common final velocity.   In every case, whether elastic or inelastic, momentum is conserved.   Particularly fascinating is the special case of elastic impact with the masses in the ratio of 3:1 and initially colliding with equal but opposite velocities.[1]   The heavier ball is stopped while the lighter ball flies back with twice its former speed.   After the second collision, the balls return to their original state, and the cycle repeats itself.

GRAVITATION

The demonstration of universal gravitational attraction requires apparatus too sensitive for the rough-and-ready work of the lecture room.   However, permanent setups may be mounted on the walls of the laboratory where the students may operate them at their leisure.

M-128. Gravitational Torsion Balance—Cavendish Experiment.   A long torsion pendulum made of a quartz fiber or a fine tungsten wire supports a mirror and light dumbbell suspension bearing two small lead balls (Fig. 40).   The whole is rigidly fixed high on the wall with an optical system of high magnifying power to show the deflections of the mirror.[2]   Sliding on parallel bars are two large lead balls, actuated from below by means of cords, so that their attractions on the suspended balls may be reversed. The period of the torsion pendulum is too long to make a determination of the gravitational constant feasible during a lecture, but the motion of the suspended system under gravitational force may be readily shown by projecting a spot of light from the mirror upon the screen.   The constants of the instrument and the theory of the experiment may be posted near by so that any interested student may actually work out the first figure of the gravitational constant by observing the deflections of the mirror. In demonstrating the principle of the apparatus, a large-scale model of the torsion pendulum may be shown and analyzed.   (M-167).

[1] LEMON, H. B., *Am. Phys. Teacher*, **3**, 36, 1935.
[2] LEMON, H. B., *Am. Phys. Teacher*, **2**, 10, 1934.

M-129. Variation of Pendulum Period with Field of Force.
Suspend an iron ball by a long wire over a large electromagnet,
concealed in a box.   Start the pendulum swinging, and then
energize the magnet.   By placing a rheostat in series with the

Fig. 40.—Cavendish balance.

magnet, the period of the pendulum may be varied over a wide
range.   This experiment simulates the variation of weight with
height and may be used to illustrate the pendulum method of
measuring the mass of the earth.   The observed variations in

period caused by the electromagnet are, of course, far greater than the variations produced by changes in g due to change in altitude.

M-130. Motion under Inverse Square Law of Attraction. Motion of one electrically charged ball in the electrostatic field of another and of one magnet in the magnetic field of another are described in A-62 and A-63. However, the motion is only a crude approximation to planetary motion because of the relatively large and inconstant component of gravitation force present.

M-131. Elliptic Motion with Conservation of Angular Momentum. A steel ball rolled in a glass funnel (M-144) or in a rigid paper cone with axis vertical will, under certain conditions, describe an elliptic motion with conservation of angular momentum and (except for frictional losses) conservation of energy. Differences in kinetic energy at "perihelion" and "aphelion" are accounted for by differences of gravitational potential energy.

WORK AND ENERGY

Most of the experiments already described may be presented from the point of view of energy. This is particularly true of the following experiments listed: 19, 37, 43–47, 82, 109, 110, 112, 161–166, 185, 216, 232–237, 239, 279.

M-132. Galileo's Pendulum Board. Hang a simple pendulum from a peg at the top of the blackboard. Pull the pendulum aside so that it makes an angle of 30 or 40° with the vertical. Draw a horizontal line at the level of the bob. Release the pendulum, and show that it rises again to this line on the opposite side. Now intercept the string supporting the bob in the middle of its swing by a pencil held firmly against the board. The bob, in spite of the shorter radius of swing, rises to the height from which it started. This is true also of the swing in the reverse direction. If the pencil is placed low enough, the bob makes a complete loop.

If desired, the apparatus can be mounted on a board about a meter square, with a dowel inserted in turn into a series of holes arranged vertically below the point of support.

M-133. Pile Driver. Dissipation of potential energy in friction and useful work may be shown by driving a nail into a block of soft wood parallel to the grain, by means of an improvised pile driver, consisting of a 1-lb steel block, 1.5 or 2 in. in diameter. The block is guided by a tube some 2 ft long into which it fits very

loosely.   It is allowed to fall vertically upon the head of the nail.
A series of 10 or 12 blows will drive the nail into the block.   A
measurable advance is shown after each blow.   An enlarged
shadow projection of the nail makes the motion clearly visible to
the class.   A rough plot of friction against length of nail in the
wood clearly emphasizes how work is the integral of force times
distance.

M-134. Brake Horsepower Test.   A standard test of the
power delivered by a motor can be carried out in a few minutes.
A pulley at least 3 in. in diameter is attached to a $\frac{1}{2}$-hp motor.
A strip of leather belt or brake-lining material about a foot long
is looped around the pulley like a belt and is attached to the hooks
of two spring balances, one of which is made fast to the ring of a
turnbuckle so that the tension on the belt may be adjusted.   The
delivered horsepower is computed from the measured values of
pulley diameter d, revolutions per second n, and difference
in tension on the balances $T_1 - T_2$, by the equation

$$\text{HP} = \frac{\pi n d (T_1 - T_2)}{550},$$

where d is in feet and $T_1 - T_2$ in pounds.

M-135. Power Developed by a Person.   A brake similar to
that described in the preceding experiment may be fitted over a
wooden disk with a metal rim about 2 ft in diameter.   A slate
disk or even an old grindstone may be substituted.   The disk is
mounted on substantial bearings and fitted with a crank.   The
tension in the brake is adjusted so that not over three turns per
second are required to absorb the power output of professor or
student.   A student may, of course, compute his own "horsepower" by measuring the time required to run up two or three
flights of stairs and by combining this observation with that of
his weight and of the height he climbs.

M-136. Power Bicycle.   The rear sprocket of an old bicycle is
firmly bolted to the end of a wooden axle, 2 ft long and 2 in. in
diameter, mounted in suitable bearings.   The axle is driven by
the chain from the front sprocket of the bicycle.   A stout rope
made fast to this axle passes over a pulley in the ceiling and is
attached to a heavy weight.   By measuring the distance the
weight rises in a given time, the power developed by the bicycle
rider may be determined.

ROTATION

For many of the experiments that follow, a rotating table with good bearings is essential. This may be a stool on which the instructor may stand or a chair suspended from a swivel in the ceiling. In some laboratories, such a stool has been constructed from the front-wheel bearing and wheel of an automobile.

Various types of motor-driven variable-speed rotator are available. A small motor, such as is used in electric fans, whose axle is fitted with a rubber stopper, is convenient for spinning gyroscopes and other apparatus. A small hand drill is sufficient for producing rotation in many instances.

M-137. Centrifugal Force vs. Centripetal Force. A wooden ball is rotated by hand in a horizontal plane at the end of a thread 2 ft long. The demonstrator holds in his other hand a long, sharp knife with which to cut the thread. While swinging the ball overhead, he discusses with the class what will happen to the path of the ball if he cuts the thread at some predetermined point. Many students have the feeling that centrifugal force is a force that will continue to act after the constraining centripetal force vanishes. The demonstrator stands in such a position that the ball would fly into the class if centrifugal force continued to act after centripetal force ceased. The ball, of course, continues tangentially after the thread is cut and may be made to strike some protected spot.

M-138. Measurement of Centripetal Force. The magnitude of centripetal force required to constrain a body to a circular path may be shown with very simple apparatus, consisting of a 20-cm length of glass or metal tube through which passes a 1-m length of fishline. To one end of the line is attached a 1-kg weight; to the other end, a wooden ball or other object weighing 50 to 100 g. The tube is held in a vertical position and moved by hand in such a way as to set the light ball rotating in a horizontal circular path. The weight is lifted from the floor or table by centrifugal force. By timing the number of revolutions per minute with the ball swinging around a circle of known radius (marked on the string), it may be shown within 1 or 2 per cent that the number of revolutions per minute is inversely proportional to the square root of the radius of rotation. The period of revolution is $t = 2\pi\sqrt{ml/Mg}$, where m and M are the small and large masses respectively, and

l is the length of the cord from the axis to the center of gravity of the revolving mass.   Commercial apparatus in which the force is measured by the extension of a spring or by lifting an axial weight may also be shown (M-177).

M-139. High-speed Chains. A loop of brass safety chain is made to fit rather loosely on a 6-in. wooden disk fastened to the shaft of a high-speed motor with controlling resistance.   The chain is gradually given a high rotary speed and then cautiously forced off the disk with a screw driver.   The rotating chain maintains its circular shape as it rolls across the lecture table. If a piece of 2-by-4 or other obstacle is placed in its path, the chain will bounce like a rigid hoop.   If a longer piece of chain, looped over the disk and an idler pulley held by hand, is set going and released, it will roll across the table, preserving its original oval shape.   The necessary centrifugal force and the normal component of the tension providing it are each inversely proportional to the radius of curvature of the chain at any point.   It is well to have a rubber mat under the drive wheel so that the chain may acquire its speed of translation quickly without scratching the table.   Caution is necessary, as these chains sometimes burst or fly off in unexpected directions.

M-140. Paper Saw. A 6-in. disk of typewriter paper spun at high speed possesses surprising rigidity.   It will sound metallic when struck and will cut through other paper.   Larger disks of Bristol board or heavier paper may be used to cut through wood.

M-141. Rotating Candle Flame. A lighted candle protected from air currents by a lamp chimney is placed on the rotating table at some distance from the axis.   The flame will be found to point toward the center of the table.   A flame placed 1 ft from the axis and rotated at 1 rps shows the effect nicely.

M-142. Paraboloid of Revolution. A cylindrical glass jar is accurately centered on a rotating table.   Colored water is placed in it, and the cylinder is rotated.   After viscous forces have brought the water to a steady state of revolution, the surface becomes a paraboloid of revolution (Fig. 41).   If the jar is just half full at the beginning, the vertex of the paraboloid will reach the bottom of the jar just as the liquid reaches its upper edge.   A short lighted candle on the end of a stick may be lowered to the bottom of the jar to show the absence of liquid at the center.

Clear water covered with colored castor oil so as to fill completely a cylindrical jar closed at the top will, on rotation, show a paraboloid of oil surrounded with water.   Any two immiscible liquids of different densities may be used.

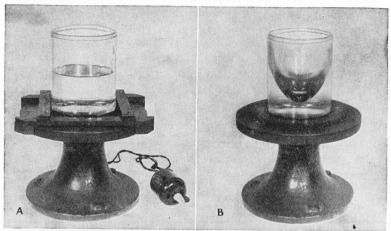

Fig. 41.—*A.* Battery jar with water at rest.   *B,* same in rapid rotation showing paraboloid of revolution.

M-143. Parabolic Mercury Mirror.   A circular pool of mercury may be rotated to make a parabolic mirror (L-25).   The focal length of the mirror is $g/8\pi^2n^2$, where n is the speed of rotation in revolutions per second.   A 6-v automobile headlight bulb is placed above the center of the mirror, and the mercury is rotated at constant speed for several minutes.   The height of the bulb is then adjusted until the reflected light just fills a circle of the same diameter as the pool of mercury.   The measured height of the bulb above the vertex of the mirror and the computed focal length should agree closely.

M-144. Motion on a Banked Curve.   A steel ball rolled down a short incline enters tangentially into a large glass funnel with axis vertical.   The ball spirals downward but rapidly increases its speed of revolution until it reaches an equilibrium level where it revolves in a horizontal plane.   As its speed diminishes owing to friction, it slowly spirals to the bottom of the funnel.   This simple experiment may be used to show why curved roadways and railroad tracks should be banked.

M-145. A variation of this experiment consists in throwing a steel ball or shooting it with a blowgun tangentially into a megaphone or other large conical tube with axis horizontal. The ball is shot toward the narrow end of the cone, but contrary to the expectations of the class, it emerges from the wide end. The initial direction of the ball should make a small angle with a generatrix of the cone. It is evident that the ball, as it spirals into the narrow end of the megaphone, encounters a component of centrifugal force directed toward the wide end. It is virtually impossible to make the ball emerge from the mouthpiece unless it is initially directed very close to a generatrix or unless the speed of the ball is *low*. High speed defeats itself.

M-146. Centrifugal Force in Pendulum Support Wire. A heavy iron ball is supported by a wire whose breaking strength is less than twice the weight of the ball. The ball is pulled aside by a force at right angles to the wire until the wire makes an angle of 60° with the vertical, whereupon it is released. The tension in the wire increases as the ball descends in its circular path, until the wire breaks. For if the ball is released and the supporting wire does *not* break, the tension in the wire becomes twice the weight of the ball when it passes through the rest position.

M-147. Flattening of the Earth. The conventional demonstration of the circular spring hoop that flattens on rotation may be varied by rotating a large ball of clay and glycerin suspended by cloth tape from a rotator. The ball will flatten perceptibly upon slow rotation, and as the speed increases, it will burst. A solid sponge-rubber ball suspended from the shaft of a motor by a short length of piano wire and spun at high speed may be deformed until the ratio of its equatorial to its polar diameter is greater than 2:1. When rotation ceases, the ball resumes its spherical shape.

M-148. Box-office Value of Centrifugal Force. A celluloid doll clothed with a full skirt, the hem of which is loaded with shot or beads, is set into rotation by a hand drill. A slight spin shows why front seats in a theater are preferred.

M-149. Stroboscopic Demonstration of Dynamic Distortion. A wheel with eight spokes is cut from sponge rubber $\frac{1}{4}$ in. thick. One of the spokes is severed near the rim of the wheel. The wheel is rotated at high speed on the shaft of a motor and is viewed first under steady and then under intermittent light

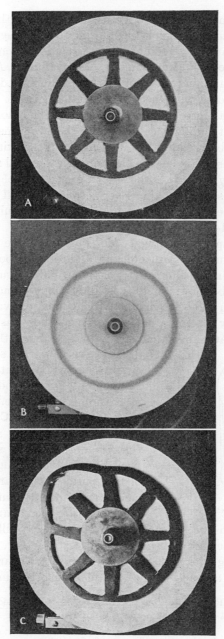

Fig. 42.—Rubber wheel with one spoke cut. A, at rest; B, rotating rapidly and illuminated with a steady light; C, same as B but under stroboscopic illumination, showing distortion.

(S-49).　The motion of the wheel is "stopped" with the strobo-scopic light, and the large distortion due to centrifugal force that failed to appear under ordinary light is made evident (Fig. 42).[1]

M-150. Speed of Rotation by Manometer. A U-shaped manometer containing water or mercury is mounted with one of its arms coincident with the axis of a rotating table.　The neces-sary centripetal force on the liquid in the horizontal tube is introduced by the difference in level in the two arms, a quantity that is easily observed by the fall of liquid in the axial arm of the U.　The depression in level of the liquid in the axial arm of the U is $\Delta h = \omega^2 r^2/4g$, where r is the length of the base of the U, and ω is the angular speed in radians per second.　It will be observed that Δh is independent of the density of the liquid filling the manometer (M-289).

M-151. Simple Centrifugal Air Pump. Three sheet-metal disks are set mutually perpendicular and rotated about a vertical axis along the intersection of two of them.　The resulting motion of the air may be shown, first, by holding a lighted match over the pole of rotation and observing how the flame is drawn downward; and second, by placing a flat paper ring, whose inside diameter is a little greater than that of the disks, around the equatorial

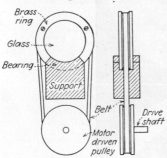

disk, where it will be supported by air pressure.　(This latter behavior is, incidentally, a good illustration of Bernoulli's principle.)

M-152. Projection Centrifuge. The clarification of a liquid by centrifuging may be shown by a projection-cell centrifuge consisting of two parallel, circular glass plates cemented in a brass ring (Fig. 43).[2]

Fɪɢ. 43.—Projection centrifuge.

The plates are 1 cm apart and 7 cm in diameter, with the space between them nearly filled with the liquid to be separated.　*Lotio alba* is satisfactory.　The cell is held between guides and supported on a brass bearing of about 90°.　There is a groove on the outside of the brass ring to take the

---

[1] Hɪᴛᴄʜᴄᴏᴄᴋ, R. C., *Elec. Jour.*, **32,** 529, 1935.　Acknowledgment is made to *The Electrical Journal* for permission to reproduce the illustrations in Fig. 42.

[2] Eʀɪᴋsᴏɴ, H. A., *Am. Phys. Teacher*, **6,** 39, 1938.

drive belt from a small motor-driven pulley.   As the cell rotates, an air bubble appears first at the center; then a halo begins to surround the bubble as the liquid clears; finally the clear liquid is surrounded by a ring of dark precipitate.

M-153. Model Centrifuge.   A glass tube 1 in. in diameter and 12 in. long is bent as shown (Fig. 44).   It is partly filled with water, and two balls, one of aluminum, the other of cork, are sealed inside it.   The cork floats in one arm while the aluminum rests at the bottom.   But when the tube is whirled, the aluminum is thrown to the outer end of one arm, while the cork floats on the *under* side of the water in the other arm, thus illus-

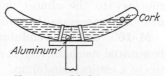

Fig. 44.—Model centrifuge; rotation causes cork to float on under side of water.

trating the separation according to densities in a centrifuge. Mercury instead of aluminum and a cork ball in each arm will show the same effect with better dynamic balance.

M-154. Whirling Bucket of Water.   Perhaps not all students are acquainted with the time-honored trick of swinging a bucket of water in a vertical circle at arm's length without spilling the water.

M-155. Dime on Coat Hanger.   A wire coat hanger hangs by its hook from the demonstrator's forefinger.   A dime is laid on the middle of the horizontal bar of the hanger, and the hanger is then whirled in a vertical plane.   With a little practice, this may be done without dislodging the coin.

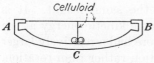

Fig. 45.—Centrifugal force trick—how can both balls be put simultaneously in the end pockets?

M-156. Centrifugal Force Puzzle. Two steel balls in a narrow box are to be caught in two indentations A and B at opposite ends of the box (Fig. 45).   One may try in vain to accomplish this result unless one knows how "to make a force act in two directions at once," simply by spinning the box about its midpoint C.   One ball goes to each end instantly.

M-157. Loop-the-loop.   A ball or small car rolls down a steep incline and thence safely around a vertical circle.   The experiment offers opportunity for the discussion of dynamic equilibrium and the minimum speed for safe passage of the top point of the circle.

M-158. Centrifugal Governor. Models of Watt's regulator or centrifugal governor are commercially available or readily constructed.

M-159. Cream Separator. A spherical glass bowl containing mercury and colored water is whirled. The mercury forms an equatorial band around the bowl, with the water in two zones above and below it (and also nearer to the axis of rotation). But contrary to the almost universal expectation of students, the mercury represents the milk and not the cream!

M-160. Conical Pendulum. A ball on the end of a cord may be rotated mechanically at steady speed to show the characteristics of a conical pendulum. The experiment offers in simple form the chief elements of dynamical equilibrium, in which the bob is balanced under the force of gravity, the tension in the strings, and the dynamic reaction (centrifugal force). The apparatus of M-138 is essentially a conical pendulum in which the centripetal force on the bob is measured by the weight hung at the center.

MOMENT OF INERTIA

M-161. Racing Rollers. Prepare two tin cans, one with a lead core surrounded by wood, the other with a wood core surrounded by lead. Simple calculations will enable one to make the masses of these cans equal. In external appearance they are identical, and a balance will show that they have the same mass; but they roll with different accelerations down the same inclined plane. The can with the lead core always wins the race; but if both cans roll up a second incline, they reach the same height. It is evident, therefore, that both had the same kinetic energy at the bottom but that the can with the lead core had a relatively larger fraction of its kinetic energy in translation rather than rotation.

In a similar manner, balls, rings, and disks may be raced down the same incline, or their times of descent over a measured distance may be taken with a stop watch. The dependence of acceleration upon moment of inertia and the distribution of kinetic energy between rotation and translation may be discussed.

M-162. Winning Ball. All solid spheres, regardless of diameter or density, descend a smooth inclined plane with the same acceleration. A hollow sphere will always lose a race with a solid sphere. But if a hollow sphere, such as a tennis ball, is filled with mercury, it will always win against a solid sphere, because a larger proportion of its kinetic energy is energy of translation. A hollow steel roller filled with mercury will likewise accelerate faster than a solid cylinder, or even than a solid sphere. The mercury partakes only partially of the rotational motion of the body. A convenient mercury-filled roller may be made by sealing mercury in a test tube that fits snugly inside a brass tube whose end plates may be soldered. The mercury is thus prevented from amalgamating with the solder or the brass.

M-163. Weary Roller. A cylindrical tube partly filled with fine dry sand or powdered tungsten will exhibit the novel phenomenon of growing weary of rolling downhill. At the start, the contents of the cylinder are tamped into one end by setting the cylinder vertically. It then rolls freely, but as it rolls, some of the powder shakes down and retards the roller by internal friction. It may even stop on the incline. The inclined plane should not be too steep. One may match such a loaded cylinder with a hollow one of equal mass and dimensions, so that the loaded cylinder may either win or lose a race, depending upon the position of its load.

M-164. Falling Spool. A spool, such as is used for wire, is allowed to fall and unwind a thread held from above. It thus spins as it falls, and its acceleration is far less than the acceleration of gravity. A spool with heavy rim (large moment of inertia) and small axle will descend very slowly. The dependence of acceleration upon moment of inertia and torque may be made evident by the use of spools having different moments of inertia and axles of different diameters. To insure rotation about the axis of the spool only, it is well to support the spool by two threads wrapped around opposite ends of the axle. Although the descent is slow, the spool will rise again nearly to the height from which it was dropped if, after descending to the end of its threads, it winds up the threads in the opposite direction. The tension in the threads is less than the weight of the spool whether it is rising or falling, as may be shown by hanging the spool from a spring balance.

M-165. Rolling Spool. A spool consisting of two brass disks 3 in. in diameter connected by a 2-in. axle $\frac{1}{2}$ in. in diameter rolls on its axle down a narrow board. Its acceleration is very small because of the large moment of inertia. A rubber mat is placed on the lecture table at the point where the disk first makes con-

tact, at which point the spool suddenly leaps forward as its
kinetic energy of rotation changes in large measure to kinetic
energy of translation.   If a second incline is so placed that the
spool rolls up it on the disks, it will be found that the spool rises
(nearly) to the level from which it started, but in far less time.

M-166. Angular-acceleration Machine.   The close analogies
between angular and linear acceleration, torque and force, and
moment of inertia and mass may be emphasized by showing the
effect of increased moment of inertia upon angular acceleration
when torque and mass remain constant.   Two equal masses
(1 kg) with setscrews are arranged to slide along a rod set perpendicular to a horizontal axle so that they may be fixed at

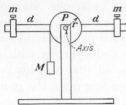

various equal distances from the axis of
rotation (Fig. 46).   A mass M tied to a
string wrapped around a pulley P of
radius r produces a torque Q that gives the
system an angular acceleration.   The
torque may be varied by changing either
M or r.   The decrease of angular accelera-

FIG.   46.—Angular ac-
celeration of the masses
m, m is produced by a
measurable torque.

tion α with constant torque but with
increased distance of the masses m from
the axis (increased moment of inertia I)
is made evident.   The device may be used, like Atwood's
machine (M-110) in translational motion, to check the
relation $Q = I\alpha$ for rotation.   For example, by timing the
descent of M over measured distances h with a stop watch, it is
possible to show that t^2 is proportional to h, that the linear
acceleration a of M is constant, and that the angular acceleration
$\alpha = a/r$ is also constant.   By using different accelerating masses
or different radii, α may be shown to be proportional to the
applied torque.[1]   Next, by varying the distance d of the movable
masses m from the axis, it may be shown that α is inversely
proportional to d^2.   Finally, if other masses m of the same figure
but of different density are used, it may be shown that α is proportional to $1/m$, and therefore that $Q = kmd^2\alpha$.

A ball-bearing bicycle hub serves as a good axle for this apparatus.   If the cross rod is made of tubing and if the masses m are
not placed too near the axis, it is possible to consider the moment

[1] The torque must be corrected for the linear acceleration of M;
$Q = Mr(g - a)$.

of inertia of the system as that of two point masses m at a distance d from the axis without introducing an error of more than 1 or 2 per cent. The apparatus may also be used for precise laboratory work.

M-167. Torsion Pendulum. The period of a torsion pendulum, $t = 2\pi\sqrt{I/Q_0}$, depends upon I, the moment of inertia of the suspended system, and upon Q_0, the torsion constant of the supporting wire. The suspended system may consist, as in M-166, of a cross rod carrying equal, movable masses whose distances from the support wire may be varied; the rod is rigidly clamped to a suitable torsion rod or wire. By changing the position of the masses by a known amount, and by timing the period of the pendulum both before and after shifting the weights, it is a simple matter to compute Q_0 and the moment of inertia from the two observed times and the known *change* of moment of inertia.[1] The torsion pendulum offers a standard method of determining the moment of inertia of an irregular object about any axis passing through its center of gravity.

M-168. Stable Axes of Rotation. A hand drill held vertically is used to rotate loops of rope or chain, supported by single wires. As the speed of rotation is increased, the object rotated assumes an axis about which its moment of inertia is maximum. The axis of rotation always passes vertically through the center of gravity of the object, even though the point of support may be some distance away. The rope or chain that otherwise hangs limp will, on rotation, take up a circular form in a horizontal plane. A stick supported from one end, or a hoop supported from a point on its periphery, will similarly revolve in a horizontal plane. If the demonstrator is adept in the use of a lariat, the same principle may be shown, or he may be successful in spinning a pie plate on the end of a stick.

M-169. Earth-Moon System. The combination of centrifugal torques that makes the chains and sticks of M-168 behave as they do may also be called upon to make a dynamic model of the earth and moon perform, demonstrating in particular how the system rotates about its common center of gravity. A 6-in. metal map globe of the earth is connected by a rigid tube 2 ft long to a

---

[1] For details of this computation see, *e.g.*, Millikan, Roller, and Watson "Mechanics, Molecular Physics, Heat, and Sound," p. 351, Ginn & Company, 1937.

smaller sphere representing the moon (Fig. 47). The system is supported by a wire attached at the midpoint of the line of centers, not at the center of gravity. When the system is set rotating by a hand drill whose chuck holds the end of the wire, the two spheres revolve in horizontal planes about the common center of gravity of the system, which may be marked appropriately to make it visible. The demonstration may be made more impressive if small lights are arranged at the upper poles of the two spheres and a third light at the center of gravity. Flashlight dry cells are enclosed in the larger globe. The light at the

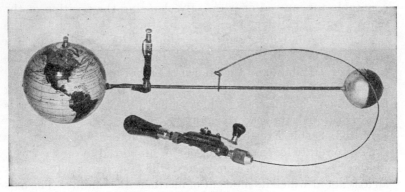

Fig. 47.—Earth-Moon system.

center of gravity remains stationary while the two lights on the globes revolve around it in small and large circles.

An apparatus consisting of two balls of different mass arranged to slide on a rod so that their common center of gravity coincides with the axis of rotation is commercially available, but its adjustment is critical.

CONSERVATION OF ANGULAR MOMENTUM

M-170. Constancy of Axis. In the absence of external torque, the angular momentum of a rotating body remains constant in both direction and magnitude. The constancy of direction may be shown by a spinning gyroscope supported in gimbals providing freedom of motion about three mutually perpendicular axes (M-192). If the axis of the spinning gyroscope is set in any chosen direction, it will maintain that direction while the stand on which it is supported is carried along a circuitous path.

M-171. A simpler apparatus consists of a 6-in. wooden disk supported by a loop of string passing through two holes drilled $\frac{1}{2}$ in. apart on either side of the center of the disk. The disk may be set into rotation in the manner of the familiar toy, by holding one end of the string loop in each hand with the disk midway between the hands. The string is twisted a few turns, and then by properly timed pulls the disk is set revolving at high speed about a horizontal axis, first in one direction, then in the other. At the instant when the disk comes to a stop before reversing its motion, the string is moved into a vertical position and again pulled. The disk reaches its highest angular speed when the cord is unwound, and while spinning it drops to the lower end of the loop. The loop is released at this end, and the spinning disk may then be swung around in almost any manner by the upper end of the loop without changing the direction of its axis, which remains vertical. This constancy of axis may be contrasted with the random motion of the disk when it is not spinning.

M-172. How the Tail Wags the Dog. The demonstrator stands upon the revolving stool and swings a baseball bat. The law of conservation of angular momentum requires that, as the bat is given angular momentum in one direction, something else must acquire equal angular momentum in the opposite direction. The result is not conducive to the maintenance of professorial dignity.

M-173. Rotary Action and Reaction. The periodic changes of angular momentum imparted to the balance wheel of a watch by its spring mechanism necessitate equal and opposite changes in some other body. This fact may be made evident by suspending a pocket watch by its ring from a nail filed to a sharp edge. If the period of the watch swinging as a pendulum from this nail is commensurate with the period of the balance wheel, a large amplitude of swing of the watch as a whole results. It is possible to bring the two periods to resonance by equipping the watch with an adjustable counterweight. The watch may also be supported in a horizontal position by a torsion wire perpendicular to its face, so that its period as a torsion pendulum agrees with the period of its balance wheel.

The same effect may be shown without the necessity of tuning by simply laying the watch face down on a smooth surface. The watch as a whole oscillates to and fro through a small angle with the period of the balance wheel. The motion may be made visible by reflecting a beam of light from a small mirror mounted perpendicularly on the back of the watch.

M-174. The axles of two machines of the type described in M-166 are connected by a spring from a window-curtain roller (Fig. 48). The spring is wound up by turning one machine in the proper direction; then both machines are released simultaneously.

Fig. 48.—Rotary action and reaction.

Their senses of rotation are opposite, and their angular accelerations are inversely proportional to their moments of inertia.

M-175. How a Cat Turns Around in Midair. After attempting in vain to turn around while standing on the rotating stool, the demonstrator shows how it may be accomplished by variation of moment of inertia. He may turn himself completely around by extending his arms, executing a turn to the left, retracting his arms, executing a turn to the right, and repeating the process a number of times. A 5- or 10-lb weight held in the hands makes possible greater change in moment of inertia and hence allows one to turn around in fewer motions. It is important to show that even though the demonstrator succeeds in moving through an angle, he has had at no time a resultant angular momentum. That is, if he stops his arm and trunk movements at any instant, his net angular velocity should be zero.

The manner in which the cat executes a turn in midair may be discussed with the aid of a wooden model consisting of two pieces of 2-by-4 representing the hind- and forequarters of the cat, with appropriately designed hind and fore feet and a head, each with proper anatomical degrees of freedom.

M-176. Pirouette. The demonstrator stands on the rotating stool with arms extended and a 5- or 10-lb weight in each hand. He is given a small angular speed by an assistant, and as he lowers his arms his speed increases greatly. Since angular momentum is conserved, the decrease of moment of inertia necessitates higher angular velocity.

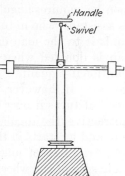

M-177. A mechanical apparatus for showing the pirouette effect is available commercially. It consists of two weights free to slide on a horizontal rod that is pivoted to rotate about a vertical axis (Fig. 49). The system is set into rotation with the weights at the ends of the rod, after which the weights are pulled toward the center by strings that pass over pulleys to a handle held at the center above the rod. As the weights approach the center, the angular speed of the system increases.

Fig. 49.—If the handle is raised while the horizontal rod is rotating, the weights are moved toward the center and the angular speed increases.

M-178. Bicycle Wheel and Rotating Stand. The demonstrator stands on a rotating stool and holds before him the front wheel of a bicycle equipped with handles on both ends of its axle. The wheel is held in a vertical plane passing through the axis of the stool. If the demonstrator spins the wheel, no rotation of the stool results; but if he then turns the spinning wheel into a horizontal plane, he will rotate in the opposite sense to the spin of the wheel. Turning the wheel over through 180° reverses his direction of motion; bringing it back to the vertical stops him. If he starts the wheel while it is held in a horizontal plane, he immediately acquires equal and opposite angular momentum. In this case, the equality of the two momenta is shown by the fact that the demonstrator stops rotating if he turns the wheel to a vertical plane while it continues to spin or if he stops the wheel while it is in a horizontal plane.

An electric motor with a flywheel mounted on the rotating stand with its axis vertical may show some of the same effects but less spectacularly.

M-179. "Quanta of Angular Momentum." It is interesting to show that angular momentum is a commodity that may be passed back and forth across the counter. The demonstrator stands at rest on the rotating stool. His assistant hands him a bicycle wheel spinning rapidly about a vertical axis. Nothing happens until the man on the stool turns the wheel over, whereupon he acquires angular velocity. He hands the wheel back to his assistant, who in turn rotates the axis through 180° and again hands it to the man on the stool. The angular velocity of the man is doubled when he turns the wheel over a second time. Additional "quanta" may be given to him by repeating the process. If, however, the assistant fails to turn the wheel over once but turns it over each time thereafter, the process becomes subtractive; the angular velocity of the demonstrator decreases to zero, and he starts in the other direction. In this manner, six or eight transfers of angular momentum may take place with a single spin of the wheel.

M-180. Baseballs or billiard balls may be thrown or caught at arm's length by the demonstrator as he stands on the rotating stool while his assistant stands on the floor. Each throw or each catch by the same hand increases the angular momentum of the demonstrator; he may decrease it or start himself in the other direction by catching the balls or throwing them with the other hand (other side of the axis). It would be less hazardous for the demonstrator to supply himself with a dozen baseballs that he may throw at a protected spot on the wall, thus illustrating by analogy the principle of the rocket car (M-119).

M-181. How to Work Up in a Swing—"Full-giant Swing." Pendular motion is a type of rotary motion and is, of course, governed by the same laws. How can one acquire large amplitude of motion in a swing without touching any external object? A simple answer to this question may be given by showing the work up of a croquet ball on the end of a long cord that passes through a screw eye in the ceiling or other rigid support (Fig. 50). It is well to attach to the cord a small wooden bead or other stop

above the screw eye so that the ball cannot descend beyond a
predetermined height, although it may be raised by pulling on the
cord.   It is possible to make the ball increase its amplitude of
swing by properly timed pulls on the cord at A as it passes
through the lowest point of its path.

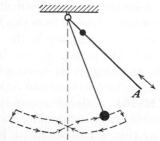

If the ball is raised a few inches each
time it passes through the bottom
point and is lowered to the stop each
time it reaches an end of its swing, it
will soon acquire a large amplitude.
Reversal of this process will diminish
the amplitude.

If, after the ball has acquired a
large amplitude of swing, the cord is
shortened sufficiently, the ball may be
made to swing over the top in a full
circle, just as the gymnast executes

Fig. 50.—By pulling the
cord at A so that the pendulum
bob follows the path shown,
its amplitude of swing is
increased.

a "full-giant" swing.   Naturally the screw-eye support must be
located so as to afford sufficient space overhead if this last
experiment is to be attempted.

M-182. A closer approximation to the actual case of a person

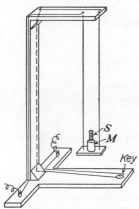

working up in a swing is afforded by
an electrically operated swing in which
the moment of inertia is changed in
proper phase by raising an iron weight
with an electromagnet.   The swing is
supported by wires a meter long that
serve as current leads to an electromagnet M (Fig. 51) situated on the seat.
A movable iron core is kept above the
magnet by a compression spring S.   A
key of the push-button type is mounted
on the base of the apparatus to enable
the operator to energize the magnet at

Fig. 51.—Model to illus-
trate work up in a swing.

will.   The swing is given a small amplitude of motion, and then as it leaves

the top of its swing, the magnet is energized, thus pulling the
iron core down (representing the crouching position of the
swinger).   As the swing passes through the bottom point,
the switch is opened, and the spring raises the iron core.   The

amplitude may thus be built up as previously described (M-181).

M-183. Reaction Engines. The earliest type of steam engine (Hero of Alexandria, 120 B.C.) was a reaction type that may be represented by a cylindrical boiler pivoted on a vertical axle. Four tubes emerge from this boiler radially, and each has a nozzle directed tangentially in the same sense. When steam is generated in the boiler, some of it is forced out through the nozzles. The escaping steam exerts a reaction upon the steam in the tube, and the boiler is set into rotation.

M-184. A simple apparatus showing the reaction principle of the rotary lawn sprinkler consists of a tall tin can mounted on a float that is ballasted with lead to keep it upright. Two tubes emerge from the bottom of the can at opposite ends of a diameter and are bent in the same sense at their ends. When the can is filled with water, the jets from the tubes react upon the can to set it in rotation. If these two tubes are closed with stoppers and water is allowed to flow out of a straight radial tube, the can is driven sidewise. Instead of the float, a thread may be used to support the can.

The reaction of an electric engine upon a circular track free to rotate has been described elsewhere (M-123).

M-185. Transfer of Rotatory Kinetic Energy by Friction. A heavy wheel (gyroscope) is pivoted on a vertical axis in a balanced framework (Fig. 52) that is supported by a thread as shown. The wheel is given a spin and the framework released. As the wheel gradually slows down because of friction in its bearings, the framework as a whole takes up rotation with conservation of angular momentum.

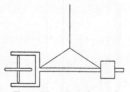

FIG. 52.—As the spinning gyroscope slows down, the framework takes up the rotation.

M-186. Paradox of Rotation. Whenever the moment of inertia I of a rotating system changes, one must examine carefully whether there is conservation of momentum ($I\omega$) or conservation of kinetic energy ($\frac{1}{2}I\omega^2$); for both $I\omega$ and $\frac{1}{2}I\omega^2$ cannot remain constant when I changes. For example, if a ball on the end of a cord is set rolling upon the lecture table and the cord is then allowed to wrap itself around a vertical rod, the ball describes a spiral path of decreasing radius. Its kinetic energy is conserved (barring frictional losses); hence, its angular momentum must decrease. In this case, angular momentum is transferred to the earth by reason of the torque applied to the rod by centrifugal force. By contrast, let the ball be given the same initial speed, but let the cord be shortened by pulling it through a hole in the lecture table. In this case, angular momentum is conserved in the ball, and the kinetic energy of the ball *increases*, even though the ball describes nearly the same path.[1] The additional energy comes, of course, from the work done in pulling the cord. The great increase in speed, both angular and linear, in this latter case is amazing.

GYROSCOPIC MOTION

M-187. Precession. Most of the phenomena of precession may be shown with a bicycle wheel equipped with handles on the ends of its axle (M-178). The wheel is given a spin by hand and one handle is slipped into a loop of string for support. When the other handle is released, the wheel precesses about a vertical axis while its own horizontal axis of spin slowly descends toward the vertical. If the precession is accelerated by pressure on the unsupported end of the axle in the direction of precession, the center of gravity rises. As the spin of the wheel diminishes, the wheel precesses more rapidly; or the precession may be made more rapid by adding a weight to the unsupported end of the axle. If the other end of the axle is supported in the loop of string, the sense of spin being unchanged, the direction of precession will reverse. From these simple phenomena, several of the important rules of gyroscopic motion may be worked out, such as the relation between directions of spin, torque, and precession and the relation between the magnitudes of spin, torque, and precession (M-188).

Since angular momentum is a vector quantity that may be conveniently represented by a vector parallel to the axis of spin, the combination of two angular momenta may be treated by the parallelogram law. Thus, whenever a gyroscope is acted upon by a torque tending to produce rotation about an axis perpendicular to the axis of spin (or of precession), the gyroscope will precess about a third axis perpendicular to the other two.

---

[1] For a more refined method of insuring duplication of path in the two cases, see R. M. Sutton, *Am. Phys. Teacher*, **4**, 26, 1936.

M-188. Fundamental Precession Equation. The fundamental relationship $Q = I\Omega\omega$, where Q is the torque producing precession, I is the moment of inertia of the spinning gyroscope, Ω is the angular velocity of precession, and ω is the angular velocity of spin, may be shown with fair precision by applying a known torque to a balanced gyroscope (Fig. 53). The movable weight W with setscrew enables one to balance the top or to apply a measurable constant torque about a horizontal axis through the pivot. The angular velocity of precession is measured directly

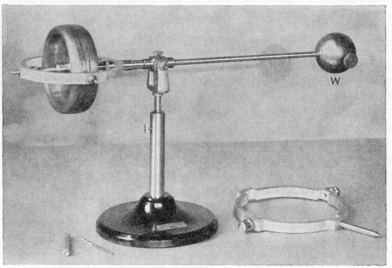

Fig. 53.—Gyroscope with movable torque weight W.

by timing the precession through one or more revolutions; the angular speed of rotation is measured by illuminating the spinning gyroscope with intermittent light from a neon lamp run on a 60-cycle circuit. Six spots are painted on the wheel at the corners of a regular hexagon whose center coincides with the axis.[1] The precession is timed for two or more speeds of spin to show that the product of these two angular speeds is constant (since moment of inertia and torque are also constant). The torque may be varied and the process repeated.

[1] For example, with the neon lamp giving 120 flashes per sec on a 60-cycle circuit, the spots will appear to lie on the corners of a stationary hexagon at wheel speeds of 20, 40, 60, 80, . . . rps.

M-189. Balanced Gyroscope. The bicycle wheel with handles
may be supported by loops of
string tied to a crossbar that is
hung by a single string from the
ceiling, so that the wheel is in
stable equilibrium whether spinning or not. In this case, the
torque that produces precession
may be applied by pushing the
ends of the axle horizontally in
opposite directions by the aid of
two sticks held in the hands (Fig.
54). Since the axis of torque is
now vertical, the axis of precession is horizontal and perpendicular to the axis of spin.

If preferred, the wheel may be
mounted with its handles between vertical guides in a framework placed on the rotating stool.
Since the stool revolves about a
vertical axis and the wheel spins
about a horizontal axis, the
wheel will precess about another
horizontal axis, and one end or
the other of its axle will rise according to the direction of rotation of the table and of the wheel.

Fig. 54.—Applying a torque to a
bicycle wheel gyroscope.

M-190. Walking Gyroscope. A heavy gyroscope is fastened

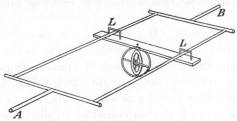

Fig. 55.—Walking gyroscope.

rigidly to a stick a foot long, with its axis parallel to the stick.
The stick hangs from two parallel horizontal rods which form

part of a cradle (Fig. 55) free to rock about a longitudinal axis AB parallel to the rods. The stick carrying the gyroscope is kept from leaving the rods by metal loops L. Now, with the gyroscope spinning, the stick may be made to progress in steps along the rod by simply rocking the cradle from side to side. When it reaches the end of the cradle, it can be made to return in a similar manner only by reversing the direction of spin of the gyroscope. It is evident that the motion is caused by a precession whose direction reverses each time the cradle is rocked. As the speed of the top diminishes, the speed of precession increases.

M-191. Maxwell's Top. A heavy wheel is arranged to spin about a pivot coinciding with its center of gravity. Thus there

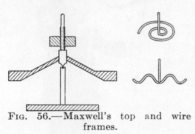

are no gravitational torques acting upon it, and it will spin steadily about any axis. If, however, a pencil is touched to the spindle of the top, the top precesses along the pencil, around the tip, and back along the other side. A helical coil of stiff wire may be placed over the spindle

FIG. 56.—Maxwell's top and wire frames.

so that the spindle follows first the inner surface of the helix and then the outer surface (Fig. 56). The performance of the top is another application of the principles of precession: for as the spindle touches any object, it tends to roll; but this in turn produces a precessional torque at right angles to the direction of rolling, thus increasing the pressure between spindle and object and making the spindle "cling" to the object, even when it is of very irregular shape. A wire bent in a sinusoidal shape makes the top execute an interesting motion.

M-192. Gyrocompass. If a gyroscope is mounted in gimbals so as to have three degrees of freedom, then, in the absence of friction, it maintains an axis fixed in space, even when it is placed upon a rotating table or otherwise turned (M-170). But if it is deprived of one degree of freedom, the gyroscope will then turn until its axis of spin coincides in direction and sense with the rotation that is given to the top as a whole. Mount the top on the rotating stand, and observe the sudden change of the spin axis through 180° when the direction of rotation of the stand is reversed, even though the motion of the stand is almost imperceptible.

M-193. Airplane Turn Indicator. If a commercial-type turn indicator is not available, a model may be shown to illustrate the principle. A gyroscope is mounted in a yoke to spin about a horizontal axis *EF*; the yoke is free to rotate about a second horizontal axis *CD* perpendicular to the spin axis (Fig. 57). If the apparatus is turned about a vertical axis *AB*, the gyroscope precesses about the yoke axis *CD* in a direction depending upon the directions of turn and of spin. In the case of the airplane turn indicator, this axis *CD* is directed longitudinally along the fuselage.

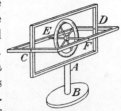

Fig. 57.—Model of airplane turn indicator.

M-194. Ship Stabilizer. There are several ways by which the stabilizing action of a spinning gyroscope may be shown. Some pieces of apparatus are available commercially (Fig. 58); others may be easily constructed. A model boat consisting of a

Fig. 58.—Model ship stabilizer.

horizontal piece of plywood with semicircular rockers is equipped with a gyroscope mounted with its spin axis vertical in gimbals so that it can precess about a transverse axis. As the boat rocks from side to side, the gyroscope precesses fore and aft. If the proper frictional torque is applied to the axis of precession, the rocking is quickly damped. Too much friction prevents precession, and no stabilizing action results; too little friction allows precession to occur but produces no damping. A paper silhouette of a ship may be added to complete the model.

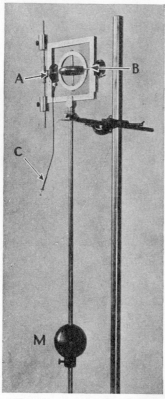

Fig. 59.—Frictional torque can be applied to the precession axis through the cable *C* to damp the motion of the pendulum.

M-195. The principle of the ship stabilizer may likewise be shown by a pendulum arrangement (Fig. 59) in which a gyroscope is held in gimbals so as to be free to precess about a horizontal axis *AB* in the plane of oscillation of the pendulum; the axis of spin of the top is vertical. The period about axis *AB* is controlled by the position of the weight *M*. Friction is applied to the axis of precession through a flexible camera release cable *C* while the pendulum is swinging.

M-196. A large-scale model is shown in Fig. 60. The demonstrator sits in the "boat," which is suspended from an overhead support so as to be free to swing like a pendulum about a longitudinal axis. He holds a handle connected to a motor-driven gyroscope by which he can control its precession. After the boat is set rocking, he may bring it to rest by four or five properly timed pumps on this handle. The converse action may likewise be shown, for the demonstrator may set himself into motion from side to side by rocking the gyroscope fore and aft.

M-197. Gyroacrobat. The stabilizing action of a gyroscope may be shown by the trapeze arrangement illustrated in Fig. 61. The top is rigidly attached to the center of a stick with its axis of spin perpendicular to the stick. Two cords are attached to the ends of this stick; midway along one cord, there is a light ring (wooden embroidery ring) through which the cord from the other end passes. The cords are thus crossed and tied to an overhead support. If the gyroscope is set spinning and then released when it sits on top of the horizontal stick as illustrated,

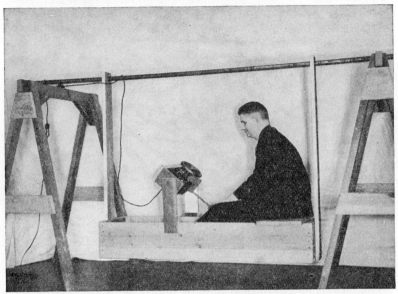

FIG. 60.—The demonstrator controls the rocking of the "boat" with the gyroscope.

it will ride in this unstable position for some time. However, if the gyroscope is released when the stick is rotated through 180°, no stabilizing action occurs, and the top promptly falls over. This experiment illustrates the most fundamental aspect of gyroscopic stabilizing, *viz.*, that there must be two degrees of instability about perpendicular axes.

M-198. Gyro Bicycle Rider. A gyroscope is mounted with spin axis horizontal and with precession axis vertical on a model bicycle. A cylindrical weight W (Fig. 62) serves for the rider's head and also serves to accelerate the precession of the gyroscope when it is out of its position of unstable equilibrium, thus introducing a righting torque. The ends of the bar AB parallel to the spin axis are connected to

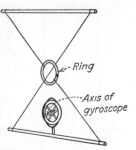

FIG. 61.—Gyroacrobat.

the handle bars of the bicycle by a parallelogram linkage *ABCD* so that as the gyroscope precesses, the front wheel is turned.

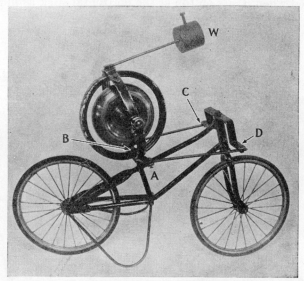

FIG. 62.—Gyro bicycle rider.

The bicycle and gyro rider may be pulled along the lecture table

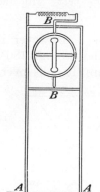

by a string, the righting action of the gyroscope lending a fantastic aspect of "intelligence" to the steering and balancing of the bicycle.

M-199. Gyro Drunken Man. Gyroscopic stabilizing may be shown by a top-heavy piece of apparatus that stands and teeters to and fro. A gyroscope is supported in gimbals with spin axis horizontal and precession axis vertical on top of a two-legged frame (Fig. 63). A lever arm attached to the gimbal frame allows the top to be turned about its axis of precession. A light spring accelerates the precession of the gyroscope whenever it departs from its position of unstable equilibrium. Thus there are axes of instability at right angles to one

FIG. 63.—The spinning gyroscope stabilizes the top-heavy framework.

another, the axis of gravitational instability *AA* and the axis of instability introduced by the spring, *BB*. Hence when the top is spinning, the apparatus stands up and teeters about its position of unstable equilibrium so long as motion is allowed to take place freely about both axes of instability.

M-200. Monorail Car. There is on the market an excellent but expensive monorail car with two heavy flywheels that spin in opposite directions. The frames carrying these wheels are geared together so that they precess through equal angles in opposite directions. The ends of the axles of the two wheels are arranged to run on tracks so as to accelerate the precession of the tops whenever they depart from their middle positions. The car will run for several minutes on a steel cable or heavy rope.

An inexpensive monorail car may be made by converting a toy gyroscope into the stabilizing element. One of the gimbal pins of the top is threaded and screwed into a short piece of brass rod. The axis of precession AB, which runs transversely across the car (Fig. 64), passes longitudinally through this brass cylinder. Thus the axis of spin and the axis of precession are mutually perpendicular. The car is equipped with two wooden or metal pulleys P so that it can run down an inclined thread or fishline. After the

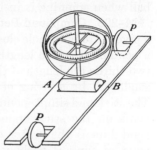

FIG. 64.—Monorail car.

top is set spinning, the car is released in an upright position, with the gyroscope axis vertical. It will run down an inclined thread the full length of the lecture room, teetering precariously from side to side. The car will right itself so long as the precessional motion of the top is allowed to take place freely. But if the amplitude of precessional motion builds up to the point where the frame touches the body of the car, the car instantly topples over.

M-201. Gyropendulum. A gyroscope is hung from one end of its spin axle by a string and is swung as a pendulum. Because of the precession introduced by rotation of the pendulum about its point of support, the gyroscopic pendulum bob executes a complex motion. If desired, a trace of this motion may be made by equipping the pendulum bob with a sand cone.

M-202. Tops. The manner in which the rolling of the peg of a top causes acceleration of precession and consequent rise of the center of gravity of the top may be demonstrated by means of a large mechanical top equipped with a rounded peg.　The promptness with which the top rises and "goes to sleep" depends somewhat upon the character of the surface on which the peg rolls; if the top is spun on a sheet of glass, for example, the peg may slip on the glass, and the top fails to rise.

An egg-shaped top will rise and spin on end if given a sufficiently high velocity of spin.　An oblate or prolate spheroid will likewise rise until its long diameter is vertical.

A hollow metal sphere with one hemisphere slightly heavier than the other will, upon being spun, precess until the heavy hemisphere is on top.　If the ball is painted half black and half white, it is then evident that the equilibrium orientation of the ball when spinning is just opposite to that when at rest.

M-203. Compound Pendulum.　A meter stick is supported on a pivot through a hole close to one end, so that it may be swung as a pendulum.　The length of the equivalent simple pendulum is two-thirds the length of the stick, as may be shown by hanging a small ball by a string of proper length from the same support. The stick and simple pendulum swing with the same period.　The point on the stick opposite the bob of the equivalent simple pendulum is the center of oscillation, which may be made the point of support without changing the period of the compound pendulum.　It is an interesting problem for the advanced student to compute the position of the axis (one-fourth the length from one end) about which the stick will swing in *minimum* time.

In a similar fashion, the equivalent simple pendulum may be demonstrated for other objects supported as compound pendulums.　Particularly interesting is the case of the hoop suspended from a point on its periphery and swinging as a pendulum in its own plane.　The length of the equivalent simple pendulum is, in this case, equal to the diameter of the hoop.　If, however, the hoop is swung in a plane at right angles to its own, the period is diminished.　The dependence of period upon moment of inertia about the axis of support may thus be emphasized.　Moments of inertia of irregular bodies may be computed by timing their periods when swung as pendulums about various axes.

M-204. Center of Percussion.　The center of oscillation of a compound pendulum is sometimes also called its center of percussion, for it is the point at which a blow may be struck without

causing reaction at the point of support.   This property may be
demonstrated in the case of the meter-stick pendulum (M-203)
by supporting it on a matchstick instead of a nail.   If the stick
is struck a sharp blow with a hammer at the center of percussion
(two-thirds the way down), there is no reaction on the point of
support.   But if it is struck above or below this point, the
matchstick may be broken.

On a larger scale, the same phenomenon may be shown by
dropping upon a movable fulcrum a 6-ft piece of 2-by-4 pivoted
at one end with a piece of $\frac{1}{4}$-in. dowel rod.   The dowel rod is
broken unless the fulcrum is located beneath the center of
percussion.

M-205. A heavy metal bar is suspended from one end by a
long cord.   Its center of percussion may be found by striking the
bar horizontally with a hammer at various points.   If the
hammer strikes opposite the center of percussion, the upper end
of the bar does not move.   If the lower end of the bar is loaded,
the center of percussion is thereby shifted farther from the point
of support, and vice versa.

M-206. Falling Chimney—Free-fall Paradox. If a stick held
in a vertical position with one end resting on the table is allowed
to topple over, each particle of it
describes a circular path.   The
center of percussion of the stick is
the point that has the acceleration of a free particle along the
path that it follows; all points
beyond the center of percussion
descend with accelerations greater

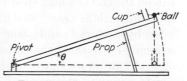

FIG. 65.—The falling stick drops
away from the ball, which is caught
in the cup.

than they would have if they were particles moving freely on their
respective paths.   In consequence of this, the stick finally reaches
a certain position below which the vertical component of the
acceleration of its end point exceeds the acceleration of gravity.
For a uniform stick, this is at such an angle that $\cos^2\theta$ is greater
than $\frac{2}{3}$, or θ is less than 35°(Fig. 65).   A mechanical gadget may
be made to illustrate this fact and to interpret the frequently
observed backward buckling of the top of a falling chimney,
which is caused, in part, by inertial reactions.

Pivot a meter stick on a horizontal axis at one end so that it is
free to rotate in a vertical plane.   At a point about 85 cm from

the axis, erect a light paper cup about 8 cm tall. Cut a slight indentation at the end of the stick to retain a steel ball when the stick is propped up at an angle of 35°. If, now, the prop is suddenly knocked out and the stick falls, the ball will fall into the cup even though the top of the cup started from a point higher than the ball. The action is quick and startling. A little trial will enable one to locate the proper position of the cup and of the prop to insure catching the ball. If a wad of paper is placed in the bottom of the cup, the ball will not bounce out to spoil the effect.

The same phenomenon may be shown more simply but less strikingly by supporting a meter stick in a horizontal position by the two index fingers. A wooden block is placed upon one end of the stick. If both ends of the stick are released simultaneously, the stick and block fall together. But if the stick is rested on one index finger and released at the end supporting the block, the stick falls away from the block as it rotates about the support. In other words, the end of the stick has a downward acceleration greater than the acceleration of gravity.

M-207. Foucault Pendulum. Many laboratories have arranged permanent mountings for a Foucault pendulum. A heavy ball on the end of a long steel wire is suspended in some convenient location, such as a stair well or elevator shaft. The ball is drawn aside by a thread, and after all motion is damped out it is set swinging by burning the thread. Its plane of oscillation may be observed to rotate slowly with respect to the floor of the room at a rate equal to the vertical component of the earth's rotation ($15°$ $\sin \lambda$ per hr, where λ is the latitude) and in the opposite sense. The rotation will therefore be clockwise in the northern hemisphere as viewed from the point of support and counterclockwise in the southern. The magnitude of the motion is readily observable in the course of an hour in middle latitudes, provided the initial plane is marked.

There are many ways of supporting the pendulum and several ways in which the rotation of its plane of oscillation may be made evident in a few minutes after it is started.

A simple and effective method of supporting the pendulum so that it may be free to swing in any plane is to use piano wire clamped at the top and passed through a circular hole, of diameter slightly larger than that of the wire, in a horizontal steel plate

rigidly mounted a short distance below the clamp.   This obviates
the necessity of using a more complex knife-edge or ball-bearing
support.

The change in plane of oscillation of the bob may be shown by
shadow projection of the motion of a small bead attached to the
pendulum wire.   The light should be placed as far as possible
from the bead.   The pendulum is started in a plane parallel to
the direction of the light so that the shadow of the bead moves
only along a vertical line on the wall.
After a few minutes, the shadow shows
an appreciable lateral motion that
increases in amplitude as time elapses,
and the component of motion perpendicular to the original plane of
oscillation increases.

M-208. A compact, permanent arrangement of Foucault's pendulum is
shown in Fig. 66.   The pendulum bob
is a 10-kg sphere hanging from the
ceiling of the room by piano wire.   The
bob swings inside a wooden box with
glass front and a slotted top to allow
free motion of the wire.   The motion
of the bob is shown by projecting the
image of a small ring of copper wire
attached to the middle of the supporting wire.   The optical system consists
of an arc and a thin condenser lens that

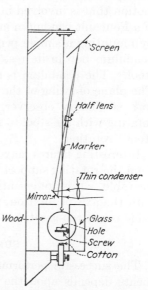

Fig. 66.—Optical arrange-
ment for Foucault pendulum.

sends a beam, by reflection from a plane mirror, past the wire ring
to an overhead screen inclined so as to be visible to all.   The
image of the marker is formed by a half lens placed close to the
wire.   On the screen are drawn two path lines at a small angle to
one another.   By adjustment of the optical system, the image of
the marker is brought to the intersection of these lines when the
bob is at rest, and the lines are so drawn that the image of the
marker is on one of the lines when the bob is drawn aside in
readiness to start.   Thus, when the bob is released, the image
of the marker moves back and forth along one path line.   The
light may now be turned off and turned on again after some
computed interval, at which time the image of the marker should

follow along the second path line. The position of the second line is, of course, optional. It will depend upon the length of time during which the pendulum is allowed to swing between observations, upon the inclination of the screen, and upon the local latitude. However, it is suggested that the lines be drawn at such an angle that the motion may be shown in twenty minutes or half an hour after starting the pendulum.[1]

M-209. Model Foucault Pendulum. The concept of relative motion that is involved in the rotation of the plane of oscillation of a Foucault pendulum may be illustrated (in exaggerated form) by mounting a simple pendulum on a rotating stool so that the pendulum bob in its rest position hangs over the center of the stool. The pendulum is set swinging, and the stool is rotated. The plane of swing of the pendulum remains unchanged relative to a stationary observer, but it would appear to an observer rotating with the stool to rotate in a sense opposite to that of the stool's rotation.

Interesting figures may be drawn if a sand pendulum is swung from the rotating support and allowed to drop sand on the rotating table. It is not essential to have the point of support coincide with the axis of rotation, provided that the speed of turning the table is not too great.

SURFACE TENSION

The successful performance of many of the following experiments depends upon the cleanliness of the glassware used and upon the quality of the soap solution.

Plateau's liquid is standard for blowing bubbles and making soap films. It consists of 1 part of oleate of soda, 40 parts of water, and 13 parts of glycerin. If prepared from free oleic acid, the formula is: 28.2 g oleic acid, 100 ml normal caustic soda solution, 300 ml glycerin, 1200 ml water. It is improved by adding 3 drops of concentrated ammonia to the above amount.

M-210. Ring Method of Measuring Surface Tension. One common method of measuring surface tension may be illustrated on a large scale by pulling a large brass ring away from the surface of water or other liquid. The ring is suspended from a light spring (Joly balance), and the extent of stretching the spring

[1] Another method of showing rotation of plane of oscillation in a few minutes is described by S. R. Williams, *Pop. Astron.*, **40**, 256, 1932.

by surface forces may be measured roughly by calibrating the spring with known weights. The magnitude of the surface tension (*e.g.*, in dynes per centimeter) is then found from the measured force divided by $4\pi r$, where r is the radius of the ring.

M-211. Surface Tension of Mercury. The large surface forces present in mercury are shown by measuring the force required to pull a razor blade out of the mercury. It is essential that the mercury wet the blade. The blade is cleaned and dipped into copper sulfate solution to form a thin layer of copper on it and then into mercury in contact with nitric acid. When a coating of mercury has been made to adhere to the blade along one of its edges, the blade may then be dipped into mercury and pulled away from the surface on the end of a Joly balance spring.

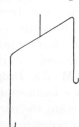

F I G. 6 7.— Frame for placing needles on s u r f a c e o f water.

M-212. Floating Metals. A needle rubbed between the fingers to make it slightly oily will float if laid carefully upon the surface of water. Razor blades, rings of wire, or paper clips are comparatively easy to float. Such metal boats may be sunk by touching the surface of the water with a drop of liquid soap. For placing needles upon the surface of water, a light wire frame (Fig. 67) is useful. It is essential that the metal objects be dry and slightly oily so that they are not wet by the water.

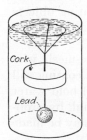

M-213. Submerged Float. A metal ring is arranged above a cork and lead float as shown (Fig. 68), so that the ring projects above the surface of the water. If the float is submerged until the ring is under water and then released carefully, the ring will no longer rise above the surface, but it will push the surface of the water up because of the buoyancy of the float. Again, a drop of soap placed upon the water will diminish the surface forces and allow the ring to break through.

F I G. 68.—If the wire ring is pushed beneath the water surface, surface tension holds it there.

M-214. Capillary Tubes. A set of connecting capillary tubes of various diameters will show that the capillary rise of water or other liquids is inversely proportional to the diameter. A similar set of tubes containing mercury will show capillary depression. (Project.)

M-215. Capillary Rise between Glass Plates. Two *clean* glass plates (30 by 50 cm) clamped together along one vertical edge and separated at the opposite edge by a thread or piece of wire are dipped into a vessel containing colored water. The water rises farthest near the clamped edge, and the curve formed by the surface of the water is a hyperbola, since the separation of the plates is proportional to the distance from the closed edge and the height of rise is inversely proportional to the separation.

M-216. Droplets in Tapered Tubes. A drop of water placed in a horizontal tapered glass tube open at both ends will move toward the narrow end of the tube. If the drop is displaced by air pressure toward the broad end of the tube, it will return when the pressure is removed. A drop of mercury in a similar tube will tend to move away from the narrow end, as may be shown by the fact that it requires a moderate air pressure to force the droplet farther toward the narrow end. (Project.) The concave meniscus of water and the convex meniscus of mercury are at the same time made evident.

M-217. Meniscus Effects. Two or three cylinders of wood or paraffin floated in a crystallizing dish containing water cling to the sides of the vessel. If more water is poured into the vessel until the meniscus is convex upward, the floating objects leave the edge and assemble at the middle of the water surface. (Vertical projection.)

M-218. Watertight Sieves. A box made of fine-mesh wire gauze dipped into hot paraffin so as to give it a thin coating will either float in a vessel of water like a boat or will hold water poured into it. However, the gauze boat may be sunk by dropping a single drop of water into it, or the gauze cup may be made to leak by touching its bottom with a wet finger.

A beaker of water may be covered with a piece of dry cheese-cloth and turned upside down without the water escaping. It is not necessary to hold the cheesecloth, as it is held in place by atmospheric pressure just as a piece of paper would be.

M-219. Various Capillary Phenomena. If the surface of water in a beaker is covered with lycopodium powder, the demonstrator may dip his finger into the water without its becoming wet.

When a paintbrush is held under water, its hairs are separated as they are when the brush is dry; but when the wet brush is withdrawn, the hairs cling together. (Project.)

Pour water down a glass rod or a wet string.

Water poured into a box constructed from typewriter paper will cause the top edges of the box to be pulled inward because of the tendency of the surface of the water to assume the minimum possible area.

M-220. When Is a Glass Full of Water? A glass tumbler is filled level with the brim with water and placed before the projection lantern so that the class can see its image. The class may be asked to guess how many 4-penny finishing nails can be dropped into the tumbler without making the water run over. With care a surprisingly large number can be introduced, because the meniscus of the water may be made to stand well above the top of the tumbler. The time consumed in performing this experiment may tax the patience of the class. The same effect may be shown by adding water from a burette or pipette until the meniscus breaks.

M-221. Change of Surface Tension with Change of Surface Conditions. Place a thin layer of distilled water in a clean flat-bottomed dish on the vertical projector. If a drop of ether or alcohol is introduced at the center of the water surface, the water draws away quickly from the spot touched and leaves a large area covered only by ether or alcohol, which quickly evaporates.

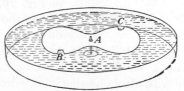

Fig. 69.—Bits of camphor at *B* and *C* cause the vane *A* to rotate.

M-222. A flat-bottomed dish containing distilled water is placed on the vertical projector. Lycopodium powder or chalk dust is sprinkled on its surface. If the surface is touched with a glass rod dipped in liquid soap, the powder is instantly swept out of the field of view. The effect is startling and unexpected. Ether vapor will produce temporary disturbances of the surface.

M-223. Bits of camphor placed on a clean water surface will dart about vigorously in random fashion over the surface because of unequal changes of surface tension produced where the corners of the camphor particles come in contact with the water. A little soap will quickly stop the motion. (Project.)

M-224. Camphor Mill. From a thin sheet of aluminum, cut a section like that shown in Fig. 69. At *A*, drill a hole large enough to slip over a long needle or piece of stiff piano wire. At *B* and *C*, cut back into the blades, and bend the cut pieces so that they will help to hold small pieces of camphor in the notches. Stick the long needle or piano wire into a flat cork weighted with lead so that it will sink in water and hold the needle vertical.

Place the aluminum blade with the camphor pieces over the pivot so that it rests on the surface of the water, supported by surface tension. The decrease in surface tension where the camphor touches the water causes an unbalanced torque that turns the blade round and round, away from the camphor.

M-225. Soap-propelled Boat. A matchstick or other light object that will float on water may be made to move about on the surface of water in a vessel as if self-propelled by simply rubbing

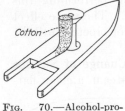

one end of the stick on a cake of soap or by inserting a particle of camphor in a split at the stern of the "boat." (Vertical projection.)

M-226. Alcohol Boat. Cut out of thin wood a small flat boat of the design shown in Fig. 70. To this fasten a small spool,

Fig. 70.—Alcohol-propelled boat.

and to the spool fasten a glass tube drawn down to a capillary and bent with its small end just at the surface of the water at the stern. Put a small tuft of cotton in the glass "smokestack," and fill with alcohol, using an eye dropper. Place the boat on smooth water, and watch it move forward under the unbalanced forces of surface tension caused by the alcohol's contaminating the water at the stern. A shallow gutter pipe may be used as a stream bed with water running in at one end and out to the sink at the other. The boat will run "upstream" at a good rate.

M-227. Duco Boat. A drop of Duco household cement will dart around the surface of a vessel of water for several minutes. Two drops will "play tag" with one another in amusing fashion, avoiding one another and executing complex rotary motions as they progress. (Vertical projection.)

M-228. Mercury Amoeba. A globule of mercury about 1 in. in diameter is placed in a shallow crystallizing dish mounted on a vertical projector. The mercury is covered with 10 per cent nitric acid. If a crystal of potassium dichromate is placed near the mercury, the mercury starts to chase the crystal vigorously as soon as the red ring of dichromate diffuses out and reaches the mercury. (This behavior is probably due to change of effective surface tension by reason of electric charge on the surface of the mercury.)

M-229. Mercury Heart. A $\frac{1}{2}$-in. globule of mercury in a watch glass is placed on the vertical projector and covered with 10 per cent hydrogen peroxide to which is added a 1 per cent solution of sodium bicarbonate until a yellow film appears upon the mercury and breaks down regularly.

M-230. A $\frac{1}{2}$-in. globule of mercury in a watch glass is placed on the vertical projector and covered with 10 per cent sulfuric acid. A few crystals of potassium dichromate are stirred in with the acid. If the surface of the mercury is now touched with an iron wire, it contracts and pulls away from the wire; but the accumulation of a surface charge makes it again expand and touch the wire, whereupon it again contracts. A rhythmic pulsation begins, which may attain considerable amplitude and vigor for several minutes. The addition of more crystals of dichromate may restore the activity of the "heart."

M-231. Pulsating Air Bubble.
Under an inverted watch glass beneath the surface of water in a vessel is imprisoned an air bubble $\frac{1}{2}$ in. in diameter. Alcohol is allowed to play upon the edge of the bubble through a bent capillary tube. The rate of flow is controlled by a screw clamp on a piece of rubber tubing connecting the capillary to a funnel (Fig. 71) and is adjusted until the bubble pulsates rhythmically.

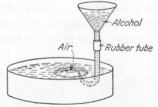

FIG. 71.—Pulsating air bubble.

M-232. Contraction of Soap Film. A soap film formed across the open end of an inverted funnel ascends toward the narrow end of the funnel, since the gain in gravitational potential energy is more than offset by the reduction of surface energy.

M-233. A U-shaped wire frame is equipped with a sliding wire link that closes the opening of the U. If a soap film is formed upon the frame, it tends to draw the wire link toward the closed end of the U. Hence, a small force is necessary to draw the link out, and upon release it will be drawn back suddenly by contraction of the film.

M-234. A cubical wire frame dipped into a beaker of soap solution shows several interesting examples of the contraction of soap films. By puncturing various parts of the film, different geometrical forms result; *e.g.*, a saddle-shaped surface may be made by puncturing the film so that it clings to the wire frame only along the four edges AB, CD, EG, and FH (Fig. 72). A film that touches nine of the edges but does not touch three mutually

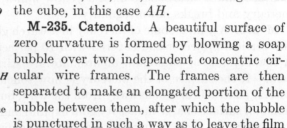

perpendicular edges that do not intersect, such as EF, CG, BD, contains a diagonal of the cube, in this case AH.

M-235. Catenoid. A beautiful surface of zero curvature is formed by blowing a soap bubble over two independent concentric circular wire frames. The frames are then separated to make an elongated portion of the

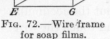

Fig. 72.—Wire frame for soap films.

bubble between them, after which the bubble is punctured in such a way as to leave the film

between the two frames. The film immediately takes on the form of a catenoid, in which there are two mutually perpendicular and equal curvatures at every point. As the frames are separated, the waist of the catenoid shrinks until a condition of instability is reached, whereupon the catenoid collapses at the center and two separate plane films are formed across the wire rings.

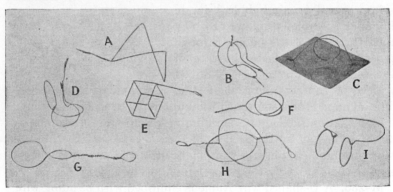

Fig. 73.—Wire frames for soap films to illustrate minimal surfaces.

M-236. Minimal Surfaces. Every soap film tends to reach a condition of minimum potential energy (M-232 to M-237) and is therefore (except for gravitational forces) a "minimal surface" for the contour presented by the frame. Many beautiful minimal surfaces are formed on appropriate wire frames. These surfaces furnish concrete illustrations of the solutions of a class of mathematical problems that has not yet yielded completely to rigorous treatment.[1] Figure 73 shows a few of the frames that form surfaces of special interest. The handles on frame *B* make it possible to change the film surface from one form to another by flexing the frame. Permanent films may be formed from collodion made somewhat thicker than the commercial grade by bubbling air through it and then allowing it to stand until all air bubbles have disappeared. The proper consistency must be determined by experiment. Care should be taken in withdrawing the wire frames from the solution. When the films have hardened, they may be sprayed with oil-base paint of any desired shade.

M-237. Ring and Thread. A wire ring has attached to it a loop of thread. It is dipped into a tray of soap solution so as to form a film within which the thread hangs limp. If the soap film is punctured inside the loop, the film on the outside of the loop contracts and draws the thread into a circle. The area of the empty circular loop is maximum for the periphery allowed by the thread; hence the area of soap film is a minimum.

M-238. Equidensity Bubbles. The demonstrator blows a soap bubble with a bubble pipe until it is 3 or 4 in. in diameter. The pipe is then connected to the gas supply, and the bubble further inflated until its mean density is that of the surrounding air. When detached from the pipe, the bubble may hover in the classroom for more than a minute. It is somewhat a matter of luck whether the bubble rises or falls after it is released from the pipe. However, it may be kept in control by gentle air currents from a piece of paper. It sometimes happens that the bubble is a trifle too heavy and begins to sink; but after it loses weight by evaporation its descent is halted, and it slowly rises to the ceiling.

M-239. Pressure within Bubble—Two-bubble Paradox. Two small bubbles are blown on the ends of a T-tube. By starting them at different times, it is possible to secure two bubbles of slightly different size. If the blowing tube is now closed and the bubbles are left to themselves, the smaller bubble will shrink because the pressure within it is greater than that within the larger bubble. Pressure within a soap bubble is greater than the

[1] COURANT, R., *Ann. Math.*, **38**, 679, 1937.

external pressure by an amount that is inversely proportional to the radius of the bubble.

M-240. Pressure within Bubble—Manometer Method. A slant water manometer that can be projected is connected by a

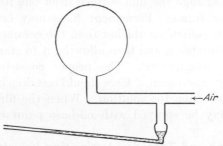

←*Air*

Fig. 74.—Measurement of pressure within soap bubble.

side tube to the tube through which a soap bubble is blown (Fig. 74). The excess pressure within the bubble may then be shown, and its dependence upon the radius of the bubble verified.

M-241. Mercury Bubbles. Air is blown into mercury under a dilute solution of ammonium chloride. Mercury bubbles rise to the surface and float for a second or so before bursting.

M-242. Drop Formation—Large-scale Model. A rubber balloon or membrane supported by a ring stand is filled with water until it is distended and constricted, very much in the form of an enormous drop.

M-243. Orthotoluidine Drop. Orthotoluidine has (at 24°C) the same density as water but does not mix with water. It is therefore an ideal substance for the formation of large drops. A large glass vessel (battery jar or aquarium) is filled with water into which salt solution is introduced to form a layer of slightly greater density at the bottom. Orthotoluidine is allowed to flow into the water very slowly through a burette, the lower end of which terminates in an inverted thistle tube (Fig. 75). A large drop of the dark liquid slowly forms and finally seals itself off by surface tension and descends toward the salt solution layer where it floats

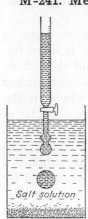

F i g. 7 5.—
Large drops of orthotoluidine in water.

in virtually spherical form. The deliberate manner in which this event takes place allows the instructor time to point out the part played by surface forces in constricting the drop, the formation of Plateau's spherule, and the oscillation of the drop as it slowly acquires its spherical form. If several drops are allowed to form in this manner, they may be made to coalesce under water by dexterously leading small drops into larger drops with a glass rod. In this way, a single drop 2 or 3 in. in diameter may be formed.

M-244. Aniline Drop. Aniline likewise forms equidensity drops when the common temperature of the water and aniline is about 25°C. In this case, no salt solution is used. About 80 ml of aniline is poured into a beaker of cool water. The aniline rests on the bottom; but if the beaker is gently heated, the aniline rises to the surface of the water, where it cools in contact with the air, and returns to the bottom in large drops, which form slowly beneath the surface of the water.

M-245. Equidensity Drops. A beaker of water is prepared with a layer of salt solution in the bottom. On top of the water is placed a drop of mineral oil or olive oil. With an eye dropper or pipette 1 or 2 ml of colored salt solution is slowly introduced into the drop of oil. The oil forms a sac separating the salt water from the fresh, and the slightly greater density of the salt water causes a large drop to form. The drops are smaller than the drops of aniline or orthotoluidine previously described, but their appearance is the same, and the necessary materials are much easier to obtain. The drops thus formed in the oil membranes sink toward the bottom of the beaker but are stopped by the denser salt solution. They may remain intact for several hours or even for days.

M-246. Spherical Oil Drop. A flat-sided bottle is half-filled with water. Alcohol is poured on top of the water, and by means of a pipette a globule of oil is introduced at the interface, where it floats in nearly spherical shape, at a level where its density is equal to that of the surrounding mixture of alcohol and water.

M-247. Variation of Drop Size with Surface Tension. A rectangular glass tank is mounted on the table of the horizontal projector and filled with water. A funnel is connected by rubber tubing to a glass tube drawn down at the end and bent through 180°; a pinchcock on the rubber tube controls the flow of olive oil and 0.5 per cent oleic acid colored with Sudan III, which is contained in the funnel. When the glass tip is held below the surface of the water and the pinchcock is opened, drops of oil about 4 mm in diameter form and ascend to the surface. If $\frac{1}{10}$-normal solution of sodium hydroxide is added to the water, the surface tension of the oil is reduced so that the drops become much smaller; the reduction may be so great that no drops form and the oil issues in a continuous stream.

M-248. Mercury Droplets. The spherical appearance of small droplets of mercury on a flat surface may be shown by horizontal projection. The coalescence of mercury droplets in a watch glass is interesting to observe when viewed by vertical projection. Clear mercury is sprayed into distilled water, where it forms many small droplets, which do not coalesce. If a few drops of acid are added, the independent droplets coalesce in random fashion, setting the resultant drops into vigorous agitation.

M-249. Water Droplets. Small spherical droplets of water may be formed on a surface that water does not wet. A piece of glass or paper covered with smoke from burning camphor or kerosene may be used to hold the droplets for horizontal projection. Droplets of spray from an atomizer may be observed to bounce when they strike the soot-covered surface.

A tumbler is filled so full that the water surface is higher than the edge of the tumbler. Water from a pipette with a small opening is allowed to strike the surface at a small angle. Tiny droplets will be seen to roll across the water surface, and some may fall off the opposite edge. Occasionally a droplet may rest for a short time on the surface before coalescing with it. (Project.)

M-250. Tears of Wine. A 25 per cent solution of grain alcohol is poured into a watch glass, arranged for vertical projection. The liquid wets the glass but, as alcohol evaporates, surface tension increases and the remaining liquid forms into droplets that run down the glass.

M-251. Castor-oil Drop. Allow castor oil to flow slowly through a tube of small aperture placed in front of the horizontal projector. The viscous liquid forms a drop slowly.

A large colored drop of castor oil[1] is formed on the surface of water. A glass rod is thrust into it, and it is dragged down under

[1] See footnote, p. 120.

the surface where it forms into a spherical drop, which clings
to the rod and slowly climbs up it until it reaches the surface,
where it again flattens out.

M-252. Liquid Drops on Surface of Liquid. Drops from the
paddle of a canoe now and then roll for several feet on a still
water surface.   The same phenomenon may be shown by horizontal projection with drops of alcohol released upon the surface
of alcohol in a dish.   If the alcohol used for forming droplets is
slightly colored, the progress of the liquid contained in the drop
may be followed even after the droplet has coalesced with the
body of the liquid.   In this case, the colored alcohol produces a
vortex ring as it proceeds beneath the surface.

M-253. Vortex Rings of Liquid. From a medicine dropper,
allow a single drop of inky water to fall into a beaker of clear
water from a height of just 1 in.   If the water in the beaker has
been standing for some time, so that its internal motions are
small, a perfect vortex ring will be seen to dart down from the
surface of the water, and its progress may be followed for 4 to
6 in. below the surface before it breaks up into a drapery of other
rings and vortex filaments.   If the water in the beaker is only
about 4 in. deep, the ring will dart to the bottom and rebound.
The height from which the droplets fall is critical.   The best
results are obtained with the height recommended.   However, if
the dropper is held so that the drop as it is nearly formed is
"picked off" by the liquid surface, a slower moving vortex ring
is formed (M-252).   Other liquids show the same phenomenon,
but water is the most convenient.

M-254. Liquid Jets. As liquid emerges vertically downward
from a circular orifice, its jet contracts in diameter (vena con-
tracta) both because of surface tension and because of the higher
speed of the liquid as it descends.   Project a portion of the jet
above the point where it becomes unstable and breaks into
droplets.   Oil shows the effect better than water.

M-255. Necklace of Droplets. Arrange a jet of water directed
at an elevation of 45° with the plane of its trajectory parallel to a
screen or wall upon which the shadow of the jet may be cast.
Adjust the water stream until the jet becomes unstable and
breaks up into drops about 8 in. from the nozzle.   If a tuning
fork is sounded in the neighborhood of the jet or touches the
stand holding the nozzle, the jet will become more stable and will
break into regularly timed droplets of equal size at some point

more remote from the nozzle. When the jet is illuminated with stroboscopic light (S-49) of the same frequency as that of the tuning fork, the stream of droplets will appear to stand still in a beautiful parabolic "necklace." If the speed of the stroboscope is altered, the beads appear to advance or return toward the nozzle.

M-256. Drop Formation Shown by Stroboscopic Illumination. A jet of water issues vertically downward from a small orifice situated just in front of the condenser lens of the projection lantern. An image of the stream is cast upon the screen by the projection lens. A cardboard disk containing a single hole is mounted at the focus of the condenser lens so that when the disk is rotated by a variable-speed motor, the light from the arc falls upon the screen intermittently. The vibration of the motor is sufficient to cause the jet to break into drops in a regular manner in synchronism with the illumination so that the image of the falling drop remains steady. By this method it is easy to demonstrate the process of drop formation, to show Plateau's spherule, and to show the oscillation of the newly formed drops.

Fig. 76.— Water from the jet forms a bubble above the cone.

M-257. Bursting Water Bubble. A nozzle directed vertically upward sends a jet of water against the apex of a conical metal cap 1.5 in. in diameter (Fig. 76). The water forms a bubble above the cap, but if one drop of ether is allowed to fall on the bubble, it bursts, owing to the decreased surface tension.

M-258. Variation of Surface Tension with Temperature. Fatty and oily substances (*e.g.*, olive oil) form droplets on the surface of hot water but spread out over the surface as the water cools. The surface tension of both water and oil decreases with rising temperature, but the rate of decrease is greater for the water. Hence a temperature is reached where the two have equal surface tensions; above that temperature, the surface tension of oil is greater than that of water.[1]

M-259. Cohesion Plates. Two well-polished plate-glass surfaces show an appreciable cohesion for one another. Let each

[1] For an extended treatment of surface films, see Wilson Taylor, "A New View of Surface Forces," University of Toronto Press, 1925.

student feel the pull necessary to separate a pair of clean dry plates 2 to 3 in. in diameter.   If a drop of water is placed between the plates, the force perpendicular to the surface required to separate them is greatly increased, although the plates may be separated laterally with ease.   (The effect in this case is undoubtedly due to both cohesion and atmospheric pressure.)

M-260. Cohesion of Water Column.   In a long tube (2 to 4 m) closed at one end, water is boiled to drive out all dissolved air.   The air is pumped out, and the tube is sealed off.   The cohesion of the water column will support it against gravity and even against rather severe inertial shocks.   Mount the tube firmly on a board for safe keeping.

M-261. Adhesion of Water to Glass.   A piece of plate glass is supported by three strings in a horizontal position from one arm of a beam balance, as shown in Fig. 77.
The plate is brought into contact with the surface of water in a beaker, after which the beaker is lowered a trifle to show that the water clings to the plate.   Sufficient weights may then be added to the

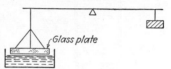

FIG. 77.—Adhesion of water to glass.

other arm of the balance to separate the plate from the water. Soft-rubber "vacuum cups" offer a convenient means of attaching the strings to the glass plate.

OSMOSIS AND DIFFUSION

Experiments on the diffusion of gases are described in A-54, A-55, and A-56, in connection with Kinetic Theory.

M-262. Diffusion of Liquids.   A tall glass cylinder (graduate) is filled one-third full of a saturated solution of copper sulfate; the upper two-thirds is filled with water.   A thin layer of oil over the water reduces evaporation.   The cylinder is placed in a location where it may be visible but free from disturbance.   The line of separation between the colored and uncolored parts of the liquid may be marked from time to time.   In the course of time, the denser copper sulfate will be found to have diffused throughout the water.

M-263. Diffusion of Liquids.   A glass tube 7 or 8 ft long and 1 in. in diameter is filled at its lower end to a depth of 6 or 8 in. with saturated copper sulfate solution, to which some crystals of copper sulfate are added. The remainder of the tube is filled with water, and the tube is then sealed. The date of filling is recorded, and the tube is kept in a vertical position as free from disturbance and from large temperature differences as possible. The progress of the color line may be marked from time to time. Such a tube may be kept for many years and exhibited annually. The slowness of the diffusion process will impress the students; for as time goes on, it may well be that the experiment was started before some of the students were born.

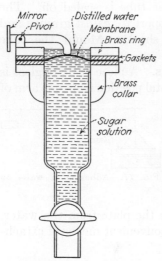

FIG. 78.—Optical osmometer.

M-264. Osmosis. A carrot or a beet into the stem of which is imbedded a glass tube securely sealed with paraffin is submerged in distilled water. The inward diffusion of the water soon causes water to rise in the tube well above the level in the vessel. Start the experiment, and keep it in evidence for several days, as the process is a slow one. Mark the level of liquid in the tube from time to time. The process is much more rapid if a cavity inside the carrot is filled with concentrated sugar solution before the top is sealed. In this case, the water may rise several feet in 24 hours.

M-265. An animal membrane or a vegetable parchment is sealed tightly over the end of a thistle tube connected to a long vertical glass tube. A saturated solution of sugar or salt is placed inside the thistle tube, and the tube is immersed in a vessel of distilled water. The level of liquid inside the thistle-tube system rises from day to day until a large pressure is attained.

Fill a small jar with dried peas, and add water until no air bubbles remain. Seal tightly. The jar will burst in a few days.

M-266. Optical Osmometer. Osmosis may be shown in the course of a lecture by means of an osmometer[1] in which the motion of the semipermeable membrane, caused by the increase in volume of liquid on one side of it, is made evident by an optical lever (Fig. 78). A brass collar is cemented to one end of a glass

[1] DWIGHT and KERSTEN, *Rev. Sci. Instruments,* **5,** 130, 1934.

tube, the other end of which is fitted with a stopcock. The membrane is held between the collar and a brass ring by three screws; leakage is prevented by rubber gaskets. The optical lever consists of a bent rod, of which one end rests on the center of the membrane and the other, which carries the mirror, is pivoted at the edge of the ring. The tube is filled with the solution to be studied, and distilled water is poured into the ring above the membrane.

LIQUIDS AT REST

M-267. Distinction between Fluids and Solids. Fluids are distinguished from solids by the ease with which parts slide over one another. A fluid cannot permanently sustain a shearing stress. If a bit of asphalt or tar is smashed with a hammer, it splinters like glass, but if the chips are placed in a watch glass, they will gradually flow out in a few days into thin wafers. On the other hand, the sand in an hourglass flows readily through the neck but comes to equilibrium in a conical pile, which never flattens out.

M-268. Distinction between Liquids and Gases. Gases are readily compressible, but the compressibility of liquids is very slight. An empty bottle used as a hammer to drive a nail would break into pieces at once. A $\frac{1}{2}$-l reagent bottle with a ground-glass stopper, if filled *completely* with water (previously boiled to expel the absorbed air), may be used with impunity to drive an 8-penny nail up to its head in a pine plank. Since the glass is backed by an incompressible fluid, it cannot yield enough to break.

M-269. Incompressibility and Transmission of Pressure in Water. A large bottle is completely filled with water and closed with a tight-fitting stopper. If the stopper is struck a sharp blow with a hammer or the heel of the hand, the bottle will be shattered. *Caution:* Hold the bottle over the sink by means of a cloth wrapped about its neck.

M-270. Compressibility of Water. Many laboratories are equipped with a piezometer of the form invented by Oersted. However, a simpler type may be constructed to demonstrate the compressibility of water. A $1\frac{3}{4}$- to $1\frac{1}{4}$-in. pipe reducer has the hole in the small end turned out so that it fits a rather heavy piece of glass tubing about 18 in. long. One end of this tube is closed; the other is slightly flared to fit the pipe reducer (Fig. 79). This tube is firmly sealed to the reducer with marine glue. A second piece of tubing, about 1 ft long and of such a diameter as to fit inside the first tube, is closed at one end and is extended at the other by about 6 in. of capillary tubing with a bore of 0.5 mm. This second tube and capillary is completely filled with air-free water and inserted in the first tube, capillary end down. About 1 cm of mercury is placed in the bottom of the outer tube and the water content of the inner tube adjusted by gentle heating so that for the temperature at which the piezometer is to be used the mercury rises a short distance up the capillary.

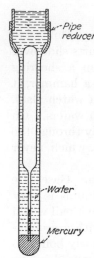

The larger end of the reducer is equipped with suitable pipe fittings so that it may be attached to a convenient faucet by means of a piece of garden hose. The whole apparatus is mounted so that the top of the mercury in the capillary may be projected on the screen. In projecting the capillary, the condenser should focus the crater of the arc on the tube. The details of the capillary will then stand out clearly in a reduced field of view. The meniscus of the mercury will easily be seen to rise and fall as the pressure in the mains is turned on and off. Regardless of changes of volume of the outer tube due to change of pressure, the inner tube is of constant volume, because the pressure upon its walls is the same both inside and out. Therefore change in the volume of the water within the inner tube, caused solely by compression, is shown by change in the position of the mercury.

Fig. 79.—Compression of water within the inner tube is shown by the rise of mercury in the capillary.

M-271. Pressure the Same in All Directions—Pascal's Law. The transmission of pressure in all directions throughout a liquid may be demonstrated by means of the pressure syringe. A spherical glass bulb blown on the end of a tube is perforated with equal small holes pointing in various directions on an equator, which is held horizontal. The tube is fitted with a piston and filled with water. This water squirts out equally in all directions when forced by the piston.

M-272. A modification of this pressure apparatus consists of a large closed metal container with several projecting tubes covered with rubber diaphragms. The container is filled with water, and no matter which of the diaphragms is pushed inward, all the others expand outward.

M-273. In another apparatus, three thistle tubes are equipped with light rubber diaphragms. The stems of the three tubes are held together with rubber bands to form a single central shaft. One tube is pointed downward, another is bent so that its diaphragm is vertical, and the third is arranged to face upward, with the centers of the three diaphragms in a horizontal plane. The diaphragms are expanded equally when the tubes and their stems are filled with colored alcohol to equal heights. When the thistle tubes are immersed in a vessel of water, the levels in the three stems are still equal. Instead of the three-tube apparatus, a single thistle tube with diaphragm may be arranged so that the diaphragm may be turned about a horizontal diameter.

M-274. Hydraulic Balance. A vertical glass tube 2 m long is connected to a rubber hot-water bottle, which is then filled with water. The level of the water in the tube is raised when a person stands on a board laid on the water bottle but the water does not squirt out of the top, as one might expect. The water rises to approximately the height of the person standing on the bottle, because his density is nearly that of water. Different individuals in the class may be "weighed" in this manner.

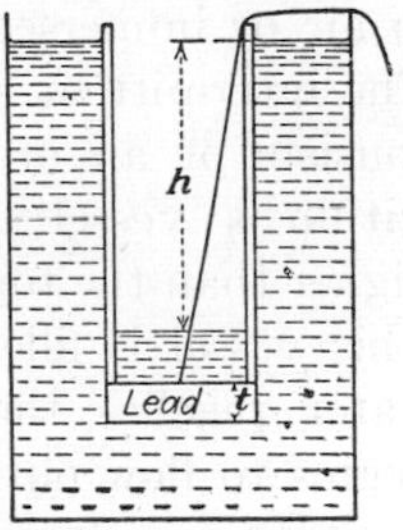

M-275. Pressure Depends on Depth. Tubes of various shapes rise from a common horizontal tube. Water is introduced, and the equilibrium level is shown to be the same in each tube.

M-276. Water pressure will hold a thin brass disk against the lower end of an empty glass cylinder held vertically in a vessel of water, but the disk falls off when water is poured into the cylinder until the level of water inside and out is the same.

FIG. 80.—Pressure depends on depth.

A disk of lead (density 11.33 g per cm³) 1 cm thick and of the same diameter as the outside of the hollow cylinder may be supported by water if the lead is about 11.5 cm or more below the surface of water outside the tube (Fig. 80). By means of a cord attached to its center, the lead may be held against the tube until sufficient depth is reached. A leather or rubber gasket between cylinder and lead will prevent leakage. When water is poured into the cylinder, the lead will fall off when the *difference* in levels h is less than 11.33 times the thickness t of the lead.

M-277. Pascal's Paradox. Two vessels made in the shape of truncated cones are identical in weight and size; one has the larger section of the cone for a base, the other the smaller. Both vessels are filled with water and placed on a platform balance. In spite of the greater force exerted on the larger base, the two vessels are in equilibrium. The bottoms of the vessels are then replaced by rubber diaphragms, and the vessels, supported by clamp stands, are lowered to the balance, so that its platforms support only the extended rubber. Equilibrium can no longer be maintained.

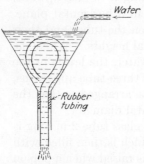

Fig. 81.—Intermittent siphon.

M-278. Siphons. A mechanical model of a siphon consists of a long flexible chain hung over a frictionless pulley. If once started, the chain will "flow" from one platform up over the pulley and down onto a somewhat lower platform.

An ordinary water siphon in air, as well as a mercury siphon in air or immersed in water, should be shown with the model. The intermittent siphon, or Tantalus cup, consists of an ordinary siphon contained within a vessel the sides of which rise higher than the top of the siphon (Fig. 81). This vessel is filled slowly, but when the water reaches the top of the siphon it begins to flow out. This action continues until the vessel is emptied; then the process repeats itself.

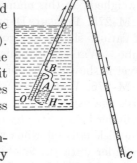

Fig. 82.—Self-starting siphon.

M-279. Self-starting Siphon. An ingenious device for starting a siphon by entrapped air is shown in Fig. 82. A bent tube bears near its end O a side arm B and a 25-ml bulb A with a small hole H. When the bulb is submerged in water, air is forced out through B by the entrance of water at H, and a column of air and water emerges from C.

As the last of the air is expelled from the bulb, the siphon flow becomes steady.

M-280. Fountain Siphon.   A delightful variant of the ordinary tube siphon may be made by connecting a flask and two tubes as shown in Fig. 83. When the level of water and the air pressure within the flask are properly adjusted, a steady stream of water shoots from the narrow orifice at C.   To start the siphon, the flask is first filled with water and then inverted in the position shown.   Air is admitted, little by little, through tube A by removing it momentarily from its reservoir, until the fountain runs freely.   The greater the difference in level between A and B, the more vigorously does the fountain play. If the flow of water is stopped at B, the fountain continues to run for a time because of reduced pressure within the flask.   It ceases to flow when the sum of the air pressure within the flask and the hydrostatic pressure above A is equal to atmospheric pressure.

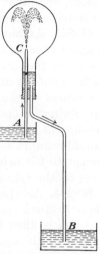

Fig. 83.—Fountain siphon.

M-281. Pressure Measurement in Siphon.   A siphon is prepared from two bent glass tubes and a T-tube connected by rubber tubing at A and B (Fig. 84.)   A mercury manometer is attached to the T-tube to measure the pressure in the upper part of the siphon.   It shows clearly that the pressure here is less than atmospheric when the siphon is in operation.   If the flow is stopped at B, the manometer measures pressure $H_1 - h$; if at A, $H_2 - h$; whereas if the siphon is running, the manometer shows an intermediate pressure that approaches $H_2 - h$ as a limit if large tubes are used to reduce loss of head due to friction.   (Here h is a correction for pressure due to the water column between T and the surface of the mercury.)

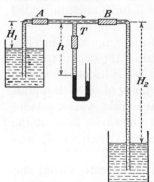

Fig. 84.—Siphon equipped with manometer for pressure measurement.

M-282. Pumps and Presses.   Glass models may be projected to show the action of the valves of suction and force pumps.   A hydrostatic press sufficiently large to break a piece of 2-by-4 timber, or a hydraulic jack fitted with a platform to lift several students, emphasizes Pascal's law of transmission of pressure.

M-283. Archimedes' Principle.   A metal or weighted wooden cylinder is turned to fit closely within a cylindrical container or bucket of the same height.   After the class has been shown the closeness of the fit, the cylinder is hung beneath the bucket from one arm of a balance.   Weights are added to the other side until equilibrium is obtained.   Now a vessel of water is brought up around the suspended cylinder until it is completely immersed. Equilibrium is destroyed but may be restored by filling the bucket to the brim with water, thus showing that the buoyant force on the cylinder is equal to the weight of water it displaces.

M-284.   Another manner of demonstrating Archimedes' principle is to use a can equipped with a spout to carry off overflow. The can is filled to the spout and brought to equilibrium on a balance.   An object *supported externally* by a thread is immersed in the water, and the displaced water is caught in a beaker standing on the table.   The balance equilibrium is maintained, showing that the weight of the displaced water is equal to the buoyant force, whether the object sinks or floats.   If an overflow can is not used, then weights equal to the buoyant force must be added to the other arm of the balance to maintain equilibrium.

A vessel of water is balanced on a platform scale, and the class is asked what will happen to the equilibrium if the instructor dips his hand into the water without touching the sides of the vessel.

M-285. Floating and Density.   A tall jar is filled with liquids of varying density: mercury, carbon tetrachloride, water, cottonseed oil, gasoline.   Objects of appropriate densities float at the interfaces: iron, bakelite, walnut, soft wood (shellacked), and cork.

Place an egg at the bottom of a tall jar filled with water, and throw a handful of salt into the water.   Sufficient salt dissolves to float the egg part way up.

M-286. Hydrometers.   The behavior of hydrometers may be shown by floating them in liquids of different densities.   A constant-weight hydrometer sinks to different depths; a constant-volume (Nicholson) hydrometer requires different weights to sink it to the fiducial point.   A Mohr-Westphal balance may be shown by shadow projection.

M-287. Instability in Flotation.   A metal boat floats in a tub of water.   Within the boat is an automaton so equipped with springs that he rises from a sitting to a standing position in response to a pull on his fishline.   The springs E and H (Fig. 85) are extended in the sitting position.   A pull on A turns B to hit the arm C and to release the catch at D.   Rotation then takes place about the knee K, until the lever I, pivoted at F, strikes the pin J.   Then the catch at M is released, the trunk of the body is free to turn about G, and the spring H pulls the body into an upright position, whereupon the boat and its occupant upset.   Critical adjustments may be made by varying the weight of the keel of the boat.

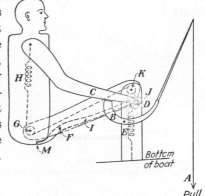

Fig. 85.—When the line is pulled the mechanical man stands up and the boat upsets.

DYNAMICS OF LIQUIDS

M-288. Inertia of Liquids. Two glass tubes about $1\frac{1}{2}$ in. in diameter and $\frac{1}{2}$ ft long, with their ends smoothed in a flame, are provided with corks. In one is placed a cylindrical piece of cork of diameter about $\frac{1}{4}$ in. less than the internal diameter of the tube. In the other is placed a cylindrical piece of lead of about the same shape.   One of the corks in each tube may be of the ordinary tapered sort; the other cork should have a small shoulder that can be pressed down so as to bear against the end of the tube.   After the two tubes are filled with water and corked, they are laid horizontally on the lecture table.   A sharp blow of a mallet on the shouldered stopper of the tube containing the cork cylinder will cause the cork to shoot forward, while a blow similarly given to the stopper of the tube containing the lead cylinder will cause the lead to move backward in the tube.

M-289. Liquid Accelerometers.   The inertia of a liquid may be utilized in various manometers for measuring linear acceleration, either vertical or horizontal (M-108), centripetal acceleration and speed of rotation (M-150), or angular acceleration (M-166).[1]

In simplest form for the measurement of horizontal acceleration, the manometer consists of a U-tube filled with mercury or water (Fig. 86a). The inertial reaction due to acceleration of liquid in the horizontal arm of the U is equalized by a difference in pressure in the two vertical arms, so that $\Delta h = La/g$, which is independent of the size of tube or density of liquid. The sensitivity of the device depends primarily upon the horizontal length L.

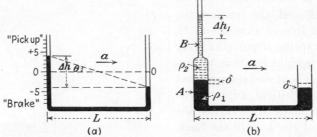

Fig. 86.—Liquid accelerometers: (a) simple form; (b) multiplying form.

For lecture purposes (M-108), it is desirable to increase the sensitivity of the accelerometer without increasing its length. This may be done by making the manometer as shown in Fig. 86b. The horizontal arm is filled with mercury, which extends into the vertical arm a short distance. The area of cross section of one arm is reduced from A to B at some point above the interface between mercury and colored water in that arm. Thus the inertia of the horizontal mercury column is equalized in large part by the change in level of water in the constricted arm of the U. The relation between change in height in this arm alone and the horizontal acceleration is then given by

$$\Delta h_1 = \left(\frac{\rho_1 A}{2B\rho_1 + (A - B)\rho_2} \right) \cdot \frac{La}{g},$$

where ρ_1 and ρ_2 are the densities of the heavy and the light liquids respectively. It will be observed that the relationship between a and Δh_1 is linear and that the instrument may be cali-

[1] SUTTON, R. M., *Am. Phys. Teacher.* **3**, 77, 1935.

brated linearly along the tube *B* directly in feet per second per second or other convenient unit, solely from a knowledge of the geometrical and density factors involved.

M-290. Water Hammer.   A water-hammer effect can often be shown by suddenly shutting off the faucet at a local sink.

A sharp metallic click is heard when water strikes the end of a glass tube from which air has been removed.   A tube 1 ft long and 1 in. in diameter is closed at one end and drawn down at the other.   Two or three inches of water are placed in the tube, and it is connected to a vacuum pump with an efficient drying system. Pumping is continued until the water boils freely at room temperature.   The small end is then sealed off.   The cryophorus tube (H-67) shows the effect nicely.

M-291. Hydraulic Ram.   Essential to the positive action of a hydraulic ram is a long feed pipe in which the water flows with high velocity.   This pipe should be 15 to 20 ft long, with a drop of 3 or 4 ft. If made of $\frac{1}{4}$-in. lead tubing, it may be coiled beneath the reservoir *R* (Fig. 87).   The valves are steel balls; valve seats at *A* and *B* are made by driving the balls against ends of the lead tubing.   The ball at *A* is retained by a cage of four wires within the air

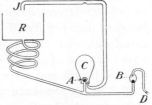

Fig. 87.—Hydraulic ram.

chamber *C* (a 1-l spherical flask).   The outlet *J* may be higher than the reservoir *R* and for convenience may be situated above *R* to help replenish the water supply.   The outlet *D* leads to the sink.

M-292. Ball on Jet—Bernoulli Effect.   A ping-pong ball may be supported on a jet of water at a height varying from 3 to 15 ft. The jet must be as nearly vertical as possible.   A piece of glass tubing drawn down to a narrow opening, not over 1 mm in diameter, serves as a nozzle.   A large basin is necessary to catch the spray if great heights are employed.

Compressed air will serve as well as water.   It is possible to support a ping-pong ball for several seconds on air from the lungs, blown through a nozzle 4 mm in diameter.   When compressed air is used, the jet may be inclined at a considerable angle.   It may be made to support a heavy rubber ball or even an ordinary screwdriver.

Instead of compressed air, a vertical jet of steam may be used. It is produced by boiling water in an ether can that is fitted with a tight cork containing a glass nozzle drawn down to a small opening.

M-293. Ball in Funnel. A ping-pong ball will be supported in the narrow end of an inverted funnel through which a jet of water or air is streaming downward.

M-294. Bernoulli Apparatus. A glass tube $1\frac{1}{2}$ or 2 in. in diameter is gradually tapered toward the center to about $\frac{3}{8}$ in. Several vertical side tubes are attached at points of different diameter along the tube. When water is sent through the tube, the effect of varying velocities of flow is shown by the different heights to which water rises in these tubes. Colored floats help to make the various water levels visible.

M-295. Card-and-spool Experiment. A pin is stuck through the middle of a card and is inserted in the hole of a wooden spool to prevent lateral motion. When one blows through the hole, the card does not fly off but presses against the spool. If a large metal disk with central hole connected to a large compressed-air outlet or tank of carbon dioxide gas is used, a similar disk is held to it with sufficient force to support a heavy weight.

M-296. Dependence of Pressure on Velocity in Air Stream. Hang two sheets of paper from the sides of a stick so that they are separated 2 to 10 cm. Blow between them, and observe how they are drawn together instead of being forced apart.

Alternatively, hang two pendulum balls a short distance apart, and blow between them. The balls immediately collide with one another. If metal balls supported by wires from a nonconducting support are connected with a lamp and 110-v supply, the collision of the balls may be made evident by a flash of the light.

M-297. Curve Balls. A throwing tool for shooting curve balls may be made from a 15-in. length of 2-in. mailing tube lined with sandpaper or from a smaller tube cut in two lengthwise and similarly lined. Ping-pong balls may be thrown from this tube with high spin velocity so as to describe "ins," "outs," "drops," or "upshoots," depending upon the manner of throwing. The ball always curves in the direction toward which its leading point is spinning.

M-298. Lift on Rotating Cylinder—Bjerknes' Experiment. Three feet of wide cloth tape is wrapped around the middle of a

paper mailing tube 2 in. in diameter and 1 ft long.   The free end
of the tape is attached to a chain of stout rubber bands fastened
to the top of the table.   The tube is laid on the table so that the
tape will unwind from the bot-
tom.   When the tube is pulled
aside horizontally and released,
the sudden unwinding of the
tape gives it high linear and spin
velocities.   If the speed is high
enough, the tube will describe a
vertical loop (Fig. 88).

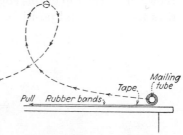

Fig. 88.—Bjerknes' experiment.

M-299. Autorotation.   An
8-in. piece of half round is care-
fully balanced on an axle AB (Fig. 89).   An air stream from an
electric fan strikes the curved face of the stick.   The stick will
rotate at high speed in *either* direction when once given a start
(see S-142).

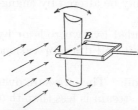

Fig. 89.—The stick is
kept rotating in either direction by an air stream.

M-300. Flettner Rotor Ship.   Upon
a light car, arranged to run on rails with
as little friction as possible, mount a
light motor with its axis vertical.   On
an extension of this axis, mount a paper
drum rotor about 1 ft high and 6 in. in
diameter.   The ends of the rotor should
be fitted with flanges that extend about
1 in. beyond the cylindrical surface (Fig.
90).   With this drum rotating rapidly, make the "ship" sail
back and forth along the track by a stream of air from an electric
fan directed at right angles to the track.   The direction of the
"ship" may be reversed by reversing
either the direction of the wind stream
or the rotation of the drum.   With the
rotor at rest, the breeze is unable to
move the car.

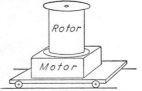

The same effect may be demonstrated
less spectacularly by balancing a motor,
driving a horizontal drum, on one pan

Fig. 90.—Model of Flettner
rotor ship.

of a platform balance.   A stream of air will raise or lower the
platform, depending upon its direction and the direction of
rotation.

M-301. Lift on an Airfoil. Hold a sheet of 8- by 11-in. type-writer paper by one edge so that the surface near that edge is nearly horizontal, while the rest of the sheet hangs limp below. Blow across the top of this edge, and observe how the whole sheet rises to a horizontal position.

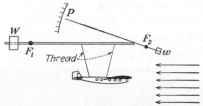

Fig. 91.—Balance to show lift on model airplane.

M-302. A model airfoil or airplane is balanced at F_1 as shown in Fig. 91. When a horizontal wind stream from an electric fan strikes it, the balance is upset as shown by motion of the pointer P balanced at F_2. The angle of attack may be altered by changing the lengths of the supporting threads.

If preferred, the airfoil may be suspended by two rods or by four wires as a pendulum, to show both lift and drag for various angles of attack.

M-303. Pressure on Surfaces of Airfoil. The pressure over the convex surface of an airfoil in a wind stream is less than that

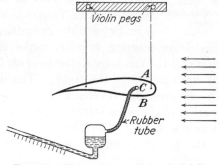

Fig. 92.—Pressure on surfaces of airfoil.

over the concave surface, as may be shown by the apparatus in Fig. 92. The airfoil is a hollow container, closed except for small holes at A and B. A slant manometer is attached at C. When the airfoil is placed in the wind stream from an electric fan, the slant manometer shows the pressure at A when B is closed and A is open, and at B when A is closed and B is open. Variations of these pressures with angle of attack may be shown by tilting the airfoil.

M-304. Aspirator and Atomizer Effect. A 6-in. length of glass tube, $\frac{1}{2}$ in. in diameter, has a constriction in the middle to a diameter of about 0.1 in. Water is run through the tube to a vessel into which the lower end of the tube dips, to reduce noise and splashing. Reduced pressure in the constriction causes dissolved air in the water to be freed and even makes the water boil. The vapor condenses below the constriction, and the hissing sound that results can be heard throughout the room.

The side tube of a water-faucet aspirator may be connected to a long open U-tube mercury manometer to show that the pressure at the constriction when water is flowing is much less than atmospheric pressure, even though the static pressure of water in the mains is greater than atmospheric.

An atomizer or insecticide sprayer may be shown. Its principle is illustrated in simple fashion by blowing through a horizontal tube across the upper end of a second tube dipping into a beaker of water. The reduced pressure caused by the rapid passage of air across the mouth of the vertical tube causes water to rise several inches above the level in the beaker.

M-305. Venturi Meter. The rate of flow of fluids is frequently measured by the type of instrument shown in Fig. 93. A manometer is attached to the flow tube CD at A and B; the area of cross section at B is less than that at A. When fluid flows through the tube

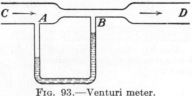

Fig. 93.—Venturi meter.

CD, the pressure at B is less than at A, as shown by the difference in level of liquid in the manometer. For air flow, water may be used in the manometer; for liquids, mercury is preferable.

M-306. Streamline Apparatus. An apparatus for showing streamlines, somewhat difficult to construct, is commercially available. It consists of a series of projection cells, with various-shaped obstacles fitting between their parallel walls and with an outlet at the bottom. These cells may be attached in turn to a double-compartment tank, one side filled with clear, the other with colored water. Through a row of holes in each of these tanks, the liquids flow into the projection cell in a series of alternate clear and dark lines, whose shape may be observed as they bend around the obstacle.

M-307. Air Flow Made Visible. A simple and effective method of rendering air streams visible consists in producing a jet of dense fog from solid carbon dioxide and water. A few pieces of dry ice are introduced into a large flask half full of warm water. The flask is closed with a stopper through which emerges a tube of large diameter. The dry ice sublimes rapidly and forms a heavy white fog. The mouth of the exit tube may be placed in the wind stream of an electric fan so that the outrushing fog is directed along the stream. Strong illumination helps to render the flow visible even in a large room. Disks, spheres, and stream-lined objects of the same cross-sectional area may be introduced into the visible stream to compare their various effects upon the flow.

M-308. Streamline Experiments. Place a lighted candle near a cylindrical obstacle, such as a large beaker or tin can. Blow the candle out by directing a blast from the lungs at the side of the cylinder diametrically opposite the candle.

M-309. A card about the size of a calling card is bent at right

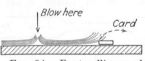

FIG. 94.—Bent calling-card turns over in upward stream-lines.

angles near its ends to form two legs about $\frac{3}{8}$ in. high. Stand the card on its legs, and invite a student to blow it over. Direct blowing between lecture table and card makes the card cling firmly to the table (Bernoulli effect).

But if the card is placed 18 in. or 2 ft away and a person blows perpendicular to the table, the card promptly turns over. In this case the streamlines curl upward after following the table for some distance (Fig. 94).

M-310. Velocity Distribution in Streamline Flow. The lower half of a glass tube 1.5 in. in diameter and 12 in. long is filled with clear castor oil. The upper half is filled with castor oil colored red.[1] Some of the clear oil is now drawn off at the bottom through a tube with a pinchcock. The rate of flow of the oil is greatest on the axis of the large tube and decreases toward the

[1] An oil-soluble dye is mixed in a small amount of carbon tetrachloride that is in turn mixed in castor oil.

walls, as is clearly evident from the shape of the interface between the clear and the colored oil.

M-311. Streamline vs. Turbulent Flow. A steel ball or a marble dropped into a tall glass graduate filled with viscous liquid (glycerin, castor oil, corn sirup, etc.) will fall slowly straight to

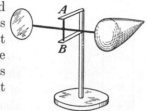

the bottom. But if the ball is dropped into water or gasoline, it soon acquires such speed that the motion of fluid past the ball becomes turbulent, so that the ball moves in a sinuous path and strikes the side of the glass cylinder before it reaches the bottom.

A hot iron ball lowered suddenly in front of a bright pinhole source of light

FIG. 95.—Streamlining reduces wind resistance.

in a dark room shows, by shadow projection, the turbulent vortices that form behind it in the air. If the ball is moved slowly, the motion of air currents is smooth and undisturbed.

M-312. Advantage of Streamline Design. A metal disk and a wooden streamlined object whose maximum area of cross section

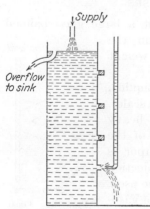

FIG. 96.—Torricelli's theorem; velocity of efflux shown by Pitot tube.

is equal to that of the disk are fastened to a stiff wire 6 in. long and balanced about a vertical wire pivot *AB* midway between them (Fig. 95). An air stream from an electric fan is directed at both objects. The streamlined body moves forward into the air stream.

If desired, the disk and the cigar-shaped object may be replaced by two toy automobiles, one streamlined, the other not.

M-313. Torricelli's Theorem. A tank with several side openings allows water to stream out in parabolic paths from which the initial velocity of efflux may be computed. More simply, the velocity may be determined by a Pitot tube, a glass tube of length equal to the height of the tank and drawn down to a small nozzle extending at right angles to the length of the tube (Fig. 96). When this tube is placed in any one of the emerging streams, the pressure that it shows is (nearly) the same as the head in the tank. It is probably worth while to show that the velocity of efflux is (nearly) independent of the size of the hole, by having two holes at the same height but of different diameters. An overflow tube and constant supply of water from the mains serve to keep the level in the tank constant.

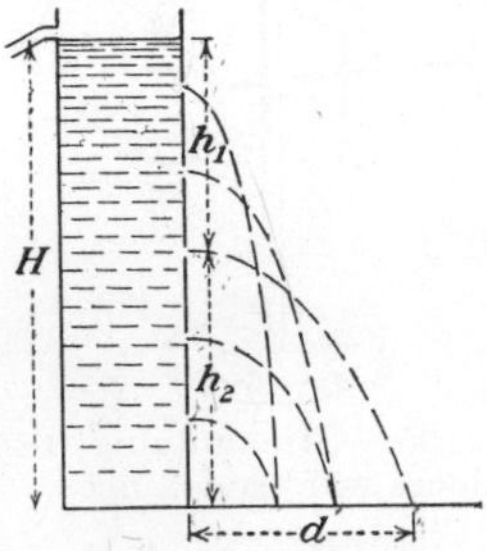

M-314. Water Parabolas. A tall reservoir, equipped with overflow tube to give constant head, is supplied with water from the mains. Water may flow from any one of several horizontal orifices, equally spaced above the table on which the reservoir stands (Fig. 97). The (theoretical) distance d at which any jet strikes the table is $2\sqrt{h_1 h_2}$, where h_2 is the height of the orifice above the table and h_1 is the pressure head. This distance is maximum when $h_2 = h_1$, *i.e.*, for a hole halfway up the reservoir.

FIG. 97.—The middle jet shoots farthest.

MECHANICS OF GASES

M-315. Gases Have Mass. Exhaust a large glass balloon with a tight stopcock. Balance it on the scales. Let the air in and show that its weight has increased about one gram per liter.

M-316. Gases May Be Poured Like Liquids. Two 500-ml beakers are balanced on the scales. Into one of them may be poured the heavy vapor of sulfuric ether until that side of the balance is depressed. The flow of vapor is readily made visible by shadow projection (L-30). Carbon dioxide may likewise be used.

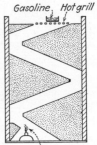

FIG. 98.—Gasoline vapor runs down the ramp and a flame strikes back.

M-317. Safety First. A teaspoonful of gasoline in an open tray is placed on a hot wire grill at the top of a "staircase" (Fig. 98). At the bottom is the open flame of a candle. In a few seconds, the heavy vapors descend the "staircase," and a flame strikes back to ignite the gasoline at the top. The front of the box representing the staircase is sealed with glass for visibility. The connection between this experiment and the all-too-frequent accidents from gasoline vapor may be emphasized.

M-318. Gas Siphon. Into a beaker on a stand about 1 ft high flows carbon dioxide from a rubber tube connected to a gas cylinder through a reducing valve. A second piece of tubing, filled with carbon dioxide, is used as a siphon to drain gas from the upper beaker into a lower one set on the table. The presence of the carbon dioxide in the lower beaker is shown by extinguishing a lighted candle set in it.

M-319. Compressibility of Air—Boyle's Law. For demonstration purposes, a large model of the Boyle's law apparatus is desirable. The scales should be graduated with broad clear lines. Both the compression chamber C, a $1\frac{1}{2}$-in. tube about 1 ft long, and the mercury reservoir R should be firmly mounted on blocks that are attached to ropes passing over pulleys and counterbalanced (Fig. 99).[1] The scales showing the pressure may be drawn on ribbons passing over spools, so that the zero of P_1 may be adjusted to the level of mercury in the compression chamber. To emphasize that it is the absolute pressure that enters Boyle's law, the left side P_1 starts from zero and gives plus and minus inches of mercury, and the right-hand scale P_2 runs from 10 to 60 in., with the local barometer reading set opposite the zero of the left scale. The stopcock in the top of the compression chamber must be carefully ground and greased to prevent leakage. Volumes are read directly from the scale V.

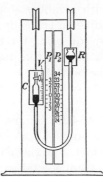

FIG. 99.—Apparatus for verifying Boyle's law.

M-320. Cartesian Diver. The diver is a test tube ($\frac{1}{2}$ by 4 in.) about two-thirds full of kerosene colored with alkannin dye (which is insoluble in water). While the finger is held over the end, the tube is inverted and dipped into water in a tall jar, and the short arm of a J-tube introduced, by which the volume of air above the kerosene may be adjusted. The tube should float with its top about 2 mm above the water surface. A little water is removed from the jar, and the top closed with a one-hole rubber stopper through which passes a glass tube attached to a length of rubber tubing. Pressure can be applied to the water surface by blowing through the rubber tube, thus causing the diver to

[1] KREIDER, D. A., *Am. Jour. Sci.*, **32**, 329, 1911.

descend. If the adjustment is right, it will be found that there is a point about halfway down where equilibrium is indifferent —below this point, the diver will continue to sink even when the air pressure is relieved. It can be brought to the surface again by sucking through the tube. The jar should be well illuminated and backed by a white cardboard.

M-321. A small medicine or perfume vial, preferably of colored glass, inverted with the proper amount of entrapped air, in a flat bottle (*e.g.*, a quart ammonia bottle) serves as the diver. The diver may be made to ascend or descend by change of pressure as previously described (M-320). However, if the bottle is closed with a rubber stopper and the air pressure within the bottle is adjusted critically, the diver may be made to ascend or descend by squeezing the bottle. The proper adjustment may be made by moving the stopper, provided that only a little air remains in the bottle.

ATMOSPHERIC PRESSURE

M-322. Simple Demonstrations. A cavity is hollowed out in the top of a cork stopper, keeping the rim of this face smooth and intact. If the cork is pressed, cavity downward, against the bottom of a tall graduate while water or mercury is poured in, the cork will remain on the bottom.

A smooth heavy object may be lifted by pressing one or more rubber vacuum cups upon it and then lifting on the cups.

Two large test tubes are chosen, one fitting nicely into the other. The larger test tube is filled with water, the smaller one inserted a little way into the mouth of the larger, and the system inverted. Water runs out, surface tension prevents the entry of air, and atmospheric pressure raises the smaller test tube.

A glass bottle is filled with water and closed with a rubber stopper through which passes a glass tube reaching nearly to the bottom. Two questions are proposed to the class: Can the bottle be exhausted (*a*) in the upright position? (*b*) in the inverted position? The answer is given by attaching it to an aspirator (M-304) in a near-by sink. This experiment is designed to show the limitation of "suction."

M-323. Magdeburg Hemispheres. Most laboratories are equipped with the standard apparatus for repeating this historic experiment. A modern modification consists of a cylinder at least 5 in. in diameter, closed with a tightly fitting piston. The cylinder is hung by chains from a rigid support. From the piston is suspended a platform on which a student may stand or sit in a chair. Upon pumping out the cylinder with a good pump, the student is lifted. Extremely low pressures are not required provided that the diameter of the cylinder is large enough. For example, the cylinder may be replaced by a bellows 2 ft in diameter, and a student may be lifted by connecting the bellows to an ordinary vacuum cleaner.

M-324. Barometer Tube. A tall vessel or tube is filled to a depth of 80 cm with mercury. Into this is dipped a glass tube with an open stopcock at the upper end. When the mercury completely fills the inner tube, the stopcock is closed and the tube withdrawn until the mercury falls away from the top, showing the barometric height. If this tube is somewhat enlarged just beneath the stopcock, a small bladder, carefully sealed, may be placed within it, and it will expand in the Torricellian vacuum.

This setup affords the opportunity to ask a catch question. If the glass tube is supported by a spring balance, does the pull on the balance equal only the weight of the tube, since the mercury is held up by atmospheric pressure? The correct answer is demonstrated.

M-325. Pressure Due to Height. A $\frac{1}{2}$-in. brass tube about 4 ft long is closed at each end. Two fine holes of equal size are bored near the ends. At the center of the tube is soldered a $\frac{1}{4}$-in. tube for connection to the gas supply. When the tube is held horizontally, the two flames issuing from the holes are the same height, but as the tube is rotated to the vertical position, the flame at the top becomes longer than the one at the bottom, because the gas used is lighter than air.

M-326. Collapse of Tin Can. A large varnish or alcohol can is heated with a small amount of water in it. When the air is thoroughly driven out by steam from the boiling water, the can is tightly corked and the heat turned off simultaneously. Upon cooling, the can collapses under atmospheric pressure; the collapse may be hastened by cooling the can with water (H-77)

A more positive procedure is to fit the can with a valve, which may in turn be connected directly to the air pump. The exhaustion is carried only to the point where the can crumples slightly. Then the can is removed from the pump, air is let in to atmospheric pressure, and the valve is closed. The can is now placed beneath a large bell jar on the plate of the vacuum pump, and the space around it is exhausted. The can is blown outward by the entrapped air.

M-327. Buoyant Effect of Air. A large cork stopper or hollow sealed glass ball is balanced against a brass weight on a simple balance placed under a bell jar. When the air is pumped out, the cork falls, showing that the air buoyed up the cork more than it did the brass weight (M-315).

M-328. Gas-filled Balloons. Balloons may be filled to any desired pressure from the gas mains by first letting the gas from the main enter an auxiliary balloon or rubber bulb. The valve to the main is closed and another to the balloon is opened so that the gas may be forced from the auxiliary bulb into the balloon. This process is repeated cyclically until the desired inflation is obtained. Using hydrogen and illuminating gas at equal pressures in identical balloons, the difference in lifting power may be shown by the load each will carry or by their relative rates of ascent without load.

PART II

WAVE MOTION AND SOUND

SIMPLE HARMONIC MOTION

S-1. Shadow Projection of Circular Motion. Simple harmonic motion is motion in which acceleration is proportional to displacement and is always directed toward a fixed point; it may be represented by the projection of uniform circular motion on a straight line in the plane of the circle. The most direct method is by shadow projection of a crank handle, such as the handle of a hand rotator. The wheel or crank is arranged to turn in a plane perpendicular to the screen or wall, on which its shadow is cast by a beam of light as nearly parallel as possible. While the handle itself moves uniformly in a circle, its shadow executes shm on the screen.

The to-and-fro motion of a piston driven by a flywheel, while not strictly simple harmonic, may be used as a first approximation.

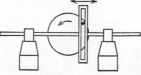

S-2. Simple Harmonic Motion Machine. Strict shm may be produced mechanically by a method sometimes used in machines, such as pumps. The

Fig. 100.—As the disk revolves uniformly, the yoke executes simple harmonic motion.

rod driving the piston carries at right angles to it a bar having a slot whose length is equal to the diameter of the driving wheel. A pin on the rim of this wheel slides in the slot (Fig. 100). As the wheel revolves uniformly, the pin describes a circle, and the slotted bar partakes only of the horizontal component of the pin's motion, which is shm. Another pin may be mounted over the center of the slot so that the pin describing the circular motion may pass under it. If desired, the whole mechanism may be concealed by a shield with circular and diametrical slots through which these two pins protrude. Colored disks may be mounted on the two pins for visibility.

127

S-3. Simple Harmonic Motion and the Simple Pendulum.
Drive the slotted yoke described in S-2 with a motor geared to
1 rps, and suspend just above it a pendulum bob adjusted to the
same period. Make the motion of the yoke and bob synchronous,
in phase, and of the same amplitude so that the two independent
motions appear to be coupled.

S-4. Projection Simple Harmonic Motion Apparatus. A
more elegant apparatus, suitable for projection, operates on the
same principle as S-2. The wheel and piston, connected by the
pin and slot as before, are now used to drive, respectively, a disk
of glass and a glass slide. On the disk is painted a circle with a
single spot; on the sliding plate are painted two lines at right

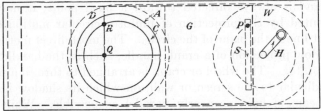

Fig. 101.—Projection slide to illustrate simple harmonic motion.

angles, with a spot at their intersection (Fig. 101). The two
pieces of glass are set together face to face, and the whole is made
to fit the slide holder of a projection lantern. When the slide is
operated, one sees on the screen a black spot moving uniformly
around the circle and another spot traversing a diameter in shm
as the projection of the first. The meaning of phase angles is
easily shown with this apparatus.

S-5. Springs and Pendulums. Mount a wheel with a white
ball on its rim with axis vertical, and drive it by a variable-speed
motor. Above the wheel hang a long pendulum, with its point
of suspension on the prolongation of the vertical axis of the wheel;
paint the bob white, and have it approximately the same size as
the ball on the wheel. Set the pendulum swinging in a vertical
plane with an amplitude equal to the radius of the wheel. By
means of the variable-speed motor, drive the wheel at such a
speed that the projection of the ball moves in step with the
pendulum, thus demonstrating that the motion of the pendulum
is simple harmonic (so long as its amplitude is not too large).

Visibility may be increased if the ball and pendulum bob are shadowed on a screen.

In a similar way, show that the vertical motion of a mass suspended by a spring is simple harmonic. In this case, mount the plane of the wheel vertical. The spring may be a coil of wire, or it may be a strip of steel held in a vise at one end and loaded at the other to reduce the frequency. In either case, the motions may be made large and observed either directly or by shadowing, or they may be made small and projected with the lantern.

S-6. Plotting Simple Harmonic Motion. When shm is plotted against time, the resulting curve is sinusoidal. This may be done point by point with any of the pieces of apparatus described in the preceding experiments for producing shm. A better way is the following. A light mirror is fixed to the side of one prong of an electrically driven tuning fork mounted in a vertical position (Fig. 102). Light from a small bright source is reflected from this mirror to a rotating mirror and thence to a screen, on

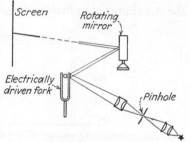

FIG. 102.—Arrangement of apparatus for producing a sine curve from a simple harmonic motion.

which it is focused by a projection lens situated between source and vibrating mirror. The rotating mirror consists usually of four mirrors arranged on the vertical sides of a cube that can be rotated about a vertical axis. The mirrors must be accurately parallel to this axis so that a reflected stationary spot of light traces the same path by reflection from each face. The cube is driven by a variable-speed rotator. With mirrors stationary, a spot of light is formed on the screen. The fork is started, and the spot executes shm in a vertical line, showing the amplitude of the motion. When the rotating mirror is started, the spot of light describes a sine curve. By changing the amplitude of motion of the fork and hence of the spot of light it can be shown that the period is nearly independent of amplitude. By shutting off current to the fork, while keeping the rotating mirror in motion, one can show damping.

S-7. Two Periodic Motions with Different Restoring Forces.
Not all periodic motions are simple harmonic. The contrast
between two somewhat similar motions is shown as follows. A
light car, running with little friction, traverses a horizontal track
raised 2 ft or more above the lecture table (Fig. 103). Strings
from each end of the car pass over pulleys and are attached to
weights as shown. The lengths of the strings are adjusted so
that with the car in the center of the track both weights W just
touch the table; thus when the car is in motion one weight is
picked up as the other is deposited on the table. The auxiliary
weights B are 20 g each (enough to keep the strings on the
pulleys) and are fastened to the strings at a distance above W
half the height of the track above the table, making this distance
the maximum amplitude of the motion. A pair of light helical

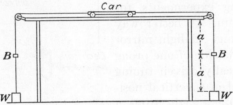

Fig. 103.—Oscillatory motion of the car produced by the weights differs from
that produced by springs.

springs are attached between the car and the ends of the track,
the weights W are lifted so that they do not act, and the car is set
in motion. The car moves more slowly as the amplitude
diminishes, but the period of its motion is independent of amplitude. The springs are then removed, and the weights W are
allowed to hang down. The car is drawn to one side and released,
whereupon it describes a reciprocating motion whose *period*
diminishes as the amplitude decreases. The weights are chosen
so that initially the period is the same as with the springs. When
springs are used, the restoring force is proportional to displacement, which is the condition for shm; but with this arrangement of
weights the restoring force is constant. From the equation
$s = \frac{1}{2}at^2$, it is evident that the period is proportional to the square
root of the amplitude in the latter case. The difference between
the behavior with springs and that with weights is remarkable.

S-8. Vibrations of Loaded Bar. A steel bar 1 m long of
rectangular cross section 1 by 2 cm is clamped at one end in a

vise, to vibrate horizontally. The other end is loaded with weights chosen so that the period of vibration may be either 1 or 0.5 sec. The bar is clamped with its wider faces vertical, and by using the two weights successively the increase in frequency of the shm with decrease in mass is shown. The bar is then set with the narrow faces vertical, and the increase in frequency with the increased stiffness of the bar is demonstrated. Lissajous figures can be demonstrated by giving the bar simultaneous horizontal and vertical displacements, releasing it and viewing it end on; the end of the bar should carry a white spot for better visibility. If the ratio of width to thickness of the bar is a small integer, the figures are relatively simple.

S-9. Mechanical Vibrator. A mechanical vibrator suitable for use in several experiments may be constructed from an old

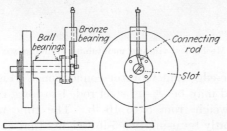

Fig. 104.—Heavy mechanical vibrator.

truck flywheel mounted with ball bearings in a heavy frame (Fig. 104). The flywheel carries two pulleys of different diameters for belt connection with a variable-speed drive. On the other end of the shaft is a rotor, along a diameter of which is cut a keyed slot. A pin in this slot serves as the crank, and the amplitude of the motion may be adjusted from 0 to about 1 cm by moving the pin. The connecting rod is of aluminum. The reciprocating motion is communicated to a rod sliding in a heavy bronze bearing carried by an arm bolted to the main frame. The bolts are set symmetrically so that the arm can be attached either vertically or horizontally. The head of the vibrating rod is threaded to take long rods, hooks, etc.

S-10. There are on the market motor-driven mechanical vibrators of adjustable amplitude and frequency such as the one illustrated in operation in Fig. 105, where it is shown maintaining standing waves in a cord (S-35).

S-11. A heavy pendulum with a steel knife-edge K resting on a flat steel plate mounted on a stout wooden stand makes a satisfactory vibrator for horizontal motion for periods between $\frac{3}{4}$ and 2 sec. Amplitude may be varied by changing the distance

FIG. 105.—Mechanical vibrator maintaining standing waves in a cord.

between knife-edge and vibrator connection C (Fig. 106). The pendulum rod may be $\frac{5}{16}$-in. steel rod, 1 m long, or more. The bob should weigh from 5 to 10 lb. The time range may be increased greatly by using two 5-lb weights that can be adjusted

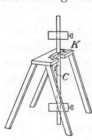

FIG. 106.—Pendulum of variable period for driving oscillators.

on either side of the knife-edge with the vibrator connection below the knife-edge. Such a pendulum can be made of convenient size with period variable from 1 to 10 sec.

S-12. A vibrator of fixed period is made by using an electric clock motor, to the shaft of which is fastened an eccentric pin that works in a slot cut in a piece of aluminum (Fig. 107). The latter is provided with two parallel slots at right angles to the central slot so as to follow only a linear component of the motion of the eccentric pin, the lateral slots sliding on two pins in a block of wood mounted on the support holding the motor.

S-13. Forced Vibrations and Resonance. A vibrator such as previously described (S-9) is arranged for vertical vibration, and a helical spring and weight are hung from the end of the vibrating rod (Fig. 108). The weight and spring are adjusted to have a period of about 1 sec; the amplitude of the reciprocating motion should be about 0.5 cm. The response curve for the driven oscillator as a function of frequency is demonstrated as follows.

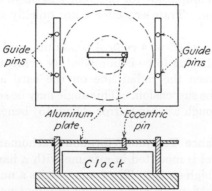

FIG. 107.—Vibrator of fixed period made from an electric clock.

The vibrator is started at a low speed, and attention is called to the small amplitude response *in phase* with the force. As the speed is gradually increased, there is an increase in response, up to resonance. The speed is then increased to about four times the resonant frequency, and the response is again of small amplitude and is found to be *out of phase* with the applied force. Free vibration may be damped out by placing the hand loosely around the spring near its midpoint. As the speed is decreased again to resonance, there is an increased response. The mechanical vibrator used in this experiment must have large inertia and fairly strong bearings, as otherwise its behavior will be distorted near resonance.

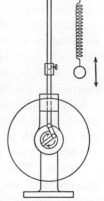

FIG. 108.—Forced vibration and resonance.

S-14. Forced Vibrations and Resonance— Phase Relations. An electric clock motor (period about 1 sec) is mounted with shaft vertical, free end down. A cork stopper is bored to fit symmetrically over the free end of the shaft; it carries a white circular card with a single black radial line. A pin is pushed through card and stopper on this line near the axis. A thread fastened to the head of the pin supports a cork ball painted white.

The length of the suspension is easily varied between a few centimeters and 1 m if the thread is pressed into a bit of soft wax on the pinhead, leaving the free end hanging down. Transient effects and final amplitude for different lengths of suspension are strikingly shown. Transient effects are quickly damped if the bob is light.

The cork bob swings as a conical pendulum, and its phase with respect to the driving force is immediately evident by observing the angle between the radial line on the card and the radial component of the suspension. This angle may be seen by viewing the motion through a large mirror set at 45° beneath the motor and pendulum.

S-15. Resonance Top and Vibration Tachometer. A heavy gyroscopic wheel is mounted in a frame with a handle so that it can be spun at high speed. The frame carries a number of metal reeds of different lengths and hence of different natural frequencies. The wheel is made slightly unbalanced, so that as it spins it gives the frame a vibration of a frequency equal to that of its spin. As the wheel slows down on account of friction, the frequency of vibration decreases, and successively longer metal reeds come into resonance with it. The principle of the vibrating-reed frequency meter, or tachometer, is thus demonstrated.

A model vibration tachometer may be made by mounting three strips of steel, each having a ball or other weight at the end, vertically in a block of wood that is beveled on its underside. This block is rocked from side to side by hand. Convenient lengths for the strips are 25, 40, 60 cm.

S-16. Impulse-driven Mechanical Resonator. A long thin bar of brass or steel with rectangular cross section is clamped at one end with its wide faces horizontal. Above the free end is mounted a glass tube drawn down so that water can issue from it in drops. The number of drops per second is adjusted to synchronism with vibrations of the bar. The vibrations can then be maintained by the falling drops, thus demonstrating how small impulses properly timed can set comparatively large masses into periodic motion of considerable amplitude.

S-17. Coupled Oscillators—Transfer of Energy. Hang a string loosely between two hooks at the same height. From the string hang two similar simple pendulums. Set one swinging, while the other is at rest. After a time that depends on the amount of coupling (tightness of the string), the second pendulum has all the energy, and the first is at rest. There is thus a periodic transfer of energy from one pendulum to the other. This may be repeated with pendulums of different masses (lead and wood). The larger mass will swing with the smaller amplitude.

S-18. Transfer of Energy from Translation to Rotation. A Wilberforce pendulum may be used to illustrate the periodic transfer of energy of translational into that of rotational vibrations. It is a long closely wound helical spring, hung vertically from a rigid support, carrying at the lower end a weight whose moment of inertia about a vertical axis may be changed by means of small weights threaded on crossarms (Fig. 109). These are adjusted until the period of the torsional vibration is equal to that of the vertical oscillation. Then when the latter motion is started by pulling down the weight and releasing it, the slight torsional twist, introduced by the contraction of the spring, builds up rotation of the bob; presently the energy is all rotational, but by the converse process it is transferred back again to the vertical oscillations and the interchange continues periodically thereafter.

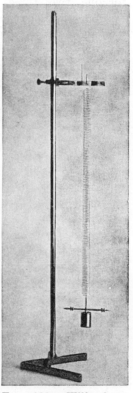

FIG. 109.—Wilberforce pendulum.

S-19. Multiple Resonance. The frequencies of the normal modes for coupled oscillators are the resonance frequencies of the system, and the number of such frequencies is equal to the number of coupled oscillators in the system. A length of piano wire is stretched horizontally between a rigid support and a mechanical vibrator capable of giving a continuous range of frequencies. Several equal masses, arranged for clamping to the wire, are affixed at symmetric points to serve for loading. With the vibrator stationary, the general free vibrations of the system and the possible modes of shm, the number of which is equal to the number of masses, are demonstrated. Then the vibrator is started, and the response for different frequencies is determined; it is found that resonance occurs at the frequencies of the normal modes, and the phase relations below, between, and above these frequencies can be shown. By repeating the process for one, two, three, and four masses, one can show that the number of resonance frequencies equals the number of masses. The masses and the tension of the wire should be adjusted so that the lowest (symmetric) frequency is about 1 cycle per sec.

S-20. Forced Vibrations and Resonance. Forced vibrations and resonance may be shown by suspending from a horizontal rubber cord a heavy driving pendulum and a number of simple pendulums of different lengths. The driving pendulum may be adjusted to any period by sliding its bob either up or down. The experiment is most striking if the driver and one simple pendulum of intermediate length have the same period. When this is the case, the amplitude of the tuned pendulum is large while the other pendulums have small amplitudes, and the pendulums of shorter period

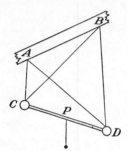

Fig. 110.—Heavy pendulum for showing forced vibration.

lead the intermediate one by progressively increasing phases whereas those of longer period have corresponding lags. The motion of the bobs may be viewed in a 45° mirror.

The free vibrations of the responding pendulums are quickly damped if the bobs are light; *e.g.*, small cork stoppers or paper cones having a mass of about 0.5 g. These light bobs can be suspended from threads passed through the supporting rubber cord with a needle. The threads are sufficiently held by friction, and their lengths may be easily adjusted. The damping of these light bobs may be decreased at any time by weighting them with several turns of lead (fuse) wire. If a second driving pendulum is hung from a cord parallel to the rubber cord, the response of the system to the two different drives will be obtained when the cords are coupled by means of a rigid connector. Instead of simple pendulums, masses suspended from light helical springs may be used. This latter type shows phase differences somewhat more clearly.

The resonant response of a watch to the oscillations of its balance wheel may be shown (see M-173).

S-21. Lord Rayleigh's model for forced vibrations is more elaborate but better adapted to these experiments than the arrangement just described. A massive pendulum CD (Fig. 110) is suspended horizontally by four steel wires from the points A and B, so that CD hangs at right angles to the direction AB. It may then be made to oscillate about the axis AB. The simple pendulum that is forced into vibration is suspended from P. Because of the large mass of the driver, the system vibrates for a long time.

WAVE MOTION

S-22. Water Waves. Waves on the surface of water are demonstrated by means of a long trough with glass sides, filled with water on which one or two corks are floated. A paddle at one end generates waves that can be seen to travel to the other end of the tank, where they are reflected. In particular the apparatus demonstrates the difference between wave motion and particle motion in the medium, since the waves move along the surface of the water but the water itself, whose motion is shown by the corks, only oscillates. It is possible to make the trough small enough for projection, but in this case one should use alcohol or other liquid of low surface tension. Standing waves may be produced by proper timing. It should be observed that the end of the tank is a loop and not a node.

S-23. Transverse Waves on Strings. The dependence of the speed of a transverse wave on a cord upon tension and upon mass per unit length may be observed by noting the times necessary for waves to travel the lengths of two similar ropes or solid rubber cords each 1 cm in diameter and 5 m long placed side by side in a horizontal plane. If both cords are under the same tension, then when they are given simultaneous sharp taps with the edge of the hand, pulses will travel the length of the cords in the same time. If one cord is subjected to a tension equal to four times that in the other, then a pulse will travel down and back one cord while it goes only to the far end of the other. If one of the cords is replaced by another that has a diameter of 0.5 cm, then when the length and tension of heavier and lighter cords are the same, the speed of the pulse will be twice as great in the latter as in the former.   The tension in each case should be made so small that the advance of the waves along the cords is slow enough to be followed easily by eye.   If gas tubing is used instead of cord, the mass per unit length may be increased by filling the tube with sand or water.

S-24. Wave Reflection at Change of Medium.   The partial reflection of pulses on cords may be shown with a cord that is 1 cm in diameter for part of its length and 0.5 cm in diameter for the remainder.   When a sharp pulse is started in the thin cord, it will be partly transmitted and partly reflected at the junction.   The reflected wave will have the same speed as the original one, a reversed displacement, and diminished amplitude (one-third as great, assuming cords having a ratio of diameters of 2:1).   The transmitted wave travels with one-half the speed, undergoes no reversal, and has two-thirds the amplitude.   On the other hand, if the pulse is started in the thick cord, the reflected wave has the same speed as the original and one-third of its amplitude, whereas the transmitted wave travels with twice the speed and four-thirds the amplitude.   Thus the amplitude of the transmitted wave *exceeds* that of the original wave even though part of the original energy is spent in producing a reflected wave.

If one of the cords is given two sharp taps in quick succession, it will be observed that the reflected pulse from the first tap passes through the direct one from the second without affecting it.

S-25. Models of Wave Motion.   There are many models and machines that may be used to demonstrate the motions of waves. One of the simplest models fits the slide holder of a projection lantern.   It consists of a frame carrying a number of wire forms bent in helixes and capable of being turned about their axes. When they are projected on the screen, they appear as waves of sinusoidal form that progress as the wire shapes are turned.   By combining several such shapes on one axis, various combinations of advancing and receding waves, standing waves and interfering waves may be shown.

S-26.   In another model, a number of small balls are fixed to the ends of a set of slender rods that can slide vertically in guides (Fig. 111).   The lower ends of the rods rest against a board cut in the shape of a sine curve.   By sliding the board beneath the rods, a wave is made to traverse the row of balls, and the relation between wave motion and particle motion is made evident.

S-27. The bottoms of the rods (all of the same length as in S-26) may rest on a series of equal disks, mounted eccentrically on a common shaft, each shifted in phase from the one preceding it by the same angle.   When the shaft is rotated, a wave moves across the row of balls.   Various elabora-
tions on this design may be constructed showing longitudinal waves, etc.

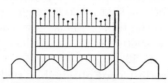

S-28. In a variation of S-26, the rods are not all of the same length but are cut so that when their lower ends stand on a flat

Fig. 111.—As the board is moved the balls show a progressing transverse wave.

surface the balls take the contour of a sine curve.   Several such sets of rods and balls may be used, illustrating waves of different wave length (Fig. 112*A*).   If the number of rods and balls in each set is the same, then the addition of several waves is shown

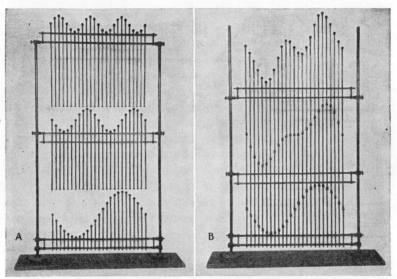

Fig. 112.—Model illustrating *A*, waves of different wave length and *B*, the addition of these waves.

by setting rods of one set on top of the balls of another set; the upper set of balls gives the form of the resultant wave (Fig. 112*B*).

S-29. Waves on Moving Cords.   Cement together the ends of a leather V-shaped belt so as to form a *smooth* joint, and place it over two pulleys, one an idler, the other driven by a variable-speed motor, the parallel portions of the belt being horizontal. The driven pulley should turn in such a direction that the least tension is in the top part of the belt. Adjust the speed of the belt so that a wave traveling along it just stands still with respect to the table. This may require speeds of the drive shaft as high as 3000 or 4000 rpm unless the tension on the belt is small.

S-30. A second method uses a 10-ft length of the heaviest and softest cord obtainable, such as is used for tying back portieres. Splice the ends together smoothly, and tie the resulting circle with a number of equally spaced threads, 2 ft long, to holes near the rim of a disk that can be rotated about a vertical axis. Accelerate the disk slowly to avoid twisting the threads until the loop of cord stands out in a circular form. When it is struck sharply, a pulse travels along it. Make the speed of rotation such that the pulse stands still with respect to the observer.

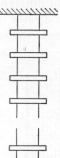

Both of these experiments demonstrate that a wave traveling in a uniform flexible string travels without change of shape and with a speed that is independent of the shape of the wave.

S-31. Modified Kelvin Wave Apparatus. The propagation of transverse waves at low speed may be shown by an apparatus consisting of a number of wooden bars 3 by 3 by 30 cm supported 8 cm apart by two stranded picture wires passing through holes in the bars 10 cm from each end (Fig. 113). The apparatus hangs from two eyelets at the ceiling so that the bars are viewed end on when the system is at rest. A torsional impulse given to the lowest bar is transmitted upward at approximately 60 cm per sec and is reflected at the top with reversal of phase.

Fig. 113.—
Twisting the
lowest cross
rod causes a
wave to move
upward along
the system.
The bars are
viewed end
on.

Hanging a weight at the bottom increases the speed. Visibility is improved by painting the ends of the bars white.

A simple damping arrangement can be made by fastening metal vanes to the lowest bar, letting them dip into a vessel of oil or water. The amount of damping is varied by changing the depth to which the vanes are immersed.

S-32. Kelvin Wave Model with Variable Damping. A more versatile wave apparatus consists of a long steel band with a number of horizontal metal crossbars carrying balls at their ends. The upper support is a vertical rod free to rotate in ball bearings; it carries a horizontal copper disk between the poles of an electromagnet (Fig. 114). By varying the current energizing the electromagnet, the damping of the wave motion at the upper end is controllable within wide limits. An impulse or a periodic motion applied to the lowest bar is transmitted up the system from bar to bar by the steel band. If the disk is fixed, the impulse will be reflected with reversal of phase. If it is free, there will be

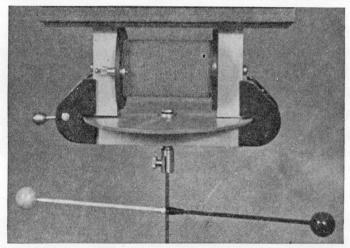

Fig. 114.—Electromagnetic damping arrangement for Kelvin wave apparatus.

reflection without change of phase. If the motion of the disk is damped, the wave will be reflected without phase change but with diminished amplitude. At one critical value of the damping, the wave energy will be entirely absorbed so that no reflected wave occurs. This is equivalent to sending the wave off to infinity.

S-33. Wave Machine. A weighted rubber tube is hung horizontally at a number of equally spaced points along its length from the ends of short horizontal bars, pivoted and counterbalanced to hold the tube straight when at rest. Friction adjustments are provided at the pivots, so that any desired amount of energy may be absorbed as the wave progresses along the tube. One end of the tube is driven by a mechanical vibrator. By varying the conditions of damping and frequency, many properties of waves can be shown (Fig. 115). The machine shows the

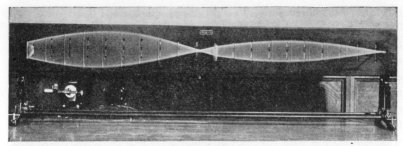

Fig. 115a.—Low pass filter made by loading cord near center to represent inductance.

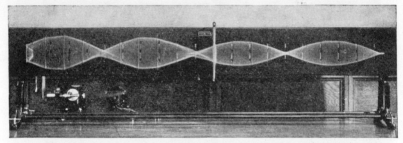

Fig. 115b.—Two springs attached at center of cord, representing capacitance—resonant frequency.

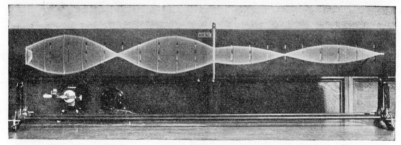

Fig. 115c.—Higher frequency than Fig. 115b; some energy passes.

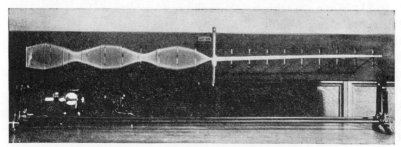

Fig. 115d.—Combination of mechanical "capacitance" and "inductance," with high impedance for frequency shown.

behavior of traveling waves; reflection at a boundary and its dependence on the rigidity of the boundary; reflection at an interface; standing waves in open and closed pipes; etc.

S-34. Standing Waves in Strings. Two similar waves traveling in opposite directions may combine to form standing waves, as may be shown by shaking one end of a rope, the other end of which is fixed. When the rope is shaken at any one of the proper frequencies, a pattern of loops and nodes appears. This principle may be demonstrated by the use of any of the various wave machines previously described or by the projection apparatus described in S-25. The slide for the projection lantern includes a set of wires arranged to show the progress of two waves traveling in opposite directions and their resultant standing wave.

S-35. Fasten a length of white clothesline to a rigid support at one end of the lecture table and to a mechanical vibrator at the other. By starting the vibrator with slowly increasing speed, show the various resonance shapes of the cord in turn, up to the fourth or fifth harmonic. Then decrease the speed of the oscillator, and watch the motion of the nodes. They spread apart, and as each one reaches the driving end a resonant response occurs. Provide for changing the tension of the cord. It should be illuminated and placed in front of a black background (the blackboard or a black cloth). If a constant frequency vibrator is used, the number of nodes and loops may be varied by changing the tension or the length.

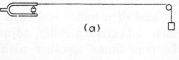

(a)

S-36. A white yarn or fishline is attached to one prong of an electrically driven tuning fork, held horizontally with the prongs in a vertical plane (Fig. 116a).

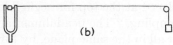

(b)

Fig. 116.—Two arrangements for producing standing waves in a cord by an electrically driven tuning fork.

The other end of the cord passes over a pulley and is weighted. As the tension of the string is increased, lower and lower harmonics resonate with the fork, showing that the fundamental frequency of the string increases with tension. If the vibrator is turned at 90° (Fig. 116b), *i.e.*, if the path of the tip of the vibrator and the string are in the same straight line, then the tension necessary to produce a given num-

ber of segments is only one-fourth as great as in the previous
arrangement, because the frequency of the string is only one-half
that of the vibrator. This second arrangement is preferable
because the vibration is all in one plane and the amplitude is
greater.[1]

The details of the motions in the several segments of a vibrating string are shown clearly and strikingly by stroboscopic
illumination. An electrically driven tuning fork, a pin driven
by an eccentric, or a flat strip of steel maintained in vibration by
an a.c. solenoid will serve for a vibrator.

S-37. Standing Waves.—If an iron wire is used instead
of a thread, it may be driven directly by an a.c. electromagnet
placed at an antinode. Another method is to pass alternating
current through a resistance wire stretched across the lecture
table and so arranged that one of its antinodal portions passes
normally through the field of a d.c. electromagnet or a strong
horseshoe magnet. If the alternating current is large enough,
the nodal points will become red hot, but the antinodes will be
cooled by their rapid motion. It is difficult to obtain stable
conditions if the heating current is too great. This experiment is
effective in a darkened room.

**S-38. Wave Machine for Both Transverse and Longitudinal
Waves.** A number of pendulums, say 15, are hung in a row from
a horizontal bar. Each pendulum consists of a spherical bob at
the end of a metal rod suspended from a steel pivot bearing.
Each rod carries a collar, adjustable with friction fit for coupling
the pendulums together with rubber bands. The collars are
placed at the top for negligible coupling; at the bottom, for close
coupling. The pendulums can be swung either in parallel planes
or all in the same plane, by turning the supporting pivots. Thus
either transverse or longitudinal waves can be shown. By means
of a fixed rod at one end to serve as a "dense" medium, reflection
can be shown. Standing waves can be set up by hand oscillation
of one end, and demonstrations given of fundamental and
harmonic vibrations corresponding to those in organ pipes.

S-39. Longitudinal Waves. A long helical spring is hung from
the ceiling or suspended in a horizontal plane by bifilar suspensions fastened every few turns along its length. If the spring is

---

[1] WATSON, F. R., "Sound," pp. 34–36, John Wiley & Sons, Inc., New
York, 1935.

stiff enough, the latter type of suspension may be unnecessary, but then the speed of a wave is high.   By compressing a few turns and then releasing them, a longitudinal wave pulse will be started.   If the end of the spring is driven by a mechanical vibrator at the proper frequency, standing waves will be set up. The details of these waves may be observed by illuminating the spring stroboscopically and casting its shadow on the screen.   If the length of wire in a spring is great compared with the length of spring itself, the velocity of the wave along the spring is given approximately by $v = (pr/2a^2)(n/2\rho)$.   In this equation, p is the pitch of the winding; r, the radius of the wire; a, the radius of each turn of the spring; n, the coefficient of rigidity; ρ, the density of the wire.   For a spring made of No. 18 copper wire of pitch

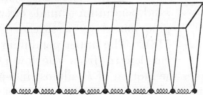

Fig. 117.—Croquet balls and springs to show progress of longitudinal waves.

1 cm and radius 5 cm, for which each turn must be supported by a thread at least 2 ft long, $v = 58$ cm per sec.   The velocity should be low for all cases where stroboscopic illumination is not used.

A uniform spring of copper wire, such as the one described in the previous paragraph, is made by wrapping wire tightly, turn against turn, upon an iron pipe.   The spring must be annealed at 400°C for half an hour, as otherwise it will be very irregular when removed from the form.   After annealing, it is stretched until the desired pitch is obtained.

S-40. A number of wooden (croquet) balls are hung from bifilar suspensions so as to swing in the same horizontal line and are connected by coil springs.   When an impulse is given to the ball at one end, a wave travels down the line.   The wave will be reflected with reversal of phase if the end ball is fixed and without reversal if it is not.   If half of the balls have greater mass than the other half, partial reflections will take place at the boundary between the two sets.   The amplitude and phase of the reflected wave and the amplitude of the transmitted wave differ when the wave goes from heavier to lighter balls from the corresponding factors when the wave goes in the opposite direction. The more massive the balls and the weaker the springs, the lower will be the velocity of the waves (Fig. 117).

S-41. Stretch a stiff helical spring across the lecture room between a rigid support and a sounding board of thin wood.

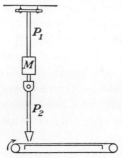

Start a pulse near the rigid support; it travels to the other end where it is heard as it strikes the sounding board. If it is of sufficient amplitude, the pulse will be reflected at the board, again at the rigid support, and will produce a second click at the sounding board.

S-42. Sand Pendulum for Compound Wave Form and Lissajous Figures. A sand pendulum is made of two pieces of gas pipe joined by a threaded coupling (Fig. 118). The upper pendulum P_1 is of different length from the lower pendulum P_2.

FIG. 118.—Sand pendulum for producing Lissajous figures and compound wave forms.

The mass M makes the motion of P_1 almost independent of that of P_2. The plane of oscillation of P_2 can be set at any chosen angle with that of P_1 by turning the coupling and then locking it with a thumbscrew. The path of the end of P_2 is traced by sand from a conical cup. A time axis is provided by having the sand fall upon an endless belt, made of black elastic cloth, which passes over rollers and a supporting platform. One of the rollers is driven by an electric motor through a worm gear reduction. This time axis is especially valuable for showing waves produced by two shm's.

For Lissajous figures, the collar supporting P_2 is turned through 90° so that the two pendulums swing in planes at right angles to each other. The moving time axis is not needed in this case.

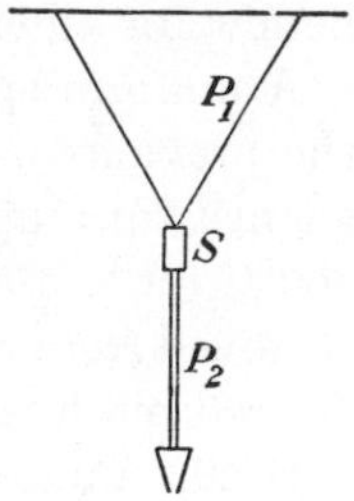

FIG. 119.—Simple sand pendulum.

S-43. A simpler form of sand pendulum for drawing Lissajous figures is made by suspending the sand container from a double cord (Fig. 119). The upper part P_1 is a bifilar suspension, and the lower part P_2 is a simple pendulum made by passing the cords through the tubular sleeve S. The advantage of this arrangement is that the ratio of the period of P_2 to that of the whole pendulum can be changed quickly by moving S. It has the disadvantage that the motion is more highly damped than in the one previously described, unless the sleeve S is massive.

S-44. Lissajous Figures. In a third method (Fig. 120), a rod of rectangular cross section is mounted in a block and the top bent over at right angles. A white ball is fastened to the bent end. By pulling the ball aside and then releasing it, a combination of vibrations is produced. If the ratio of the lengths of the two portions of rod is properly chosen, the ball will traverse a repeating path, except for damping. Illuminate the ball.

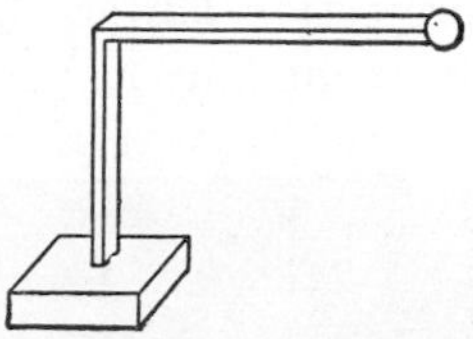

Fig. 120.—When the ball is plucked, it executes Lissajous figures.

S-45. Lissajous figures of large size may be obtained by successively reflecting upon a screen a beam of light from mirrors attached to the prongs of two electrically driven tuning forks vibrating in planes at right angles to each other. If the forks have slightly different periods and equal amplitudes, the resulting figure will change slowly from a straight line through an ellipse to a circle and back again to a straight line perpendicular to the first. The optical arrangements are shown in Fig. 121. Instead of tuning forks, two flexible sticks 50 cm long with mirrors attached to their free ends are clamped in vises. They may be used either in the same plane for showing compound wave forms or at right angles for showing Lissajous figures.

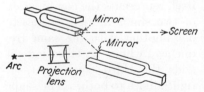

Fig. 121.—Arrangement for projecting Lissajous figures produced by two tuning forks vibrating at right angles to each other.

S-46. Harmonograph for Describing Lissajous Figures.

A more elaborate but very instructive piece of apparatus may be constructed if facilities are available. Two bars are made to vibrate at right angles with each other by means of cams. The bars carry mirrors at their ends, from which light is reflected to a screen. The two spots so formed execute shm's at right angles to one another. A third spot, formed by light reflected from both mirrors, executes a motion that is the combination of the two shm's. By means of color filters, the three spots are given distinctive colors. The machine is driven by hand, so that the motions are slow enough to be followed by the eye. A simple gearshift permits varying the ratio of periods of the two oscillating bars to give several simple fractions and their corresponding closed Lissajous figures.

S-47. Harmonic Curves in Space. An apparatus for showing certain harmonic curves in space may be constructed as follows. A paper card with a vertical slit is driven in the slide position of a projection lantern by a vibrator so as to execute shm. Light from the lantern passes through the slit in a plane vertical sheet

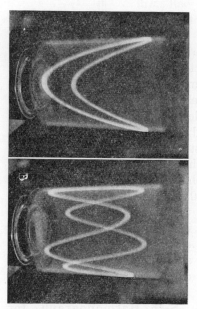

that performs shm in a direction perpendicular to itself. A white-enamelled pencil is mounted in the flat end of a motor pulley so as to generate a cylinder when the motor runs (Fig. 122). The motor is set with axis horizontal in front of the lantern. The sheet of light intersects the cylinder generated by the pencil so as to produce sine curves wrapped around a cylinder. The circular motion itself represents the combination of two shm's at right angles to one another with the same frequency, while the vibrating slit adds the third component, at right angles to both. The shape of the curve depends upon the frequency of vibration of the slotted card with respect to that of the pencil.

FIG. 122.—Harmonic curves in space.

S-48. A more elaborate apparatus permits varying the frequency of all three components within limits. Three synchronous motors are used, which may be two-, four-, and eight-pole. The two-pole motor carries an eccentric pin, fitted with a very small pulley sheave, over which is looped a strong fishline. The string is cemented to a small card near one end and continues to a rubber band. The card has a narrow slot at right angles to the string. Rotation of the motor produces a vibratory motion in the card that is very nearly simple harmonic, since the card is far from the driving pin. A similar arrangement is used to drive a second slotted card, above the first and parallel to it, but moving in a direction at right angles to the motion of the first. In the arrangement shown in Fig. 123, both cards C are driven by the motor M_1. The speed of eccentric E_2 may be changed by adjusting the speed control S; alternatively, the fishline loop may be transferred to the eccentric E_3 on motor M_2. The two cards are carried by horizontal slotted guides just above the condenser lens of a lantern arranged for vertical projection. A pencil of light

FIG. 123.—Motor drive for projecting three-dimensional Lissajous figures.

passes through the two slits and falls on a small white card driven by a third motor in shm along the direction of the light beam. Thus the spot of light seen on the card executes a motion that is the resultant of three mutually perpendicular shm's. The motor of lowest speed should be used to drive the screen, since windage is a source of trouble; for the same reason the card should be small and braced in the back with triangles of cardboard cemented to the reciprocating shaft, which is of wood with very light inset metal bearings.[1]

S-49. Ripple Tanks. Many wave phenomena in two dimensions are easily shown by ripple tanks, of which several designs

[1] Dod, W. C., *J. Acoust. Soc. Am.*, **6**, 279. 1935.

have been proposed.   Because of the importance of this demonstration technique, more than average detail is given in the following pages, so that those who wish to refine their own procedures may do so.   A ripple tank consists essentially of a shallow tray filled with a liquid on the surface of which ripple patterns are set up and made visible by projection, by either reflected or transmitted light.   Mercury seems to give very satisfactory results, and of course the waves are projected by reflection. Water, however, is much simpler to work with and gives good results; projection is usually by transmission.

The tank may be small enough to fit on the vertical projection attachment of a lantern, but it is better to use a larger one, as much as 1 m square.   The sides of the tank may be made of angle iron, with a sheet of clear glass for the bottom, the seams being filled with asphaltum paint or picein cement to make joints water-tight. Wedge-shaped strips of wood with a bevel of small angle should be used around the edges of the tank

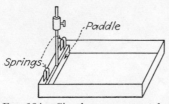

Fig. 124.—Simple arrangement for generating plane parallel waves.

to damp out reflections from the sides.   The tank is set on a stand above the table.   Best results are secured by projecting vertically onto the ceiling or by a 45° mirror onto a screen.   It is possible, however, to project obliquely straight through the tank onto the screen, although in this case the patterns are distorted.

There are many methods of generating waves and ripples. Probably the simplest is a generator of parallel plane waves.   It consists of a strip of wood mounted parallel to one side of the tank on two inverted U-shaped springs (Fig. 124); the strip dips into the water where its vibration sets up a series of ripples. From the center of the strip rises a vertical rod carrying a sliding weight by which the frequency of the generator can be changed. A paddle actuated by a mechanical vibrator is satisfactory for simple harmonic waves, provided that the vibrator is on a different support from the tank; otherwise the vibrations of the machine set up disturbing patterns in the water.

For the production of ripples, an electrically driven tuning ork may be used, equipped with a stylus to dip into the water.

The ripples may also be produced electrically. One terminal of a small spark coil or of a transformer is connected to a wire dipping into the water, the other to the tank. The form of the ripple is different in the two cases: the transformer produces very nearly a sine wave, while the spark coil produces a sharp pulse. As the ripples advance, however, this difference disappears, and the two methods have the same result except that the frequency can be changed with the coil but not with the transformer.

A third method, which is very satisfactory, is to use a periodic blast of air. A bicycle hand pump having a bore of 2 cm and driven with a stroke of 1.5 cm works well. However, the eccentric drive for such a reciprocating pump is a source of vibration that may disturb the pattern. This trouble may be avoided by using

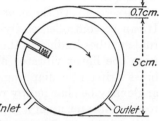

Fig. 125.—Rotary air pump for generating ripples.

a rotary pump (Fig. 125). The vane, which bears against the outer part of the air chamber, is of hard rubber so that it quickly wears to a good fit. A spring may be placed in the slot under the vane to insure its moving outward, or, if the vane is weighted by a lead plug, centrifugal force will keep it out at all times. The machine work on the pump should be good, but it is not necessary to have exceedingly close fits of the various parts, particularly if the pump is run at more than 1200 rpm.

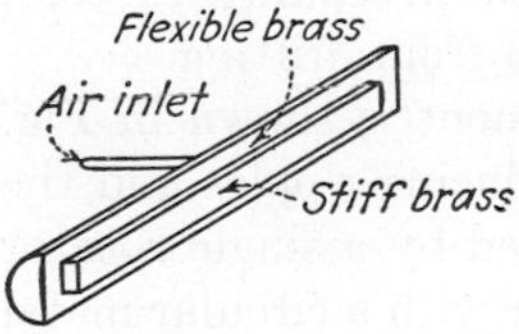

Rubber tubing connects the pump to glass tubes attached to the edge of the tank in such a way that they can be moved about to bring the air puffs to any part of the water surface. The point sources are glass tubes 0.5 mm in inside diameter cut off square at the ends and mounted several millimeters above the water surface. The source for linear waves is made from half a brass tube 30 cm long by 4 cm in diameter. The ends (Fig. 126) are of heavy brass plate soldered to the tubing, and the front is a diaphragm of sheet brass or phosphor bronze 0.25 mm thick. The center of the diaphragm is stiffened by a brass strip 27 cm long, 12 mm

Fig. 126.—Generator for linear waves.

wide, 3 mm thick. This diaphragm, intersecting the water surface and moving as a unit, generates plane waves. The pump connection, a brass tube, has one end fastened into the center of the back of the source and the other end resting upon one edge of the tank.

The definition of the images of the ripples depends upon the divergence of light from the stroboscope slots at the ripple tank, the amplitude of the ripples, and the distance from the ripple tank to the screen. Of these, amplitude is usually the most important. It can be controlled easily by means of screw pinchcocks on the rubber tubes leading to the source. The definition of the ripples from the linear vibrator also depends upon the angle that the brass strip on the diaphragm makes with the water surface. The angle may be changed by resting the free end of the tube leading to this vibrator upon a bracket supported on thumbscrews.

For viewing and for projection, light from a source of small area (d.c. carbon arc or an airplane headlight lamp, 12 v and 35 amp) is focused upon the slits in a stroboscope disk and is reflected by a 45° plane mirror (or 90° glass prism to avoid double image) up through the ripple tank to another 45° mirror. The stroboscope disk may be driven by a variable-speed motor (E-232), but results are more satisfactory if it is driven by the same motor that drives the pump. It should, however, be connected to this motor by means of a planetary gear system, so that the disk may be stopped or run faster or slower or in synchronism with the pump without changing the speed of the driving motor.[1] With separate motors, it is very difficult to keep the wave pattern from drifting.

A simple, complete ripple-tank arrangement is shown in Fig. 127, in which the air-puff impulses for producing ripples and the stroboscopic illumination are both controlled by a single rotator (hand or motor driven) (E-232). A rotator with a circular metal plate *D*, having near its rim a circle of evenly spaced holes (such as the siren disk in S-120), is provided with a shield of blackened cardboard or metal 2 or 3 in. square, with a hole in the center of the same size as the holes in the siren disk. The hole in the shield is opposite the line of holes in the plate. Two brass tubes *A* and *B* are supported in a line perpendicular to the plate with the row of holes between them and are adjusted to be as

---

[1] For details of the tank system and planetary transmission, see W. Baldwin, Jr., *Rev. Sci. Instruments*, **1**, 309, 1930.

close to the plate as possible without touching it when the plate
is in rotation.   Compressed air emerges from a fine hole in tube
A.   Tube B is connected by a rubber tube $\frac{1}{4}$ in. in diameter to a
glass nozzle with suddenly tapering end that can be mounted at
any desired position over the ripple tank.   The system is set in
front of the projection lantern so that the light is condensed upon
the opening in the fixed screen, the interrupted light being
reflected by a mirror through the ripple tank and projected upon
the screen.   A useful feature of the apparatus is the ease with
which frequency of ripples and light may be changed.   This is
especially valuable when showing diffraction effects.   If it is

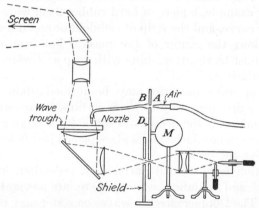

Fig. 127.—Ripple tank with intermittent air blast and stroboscopic illumination
controlled by a single motor.

desired to change the phase of the ripples relative to the light, the
air-tube system may be mounted on a sleeve (not shown in
Fig. 127) concentric with the axis of the siren disk.

Besides the production and propagation of waves and ripples,
the ripple tank is very useful for showing interference, reflection,
refraction, diffraction, and other wave phenomena.   For interference, two sources are required.   They may be of any of the
types previously described; if they are air blasts, they should
come from the same pump.   For reflection at various curved
surfaces, obstacles of the desired shape and size are put in the
path of the waves.   They may be solids that do not float or strips
of celluloid or sheet metal bent to the proper curve and held in
any convenient support.   Diffraction gratings may be cut from

sheet metal.   For refraction, the obstacle is made from a sheet of
clear glass in the shape of a lens or prism and is submerged just
below the surface, so that a shallower layer of water lies in the
path of the waves.   The depth of the water layer may be controlled by placing the obstacle on a glass table that is supported
by three thumbscrew legs.   Refraction effects are best seen by
using low-frequency waves viewed without a stroboscope.

To reduce the confusion resulting from refraction of light by
the water meniscus at the face of the obstacle, a mask should be
provided for each obstacle.   The masks are made from any
opaque material that will not float (*e.g.*, hard rubber) and are
cut 1 cm wider than the obstacle on each side.   For a curved
mirror, for example, a piece of hard rubber 2 cm wide is cut with
the proper curve, and the strip of celluloid or metal mounted in a
slot cut along the center of the mask.   For best results, the
obstacles must be clean; washing with soap and water to remove
grease is sufficient.

Images of wave patterns may be formed upon an opaque
screen some distance away or upon a transluscent screen placed
near the tank or, if the demonstration is for a small group, upon
a piece of ground or flashed opal glass placed just below the plane
mirror above the tank.

In addition to the usual patterns of reflection, interference,
diffraction, and standing waves, there are several others of
interest.   The Doppler effect in waves on water may be shown by
moving a point source horizontally.   The waves thus formed are
circular but not concentric, being crowded together in front of the
source and spread apart behind.   If the speed of the source is
greater than the speed of the ripples, a "bow wave" is formed.
If plane waves are sent through rows of nails regularly placed,
"Laue spots" may be obtained.   Wave groups are obtained if
two sets of ripples are produced simultaneously by blasts from
two pumps operated at different speeds.   The formation of a
plane wave by a number of circular waves having their centers on
the same straight line—Huygens' construction—may be shown
by using a row of point sources.

SOUND

S-50. A Sounding Body Is in Motion.   Two tuning forks of the
same frequency, mounted on resonance boxes, are set up some

distance apart. A pith ball hanging from a thread touches the
prong of one fork, and the other is set into vibration. The first
fork responds by resonance, and the pith ball is thrown aside
(shadow projection). When the second fork is stopped, the first
is heard, thus showing that the sound accompanies the motion.
For a large group, a mirror may be fastened to one prong of the
resonating fork; a spot of light reflected from this mirror to a
screen will dance as the fork sounds. Tuning forks may be
passed around the class, so that the students may see their
vibration when sounding or feel it by pressing the fork lightly to
the finger tips or cheek. A rod may be clamped in the middle,
and a pith ball hung so as to rest against one end. When the
other end is stroked longitudinally with a rosined cloth, so that
the rod emits a sound, the pith ball is thrown aside.

In all of these experiments, it must be obvious to the student
that the source is performing vibratory motion. That this is shm
or approximately so can be shown by the optical method of S-6
where light from a strong source is focused upon a screen by way
of a mirror on the prong of a fork and a rotating mirror. When
both mirrors are at rest, a spot of light is seen on the screen.
When the fork is set in vibration, the spot spreads out into a line,
and the fork is adjusted until the line is vertical. When the
rotating mirror (with axis vertical) is set in motion, the path of
the spot has the form of a wave, which shows that the motion is
periodic; and the fact that it is a sine wave demonstrates that
the motion is simple harmonic. A permanent record of the
motion of a fork may be obtained by causing a stylus attached to
one prong of the fork to produce a trace upon wax-sensitized
paper or a coated glass plate moving at right angles to the plane
of vibration. The coating material for the plate may be lampblack in alcohol or whiting in water. The latter is less messy.
(Project.)

S-51. Show the details of motion of a vibrating fork by stroboscopic illumination. Cast the shadow of the fork on the screen
by intermittent light. Hold the fork at some point near the
screen, or clamp it in the slide position in a projection lantern.
The former method is simpler but is effective only with forks
having long narrow prongs and large amplitude.

S-52. Material Medium Necessary for Transmission of Sound.
A bell jar, to be set on the plate of a vacuum pump, is provided

with two electric terminals.   An electric bell is suspended from these terminals by very flexible springs, which serve also to conduct current to the bell.   With air in the bell jar, the bell is set ringing; the sound of it is easily heard.   The pump is then operated, and as the pressure of the air is reduced the intensity of sound from the bell decreases, until at sufficiently low pressure it may become inaudible.   The suspension of the bell must be very flexible to avoid transmission of sound through it to the bell jar. It may be well to suspend the bell by thin rubber bands and to conduct the current to the bell by coiled leads of fine wire.

A substitute for the bell jar, probably more convenient, is a glass bottle with a mouth wide enough to admit the bell.   A rubber stopper is used to seal the bottle.   The stopper is bored with three holes, for the metal air cock and the electric leads. The two leads, serving also as supports for the bell, are machine screws provided with washers on each side, which are drawn down tight with a nut.   If the holes are smaller than the parts to be inserted, the joints will be tight.

Instead of an electric bell, a small table bell is hung from the stopper by a piece of rubber tubing.   The bell is rung by shaking the bottle.   The bottle may be passed around the class before evacuation and again afterward.   A little sound is likely to be transmitted by the relatively heavy supporting system of the bell.

S-53. Sound Is Wave Motion.   The fact that the sound of an electric bell operating within an air-filled closed bottle can be heard on the outside is proof that sound is not a transfer of material particles.   The student has often had the converse experience of being within the bottle (a closed house) and hearing the sound outside (street noises).   Thus it appears that sound must be a wave motion; *i.e.*, the transfer of energy by disturbances in a medium.

S-54. Slow Mechanical Transmission of Sound Waves.   A long helical coil of fine steel wire of very small diameter transmits sound at low speed (see S-39).   A card set into the coil near one end serves as receiving diaphragm.   A person speaks a word or two onto this card.   After an appreciable time, the sound is quite faithfully reproduced by a second card at the far end of the coil.   The arrival of the words there is preceded by a slight scratching sound, due apparently to minute disturbances that travel somewhat faster than the main waves.

SOURCES OF SOUND

S-55. Tuning Forks.   The sound from steel forks usually dies away quite rapidly, although modern forks of special alloys have a very small decrement and are audible for 3 or 4 min. after being struck.   They owe this property to low internal friction.   A comparison of the performance of two forks, steel and alloy, mounted on similar resonator boxes, would suggest that most of the energy of the steel fork is dissipated by internal friction in the fork itself, rather than by the resonator box.

When a tuning fork is struck or bowed, its fundamental frequency is usually accompanied by audible harmonics, of which the second is the most pronounced.   If the fork itself is presented to the mouthpiece of a phonelescope (S-78), the presence of harmonics is shown by the complex wave form.   But if the fork is mounted on a resonator, the wave due to sound from the resonator box shows a pure sinusoidal form.

S-56. Electrically Driven Tuning Fork.   For continuous sound, a fork must be driven electrically.   The usual method of mounting a solenoid between the prongs of the fork and then interrupting the current by means of the vibrations of the fork itself is not very satisfactory because of the clatter of the make-and-break mechanism.   A much better, though more elaborate, way is to drive the fork by means of a vacuum tube circuit.[1]   The fork is driven by an electromagnet, and the circuit includes an acoustic link consisting of a telephone mouthpiece as a microphone pickup (Fig. 128).

S-57. Organ Pipes and Whistles.   Organ pipes are among the simplest forms of sound source, but for continuous operation they require a source of compressed air.   Bellows, either hand- or foot-operated, may be substituted for a power blower.   For blowing several pipes, a wind chest with a number of openings, preferably controlled by key-operated valves, is convenient.

Whistles of various types are useful, particularly for high-pitched sounds, either audible or supersonic.   These sounds, being of short wave length, are very satisfactory for experiments

[1] For further details, see Williamson and Eisenbeis, *Am. Phys. Teacher*, **4** 91, 1936.

in reflection, interference, and diffraction (S-90). Moreover, a sensitive flame is a good semiquantitative detector of such sounds. The Galton whistle is well known. The length of the vibrating air column can be changed by means of a piston moved in and out by a calibrated screw. The whistle is usually blown with a rubber bulb attached to the open end of the tube.

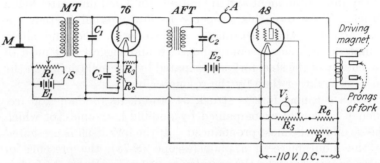

Fig. 128.—Electrically driven tuning fork. M, telephone microphone; MT, microphone transformer; AFT, audiofrequency transformer. The microphone and the tuning fork are acoustically coupled.

S-58. High-pitched Whistles. Another form of whistle is easily made from a short length of brass tubing. A notch is cut near one end with a file to provide the lip of the whistle (Fig. 129a). A piece of machine screw, flattened on one side, is screwed into this end of the tube, to produce a flat stream of air. The other end is closed with another screw, ground flat on the end, by

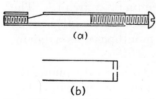

Fig. 129.—(a) Whistle of variable frequency; (b) bird call.

means of which the length of the air column can be changed. If the tube is small and the vibrating column short, the frequency of such a whistle may be made very high (supersonic). Two such whistles are conveniently connected to a single blowing tube by means of a glass T-tube. They are useful for showing beats and beat notes (S-107). They do not require much air and can easily be blown by the mouth.

S-59. Bird Call. The bird call is a tube about 4 cm long and 1 cm in diameter, of brass or tin plate, closed at one end by two parallel plates, 2 mm apart (Fig. 129b). Through these plates are bored small central holes, about 0.5 mm in diameter. The two holes must face each other exactly. The dimensions may be varied considerably, but the smaller the tubes and the finer the holes, the higher is the pitch.

S-60. Directional Sound Source. For a number of experiments, a shrill whistle must be mounted so that the emitted sound is confined to one direction. The mounting shown in Fig. 130 is satisfactory. The tube is of cardboard or brass, plugged with cotton to reduce standing waves and resonance. Several different cardboard megaphones are made to slip over the open end of the tube. If one megaphone is a long narrow cone with the open end of diameter greater than the wave length, the system will be an effective emitter and director of sound, and most of the energy will be confined to the axis of the cone.

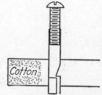

FIG. 130.—Directional sound source.

S-61. Singing Tubes. These tubes are particularly useful where compressed air is not available. A tube open at both ends is mounted vertically to enclose a pinhole gas flame (Fig. 131). The position of the jet in the tube is important. The distance of the base of flame from the lower end of the tube must be between 0 and $\lambda/4$ or between $\lambda/2$ and $3\lambda/4$ but not between $\lambda/4$ and $\lambda/2$. A point slightly less than half the length of the tube above the

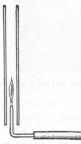

FIG. 131.—Singing tube.

lower end seems to be the best place for the flame to excite the fundamental. If the tube does not start to sing when the flame is inserted, the gas flow should be decreased until it does. After singing starts, the flow may be increased again. The pitch of the note may be changed by changing the effective length of the tube by sliding a paper or metal extension over one end. Great changes in length cannot be made without readjusting the position of the jet.

S-62. A vertical tube will sing when a piece of metal gauze is placed in the lower half (best about a quarter of the way up) and heated with a flame. The tube begins to sound soon *after* the flame is withdrawn and continues until the gauze has cooled to the temperature of its surroundings. If the gauze is electrically heated, the sound is continuous. The tube ceases to sound when laid on its side but starts again when set upright. A length of stovepipe 5 or 6 ft long or a cast-iron water pipe, when made to sing in this way, will emit a powerful low-pitched tone. If a stream of warm air is sent up a vertical tube in the upper half of which is placed a cooled gauze, a sound will be emitted. This sound will be continuous if the gauze is cooled by circulating cold water in small pipes on which the gauze may be woven, while hot air rises from a candle or gas flame at the bottom of the tube.

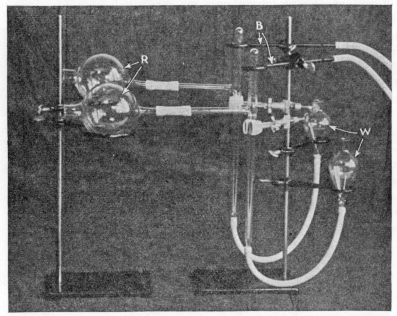

Fig. 132.—Knipp tubes with resonators R and water reservoirs W for varying the pitch. The tubes are heated by ring burners B.

S-63. Knipp tubes are singing tubes of a special form. They consist of a short length of glass tube set in the closed end of a larger tube and held coaxial with it by means of small glass studs. The closed end is heated, and the tube soon begins to sing. Variants include methods of changing the resonating length and of reinforcing the tone with resonators.[1] Strong beats may be produced by using two tubes as shown in Fig. 132. The pitch of each tube is controlled by adjusting the water level by the flasks W.

[1] Dimensions may be found, *e.g.*, in F. R. Watson, "Sound," p. 214, John Wiley & Sons, Inc., New York, 1935.

S-64. A flame can be used to maintain the vibration of an air column. A gauze is placed at the lower end of a vertical tube and gas from a burner is lighted *above* the gauze. The gauze must be rather fine; the coarsest that can be used is 16 mesh for copper and 20 mesh for iron, which is a poorer conductor of heat.

S-65. Shrieker. Insert a tube ½ in. in diameter and 12 in. long into a flask or bottle nearly full of water. Blow across the mouth of the tube to evoke a loud note of descending pitch as the water level within the tube is forced downward by pressure of the air stream. Strong rhythmic blowing, so timed as to build up the surging of water within the tube, will generate shrill fluctuating tones loud enough to awaken even the sleepiest student.

S-66. Nonresonant Air Jet. Compressed air issues from the flattened end of a tube and strikes against a thin metal strip placed edgewise in front of it (Fig. 133). There are many frequencies of rather low intensity present in the turbulent air about the strip. These frequencies may be varied somewhat by moving the strip toward or away from the tube and by changing the flow of air. The energy of the sound appears to be concentrated in a few frequencies if a wire of circular cross section is used instead of a flat strip. This type of source is particularly useful for showing that all enclosed air columns—milk bottles, cocoa cans, conch shells, etc.—have characteristic frequencies. The flattened tip may be a small fishtail burner top closed somewhat more than usual by pressing it in a vise.

FIG. 133.—Nonresonant air jet for exciting resonance in various vessels.

S-67. Point Source of Sound. A metal rod, *e.g.*, a steel drill rod, is supported at its center between pivots. Attached at the midpoint of the rod is a bent lever. A spring, under a tension of 500 g or more, holds one end of the rod in contact with a small bakelite pulley ½ in. in diameter (Fig. 134). As the pulley is rotated by a variable-speed motor, its frictional bowing sets the rod into violent longitudinal vibration with the natural frequency of the rod. For still greater intensity, the other end of the rod may be enclosed in a short tube of metal or paper adjusted so that the resonant frequency of the cuplike cavity is the same as that of the rod.   This resonator is then fastened securely to the rod.   The motor is enclosed in a sound-proof box and the exposed

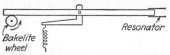

end of the rod serves as an intense point source of sound of a definite frequency.   The frequency is not sensitive to small changes in motor speed or spring tension.

FIG. 134.—Point source of sound.

S-68. Audio-frequency Oscillator.   Numerous tube circuits have been designed for generating electric currents of audio frequency.   The oscillator shown in Fig. 135 is given for its simplicity rather than for its stability or purity of wave form.   It is quite satisfactory for demonstration purposes when its output is fed to an amplifier (see A-81) and loudspeaker.   A triode (almost any type), two audio transformers, and a condenser are connected as shown.   The secondary S_2 of the second transformer is connected to the input of the amplifier.   If oscillation does not occur

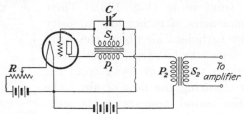

FIG. 135.—Simple audio-frequency oscillator circuit.

when the filament of the tube is hot, reverse the terminals of S_1, which controls the grid of the triode.   Frequency may be varied by changing the capacitance of the condenser C or (within limits) by changing the heating current in the filament by the rheostat R.[1]   A more elaborate beat-note oscillator is described in A-27.

SOUND DETECTORS

S-69. Sensitive Flames and Jets.   For demonstration work, the most satisfactory detector of sound is the sensitive flame

[1] Circuits for beat-note, magnetostriction, and piezoelectric oscillators will be found in modern texts on radio or sound; *e.g.*, OLSEN and MASSA. "Applied Acoustics," P. Blakiston's Son & Co., Inc., Philadelphia, 1934; DAVIS, A. H., "Modern Acoustics," The Macmillan Company, New York, 1934; RAMSEY, R. R., "Fundamentals of Radio," 2d ed., 1935, and "Experimental Radio," 4th ed., 1937, Ramsey Publishing Company, Bloomington Ind.; etc.

(properly, the sensitive *jet*, since the flame is not primarily responsible for the sensitivity—the jet is lighted simply to make it visible and to get rid of the gas). A sensitive flame is a tall, steady flame, which becomes turbulent and shortens when disturbed by high-pitched sound. A piece of glass tubing 1 cm in diameter is heated and drawn out into a cone with a diameter of less than 1 mm. The tube is then cut off square at this narrow section, connected to the gas mains, and rigidly mounted in a vertical position. The gas is lighted at the tip, and the gas flow is adjusted to a rate just below that at which the flame becomes turbulent. The tip is then filed *gently* with a fine file until maximum sensitivity (as tested by a shrill whistle) is obtained. If filing is continued, the sensitivity will alternately decrease and increase.

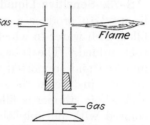

FIG. 136.—Sensitive flame using a Bunsen burner.

A tube prepared by filing in this manner will also produce a sensitive jet of gas or liquid; a gas jet is more sensitive than the flame and at a very much lower gas pressure. This may be shown by casting the shadow of the tube on a screen by light from a point source, adjusting the flame to sensitivity, and then extinguishing it while the gas is still turned on. The pressure may then be reduced without destroying the sensitivity of the jet, as can be seen by the behavior of its shadow. It will be sensitive to the same sounds as those to which the flame responded.

S-70. Another form of sensitive flame is shown in Fig. 136. An ordinary Bunsen burner is fitted with an open hood of brass tubing, $\frac{3}{4}$ in. in diameter, held at the bottom by a cork bored to take the tube of the burner so that the hood extends 1 in. above the burner. Just above the top of the burner tube two holes, opposite each other, are bored in the hood. A glass tube is drawn down to a small opening and inserted a little way into one of these holes. It is connected to the gas supply, gas is turned into the burner also, and the jet is lighted at the second hole in the hood. Both gas streams are adjusted until the jet is barely stable, in which condition it is very sensitive.

S-71. A third method is to hold a copper gauze 5 cm above a sensitive jet and light the gas above the gauze. The gauze should be no coarser than 16 mesh, and 32 mesh is better.   It should be about 15 by 15 cm.   The sensitivity can be varied by changing the gas pressure or by changing the position of the gauze.[1]

S-72. Sensitive flames, such as those first described by Rayleigh, Tyndall, and others, are similar to the ones described in the foregoing paragraphs.   A Bunsen burner with a long upright tube—about 5 in.—can be made sensitive to rather low-pitched sounds such as those from speaking or coughing.   The air holes at the base of the burner are closed tightly, and the gas pressure is reduced until the flame becomes lopsided, in which state it is sensitive.

S-73. Sensitive Liquid Jet.   The tube described in S-69 may be used to produce a sensitive jet of liquid.   An aquarium is filled with water to which a few drops of hydrochloric acid have been added.   The tube used to produce the sensitive flame is inverted and supported rigidly above the aquarium so that the orifice is just below the surface of the water.   A flask closed with a two-hole stopper is filled with a solution of sodium hydroxide colored with phenolphthalein.   A tube projecting through one hole of the stopper nearly to the bottom of the flask is connected with the sensitive jet; a tube through the other hole runs to the water main.   Water is allowed to flow very slowly into the flask, driving the red phenolphthalein solution through the nozzle into the water in the aquarium.   The jet extends into the water for a short distance and is then clarified by the acid.   It is very sensitive, responding to light taps on the tank or desk.   If water is allowed to drop into the flask from the main, each drop, as it falls, will disturb the jet at the orifice, and the red liquid will form in concentric rings around the orifice at the surface of the acid solution.   These experiments show conclusively that it is the jet and not the flame which is sensitive.

S-74. A somewhat simpler experiment consists in placing a vibrating tuning fork against the tube from which a water jet issues.   The jet is broken up into drops regularly spaced.   If these fall against a drumhead—the bottom of a tin pail will

[1] Three burners especially designed for natural gas or natural gas enriched with benzene are described by R. C. Colwell, *Rev. Sci. Instruments*, **1.** 347, 1930.   For a theoretical discussion of sensitive jets, see E. G. Richardson, "Sound," Longmans, Green & Company, New York, 1935.

serve—a note of the same frequency as the fork results. It is especially interesting to back-couple the drumhead to the jet with a wooden or metal rod. The oscillations are then self-sustaining. This is a good experiment for showing by analogy the effect of plate-grid coupling in an oscillator tube (S-68 for example). This experiment is not unlike M-255. The "necklace of droplets" effect may be seen by stroboscopic illumination.

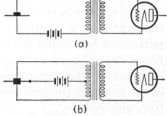

FIG. 137.—Circuits for connecting (a) single-button and (b) double-button microphones to amplifier.

S-75. Microphones. In many experiments where it is desired to amplify sound to make it audible to a large class, modern electro-acoustic systems are excellent. For general ruggedness and high output, the carbon-granule micro-phone is most satisfactory. It is connected to an amplifier through an audio-frequency transformer as shown in Fig. 137, and the output of the amplifier is connected to a loudspeaker or oscilloscope (or both).

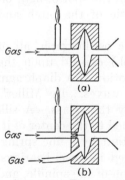

FIG. 138.—Two types of manometric-flame capsule; (a) simple form; (b) with needle valve.

SOUND ANALYZERS

S-76. Manometric Flames. Two types of capsule for manometric flames are shown in Fig. 138. In both cases, the diaphragm is of thin rubber, and the space on one side of it communicates with the gas inlet. The gas emerges from a small nozzle where it is burned. Sound waves imping-ing on the other side of the diaphragm periodically change the pressure of the gas, thus producing changes in the height of the flame. One type differs from the other in having two gas inlets and a very small wire that extends from the center of the diaphragm to act like a needle valve in the cone-shaped orifice. Thus the vibrations of the diaphragm change the gas pressure and the size of the orifice at the same time. The sensitivity of the flame may be altered by varying the flow of gas in each of the two tubes. The gain in sensitivity by use of the valve is partly offset by the extra load on the diaphragm and consequent loss of response at high frequencies.

The flame is viewed in a rotating mirror. The mirror may be cubical in shape, with four vertical faces; for good results the faces must all be accurately parallel to a vertical axis about which the cube turns. A better mirror is obtained by front silvering both sides of a plane parallel piece of glass, which is then mounted in a frame fitting the rotator, parallel to the axis of rotation. Such a mirror can be rotated at higher speed, with steadier image of the flame, than the cubical mirror. If the frequency of the sound is not too high, the mirror may be dispensed with and the variations in the height of the flame may be seen by moving the head rapidly from side to side.

S-77. Phonodeik or Phonelescope. A very simple method of showing the complex nature of sound waves is to reflect a parallel beam of light onto a rotating mirror and thence to a screen from a small lightweight mirror cemented to the center of a diaphragm of thin rubber covering one end of a tubular carton. When a note is sung into an opening in the side of the tube, the diaphragm vibrates, and the motion of the mirror causes the spot of light on the screen to move in figures characteristic of the pitch and quality of the note.

S-78. There are many forms of acoustic oscillograph, all of which (except the cathode-ray oscillograph) depend upon the communication to a small mirror of the motion of a diaphragm set into vibration by impinging sound waves. In Miller's phonodeik,[1] the diaphragm is of extremely thin glass. A silk fiber or a very fine platinum wire is attached to the center of it, wrapped once around a spindle, and kept taut by a fine spring. The spindle carrying the mirror is mounted in jewel bearings. Vibration of the diaphragm causes a rotation of the spindle, and the consequent linear oscillation of a spot of light reflected from the mirror is spread out by a rotating mirror or photographed on a moving film. The phonelescope operates on virtually the same principle but is more rugged and less sensitive.[2]

[1] For details, see D. C. Miller, "Sound Waves, Their Shape and Speed," The Macmillan Company, New York, 1937.

[2] DORSEY, H. G., *J. Optical Soc. Am. and Rev. Sci. Instruments*, **6**, 279, 1922. The device is obtainable from Capital Apparatus Works, Box 582, Washington, D. C.

Other forms differ from this chiefly in the manner of supporting and driving the mirror and in delicacy of construction.   In one (Fig. 139), the mirror is supported along one edge by a fiber cemented to it.   The opposite edge is cemented to the fiber running to the center of the diaphragm. This construction elimi-
nates the bearings and their friction
and also the friction due to the
bending and unbending of the fiber
wrapped around the spindle.

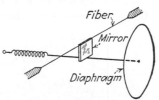

Fig. 139.—Phonodeik mirror supported by single fiber.

In another form, bearing friction is eliminated by supporting the spindle N (a No. 12 cambric needle) by two fine tungsten wires wrapped around it at its ends and kept taut by springs S; there is, of course, friction in the wires as they bend, and friction between adjacent turns (Fig. 140).   The

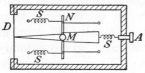

Fig. 140.—Phonodeik mir-
ror mounted on spindle, supported by fine wires.

diaphragm D is connected to the spindle by two other tungsten wires.   The position of the mirror M is adjusted by a screw A.

In still another form, rolling friction is substituted for sliding.   A nonmag-netic spindle lies on the polished pole pieces of a horseshoe magnet.   On top of the spindle rest the two prongs of a light steel fork (Fig. 141) whose stem is attached to the center of the diaphragm.   The apparatus may be made large and sturdy if the mirror is driven by a dynamic loudspeaker.   The tone to be analyzed is fed to an amplifier and thence to the loudspeaker.   The construction and adjustment of the moving parts are simplified by the fact that a large amount of power can be supplied to the speaker.

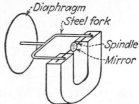

Fig. 141.—Phonodeik mir-
ror on spindle supported by
magnet; only rolling friction
present.

An especially rugged phonodeik may be made by driving a 3- by 5-mm mirror with a dynamic loudspeaker.   The mir-ror is mounted on a slender steel shaft and is driven by a thread from the loudspeaker diaphragm, wrapped once around a small pulley, 5 mm in diameter, on the steel shaft.[1]

[1] For further details see C. G. Kretschmar, *Am. Phys. Teacher*, **4**, 90, 1936

The optical system used with a phonodeik is of prime importance. A very satisfactory one is shown in Fig. 142. All parts are mounted in a light-tight box. The front of the box has a ground-glass or flashed-opal screen 40 cm long by 25 cm high. The rotating mirror and its driving motor are mounted on felt and sponge rubber so that their vibrations do not affect the phonodeik

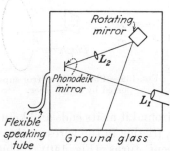

FIG. 142.—Optical system for use with phonodeik.

element. The flexible speaking tube leads to the phonodeik diaphragm. Since this tube has several resonance frequencies, the system has several peak responses. The change when a tube of different length is substituted is quite marked. L_1 is a spherical lens of about 25 cm focal length, and L_2 a cylindrical one of 35 cm focal length. The light source is a carbon arc or an oscillograph lamp (size of coiled filament 3 by 1.5 mm) that takes 11 amp at 3.5 v from the secondary of a transformer whose primary is connected directly to a 110-v a.c. line. Either source is satisfactory for demonstration to a group of 40 or 50 persons in a moderately lighted room. The rotating mirror is run at constant

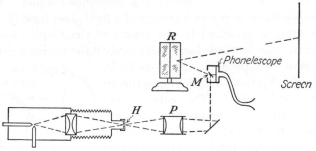

FIG. 143.—Lecture-table arrangement of apparatus for use with phonelescope.

speed; the speed that serves best over the frequency range 128 to about 2500 vps is determined by trial, and a fixed resistor is put in series with the motor to hold it at that speed. The system as a whole is portable.

The lecture-room arc lamp may be used as a source of illumination for the phonelescope with the various parts spread out on the

lecture table so that all are visible. The arrangement is shown
in Fig. 143. The light of the arc is focused upon a small hole H
in a metal cap, and the image of this hole is cast upon the screen
by the projection lens P, the light passing to the screen by reflection from the phonelescope mirror M and the rotating mirror R.
Care should be exercised to exclude all stray light.

S-79. Cathode-ray Oscilloscope. If facilities are available,
excellent results can be simply obtained with a cathode-ray
oscilloscope. A phonograph and pickup or a microphone is used
and the current amplified and fed to the oscilloscope or a loudspeaker or both at once. The larger the face of the oscilloscope
tube the better, particularly where the class is large (A-71).

TRANSMISSION OF SOUND

S-80. Speed of Sound in Air. The direct measurement of the
speed of sound as distance divided by time, which may be under-
taken out of doors, is not feasible within the lecture room; hence
indirect methods must be used. A glass tube 1 m long is mounted
vertically. From the bottom, a rubber tube leads to a reservoir
filled with water, for varying the water level in the tube. A
vibrating tuning fork is held above the open end of the tube, and
the length of the air column adjusted by changing the water level
until resonance is reached. Then from frequency of the fork and
wave length as determined from length of resonating column
(with correction for size of tube), the speed of sound is
calculated.

S-81. Velocity of Sound by Toothed-wheel Method. The
method first used by Fizeau[1] for determining the velocity of light
may be used in simplified form to determine the velocity of
sound. A high-pitched whistle S surrounded by a box D lined
with balsam wool sends sound through aperture A_1 into the long
box B where it is reflected from the end M (Fig. 144). The box B
is made in two telescoping sections, each 1.5 m long. Sound
emerges from aperture A_2 to affect a sensitive flame F (S-69). A
toothed wheel of plywood W, 60 cm in diameter, is driven by
motor R (E-232). The motor speed, distance traversed by
sound, and number of teeth on the wheel may be varied inde-

---

[1] For Fizeau's account, see W. F. Magie, "A Source Book in Physics,"
p. 340, McGraw-Hill Book Company. Inc., New York, 1935.

pendently; and the conditions may be adjusted until sound is "eclipsed" and does not affect the sensitive flame.[1]

S-82. Speed of Sound in Metals. The speed of sound in a solid rod can be determined by the Kundt's-tube method. A rod of brass or iron is clamped horizontally at its midpoint. One end of it carries a disk of cork or other light material fitting loosely in a long glass tube and serving as a piston. The glass tube contains cork dust or lycopodium powder. The metal rod is stroked longitudinally with a rosined cloth, thus setting it into vibration with a node at the middle, where it is clamped, and a loop at each

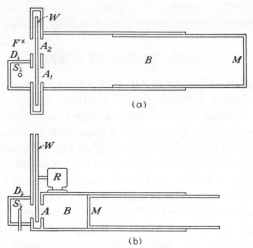

Fig. 144.—Velocity of sound by Fizeau's toothed-wheel method.

end. The length of air column in the tube is adjusted until resonance is obtained, at which maximum agitation of the dust occurs. The dust then piles up at the nodal points, a half wave length apart. From the measured wave length and the known speed of sound in air, the frequency can be found, which, multiplied by the wave length (twice the length of the rod) gives the speed in the metal. The mechanical drive described in S-67 may be found convenient.

S-83. Effect of Air Temperature on Speed of Sound. Two organ pipes, tuned to the same pitch, are blown from the same source simultaneously. When the temperature of the air within one pipe is raised by means of a heater coil, beats result between

[1] For further details, see H. K. Schilling, *Am. Phys. Teacher*, **4**, 206, 1936.

the notes of the two pipes, showing a change in pitch in the heated pipe on account of a change in the speed of sound.

S-84. The same effect is more easily shown with a pair of high-pitched metal whistles (S-58) blown from a single source by attaching them to a T-tube. The whistles are tuned to unison (absence of beats). When one whistle is heated with a match flame, the pitch rises because of increase in speed of sound with rise of temperature, and rapid beats are heard.

S-85. Effect of Medium on Speed of Sound. Two closed vertical organ pipes are connected to the same source of compressed air and adjusted to unison. One is then filled with hydrogen, whereupon beats result from the change in speed of the sound in that pipe.

One end of a long piece of gas tubing is attached to a whistle (S-58) and the other to a gas outlet. The pitch of the whistle suddenly rises when the gas reaches it. (A similar change in pitch occurs when a Bunsen burner is turned on.) If the tube is disconnected from the jet and blown with the mouth, there will be a decided drop in pitch at the moment when all the gas is expelled and air reaches the whistle.

S-86. Fill the lungs with hydrogen or helium, and speak or sing. One must take the hydrogen from a tank so as to get enough of it. The change in quality of the speaker's voice is very pronounced, on account of the increase in frequency of all pitches originating in the vocal cavity, although the fundamental pitch determined by the vocal cords remains unaffected. This experiment never fails to bring down the house.

S-87. If there is available a railroad track, an iron fence, or other continuous length of metal bar or pipe, a striking qualitative experiment can be performed. A sharp blow with a hammer is struck against the rail, and observers some distance away can detect the difference in time required for the sound to travel through the air and through the rail. The distance should be as much over 200 ft as convenient.

S-88. Attenuation in the Medium. Let the student hold one end of a metal or wooden rod against one ear and the end of a rubber tube of equal length against the other. Touch the far ends of these with the stem of a vibrating tuning fork. The sound is transmitted with less energy loss along the wood or metal than along the rubber.

For a large group, this attenuation may be shown as follows. Mount the stem of a tuning fork in a block of wood. Then, with the fork in vibration, establish contact between the bottom of the block and a sounding board—the desk top—through various materials. Suggested materials are a wooden rod, a metal rod, a beaker of water, a solid rubber block, a block of porous rubber (bath sponge), absorbent cotton, balsa wood, etc.

S-89. Attenuation of Sound in Carbon Dioxide. Sounds of high pitch, above about 8000 cycles, are greatly attenuated in carbon dioxide. Direct a high-pitched sound source, such as a vacuum-tube oscillator and loudspeaker or telephone receiver (S-68) or the point source (S-67) into one end of a 2-in. water pipe 10 ft long. A tone of 8000 cycles is readily transmitted through the pipe when it is filled with air but is reduced almost to inaudibility when the pipe is filled with carbon dioxide. For tones below 2000 cycles, the gas is nearly as "transparent" as air. This "anomalous" absorption is explained on the basis of energy transfers during molecular collisions. Similar experiments reveal that hot air of desert humidity (10 to 15 per cent *relative* humidity) is relatively "opaque" to high-pitched sounds, whereas the cold dry air of the arctic is relatively "transparent."

WAVE PROPERTIES OF SOUND

S-90. Many of the fundamental properties of waves, often met experimentally only in optics, may be demonstrated effectively by sound waves generated by a shrill whistle, with wave lengths varying from 2 to 8 cm. The whistle should be operated by compressed air at steady pressure as measured by a manometer in a side arm; the intensity should be as low as the experiment will allow, to reduce secondary effects due to reflection from the floor, walls, etc. The detector may be a sensitive flame, or a crystal microphone with amplifier and oscilloscope. The latter arrangement is shown in Fig. 145. Numerous "optics" experiments are possible. Several are suggested in brief by the diagrams in Fig. 146. The great advantage of this method of showing wave phenomena lies in the ease of adjustment and the large scale of slits, apertures, and mirrors that can be used. The box that encloses the source is lined with cotton or balsam wool. Slits and apertures cut from plywood are used to close the end of the box. "Half-silvered mirrors" are made from window screening that has been painted to increase reflection.

These wave experiments are of two types, those with exposed source and those in which the source is enclosed in a soundproof

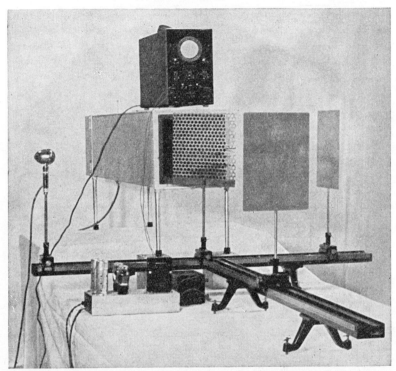

Fig. 145.—Apparatus for demonstrating wave properties of sound. As shown in this figure, the partial reflector and two plane reflectors are arranged for demonstrating the principles of the Michelson interferometer. The source of sound is in the box at the rear. The microphone stands at the left. As one or the other of the plane reflectors is moved, maxima and minima are detected by the variations in amplitude of the motion of the spot on the oscilloscope screen.

box. In the diagrams of Fig. 146, X represents the source, M the microphone or sensitive flame. The arrows indicate the motions suggested for the different parts.[1]

S-91. Reflection and Transmission at a Plane Surface. Whistle and detector are placed some distance apart in a line

[1] For further details, see H. K. Schilling, *Am. Phys. Teacher*, **4**, 206, 1936; Schilling and Whitson, *Am. Phys. Teacher*, **4**, 27, 1936; and a complete survey by H. K. Schilling, *Am. Phys. Teacher*, **6**, 156, 1938.

parallel to the plane of the reflector, which is vertical. By turning the reflector, the equality of angles of incidence and reflection can be shown. In this experiment, it is necessary that all the

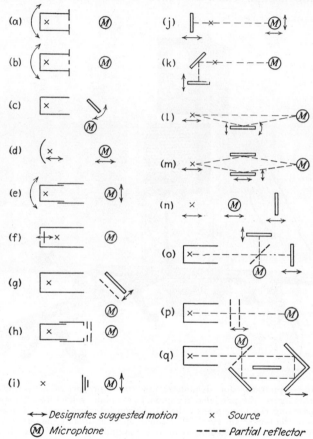

→ *Designates suggested motion*   × *Source*
Ⓜ *Microphone*   ---- *Partial reflector*

Fig. 146.—Various ways of arranging the apparatus of Fig. 145. (*a*) Single slit diffraction; (*b*) double slit interference; (*c*) simple reflection; (*d*) focusing of waves by curved reflector; (*e*) telescoping sound box for changing distance between source and opening; (*f*) variation of sound output by adjustment of reflector at back of box; (*g*) thin-film interference; (*h*) zone plates; (*i*) Arago's bright spot; (*j*) standing waves; (*k*) simplest interferometer; (*l*) Lloyd's mirror; (*m*) double Lloyd's mirror; (*n*) standing waves; (*o*) Michelson's interferometer; (*p*) Fabry-Perot interferometer; (*q*) complex interferometer.

sound energy be propagated along one line. Therefore the whistle should be enclosed as described in S-60 and a conical megaphone placed on the end of the mount. If this is insufficient, paper tubes may be used to define the directions of both the incident and the reflected beams, or the whistle may be placed at the focus of a parabolic mirror. A hissing a.c. arc makes a good source of sound since the light path shows also the path of the sound. Whether or not all these precautions are necessary depends so much on the presence and disposition of other reflectors that no general rule can be given. The reflector must be large compared with the wave length. Various materials can be used: a wooden drawing board; cardboard; cellophane; felt; cloth, first dry and then wet. The last is a poor reflector in the first case but a good one in the second. If a second flame is placed behind the reflector, some indication of the transmission can be obtained. In this case, the reflector must be large so that the flame will not be affected by diffracted waves. The heated air column rising above a row of burners serves also as a reflector.

S-92. Curved Reflectors. Place the flame and whistle several meters apart. Reduce the intensity of the whistle until the flame does not respond even with a plane reflector behind it. Then replace the plane reflector with a curved one arranged so that flame and whistle are at conjugate points. With both flame and whistle at the focal points of two mirrors, the sound may be sent over great distances and still cause appreciable response. In these experiments, the whistle should be free, *i.e.,* without megaphone.

S-93. A watch is placed at the focal point of a mirror, and the sound of its ticking is projected in a beam that may be swept across the class by turning the mirror.

S-94. In a room with curved walls, particularly under a dome, the phenomenon of the "whispering gallery" may be demonstrated. The observer stands with his ear near the wall at some point. If another person standing close to the opposite wall and facing parallel thereto speaks, he can be heard by the observer although persons in the middle of the floor cannot hear him. The sound appears to "creep" around the wall by repeated reflections. The experiment, however, is most effective within a dome, for here the inward slope of the walls keeps the sound down to the level of the observer by reflection between wall and floor. When a screen is placed against the wall and perpendicular to it, no sound reaches the observer. This effect can, of course, also be demonstrated with a whistle and flame. It is due to reflection, but source and receiver are not at conjugate foci of a spherical mirror, which appears to be the usual explanation.

S-95. Refraction. Make a lens for sound by cementing together the edges of two circular sheets of cellophane, 18 to 24 in. in diameter. Mount them in a circular frame of somewhat smaller diameter, and fill the space between them with carbon dioxide. Place a whistle and a flame at the conjugate points of this converging lens. Reduce the intensity of the whistle until there is little or no response of the flame when the lens is not present; then insert the lens. The focal length of a double convex lens filled with carbon dioxide is almost exactly twice the radius of curvature of the faces. The whistle should not have a megaphone in this case. Whistle and flame must be accurately located.

S-96. Direct a parallel beam of sound from a curved mirror or a lens toward a distant flame, which responds to it. Interpose a prism of carbon dioxide between source and flame. Move the flame to one side to find a spot where it will again respond. Since the angular deviation of the beam is small, the distance from the prism to the flame must be large to get an appreciable linear displacement of the beam, and the flame should be at the focal point of a lens or a mirror for good response.

S-97. Set up whistle, flame, and drawing board so that response of the flame occurs only when the angle of incidence equals the angle of reflection (S-90). Now allow carbon dioxide, hot air, or any gas with a different density from the air in the room to pass through the path of the incident beam. The refraction and reflection of the new medium will "scatter" the sound. The carbon dioxide can be poured into the beam from a sprinkling can.

S-98. Diffraction. A whistle and a spherical mirror are arranged to produce a parallel beam, which is interrupted by a drawing board in such a position that a sensitive flame behind it does not respond to the whistle. When the board is withdrawn sidewise, some point will be found at which the flame will respond even though it is still situated within the geometrical shadow of the board.

Instead of moving the obstacle, successively narrower pieces of cardboard may be substituted for it until the flame responds even though it is centrally located within the shadow.

S-99. A cardboard sheet with a slit is placed in the parallel beam as an obstacle. The sensitive flame is moved from side to side, and the width of the slit is varied to show the extent of the diffracted beam, which becomes greater as the slit is narrowed.

S-100. Attach a megaphone of rectangular cross section to a whistle. Make the longer dimension of the opening about $\frac{3}{2}\lambda$ and the shorter about $\lambda/3$. Place a flame at some distance from the megaphone and to one side of the axis. Adjust either flame or whistle until there is little or no response when the shorter dimension of the megaphone is vertical. Then turn the megaphone through 90° until its long dimension is vertical. The flame will now respond; for, owing to diffraction, most of the sound energy is confined to the plane perpendicular to the longer dimension.

S-101. Interference. Two megaphones with rectangular apertures, about a foot apart, are connected to an enclosed whistle by a T-tube connection. The two megaphones are parallel to each other with their smaller dimension horizontal. A sensitive flame is moved about to investigate the interference pattern.

S-102. Two identical loudspeakers fed from the same audio oscillator and amplifier are mounted on the ends of a 12-ft board that can be turned about a vertical axis. The interference pattern is projected into the room and can be moved about the class by turning the arm. This pattern may be compared with the pattern produced in the ripple tank by a double source.

S-103. A high-pitched whistle or other source of sound is set in front of a mouthpiece communicating with two U-tubes through a T-tube connection. The other ends of the U-tubes are joined by a second T-tube to a tube leading to an earpiece. The length of one of the U-tubes can be varied by means of a sliding section. When the two sound paths formed by the tubes differ by an odd number of half wave lengths, interference reduces the intensity of the sound reaching the earpiece. If a microphone is substituted for the earpiece and used to drive an amplifier and a loudspeaker, the effect becomes audible to the class as a whole.

S-104. Send a parallel sound beam against a cardboard sheet having two parallel slits, and using a sensitive flame, investigate the region behind the slits for interference.

S-105. Standing Waves. Standing waves are obtained when a sound beam is incident normally on a reflector such as a drawing board. A sensitive flame will show nodes and loops between the source and the reflector, and will have maximum response at the loops or antinodes.

Two sheets of beaverboard are set up facing one another about 2 m apart. In the center of one is mounted a loudspeaker connected to an amplifier fed by a 1000-cycle oscillator. The separation of the two boards is adjusted until the condition for standing waves has been found. A sensitive flame moved back and forth between the baffles will show the existence of loops and nodes. The flame may be mounted on a long arm whose support should be independent of the baffles.

S-106. Beats. Interference between waves of different frequencies produces the fluctuations of intensity called beats. This may be shown by reflecting light successively from mirrors attached to the prongs of two electrically driven tuning forks of slightly different frequencies, whose prongs are vibrating vertically, thence to a rotating mirror and to a screen (Fig. 147). Beats are produced audibly from two sounding forks or pipes or strings of slightly different frequencies.

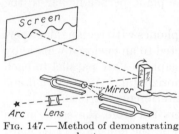

Fig. 147.—Method of demonstrating beats.

S-107. Beat Notes. Two high-pitched whistles, such as those described in S-58, are connected to a T-tube and blown simultaneously. If they are started in unison and the frequency of one of them is then changed, the difference in frequencies soon becomes sufficient to produce a musical beat note, which rises and falls in pitch as the frequency difference is changed. If the pitch of one whistle is carried above the limit of audibility while that of the other is still within the audible range, or if both are carried to supersonic frequencies, the ear no longer hears the beat note, but a sensitive flame responding to the whistles will emit an audible note of the beat frequency.

S-108. Longitudinal Vibrations in Strings. A string vibrating longitudinally is a poor radiator of sound, because as it moves it sets up two trains of waves differing in phase by practically 180°. A string is held in one hand while the thumb and a finger of the other are passed along it. No sound is heard. But let the string be fastened to the center of a diaphragm stretched across the open end of a cylinder—parchment or heavy paper on a tin can is good—and now the sound can be heard at a distance, particularly if the string is rubbed with rosin. By choosing the proper-sized can and by slipping the fingers along the string in jerks, the device can be made to bark like a dog.

S-109. Interference Pattern of Tuning Fork. A tuning fork held in the hand and struck with a rubber mallet emits a feeble sound audible for only a few feet, owing to destructive interference between different trains of waves generated by the fork. Such interference is easily demonstrated by rotating a vibrating fork near the ear. Four distinct minima are observed for each revolution of the fork. It is possible to eliminate much of the interference and make the fork sound loudly by holding it in front of a slit cut in a piece of cardboard. The fork should be held close to the cardboard but not in contact with it, with the plane of its prongs either parallel or perpendicular to the cardboard. A slit having dimensions approximately equal to those of one prong of the fork works admirably, and the fork sounds almost as loud as if it were mounted on a resonator box.

S-110. Forced Vibration. Sound a tuning fork in air, and then set the table top or blackboard in vibration by pressing the stem of the fork against it. Next strike two similar forks with equal force simultaneously. Press the stem of one against the table, and hold it there until the sound is no longer audible. Then press the stem of the other fork, which has been vibrating in air all this time, against the table. The second fork will still emit sound. This shows that the rate of energy dissipation of the first fork while held against the table was greater than that of the second fork, which acted only on the air.

A familiar trick consists in exciting the prongs of a dinner fork by pinching two tines between the thumb and first finger. The operator then pretends to "carry the sound" on his finger tips to a tumbler of water. At the instant he "deposits the sound" in the tumbler, he presses the handle of the fork inconspicuously upon the table top, whereupon the sound of the vibrating fork is heard for the first time.

S-111. Musical Resonators. Pour water into a tall jar, and observe how the pitch rises as the air column shortens. Pour water into several thin-walled tumblers arranged in a row, and draw a knife or a piece of wood across the tops of the tumblers. By adjusting the depth of water in each, the tumblers may be tuned to the musical scale. Similarly, stoppers may be pulled from a series of test tubes or bottles filled to different depths with water. For a musical effect, the stoppers should be pulled out in quick succession, which can be done by fastening them to a hinged arm. Small bottles are more easily held in a rack than tubes.

S-112. Closed-tube Resonator. Direct the nonresonant air jet (S-66) across the mouth of a milk bottle, tin can, or other container to evoke characteristic pitches, or simply blow across the mouth of a flask or bottle.

Support a vibrating fork over an adjustable air column (resonance tube), and adjust the length of column until resonance occurs (S-80). Show that there are several resonant lengths, which are odd multiples of the shortest resonant length. The easiest way to change the length of air column is to fill the tube with water and then to let it run out through an opening at the bottom provided with rubber tube and pinch clamp. Minor adjustments of air column length may then be made by squeezing a rubber bulb attached to a side arm.

S-113. Open-tube Resonator. The same experiment may be performed with a tube open at both ends. The length of the tube may be adjusted with a paper extension held in position by a rubber band. For a given fork, the open tube at resonance will be approximately twice as long as the closed one.

S-114. Conical Resonator. A vibrating fork held over the end of an open organ pipe of the same pitch causes the pipe to resonate. Helmholtz resonators may be used in the same way. The frequencies of two resonating tubes of the same length but of different areas are different. If the tube is circular in cross section and closed at one end, $0.6r$ must be added to the tube length to secure the "effective length." For one open at both ends, the correction is $1.2r$. In both cases, it is assumed that r, the tube radius, is small compared to the wave length. If the tube is conical and open at the ends, the slant height and not the length parallel to the axis must be used. If the pipe is only slightly conical, the difference between it and a parallel-sided pipe is in second order terms only. In a conical pipe closed at both ends, the nodes are not equidistant, but slight conicality has only a second-order effect. The cones here described are assumed to be truncated ones. If a complete cone—*i.e.*, one continued to the vertex—is used and the base is closed, the frequencies are inversely proportional to the slant height, and the overtones are not harmonics. An interesting case is that of a complete cone with base open. Here we have a conical tube *closed* at one end and *open* at the other, but the frequency of its fundamental and its full harmonic series are exactly those obtainable from a parallel-sided pipe of the same length and *open at both ends*. This can be shown with a series of forks having the ratios 1:2:3, etc., the lowest of which has the same frequency as the fundamental of some parallel-sided pipe open at both ends. A full cone open at the base is made so that its length (slant height) is equal to that of the pipe plus end corrections. Both cone and pipe respond to the same forks. The theory of the conical resonator is not simple. The range of frequencies to which this conical pipe responds is rather broad. However, the experiment is valuable in emphasizing the fact that the elementary analysis for finding the fundamental of a pipe is far from general in its application.

S-115. Resonant Response of Tuning Fork. Two tuning forks of the same pitch, mounted on resonance boxes, are set some distance apart with open ends facing one another. If either fork is struck and then silenced a few seconds later, the other fork will be heard. There is no such response when one fork is slightly weighted. The sound from the responding fork is much louder if the responding system is held in the hand instead of being allowed to remain on the table.

S-116. Resonant Response of Strings. Three strings are tuned on a sonometer (S-131) so that the frequency of the first is slightly above, of the second equal to, and of the third slightly below the frequency of a fork. A small paper rider is placed on the center of each string, and the stem of the vibrating fork is held against the sonometer box. The rider of the second string will be thrown off, but the other two will remain, showing that the tuned string responds most vigorously.

S-117. Resonant Response of Vocal Cavities. The artificial larynx designed by the Bell Telephone Laboratories demonstrates the resonance of the oral cavity. The squawking whistle from a toy balloon offers a simple substitute; it consists of a thin rubber band $\frac{3}{16}$ in. wide stretched tightly across the mouth of a

¼-in. tube about 1 in. long. The operator fastens a length of
rubber tubing to the squawker, puts it in the back of his mouth
and to one side, and blows it with compressed air from a tank or
balloon. He then talks without using his vocal cords. The
quality is poor, but he can imitate a baby perfectly with such easy
words as "mama" and "papa."

MUSICAL SOUNDS

S-118. Semimusical Sounds. This class of sounds includes
those in which the quality is so poor that only by courtesy can
they be called musical; yet they are not noises because their
source is a series of regular impulses. Such sounds are produced,
for example, by drawing the thumbnail or a stiff card across the

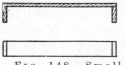

cover of a cloth-bound book, or by pulling
one piece of silk at uniform speed over
another piece. A piece of cloth of uniform
weave—muslin or silk—when ripped will
give a sound of definite pitch, depending
upon the speed of ripping. A familiar
example is the high-pitched ringing sound
produced when a shot is fired in an empty
stadium, or that heard when driving in an
automobile near a row of regularly spaced

F ɪ ɢ . 148.—S m a l l
benches of various
lengths may be made
to produce semimusical
sounds of different pitch
when slid along the lec-
ture table.

posts, or when walking near a picket fence. When a piece of
tin (not tinned iron) is bent quickly, it emits a "cry." Several
small benches made by nailing three pieces of wood together, as
shown in Fig. 148, will vibrate when pushed longitudinally along
a table top. By adjusting their lengths, they may be tuned
to give recognizable pitches. Countless other examples may be
found in common noises about the laboratory.

S-119. From clear-grained hard wood, cut eight sticks each
about 3 cm wide by 0.5 cm thick and having the following lengths:
22.0, 22.8, 24.2, 25.8, 27.2, 28.3, 29.5, 30.5 cm. Drop these
sticks onto the table or floor in rapid succession, to obtain the
notes of the diatonic scale. These sticks may be hung up and
played like a xylophone by tapping their centers. Two strings
are attached to each stick at its nodal points. For bars with
free ends, such as these, the two nodes for the fundamental are at
distances of 0.2232 times the length from the ends. The pitch of

any bar may be raised by shortening it; it may be lowered by making one or more shallow crosscuts with a saw near the middle.

S-120. Musical Sounds—Pitch and Frequency. The siren disk is an important instrument for the study of musical intervals and of the relation of pitch to frequency. A disk of metal has a number of concentric rows of regularly spaced holes. It is rotated at uniform speed, and an air blast is directed against one row of holes. The sequence of regular puffs of air issuing from successive holes produces a musical note whose frequency can be calculated from the speed of rotation and the known number of holes. The frequency may be increased by increasing the speed of rotation of the disk (E-232) or by blowing the air through a row containing more holes. A complete octave may be played if the numbers of holes in the successive rows are 24, 27, 30, 32, 36, 40, 45, 48. There should be one row of irregularly spaced holes for producing noise. Although the pitches emitted by all rows rise with increase in speed of rotation, the musical intervals between them remain unchanged. Chords may be played by blowing through more than one row of holes at a time.

S-121. Savart Wheel. An experiment similar to the preceding consists in holding the edge of a stiff card against the rim of a toothed wheel rotated on a shaft. If several wheels with different numbers of teeth are placed on the same shaft, different pitches can be obtained with the same speed of rotation; or the pitch can be changed by changing the speed. A wheel with irregularly spaced teeth will give only a whirring sound without recognizable pitch.

S-122. Audible Range of Sound. The upper limit of audibility can be determined approximately by whistles, tuning forks, or steel bars tuned to high frequencies. Extraneous noise, especially in the case of whistles, makes the determination somewhat unreliable. For better results, a beat-frequency oscillator (A-27), giving frequencies from 10 to 30,000 cycles per sec, is connected to a loudspeaker through an amplifier and attenuator.

S-123. Tone Quality. An oscillator giving a pure tone is connected through an amplifier with a loudspeaker and a cathode-ray oscilloscope, which shows that the pure tone is produced by a sine wave disturbance. It is possible to use the Bell Telephone Laboratories pure-wave records with phonograph pickup instead of the oscillator.

Bell Telephone Laboratories records showing dependence of tone quality upon harmonics are very instructive.[1] In place of these records, one may use a microphone or phonograph pickup, high- or low-pass filter, amplifier and loudspeaker. By cutting the filter in and out, the tone quality can be changed.

A series of organ pipes can be tuned to give the harmonics of a fundamental. The pipes should be wide, open pipes, so as to reduce their own harmonics. It requires careful tuning to make the pipes accurately harmonic, and not more than seven or eight can be used. They are all sounded together and then removed one by one to show the effect of suppressing various harmonics.

S-124. Using a phonelescope, or a microphone, amplifier, and cathode-ray oscilloscope (S-78, 79), demonstrate the connection between wave form and tone quality. The characteristic wave forms of vowels sung at the same pitch may be shown. But it should be noted that phase shifts among the harmonics may cause dissimilarity of wave form but not necessarily dissimilarity of sound quality, as can be shown from the appearance of the wave form for the same vowel sung at different pitches.

S-125. Using a microphone and oscilloscope, demonstrate the wave form of the tone from a tuning fork. This is not in general a pure sine wave, especially if the fork is struck sharply, as is at once evident on the oscilloscope screen. If the fork is mounted on a resonance box and the open end of the box is turned toward the microphone, the oscilloscope indicates that only the fundamental is reinforced. The harmonics usually present after the fork has been struck may be damped by touching the fork near the base of the prongs.

S-126. Organ Pipes. The part played by resonance in the production of a musical tone is well demonstrated by an organ pipe. Show a series of open and closed pipes of different lengths, or better two such pipes of variable length. At least one pipe should have a series of holes bored in the side of it, the spacing being such as to give the notes of the diatonic scale. It is played as a clarinet. The pipe must not be too long, else the spacing of the holes will be too great for fingering. A set of Pan pipes also may be demonstrated.

[1] These records are obtainable from Bell Telephone Laboratories *Bur. of Pub.*, 463 West St., New York.

S-127. Standing Waves in a Pipe.   The production of standing waves in a Kundt's tube has been described in S-82.

An organ pipe is made with one wall of flexible material— rubber or cellophane.   The pipe, laid on its side, is sprinkled with sand, which indicates the nodes of pressure within the sounding pipe by piling up at these points.

S-128. A slender resistance wire (*e.g.*, No. 30 chromel) is mounted along the axis of a long glass tube, one end of which is closed.   It is kept under tension by a spring so that, even when it is heated electrically, it does not sag.   The wire is heated to a bright red.   A shrill whistle is blown at the open end of the tube. When either the pitch of the whistle or the length of the tube is adjusted so that standing waves are produced, the hot wire shows clearly by its alternate regions of high and low luminosity where the nodes and loops of velocity are located.

S-129. If sand is sprinkled on a thin membrane like cellophane stretched over a small ring and the ring is lowered into a sounding pipe having at least one transparent side, then the motion of the sand indicates the *velocity* loops and nodes of the air within the pipe.   It is well to overblow the pipe so as to use harmonics rather than the fundamental, thus obtaining more nodes.

S-130. A galvanized-iron pipe 4 m long and 10 cm in diameter (like that used for rainspouts) is closed at one end with a membrane of rubber or cellophane, and the other end is attached to a gas pipe.   A line of holes 1 mm in diameter and 4 cm apart is drilled along one side of the tube for its whole length.   A source of sound is placed near the membrane, and the gas issuing from the row of holes is lighted.   The flames are of maximum height at the pressure antinodes but minimum at the nodes.   If the tube is viewed with the aid of a rotating mirror, it will be observed that all of the flames fluctuate in height but that the maximum fluctuation occurs at the pressure antinodes.   For maximum response, standing waves should be produced in the pipe, by using as the source a loudspeaker driven by a variable-frequency oscillator (A-27) or by tuning the pipe to a source of constant frequency.

Another way to show the vibrations in an organ pipe is to mount a row of manometric-flame capsules (S-76) in the wall along its length.   The flames are viewed in a rotating mirror.

S-131. Sonometer. A sonometer is a long hollow box along the top of which are stretched one or more strings rigidly attached to the box at one end, with provision at the other for changing their tension.   The length of each string can be changed by moving a bridge under it.   With such an instrument, the effect of length, tension, diameter, and kind of material on the pitch of a vibrating string is demonstrated.   A sonometer wire may be used to show the harmonics of a vibrating string.   If the string is plucked near one end and stopped at one-half, one-third, one-fourth, one-fifth, etc., of its length, the second, third, fourth, fifth, etc., harmonics are brought out.   If a sharp-edged piece of soft rubber (an eraser) is used to stop the string, it is possible to make 10 or more harmonics successively audible in this manner.

S-132. Vibrating Strings.   The motion of a string is always periodic, no matter how the motion may be started.   The motion

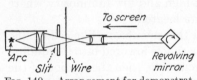

FIG. 149.—Arrangement for demonstrating vibrations of a wire.

of a sonometer wire may be made visible by illuminating it stroboscopically and projecting its shadow on a screen (S-133).   Another method is to illuminate a short segment of it by light passed through a slit, the light then going to a revolving mirror and thence to a screen, where the motion of the wire is made evident by its shadow (Fig. 149).

S-133.   The motion of any portion of a vibrating string may be shown by stretching it across the slide position of a lantern and limiting the light beam to a slit 1 mm wide placed behind the string.   The length of the string is perpendicular to the longer dimension of the slit.   The light falling on the screen is interrupted by a stroboscope disk.   The difference in character of the sound produced by bowing, plucking, and striking a string can be demonstrated by this method.   Best results are obtained with a good gut string.

S-134. Rubber-band Harp.   The pitch of a vibrating rubber band is only slightly changed by great increase in tension (and hence in length).   If a rubber band is repeatedly plucked while being stretched, its pitch will be observed to change very little. Several rubber bands may be fastened to two bars set at an angle to one another, so that the original lengths of the bands are different.   As the bars are moved apart, changing the lengths of the bands, the individual pitches remain nearly the same,

although they may differ from one band to another.   Thus, in the
equation for frequency of a vibrating string, $n = \dfrac{1}{2L}\sqrt{\dfrac{T}{M}}$, n (the
frequency) is nearly constant for large changes of length L and
tension T, since T is proportional to L, and M (mass per unit
length) is inversely proportional to L.[1]

S-135. Vibrations of Bars.   A 4-ft steel bar of rectangular
cross section, having a fundamental frequency of about 1 vps, is
held vertically by its lower end in a clamp attached to and driven
by a mechanical vibrator.   The bar, with one narrow face
scratched horizontally with sandpaper, is set against a black
background and strongly illuminated.   The oscillator is set in
motion, and its speed gradually increased, so that the bar
vibrates with the fundamental frequency and the first two or
three overtones.   The overtones are not harmonic, and the nodes
are not evenly spaced.

S-136.   A thin rod $\frac{1}{8}$ in. in diameter and 4 ft long is soldered
securely into a short section of heavier rod ($\frac{1}{2}$ in.) and clamped in
a vertical position.   The rod is held between the thumb and
fingers at a point about 1 ft above the support and bowed with a
bass-fiddle bow on its lower segment.   There result tones that
can be varied in frequency by changing the position of thumb and
fingers.   Resonant vibrations can be shown by holding the rod at
nodal points and plucking it between nodes.

S-137. Vibration of Plates.   A metal plate is held horizontally
in a clamp at its center and covered with lycopodium powder or
fine sand.   It is set in vibration by striking or bowing.   If while
the plate is being bowed it is touched lightly with the finger at
some point, all modes of vibration will be damped out except
those having nodal lines passing through the point touched.   The
position of the nodal lines of vibration is indicated by the massing
of the powder along them.   The shape of the figures depends
upon the positions of stopping and of bowing.   Either round or
square plates may be used, but the latter give more interesting
figures (Fig. 150).   The figures may be made visible to a large
group by reflecting them with a 45° mirror or by using glass plates
and projecting the figures onto a screen by light passing upward
through the plate.

---

[1] Sudden changes in length are accompanied by slight changes of pitch
owing to changes of temperature of the rubber (see H-173).

S-138. The previous setup (S-137) may be reversed by supporting the edges of the plate on a rubber pad in the form of a ring, soldering a nail to the center of a telephone diaphragm, and allowing the nail to press against the plate. The frequency of the vibrator is varied by changing the frequency of the source of alternating current (vacuum-tube oscillator and amplifier) until nodal lines appear faintly, and these are then emphasized by putting matchsticks under the plate beneath these lines. The experiment shows some of the types of vibration of drums, telephone and loudspeaker diaphragms.[1]

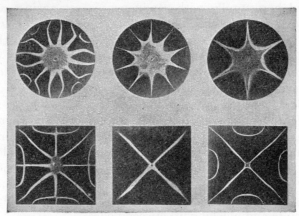

Fig. 150.—Chladni figures.

S-139. Suspend four pith balls so that they touch lightly against the rim of a hemispherical bowl of glass or a large goblet. Space the balls equally about the rim, and bow the bowl at a point halfway between any two of the balls. Then bow at some other point. In the first case, the balls do not move because they are at the nodes, but in the second case they do.

S-140. Aeolian Sounds. A current of air—such as the wind—moving past a wire will set it into vibration because of the formation of eddies first on one side, then on the other. A shallow vessel, such as a washbasin, is set on a rotating table and filled with water. Above it and near the periphery is hung a pendulum of short period, arranged so that the bottom of the pendulum bar dips into the water. The period is made adjustable by a sliding weight, and the pendulum is mounted to swing only along a

[1] COLWELL, R. C., *Phil. Mag.*, **12**, 320, 1931.

radius of the circles in which the water moves, that is, across the direction of motion of the water. The vessel and water are set into rotation, and when the speed is brought up to the right value, the oscillations of the pendulum will be seen to reach a maximum, being less for either higher or lower speeds. (See also M-311.)

S-141. An aeolian harp works on the same principle. A number of strings stretched side by side are tuned to the same very low pitch. As the wind blows over them, various harmonics respond for different wind speeds, and if the strings are of different thicknesses the wind note will not be the same for all of the strings at the same time. If the wind note corresponds to a natural frequency of the strings, then resonance will cause the strings to vibrate strongly. Most of the overtones of the strings are in harmony with one another, because the strings are all tuned to the same pitch, which is taken low so that the wind excites overtones rather than the fundamental. However, the odd harmonics beginning with the seventh are discordant and account in part for the peculiar character of the rising and falling music.

A simple framework is mounted on a whirling table so that it can be turned rapidly. It carries one or more vertical wires, which are thus moved rapidly through the air and produce the same singing notes as if the air blew over them. If the wires are of different diameters but tuned to the same fundamental frequency, they will emit different notes, lowest for the wire of greatest diameter.

FIG. 151.—Wind notes produced near the wire are communicated to the ear through the tube.

S-142. A piece of glass tubing is drawn down to a small opening (Fig. 151). A piece of wire (No. 18) is fastened to it so that it stands across the axis of the tube about $\frac{1}{4}$ in. in front of the small end. A length of rubber tubing leads from the larger end of the glass to the ear. When the wire is held in a draft such as passes through the opening of a nearly closed door or window, the wind note is easily heard. The eddies formed as the wind passes the wire are caught by the small end of the glass tube, and the sound produced is carried to the ear.

S-143. The Australian "bull-roarer" operates by the autorotation (M-299) of a flat plate in an air stream. A thin piece of wood or aluminum about 1 ft long by 2 in. wide with rounded ends is tied at the center of one end to a piece of good quality string or linen tape. As it is whirled, it twists the string until it can twist no farther, when it untwists. The loud noise that it produces is due to the generation of eddies in the air.

S-144. Radiation of Waves. The way in which waves are radiated from a source is well demonstrated by the use of the ripple tank (S-49). Waves spread out more from a narrow paddle than from a wide one. The spreading from a small paddle is reduced by placing a bar on each side of it (Fig. 152) to act as a baffle. Two parallel bars illustrate transmission in tubes and small radiation from the open end. Two bars at a small angle with vertex near the source illustrate improvement in radiation produced by flaring the tube, making a horn. Too large a flare reduces the radiation, as is shown by spreading the bars farther apart. By changing the frequency, the increased directionality of short waves can be demonstrated.

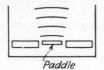

Paddle

S-145. The corresponding properties of loudspeakers can be demonstrated by arranging a phonograph and pickup and a beat-frequency oscillator to be fed independently through an attenuator and amplifier to any one of four horns—a dynamic speaker with baffle, a short exponential horn (4 to 6 ft), a long exponential horn (8 to 12 ft), and a horn unit without the horn.

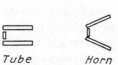

Tube   Horn

Fig. 152.—Arrangement of paddle and baffles in ripple tank to illustrate radiation of waves.

With the phonograph, the quality of all four can be compared. With the oscillator, the comparison can be made at different frequencies. At high frequencies, the horns and the hornless unit are about the same except for directionality, and the dynamic speaker is not so good. At low frequencies, first the hornless, then the short horn, cut off transmission. There is a sharp cutoff for the short horn as the frequency decreases.

S-146. Absorption of Sound—Reverberation. Use Bell Telephone Laboratories records of reverberation and echo.[1] Use a loudspeaker with decibel attenuator to measure the reverberation time of the lecture room for different intensities; then plot a curve of reverberation time. The reverberation time is defined as the time required for the sound level to drop 60 db or to one-millionth of the original intensity.

[1] See footnote, p. 184.

S-147. A loudspeaker is attached to one end of a brass tube 4 to 6 in. in diameter and 6 ft long. The other end is closed with caps of various materials, hard or absorbing. Near the capped end is made an opening, opposite which is set a microphone connected to an amplifier and meter. With a warble tone or a phonograph record (not a pure tone) to drive the loudspeaker, the length of time required for the sound to die out can be measured for different kinds of cap material. The intensity dies out exponentially; loudness dies out linearly. The slope of the loudness vs. time curve is inversely proportional to the reverberation time, which can be shown also to be inversely proportional to the absorption coefficient of the material of the end cap.

S-148. Sound Waves in an Auditorium. A cross-sectional model of a theater is cut out of a piece of thick wood or other material and laid in a ripple tank. Pulse waves originating at the stage are produced with a mechanical dropper. The way in which the waves are scattered and reflected by the walls is observed. Smooth walls may give rise to echoes, while broken wall surfaces spread the sound out more uniformly. Walls of certain shapes may focus the sound, producing bad echoes and dead spots. Cross-sectional models of a local auditorium are suggested.

S-149. Scattering of Sound. A brass disk, greased, is used in the ripple tank as an obstacle for a train of waves. The paddle should be wide enough to produce a directional beam of waves. The generator for linear waves (Fig. 126) is suggested. By changing the frequency the wave length is changed, and the difference in scattering for different wave lengths is observed. Long waves scatter in all directions; short waves scatter principally forward.

S-150. Doppler Effect. Change in pitch due to motion of the observer with respect to the source of sound is familiar to all. It may be demonstrated in several ways. A 2000-cycle tuning fork may be struck and then swung rapidly away from the class. A better way is to mount a reed on the end of an arm attached to a rotator, so that the reed is moved rapidly in a circle. The alternate rise and fall in pitch as the reed approaches or recedes from the class is apparent. The same effect may be observed by blowing a shrill whistle while it is swung in a 3-ft circle on the end of a rubber tube. A loudspeaker may be mounted on a rotating arm with counterweight and a 2000-cycle note supplied to it (see also S-49).

S-151. An amusing mechanical analogue of the Doppler effect may be shown by driving an endless string stretched over two pulleys separated by the length of the lecture table. A student drops paper riders periodically onto the string at one end. The instructor picks up the riders at the other. If one moves with respect to the other, the period of picking up riders is altered. This experiment shows clearly the difference in the effect for moving observer and moving source. Timing may be done with a metronome.

S-152. Direction Judgment of the Ear. For *low-pitched sounds*, locating the source depends upon the *phase difference* of the sound waves arriving at the two ears. Two small funnels are attached to a T-tube by rubber tubes several feet long, one tube being about 1.5 times as long as the other. The funnels are put over the ears, and the open end of the T is tapped with the finger. The sound will seem to come from the side of the shorter tube. The two tubes may be replaced with the two U-tubes described in S-103.

S-153. For *high-pitched sounds*, the location depends upon the *difference in intensity* at the two ears due to the sound shadow cast by the head. The following experiment shows the existence of such a shadow. Extend the right arm directly out to the right of the body. Rub the thumb and fingers of the right hand over one another. This produces a series of high-pitched sounds of low intensity that can be heard in a quiet room. Now close the right ear with the left hand or with cotton. The sound will not be heard by the left ear. Repeat, but now hold a tuning fork of low pitch in the right hand. The left ear hears this. This experiment, which involves diffraction, is not so conclusive as it might be; for the loudness even for low-pitched sounds is much less when the right ear is closed.

PART III

HEAT

THERMOMETRY

H-1. Temperature Diagram. A temperature diagram ranging from absolute zero to 6000°K is painted on a board as long as convenient. In a small room, a 3-m diagram showing 20° per cm will serve. Upon this scale are indicated several fixed points for reference, such as the boiling point of liquid air, 88°; freezing point of water, 273°; boiling point of water, 373°; boiling point of mercury, 630°; melting point of gold, 1336°; melting point of iron, 1808°; melting point of tungsten, 3643°; temperature of a carbon arc, 4000°; surface temperature of the sun, 5500°. On such a diagram, the whole range of atmospheric temperature covers only about 5 cm. It may be desirable to paint another diagram on the same board which shows a six-fold magnification of the range from 0 to 1000°, so as to compare the Kelvin, centigrade, and Fahrenheit systems within a range more commonly encountered.

These diagrams should be painted on a white background, with clear black lines at least 3 to 5 mm wide and correspondingly visible lettering; they should be mounted vertically if possible, with the zero as high as convenient. The region of common atmospheric temperature may be indicated by a red bracket.

Such diagrams as these convey some idea of the limited range of human temperature sense, and they serve as a natural introduction to the discussion of thermometry. It is somewhat startling to consider that the temperatures of some of the hotter stars would have to be represented on the 6000° diagram by points outside the lecture room.

H-2. Thermometers. A discussion of thermometry may be illustrated by an exhibit of several types of temperature-measuring device, which may well include mercury thermometers of various ranges and sensitivities, air thermometers, differential thermometers, resistance thermometers, bimetallic thermometers, thermocouples, and optical pyrometers. The laboratory may

193

possess specimens or charts from manufacturers showing mercury thermometers in various stages of manufacture.

H-3. Historically, the Galileo air thermometer is of interest.

It may be constructed simply from a 200-ml flask with a single-hole stopper into which is inserted a tube dipping vertically into a beaker of colored water (Fig. 153). The flask is heated gently with a Bunsen burner until a few bubbles of air emerge from the tube. As the flask cools, water rises in the tube. Its level may be made to change visibly by heating the bulb with the hand, cooling it with ice, etc. It is evident that in Galileo's thermometer falling temperature is accompanied by a rising thermometer! A modified form of this thermoscope may be made by bending the vertical tube into a U

Fig. 153.— and filling it partly with colored liquid. A third form
Galileo's air of air thermoscope consists simply of a flask contain-
thermoscope. ing a small amount of colored water; a glass tube
passing through a tight stopper projects some distance above the flask and dips into the liquid (Fig. 154). A few bubbles of air blown through the tube will cause the liquid to rise to a convenient height above the stopper. In large rooms, it may be necessary to project an image of the meniscus to show changes of level with change of temperature of the bulb; other- wise, the vertical tube should be backed with a white card.

H-4. Constant-pressure Air Thermometer. A 200-ml flask is equipped with a single-hole stopper and a tube projecting horizontally (Fig. 155). Into the tube is introduced a globule of mercury to separate the air in the flask from the outer air.

Changes of temperature of the bulb cause the
mercury globule to move laterally because of changes
of gas volume at constant pressure. (Project.)

Fig. 154.—
Simple air
thermoscope.

H-5. Constant-volume Air Thermometer. For demonstration purposes, an air thermometer of the constant-volume type may be arranged from a glass bulb to which a vertical glass tube is con- nected by pressure tubing (Fig. 156). Mercury is introduced into the tube to a fiducial point by raising or lowering the vertical

tube to change the pressure. It is generally sufficient to show
that changes of temperature produce changes of pressure. More

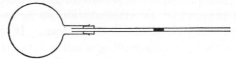

FIG. 155.—Simple constant-pressure air thermoscope.

accurate use of such thermometers may be reserved for the
laboratory.

H-6. Lecture-table Thermometer. The thermocouple is an
eminently satisfactory device for demonstrating temperature
differences. Even though the principles
involved are not discussed until later in the
course, the student should be given confidence in the temperature scale that
thermocouples afford. It is comparatively
easy to construct a large-scale thermometer
that will read temperatures directly by connecting a thermocouple to the lecture-room
galvanometer. The thermocouple consists
of a 1-m length of No. 24 constantan wire
soldered to copper leads from the galvanometer. One junction is kept in a beaker or,
better still, a Dewar flask, containing ice
water, while the other may be moved to any
point where temperature is to be measured.
With such a thermocouple and a sensitive
lecture-room galvanometer with suitable
scale, temperatures may be read to the
nearest degree even by a large class. Double
or triple junctions may be used if greater
sensitivity is desired. The sensitivity and
setting of the thermometer may be adjusted
by a resistance box or an inexpensive radio
potential divider, simply by putting the
warm junction into a beaker of hot water

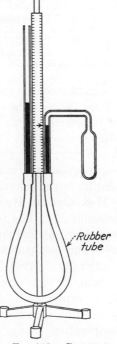

FIG. 156.—Constant-
volume air thermom-
eter.

and changing the resistance until the scale reading agrees
with the reading of a mercury thermometer held in the
same beaker (Fig. 157). This adjustment may be made

before the lecture begins and may be easily repeated if a thermocouple of different sensitivity is used. The performance of a thermocouple thermometer may be determined by a moderate amount of experimentation so as to select the factors suitable for any particular lecture room. It is an instrument of great flexibility for measuring small or large temperature differences as well as for showing ordinary temperatures with sufficient precision. It is more satisfactory to let the student read temperatures for himself than to have him rely upon the instructor for such information. Some laboratories are equipped with mercury thermometers suitable for projection, but even these lack the convenience and adaptability of the thermocouple thermometer.

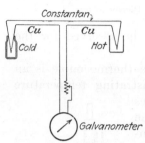

FIG. 157.—Copper-constantan thermocouple as lecture-table thermometer.

H-7. Since the class is introduced to the thermocouple thermometer before it encounters thermoelectricity, it may be suitable at first to make up two simple thermojunctions as the class watches by twisting a piece of copper wire about each end of a piece of constantan wire and to demonstrate the thermoelectric effect simply by causing the lecture-room galvanometer to move to left or right by differential heating of the junctions.

H-8. Optical Pyrometry. The principle of optical pyrometry may be introduced by showing the changes in color and brightness that occur in an electrically heated iron wire as the current in it is gradually increased. This experiment, which shows a qualitative dependence of color upon temperature, may be followed by

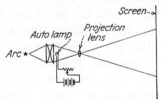

FIG. 158.—Arrangement for showing principle of optical pyrometer.

another that emphasizes the color-matching principle of the pyrometer. Place a smooth, clear glass, 6-v automobile lamp in the focal plane of a projection lantern (Fig. 158). Connect the lamp with a variable source of emf to control its brightness. At low voltage, the filament of the bulb will show dark against a bright background; but as the voltage is increased, the filament disappears and finally reappears bright against the background of the lantern illumination. In case an arc light is used in the lantern, severe overloading of the lamp will be required, and it is advisable to use an amber filter between the arc and the headlight bulb to reduce the intensity of the background radiation from the arc (L-99).

EXPANSION

H-9. Linear Expansion. A long wire is stretched between supports on the lecture table and heated electrically. A rheostat R, of 20-amp capacity, is included in the circuit (Fig. 159). When R is 3 ohms, a 6-ft length of No. 20 nichrome wire will be

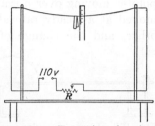

Fig. 159.—Expansion of a wire.

heated to a bright yellow color on a 110-v line. The expansion and consequent sagging of the wire are made visible by hanging over it a white strip of asbestos or a small card held by a paper clip. If an iron wire is used, the sagging is temporarily checked near 800°C, the recalescence temperature, at which occurs a change in the crystal form of the iron. The reverse effect occurs on cooling. A vertical scale placed behind the wire may help to make its motion more evident (see E-104).

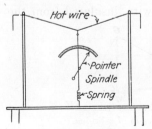

Fig. 160.—Model of hot-wire ammeter.

H-10. The expansion may also be shown if one end of the wire is passed over a pulley and kept taut by a weight or spring. A large pointer on the pulley indicates its motion.

H-11. A third method that illustrates the principle of the hot-wire ammeter may be shown at this point in the course as well as later when current-measuring devices are discussed (E-171). A short link of wire is attached to the center of the long heater wire (Fig. 160). A thread from the link is wrapped once or twice around a spindle carrying a light, balanced pointer and is kept taut by a weight or spring. Expansion of the wire is indicated by motion of the pointer. This method also may be used to show the recalescence of iron (H-9).

H-12. The expansion of rods or tubes of various metals, such as brass, iron, aluminum, invar, is shown by a number of standard pieces of apparatus. The specimen is clamped at one end; the other end rests on a needle free to roll on a glass plate or smooth surface (Fig. 161). The needle carries a straw or other light pointer moving over a scale. The flame of a Bunsen burner is moved at a steady rate along the sample from one end to the other, and the change of the indicator needle noted. More

accurate results are obtained with tubes heated by steam from a flask or hypsometer, so that a definite temperature rise occurs and expansions of different tubes can be compared.

Fig. 161.—Linear-expansion apparatus.

H-13. Bending Glass by Expansion. A strip of plate glass is held in a vise and heated gently on one side by a Bunsen burner. It bends toward the cooler side because of expansion, and the motion may be magnified by reflecting light from a mirror cemented to the cold side.

H-14. Linear Expansion—Bridge Model. The "roadway" *ABC* (Fig. 162) is made of two pieces of brass, each 30 by 4 by 0.2 cm, hinged at *B*. The ends at *A* and *C* are slotted and can be either locked in place by wing nuts or left free to slide. Two parallel cables *EFBGH*, of No. 18 iron wire, insulated from the

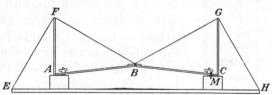

Fig. 162.—Model to illustrate expansion of a bridge.

"roadway" and towers, are heated by an electric current. The consequent sagging of the bridge can be observed directly, or it may be magnified by use of a mirror *M* on a needle under one end of the bridge, the other end being locked. The expansion of the roadway itself may be shown by locking both ends and heating it with a Bunsen flame, thus causing the supporting wires to slacken visibly.

H-15. Ball and Ring. A metal ball that when cold will pass through a snugly fitting ring cannot do so after being heated even a few degrees, but will pass through if the ring is also heated.

H-16. Shrink Fit. The principle of shrink fits is illustrated by making a brass ring of square cross section, 5 by 5 mm, which will just slip over the small end of a slightly tapered steel bar 2 cm in diameter. When the ring is heated, it will slip farther onto the bar, where it will bind tightly upon cooling. The ring and bar are then passed around the class to let each student attempt to pull them apart. They are easily separated when both ring and bar are heated.

H-17. Forces Involved in Expansion. An iron or a brass bar B (Fig. 163), of square section 2 cm on a side, is held in a strong cast-iron yoke Y. Through a hole in one end of the bar passes a short cast-iron peg C, 5 mm in diameter, which bears

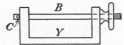

FIG. 163.—The rod C is broken as the heated bar B contracts on cooling.

against the shoulders of the yoke when the large nut at the other end of the bar is tightened. The bar is heated several hundred degrees, the nut tightened, and the whole system allowed to cool. The peg will be snapped by the strain. The bar can also be arranged with two holes and two nuts so that one rod is broken while the bar is being heated and the other while it is cooling.

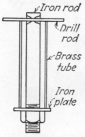

FIG. 164.—Expansion of the brass tube breaks the drill rod.

H-18. A second method is shown in Fig. 164. A 1-in. iron bar, about 10 in. long, has a transverse hole drilled near one end; the other end is threaded to take a heavy nut, bearing against a thick iron plate 2 in. in diameter, on which rests a 7-in. length of brass tube, 1.5 in. in diameter with $\frac{3}{16}$-in. walls. A $\frac{5}{16}$-in. drill rod is hardened by heating to redness and quenching in water. The rod is slipped through the hole in the iron bar, and the nut tightened until the brass tube presses against the rod. The hole in the bar should afford sufficient clearance for the drill rod and should be reamed out on both ends so as to increase the leverage. When a Bunsen burner is used to heat the outer brass pipe, the expansion breaks the steel drill rod. It is wise to use a barricade, as the pieces may fly out with some violence.

H-19. Linear Expansion of Rubber.

Stretched rubber contracts upon heating because of increase in its Young's modulus. This fact may be simply shown by hanging a 100-g weight from a rubber band and heating with a radiant heater. On a larger scale, a piece of $\frac{1}{4}$-in. thin-walled rubber tubing 1 ft long is stretched by a weight W (Fig. 165) to at least twice its original length. When the metal tube T surrounding the rubber is heated strongly with a Bunsen burner, the weight W will be raised about 2 cm. The motion is magnified by a 1-ft aluminum pointer P, which should be capable of vertical adjustment to allow for the elastic yield in the rubber.

H-20. Rubber-driven Pendulum.

A steel bar, about 15 in. long (Fig. 166), carries heavy

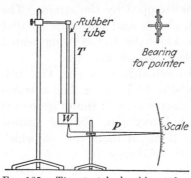

Fig. 165.—The stretched rubber tube contracts upon heating.

Fig. 166.—Rubber-driven pendulum.

cylindrical weights at each end. Nine inches above the lower weight is set a knife-edge, at right angles to the bar. Below the upper weight is a collar, adjustable by means of a setscrew, carrying a 3-in. length of $\frac{3}{4}$-in. bar on each side. The two ends of the knife-edge rest on a flat plate at the top of a support rod, the plate being notched to take the bar of the pendulum. The collar is adjusted so that the pendulum is unstable in a vertical position. It is kept from swinging over by two or three stout rubber bands, stretched between a peg on the bottom weight and another on a collar on the support rod, as shown. This collar should be adjusted so that when the pendulum swings over to about the angle shown, the rubber bands are stretched to about four times their original length. The support rod also carries a sheet-metal shield, behind which is placed an electric heater, in such a position that its heat falls on the rubber bands when the pendulum is in the position shown. The rubber contracts and pulls the pendulum toward the erect position. Beyond this position, the rubber is shielded from the heat. The pendulum oscillates with a period of about 3 sec. This apparatus demonstrates the same characteristic of stretched rubber as that illustrated by the previous experiment; its automatic operation makes it suitable for a museum exhibit.

H-21. Differential Expansion. The simplest way of demonstrating differential expansion is to use a compound bar, made by welding or riveting together two 25-cm strips of metal (*e.g.*, brass and invar steel) that have different coefficients of expansion. If the bending that occurs when the bar is heated in a Bunsen flame is not visible to the class directly, it may be magnified by shadow projection.

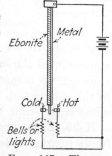

FIG. 167.—Thermostat circuit.

H-22. A bimetallic-strip thermostat may be arranged with electrical contacts, so that a light is flashed or a bell rung, either on heating or cooling or both. By careful adjustment, a thermostat of metal and ebonite can be made so sensitive that it can be operated by the radiant heat from the hand held 3 to 4 in. above it. Or it may be heated with a lamp and cooled with an electric fan. A suitable circuit is shown in Fig. 167.

An electric sign flasher, or "blinker," may be shown, and its operation exhibited. The thermostat from an automatic electric iron, disk or strip type, that snaps on and off through positions of unstable equilibrium, is another variation. The switch may be used to control an electric light that goes out when the switch is heated externally by a Bunsen burner.

H-23. A gridiron pendulum of constant effective length may be built of tubes of brass and zinc, arranged so that steam may be passed through them, and the effect of the differential expansion of the metals shown. The pendulum may be shown in conjunction with a simple pendulum, consisting of a spherical bob supported by two iron wires that are heated by an electric current. The simple pendulum is hung so that the bob swings just above the lecture desk when the wire is cool; on heating the wire, the bob scrapes the table.

H-24. Trevelyan Rocker. A brass or copper rocker, of the shape shown in Fig. 168, is heated in a flame to 100 or 200°C. It is then laid on a cool lead support. The rocker oscillates rapidly for several minutes. Both rocker and support should be polished with fine emery paper at the points of contact. On a lecture desk, the rocking produces enough noise to be audible to a large class.

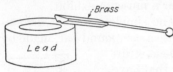

FIG. 168.—Trevelyan rocker.

If desired, a small mirror may be set on the rocker, and a beam of light reflected to the wall, thus making the motion apparent. The rocking is due to rapid local expansion of the lead under one edge of the rocker, tipping it so that the other edge makes closer contact with the lead. The alternate expansion and contraction thus set up make the rocking continue. The use of "dry ice" in this connection is not recommended, for although the audible effect is the same the cause is not (see H-52).

H-25. Expansion of Fused Quartz. The low expansion of fused quartz is demonstrated by heating a piece of tubing or other quartz ware to redness in a Bunsen flame and then plunging it into water. It is not harmed, whereas an ordinary glass tube will be shattered by similar treatment, even though it is heated to a lower temperature. Pyrex glass and ordinary soft glass may be compared for a smaller temperature change.

H-26. Prince Rupert Drops. Droplets of molten glass that have been suddenly cooled exhibit extraordinary strength when subjected to blows from a hammer; but when the tip of the droplet is broken so as to upset the equilibrium of strains within it, it flies into powder. The droplet should be enfolded within a pocket handkerchief to prevent injury from flying glass.

H-27. Expansion of Liquids. A number of test tubes are held side by side in a wire or wooden rack and arranged in front of the lantern for shadow projection. They are nearly filled with equal volumes of various liquids: alcohol, benzene, glycerin, turpentine, water, mercury. When a glass vessel containing hot water is raised around the tubes so as to heat the liquids, the different expansivities are shown by the differences in the levels assumed by the liquids. The motion of the meniscus may be magnified considerably by equipping each test tube with a single-hole stopper and a glass tube of small bore. Care should be taken to exclude air bubbles.

H-28. Expansion and Maximum Density of Water. A pyrex bulb of the design shown in Fig. 169 has one junction of a thermo-couple sealed into a side arm situated at A. The bulb is filled with distilled water at about 35°C, and the stopper B is inserted, so as to eject all air bubbles and fill the stem with water. It is placed in an ice bath for an hour before class time; when desired, it is withdrawn and put in the lantern so as to project the level of the water in the stem, and the thermocouple is connected to the lecture-room galva-nometer. The class watches the level of the water in the stem and the galvanom-eter deflection as the temperature rises, observing the temperature at which the level of the water is lowest.

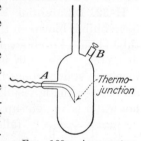

FIG. 169.—Apparatus for showing expansion and maximum density of water.

H-29. The bulb used in the preceding experiment may be replaced by a quartz flask of 100-ml capacity. Through a stopper in the neck are inserted a thermocouple and a capillary tube, 15 cm long with 1-mm bore. The flask is filled with distilled water, air bubbles being carefully removed with a wire, and the stopper is adjusted so that the water level stands well up in the capillary tube. The flask is cooled and projected as in the previous experiment. It is well to have a transparent glass scale held to the capillary by rubber bands, so that the changes in level may be followed more readily. With the dimensions given, the water meniscus drops 5 or 6 mm before it begins to rise. The preliminary contraction and beginning of the expansion require about 10 min. The expansion of a quartz flask is so slight that practically all the volume change is due to the water. With a pyrex flask, the rise of the water meniscus is slightly delayed. However, it is possible to compensate for the expansion of a 100-ml pyrex flask by putting 5.3 ml of mercury into it.

H-30. Maximum Density of Water. A jar of water, 35 cm high, has 15 cm of ice floating on top. A thermometer with bulb at the bottom of the jar, or a thermojunction at the same place, shows that the temperature at the bottom of the jar does not fall below 4°C, the temperature of maximum density of water.

H-31. The familiar Hope apparatus may be used, with a freezing mixture of cracked ice and salt surrounding a tall jar of *ice water* at its midpoint. The water at the top may freeze while the water at the bottom ceases to change temperature at 4°C, as shown by a thermometer or a thermocouple.

H-32. Differential Expansion of Liquid and Container. A 5-cm bulb is blown on the end of a soft-glass capillary tube. The tube should be about 15 cm long, with a bore about 1 mm in diameter. The bulb is filled with clean mercury, so that the meniscus stands about halfway up the tube. The position of the meniscus is made visible to the class by projection. A beaker of hot water is brought up around the bulb. The mercury level first falls, then rises.

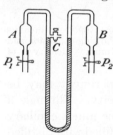

FIG. 170.—Apparatus for showing equality of pressure-temperature coefficients of two gases.

A similar result may be obtained by using water in a small flask or bottle with a 2-mm tube inserted through a rubber stopper. The reverse process, obtained when the hot bulb is immersed in ice water, may also be shown. The student may observe the same phenomenon in the laboratory with a thermometer.

H-33. Expansion of Gases. The expansion of gases has already been mentioned in the section on thermometry, in connection with the demonstration of various types of air or gas thermometer (H-4, 5). To show that different gases have the same coefficients of pressure increase at constant volume, two bulbs, not necessarily of equal size, are connected with the two ends of a U-tube containing colored liquid. Both bulbs are provided with pinchcocks (Fig. 170). Illuminating gas is introduced into bulb A through pinchcock P_1, thus driving the air out at C; after a few moments, the escaping gas may be ignited. Close C, P_1, and P_2, and adjust any slight difference of pressure that may exist between A and B by valving at C. This whole operation may be performed during the class period so that the students may see that one bulb is filled with illuminating gas, the other with air. First, heat one bulb by hand to show movement of the liquid as a result of pressure increase due to temperature increase. Both bulbs are then immersed in a vessel of hot water, so that they rise to the same temperature. The liquid in the U-tube may be disturbed at first owing to unequal conduction of the glass bulbs and of the gases, but it eventually returns to its initial position, showing that the pressure increase in both gases is the same. Other gases may be used if available. If the two pressures are not the same at the beginning, the level of the liquid will be different when temperature equilibrium is reached.

H-34. The equality of the coefficients of volume increase at constant pressure may be shown by using two bulbs of equal size, filled with different gases, as constant-pressure thermometers (see H-4). The two bulbs are immersed in a water bath to show equal motions of the mercury globules.

SPECIFIC HEAT

H-35. Contrasting Specific Heats. A disk of iron and a light metal vessel containing water are adjusted to have the same mass. This condition may be emphasized simply by hanging them on opposite ends of an equal-arm balance (meter stick and fulcrum). The area of the disk is the same as that of the bottom of the vessel. Two similar Bunsen burners are adjusted to give flames as nearly as possible equal and are set, one under the iron, the other under the vessel of water; or a single hot plate may be used to heat both. After a few minutes, the lecturer dips his fingers into the water and sprinkles a few drops on the iron disk. The drops sizzle and quickly boil away, thus demonstrating that the iron is much hotter than the water. Equal quantities of heat put into equal masses of different substances do not in general produce equal increases of temperature. The demonstration thermocouple may also be used to show the difference in temperature, one junction being held in contact with the iron, the other in the water.

H-36. Comparison of Specific Heats of Metals. Several cylinders of the same diameter (2 to 3 cm) are cut from rods of different metals (Al, Fe, Cu, Sn, Pb) and adjusted to have the *same mass*, approximately 100 g. It is well to emphasize this point by weighing the cylinders before the class on a rough balance. The cylinders are all provided with small hooks in the top, by which they are tied with threads to the ring of a ring stand. They are all heated in hot paraffin or oil to, say, 150°C and then simultaneously removed from the oil and set on a flat disk of paraffin, 0.5 cm thick, which has previously been molded in a pie plate and removed by gentle heating. The depth to which each mass melts its way into the paraffin is an indication, in large part, of the amount of heat liberated by the cooling metal. If some of the masses melt holes completely through the paraffin disk, the class can observe the difference in the times at which the masses drop through the disk. The conclusion is that different amounts of heat may be given out by equal masses in cooling through the same temperature range.

H-37. A variation of the previous experiment is to heat the cylinders in boiling water and then to lower them into separate small beakers (200 ml) containing equal masses of water at room temperature. Similarly 100 g of mercury may be used. The demonstration thermocouple shows successively the different resulting temperatures. Finally 100 g of boiling water is poured into another beaker of water; the resulting temperature is much higher than any of the preceding.

H-38. Ice Calorimeter. Place four or more similar glass funnels in a rack, and fill them with finely cracked ice. Place beneath them an equal number of similar glass graduates, attached to a board so that all can be emptied at once (Fig. 171). This operation is easily performed if the bases of the graduates are set in shallow holes in the board and retained by two strips of wood screwed to the board, one on each side of the row of graduates. Equal masses of different metals, hung by threads from a wooden rod and properly spaced to correspond with the funnels, are heated in boiling water (either in a long tank or in separate beakers, if necessary). After the ice has cooled the funnels so that all are dripping slowly and alike, the graduates are emptied of the accumulated water, and the hot metal masses are lowered into the funnels. One funnel is left empty as a control. Melting of the ice occurs quite rapidly at first. As soon as the metals are cooled, as indicated by the slowing down of the melting, the graduates are removed, and the respective volumes of

water read.   The volume of water in the control graduate is sub-
tracted from each of the other volumes.   Thus amounts of water
proportional to the respective specific heats are determined.   By
assuming a value for the heat of fusion of ice, approximate values
of the specific heats of the metals may be calculated.

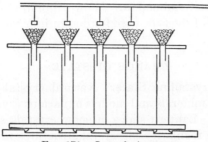

Fig. 171.—Ice calorimeter.

H-39. Specific Heat—Method of Mixtures.   Different known
masses of hot and cold water are mixed in a large beaker.   The
class calculates the temperature of the mixture from the known
temperatures of the two masses of water and compares the
calculated value with the value observed on the demonstration
thermocouple.   Large quantities of water should be used, so that
the heat capacity of the beaker may be neglected.

H-40.   Measured masses of different substances (*e.g.*, lead shot,
glass beads, copper shot) may be heated in copper cups immersed
in a steam bath and then poured into different calorimeters containing known masses of water.   Temperature of the hot substances and initial and final temperatures of the water in each
calorimeter are recorded, and from the data obtained the various
specific heats are computed.

H-41.   A differential thermoscope is made as follows.   Two
similar Dewar flasks, unsilvered and unevacuated, have outlet
tubes sealed into the outer wall of each flask.   The outlet
tubes are joined by means of rubber tubing to the two arms of a
U-tube containing colored water or other indicating liquid.
Equal volumes of water at room temperature are poured into the
flasks.   Then the same *masses* of mercury and of water at 100°C
are poured into the respective flasks.   The motion of the indicating liquid shows qualitatively the difference in the heat capacities
of the mercury and the water.

If Dewar flasks cannot be procured, wide-necked boiling flasks may be substituted; a side tube is sealed onto each, and a test tube, as large as possible, is set in the neck of each, the joint being made airtight with wax or with a short length of rubber tubing slipped over the test tube.

H-42. Heat of Combustion. Show a bomb or a continuous-flow calorimeter of the type used for determining heating values of fuels and foods.

CHANGE OF STATE

H-43. The Crystalline State. Natural crystals of rock salt, quartz, or other minerals and models of various crystal structures may be shown. Lantern slides of snow crystals show beautiful examples. The regularity of crystal structures may be pointed out as evidence of molecular patterns.

H-44. Crystallization. A thin layer of sulfur is melted on the flat bottom of a crystallizing dish, which is then set on the lantern for vertical projection. In a few seconds, crystals are seen to branch out from the sides of the dish.

A clean lantern-slide cover is wet with a saturated solution of ammonium chloride and warmed over a flame. It is placed in the slide holder of a projection lantern before crystallization starts. Crystallization proceeds rapidly, especially if the lantern is warm.

H-45. The crystallization of sodium acetate or sodium hyposulfite from concentrated solution may be shown. Crystallization may be started by inoculation with a small crystal. The growth of a "lead tree" by electrolysis (E-195) may also be shown at this time as an example of crystallization. Beautiful effects may be obtained by showing crystallization under polarized light (L-122).

H-46. Cooling Curve during Freezing. One hundred grams of tin are melted in a crucible, and the melting point determined with a 0 to 360°C thermometer or with the demonstration thermocouple. The tin is heated initially to 300°C, and the temperature is read every 30 sec. The tin cools to 160°C in about 10 min, but for half this time the temperature remains near 230°C during freezing of the tin. A cooling curve may be plotted directly on the blackboard point by point as readings are taken.

H-47. Wood's Metal. A metal that will melt in hot water (65.5°C) may be made by melting together 4 parts by weight of bismuth, 2 parts lead, 1 part tin, and 1 part cadmium. Tea-spoons cast from this metal will melt in hot tea.

H-48. Heat of Crystallization and Undercooling. Melt 150 cm³ of sodium acetate in a 300-ml flask, and allow it to undercool. (Prepare two or three flasks, as crystallization is almost sure to start in one of them before the lecturer is ready for it.) When a minute crystal of sodium acetate is dropped into the flask, crystallization takes place rapidly, and the temperature rises to the freezing point, as is readily shown with the demonstration thermocouple. A concentrated solution of sodium sulfate is likewise satisfactory.

H-49. Another method is to melt photog-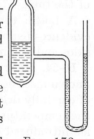
raphers' hypo (sodium thiosulfate) in a beaker and pour it into an unsilvered, unevacuated Dewar flask with a side arm. A U-tube ma-nometer with colored liquid indicator is attached to the side tube (Fig. 172). If undisturbed, the hypo will cool to room temperature without solidifying. When a small crystal of hypo is added and the undercooled liquid is stirred gently,

Fig. 172.— crystallization sets in, and the temperature rises Double-walled to the freezing point. The evolved heat warms flask with ma- the enclosed air as indicated by the motion of as a thermo- the colored liquid in the manometer. The hypo scope.
may be remelted by heating the flask in boiling water.

H-50. Heat of Solution. Heat is evolved if sulfuric acid is dissolved in water; cooling results if hypo or ammonium nitrate is dissolved in water. The apparatus used in the previous experi-ment is suitable for showing either of these effects; or the acid and hypo may be dissolved in separate beakers, into which are put the two junctions of the demonstration thermocouple, protected from contact with the liquids. In the latter case, one solute should be dissolved first, with the other beaker full of water, and the temperature change shown. When the second solute is dissolved, there is an increase in temperature difference.

H-51. Sublimation. The direct change from solid to vapor is shown by the evaporation of carbon dioxide snow or "dry ice." Carbon dioxide in the liquid state can be obtained only under pressure (see H-59).

H-52. The evolution of gas from solid carbon dioxide (due to heat absorbed from metal in contact with it) may be used to give rise to an interesting mechanical effect similar in result but not in cause to the operation of the Trevelyan rocker[1] (H-24). Rest one end of an iron rod on a piece of dry ice, the other end of the rod on the lecture table. Jar it a little. There ensues a high-pitched vibration. A silver teaspoon is a good substitute for the iron rod.

H-53. Hold a few pieces of camphor in the closed end of an inverted test tube by means of a piece of wire gauze. Warm the camphor gently with a Bunsen flame to accelerate its evaporation. The vapor will condense in the solid state on the cooler portions of the tube. (Project.)

A bottle that contains gum camphor will sometimes show evidence of sublimation by the presence of camphor crystals on its sides and stopper.

H-54. Heat of Fusion of Ice. Into a calorimeter containing a known mass of water at a known temperature drop several grams of carefully dried ice. Stir the mixture until all ice is melted and the temperature is uniform throughout. Determine the mass of ice introduced by weighing the calorimeter again, and calculate the heat of fusion from the observed masses and temperatures involved.

H-55. Expansion on Freezing. Bismuth is melted in a heavy pyrex test tube and allowed to cool. As it freezes, a hummock rises on the surface, thus indicating expansion. (Project.) For permanent use, the tube containing the bismuth may be evacuated and sealed off. The tube should be heavy-walled pyrex, 1 cm in diameter and 30 cm long, and should contain 10 cm of bismuth. An air jet directed vertically at the bottom of the tube containing molten bismuth will freeze it in about 3 min. A more pronounced hump may be raised by first freezing the meniscus.

H-56. Ice Bomb. A 3-in. cast-iron bomb is filled with freshly boiled water—preferably boiled *in* the bomb so as to remove all air bubbles—and closed with a tight screw plug, care being taken to exclude air. When packed in a freezing mixture of ice and salt in a chalk box, the bomb breaks in half an hour. It is well to protect the class by using a strong outer container, as sometimes the breaking is explosive. Timing may be made more definite if the bomb is cooled to 4°C in an ice bath before putting it in the

[1] HAGENOW, C. F., *Rev. Sci. Instruments*, **2**, 194, 1931.

freezing mixture. The lecture experiment may then be started so that the bursting will occur at a time which the lecturer can predict approximately, thus eliminating delay and prolonged suspense.

H-57. Effect of Pressure on Melting Point of Water—Regelation. Substances that expand upon freezing show a lowering of melting point under pressure. Two small flat blocks of ice may be pressed together in the hands; when pressure is released, they are found to be frozen together quite firmly.

A block of ice, at the melting point, is supported above the sink; and a loop of wire, heavily weighted, is hung over it. A steel wire 0.7 mm in diameter (B & S No. 21) weighted with 25 kg will melt through a piece of ice 12 by 20 cm in a little less than an hour. A steel wire 0.3 mm in diameter (B & S No. 30) weighted with 20 kg will cut through a 10-kg block in half an hour. The plane cut through the ice by the wire is visible because of the collection of many minute air bubbles. At the conclusion of the experiment, the block of ice may be shattered on the floor to show that it breaks no more readily where the wire passed than elsewhere. Iron and copper wires of the same size and under the same tensions require different times to cut through the same block of ice because of their different heat conductivities.

A small block of ice, say 1 by 1 by 6 in., set on the open jaws of a wooden clamp, may be used if desired. In either case, the loop of wire may be replaced with a single length, weighted at each end.

H-58. A cylinder 2 in. long is cut from mild steel shafting 2 in. in diameter and bored with a 1-in. hole. A plunger 2.5 in. long and a plug 0.25 in. thick are cut to fit the hole closely. The pieces are first cooled in ice water, and the cylinder is filled with finely cracked ice. The plug and plunger are inserted, and the cracked ice compressed strongly in a vise. Upon removal from the vise, a solid, hard cylinder of ice may be pushed out of the hole. (If snow is available, it may be used instead of the cracked ice.)

H-59. Liquid Carbon Dioxide from Solid by Pressure. A strong glass bulb with a 1-cm^2 neck is securely waxed into a hole through a brass plate (Fig. 173). It is filled with dry ice, and a cork inserted. The cork is held in place by a 5-kg weight placed on a brass platform. The pressure of melting carbon dioxide is about 5 atmos (5 kg per cm^2). After the carbon dioxide is partly melted, the weight is lifted slightly, whereupon instantaneous freezing of the liquid accompanies the sudden outrush of gas. The bulb is housed within a glass cylinder containing a little phosphorus pentoxide to prevent frosting of the glass. A 60-w lamp furnishes heat for melting the solid carbon dioxide as well as light for greater visibility.

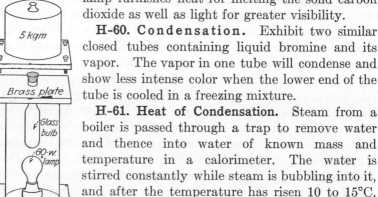

H-60. Condensation. Exhibit two similar closed tubes containing liquid bromine and its vapor. The vapor in one tube will condense and show less intense color when the lower end of the tube is cooled in a freezing mixture.

H-61. Heat of Condensation. Steam from a boiler is passed through a trap to remove water and thence into water of known mass and temperature in a calorimeter. The water is stirred constantly while steam is bubbling into it, and after the temperature has risen 10 to 15°C, the steam tube is removed. Determination of the new weight of the calorimeter and water shows the mass of steam introduced, and the heat of condensation is readily determined from the masses and temperatures involved.

Fig. 173.— Apparatus for showing carbon dioxide in liquid state.

H-62. Cooling by Evaporation. Ethyl chloride is squirted on the bulb of a simple air (or other) thermometer; marked cooling results. Water in a small evaporating dish is easily frozen in this way.

H-63. A drop of water is placed under a large thin watch glass resting on a cork. An air jet is arranged to blow across the surface of ether in the watch glass, or the whole may be placed under a bell jar and pumped. In about a minute, the ether will have evaporated, and the glass will be frozen to the cork. A metal thimble may replace the watch glass, the top of the cork being slightly hollowed out to receive it, but the time of freezing is slightly greater in this case.

If ether vapor cannot be tolerated in the room, the method illustrated in Fig. 174 may be used. Illuminating gas is bubbled through the ether, and the emergent gases are burned. *Caution.*

H-64. A small wide-mouthed bottle full of carbon disulfide is plugged with a wad of finely shredded black paper wet with the carbon disulfide and dipping into it like a wick. Rapid evaporation from the large surface cools the paper, thus allowing water vapor in the air to condense and form snow crystals on it.   A few minutes is enough for formation of frost.   *Caution:* The vapor of carbon disulfide is highly inflammable and poisonous.

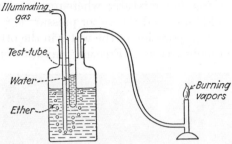

Fig. 174.—Gas bubbling through the ether cools it and the water; the vapors are burned.

H-65. Carbon Dioxide Snow.   A fresh tank of compressed carbon dioxide is supported in an inverted or inclined position with nozzle downward, and a chamois, flannel, or burlap bag of several thicknesses is tied over the outlet.   Open the valve wide, and allow the carbon dioxide to escape rapidly.   Carbon dioxide snow is formed in the bag by rapid expansion and evaporation. The noise of the rapidly escaping gas is very exciting.   The rapid vaporization removes heat from the air, the nozzle, and a portion of the liquid carbon dioxide not yet vaporized, thus freezing the central portion of the stream.

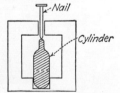

Fig. 175.—When the seal is broken, the sudden expansion of carbon dioxide cools the steel bulb.

H-66.   An economical way of showing cooling by expansion is to use the small steel bulbs of carbon dioxide made for charging soda-water siphons.   These are sold under various trade names at most drugstores for a few cents each.   A simple wooden frame (Fig. 175) may be constructed to hold a bulb in a vertical position, with a nail directed at the seal.   A sharp blow on the nail breaks the seal and allows the gas to escape.   The resulting low temperature may be shown by a thermojunction taped to the bulb, or the bulb may be passed around the class.   These bulbs contain insufficient gas to produce carbon dioxide snow, but frost will form on the outside owing to condensation of water vapor from the air.

H-67. Cooling by Evaporation—Cryophorus. A J-tube 2 cm in diameter and 30 cm long has a 5-cm bulb on each end. One of the bulbs is half filled with water, and the system is evacuated and sealed. With all the water in one bulb, the other bulb is immersed in a freezing mixture; whereupon water vapor condenses in the cold bulb, and the vapor pressure is reduced. The consequent rapid evaporation of the water in the other bulb cools it, and it eventually freezes. Freezing mixtures of ice and salt

Fig. 176.—Cryophorus.

are satisfactory provided that the tube is agitated to prevent undercooling; solid carbon dioxide (dry ice) in alcohol or liquid air will cause freezing more quickly, regardless of undercooling. Freezing of the water should not be prolonged, as the glass may crack.

H-68. Another form of cryophorus is a flask whose bottom is concave, so as to make a dish when the flask is inverted. The flask is half filled with water, evacuated, and sealed (Fig. 176). Finely crushed dry ice mixed with alcohol, for better contact, is placed in the concavity. The water in the flask freezes quickly.

H-69. Freezing Water by Evaporation—The Triple Point. Of the many ways of showing this experiment, the following is suggested as one of the best. A 500-ml flask is connected through a ground joint to a vessel half filled with concentrated sulfuric acid and to a vacuum pump (Fig. 177). Fifty milliliters of tap water in the flask should boil vigorously a few seconds after the pump is started and should freeze in 2 or 3 min. If the experiment is not successful, it is probable that (barring leaks) the water is undercooled, in which case shaking the flask will usually bring about freezing. A thermojunction or thermometer in the flask enables one to follow the temperature changes. With rapid pumping, it is possible to undercool the water as much as 10°C.

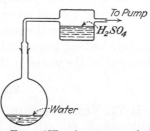

Fig. 177.—Apparatus for demonstrating the triple point of water.

H-70. A somewhat simpler arrangement for the same experiment is shown in Fig. 178. A watch glass is set on a wire triangle over an evaporating dish containing concentrated sulfuric acid. A small quantity of water is placed in the watch glass and covered with another watch glass. The bell jar is set in place with a rubber gasket, and the pump started. With a motor-driven pump, 4 to 7 min is needed to freeze the water. The image of the watch glass should be projected on a screen (with a water cell in front of the lantern condenser to absorb the heat from the arc). Bubbles of steam may be seen breaking through the freshly formed ice.

The function of the acid is to absorb the water vapor, and it must be concentrated. It should not be used more than two or three times. After demonstrating the formation of ice at the

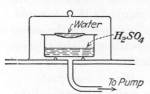

Fig. 178.—Another arrangement of the apparatus of Fig. 177.

triple point, it is interesting to use the demonstration thermocouple to show the high temperature attained by the acid.

H-71. Five milliliters of distilled water is placed in a clean test tube into which a thermojunction is inserted. The tube is placed in a mixture of alcohol and ice at −5°C or cooler (20 ml of alcohol added to 200 cm³ of crushed ice). The water in the test tube is stirred until a temperature of about 3°C is reached, when it is left to stand quietly. It will undercool to about −4°C. When this temperature has been reached, the tube may be removed from the cooling mixture and shown to the class with the water still in the liquid state (project or shadow). A slight disturbance of the water causes it to freeze, and the temperature is observed to rise promptly to 0°C. If shaking fails to start the freezing, a small bit of ice dropped into the tube will start it. It is important for the success of the experiment that the freezing mixture be kept from coming up around the test tube higher than the level of the water in the tube.

VAPOR PRESSURE

H-72. Vapor Pressure—Pulse Glass. A glass tube 15 cm long with a bulb at each end is partly filled with a colored volatile liquid under reduced pressure. If one bulb is warmed in the hand, the increased vapor pressure forces the liquid into the other bulb in a series of pulses.

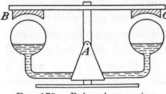

Fig. 179.—Pulse-glass engine.

H-73. Pulse-glass Engine. A pulse glass is supported in a stirrup (Fig. 179) so that it can rotate about an axis perpendicular to the plane of the diagram. At *B* and *C* are pads of cotton soaked in ice water or ether or carbon disulfide and thus cooled by evaporation. A bulb in contact with *B*, say, is cooled, the vapor pressure in it is lowered, liquid is driven up into it by the vapor pressure in the other bulb, and the glass is overbalanced. Repetition of the process then occurs at *C*, and a reciprocating motion results. A piece of ice may be substituted at each end for the cooling pads.

H-74. Vapor Pressure of Water at the Boiling Temperature. A J-tube (Fig. 180), open at the upper end, contains mercury and water. It is inserted through one hole of a two-hole rubber stopper into a 2-l flask containing a few hundred cubic centimeters of water. When the water in the flask is boiled, the steam from it escapes through the second hole, and the mercury in the two arms of the J-tube comes to the same level. Hence the vapor pressure of the water in the closed arm of the J (which is at the temperature of boiling water) is 1 atmos. (Project.) The

sealed end of the J-tube is filled with clean mercury so that all
air is excluded from it and so that the mercury extends a short
distance above the bend into the open arm of the J.   Boiled water
is poured on top of the mercury, and by judicious tilting a little
of it is allowed to flow around the bend into the closed arm.   Care
must be taken that no air is introduced with the water.   Surplus
water above the free surface of the mercury
may be soaked up with filter paper or
boiled away

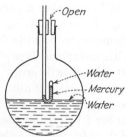

**H-75. Boiling Water at Reduced Pres-
sure.**   Boil water vigorously in a round-
bottomed 1-l flask for about a minute to
drive out air.[1]   Remove the flame, and
quickly insert a tight rubber stopper.
Invert the flask, supporting it in a clamp
or ring.   It is well to submerge the stopper
in a beaker of water in order to prevent the

Fig. 180.—Vapor pres-
sure of water.

entry of air.   The water in the flask may be made to boil
repeatedly by pouring cold water over the outside or by applying
ice to it.   A thermometer or thermojunction may be added to
show that the temperature of the boiling water is far below 100°C.

H-76.   The same effect may be shown by connecting a flask
partly filled with warm water to an aspirator or vacuum pump.
The water boils when the pressure is reduced sufficiently, but
boiling stops immediately when air is readmitted.

H-77. Vapor Pressure of Water at Room Temperature.   A
small amount of water in a 5-gal oilcan is boiled for a few minutes
to drive out air.   The flame is removed and a tight stopper
quickly inserted.   As cooling progresses, the vapor pressure
within the can diminishes, and it soon buckles under the pressure
of the atmosphere.

**H-78. Vapor Pressure of Water at High Temperature—Steam
Bomb.**   The vapor pressure of water above 100°C mounts rapidly
when the vapor is confined, as may be shown by heating water in
a corked test tube or by means of a simple "bomb."   One end of
a piece of 5-mm glass tubing is sealed, and the open end is drawn
out to a capillary a short distance from the sealed end.   While
the glass is still warm, the tip of the capillary is dipped into a
beaker of water; thus, upon cooling, the tube may be filled with

[1] *Caution:* A flat-bottomed flask is likely to break under reduced pressure.

water, and the tip of the capillary sealed off with a needle flame. If such a bomb is placed on a wire gauze over a Bunsen flame, it will explode violently in about 30 sec. *Caution:* Surround the bomb with a piece of iron pipe to stop flying fragments of glass.

H-79. Artificial Geyser. A conical tube of galvanized iron some 12 cm in diameter at the bottom, 4 cm at the top, and 1.5 to 2 m long makes a good model that approximates the working of some geysers. At the top is a conical catch basin 1 m or more in diameter to provide for return of the water. The tube is filled with water and heated by several Bunsen burners. After 15 or 20 min, it will erupt and will repeat thereafter at intervals of approximately 2 min. A pair of electric immersion heaters may be more convenient, but the time required for getting up steam is longer (1 hr), and the period is about 5 min. The geyser shoots high into the air; therefore it is convenient to drop the tube through a trap door in the floor of the lecture room, letting the catch basin rest on the floor.

H-80. A brass tube 0.5 in. in diameter and 6 ft long has one end soldered into the top of a cylindrical vessel 10 in. long and 4 in. in diameter. This vessel may be made of a large tube with end plates soldered on. To the upper end of the small tube is soldered the cover of a garbage can about 2 ft in diameter. The tube and cylindrical vessel are filled with water and set on a tripod. Two Bunsen burners of the Meker type are used to heat the vessel of water. It is desirable, though not necessary, to make the model more stable by using a tall clamp stand and single clamp at the center of the tube. The eruptions occur at intervals of about 3 min. The water and steam rise to a height of 3 or 4 ft.

H-81. Vapor Pressure. Place four barometer tubes containing mercury side by side, with their ends dipping into a well of mercury. By means of a curved pipette or dropper, inject into one tube a few drops of water. The mercury column at once falls some 2 cm. Alcohol is introduced into the second tube and shows a vapor pressure of 6 cm or more, while ether in the third shows a vapor pressure of perhaps 40 cm. Enough liquid must be introduced in each case so that some remains visible on top of the mercury. The fourth tube, showing the barometric pressure, is for comparison. With a Bunsen flame, warm the liquid above one of the columns, and show the increase of vapor pressure as the temperature rises.

H-82. A pyrex tube 1 cm in diameter and 1 m long is sealed into a cylindrical bulb 3 cm in diameter and 15 cm long so as to reach nearly to the bottom (Fig. 181). With the top open, partly fill the bulb with the test liquid, *e.g.*, alcohol. Boil the liquid to drive the air from the tube. Then, while still boiling, dip the open end into mercury and allow the latter to be sucked in. Adjust the mercury in the tube so that it has the same level as that in the bulb. Evacuate the tube, and seal off. Similar tubes may be made using water, glycerin, or other test liquids. The bulbs are immersed in hot water, and the vapor pressures at various temperatures may be observed directly. It is instructive to show that when alcohol in an open beaker boils in the water bath, the tube containing alcohol shows 1 atmos pressure; and that at higher temperatures, its vapor pressure exceeds 1 atmos.

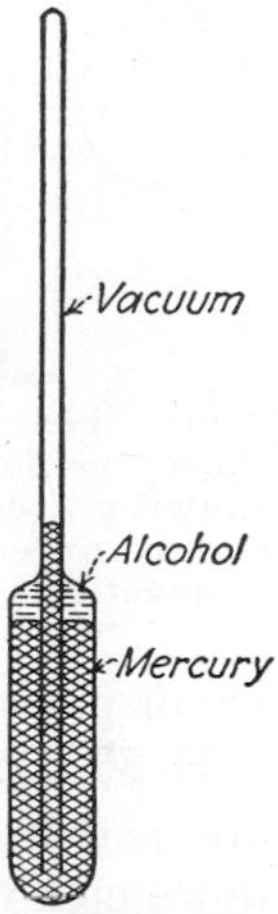

H-83. Vapor Pressure of Water—Bumping. A tube of the same form as that shown in Fig. 181 but open at the top contains distilled water above the mercury in the bulb. If the water is free from dirt and air, it may be heated in an oil bath well above 100°C without boiling. Then suddenly a vapor bubble forms, and the mercury column springs up about 20 cm.

Fig. 181.— Tube for showing vapor pressure of alcohol or other liquid.

H-84. Free and Retarded Evaporation. The final *pressure* of a saturated vapor depends only upon its temperature and is independent of the presence of other gases or vapors; however, the *time* required for the vapor to reach its final pressure is dependent upon the presence of other gases, being longer if other gases retard evaporation. The contrast between free and retarded evaporation may be shown by the following experiment.

A spherical flask is closed with a tight-fitting two-hole rubber stopper, through one hole of which passes the stem of a thistle tube or small funnel provided with a stopcock. A tube passing through the other hole communicates with an open mercury manometer. With the stopcock open, the manometer indicates no pressure difference between the inside and outside of the flask. A few milliliters of ether or alcohol are then introduced into the flask through the funnel and the stopcock is closed quickly. The partial pressure of the vapor builds up slowly as shown on the manometer.

Likewise, if a second spherical flask is connected with a mercury

manometer sufficiently long to show barometric height and if the flask is evacuated through stopcock A (Fig. 182) before the liquid is introduced through stopcock B, the vapor pressure reaches its maximum very rapidly, and the two cases may be contrasted. If sufficient liquid is introduced to produce saturation, the final vapor pressure is the same in each case.

FIG. 182.— Apparatus for showing free and retarded evaporation.

H-85. Vapor-pressure Fountain. A small glass vial or test tube, containing ether, is attached to a glass tube passing through a single-hole stopper nearly to the bottom of a flask (Fig. 183). The glass tube is drawn down to a small aperture at the top. When the flask is half filled with warm water and the vial of ether is immersed in it, ether vapor pressure causes a stream of water to issue from the orifice.

H-86. Comparison of Vapor and Gas. Two barometer tubes are fastened to a board, painted white, that can be moved up or

down on a vertical stand equipped with stops. The tubes are filled like barometers; but one contains a little air above the mercury, and the other contains alcohol and alcohol vapor. They dip into a deep well of mercury (a hydrometer jar). When the tubes are moved up and down, the mercury level in the tube containing alcohol remains constant, indicating constant vapor pressure independent of volume, while the level in the tube containing air changes, its volume being inversely proportional to pressure. A third tube may be used as a comparison barometer if desired.

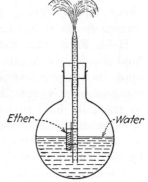

FIG. 183.—Vapor-pressure fountain.

The same effect may be shown by tilting the tubes instead of lowering them into a reservoir of mercury. In this case it is necessary to measure heights from some plane, such as the table.

H-87. Vapor Pressure of Solutions. The vapor pressure of aqueous solutions of solids is lower than that of pure water, as is shown by the fact that such solutions must be raised to a higher temperature to boil, *i.e.*, in order to exert a vapor pressure of 1 atmos. Boil a salt or sugar solution in a beaker, and show with the demonstration thermocouple that the temperature of the boiling liquid is above 100°C. With one junction in a beaker of boiling water and the other in the boiling solution, the elevation of the boiling temperature in the latter is immediately apparent.

H-88. Partial Pressure—Cooling by Expansion. Introduce a very small amount of smoke from a burning match into a 1-l flask. Pour a few milliliters of alcohol into the flask, quickly close it with a stopper, and shake it vigorously. Vaporization of the alcohol increases the pressure within the flask. Hold the flask in the beam of the lantern, and remove the stopper. The gases, which rush out with an audible noise, are cooled by expansion, and the flask is filled with dense fog.

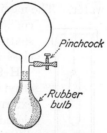

FIG. 184.—Apparatus for showing cloud formation.

H-89. Cooling by Expansion—Effect of Nuclei on Condensation. A 1- or 2-l flask has a side tube on its neck, fitted with a rubber outlet tube and pinchcock (Fig. 184). The rubber bulb from, say, a battery filler is fastened tightly over the neck of the flask, and bulb and neck are filled with water. Set the inverted flask against a black background, and illuminate from one side with the beam from a lantern. Pressing the bulb compresses the air in the flask; releasing the bulb permits expansion, cooling, and condensation of water vapor. The air in the flask is first made dust free by repeated condensations. In this condition when pressure on the bulb is suddenly released, only a few large drops are formed. Open the pinchcock, and allow a small amount of smoke to enter from a burning match or cigarette. Shake the water around to disperse the carbon particles. Expansion now produces a dense white cloud. The experiment illustrates cooling by expansion with consequent increase of the relative humidity to the saturation point, and the importance of nuclei for condensation. It shows many of the physical principles underlying the Wilson cloud chamber (A-116).

The flask may also be connected to a vacuum pump capable of reducing the pressure rapidly to about 5 cm of mercury; or a large bell jar may be used on the pump plate, with a wet cloth inside to furnish the necessary water vapor.

H-90. Critical Temperature. The experiment showing the disappearance of the meniscus in an ether tube at the critical temperature is a good one, but it is dangerous; special measures should be taken to protect both the class and the lecturer. The manufacture of ether tubes for this purpose has been practically discontinued because of the danger involved. Liquid carbon dioxide in a heavy-walled glass tube can be used. The tube is mounted in a glass vessel from the bottom of which a rubber tube runs to another vessel containing water at about 40°C, which can be raised so that the carbon dioxide is surrounded by the warm water. The meniscus vanishes upon heating and reappears upon cooling, as shown by projection. Iron plates or shatterproof glass should be used to protect both the class and the demonstrator.

Fig. 185.—Critical temperature tube with protecting hood.

H-91. A critical-temperature tube containing ethyl chloride is made as follows. A glass tube of external diameter 1 cm, internal diameter 0.5 cm, is closed off at one end and drawn down at the other. The length is about 8 cm. It is filled somewhat more than half full of ethyl chloride from a standard cylinder available at any medical-supply house. Ethyl chloride boils at 12.2°C, but by means of an ice pack the tube is kept cool while the constricted end is sealed off with a fine flame. A small hook or loop is made of the thick glass at this end of the tube. When completed, the tube should be about half full of liquid; the remaining space is largely filled with vapor. The tube is placed in an iron pipe, which is always to be used for safety. The pipe is 20 cm long and 3 cm in diameter; each end is closed with a cap screwed on loosely (Fig. 185). Two rectangular windows 1 by 5 cm are cut in the pipe on opposite sides. A hook is screwed into the inside of one of the caps so that when the pipe is clamped in a vertical position, the ethyl chloride tube may be hung from it. When this pipe is supported by a clamp stand in front of a lantern, the image of the ethyl chloride tube can be projected through the

windows onto a screen.   The iron pipe is heated uniformly with a
Bunsen burner.   The meniscus in the tube gradually becomes
flatter as the temperature rises and the surface tension diminishes.
There will also be some boiling of the liquid.   At the critical
temperature (187.2°C, 52 atmos), the meniscus becomes a hazy
dark streak across the tube and then disappears.   The heating
should be discontinued immediately.   In about a minute, the
meniscus reappears.

H-92. Dew Point and Humidity.   Exhibit hygrometers, wet-
and dry-bulb thermometers, sling psychrometer, and dew-point
apparatus.   In using the wet- and dry-bulb hygrometer, point
out the necessity of fanning to secure correct results.   Weather
Bureau instructions may be followed.[1]   In place of such apparatus, the demonstration thermocouple may be used, with one
junction dry and the other sur-
rounded by a wet wick.   The relative humidity in either case is
obtained from the usual charts or
tables.

H-93. The demonstration of dew
point with the usual laboratory
apparatus is on too small a scale for
the large classroom.   The experiment may be adapted for demonstration, however, by placing ether in a
container having a flat side of
polished metal A (Fig. 186), from

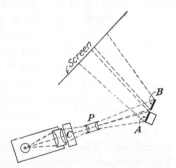

Fig. 186.—Method of projecting
dew-point apparatus.

which light from the lantern is reflected to the screen through
the projection lens P, a water cell C being placed in front
of the condenser to absorb heat from the arc.   A second
polished metal plate B, not cooled, may be arranged to throw
another reflected image on the screen alongside the first.   Upon
cooling the plate A by rapid evaporation of ether, the formation of
dew changes the brightness of the first reflected beam.   The
temperature is obtained with the demonstration thermocouple.

H-94. Charts and Models.   Various charts and diagrams may
be exhibited as desired: melting points, vapor pressure-temperature curves, boiling points, triple-point diagram, critical tempera-

[1] Marvin, C. S., *U. S. Dept. Agr.*, *Weather Bureau Bull.* 235, Govt.
Printing Office, 1915.

ture, diagrams of refrigerating systems, air-conditioning charts. Slides showing the progress of a storm for successive days may be made by photographing weather maps on which the isobars and isotherms have been retraced in black ink. Models of thermodynamic surfaces showing phase regions in three dimensions are very instructive.[1]

LOW TEMPERATURES

For moderately low temperatures, freezing mixtures of salt and ice, concentrated nitric acid and ice, etc., may be used. Still

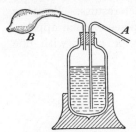

FIG. 187.—Simple method of removing liquid air from Dewar flask.

lower temperatures are obtainable with solid carbon dioxide (cake or snow) and with liquid air. By judicious planning, 1 or 2 l of liquid air may be made to perform a large array of experiments in the course of a class period. Dry ice is safer, less expensive, and in general more easily obtained and it is satisfactory for the performance of many of the experiments that follow if it is crushed and mixed with alcohol to form a thick "mush."

Care must be used in handling both solid carbon dioxide and liquid air. The mush of dry ice and alcohol is dangerously cold and is tenacious when it comes in contact with the hands. Many liberties can be taken with liquid air, but it should be constantly borne in mind that it is (unless fresh) almost pure oxygen. Hence it makes virtually explosive mixtures with alcohol, ether, acetone, cotton, etc. Always use it in small quantities with adequate safeguards against fire or explosion.[2]

Liquid air is always retained in Dewar flasks (see H-166, 167) to prevent rapid loss from evaporation. Pouring it from the flask is not advisable, as the lip of the flask may be cracked by sudden cooling. The device shown in Fig. 187 is convenient for removing any desired quantity. The atomizer bulb B is squeezed to increase air pressure within the flask so as to force liquid air out through tube A.

[1] For example, those described by F. L. Verwiebe, *Am. Phys. Teacher,* **3,** 179, 1935.

[2] For further directions, see H. P. Cady, *J. Chem. Educ.,* **8,** 1027, 1931.

H-95. Dry Ice. Solid carbon dioxide ($-78.5°C$) may be purchased in cakes for a few cents a pound or made during the class period by the method previously described (H-65). The rapid sublimation of dry ice has been described (H-52). It may be demonstrated by placing a cake of dry ice on a smooth marble-topped table, where it chatters owing to the formation and escape of vapor. Almost any piece of metal in contact with dry ice at moderate pressure emits a high-pitched buzzing sound. A tuning fork may be excited in this way.

H-96. Temperature of Liquid Air and of Solid Carbon Dioxide. A pentane thermometer or, more simply, the thermocouple may be used to show these low temperatures. The demonstration may be carried out stepwise: junction A in boiling water and junction B in ice water; A in a freezing mixture (the galvanometer deflection will be in the opposite direction unless a reversing switch is used); B in dry ice and alcohol; A in liquid air. Fresh liquid air is a little colder than air from which the nitrogen has largely boiled away. Paper coated with bi-iodide of mercury (or a glass tube filled with it) changes from red to yellow on cooling in liquid air.

H-97. Expansion of Solid Carbon Dioxide. Place some small pieces of dry ice in a test tube, and cover the mouth of the tube with a toy balloon tied securely to avoid leakage. As the carbon dioxide turns to gas, it inflates the balloon. By contrast, the balloon may be collapsed again by inserting the test tube in liquid air to freeze out the carbon dioxide.

H-98. Air Pressure at Low Temperature. When the bulb of a small thermoscope is immersed in liquid air, the decrease of pressure in the bulb is strikingly large. The thermoscope consists of a glass bulb about 4 cm in diameter on the short arm of a J-tube 75 cm long. The long arm, directed downward, has its open end submerged in a small beaker of mercury. The effect is less striking with a mixture of carbon dioxide and alcohol.

H-99. Behavior of Common Substances at Low Temperature. A flower is quickly frozen by dipping it into liquid air; its appearance is unchanged, but it is very fragile and shatters at a touch. Pieces of red meat, wieners (in place of fingers!), thin rubber tubing, and sheet iron when cooled in liquid air break to bits under a sharp hammer blow. A hollow rubber ball frozen and thrown against the wall shatters spectacularly; the pieces regain their elasticity as they warm up.   A hollow rubber doll may be given a "bath" in liquid air and shattered in similar fashion.   A rubber sponge frozen in liquid air may be sawed in two like a block of wood.   Alcohol placed in a beaker set in liquid air becomes highly viscous.   A pencil makes no marks when its tip is at liquid-air temperature.

H-100. Lead Bell.   A small bell made of thin lead sheet and provided with a wood or ebonite handle gives a dull sound at room temperature but tinkles musically when cooled to liquid-air temperature.   A second bell, not cooled, may be sounded for comparison.   A plate of lead suspended from one corner by a wire and struck with a wooden mallet serves equally well.   A coiled spring made of solder or fuse wire (15 to 20 turns, 1 in. in diameter) will support a weight and will oscillate when cold; if it is warmed locally with a match or even by breathing upon it, it stretches at that place.

H-101. Mercury Hammer.   Pour mercury into a safety-match box with a piece of wood inserted to serve as a handle. After the mercury is frozen, remove the box, and drive nails into soft wood with the solidified mercury, which has much the character of lead at ordinary temperatures.   Then "pour" the hammer back into the mercury bottle, simply by placing it in a funnel and allowing it to melt.

H-102. "Ice Stove."   When liquid air is poured into a hole in a block of ice, the ice cracks around the hole.   Liquid air in a pyrex beaker or teakettle set on a cake of ice boils vigorously, and the beaker usually freezes to the "ice stove."   A little alcohol added to the liquid air makes dense clouds of vapor.

H-103. Electrical Resistance at Low Temperature.   A 6-v automobile lamp, a 6-v storage battery, and a resistance coil of iron or nickel wire (not alloy) are connected in series, the resistance being such that the lamp glows dull red.   When the resistance coil is immersed in liquid air, the lamp glows brightly.

H-104.   A 3-v flashlight bulb is connected in series with a 4.5-v C-battery and a compact coil of fine copper wire of sufficient resistance to make the light glow a dull red.   When the coil is immersed in liquid air, the lamp glows brightly.   This arrangement is convenient to handle and has the advantage that no external connections are required and all of the apparatus can be held in the hand.

H-105. Spheroidal State. Pour liquid air over the table or on the back of the hand. The air film formed by evaporation insulates the hand and prevents it from being injured. Many lecturers take a small quantity of liquid air into the mouth, rolling it about on top of the tongue and puffing out clouds of frost. *Caution:* Do not swallow or allow to touch teeth with fillings.

H-106. A brass or iron ball, 1 to 2 in. in diameter, mounted on a light metal rod with an insulating handle, is held beneath the surface of liquid air in a transparent Dewar flask. The spheroidal state protects the liquid air at first, so that only moderate boiling occurs; but when the liquid air wets the ball, sudden rapid ebullition takes place. After the ball is cooled, it is removed from the liquid air and held in a Bunsen flame, where it quickly becomes covered with a layer of frost, owing to condensation of water vapor and carbon dioxide from the flame (see also H-134, 135, 136).

H-107. Filtering Liquid Air. A piece of filter paper is creased so that the cone is rigid enough to be used without a funnel. Liquid air poured into it runs through rapidly, and crystals of ice and carbon dioxide are retained. A felt hat may be used as a filter in the same way.

H-108. Density of Liquid Air. A large open glass vessel is filled with water and strongly illuminated. A small quantity of liquid air is poured onto the water, where it moves about turbulently. As the nitrogen boils away and the liquid air becomes richer in oxygen, globules of it sink and oscillate up and down because of convection currents and ice formation.

H-109. Liquefaction of Air at Atmospheric Pressure. A test tube containing liquid air is connected to a vacuum pump and placed inside a larger tube through which a slow current of air can be passed (Fig. 188). When the pressure over the liquid air is reduced by rapid pumping, the evaporation cools the liquid so

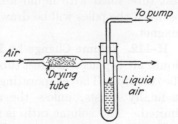

FIG. 188.—Liquefaction of air at atmospheric pressure.

that air from the room condenses on the outside of the tube and runs down in drops. Solid nitrogen (melting point −210°C) can be produced if the air in the tube is pumped rapidly enough. An image of the test tube should be projected on the screen, so that the class can see the formation of drops of air condensed at atmospheric pressure. It is necessary to cool the larger tube in liquid air before starting the pump.

H-110. Liquefaction of Air under Pressure. A bicycle pump is attached to an inner-tube valve and a large test tube so that

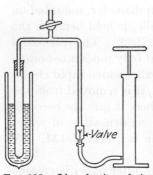

Fig. 189.—Liquefaction of air under pressure.

the air in the test tube may be put under pressure. The tube is introduced into a Dewar flask of liquid air (Fig. 189) where, because of the increased pressure, the air within the tube condenses. Liquefaction may be continued as long as the test tube is kept at liquid-air temperature and the bicycle pump is operated. Sufficient liquid air may be made to pour out, or its presence may be shown by making it blow up a small balloon attached to a side arm with stopcock.

H-111. Magnetic Properties of Liquid Oxygen. Liquid air is poured into a loop of paper held between the pole pieces of a strong electromagnet; when the paper is removed, liquid oxygen sticks to the pole pieces until it evaporates. The pole pieces should be conical and set close together. (Project.) A small test tube filled with liquid air and hung just outside the space between the poles will be drawn between them on energizing the magnet.

H-112. Volume Change by Evaporation. A small quantity of liquid air is placed in a test tube, and a toy balloon is slipped over the mouth. The evaporating air blows up the balloon until it finally bursts, unless the amount of air used is purposely limited. The volume ratio is about 800:1.

H-113. A model steam engine may be run with liquid air in a test tube connected to the boiler.

H-114. A fountain may be made from a flask having a side arm on the neck. A glass tube slightly drawn down at the top is inserted into the neck of the flask through a tight stopper. A

test tube containing liquid air is connected by another stopper
to the side arm.   Water placed in the flask is forced out much
more strongly than can be done by blowing into the side arm.
The arrangement shown in Fig. 183 may also be used, with liquid
air instead of ether in the vial.

H-115. A strong test tube half-filled with liquid air may be
used as a gun to shoot corks around the class.   Such a popgun
may be equipped with a stopcock on a side arm to allow the
evaporating air to escape (Fig. 190).   The cork is ejected about
2 sec after closing the stopcock.   A more elaborate but safer
"cannon" may be constructed of a
15-in. section of 2-in. iron pipe capped
at the lower end and mounted vertically on a solid base.   A few hundred
milliliters of liquid air is poured into
the pipe, and a tight cork is driven
in with a hammer to be blown out
explosively.   Dexterous lecturers

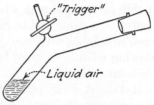

Fig. 190.—Liquid-air popgun.

sometimes use this pipe from the shoulder as a gun, introducing
a test tube containing liquid air so that rapid evaporation occurs
only when the gun is tipped to spill the liquid air into the gun
barrel.

H-116. Absorption of Gases by Cooled Charcoal.   A test tube
containing coconut charcoal is closed with a one-hole stopper,
from which a bent glass tube 80 cm long dips into a beaker of
mercury.   The test tube is cooled in liquid air, and the absorption
of the air in it is shown by the rise of mercury in the tube almost
to barometric height.   A similar tube without charcoal should be
used as a simple thermoscope for purposes of comparison (H-98).
A more elaborate setup is to connect three glass charcoal traps
(1 by 6 in.) with mercury manometers.   After baking and pumping the traps, they are filled with carbon dioxide, air, and hydrogen, respectively, at atmospheric pressure.   When the traps are
cooled in liquid air, the manometers show that the carbon
dioxide is all condensed, the air strongly absorbed, and the
hydrogen only slightly absorbed.   The traps should be made of
pyrex glass to decrease the possibility of cracking.

H-117. A discharge tube with a bulb containing coconut
charcoal sealed onto it is evacuated to a pressure of 2 or 3 mm.
An induction coil connected to the tube will produce a diffuse

violet discharge at this pressure. When the charcoal tube is immersed in liquid air, the discharge passes through all the stages associated with rapid improvement of the vacuum. In the final stage, the vacuum may be so good that the discharge will no longer pass.

H-118. Chemical Activity of Liquid Oxygen. A slow-burning, almost fireproof piece of felt, or a cheap cigar, burns vigorously after saturation with old liquid air, which is rich in oxygen. A shallow layer of alcohol burning quietly in an open pan burns almost explosively when a little liquid air is (*cautiously*) added. A thin carbon rod with a bit of sulfur on the end to aid ignition is heated in a flame and burns vigorously when placed in liquid air; even iron (thin wire, pen points) may be burned in this way. A glowing splinter of wood bursts into flame when held in a beaker containing liquid air.

H-119. A small piece of potassium is dropped onto water to demonstrate its great chemical activity in liberating hydrogen from the water. A bit of potassium cooled in liquid air and dropped onto water shows no effect at low temperature, but it will explode after it has warmed up. Protect the class by a sheet of safety glass.

H-120. Having previously lighted a cigarette in a long holder, the lecturer takes a small quantity of liquid air into his mouth, inserts the holder between his lips, and *blows outward*. The cigarette burns to a cinder with amazing rapidity.

H-121. Steel wool is packed into a galvanized-iron box 2 by 2 by 1 in. cut from sheet metal. A liberal quantity of liquid air is poured into the box and is allowed to boil away for about 15 sec. The steel wool may be ignited by applying a lighted match to it; it burns vigorously with intense heat and melts a hole through the bottom of the sheet-iron container. For safety, the experiment should be performed upon a thick piece of asbestos, with a sheet of plate glass set up to protect the class from flying sparks.

TRANSFER OF HEAT

H-122. Conduction in Solids. Several bars of the same length and cross section but of different metals are fitted tightly into a block of copper and heated at their common junction point. The relative conductivities are indicated by the ignition of match heads inserted in holes in the ends of the bars. Other inflammable material may be used, or a temperature-indicating paint[1] may be applied to each bar. More precisely, the rise in temperature in any rod is proportional to $1/dc$, where d is density and c is specific heat. Therefore rods of brass, copper, iron, and German silver may be used, for which the product dc is nearly constant, whereas zinc, aluminum, and lead have distinctly different values for this product.

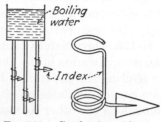

Fig. 191.—Conduction of heat in metal rods.

A simpler but cruder manner of showing the same effect consists of wiring together the ends of copper and iron rods and inserting the junction in a Bunsen flame. After a few moments of heating, press the head of a match firmly against each rod, and advance it slowly from the cool end toward the flame until it ignites. The match in contact with the copper rod will ignite much farther from the source of heat than that in contact with the iron, because of the greater conductivity of the copper.

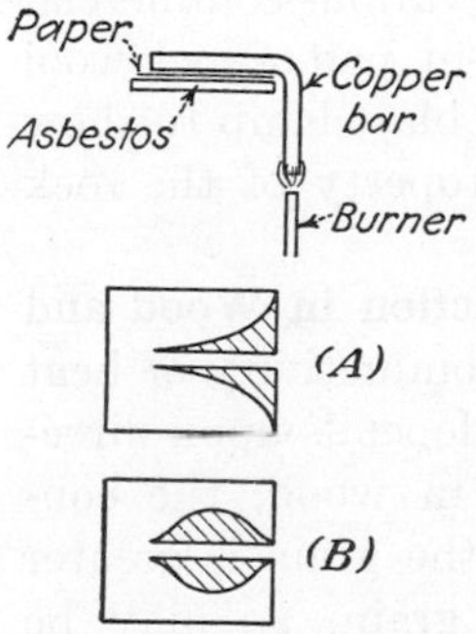

H-123. The progress of heat through a bar, one end of which is heated, may be indicated by the dropping off of 10-penny nails held by wax or of lead shot stuck on by paraffin at regular intervals along the bar. In this case, it is important to protect the bar from the direct radiation of the Bunsen burner.

H-124. Rods of brass, steel, and copper, each 2.5 mm in diameter, are soldered to the bottom of a metal vessel (Fig. 191). On each rod is placed an indicator consisting of two or three turns of wire attached to a pointer. The indicators fit loosely upon the rods but are kept from slipping down by a small amount of paraffin melted around the turns. Boiling water is poured into the vessel, and the pointers descend as the high-temperature front advances and

Fig. 192.—Conduction of heat shown by patterns on temperature-indicating paper.

---

[1] Lea's salt $Ag_2HgCl_2I_2$. Several temperature-indicating paints are sold by Efkalin Co., 15 Moore St., New York, N. Y.

melts the paraffin. The distances that the indicators travel are roughly proportional to the conductivities of the metals.

H-125. A simple apparatus (Fig. 192) consisting of a bent copper bar placed with one end upon a piece of temperature-indicating paper backed by a strip of asbestos serves to show the progress of temperature elevation. First heat the bar with a Bunsen burner until pattern *A* is formed; then cool the bar with tap water until pattern *B* appears.

H-126. Davy Safety Lamp. The high conductivity of copper and its application in the Davy safety lamp are commonly shown by igniting the gas from a Bunsen burner beneath a fine copper wire gauze. A flame on either side of the gauze will not strike through to the other side until the gauze itself becomes red hot. It is interesting to use two or three gauzes above one another, separated by a centimeter or two, and to split the flame into two or three pieces. For example, the flame may burn below the first gauze and above the second, with no flame between the two. A Davy safety lamp may be exhibited. With a flame burning inside the lamp, a stream of illuminating gas may be directed at the lamp without being ignited outside the gauze.

H-127. Heat Insulation. Show samples of various commercial insulating materials. Place a penny upon a $\frac{1}{2}$-in. pad of rock wool lying on the hand, and heat it red hot with a blast lamp to show the insulating property of the rock wool.

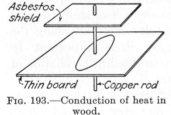

FIG. 193.—Conduction of heat in wood.

H-128. Conduction in Wood and Crystals. The conductivity of heat in most crystals depends upon direction. Likewise, in wood, the conductivity along the grain is greater than across the grain, as may be shown by the following experiment. A copper rod, 1 cm in diameter, is fitted through the center of a thin board and is equipped with an asbestos shield, as illustrated in Fig. 193. The board is coated on one side with paraffin. When the upper end of the copper rod is heated in a Bunsen flame, the paraffin melts in the form of an ellipse, typical of conduction in anisotropic bodies.

H-129. Comparison of Conductivities of Wood and Metal. Wrap a sheet of paper tightly around a cylinder made of sections of brass and wood carefully fitted together, and hold the junction in a Bunsen flame while rotating the cylinder. The paper will quickly char where it is in contact with the wood. It is protected where it is in contact with the brass because of the relatively high conductivity of the metal.

H-130. High Conductivity of Copper or Silver. An entertaining demonstration consists in applying the lighted end of a cigarette to a pocket handkerchief placed over a coin. The handkerchief is uninjured, whereas a hole is quickly burned through it if the coin is removed.

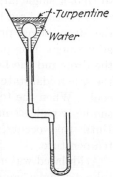

FIG. 194.—Poor conduction of heat in water.

H-131. Poor Conductivity of Water. Retain a piece of ice in the bottom of a large test tube full of water by means of a piece of wire gauze or a helical coil of wire. The water in the upper part of the test tube may be boiled in a Bunsen flame without melting the ice.

H-132. The bulb of an air thermometer is inserted in a funnel (Fig. 194); the junction is made watertight by a small piece of rubber tubing. The funnel is filled with sufficient water to cover the bulb to a depth of 3 mm. On top of the water is poured a layer of turpentine, alcohol, or ether. Upon igniting the inflammable layer, the air thermometer shows little effect, thus indicating the poor conductivity of water. To emphasize the contrast of temperatures above and below the surface of the water, the lecturer may ignite pieces of paper in the flame or boil water in a beaker held above it.

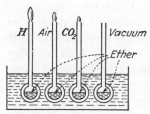

FIG. 195.—Poor conduction of heat in gases. The double-walled vessels contain various gases through which heat is conducted to the ether at different rates, as shown by the heights of the flames.

H-133. Conduction in Gases. Four small double-walled bulbs filled with equal volumes of ether and with their outer shells containing various gases are placed in a vessel of boiling water (Fig. 195). The relative conductivity of the gases is shown by the length of time before the ether vapor can be lighted above each bulb and by the height of the flame.

H-134. Spheroidal State—Poor Conductivity of Gases. A metal plate slightly convex upward is mounted horizontally in the field of a projection lantern. A long glass tube drawn down at one end contains a little water and is supported in a clamp stand so that a single large drop of water hangs from the orifice. The plate is heated red hot and the drop lowered onto it, the image of the drop being projected on the screen. By careful optical adjustment, it is possible to show that there is a space between the drop and the hot plate. While the drop is resting quietly in the spheroidal state, the flame is removed and the plate allowed to cool. When the temperature becomes sufficiently low, the drop suddenly makes contact with the plate and boils vigorously away. Until this occurs, the water remains slightly below boiling temperature.

Acidulated water may be used, and a wire run down the glass tube to make contact with the drop, so that when the drop touches the plate it closes an electric circuit and rings a bell.

H-135. A wet finger can be dipped into molten lead or boiling mercury without injury, since the finger is protected momentarily by a layer of water vapor.

H-136. A small nugget of silver heated to redness may be plunged into a vessel of water without causing boiling for a second or two, since the water is protected by a steam film. Sudden and violent boiling then occurs. (Project.)

H-137. Convection in Gases. A point source of light, such as an arc without condenser lenses, illuminates a screen 20 or 30 ft distant. A lighted Bunsen burner or a match is held midway between the source and the screen. Upon the screen will appear the shadows of turbulent, rising air currents, similar to those commonly observed around a hot stove or a bonfire. A tin can containing dry ice or even ice water shows descending currents. A 1-ft length of 3-in. pipe, heated strongly in a Bunsen flame and held end on toward the screen, shows convection currents that hug the pipe closely and rise above it in streamline fashion. An electric hot plate shows various effects when held horizontally or vertically in the light beam.

H-138. The transfer of heat by convection across "dead-air" spaces in buildings may be similarly demonstrated by shadow projection by placing in the beam a metal box 1 ft square, with front and back of window glass (Fig. 196). One side of the box is heated electrically, and the opposite side is cooled by tap water. Circulating convection currents will be visible. It is suggested that the box be provided with an accessory wooden or cardboard grating that may be inserted by removal of the lid, so as to divide the space between the two walls into a number of small cells, thus breaking up the convection currents into numerous smaller currents. The extension of this principle to the problem of heat insulation is obvious.

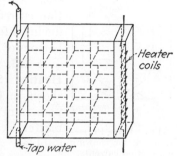

FIG. 196.—Transfer of heat by convection.

H-139. Two similar lamp chimneys or glass tubes fit over holes in a metal container (*e.g.*, two pie plates soldered together). A short piece of candle is lighted and placed under one chimney so that the flame is visible (Fig. 197). Smoke from a bit of glowing paper held above the other chimney flows downward into it, giving evidence of a strong convection current. The candle soon goes out if either chimney is covered.

H-140. A variation of the previous experiment consists in placing a short lighted candle under a single lamp chimney, set in

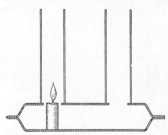

FIG. 197.—The candle goes out if convection currents are stopped.

a dish of water to exclude air at the bottom. The candle continues to burn if the air column in the lamp chimney is divided into two parts by a metal vane. Again the convection currents may be demonstrated by allowing smoke to go down one side and up the other. When the metal vane is removed, the candle goes out.

H-141. Convection in Liquids. Fill a small projection cell with ice water, and place it in the lantern with its image slightly out of focus. By means of a medicine dropper or pipette, introduce carefully a little hot water near the bottom of the cell, and observe the rising convection currents. Likewise, cold water introduced on the surface of a cell filled with hot water will show descending currents.

H-142. A projection cell is made by clamping a curved piece of rubber tubing between two plates of clear glass a little larger than lantern slides (Fig. 198). A small spiral of resistance wire is placed in the bottom of the cell with its leads passing between the rubber tube and the glass. The cell is filled with water and placed before the condenser lens of the lantern. When an electric current heats the resistor, the ensuing convection currents may be made visible by introducing a few drops of colored liquid near the bottom of the cell through a pipette.

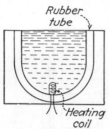

FIG. 198.—Projection cell for showing convection currents.

H-143. Convection in Liquids—Model Heating System. The glass tube *ABCD* shown in Fig. 199*a* is filled with a solution of potassium permanganate or other coloring matter, care being taken to exclude air bubbles. The upper cylinder is filled with clear water to a level just above *A*. Upon heating the tube at *E* with a Bunsen burner, currents are set up as indicated by the mushrooming of colored solution out of the end *A*. Use a white background and strong illumination.

H-144. A rectangular glass tube with aperture at *A* (Fig. 199*b*) is filled with water and heated at *B*. A few permanganate crystals at *A* will show by the coloring they impart to the water that circulation is taking place in a counter-clockwise direction. Illuminate against a white background.

H-145. A more elaborate model of a heating system may be made by connecting a 500-ml flask to an "expansion chamber" by means of a large vertical tube in parallel with a "radiator" consisting of five 3-in. turns of ¼-in. copper tubing painted dull

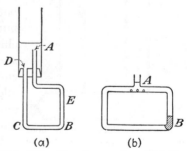

FIG. 199.—Two forms of model heating system.

black. The lower end of this tube is tapered and projects into the flask as shown in Fig. 200. Heat is applied to the lower flask, and as the water begins to circulate, a few drops of colored liquid (potassium permanganate solution) are introduced near the downflow tube at *D*. The circulation of the water is thus made visible.

H-146. Conduction and Convection. A platinum wire with leads passing through a solid rubber stopper is introduced into a glass flask and heated electrically to a dull red. If now the flask is evacuated, the wire glows more brilliantly because of reduced heat losses, even though the voltage across the wire is kept constant. This experiment illustrates in simple fashion the principle of the Pirani vacuum gauge.

H-147. Water may be boiled in a paper container over a Bunsen burner. The container may be made by folding a piece of typewriter paper so as to form a vessel 10 by 10 by 2.5 cm and fastening the corners together with paper clips. The paper may burn down as far as the surface of the water, but no farther.

RADIATION

H-148. Rectilinear Propagation of Radiation· The straight-line propagation of radiation may be demonstrated as follows. Two sheets of tin foil A and B are hung 10 cm apart. A star-shaped aperture is cut in B (Fig. 201). The right-hand surface of A is blackened, while the left-hand surface is coated with paraffin. An intense source of radiation, such as a white-hot ball, 400-w lamp, or carbon arc, is placed at C. The paraffin on A melts in the shape of a star, the sharpness of whose edges depends largely upon the size of the source of radiation.

Fig. 200.— Model heating system with "radiator."

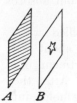

F I G. 201.—Rectilinear propagation of radiation.

H-149. Reflection of Radiation. A sheet of polished metal (*e.g.*, aluminum) may be used as a reflector to cast the radiation from an electric heater upon a thermopile shielded from the source. A plate-glass mirror of equal area substituted for the metal gives a much smaller deflection of the galvanometer because of absorption of infrared radiation in the glass.

If the radiation from a hot source is allowed to fall directly upon a thermopile placed several feet away, the resulting galvanometer deflection may be greatly increased by introducing a long shiny metal tube between the two.

H-150. Focusing of Radiation. Many laboratories are equipped with a pair of large parabolic reflectors for use in heat, sound, and light experiments. The two reflectors may be arranged several meters apart so that the radiation from a red-hot iron ball placed at the focus *A* of one reflector comes to a focus at *B* after reflection from the second. Point *B* may be located by observing the visual image of the red-hot object. At *B* is placed a bimetallic thermostat arranged in series with a dry cell to ring a bell or turn on a light. If the mirrors are good ones, it may be possible to ignite a match held at *B* when a red-hot ball or radiant heater supplies heat at *A*. A third and rather startling indicator at *B* consists of a toy balloon filled with an explosive mixture of hydrogen and oxygen. Screens of glass or other absorbent material may be interposed between the two mirrors. A sheet of black cellophane transmits the infrared but cuts out practically all the visible radiation.

H-151. Focusing of Infrared Radiation. Place a 250-ml spherical flask full of an opaque solution of iodine in carbon disulfide immediately in front of the projection lens of an arc lantern. The flask serves as a crude lens that focuses the infrared from the arc but cuts off all visible radiation. It is very easy to locate the focus of the system by moving the hand about in front of the flask. (If you don't say "Ouch," get a hotter arc!) A piece of black paper held at the focus will glow and catch fire; blackened safety matches will be ignited at the same spot. By contrast, a water-filled flask passes visible radiation but absorbs infrared. Its focus is not nearly so hot (L-113).

H-152. Ice Lens. Fill to the brim with distilled water, recently boiled, two large watch glasses, preferably about 4 in. in diameter. Place them in the ice-cube compartment of a refrigerator, to make two plano-convex ice lenses. After they are frozen, slip them, with or without the watch-glass molds, into a frame prepared to hold them, flat face to flat face, as a biconvex lens. Introduce the lens into the beam of an arc light, and focus radiation upon a match head or piece of black paper. The ice lens will last longer if a water cell is introduced between the arc and the lens.

H-153. Greenhouse Effect. A wide-mouthed bottle is fitted with a single-hole stopper through which a thermometer is inserted. The bottle is partly surrounded by cotton waste and placed out of doors in direct sunlight for several minutes, after which it is brought into the lecture room, and the temperature within the bottle is read and compared with the outdoor temperature. In general, there will be a surprisingly large difference.

H-154. Selective Absorption of Radiation. A projection lantern with a 1000-w bulb supplies enough heat at the focus of its condensing lens to set off a match, provided that the head of the match is first blackened with a lead pencil. It is interesting to substitute for the match the clear glass bulb of a thermoscope (H-3). The fluid of the thermoscope indicates no rise of temperature, since the clear glass absorbs practically no radiation still present in the light from the arc. If, however, the bulb is covered with a hood of black paper or otherwise blackened, a large temperature rise occurs.

H-155. Heat from a radiant heater or Bunsen flame is allowed to fall upon a sensitive thermopile connected to a lecture-room galvanometer. When various screens are interposed between the source and the thermopile, the reductions in the galvanometer deflections show their relative absorptions. Quartz, rock salt, an opaque solution of iodine in carbon disulfide in a quartz vessel are relatively transparent; glass, water, etc., are opaque. A nickel oxide glass (Corex red-purple) transparent to infrared has been perfected.[1] Black bakelite, opaque to visible radiation, is semi-transparent to infrared.

H-156. Surface Radiation. The relative radiations from various surfaces at the same temperature may be readily shown by use of a Leslie cube, *viz.*, a cubical brass box into which hot water may be poured or through which steam may be passed. The faces of the cube differ from one another; for example, they may be black, white, polished, painted, or cloth-covered. One may compare the radiations of the surfaces by turning them successively toward a thermopile and by observing the galvanometer deflections. The roughness of the radiating surface is an important factor, and the common conception that "black" objects invariably radiate and absorb better than white ones needs modification. For instance, if two surfaces of a Leslie cube are covered with shiny black cloth and coarse white cloth, respectively, the white cloth radiates more than the black. Hence, at

[1] Filters of many kinds may be obtained from Corning Glass Co., Corning, N. Y.

low temperatures, white may be as good a radiator or absorber as black. In sunlight, white clothes are cooler than black; but indoors, white and black are probably equally warm or cool.

H-157. Two tin cans of equal size (about 0.5 l) are filled with hot water at the beginning of the hour. One can is smooth, the other is covered with one layer of asbestos paper. After the cans have stood for a while, the water in the asbestos-covered can is found to be *cooler* than that in the shiny can, as may be indicated to the class by inserting one junction of the demonstration thermocouple into each can. The reduction of heat loss due to low conductivity of the asbestos is more than offset by the increased loss by radiation due to roughness of the surface.

H-158. Black-body Radiation. A piece of graphite and a piece of white-porcelain evaporating dish, both heated to red heat, show comparable radiations since both are virtually "blackbody" radiators at high temperature.

A porcelain dish with a pattern or design is heated in a blast lamp to high temperature. The pattern glows bright against a darker background of "white" porcelain, showing that the pattern, which absorbs radiation better than the porcelain, also radiates better.

H-159. Surface Absorption. The junctions of the demonstration thermocouple are enclosed in glass tubes so that they may be covered with small black or white caps. A radiant-heater unit is placed midway between the two junctions so as to radiate energy to them equally. If two white caps or two black caps are used, no temperature difference is indicated. But if a white and a black cap cover the two junctions, the thermocouple indicates that the black cap absorbs more radiation than the white.

H-160. Black and white surfaces absorb radiation from incandescent sources differently, but they may absorb the far infrared from cooler sources equally. This fact may be shown by exposing a special thermocouple first to an arc light and then to a vessel of hot water. The thermocouple consists of a sheet of copper foil 4 by 8 cm with two constantan wires soldered to the back (Fig. 202). Half of the sheet is whitened by applying a suspension of plaster of paris in alcohol; the other half is blackened with smoke from burning camphor or with a suspension of lampblack in alcohol. The constantan wires are connected to the lecture-room galvanometer, and the foil is exposed to the radiation of a carbon arc (the "sun") at 1 m distance. The black junction is warmed more than the white. If the sheet is now placed at a distance of 20 to 30 cm from a Leslie cube full of hot water, the blackened metal absorbs no better than the white.

H-161. A Leslie cube with two opposite faces blackened is filled with hot water or heated by passing steam through it. It is placed midway between the two bulbs of a differential thermoscope constructed by connecting two test tubes with a horizontal glass tube containing a globule of mercury. If one tube is painted black while the other is left clear, the motion of the mercury in the connecting tube shows that the black tube absorbs radiation more than the other.

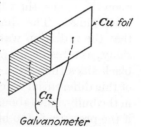

Fig. 202.—Copper-constantan thermocouple for showing absorption of radiation by white and black surfaces.

H-162. Absorption of Radiation. A white card, blank on one side, has some characters in India ink upon the other side. After the card is shown to the class, it is exposed to a hot electric-light bulb or to radiation from a carbon arc, with the inked side toward the source. The card will char locally so that the characters become permanently visible on the reverse side.

H-163. Comparison of Radiation and Absorption. Two Leslie cubes connected to a horizontal tube with a mercury globule in it form a differential thermoscope; a third Leslie cube containing hot water is placed between the first two (Fig. 203). If a polished face of the center cube faces a blackened face of one of the side cubes, while a blackened face of the center cube faces a polished face of the other side cube, no motion of the mercury globule occurs. The negative result of this experiment is important in that it furnishes an experimental basis for the principle that good radiators are good absorbers and poor radiators are poor absorbers.[1]

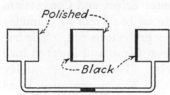

Fig. 203.—Comparison of radiation and absorption.

[1] For the details of the reasoning leading from this experiment (Ritchie's experiment) to Kirchhoff's law of radiation, see F. K. Richtmyer, "Introduction to Modern Physics," 2d ed., p. 197, McGraw-Hill Book Company, Inc., New York, 1934.

H-164. Crookes' Radiometer. The well known Crookes' radiometer may be used as a detector of radiation in many of the experiments already described. This interesting device consists of a light paddle wheel with four very thin vanes blackened on one side and polished on the other. The wheel is mounted in glass bearings inside a partly evacuated bulb. When radiation falls upon the vanes, the wheel revolves as if the radiation repelled the black sides. The simplest explanation[1] of this phenomenon is that the radiation warms the black sides slightly more than the shiny; as a result, air molecules rebound more vigorously from the black sides than from the shiny, and the wheel revolves because of this differential reaction. It is important to have the pressure in the bulb right (about 1 mm) because viscosity retards the wheel if the pressure is too high, whereas there is insufficient reaction if the pressure is too low.

If a radiometer is allowed to run under direct sunlight for several minutes, it may be found to run backward for a short time after it is removed to the shade. This is doubtless due to the fact that the black surfaces of the vanes radiate so rapidly that they cool below the temperature of the shiny surfaces, thus reversing the previous condition. In the presence of a cake of dry ice, the radiometer will likewise run backward.

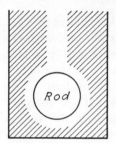

Fig. 204.—Radiometer effect and convection.

H-165. Radiometer Effect and Convection. A short length of brass bar 1 cm in diameter is cut to slip into a projection cell. The bar is heated in a Bunsen flame and lowered into the cell by a fine wire. The cell is previously filled with a dense cloud of smoke. The appearance is as indicated in Fig. 204. The clear space around the rod is caused by the radiometric repulsion of smoke particles, and convection currents cause the clear space to extend upward.

H-166. Dewar Flask. Silvered and unsilvered Dewar flasks may be exhibited; also unevacuated and poorly evacuated flasks. By pouring equal volumes of liquid air into these vessels and observing the relative rates of evaporation, the various factors of conduction, convection, and radiation may be sorted out. If

[1] For a more exact explanation, consult Kennard, E. H., "Kinetic Theory of Gases," McGraw-Hill Book Company, Inc., 1938.

desired, separate thermojunctions may be taped to the outsides of the various flasks, placing all cold junctions in a common recepta-cle of ice water. Equal volumes of hot water may then be poured into the different flasks, and the various temperature rises may be noted by connecting the thermocouples successively to the lecture-room galvanometer.

H-167. An unevacuated, unsilvered Dewar flask is connected to a pump. It is evacuated, and the inner chamber filled with liquid air. After boiling has subsided, air is allowed slowly to enter the space between the walls. The liquid starts boiling vigorously again, and frost appears outside.

H-168. Kinetic Theory. A number of experiments demon-strating kinetic theory principles will be found in Part VI (see A-41 to A-61).

HEAT AND WORK

H-169. Heat from Friction. A metal tube 1 cm in diameter is mounted in a vertical position on the hand- or motor-driven rotator. Ether, alcohol, or water is poured into the tube, which is then tightly corked. A wooden clamp is made to fit snugly about the tube. When the tube is spun, the heat generated by friction with the clamp increases the temperature of the liquid until its vapor pressure shoots the cork out explosively.

H-170. Sparks struck by flint and steel, or sparks generated by holding a piece of steel against a spinning grindstone, are good evidence of the transformation of work into heat. A fire may be kindled by the use of tinder, or gunpowder may be ignited.

H-171. Fire by Friction. Generating fire by the primitive bow-and-drill method is an interesting application of thermo-dynamic principles. A board of elm, soft maple, or other *dry*, non-gummy wood, 1 by 10 by 60 cm, is bored with a $\frac{1}{2}$-in. machine drill to make a series of shallow holes 5 mm deep near one edge. Notches are cut between the edge of the board and the centers of the holes. The other parts of the apparatus are a bow 75 cm long with a stout leather thong, an eight-sided wooden spindle 1.5 cm in diameter and 25 cm long, and a metal block with a conical hole to serve as an upper bearing for the spindle. A handful of absorbent cotton previously dried by heating in a metal beaker is placed on a chalk-box cover and clamped beneath the notched board. The upper bearing is lubricated with vase-line, and the spindle is inserted with the leather thong wrapped once around it. A few minutes of hard work with the bow will produce considerable smoke and a small live coal of charred wood dust.   The notched board is unclamped; the coal is picked up in the middle of the dry cotton and swung vigorously at arm's length until it bursts into flame.   The lecturer usually gets nearly as hot as the wood dust!

H-172. Heat from Work.   Ten-centimeter pieces of No. 14 iron wire may be passed about the class, and each student may observe the temperature rise that results from his bending the wire back and forth in the process of breaking it in two.

H-173.   Thin rubber bands may be used to furnish an illustration of adiabatic expansion and contraction.   Each member of the class is provided with a fresh rubber band.   By putting it to his lips, he may observe the temperature changes that occur during extension and contraction.   The contraction of the rubber band is analogous to the expansion of a gas; for in both cases, external work is done at the expense of internal energy, and cooling results. (It is possible that change of state also accompanies the deformation of rubber.)

H-174.   A thermojunction made by spot-welding together a nichrome and an iron wire is inserted into a jug one-quarter full of mercury.   The junction is connected to the lecture-room galvanometer by long flexible copper leads so that the bottle of mercury may be shaken vigorously.   After a few minutes of shaking, the mercury shows a distinct rise of temperature.   This experiment is purely qualitative and is not subject to numerical computation.

H-175.   A 250-g slug of lead with an iron handle is pounded vigorously with a heavy hammer on a hardwood block.   The rise in temperature may be shown by a thermojunction either buried in the lead or brought into contact with it.

H-176. Mechanical Equivalent of Heat—Shot Tube.   One or two kilograms of lead shot at room temperature is poured into a long, stout mailing tube, which is then securely corked at both ends.   The tube is inverted rapidly a number of times so that the shot rushes from one end to the other.   After 100 or more inversions, the shot is poured out, and its temperature rise measured by a sensitive thermometer or thermocouple.   The rise in temperature multiplied by the mass of the shot and its specific heat gives a measure of the heat developed, while the product of the number of inversions, the mass of the shot, and the height of fall (length of tube) gives the work done. Numerical values for the mechanical equivalent of heat calculated from this experiment are in good agreement with those obtained by more refined means.

H-177. Mechanical Equivalent of Heat. A numerical value of Joule's equivalent J may be determined as a lecture experiment by using Searle's revolving-drum apparatus. It is important to draw a simplified diagram of the apparatus on the blackboard to give the class an understanding of its operation (Fig. 205). Members of the class may calculate J from the data obtained. The experiment requires 5 to 10 min.

FIG. 205.—Searle's revolving-drum apparatus for determining the mechanical equivalent of heat.

A large-scale model may be made in which heat is developed in a brake as a heavy weight descends to the floor.

H-178. Mechanical Equivalent of Heat. A $\frac{1}{4}$-hp motor is suspended by two parallel wires, of length l separated by distance d, that serve both as current leads and bifilar suspension (Fig. 206). The axis of the motor is vertical, and from the end of its shaft is suspended by means of a No. 14 steel wire a metal drum that revolves with small clearance inside the cup of a calorimeter. The calorimeter is filled with sufficient water to cover the drum, and the motor is driven for a few minutes, during which the temperature of the water rises several degrees because of frictional work expended in the calorimeter. The torque Q applied to the revolving drum is determined from the weight of the motor W

and the angle ϕ through which the motor turns about the vertical when in operation, as shown by a pointer or optical lever $Q = \dfrac{Wd^2}{4l} \sin \phi$.* A revolution counter gives n, the number of turns of the drum, and the heat delivered to the calorimeter and water is measured in the usual way by observing temperature

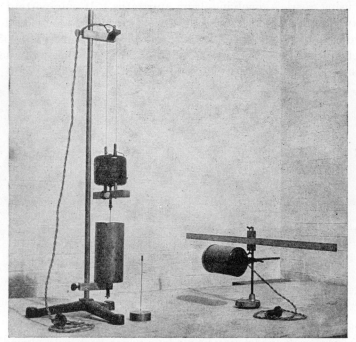

Fig. 206.—Apparatus for determining mechanical equivalent of heat.

change $(T_2 - T_1)$ and mass of water, M_w, and of calorimeter, M_c. The mechanical equivalent of heat may then be determined by

$$J = \frac{2\pi n Q}{(M_w + sM_c)(T_2 - T_1)},$$

where s is the specific heat of the calorimeter.

H-179. Heating by Compression—Fire Syringe. A stout glass tube 2 cm in diameter with 1-cm bore and 20 cm long, closed

* A more rigorous value of torque is $Q = \dfrac{Wd^2 \sin \phi}{4\sqrt{l^2 - d^2 \sin \dfrac{\phi}{2}}}$, but the term $d^2 \sin \phi/2$ is usually very small in comparison with l^2 and can be neglected.

at one end, is equipped with a tight-fitting plunger.   Into the end
of the plunger may be inserted a small piece of guncotton or cotton
dipped in ether or acetone.   A quick compression will ignite the
cotton.   If the syringe fails to work, remove the plunger, blow
out the tube, and try again.   A brass tube will work equally
well, but the flash, which occurs under compression, is not
visible.

H-180. Heating by Compression.   A heavy-walled glass tube
about 3 cm in diameter and 30 cm long is fitted with an airtight
piston.   The shaft of the piston slides freely through a cork in the
upper end of the tube.   The lower end is closed with an ebonite
plug, through which pass 18 fine wires (No. 31 to 36) alternately
nickel and iron.   The ends of these wires are soldered together in
pairs to form a thermopile, with nine junctions inside the tube.
The outside junctions are protected with sealing wax, and the
plug is mounted in a suitable wooden base with two binding posts
for the thermopile terminals, which are connected to the galvanometer.   When the piston is pushed down quickly, a galvanometer
deflection occurs.   It may be shown by heating the thermopile
with a lighted match that the deflection is such as would be
caused by a rise of temperature inside the tube.

**H-181. Temperature Changes Due to Expansion and Com-
pression.**   Two equal lengths of No. 40 enameled copper wire
2.5 m long (8 ohms resistance) and two lengths of insulated
constantan wire of the same resistance are soldered alternately
end to end, and the resultant long loop is wound in a single-layer
coil about one end of an ebonite rod 1 cm in diameter and 15 cm
long.   Four strips of copper foil are soldered to the junctions so
as to make a Wheatstone bridge.   They are fastened to binding
posts at the other end of the ebonite rod.   The bridge is mounted
in a 1-l flask with a side tube in the neck, the ebonite rod passing
through a tight-fitting stopper with the binding posts outside.
The lecture-room galvanometer and dry cells are connected in
the ordinary manner of the Wheatstone bridge, and a balance is
secured by shunting one arm of the bridge with a resistance box.
(The proper arm must be discovered by trial.)   A rubber bulb
such as is commonly used on battery fillers is connected to the
side arm of the flask.   Compression of the air within the flask
causes the galvanometer to swing in one direction, whereas
expansion causes it to deflect the other way.   Gently warming

the flask with a burner serves to show that the first swing was caused by a rise of temperature in the gas.

H-182. Models. Model steam engines, turbines, gas engines, and motors may be shown during the discussion of the relation between Heat and Work. Miniature working models of steam and internal-combustion engines are obtainable commercially. A model steam engine may be run by liquid air.

The action of an internal-combustion engine may be shown, in part, by exploding gasoline in a coffee can. An automobile spark plug is fastened securely in the side of the can and connected to an induction coil. A few drops of gasoline (quantity determined by trial) are introduced, and the lid is placed on the can. After shaking the can to mix gasoline vapor and air, the demonstrator ignites the explosive mixture by closing a switch in the primary circuit of the induction coil.

PART IV

ELECTRICITY AND MAGNETISM

ELECTROSTATICS

E-1. Electric Charges on Solids Separated after Contact. A hard rubber rod or a stick of sealing wax is rubbed with fur and then placed in a stiff aluminum-wire stirrup hung by a silk thread. The suspended rod will move away from another rod that has been rubbed with fur but toward a glass rod that has been rubbed with silk. This behavior is interpreted in terms of two kinds of charge and the forces exerted between them. Positive electricity is defined (arbitrarily) as that which appears on glass when rubbed with silk.

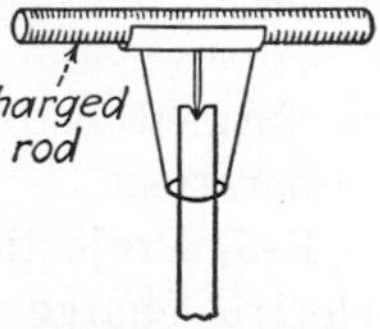

Another method of supporting a charged rod so that it is free to turn is shown in Fig. 207. The rod is laid on a metal trough to which is attached a pivot supported by a vertical rod. The trough also carries a wire framework that forms a collar surrounding the support rod and so prevents the charged rod from falling.

Charged rod

FIG. 207.—Torque-free support for charged rod.

A 10-ft plank (well dried) is suspended by a wire or strong cord at the middle so that it hangs horizontally. An ebonite rod is rubbed with fur and one end of the plank also brushed with the fur. The plank is set into rotation by repulsion when the charged rod is brought near to its charged end.

E-2. Large-scale Electroscopes. There are many ways of detecting the presence of a charge on a body; all depend on the forces exerted between charges. In this sense, small bits of paper or pith, cork filings, sawdust, and other light objects attracted toward charged bodies are electroscopes, as are also the torsion pendulums described in E-1.

An "electrical pendulum" consists simply of a small ball of pith or a ping-pong ball, coated with metallic paint and suspended by a long silk thread. It is a more sensitive detector of charge than the torsion pendulum. An inverted electrical pendulum is made by tying a gas-filled balloon to the table top or to the floor by a thread 3 or 4 ft long. The balloon is charged by rubbing on the demonstrator's hair, or by stroking with cat's fur.

Two gilded ping-pong balls are hung from the same point on a sealing-wax rod by fine wires. When the system is charged, the balls fly apart, and the magnitude of their separation may be made an indication of the amount of the charge, on an arbitrary scale. Two similarly treated rubber balloons separate in the same way.

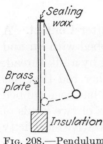

FIG. 208.—Pendulum electroscope.

A simple and sensitive electroscope is provided by suspending a gilded ping-pong ball by a No. 40 copper wire, which passes over a piece of sealing wax for insulation and is connected to an insulated plate of brass or aluminum mounted vertically so as to be tangent to the ball when the system is uncharged (Fig. 208). This arrangement permits many electrostatic experiments to be performed before a large class without the use of projection apparatus.

E-3. Projection Electroscopes. In the gold-leaf electroscope, electric charge is detected either by motion of two gold leaves hanging vertically beside one another or by the motion of one leaf hanging beside a fixed plate. In either case, the charge to be detected is communicated to the leaves from an external knob, insulated from the protecting case of the instrument. Students may be encouraged to make their own electroscopes. A glass jar with a tin top, a rubber stopper for insulation, a long nail, and a piece of aluminum foil (chewing-gum or candy wrapper) are sufficient. The rubber stopper is set in a hole cut in the top of the jar, and the nail is pushed through a hole in the stopper. The aluminum foil is fastened to the nail by wrapping it with a piece of fine wire.

In using the gold-leaf electroscope before a large class, place it near the condensing lens of a projection lantern, and cast an image of the leaves upon the screen (L-1). An erecting prism is useful but not necessary. Shadow projection of the whole electroscope has the advantage of showing the class both the motion of the leaves and the operator's manipulations. The electroscope may safely be charged by contact with a proof plan-that has been touched to a charged rod.   (Charging by induction is described in E-23.)

A simple projection electroscope is made with a cylinder of thin paper in place of the gold leaf.   This cylinder, made conducting with India ink, is attached to a metal rod projecting through the top of the case and insulated from it with sulfur or other dielectric. A convenient case may be made of a 3-in. length of brass tubing, 4 in. in diameter, with glass windows cemented on the ends, and mounted on a suitable stand to fit the lantern.   The instrument may be made into a vibrating electroscope of the Zeleny type by including in the case a metal block placed so that the leaf will strike it when sufficiently deflected.   This block is grounded to the case, so that when the cylinder strikes it, its charge is lost and it falls back.   If charge is being continuously supplied to the electroscope knob, the cylinder will vibrate at a rate proportional to the rate of supply of charge, *i.e.*, to the current.

Caution: When an electroscope is connected to a battery or other source of potential capable of giving a relatively large current, a high resistance should be put in series with the electroscope for its protection in case the leaf should strike the case or a plate attached to the other terminal of the source.   A resistance that limits the maximum current to 1 ma will in general suffice.

E-4. Electroscopes and Electrometers.   For many purposes, the large-scale and sturdy electroscopes previously described (E-2 and 3) are adequate.   Other more sensitive types of electrostatic instrument are useful for experiments where voltages, minute charges, or ion currents must be measured.

The electrostatic voltmeter (Braun) consists of an aluminum vane balanced in a vertical position near a fixed vertical metal rod mounted on an insulator.   When rod and vane are charged, the vane rotates under repulsive forces of electrostatic origin, and its new equilibrium position depends upon the charge and hence upon the potential of the system.   The instrument may be calibrated directly in volts from, say, 0 to 2000 v.   The moving-vane-and-rod assembly may be used separately from the case to serve as an indicator of charge wherever a leaf electroscope is needed (Fig. 209).   (Shadow projection.)

The oscillating-leaf electroscope (Zeleny[1]) is useful for indicating ion currents.   It consists of a wide leaf suspended from an

[1] ZELENY, J., *Phys. Rev.*, **32**, 581, 1911.

insulated support close to an insulated stationary plate (Fig. 210). When a potential is applied to the plate, the leaf is charged by contact and is repelled. As the leaf loses charge, it again comes in contact with the plate, and the process repeats itself. The rapidity with which the leaf oscillates is proportional to the current reaching the exterior terminal connected to the leaf. Motion of the leaf is shown by shadow or image projection.

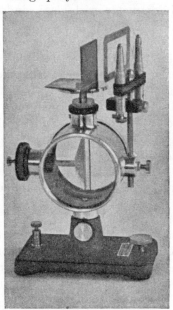

Fig. 209.—Braun electro-
scope.

Fig. 210.—Zeleny electroscope.

For the measurement of very minute charges and potential differences, the demonstrator may use a quadrant or a string electrometer. Inasmuch as these instruments are rarely used except in advanced electrical or research laboratories, the reader is directed to any text on experimental atomic physics for details of their adjustment and calibration.

E-5. Conductors and Insulators. By means of a wire, connect the electroscope to a conductor mounted on an insulating stand. If necessary, support the wire by pieces of glass tubing fitted into wooden bases. Charge the conductor by means of a proof plane and charged rod. The consequent divergence of the electroscope leaves shows that the wire conducts charge. If a silk thread is used in place of the wire, the insulating property of silk is demonstrated. If a dry cotton thread is used, it will ordinarily be sufficiently nonconducting to prevent flow of electricity to the electroscope. If, however, the moistened fingers are run along the thread, it becomes a poor conductor; a thread moistened with salt water shows some conductivity even after it has dried.

Although the subject of capacitance has not usually been discussed at the time this demonstration is used, it is nevertheless interesting at this point to show poor conductivity by connecting one insulated conductor A (Fig. 211) to the electroscope E with a wire W, at the same time connecting A to a second insulated conductor B by a cotton thread T that has been wet with salt water and then allowed to dry. If the conductor B is given a charge, the divergence of the electroscope leaves is gradual because of the time required for sufficient charge to flow along the cotton thread to charge both A and E. (The rate of charging E is greater if B is connected directly to E without the presence of A.) Then, after the electroscope has reached its full deflection, B may be grounded, and the electroscope leaves come together slowly. The

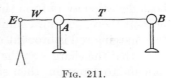

FIG. 211.

time required for these effects can be shortened by running the moistened fingers along the cotton thread, if the latter is not already a sufficiently good conductor.

E-6. Attraction and Repulsion. When a rubbed ebonite rod is dipped into a container filled with dry cork filings, a surprisingly large mass attaches itself to the rod. After a short interval of time, one may notice some of the particles of cork being forcibly ejected because of the repulsive forces between them and the rod. At first, the attraction between the negative charge on the rod and the induced positive charge on the cork particle predominates; but when the cork particle becomes charged by conduction from the rod, the force of repulsion between similar charges is shown. "Familiarity breeds contempt!" If the demonstration is carried out with strong illumination against a black background, the trajectories are visible at a distance.

E-7. Force between Charges—Coulomb's Law. Two pith balls of equal mass are aluminum painted to improve their conductivities and are suspended by silk threads, the upper ends of which are attached to a common point on a horizontal support rod as in E-2. The pith balls are charged by contact with a hard rubber or a glass rod, and after the first contact their efforts to keep away from the rod are amusing and instructive. The distance between the pith balls, their masses, and the lengths of the supporting threads may be given to the class as data for computing the charge on each ball, provided that the charges on the two balls are assumed to be equal. This demonstration assumes Coulomb's law and furnishes a link between Mechanics and Electrostatics.

E-8. Electrostatic Induction. A cylindrical conductor with hemispherical ends, mounted on an insulating stand, is provided with two wire supports, one above each end, from which metallized pith balls are hung by silk threads so as just to touch the ends of the conductor when it is uncharged. When a charged rod is brought up toward one end of the conductor, the pith balls are both deflected away from the ends, showing that charges are now present there.   A third similar pith ball charged by contact with the charging rod is brought near each of the other balls in turn to show that the charges on the ends of the conductor are of opposite sign and to determine their signs with respect to that of the charge on the rod.

E-9. A charged rod is held by a wooden support near a conductor on an insulating standard. Using the electroscope and proof plane, demonstrate that the conductor was uncharged before the charged rod was brought near; that there are charges on the conductor separated by induction; and that the conductor is uncharged after the inducing charge has been removed, provided that only small and nearly equal amounts of the induced charges have been removed for testing purposes. The fact that there are induced charges on the conductor may be demonstrated by bringing the proof plane into contact with the conductor and then transferring the charge received by the proof plane to the electroscope. The fact that the charges induced on opposite ends of the conductor are opposite in sign is shown by giving the electroscope a charge and then conveying a sample charge from each end of the conductor to the electroscope by using the proof plane. In one case, the divergence of the leaves increases; in the other, it decreases. By similarly testing the inducing charge, it can be shown that the charge induced on the nearer end of the conductor is of opposite sign.

E-10. Electrophorus. The electrophorus, described in all elementary textbooks, is easy to make. Melt a layer of sealing wax in a pie plate, and let it harden. Provide a flat metal disk, slightly smaller than the surface of the wax, with an insulating handle of pyrex or ebonite. Give a negative charge to the wax by rubbing it with fur. Place the disk in contact with the charged wax, which induces a positive charge on the lower side and a negative charge on the upper side of the disk. The usual method of removing the induced negative charge is for the demonstrator to touch the disk with his finger. A variation of this method is to use a neon-discharge-tube "wand," which is held so that the hand makes contact with one electrode. Touch the electrophorus disk with the other electrode of the tube. When the negative charge flows to ground through the demonstrator's body, the neon tube flashes brilliantly. A second flash is obtained by similarly touching the wand to the charged disk after it is removed from the wax plate. For best results, the metal disk should be at least $\frac{1}{8}$ in. thick, with its edge smoothly rounded.

E-11. Mechanical Work and Energy of Charge. Work is required to separate the unlike charges in the electrophorus. Suspend an electrophorus disk by its insulating handle from a sufficiently sensitive helical spring. With the disk initially uncharged, lower it onto a hard rubber plate. Without touching the upper plate to any conducting material, slowly raise it again. The extension of the spring remains unchanged. Now with the plates again in contact, remove the charge induced on the upper surface of the upper plate by touching it with the finger. The force now needed to separate the plates is more than the weight of the disk, as shown by the increased stretch in the spring. Thus work must be done in separating the unlike charges.

E-12. Electret. An electret is an interesting variation of the usual electrophorus. Essentially, an electret is a sheet of dielectric that retains an electric moment after the externally applied electric field has been reduced to zero. It is somewhat analogous to a permanent magnetic sheet, but the analogy is not very close, as will appear presently.

To prepare an electret, it is necessary to produce an electric field strength of about 10,000 v per cm in a molten dielectric and to maintain this field while the dielectric is solidifying. A pyrex pie plate makes a good container for casting the dielectric. A sheet of tin foil is spread evenly on the bottom of the plate so as to extend over the edges of the plate to serve as connection for one terminal of the high-voltage source. A few short pieces of pyrex tubing are placed on the surface of the tin foil, to support at the proper distance above it a brass disk that serves as the other electrode. The separation of electrodes should be such that the high potential source to be used will produce a field of abcut 10,000 v per cm. A full-wave rectified a.c. source, unfiltered by condensers or inductors, may be used. A potential difference of 2200 v average value with a distance of 2 mm between electrodes is satisfactory.

A tin pie plate may be substituted for the pyrex as a mold for the dielectric, the wax poured in, and a second pie plate floated on it in place of the brass disk. The upper plate must be kept from touching the lower one at the edges by insulating stops.

As a dielectric, one may use a mixture of two parts Carnauba wax, two parts rosin, and one part beeswax, the last to make the casting less brittle. These ingredients should be melted and mixed in a separate dish, then strained through cheesecloth into the pie plate. The plate may be placed over a wire screen on a tripod stand to allow application of a little heat in case the mixture has solidified after it has been poured into the plate and the upper electrode has been lowered into position. A piece of pyrex tubing attached at the center of the upper disk provides a handle. The bottom surface of this disk should be covered with tin foil, to prevent the mixture from sticking to the disk on cooling. The electric field is maintained until the mixture is cool. It is well to record the polarities of the electrodes. After the mixture has solidified and the high-voltage source has been disconnected, the tin foil may be removed from the upper disk. To keep moisture off the surface of the electret, it should be stored in a dry place, and the bottom tin foil should be connected to the brass disk when not in use, to prevent a layer of ions from gathering on the surface of the electret.

In use, the brass disk is operated exactly like the disk of an electrophorus. During the first few days after preparation, the upper surface of the electret has a charge of electricity opposite in sign to that given the brass disk by the high-voltage source. In one or two weeks, this charge will reduce to zero and then reverse. The magnitude of charge will increase for several days, until after a period of about four weeks it reaches a maximum. The potential of the brass disk, after it has first been grounded and then removed from an electret such as this (2 mm thick) is sufficient to pass a fair-sized spark a distance of 1 cm to a grounded conductor. It is probable that the electret will retain its electric moment for several years provided that it is kept in a dry place. During the summer months, it may be necessary to keep it in a calcium chloride drying chamber.[1]

E-13. Electrostatic Induction—Faraday's Ice-pail Experiment. This well-known experiment proves the equality of the induced and the inducing charges. A hollow conductor open at the top (a tin can will do) is mounted on an insulating stand and connected to an electroscope. A metal ball hanging by a silk thread is given a charge of known sign by contact with a charged rod or electrophorus disk. The ball is then lowered into the hollow conductor without touching it. The divergence of the electroscope leaves demonstrates the presence of an induced charge on the outside of the conductor. The demonstrator may call attention to the fact that the divergence of the leaves does not change as the inducing charge is moved about inside the conductor, thus showing that all of the lines of force from the inducing charge end on the inside of the conductor, regardless of the location of the inducing charge, provided that it is not too near the opening. If the ball is removed without touching the conductor, the electroscope leaves collapse, showing that no charge was transferred to the conductor. But if the ball is allowed to touch the bottom of the hollow conductor, the fact that there is no further change in the divergence of the leaves indicates that there must have been a charge induced on the inside of the hollow conductor exactly equal to that on the ball. This equality is further proved if the ball is withdrawn, the electroscope then discharged, and the ball returned to its original position within the hollow conductor without having been in contact with any body outside the conductor. The electroscope now shows no divergence, demonstrating that the ball was completely discharged by contact with

---

[1] EGUCHI, M., *Phil. Mag.*, **49**, 178, 1925; JOHNSON and CARR, *Phys. Rev.*, **42**, 912, 1932; EWING, M., *Phys. Rev.*, **36**, 378, 1930; GOOD, W. M., *Phys. Rev.*, **53**, 323, 1938.

the inside of the hollow conductor and establishing the equality between the inducing and the induced charges.

E-14. Equality of Charges on Solids Charged by Contact. The simple Faraday ice-pail apparatus (E-13) allows one to show that the two charges produced by contact between dissimilar bodies are equal and opposite in sign. A hard rubber rod has a piece of woolen cloth wrapped around one end and securely tied. This rod and another one having nothing attached to it are held inside a hollow conductor connected by a wire to an electroscope. When the end of the plain rod is rubbed against the woolen cloth, the electroscope leaves do not diverge; but if either rod is withdrawn, there will be a divergence of the leaves, of the same amount. The experiment may be varied by rubbing the two rods together outside the conductor, then inserting one after the other separately, then both together (see also E-52).

E-15. Charging Paper on Slate. It is well to show that the materials so far used in the production of electric charges are not exceptional in this respect. If a sheet of paper is held against a slate blackboard and rubbed with the hand or struck with fur, the paper becomes charged and will stick to the board because of the induced opposite charge on the board. It is of interest to remove the paper and to watch it return to the board when released nearby. The sign of the charge on the paper may be determined by carrying it to the vicinity of a charged electroscope (E-24).

E-16. Electrically Charged Student. If a student stands on an insulated platform—an inverted battery jar will do—and is struck several times on the back with a piece of fur, his body becomes charged to a potential of several thousand volts above ground, and a 2-cm spark can be drawn from knuckles or ear, greatly to the amusement of the class. If the student holds a key tightly in his hand, sparks may be drawn from the key without causing him discomfort. The instructor may present to him a grounded Bunsen burner and let him ignite the gas by the spark. The sign of the charge on the student may be tested by a proof plane and an electroscope to which a known charge has been given (E-24).

E-17. Charging Metals by Contact. The charging of metals by contact may be shown and the signs of the charges determined. It is only necessary that the metal be held by an insulating handle and be rubbed with wool. If a hard rubber rod with woolen cloth attached (E-14) is used, then the sign of the charge on each body is easily determined by placing it within the ice pail (E-13), provided that the electroscope has been given a charge of known sign; in this case, increased or decreased divergence of the electroscope leaves indicates the sign of the unknown charge (E-24). If a substance in the following list of materials is rubbed with one below it in the list, it becomes charged positively, the other substance negatively: fur, wool, quartz, glass, silk, wood, metals, hard rubber, sealing wax, rosin, sulfur, guncotton. Surface conditions may change the above order to some extent.

E-18. Neon Discharge from Rug Scuffing. Charges may also be separated by several other means, such as rubbing dry paper with the hand, passing a rubber or bakelite comb or fountain pen through the hair or rubbing it on the sleeve, drawing a rubber band across the edge of a board or desk. Charging the human body by scuffing the feet across a rug is a familiar parlor trick that may be varied by discharging the accumulated charge through a neon discharge tube. The operator holds one end of the tube and, after scuffing his feet on a rug, presents the other end of the tube to an uncharged person or, better still, to a radiator or other grounded conductor.

E-19. Electric Charges from a Stretched Rubber Band— Charging Electroscope by Contact. A piece of stiff wire is bent into the form of a miniature violin bow, and rubber stoppers are fitted over its ends. An ordinary rubber band becomes charged positively when stretched across the ends of this frame. This charge may be conducted to an electroscope by sliding the band along the knob. The device is convenient because any desired quantity of charge may be obtained by sliding a suitable length along the knob. If the stretched rubber band is rubbed along a grounded conductor, the positive charge will be removed; after the band has been allowed to contract to its original length, it will be charged negatively, thus enabling one to conduct a negative charge to the electroscope.

E-20. Charging by Contact between Glass and Mercury. The charging of a solid and a liquid may be shown with an evacuated glass tube containing a small quantity of mercury. A glass tube about 2 cm in inside diameter and 60 cm long is drawn down to a capillary at one end. The mercury is introduced into the bottom of the tube.   Connection is made to a pump, and the tube is evacuated.   During evacuation, the tube may be heated with a flame, and the mercury boiled to expel air.   The tube is then sealed off at the capillary.   When the tube is shaken, potential differences are developed sufficient to cause a luminous discharge, but the luminosity is not great enough to make the demonstration effective in a large auditorium unless it is quite dark.   It is well to hold the tube in a horizontal position while shaking to avoid the mercury-hammer effect.

If facilities are available, the experiment may be varied by the introduction of neon.   A glass tube 5 mm in diameter and 25 cm long is sealed at one end, and a small quantity of clean mercury put in it.   It is evacuated thoroughly, and neon gas is admitted to a pressure of a few millimeters, after which the tube is sealed off.   Upon shaking the tube, the characteristic neon discharge may be observed in a dark room.   The effect is enhanced if the tube is constricted at a number of places along its length so as to increase the contact of mercury with glass as it is shaken from one end of the tube to the other.   The neon must be pure, otherwise the color is muddy.

E-21. Mercury-glass Charging Wand.   The effect described in E-20 is employed in a simple charging rod to replace the more usual rubber or glass ones.   A glass tube 30 cm long and 1 cm in diameter containing a little mercury is evacuated and sealed. One end is covered with tin foil or platinized.   When mercury is allowed to run from one end of the tube to the other, it acquires a positive charge; when it is run into the platinized end, a negative charge is induced on the glass, and a positive charge appears on the metallic coating.   A negative charge may likewise be obtained by grounding the metallic coating and then allowing the mercury to run back to the other end of the tube.   The rod may be used to obtain *either* positive or negative charge for charging an electroscope by contact or induction; the potential of the charge on the metal coating is sufficiently high to produce a flash in a neon bulb.[1]

E-22. Charging by Change of State.   Many substances become charged upon solidification.   Sulfur is melted in a glass dish, and some of it is taken up on the end of a glass rod where it is

---

[1] HOPFIELD, J. J., *Rev. Sci. Instruments*, **2**, 756, 1931.

allowed to solidify.   If it is held near an electroscope, it can be shown to acquire a negative charge.

E-23. Charging Electroscope by Induction.   Hold a charged rod near the knob of an electroscope.   A charge of opposite sign is induced on the knob, while a charge of the same sign is induced on the electroscope leaves.   Charge on the leaves is conducted away by touching the knob (grounding) while the inducing charge is near.   Break the ground connection, and remove the inducing charge.   The electroscope is thus left with a permanent charge of sign *opposite* to that of the inducing charge.   Any insulated body may be similarly charged by induction, giving a resultant charge opposite to that brought near it.

E-24. Identifying Positive and Negative Charges.   The electroscope charged with electricity of known sign, either by contact (E-19) or by induction (E-23), may be used for testing the sign of an unknown charge.   A charge of the same sign as that on the electroscope, when brought near the knob, will cause increased divergence of the leaves, while a charge of opposite sign will cause decreased divergence.   It is instructive to bring a charge of opposite sign so close that the leaves not only collapse but begin to diverge again.   In determining the sign of an unknown charge, one must remember that the approach of any grounded conductor, for example, the demonstrator's hand, toward the electroscope knob, will cause decreased divergence of the leaves since some of the charge on the leaves flows to the knob as a result of the attraction caused by the charge induced on the grounded conductor (condenser effect).   This difficulty is largely avoided if the charge being tested is brought up on a proof plane attached to the end of a long pyrex rod.   Another source of trouble is the charging of the demonstrator's body, especially in dry weather and on dry wood floors.   This charge can be removed by touching a gas or water pipe.

E-25. Kelvin Water Dropper.   Two tin cans A and B (Fig. 212), with tops and bottoms removed, are mounted on insulating supports above two other cans C and D with perforated bottoms, also insulated.   The cans are connected electrically as shown, with one pair connected to a vibrating-leaf electroscope (E-4) with case grounded.   The arms of a glass T-tube are bent at right angles, and the tube is mounted so that water may drip from both arms through the upper cans without touching them and may then be caught in the lower cans, whence the water runs off to the sink; the flow of water is regulated with a pinchcock. As they leave the glass, the water drops are charged, and charges build up by induction and contact so that the electroscope leaf is deflected until it strikes the grounded stop in the case. As dropping continues, the leaf oscillates, about twice a second. The sign of the charge on each of the conductors should be tested by presenting the electroscope to each in turn. A large potential difference can be generated by this simple electrostatic machine.

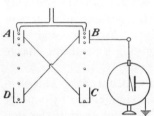

FIG. 212.—Kelvin water dropper.

A "dry water dropper" has been constructed, in which $\frac{1}{2}$-in. steel balls are dropped instead of water droplets. The balls are dropped over and over again as they are returned to their upper elevation either mechanically or by hand.

E-26. Toepler-Holtz and Wimshurst Machines. An electrostatic machine (frequently called "influence," "induction," or "static") is really a continuous-action mechanical electrophorus (E-10). Such machines may be shown at any time after the simple experiments on electric induction are performed. They are useful for subsequent demonstrations, since they are more effective charging devices than the electrophorus or electret. By increasing the distance between the two knobs, to delay the spark discharge, higher potential differences can be built up. Much larger charges can be stored before the spark discharge occurs by connecting the knobs to Leyden jars, which are usually component parts of the machines. Proof plane and electroscope may be used to show that the knobs are oppositely charged (E-24). A card or a thin sheet of glass may be punctured by the passage of a spark through it; however, the spark will in general go around the edge of a thick piece of glass.

E-27. Van de Graaff Generator. The principle of generating high potentials by the mechanical separation of electric charges, upon which the operation of the Kelvin water dropper (E-25) is based, is likewise shown in the Van de Graaff electrostatic generator. A small model of this generator may be constructed at low cost. The generator consists of one or more endless belts of silk or paper driven at high speed by a motor. The belts become charged when they pass pointed wires connected to a 10,000-v transformer and kenotron rectifier and carry their charge to the inside of an insulated sphere, where they give it up to other pointed wires connected to the sphere and return "for another load." The insulated sphere thus acquires charge, and its potential builds up to a high value, higher in general than can be obtained by an ordinary rotating-plate static machine. The charging transformer and rectifier can be omitted, and the device can be made self-sustaining when once started by a static

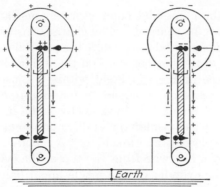

Fig. 213.—Van de Graaff electrostatic generator.

charge by using two insulated spheres and two belts, with appropriately arranged points as shown in Fig. 213.[1]

DISTRIBUTION OF CHARGE ON CONDUCTORS

E-28. Location of Charge on Insulated Hollow Conductors. A hollow conductor on an insulating stand is charged by contact with the electrophorus disk. With proof plane and electroscope, show that no charge is given to the proof plane when it is touched to the inside of the conductor, but that a charge is received by contact with the outside.

A cone-shaped linen bag, generally called a "Faraday's bag," has its base attached to a ring on an insulating stand and has two silk threads attached to its apex, by which the bag may be pulled inside out. The bag is given a charge, and the proof plane is used to show that the charge is wholly on the outside. The bag

[1] For further details, see Van de Graaff, Compton, and Van Atta, *Phys. Rev.*, **43**, 153, 1933.

is then pulled inside out and the proof plane again used to show that there is still no charge on the inside.

E-29. Surface Distribution of Charge.   An egg-shaped conductor on an insulating stand is charged.   Proof plane and electroscope are used to compare charge densities at various points on the surface of the conductor.   It is found that the charge density (and hence the charge acquired by the proof plane) is greatest at the point of greatest curvature.   (Care must be exercised that the proof plane itself does not disturb the charge distribution by its presence.)

Instead of the ellipsoidal conductor, an insulated aluminum cooking pan may be charged.   The charge density is greatest at the corners and edges and least where the pan is flat, being greater on the outside of the bottom than on the inside of it.

E-30. Absence of Electric Field within a Closed Conductor. A cylinder of coarse-mesh screen (galvanized-iron wire of $\frac{1}{4}$-in. mesh serves well) about 4 in. in diameter and 8 in. long, open at both ends, is set on an insulated metallic plate connected with one terminal of the electrostatic machine.   A metal-coated pith ball is suspended by a fine wire from the top of the cylinder so as to hang against the cylinder on the inside about half-way down, a similar ball being suspended from the top so as to hang about half-way down on the outside.   When the machine is started, the outer ball deflects outward, the inner one remaining motionless.   In the absence of an electrostatic machine, the electrophorus may be used.

E-31. Electric Shielding.   Since charges reside on the outside of conductors, an electroscope, whether charged or uncharged, when enclosed within a conducting surface will be unaffected by outside charges.   The shield may be a closed metal vessel but need not be continuous.   A cage made of heavy wire screening is entirely effective.   Charges may be brought near the screen and, if it is grounded, sparks may be passed to it without affecting the electroscope within.   Project the image of the electroscope leaves to show the absence of any effect.

E-32. Discharge of Electricity from a Point.   A thin sheet of metal is rolled into a sharp-pointed cone and attached to a conductor on an insulating support.   The hollow conductor used in E-28 is convenient, since the metal sheet may be cut in such a shape that a strip will extend from the base of the cone, the strip being bent into a hook to hang over the edge of the opening in the hollow conductor. Another conductor, also on an insulating support, is placed about 5 cm from the vertex of the cone and is charged either by use of the electrophorus disk or by the electrostatic machine. Charges are induced on the conductor carrying the cone. If the inducing charge is now removed, it can be shown by proof plane and electroscope that the conductor carrying the cone has acquired a net charge of the *same* sign as that of the charge on the other conductor, owing to the escape of charge from the conical point. This experiment may be contrasted with E-23, where an *opposite* sign of charge results.

E-33. A charged conductor is connected to an electroscope and contact made with the blunt end of a carefully insulated darning needle, so that the needle projects perpendicularly from the surface of the conductor at the place of contact. The deflection of the electroscope falls to zero.

E-34. A tinsel tassel is hung from one knob of a static machine, and the machine is started. The strands of the tassel stand apart because of repulsion, but when the point of a needle held in the hand or otherwise earthed is brought near the tassel, the strands collapse. If the needle is not earthed but is held in an insulated handle, its effect is negligible.

E-35. If a point attached to one knob of a static machine is brought near an insulated uncharged conductor, the conductor becomes charged, as may be demonstrated by bringing it near an electroscope.

E-36. The lecture-room galvanometer is connected to one knob of the static machine and to a wire suspended from an insulated support so as to hang over the other knob to form a vertical air gap, shorter than that between the knobs (Fig. 214). The galvanometer deflects widely, owing to the invisible brush discharge between the dangling wire and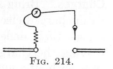

FIG. 214.

the adjacent knob. With point terminals on the static machine, this brush discharge may be seen in a darkened room. The galvanometer should be protected by using a 0.5-megohm series resistor and disconnecting the condensers of the static machine.

E-37. "Electric Wind." A candle flame held near a pointed conductor connected to the *positive* terminal of a static machine is strongly repelled from the point *as if* a breeze of ions were actually issuing from the point. If the flame is held near the negative terminal, it is attracted toward it. The phenomenon is one of electrostatic repulsion and attraction rather than of any strong ion current issuing from the positive point. In the luminous part of the flame, positive ions predominate.

E-38. Electric Reaction Wheel. The "electric whirl" is another device illustrating discharge from a point. Two wires are crossed at their midpoints, and their pointed ends are bent at right angles so that they form a swastika. The device is pivoted at the crossing and connected to either terminal of a static machine. Rapid rotation is caused by reaction forces due to the repulsion of ions from the points.

E-39. "Electric Chimes." This is an old demonstration, but still effective. The action depends on attraction and repulsion of charges, involving induction. It may be understood by reference to the case of two bells supported at the same level, with a small metal clapper (ball) suspended by an insulating thread midway between them. One of the bells is connected with one knob of an electrostatic machine or a charged Leyden jar, while the other is earthed. Attraction between the charge on the first bell and that induced by it on the clapper causes the latter to strike the bell. The clapper now becomes charged with the same sign as the bell and is repelled with enough force to strike the earthed bell, to which it loses its charge. The process is repeated indefinitely, as long as the charge is maintained on the first bell.

E-40. Effect of Intervening Medium on Force between Charges. Bring a charged insulated conductor near the knob of an uncharged electroscope; the induced free charge on the leaves causes their deflection. Without touching the electroscope or moving the charged conductor, insert successively between the two, without touching either, sheets of equal thickness of glass, paraffin, shellac, hard rubber. When each of these sheets is introduced, the deflection of the electroscope leaves decreases a little, and when the sheet is removed the deflection rises to its former value.

E-41. Water Jet. This experiment involves not only induction but surface tension and adhesion. A stream of water flows from a small glass nozzle with a 2-mm orifice, inclined at 10° from

the vertical. The pressure is adjusted until the jet rises upward
2 or 3 ft and falls into the sink. The normal jet is smooth near
the orifice but becomes unstable and breaks into drops near the
top of the arc. Surface-tension forces predominate. If a
charged rod is brought toward the jet, about on a level with the
nozzle, forces of adhesion are in part counteracted by electrostatic
repulsion of like induced charges on nozzle and water, and the
charges induced on the water tend to counteract surface tension
along the jet. The form of the stream is then seen to change,
until the jet is smoothly continuous from nozzle to sink, with
apparently circular cross section at all points. If the rod is
moved still closer, the jet bends toward the rod because of electrostatic attraction between the charged rod and the induced charge
on the water. If the charged rod is brought very close to the jet,
the induced charge is increased to such an extent that the jet
breaks up into small droplets which fly away from each other and
of which some may even be drawn backward around the rod.
This dispersion of the drops is much more pronounced than in
the normal jet, because of positive repulsion due to electrostatic
charges. (See also A-120.)

E-42. Movement of Charged Material along Lines of Force.
Connect the static machine with the handle of a small metal ladle
provided with a lip, such as is used to pour Babbitt metal. Hold
the ladle by a dry wooden stick attached to its handle, and melt
in it some rosin. Hold the ladle a foot or so above a paper spread
to cover a large area on the lecture table, and keep it well
away from the clothes. Now start the static machine, with
condensers attached and spark gap set at 3 in., and slowly pour
the molten rosin from the lip. The result is somewhat spectacular. Tiny streams of electrified rosin spurt from the edge of the
lip, almost in straight lines, apparently in defiance of gravity.
They keep well apart from each other, striking the paper and
solidifying into droplets. The jets follow the field, whose lines
run quite straight out from the edge of the ladle to an appreciable
distance. Gravitational forces are small compared to electrostatic near the ladle. The jets collapse whenever a spark occurs
between the knobs of the static machine, but they stiffen again
as the charge on the ladle builds up. A synchronous pulsating
behavior can be noted in an electroscope placed in the same field
(E-52). Solidified remnants of the directed jets may be found

attached to the edge of the ladle at the conclusion of the experiment. Use shadow projection.

E-43. Movement of Charged Particles in Electric Field. Support two small metal plates horizontally on insulating stands, one about 1 cm above the other, and connect them to the terminals of a static machine. Sprinkle aluminum powder on the lower plate. When the machine is operated, the powder acquires the charge of the lower plate and is repelled to the upper plate, where the sign of its charge is reversed and it is driven downward. Thus there is a continual stream of particles in both directions, which may illustrate by analogy the conduction of electricity through a gas by ions. The motion is made visible by shadow projection.

The same effect may be shown on a larger scale. A glass bell jar with a metal terminal in the top rests on a wooden base on which is laid a metal disk. The disk and upper terminal are connected to the terminals of a static machine. When the machine is operated, metallized pith balls inside the jar rise and fall between the terminals.

E-44. Mapping Field of Force with Epsom Salt Crystals. Two disks of tin foil 1 cm in diameter are cemented to a glass plate that is set in a lantern arranged for vertical projection. A narrow strip of foil is left attached to each disk for electric contact by fine wires to the terminals of a static machine. When the machine is operated, an electric field is set up between the disks. The lines of force of this field are made "visible" by sprinkling fine epsom salt crystals on the glass plate through a wire sieve. The plate is tapped to assist in the alignment of the crystals.

E-45. Mapping Field of Force near Electrified Bodies with "Electric Doublet." Two pith balls are aluminum painted and thrust over the ends of a thin glass rod about 6 cm long. One end of a silk thread about 50 cm long is attached to the middle of the glass rod, and the other end to a short wooden rod. Two conductors on insulating supports are connected to the terminals of a static machine and charged. One of the pith balls is given a positive charge by contact with one of the conductors, and the other is given a negative charge in the same manner. If the "electric doublet" so produced is held in the region of a charged conductor or set of conductors, the doublet will point in a direction tangent to a line of force. By "fishing" in various places, the electrostatic field can be mapped.   If aluminum paint is used on one pith ball and bronze paint on the other, the positive directions of lines of force may be shown more readily.

E-46. Human Electroscope.   A student (with fine dry hair) stands on an insulating stool and takes hold of one terminal of the static machine (previously discharged to prevent shock).   When the machine is run, his hair tends to rise and extend along the lines of force of the field about his head.   This hair-raising experience is accentuated by placing a grounded metal plate horizontally above his head at a distance greater than the spark gap. Each time a spark passes, this "hair electroscope" will collapse, then rise again.   There is no danger to the student if the terminals of the spark gap are short-circuited before he takes hold.   He will have no unpleasant shocks so long as he continues to hold to the terminal, but he may experience sparks if he lets go or touches grounded objects.   It is best to cut out the condensers during this experiment.

E-47. Discharge through the Body.   Two students *A* and *B* stand on two insulated platforms, and each grasps one of the knobs of a static machine (previously short-circuited).   (If condensers are used, they should be of small capacitance.)   A third student *C* stands on the floor and so is earthed.   After the machine is started, *C* touches *A*, and a small spark passes.   He removes his hand from contact with *A* and similarly touches *B*, and another small spark passes.   Then *C* touches *A* while still in contact with *B*, and a large spark passes, since there now occurs an almost complete neutralization of the charges on the machine. The smaller sparks indicate partial discharges to earth, the rest of the charge in each case being bound by the attraction of the opposite charge on the other terminal.

E-48.   All the students in the class join hands and form a line around the sides of the lecture room.   The student at one end of the line makes contact with one knob of the static machine.   At the other end of the line, a spark gap is formed between the other knob of the machine and a metal rod held in the hand of the last student.   This student closes the gap.   All the class now feel what they previously only saw and heard, the effect of spark-gap length (between knobs of the machine) on the charge and voltage.   *Caution:* Keep the charge small by using a small condenser.   Remember that even a $\frac{1}{16}$-in. spark requires about

5000 v.   Encourage the students to grasp hands *tightly* so that sparking shall occur only at the end of the line.

E-49. Voltage Measured by Length of Spark. Connect an electrostatic voltmeter (E-4) to the ball terminals of a static machine with condensers, and note the reading just prior to the spark discharge.   Repeat a number of times, varying the spark gap.   Compare the observed value with that usually given, *viz.*, 30,000 v per cm in air at atmospheric pressure.

E-50. Discharge of a Conductor by Surrounding Gaseous Ions. A charged conductor (positive or negative) is connected with an electroscope.   When a flame (candle or lighted match) is brought near it, the deflection of the electroscope falls rapidly to zero, showing that the charge has been dissipated.   The electroscope is quickly discharged by blowing the gases of combustion from a flame upon the conductor.   A sample of radium gives the same effect (A-112), and so do x-rays (A-103).

E-51. Ions Formed in Flame. Two metal plates supported vertically on insulating stands are set parallel and 2 to 3 cm apart and are connected to the terminals of a static machine.   A candle flame is held just beneath the plates.   The hot gases rising between the plates are made visible by shadow projection (H-137). When the static machine is operated, the gases will be seen to divide into two streams as ions of opposite sign are attracted to the charged plates.

E-52. Extent of Electric Field. An unshielded electroscope is set several feet away from a static machine (with condensers) and a 2-in. spark gap.   As the machine builds up charge, the electroscope leaves rise; when a spark occurs, they fall, although not completely, as the field immediately begins to build up again. This experiment demonstrates strikingly the existence of an appreciable field at relatively large distances from the charges. (A radio receiving set with loudspeaker may be used as a sensitive detector of sudden changes of field.)

With the condensers out and the spark gap several inches long, test the signs of the charges on the knobs by charging the electroscope, held near one of the knobs, by induction.   Then discharge the knobs by contact, and note, by the absence of the deflection of the electroscope brought near them, the absence of charge.   This is a simple experiment but fundamental, since it shows that the two charges, simultaneously produced, are equal in amount and opposite in sign. (Compare E-14.)

E-53. Energy in the Discharge. The knobs of the static machine are set a few centimeters apart, and some alcohol in a spoon is held just below the gap. When a spark passes, it ignites the alcohol, directing attention to the heat in the spark and so to the potential energy stored in the charges. Gas flowing from a grounded Bunsen burner may be ignited by a spark from the charged disk of an electrophorus. Powder in a toy cannon may be exploded by passing a spark between terminals buried in the charge.

E-54. Heat Generated by Spark. A glass tube with side arm as shown in Fig. 215 is mounted vertically. Ball electrodes project through tight rubber stoppers in each end of the larger tube. Water fills the tube nearly to the level of the lower knob. When a spark from a static machine (with condensers in) is passed between the knobs, the expansion of the air drives the liquid into the side tube.

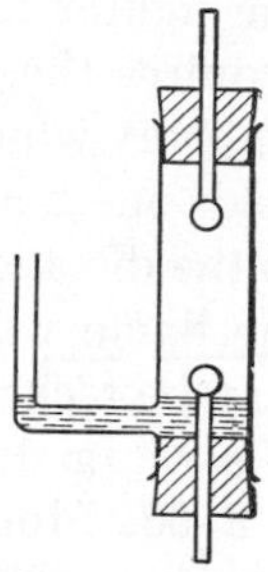

Fig. 215.— When a spark passes between the balls, the heat generated expands the air and forces the water into the side tube.

E-55. Gas Explosion by Spark. An insulated terminal or automobile spark plug is mounted in the wall of a metal vessel so that a spark may be made to pass between the terminal and the wall. The vessel is filled with an explosive mixture of hydrogen and oxygen and is corked. The terminals of the spark gap are connected to the knobs of a static machine. When a spark passes, the gases explode and blow the cork out. An explosive mixture of gasoline vapor and air may be more readily obtained (H-182).

POTENTIAL AND CAPACITANCE

E-56. Electric Potential. As an aid in teaching the idea of potential, one may charge an insulated conductor either with the static machine or with the electrophorus disk. The work done in bringing additional charge of like sign from a distance up to this conductor may be illustrated by bringing up a similarly charged pith ball hanging by a silk thread from any convenient support. As the demonstrator moves the charged pith ball toward the conductor, it is evident that work must be done against the observed repulsive force between the conductor and the pith ball.

E-57. Mapping Potential Field. Charge a large metal sphere, and suspend it by an insulating string as far as possible from other objects. Attach a small metal alcohol lamp or a cigarette lighter to the end of a long, insulating handle (preferably rubber). Run a wire from the metal lighter to one side of an electrostatic voltmeter, and ground the other side of the meter. The flame of the lighter ionizes the surrounding air, and the lighter rapidly acquires the charge necessary to bring it to the potential of the point at which it is held. By moving the lighter about in the field, one may show that the potential is inversely proportional to the distance from the center of the charged sphere. Ions from the flame will in time neutralize the charge on the sphere. It may be recharged from time to time by touching it with the knob of a charged Leyden jar.

E-58. Model of Potential Field. Stretch a sheet of rubber dam horizontally midway between the table and a glass plate set

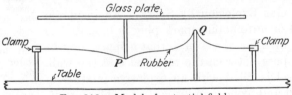

FIG. 216.—Model of potential field.

15 in. above it. The plane of the dam represents a region of uniform potential, which may be taken as zero. At some point Q (Fig. 216), push the dam up by a $\frac{1}{2}$-in. dowel rod, rounded at its upper end, to represent an increase of potential due to the presence of a "positive charge." Magnitude of charge is proportional to the length of dowel rod above the zero level of the dam. The potential diminishes on all sides, at a rate roughly proportional to Q/r. "Negative charges" may be introduced into the field by inserting dowel rods between the dam and the glass plate, as at P, thus introducing depressed regions of negative potential. Positive and negative electrical potentials are here represented by gravitational potentials, positive and negative with respect to the zero level of the dam. The potential difference between any two

points is, of course, represented by the vertical distance between them. The field strength or potential gradient at any point is represented by the *slope* of the rubber-membrane surface at that point. Gravitational equipotential ("level") surfaces intersect the dam in contour lines, which, when projected on the zero plane, represent the traces on that plane of the electrical equipotential surfaces due to coplanar charges. Combinations of rods or objects of various cross sections may be used to show the potential field about various combinations of charged conductors. The motion of charged particles in electric fields (*e.g.*, as in a triode vacuum tube) may be shown by rolling small balls or shot on such potential models (see A-83).

E-59. Potential of a Conductor during Discharge—Electroscope as Potential Indicator. A conductor on an insulating support is connected to a Braun electroscope (E-4) in the lantern field. The conductor is charged by sparks from the electrophorus disk until the electroscope vane stands out at an angle of 45° or more. When the vane has stopped oscillating, connection is made between the charged conductor and one terminal of the electric chime (E-39), the other terminal being grounded. This connection may be made by means of a wire attached to the end of a glass rod and held in contact with both the conductor and the terminal of the chime. The kinetic energy gained by the brass ball in moving from one bell to the other is dependent upon the charge imparted to the ball when in contact with the first bell, which depends upon the potential of the conductor. Since the intensity of the sound is dependent upon this kinetic energy, the gradually decreasing sound intensity shows the slow decrease in potential of the conductor during discharge.

The Braun electroscope is included in the experiment to show that the deflection of an electroscope is an indication of the potential of a conductor. While the potential of the conductor in this experiment decreases, the electroscope vane returns slowly toward its undeflected position.

E-60. Potential of Charged Sphere. A conducting sphere is supported on an insulating stand, and three small electroscopes are attached to it at points 90° apart on a horizontal plane through the center. The electroscopes consist of pairs of small pith balls, aluminum painted, hung from the sphere by *conducting* threads. When the sphere is charged, the three electroscopes show the

same deflection.   When the sphere is discharged, the deflections
vanish.   Now a second charged sphere is brought near the first,
but not touching it, with its center on the diameter connecting
two of the electroscopes.   These two will show equal deflections,
on account of the equal, though opposite, charges induced on the
first sphere.   The third electroscope, which is midway between
the other two, will show no deflection.   Nevertheless, the sphere
is a conductor and must therefore be at the same potential
throughout.   Since, however, the electroscopes obviously have
different deflections, we must conclude that there has been a
redistribution of charge on the sphere.   If an earthed metal
plate is brought up near one of the electroscopes showing a
deflection, the deflection decreases, while a similar plate brought
up to the middle (undeflected) electroscope will cause it to deflect.
Redistribution of charge on the sphere because of the presence
of the earthed plates may make the deflections of the three
electroscopes equal.

**E-61. Comparison of Charges on Spheres at Same Potential—
Capacitance.**   Two conducting spheres of diameter about 2 cm
and 4 cm respectively are equipped with pyrex rod handles.
The spheres may be made of wood or cork, aluminum painted.
They are charged to the same potential by touching them
simultaneously to a large charged conductor or to one terminal
of a charged Leyden jar.   They are then introduced separately
within a hollow conductor connected to an electroscope (E-13),
without touching the walls of the conductor.   The divergences
of the leaves of the electroscope serve to compare qualitatively
the magnitudes of the charges on the two spheres.   The larger
sphere will, of course, bear the larger charge, although the
potentials of the two spheres are equal.

E-62. Elementary   Condenser.   Charge   an   8-in.   insulated
metal sphere with several sparks from the electrophorus (E-10).
It will be noted that successively weaker sparks pass to the sphere
as charging proceeds, for the potential of the sphere rises.   Discharge the sphere to ground, and observe the character of the
spark.   Place near the sphere a conductor, such as a parabolic
reflector (H-150).   This second conductor is at first insulated.
The capacitance of the sphere has now been increased somewhat,
and many more strong sparks may be passed to it from the electrophorus.   Remove the neighboring conductor, and again dis-

charge the sphere to ground. A more intense spark is observed.
Finally, replace the neighboring conductor, but this time ground
it, and repeat the previous charging and discharging process.
The capacitance is greatly increased, and a large number of
sparks may be passed to the sphere because its potential rises
slowly with increasing charge.

E-63. Leyden-jar Condenser. A Leyden jar with outer coating grounded is charged by bringing the electrophorus disk close
enough to the knob of the jar for a spark to pass. After a number
of small charges have been given to the jar by successive applications of the electrophorus disk, the inner and outer coatings of
the jar are connected by a pair of discharge tongs, whereupon a
noisy, bright spark passes. The tongs are removed, and after
a few seconds they are again used. A second, weaker spark will
be observed, showing that the condenser coatings have acquired
a "residual charge" in the short interval between the first discharge and the second application of the tongs.

The Leyden jar may be discharged through the class as
described in E-48. Use discretion! A small charge is sufficient
to give the students a jolt.

E-64. Dissectible Leyden Jar. A Leyden jar whose inner and
outer coatings can be removed is charged, and the electrodes are
then removed from the glass. When they are brought into
contact with one another, no spark passes; but if the jar is reas-
sembled, it may be discharged in the usual manner, showing that
the energy of the charge resides in the dielectric.

E-65. Bound Charge on Leyden Jar. The two coatings of a
charged Leyden jar on an insulating stand can be grounded
alternately with only small loss of charge. This process may be
repeated a number of times, but when the two coatings are
finally connected, a vigorous spark is obtained. Thus *either*
coating of the jar may be put at ground potential (or any other
potential) without affecting the *potential difference* between the
coatings.

**E-66. Positive and Negative Charges on Dielectric—Lichten-
berg Figures.** A charged Leyden jar is held in the hand by the
outer coating, and with the knob a pattern is traced on a plate of
dielectric, such as shellac or hard rubber. The jar is then set on
an *insulating* stand, and the hand is transferred to the knob,
without discharging the jar, so that a corner of the outer coating

may be used to trace another pattern on the dielectric. The dielectric plate is then sprinkled with a mixture of litharge (red lead) and flowers of sulfur, well dried and shaken together, so that the litharge particles become charged positively by friction and the sulfur particles negatively. The litharge then adheres to the pattern traced by the negative electrode of the Leyden jar, and the sulfur to that traced by the positive electrode. The two patterns are easily distinguished by the difference in their colors as well as by their character; the yellow pattern has many branching lines, while the red appears in small circular spots. The principle of this experiment has recently been adapted to the measurement of the very high voltages of lightning.

E-67. Addition of Potentials. Connect three or four similar Leyden jars in parallel, and charge them by the static machine. Discharge them simultaneously, and note the length and intensity of the spark. Again charge them in parallel, place on individual insulating stands, and connect in series. The potential difference between the end terminals is now the sum of the potential differences of the individual jars, and a much longer but less intense spark will be obtained. This simple method of "multiplying potentials" is frequently used for obtaining high voltages from low.

E-68. Condensers in Series and Parallel. Connect four similar Leyden jars in parallel, and charge them by a static machine. Disconnect one of the four and discharge it; then discharge the other three together. Since the potential difference across each jar is the same, the difference in the "fatness" of the sparks comes from a difference in quantity of charge. Now connect the three jars in *series* and the fourth in parallel with the three, and charge as before. Disconnect the one jar, and discharge it; then discharge the three that are in series. The length of spark is the same in the two cases, but in the latter case the spark is much weaker because of reduced capacitance due to the series connection. Similar to this experiment and to E-67 is another experiment (E-262) performed with a ballistic galvanometer and condensers charged at low voltage.

E-69. Parallel-plate Condenser. A convenient demonstration condenser consists of two metal plates mounted parallel to each other on insulating supports, one of the plates being movable. An easily constructed form consists of two rectangular sheets of metal, about 12 by 20 cm, tacked to two blocks of wood resting on a sheet of glass for insulation. The sides of the two plates facing one another are coated with shellac for insulation. One condenser plate is connected to the knob of an electroscope with grounded case; the other plate is grounded. The plate connected to the electroscope is charged, and the divergence of the electroscope leaves indicates the potential difference between charged plate and ground. If the plates are brought close together, the divergence of the electroscope leaves decreases. If the distance between the plates is increased, the increased potential difference is shown by the electroscope. This experiment emphasizes the fundamental relationship among charge, potential, and capacitance, $Q = VC$. The charge upon the insulated plate is constant; the potential must therefore increase with decrease of capacitance, and vice versa.

This principle is frequently used in "potential multipliers" to detect small potential differences by electroscopes or electrometers (E-71 and 116). A convenient substitute for the parallel plates described above is a radio condenser with a set of rotating plates. One set of plates is grounded; the other set is connected to the electroscope and charged.

E-70. Dielectric Constant and Capacitance. The apparatus described in E-69 may be used to make a rough determination of the dielectric constant of an insulator. The divergence of the electroscope leaves is decreased when a sheet of insulating material is inserted between the plates (E-40). If pieces of plate glass, hard rubber, and paraffin of approximately the same thickness are used separately, with the distance between the condenser plates fixed and only a little more than the thickness of the dielectric sheets, the relative effects of the different materials may be observed. Any charge on the test sheets may be removed by passing a flame quickly over their surfaces before they are inserted between the condenser plates.

E-71. Condensing Electroscope. Small electrostatic charges may be detected by an electroscope and variable condenser. One of the plates of a parallel-plate condenser is earthed; the other plate is connected to an electroscope in the lantern field, and a sheet of mica or of paraffined paper is used as a dielectric (Fig. 217). If a charge too small to deflect the electroscope is given to the insulated plate, a deflection is produced when the upper plate is lifted from the sheet of dielectric, because of a decrease in the capacitance of the condenser. Attention is called to the fact that charges are sometimes developed on the surface of a sheet of mica by slight rotations of the disk. These charges may be removed by holding the mica momentarily over a flame.

The capacitance of the pair of plates may be greatly increased by grinding the disks together with fine emery until the ground

FIG. 217.—Condensing electroscope.

surfaces appear uniform, after which the disks are cleaned and dried. One of them is dipped in thin shellac to form an insulating layer on its ground surface. This disk is mounted on the knob of an electroscope, or on an insulating stand with a wire running from disk to electroscope. The other disk is provided with an insulating handle of sealing wax or hard rubber.

E-72. Contact Difference of Potential. To demonstrate contact potential difference one needs, in addition to the condensing electroscope (E-71), a plate of copper and one of zinc, both on insulating handles. The copper plate is earthed, and the zinc plate is laid upon it, their surfaces being close together. The potential of the zinc while in contact with the copper is of the order of 1 v above that of the copper, and a positive charge is given to the zinc. The zinc plate is then removed from contact with the copper and touched to the insulated plate of the condenser. Some of the positive charge is conveyed to the insulated condenser plate, but it does not deflect the electroscope because the amount of charge so conveyed is too small. With condenser plates about 15 cm in diameter and zinc and copper plates about 8 cm in diameter, it is necessary to repeat the operation of touching the zinc to the copper plate and to the insulated condenser plate about thirty times to make an ordinary electroscope show a distinct deflection, when the capacitance of the condenser is decreased by the removal of the grounded plate. The sign of the charge given to the electroscope should be tested to show that it is positive. The experiment may then be repeated with the zinc plate grounded and the copper plate used to charge the electroscope, in which case the charge on the electroscope is negative.

Other materials may be used to demonstrate larger contact potential differences. For example, a block of paraffin dipped

into distilled water in an insulated can and removed will be found
to have acquired a negative charge, leaving an equal positive
charge on the water.   Quartz dipped into mercury acquires a
positive charge.

E-73. Dependence of Capacitance on Area.   An insulated
hollow conductor with open top is connected to an electroscope.
A piece of brass chain about 1 m long is coiled within the hollow
conductor, one end of the chain being attached to a pyrex rod
about 50 cm long.   The conductor is charged, and the chain
slowly lifted out.   The electroscope leaves slowly collapse,
because of the decreasing potential of the conductor resulting
from an increase in its surface area, but return to their original
deflection when the chain is lowered into the conductor again.
Telescoping metal tubes may be used to
produce the same effect.

E-74. Another method is to cement one
edge of a long rectangular sheet of tin foil
to a horizontal pyrex rod supported in
notches cut in the upper ends of two
vertical pieces of wood, the lower ends of
which are attached to a wooden base.
One end of the pyrex rod is bent to form
a crank.   When the rod is rotated, the
tin foil is wound up like a curtain.   A small brass rod is cemented
to the lower edge of the tin foil, to keep the foil under slight tension, and a fine wire is attached to it to connect the sheet of foil
with an electroscope.   If the foil is charged, the divergence of the
electroscope leaves is an indication of the potential.   As the foil is
rolled up, the potential increases, showing clearly the dependence
of the capacitance on the area.   An insulated window-shade
roller may be used in place of the glass crank.

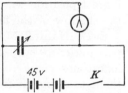

Fig. 218.—Radio tuning
condenser and electroscope
arranged to show change of
potential with change of
capacitance.

E-75. A still simpler method of changing capacitance with
change of area is with a plane-plate radio condenser with rotating
plates.   One set of plates of the condenser is connected to an
electroscope, and, when set for maximum capacitance, the condenser is charged by a 45-v B battery.   The switch K (Fig. 218)
is opened, the plates are rotated toward minimum capacitance,
and the divergence of the electroscope leaves indicates an increase
of potential.   This simple device may be applied to E-71, 116,
etc.

MAGNETISM

E-76. Indicator for Magnetic Effects. In showing magnetic experiments, it is important to have some clearly visible indicator whose function is similar to that of an electroscope in electrostatic experiments. A large compass needle swinging in a horizontal plane on a jeweled bearing serves well. Two paper flags of different color will enable students at a distance to distinguish between north and south poles of the needle. For still greater visibility, one may use a large dipping needle swinging in a vertical plane about a horizontal axis mounted in jeweled bearings. If possible, the needle should be placed to swing in an east-west plane perpendicular to the magnetic meridian so that its rest position will be horizontal. Paper flags may be used, or the shadow of the needle may be projected.

E-77. Natural Magnets. Two pieces of magnetite are held in paper stirrups suspended by threads. These natural magnets or lodestones come to rest in the magnetic meridian. If one of them is removed from its paper stirrup and brought near the other, the repulsions between like poles and the attractions between unlike poles will be evident. For large classes, the directional effects may be shown by attaching light paper arrows to the lodestones or by using the magnetic indicator (E-76). A piece of magnetite picks up small tacks. Iron filings cluster about certain regions commonly called "poles." (Shadow projection.)

E-78. Magnetization by Contact. A steel knitting needle may be magnetized by stroking it with a piece of lodestone (or any permanent magnet). This experiment is of some historic interest, since for centuries the magnetic needles of mariner's compasses were magnetized by contact with natural magnets. If the steel knitting needle is already magnetized, it may be demagnetized sufficiently for the present purpose by passing it through a solenoid connected to an a.c. line. After such a needle has been magnetized by contact with a piece of lodestone, it too will pick up tacks and iron filings.

E-79. Magnetization by Contact. To induce four poles in a knitting needle, support it horizontally with its ends resting on the north poles, say, of two similar bar magnets, and stroke it with the south pole of a third magnet, beginning at one end of the needle and lifting the magnet away from it near its center, then repeating, in the reverse direction, on the other half of the needle. The needle will then have a south pole at each end and two north poles close together at the center.

E-80. Magnetization by Mechanical Disturbance in Earth's Field. A magnet may be made by hammering a soft iron bar held parallel to the lines of force of the magnetic field of a solenoid or of the earth. A bar of permalloy is magnetized simply by holding it parallel to the earth's field, and it will change polarity upon reversal end for end. The polarity may be tested with a compass needle (E-76).

E-81. Isolated Pole. The condition of a single "isolated" pole can be approximated by passing a long bar magnet (knitting needle) through a cork and floating it vertically in water, the upper end of the needle being much nearer the cork than the lower, for stability. The lower pole is now so far from the upper that one can lead or propel the magnet about with another isolated pole (a similar needle held in the hand), approximating closely the action of two ideally isolated poles on each other.

E-82. Induced Magnetic Poles. A chain of nails or tacks may be supported from a magnet, each in turn becoming a magnet by induction. The polarity of the end of the chain may be tested with a compass needle (E-76).

E-83. Magnetization by Current. A solenoid is connected to a source of direct current. A piece of steel, initially unmagnetized, is magnetized by placing it in the solenoid. As a sample of steel, one may use a demagnetized compass needle with a pivot bearing or a steel knitting needle supported in a wire or paper stirrup by a thread. When in the demagnetized state, neither of these needles shows any distinct tendency to align itself in the earth's magnetic meridian, but after magnetization the needle becomes a magnetic compass.

E-84. Strong Permanent Magnets. Strong permanent magnets of cobalt steel may be shown, and their magnetization emphasized by using one of them to pick up a cluster of nails. Two 35 per cent cobalt-steel magnets about 6 by 6 by 35 mm are so strong that one of them may be supported in the air at a distance of 1 or 2 cm above the other by the repulsion between like poles. One magnet is attached to a wooden base; end guides for the second magnet are made of celluloid films bent into half

cylinders and held by large brass pins driven into the base.
These guides are necessary to prevent motion of the hovering
magnet in a horizontal direction, since it cannot be in stable
equilibrium under magnetic and gravitational forces alone. A
suggestion of mystery may be added, if desired, by concealing the
first magnet. (Project.)

Forces between magnets may be demonstrated with two
cylindrical cobalt-steel magnets. They are laid on the table and
rolled toward each other. If the magnetic axes agree in sense,
the magnets will be repelled as if by an elastic collision; if the
axes are opposite in sense, the magnets will be strongly attracted.
If they are held together with like poles adjacent and then
released, they will roll away from each other. If one is at rest on
the table and the other is rolled toward it, so as to repel it, the
first starts rolling away, and the second stops. Interchange of
momentum may thus take place without actual contact between
the magnets.

E-85. Which Is the Magnet? Show two similar bars of iron,
one magnetized, the other not. Ask the students how to discover
(without other equipment) which bar is magnetized. Evidently
this question cannot be answered by touching the ends of the bars
together, for they invariably show only attraction for one
another. But if the end of one bar is presented to the middle of
the other, there will be attraction when the magnetized bar
touches the middle of the unmagnetized, but not when the two
bars are interchanged.

E-86. Magnetic Balance. A permanent magnet is balanced on knife-
edge bearings. A second magnet is
placed below it, in such a position

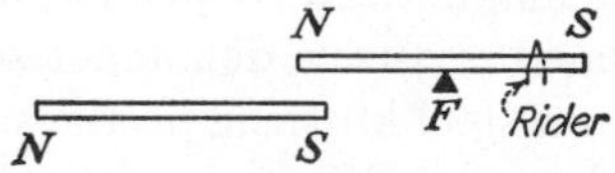

Fig. 219.—Magnetic balance.

that one pair of like poles is a few centimeters apart, while the
other pair is far enough away so that forces due to these
poles are negligible (Fig. 219). The balanced magnet is restored
to equilibrium by means of a rider. The magnitude of the force
of repulsion or attraction may be determined from the position
of the rider and its mass. By measuring the distance between
the poles, the inverse square law may be roughly verified; it
should be noted, however, that the poles are not exactly at the
ends of the steel bars.

E-87. Determination of Pole Strength from Law of Force.
Two similar steel knitting needles are magnetized equally in the
same solenoid. They are suspended by light threads about 25 cm
long from each end, so that like poles are adjacent. The magnets
hang horizontally and parallel, and the threads from the north
ends meet at a common point, as do those from the south ends.
The needles then repel each other to a distance of a few centimeters. If the masses of the needles are equal and known,
together with the length of the threads and the distance between
the magnets, then the pole strengths (assumed equal) may
be computed from the inverse square law. This experiment
may be made a connecting link between the subjects of Mechanics
and Magnetism.

E-88. Magnetic Induction. A bar of soft iron held near a
strong permanent magnet becomes a magnet by induction (F-82).
Tacks will cling to the ends of the bar as long as the permanent
magnet is near enough to magnetize it by induction, but the tacks
will fall when the permanent magnet is removed.

The inducing magnet and the piece of soft iron are held with
their axes collinear. A compass needle (E-76) shows that the end
of the soft-iron bar more distant from the inducing magnet
has a polarity of the same sign as the magnetic pole on the nearer
end of the permanent magnet. This effect may be compared
with that of electrostatic induction (E-8).

E-89. Magnetic Fields Shown by Iron or Permalloy Filings.
Strips of magnetized clock spring or other thin steel are sealed
between two glass plates, whose edges are bound with gummed
tape. The plates are placed horizontally in the field of a lantern
arranged for vertical projection. Iron filings sifted over the top
plate become magnetic by induction and when the plate is
lightly tapped they arrange themselves along the lines of force.
In this manner, the fields between like poles, unlike poles, and
that produced by induction in soft iron may be shown on the
screen. Small letters *N* and *S* of black gummed paper may be
attached to the inside surface of one of the glass plates near the
ends of the steel strips to indicate polarities.[1]

[1] Magnaflux powder is an excellent material for showing magnetic fields
in this and similar experiments. It is supplied by Magnaflux Corporation, 25 West 43d St., New York. N. Y.

E-90. Mapping Field of a Magnet. Show the lines of force in the field of a permanent horseshoe magnet by supporting two small parallel equal bars of soft iron vertically in a projection cell in which iron filings are suspended in a mixture of equal parts of glycerin and alcohol. The upper ends of the iron bars project equal distances above the liquid, and the poles of the magnet are placed against them. (Project.)

E-91. Theory of Magnetization. The molecular theory of magnetization may be illustrated by a model consisting of several short magnets free to turn about vertical axes on pivots set in a wooden base. The magnets are first arranged in random orientation. A magnetizing field is then produced by means of one or two strong cobalt-steel magnets, whereupon the short magnets align themselves with the direction of the magnetizing field.

The experiment as just described is not suitable for showing to a large class, unless the magnets are mounted on a glass plate for vertical projection. A modification of the demonstration is obtained by using several short magnetic needles in random orientation on a ground-glass plate a few inches above the poles of an electromagnet. Steel phonograph needles may be broken into two pieces, and the pieces magnetized by contact with a strong electromagnet. The images of the needles are formed on a screen by the vertical projection lantern. As current in the electromagnet windings is gradually increased, the short magnetic needles align themselves discontinuously in a manner suggestive of the alignment of elementary magnets in the Barkhausen effect (E-94).

E-92. Elementary-current Model of Magnetization. An apparatus consisting of coils carrying current, with no iron whatever, is used as a magnetization model (Fig. 220). The magnetizing field is provided by a current of from 0 to 20 amp flowing in a large solenoid. The elementary magnets are small coils of wire supported by pieces of twine. The restoring torques that produce random orientation of the coils in the absence of a field are supplied by small helical springs, which also serve as current leads. A top view of the model is possible with the aid of a 45° mirror placed above it. The model may be operated on alternating current if direct is unavailable, since reversal of current in both the large solenoid and the small coils leaves the direction of torque on the latter unchanged. This model, which depends upon the interaction of currents, is in keeping with modern theories of magnetization.[1]

E-93. Breaking a Magnet. If a slender piece of magnetized hard steel is grasped with two pairs of pliers, it may be broken into smaller pieces. The indicator needle (E-76) will show that each piece is a complete magnet and that a pair of opposite poles appears at each break. Bars of steel with transverse cuts to facilitate breaking may be purchased, or knitting needles may be hardened for this purpose and magnetized by an electromagnet prior to use.

Fig. 220. —Elementary-current model of magnetization.

E-94. Barkhausen Effect. Discontinuities in the magnetization of iron due to sudden realignment of submicroscopic groups of elementary magnets during the growth of the magnetizing field may be demonstrated by placing a soft-iron core within a solenoid having several hundred turns of fine wire. The two ends of the winding are connected to the input of an audio amplifier and loudspeaker (A-85). When a bar magnet is thrust toward the soft-iron core, the elementary magnets align themselves intermittently in the direction of the magnetizing field. As each group of magnets turns over, a feeble emf is induced in the solenoid. There results a rasping sound in the loudspeaker, which may be changed by altering the rapidity of approach of the permanent magnet. There is a difference in the sound when a hard-steel core is used in place of the soft iron. A greater effect

[1] For further details, see F. W. Warburton, *Am. Phys. Teacher,* **4,** 213, 1936.

may be obtained if both core and coil are made short so that they can be inserted between the ends of a U-shaped magnet, which may then be rotated through 180° to reverse the polarity.

E-95. Retentivity. The retentivity of soft iron may be shown by attracting to the pole pieces of an inverted U-shaped electromagnet a soft-iron bar. When the current is stopped, the bar will continue to cling to the iron core; but if the bar is pulled away, the magnetic induction in it decreases to such an extent that it will no longer be held against the pole pieces when returned to them.

E-96. "Pulling Magnet." A piece of demonstration apparatus known as a "pulling magnet" shows the force between two pieces of magnetized iron and the retentivity of iron somewhat better than the electromagnet and iron bar of E-95. The pulling magnet has a soft-iron core in the form of a split toroid with polished contact surfaces. A few turns of wire are wound around one half of the toroid. So long as current is supplied, by a single dry cell, the iron is so strongly magnetized that it is difficult or impossible for two students to pull the two halves of the toroid apart. Handles may be attached to the toroid halves to facilitate pulling. To show retentivity, the two sections are fitted together and magnetized by the current. After the current is stopped, it is still difficult to separate the halves, but once separated and replaced, no appreciable force is needed to separate them a second time. The iron may remain magnetized for months, because of the excellent fit between the two sections of the toroid, which leaves no free poles to cause a demagnetizing effect.

E-97. Influence of Area of Contact between Pieces of Magnetized Steel on Tractive Force. When two plane surfaces of magnetized iron are in contact, the force required to separate them is $F = B^2A/8\pi$, where B is the magnetic induction and A is the area of contact. Expressing B in terms of flux ϕ, the equation becomes $F = \phi^2/8\pi A$. From this equation, it is evident that the force is inversely proportional to the area of contact, provided ϕ is independent of this area. In the experiments to be described, this condition is not strictly fulfilled, but the variation of ϕ with area is small enough to enable one to show a large increase in F accompanying a *decrease* in A.

For a demonstration of the effect with a permanent magnet, one may turn a truncated cone on one end of a piece of drill rod

15 cm long and 1 cm in diameter. The diameter of the small end of the cone and its height may each be 0.5 cm. After the rod is machined and the ends lapped, it is glass hardened and permanently magnetized. The large end of such a rod will lift a 200-g piece of iron, whereas the small end will lift a 600-g piece. Another way to show these forces is to hang the magnet from a spring balance and to measure the forces necessary to separate each end of the magnet from a heavy piece of iron.

E-98. In the following demonstrations, an electromagnet (Fig. 221) is used. Its core is a piece of cold-rolled steel 40 cm long and 4.5 cm in diameter. The winding consists of 1500 turns of No. 16 wire wound on a brass form. A magnetizing current of 2.5 amp is used in this experiment and in E-99.

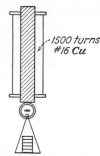

An iron ring 3.3 cm in diameter outside, 2.7 cm in diameter inside, and 0.3 cm thick is shrunk over a brass disk, in the center of which is screwed a brass hook. When the face of the disk is against the core of the electromagnet, the magnetic force between the ring and the core will support a load of 115 g. When the curved edge of the ring is in contact with the core, a load of 800 g may be supported. In this case, a string is passed through a hole drilled near one edge of the brass disk, so that the ring may be pulled away from the core without tipping.

FIG. 221.—The iron ring will support a greater load in the position shown than when placed horizontally against the magnet pole piece.

E-99. A soft-iron bar 15 cm long and 1 cm in diameter has a truncated cone turned on one end, as for the bar magnet previously described (E-97). Holes are drilled through the bar near each end for the attachment of strings by which weights may be supported. When the large end of the bar is in contact with the core of the electromagnet (E-98), the mass that can be supported is about 100 g; when the small end is in contact with the magnet, about 3400 g may be supported.

E-100. Magnetization and Hysteresis Curves for Iron by Magnetometer Method. The magnetometer provides a simple and direct means for determining the intensity of magnetization of a sample of iron or steel and its hysteresis curve without using a ballistic galvanometer. The magnetometer is a short magnetic needle suspended by a fiber of unspun silk, with a small mirror attached.   A small damping coil in series with a dry cell and a key is placed near the magnetometer; the needle can be brought to rest by timely tapping of the key.

The iron or steel sample is a rod about 1.5 cm in diameter and 40 cm long.   It is magnetized by a solenoid of 850 turns of No. 22 wire wound on a piece of fiber tubing 75 cm long.   The sample rod is placed in the center of the solenoid, which is in an east-west position and either east or west of the magnetometer.   The distance between magnetometer and center of rod is chosen so that the deflection of the spot of light reflected from the mirror will remain on the scale for the highest value of magnetization

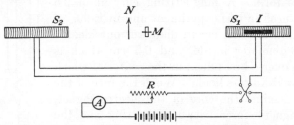

Fig. 222.—Magnetometer method for showing hysteresis of iron bar at *I*. The magnetometer *M* is midway between the magnetizing solenoid S_1 and the compensating solenoid S_2.

that is to be used.   The rod is now removed from the solenoid in order that the magnetic field produced at the magnetometer by the current in the solenoid may be compensated for, by adjusting the position of another solenoid connected in series with the first and placed in an east-west position on the opposite side of the magnetometer.   The arrangement of solenoids and circuit is shown in Fig. 222.

A rheostat and an ammeter are included in the circuit.   The demonstrator should mark those positions of the rheostat that give the various currents he expects to use, since it is not possible to decrease the magnetizing current when taking readings on the magnetization curve without introducing errors due to hysteresis.

After the sample is demagnetized (E-127), it is placed in position in the magnetizing solenoid.   The switch is closed to give the first of the chosen values of magnetizing current, and the deflection of the magnetometer needle is noted.   The rheostat is then changed to give the next value of current, and so on up to the highest value to be used. From this point, the hysteresis loop may be run by reducing the current in steps to zero, reversing its direction through the solenoids, increasing it in steps in the opposite direction to the same maximum value as before, and returning to the starting point. Since for demonstration purposes, absolute values of magnetization are unimportant, it is sufficient to plot magnetometer deflections against corresponding magnetizing currents. If small-angle deflections of the magnetometer are used, it is permissible to consider magnetization proportional to deflection; actually, the field produced by the magnetized sample is proportional to the tangent of the angle of deflection.

E-101. Hysteresis of Iron Shown by Cathode-ray Oscilloscope. A cathode-ray oscilloscope may be used to show hysteresis of the

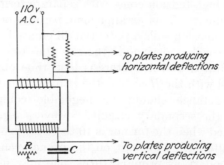

FIG. 223.—Circuit for showing hysteresis in a transformer core by cathode-ray oscilloscope.

iron in a transformer core. The connections are shown in Fig. 223. The primary of the transformer is connected in series with a rheostat from which one may pick off a potential difference proportional to the primary current and hence proportional to the magnetizing force H in the iron. This potential difference is applied to the oscilloscope plates producing horizontal deflection of the cathode-ray beam. Hence the abscissae of whatever figure is shown on the fluorescent screen will be proportional to instantaneous values of H in the iron.

The secondary of the transformer is connected to a resistor in series with a condenser. The instantaneous potential drop across the condenser should be small compared with that across the resistor. When this condition is fulfilled, the potential drop across the condenser is proportional to the instantaneous value of B. Hence if the oscilloscope plates producing vertical deflections are connected to the terminals of the condenser, the ordinates of the figure on the fluorescent screen of the tube will be proportional to B. This figure is the Lissajous figure resulting from the combination of two shm's at right angles to each other and differing in phase by either 0 or 180°, depending upon the accidental choice of polarity in connecting one of the two pairs of plates. The phases should be the same to give the hysteresis loop as it is usually plotted. If the phases are not the same, the resultant figure will be a mirror image of the customary loop. By reversing the connections to one of the two pairs of plates, the desired orientation of the loop may be obtained.

A small demonstration transformer that has two low-tension coils and two high-tension coils, with separate terminals for each coil, is convenient. This arrangement permits one to apply to one of the low-tension coils a potential difference larger than that for which the coil is designed; thereby the iron may be magnetically saturated and a hysteresis loop thus obtained that is nearly parallel with the H-axis at the two ends of the loop. The capacitive reactance should be negligible compared to the resistance in the secondary circuit; however, a good hysteresis loop is obtained when the former is 10 to 15 per cent of the latter. With 110-v alternating current on the primary and about twice as many secondary as primary turns, one may use about 1000 ohms for R and about 20 μf for C. A fair hysteresis loop is obtained with only 10 μf.

E-102. Paramagnetism and Diamagnetism. Many substances are sufficiently affected by a strong magnetic field to show a tendency to set themselves either parallel or perpendicular to it. Samples in the form of small cylinders are hung between the pole pieces of a magnet by suspension threads that are free from twist. For all except the ferromagnetic materials, the forces are so small that it is necessary to have a moderately strong and nonuniform magnetic field. A U-shaped electromagnet with an iron core, 2.5 cm in diameter and 40 cm long, magnetized by about 15,000 ampere turns and provided with pole pieces 2 cm apart, will supply a sufficiently strong field; and if one of the pole pieces is flat while the other is pointed, the field will be sufficiently nonuniform. For showing the experiment to a large class, the vertical projection lantern may be used to form on the screen images of the pole pieces and of the suspended sample of material. A cylinder of nickel aligns itself parallel to the direction of the field. So does a cylinder of aluminum, though the force on it is much weaker. Diamagnetic substances, such as bismuth and glass, will set themselves across the field. The paramagnetic property of a solution of ferric chloride may be shown by suspending in the field a short sealed glass tube containing the liquid. The tube thus suspended takes a position parallel to the field, although an empty glass tube takes the perpendicular position. Liquid oxygen is paramagnetic (H-111). One should be careful to distinguish between true paramagnetic and diamagnetic effects and effects due to eddy currents. Samples of copper or aluminum placed in a *changing* magnetic field show pronounced deflection due to electromagnetic induction.

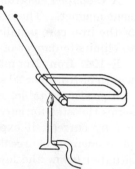

E-103. Effect of Temperature on Magnetic Properties of Nickel. A 3-mm nickel rod slightly longer than the distance between the ends of a strong U-shaped magnet is suspended from a horizontal support in a horizontal position like a pendulum by means of two

Fig. 224.—The nickel rod is attracted to the magnet when cool but falls away when heated.

asbestos strings or fine copper wires (Fig. 224). The rod, when cool, is attracted by the magnet and thus displaced from its lowest position. A Bunsen flame is placed near the magnet and in such a position that the nickel rod becomes heated while it is held aside by the magnet. When heated, the nickel loses its paramagnetic properties, and the magnet no longer holds the rod. The rod therefore breaks away from the magnet and leaves the Bunsen flame. Upon cooling, the permeability of the rod increases, the magnet attracts the rod to its first position, and the cycle is repeated.

It is helpful to have a glass cylinder or a sheet of metal in such a position that the rod will swing against it when it breaks away from the magnet. This makes an audible event in each cycle, and limits the amplitude of swing. It is necessary to protect the magnet against excessive heating.   The ends of the nickel rod should be wound with asbestos, and the poles of the magnet may be protected by using the same material.   The asbestos not only protects the magnet, but it also secures a more frequent repetition of the cycle since it prevents the nickel from making contact with the ends of the magnet, thus making it easier for the rod to break away.   A still better precaution against over-heating is to put the magnet in a shallow aluminum pan containing enough water to cover it.   This furnishes perfect protection against overheating, and at the same time demonstrates that magnetic fields are not screened by aluminum.

A U-shaped electromagnet may be used in place of the permanent magnet.   The field produced by it is stronger, and the ends of the iron core usually project far enough beyond the windings to eliminate danger of damage from heat.

E-104. Iron Nonmagnetic at High Temperature.   Hang a length of No. 16 or 20 soft-iron wire from two rods at opposite ends of the lecture table, connecting it to a 110-v d.c. source with series rheostat for current control.   When the wire is heated red hot by current, it expands and sags, showing, incidentally, the phenomenon of recalescence (H-9).   If an electromagnet is situated below the lowest point of the wire and slightly to one side, the wire will be drawn aside when magnetic, and its motion can be seen in a mirror set at 45° above the wire.   Thus it is possible to show the restoration of magnetic properties as the wire cools through the critical temperature at which recalescence occurs.   This temperature varies somewhat for different samples of iron but lies between 690 and 870°C.

E-105. Magnetic Screening.   A collection of nails or of iron screws is placed in a shallow crystallizing dish on a box high enough above the lecture table for good visibility.   Just over the nails there is a horizontal sheet of glass, then a space of about 1 cm, then another sheet of glass, and finally the poles of an electromagnet in contact with the second sheet of glass.   The current in the magnet is adjusted to draw the nails against the first sheet of glass.   If a sheet of iron is now inserted in the space between the two sheets of glass, the magnetic field will be screened, and the nails will drop.   Magnetic screening cannot be made so complete as electrostatic screening; however, a sheet of iron about 3 mm thick will screen effectively enough for the present purpose.   The second sheet of glass is used to facilitate the removal of the iron sheet while the magnet is energized. Except for this purpose, it may be dispensed with. The demonstrator may use sheets of various substances such as brass or fiber, to show that effective screening is exclusively a property of iron.

E-106. By the attraction of a magnet placed above it, hold in mid-air a nail anchored to the table top with a string. When slabs of nonferromagnetic material are placed between nail and magnet, no change in the supporting force is apparent. When, however, a sheet of iron is interposed, the nail falls.

E-107. Magnetic Screening. Suspend a soft-iron bar or rod horizontally by two long threads. A long pointer is attached to the bar. Near one end of the bar and in line with it is placed a bar magnet close enough to displace the soft-iron bar from its equilibrium position. If now a sheet of iron is inserted between the two, the force of attraction is diminished, and the motion of the bar is made evident by the motion of the pointer across a scale. An optical lever may be used if preferred.

E-108. Shunting Magnetic Flux. Pick up a $\frac{1}{2}$-in. steel ball on the end of a strong bar magnet. Then lay a nonmagnetized bar of soft iron against the bar magnet, and slide it toward the suspended ball. As the end of the soft-iron bar approaches the ball, the ball drops off, since much of the magnetic flux is now shunted through the bar to the other pole of the magnet. A bar of permalloy serves admirably for "by-passing" the magnetic flux. Show, by turning the bar end for end, that the effect is independent of its direction.

E-109. Magnetostriction. The length of a rod of nickel or steel changes slightly when the rod is magnetized. Although the change is only of the order of 1 part in 500,000, it is, nevertheless, quite easy to demonstrate this minute effect to a large class. A rod of nickel about 6 mm in diameter and 20 cm long is placed within a short solenoid so that one end of the rod is in contact with a wooden plug inserted into the end of the solenoid. The other end of the rod extends a short distance beyond the open end of the solenoid and touches a brass rod that acts as a lever to magnify the change in length of the nickel rod (Fig. 225). A nail is passed through a hole in the lever and driven into a block of wood to serve as fulcrum. The lever may be 4 mm in diameter and 50 cm long, with the short arm 2 cm. A thread attached to the end of the long arm is wrapped once around a spindle free to rotate and is kept taut by a small weight. With a spindle of diameter about 2 mm, its rotation may be about 1° when the solenoid is energized. This rotation is best made visible by reflection of a beam of light from a small mirror attached to the spindle.

Nickel decreases in length when magnetized. The cobalt steel developed during the past few years for permanent magnets of high magnetization intensity shows a relatively large magneto-striction effect. This material increases in length when magnet-ized. A rod of 35 per cent cobalt steel about 20 cm long, when used in the arrangement just described, will lengthen enough to rotate the mirror on the spindle about 2°. When demonstrating an increase in length, it is neces-

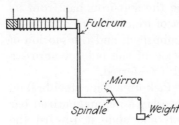

FIG. 225.—Arrangement for showing magnetostriction.

sary to show that the effect is not due to heating by the solenoid current. Heating may be reduced by wrapping the rod in paper. The fact that change in length resulting from magnetization is immediate shows that it is not caused by heating.

If alternating current is used in the solenoid, the spot of light becomes a line as the alternate expansion and contraction of the rod cause it to move in periodic motion on the wall. This also shows that the effect cannot be due to heating. If desired, a rotating mirror may be used to spread the light path into a sine curve (S-76).

E-110. Magnetic Heat Motor. A piece of magnetic alloy (70 per cent Fe, 30 per cent Ni) in the form of a thin strip is wrapped around the rim of a wheel. The wheel must be well balanced, and its bearings must have very little friction. The rim is placed between the poles of a 17 per cent cobalt-steel U-magnet with pieces of soft iron on the ends of the U to make the air gap just wide enough to allow the passage of the wheel rim. An automo-bile headlight lamp with a reflector is arranged to heat by radia-tion the portion of the metal strip just above the magnet. The permeability of this portion of the strip is reduced by rise in temperature, and the unheated portion of the strip is therefore drawn into the gap between the poles. The heating action continues, and the wheel slowly rotates. The effect will be enhanced if the heat from a small carbon arc is focused on the tape just above the air gap. The wheel must turn very freely, and the magnetic field must be strong, with a steep gradient of field intensity. For a museum exhibit, a further element of mystery may be introduced by concealing the source of radiation behind infrared filters.[1]

E-111. Terrestrial Magnetism. The alignment of a compass needle in the magnetic meridian is easily shown (E-76). To show approximately the declination at any location on the lecture table, a true north-south line should be established and made permanent by marks on two walls of the room. Such a line may be established from a large-scale map that gives the orientation of the building or a street near it; or the line may be established from the shadow cast by the edge of a window at local apparent noon, which can be determined from the longitude of the place and the equation of time as given in a nautical almanac. Draw a chalk line on the lecture table or stretch a piece of light cotton cord across it in the true north-south direction. With the compass needle just over the chalk line or just under the cord, the declination on the lecture table may be determined accurately by using a protractor, and the magnetic meridian may be marked on the table.

The inclination is read directly from the dip-needle apparatus. It may be noted that the direction of the earth's field at a point on the lecture desk is likely to differ from that given by the tables for the place in question, on account of the presence of iron gas and water pipes, radiators, etc.[2] The vertical and horizontal components of the earth's field may be determined with the earth-inductor (E-222).

E-112. Magnetic Induction in Earth's Field. A 1-m length of $\frac{1}{2}$-in. water pipe, held parallel to the lines of force of the earth's field and struck with a hammer, becomes magnetized by induction (E-80), as can be shown by presenting its ends to a compass needle; in the northern hemisphere, the lower end of the pipe repels the north end of the needle. When the pipe is turned end

---

[1] MILLS, J., *Am. Phys. Teacher*, **5**, 40, 1937.

[2] Maps showing the magnetic elements, declination, dip, and horizontal intensity over the surface of the earth may be purchased from the Hydrographic Office, U. S. Navy Department, Washington, D. C.

for end, it retains its polarity until it is struck again, whereupon the polarity reverses.   If the iron has an objectionable amount of permanent magnetization, it may be demagnetized and made magnetically soft by bringing the whole pipe to a dull red heat and allowing it to cool slowly.

A permalloy rod shows induced magnetization in the earth's field much more strongly than iron.   This material has a high permeability in weak fields.   The lower end of the rod always repels the north end of a compass needle provided that it is not held so close to the needle that the latter, rather than the earth's field, controls the rod's magnetization.   A permalloy rod will pick up pieces of permalloy ribbon when the rod is parallel to the earth's field and will drop them when it is turned perpendicular to the earth's field.

CURRENT ELECTRICITY

It is important to give the student a clear idea of the close connection between static and current electricity so that he does not regard them as independent.   For that reason, a number of experiments have been included to enable the instructor to show clearly the relationship between the two subjects.

E-113. Potential Drop along a Conductor with Current from a Static Machine.   One end of a stick of wood about 2 cm square and 3 m long is held in an earthed metal clamp; the other end is suspended above the lecture table by a cord.   A metal clamp is attached to the insulated end, and a wire connects the clamp with one terminal of a static machine, the other terminal of the machine being grounded.   An electroscope serves as an indicator of potential at various points on the stick between the ground connection, where the potential is zero, and the insulated end, where the potential is a maximum.   The electroscope case must be grounded.

If several electroscopes are at hand, the simplest method is to twist four or five wires tightly around the stick, spacing them uniformly between the two ends.   An electroscope is then connected to each of these wires.   A few turns of the static machine will supply the necessary potential.   The electroscopes announce the arrival of charge at the points on the conductor to which they are connected.   The greater time needed for flow of charge to the more distant points is clearly shown.   If the static machine has its terminals connected to the condensers usually mounted on the base of the machine, then enough charge will be stored during a few turns of the plates to bring the current in the stick to a steady value and to maintain that value for a considerable time. The various electroscopes then indicate the potentials of the uniformly spaced wires, while the potential drop along the conductor is clearly demonstrated.

If the experiment is shown to a large class, a projection electroscope should be used. One method of procedure is to wrap strips of tin foil about 5 cm wide around the wood at the points where potentials are to be indicated. These strips are tied on by thread or fine wire, and a piece of coarser wire is twisted tightly around each strip near its center. The electroscope is connected to one of the wires to show the time required for the potential to reach a steady value. After the steady value is reached, the electroscope may be connected to each wire in turn, starting at the end joined to the static machine, to show the potential drop along the stick. The tin-foil strips are needed to furnish the necessary contact and to accumulate enough charge so that the deflection in the electroscope is not dependent upon the time during which the contact is made. The wire leading to the electroscope should be attached to an insulating handle to avoid discharging the tin-foil strips.

There is another method of performing this demonstration. Tin-foil strips and wires around the stick are not used, but the fine wire leading from the electroscope is attached to a metallic conductor with an insulating handle. The discharge tongs commonly used with Leyden jars are suitable. The demonstrator moves the conductor along close to the wooden stick, keeping it as nearly as possible at a uniform distance from the stick. The charge induced on the electroscope is then proportional to the potential of the region of the stick just opposite the conductor. The advantage of this method is that the continuously varying potential is shown. The disadvantage lies in the difficulty of keeping the electroscope lead wire away from the top of the lecture table.

With any of the three procedures described, it is well to show that all points on the stick come to the same potential when there is no current, as is the case when both ends are insulated. It is also desirable to show that any two points come to the same potential when they are connected by a wire. A Zeleny electro-scope used as a current indicator shows the effect of putting two sticks in series, then in parallel.

E-114. Water Analogue of Current and Potential. The filled reservoir *J* (Fig. 226), corresponding to a charged Leyden jar or other condenser, has leading from it as a conductor a 1-mm capillary tube *C*, placed horizontally. A pivoted spoon *S* fills periodically with water, dumps, and repeats, corresponding to the needle of the Zeleny electroscope. The rate of water flow (current) is proportional to the pressure head in the reservoir (potential difference in condenser). A pressure drop exists along the line, as indicated by the gauge *G* (voltmeter or electroscope), which should be of at least 5-mm bore to avoid capillary effects.

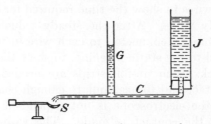

Fig. 226.—Water analogue of current and potential.

The rate of flow is affected by the length of the conducting tube and the cross section of its bore. Stopping the flow stops the current and brings the pressure to the same value at all points along the conductor, as indicated by the equality of levels in *G* and *J* (all points at the same potential). While the water analogue holds in many respects, too much must not be expected from it.

E-115. Electric Charges from Dry Cells. An electroscope may be charged by a number of 45-v B batteries in series. By chang-ing the number of batteries, the additive nature of potential may be shown. Use a protective high resistance in series with the batteries to limit current in case of short circuit.

E-116. Identification of Charge from Dry Cells. The upper plate of a condensing electroscope is earthed and also connected to one terminal of several dry cells in series. The lower plate is touched momentarily by the other terminal of the dry cells. The condenser is thus charged, but no deflection of the electroscope is observed, since the potential supplied by the dry battery is much too small.   However, as the capacitance of the condenser is decreased by the removal of the upper plate, the potential of the insulated plate increases, and the electroscope leaves show a deflection.   The sign of charge on the insulated plate should be determined by bringing a charged glass or rubber rod near the electroscope (E-24).   In this way, the demonstrator may prove the charge obtained from the carbon terminal of a dry cell to have the same sign as the charge on glass that has been rubbed with silk, which is, by definition, positive.

The condensing electroscope used in this experiment may be of the horizontal-plate type (E-71), the vertical-plate type (E-69), or the multiple-plate radio-condenser type (E-75).

E-117. Electrostatic Motor.   A relatively large static machine is connected to a smaller one.   When the larger machine is turned, the energy is sufficient to operate the smaller one as a motor.   The drive belt should be removed from the smaller machine to reduce friction.   A similar experiment may be performed with a single machine and a battery of about four Leyden jars connected in parallel.   The machine is first turned to charge the condensers.   The drive belt is then removed, whereupon the machine stops and then reverses its direction of rotation because the stored energy is being given back.   (The experiment with one machine used to turn another is analogous to that of a generator operating a motor, while the experiment with a single machine and battery of Leyden jars is analogous to that of a generator used for charging a storage battery, the battery subsequently being used to operate the generator as a motor.)

E-118. Heating Effect of Current from a Static Machine.   A piece of wood about 1 cm² in cross section and 20 cm long has several turns of copper wire wrapped tightly around each end. The wire should be tight enough to press firmly into the wood. As a preliminary test, the terminals should be connected to the static machine with a microammeter or galvanometer in the circuit, one terminal of the instrument being earthed.   This is to make sure that at least half a watt will be dissipated in heat.   The potential drop may be estimated from the sparking distance between the terminals of the machine (30,000 v per cm).   It is likely that the resistance of the wood will be too high to develop the necessary amount of heat.   In this case, one may decrease the length of the stick or soak the wood in a salt solution, afterward drying it. If the latter is done, enough moisture will remain in the wood to increase its conductivity far above the former value.

After adjusting the resistance of the wood to a value that will ensure maximum heating with the particular static machine available, the stick is placed within a glass tube not much larger than the wood. Both ends of the tube are closed by tight stoppers through which pass the ends of the stick (Fig. 227). An arm of a U-shaped water manometer is inserted through one stopper. For a small class, the water may be colored to improve visibility; for a large class, the U-tube should be projected.

FIG. 227.—Current from the static machine heats the wood, and the resulting expansion of the air in the tube is shown by motion of the liquid in the manometer.

Provided that the power is half a watt or more, there is no difficulty in showing the heating effect accompanying the operation of the static machine by the rise of water in the open column of the U-tube. It is essential that there be no leaks. The stoppers may be sealed with sealing wax if necessary to prevent the escape of air.

E-119. Electric Currents from Voltaic Cells. Exhibit a few types of voltaic cell, and show the heating and magnetic effects of currents obtained with these cells. The current from a few voltaic cells in series is sufficient to bring a short loop of iron or nichrome wire to the temperature of incandescence. Show the magnetic field near a conductor by holding over a compass needle (E-121) a straight copper wire connected to the terminals of a single cell.

E-120. Elementary Storage Cell. Connect two lead plates in a glass jar containing 30 per cent sulfuric acid to the middle terminals of a d.p.d.t. switch. Connect two of the other terminals of the switch to two or three dry cells in series for charging the storage cell. Connect the two remaining terminals of the switch to a 1.5-v flashlight bulb. After the lead cell has been charged by the dry cells for a few minutes, the switch is thrown over to connect the cell to the flashlight bulb. A center-zero ammeter shows that the direction of current during charge is opposite to that during discharge.

E-121. Oersted's Experiment. A straight wire is stretched horizontally in the magnetic meridian just above a pivoted compass needle (E-76). When there is current in the wire from several dry cells in series or from a storage cell, the compass needle turns, in a direction that depends upon the direction of the current through the wire, and through an angle that depends upon the current strength. This simple experiment may be made the basis for discussion of the rules of direction of magnetic field with respect to direction of (conventional) current.

It is of interest to show that similar magnetic effects are produced whether the current be in a metallic conductor, in a long tube containing an electrolyte, or in a gaseous discharge tube. Direct current must, of course, be used. All three types of conductor may be connected in series to insure equality of current.

E-122. Magnetic Field Due to Current in a Long Straight Conductor. A simple method of demonstrating the circular field due to current in a long straight conductor is to stretch a long wire vertically above the lecture table. A heavy copper wire may pass through a hole in the table, or it may pass close to the edge of the table. The current needed is 50 amp or more. Such a large current may be supplied by an Edison battery without damage to the battery, or it may be provided (with some risk of damage) by a 6-v lead storage battery. A compass needle with paper flags may be used to show the direction of lines of force due to the current and to show that the magnetic field is concentric with the conductor. A dipping needle may be used to explore the field about a long horizontal conductor. In either case, the needle indicates a field that is the resultant of the field produced by the current and one component of the earth's magnetic field.

E-123. Magnetic Field about Various Conductors. Three glass plates arranged for vertical projection are convenient for showing magnetic fields about current-carrying conductors. In the first, a vertical wire passes through a hole in the glass plate. Since the lantern lenses limit the length of the vertical portion, the direction of the conductor must change not far below and above the glass plate. The magnetic fields produced by current in the connecting wires will distort to some extent the circular field due to current in the vertical wire. The magnitude of this disturbing effect is reduced by running the two lead-in wires parallel.   Several turns of wire may be used to reduce the current required.

In the second, two parallel wires are arranged with connecting wires extended on opposite sides of the glass plate.   They may be used to show the field surrounding two parallel conductors carrying current either in the same or in opposite directions.

In the third, several turns of wire are passed through two holes in the glass plate to form a coil whose plane is perpendicular to the plate while its center lies in the plane of the glass.   With it, the field surrounding a circular coil carrying current may be shown.

To show the direction of field at several points, one may use a number of small compass needles.   Small compasses about 1 cm in diameter are available but cannot be used for projection without modification because the cases in which the pivots are mounted have opaque bottoms.   However, the needles and their pivots may be removed from the cases for mounting on microscope slides.   A few of these needles arranged on a circle with the wire or coil at the center show the circular character of the field about such a conductor.

Finally, fine iron filings may be sifted on the glass plate and the plate tapped to facilitate orientation of the filings.   Greater current is required in this case.

E-124. Magnetic Field Produced by Current in a Circular Coil—Tangent Galvanometer.   The field at the center of a circular coil has an important application to the definition of the unit of current strength.   A large circular coil placed in the plane of the magnetic meridian is used, and a compass needle with a paper flag is placed at the center of the coil.   The current in the coil is proportional to the tangent of the angle through which the needle is deflected.   A rheostat should be used for varying the current, and it may be well to have a shunt in the circuit, to which the terminals of the lecture galvanometer or an ammeter may be connected.   This experiment establishes a connection between current strength and the horizontal component of the earth's field.   It also introduces the lecture (d'Arsonval) galvanometer as a current-measuring instrument, which may be calibrated in terms of the tangent galvanometer.

E-125. Field Produced by Current in a Solenoid.   To show that a solenoid is magnetically much like a bar magnet, two layers of wire are wound on a mailing tube. Beginning at a point about 5 mm from the center, the winding proceeds to the nearer end of the mailing tube; then it extends to the other end of the tube, whence it returns to a point about 5 mm from the center of the tube and 1 cm from the beginning of the winding. Lengths of wire are left at the beginning and end of the winding, to serve both as current leads and as a bifilar suspension by which the solenoid may be hung horizontally. When current is established, the solenoid turns into the magnetic meridian. A reversing switch should be included in the circuit. A compass needle demonstrates the polarity of the solenoid, and a bar magnet shows that forces are exerted on a solenoid by a magnet. The insertion of an iron core in the suspended solenoid makes its magnetic effects much more pronounced.

E-126. Electromagnet. An ironclad electromagnet, whose energizing coil is surrounded by iron, may be shown as a model of the large commercial lifting types. It is impressive to lift a large weight by using a few dry cells as source of current. With current from a single dry cell, through some 25 turns of wire, the magnet is able to support a load of over 200 lb.

E-127. Magnetization and Demagnetization. With direct current, magnetize a steel rod inside a coil. Then with alternating current, demagnetize the same rod in the same coil, starting the current at a value approximating that of the direct current and reducing it to zero by a potential divider.

FIG. 228.—Circuit for magnetization and demagnetization of iron specimens.

Iron filings may be used as a detector of magnetization. A d.p.d.t. switch permits rapid change from direct to alternating current (Fig. 228).

E-128. Force on Core of Solenoid. A large solenoid capable of carrying a heavy current, such as one of the coils of an electromagnet, is laid horizontally on the lecture table and connected to a d.c. source through a switch. One end of an iron or steel rod, such as a laboratory support rod, is inserted in the solenoid. When the switch is closed, the rod is violently drawn into the coil, as if by suction, and may oscillate several times before coming to rest. This shows that magnetic material tends to move into the part of a magnetic field that is most intense. If the demonstrator is quick enough, he may be able to open the switch just as the rod reaches the center of the solenoid, so that its momentum throws it out the other end.

E-129. Magnetic Field Due to Current through Coil. A cylindrical projection cell is made by cementing flat glass plates to the ends of a short piece of large-diameter glass tubing, in which a lateral hole has been made.   The cell is filled with a half-and-half solution of glycerin and alcohol in which iron filings are suspended by thorough shaking.   The cell is wound with a helix of several layers of wire.   A beam of light is passed longitudinally through the cell.   When direct current is sent through the coil, the iron filings orient themselves parallel to the field and at right angles to the plane of the coil, thus permitting more light to pass to the screen.   The same cell may be placed between the poles of a strong electromagnet to show the form of magnetic field produced (E-89).

E-130. Resultant of Uniform and Circular Magnetic Fields. On either side of the vertical wire used in E-123, place soft-iron

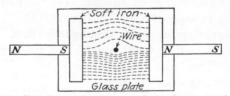

Fig. 229.—Resultant of uniform and circular magnetic fields.

bars backed with strong permanent magnets to produce a uniform field (Fig. 229).   Show the resultant of this field and that due to current in the wire by sprinkling iron filings on the glass plate.

FORCES ON CONDUCTORS IN MAGNETIC FIELDS

E-131. Force on Conductor Carrying Current Perpendicular to Magnetic Field.   A narrow strip of lead foil hangs vertically between the poles of a U-shaped permanent magnet.   (A length of Christmas-tree decoration with its ends attached to slender brass rods makes a good conductor for this purpose.   It is flexible and easily seen by a class of average size.)   The foil should be slack in order that it may move several centimeters at the moment when current starts.   A few dry cells connected in series with it and to a reversing switch will supply sufficient current to show the force on the conductor.

E-132. Two glass U-tubes filled with mercury are connected by an inverted U-shaped segment of large-diameter aluminum wire (Fig. 230). This wire is set between the poles of an electromagnet perpendicular to the strong magnetic field. When a storage battery is short-circuited through the aluminum wire, the wire hits the ceiling.

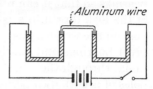

FIG. 230.—The aluminum wire is situated transversely in a strong magnetic field, so that a heavy current throws it violently upward.

E-133. Electromagnetic Swing—Ampère's Experiment. A U-shaped wire is supported by mercury cups or wire loops as shown in Fig. 231. One pole of a vertical bar magnet is placed just below it. When a current passes through the wire, it is moved to one side. By proper timing of current impulses, a pendulum motion is built up.

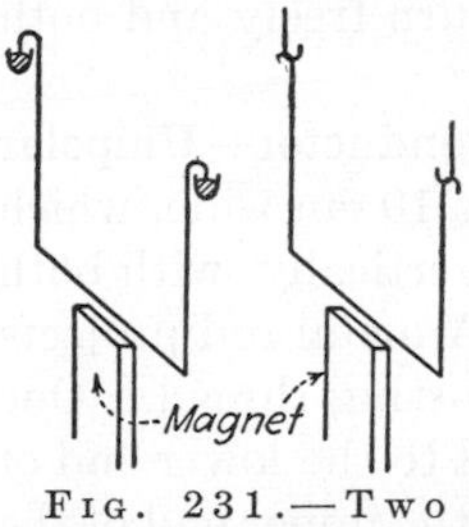

FIG. 231.—Two methods of supporting a wire for Ampère's experiment.

E-134. Magnetic Grapevine. Suspend a very flexible wire alongside a vertical bar magnet. When there is current in the wire, it wraps itself around the magnet. Reversing the current unwinds the wire and makes it wrap in the opposite direction. Braided Christmas-tree tinsel is suitable.

E-135. Rolling Rod in Field of Magnet. An electromagnet or a strong bar magnet is arranged to produce a vertical magnetic field. Two parallel brass rods are supported horizontally (Fig. 232), one on each side of the poles of the magnet, so as to form a track. A third brass rod laid across the track is free to roll along it between the poles of the magnet. A battery is connected through a reversing switch to the parallel rods. The

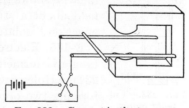

FIG. 232.—Current in the transverse rod causes it to move across the magnetic field.

current in the rolling rod is thus perpendicular to the field, and the rod will roll under the action of a force parallel to the track.

As the direction of the current is periodically reversed, the rod rolls back and forth along the track.

E-136. Barlow's Wheel. A copper disk is mounted on pivot bearings so that it can rotate in a vertical plane. The lower edge of the disk dips into a pool of mercury connected to one binding post on the wooden base, and connection is also made between the pivot bearings and another binding post, so that current will be radial through the wheel. The disk is free to rotate between the poles of a U-shaped permanent magnet placed so that the current is approximately perpendicular to the direction of the magnetic field. Current is supplied by a few storage cells connected through a reversing switch. The interaction of magnetic field and current causes a slow rotation of the disk. By tracing the direction of the current along the radius of the disk and by knowing the direction of the magnetic field, one may verify the motor rule. For successful results, the disk must turn freely and both disk and mercury must be clean.

E-137. Force on Magnet in Field of Conductor—Unipolar Motor. Suspend from a thread a light frame 10 cm wide, which holds two long, magnetized knitting needles vertically, with both south poles directed downward (Fig. 233). A metal rod projects upward from the table in line with the supporting thread. One terminal of a 6-v storage battery is connected to the lower end of the rod; the other terminal is connected with the upper end of the rod by a flexible wire held in the hand, so that the contact may be broken and the wire drawn aside to permit passage of each needle as it comes around. By proper timing of current impulses, the

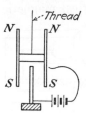

FIG. 233.—Unipolar motor.

needles are set into rotation. This experiment likewise shows the circular nature of the magnetic field about a straight conductor (E-123) and its effect on "isolated poles."

E-138. Electromagnetic Balance. An open rectangle is formed of heavy aluminum wire (Fig. 234). Holes are drilled part way into the wires forming two opposite sides of the rectangle, and the wire frame is balanced in a horizontal plane on pivots fitting into these holes, the two standards being conductive. The wire may be bent slightly at points over the pivots in order that the frame may be in stable equilibrium. The free ends of the wire are not in contact.

The side of the rectangle opposite the free ends is in the horizontal magnetic field of a U-shaped permanent magnet or an electromagnet. A battery is connected through a reversing switch to the two pivots. Current through that part of the rectangle that is perpendicular to the field will disturb the balance of the frame.

E-139. Vibrating Lamp Filament. A long tubular lamp with a straight filament carrying an alternating current is held between the poles of a strong U-shaped magnet. The filament will vibrate with sufficient amplitude to show an apparent widening. For a large class, a magnified image of the filament may be formed on a screen by means of a lens or a concave mirror. The shadow of the magnet may also be seen on the screen, but enough of the filament extends beyond the magnet to show vibration satisfactorily.

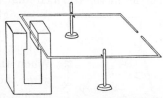

Fig. 234.—Electromagnetic balance.

E-140. Vibration of Wire Tuned to Alternating-current Frequency. A brass sonometer wire (S-131) is stretched horizontally and tuned to resonance with the a.c. frequency. A strong U-shaped permanent magnet or an electromagnet is placed near one end of the wire so that its field is perpendicular to the wire. When there is an alternating current in the wire, the wire will vibrate, and by adjusting either the tension on the wire or its length, the tuning may be improved. The motion of the wire may be shown by stroboscopic illumination (S-49). A long wire may be used, and the current in it may be increased to the point where the wire glows red at its nodal points (S-37).

E-141. Electromagnetic Circuit Breaker. A straight vertical copper wire about 25 cm long hangs so that it may swing like a pendulum. The upper end of the wire may be soldered perpendicularly to a slender finishing nail, the two ends of which rest in grooves in wooden supports. The lower end of the vertical wire dips into a small pool of mercury. A U-shaped magnet is placed near the lower end of the wire in such a position that the magnetic field between its poles is approximately perpendicular to the wire. One terminal of a storage battery makes contact with the supporting nail through a flexible lead; the other makes contact with the pool of mercury. When current is sent through the wire, the electromagnetic force causes it to swing away from the pool of mercury, thus breaking contact. It will then swing back, and the cycle will be repeated.

E-142. Elementary Motor. A vertical solenoid or a bar magnet carries at the top a circular trough containing mercury (Fig. 235).

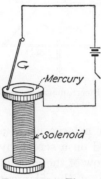

FIG. 235.—Elementary motor.

A straight copper wire is suspended loosely from a point on the axis of the magnetic field so that its lower end dips into the mercury. When there is current in the oblique copper wire, the wire rotates in the trough, like a conical pendulum.

E-143. Torque on a Coil. A wire frame, in the shape either of a rectangle or of a circle, is mounted on bearings so as to be free to rotate about a vertical axis. (This apparatus is sometimes called Ampère's frame.) A magnetic field may be supplied by two strong bar magnets held by wooden clamps in such a manner that the field in the space occupied by the wire frame shall be as strong as possible.

The torque on the coil is demonstrated by connecting it to a few storage cells, preferably through a reversing switch. If the demonstrator is quick enough, he may be able to reverse the direction of current through the coil at suitable times during each revolution and thus obtain a continuous rotation of the coil. This reversal process is carried out automatically by the commutator of a d.c. motor.

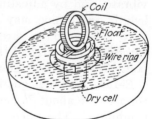

FIG. 236.—Floating coil.

E-144. Floating Coil. An annular wooden float supports a coil of wire in a vertical plane (Fig. 236). A flashlight cell, also supported by the float supplies current to the coil. The apparatus floats on water in a large glass jar. It is prevented from sticking to the jar by a wire ring slightly larger in diameter than the float and supported by it a short distance below the water surface. This arrangement provides a current-carrying coil free to rotate about a vertical axis, useful for showing torque due to a magnetic field. A soft-iron bar is supported horizontally over the jar near the coil. A bar magnet is then brought into contact with one end of the soft iron. With the proper orientation of the bar magnet, the coil will float away from the soft iron, turn around, and come back to it.

E-145. d'Arsonval Galvanometer. A large model d'Arsonval galvanometer may be constructed from a coil and a U-shaped magnet. The dimensions of the model depend on the size of the magnet, which should be as large as possible to ensure good visibility. The coil is made by winding fine wire on a rectangular frame. The coil is shellacked and removed from the frame, and the turns tightly bound together with silk thread. A cylindrical piece of soft steel fitting loosely inside the coil is mounted midway between the poles of the magnet, which are clearly marked N and S to show the direction of the magnetic field. A mirror is attached to the coil, and the latter is suspended in the magnetic field. Coarse phosphor-bronze ribbon is suitable for the suspension.

An image of a lamp filament is formed on a screen after reflection from the galvanometer mirror. A dry cell in series with a variable resistance may be used as the source of energy. The coil deflection is shown to be inversely proportional to the resistance of the circuit.

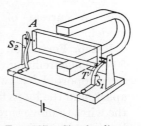

FIG. 237.—Simple direct-current motor.

E-146. Simple Direct-current Motor. A rectangular coil of wire is mounted on a longitudinal axle running in oiled bearings (Fig. 237). One terminal of the coil is connected to the axle; the other protrudes as a stiff wire T, which makes contact each revolution with the spring brass strip S_1. A single dry cell is connected to S_1 and to a second brass strip S_2, which makes contact with the axle at A. The coil may be made to run continuously in the field of a horseshoe magnet by the periodic impulses given to it by the current whenever T makes contact with S_1. A small flywheel on the axle assures continued motion between impulses. The direction of motion may be reversed by turning the magnet over or by reversing the battery terminals. Simple motors and generators of this type with commutators for a.c. or d.c. operation are available at scientific supply houses.

E-147. In a more elaborate model motor, the armature consists of one or more turns of heavy copper wire wound in a circular coil about 25 cm in diameter (Fig. 238).   This is mounted in ball bearings so that it may rotate about a vertical axis with minimum friction.   The ends of the coil are soldered to the strips of a two-segment commutator made from a short piece of brass tubing fitted over a piece of fiber tubing, riveted on, and then separated into two segments by cutting with a hacksaw.   The commutator is more easily seen by the class if it is on the upper side of the armature coil.   As brushes, one may use two strips of thin spring brass or copper.

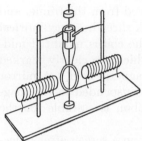

FIG.   238.—Model direct-current motor.

The field is furnished by two solenoids mounted with their axes horizontal. Each solenoid is about 25 cm long and has an iron core 4 cm in diameter.   If the solenoids are made of wire of a size nearly the same as that in the armature coil, the model motor may be operated as a series machine.   It may be shown that changing the brush connections changes the direction of rotation of the coil.   A current of 15 to 20 amp is needed to operate the model.

E-148. Forces on Parallel Conductors.   Two straight wires 50 cm long are hung vertically by loops at their upper ends, which are supported by two brass pins.   The wires are about 1 cm apart, and the loops fit loosely enough to permit the lower ends of the wires to move through horizontal distances of 1 or 2 cm.   The lower ends dip into a pool of mercury.   The brass pins and the mercury are connected to separate binding posts, so that current can be sent through the wires in the same or in opposite directions.

When currents in the two wires are in the same direction, the attractive force causes the wires to move toward each other. When currents are in opposite directions, repulsion between the currents is shown.   The current should be 15 or 20 amp; but the forces are nevertheless small, and for a large class it is advisable to project the wires on a screen.

E-149.   Four or five feet of flexible copper wire (*e.g.*, No. 36 s.c.c.) is connected to terminals 2 in. apart so as to hang in a long narrow loop.   The loop is connected in series with a resistor such as is used with the lecture-room arc lamp.   When there is a large current the loop opens.

Two circular coils, suspended in parallel vertical planes by long lead wires, show attraction or repulsion depending upon whether the currents traverse them in the same or in opposite senses.

E-150. Dancing Spring. Another device for showing the attractive forces between parallel currents in the same direction is a helix of fine spring brass wire hanging in a vertical position. The lower end of the wire dips into a pool of mercury. When current is sent through the helix, the attractive forces between adjacent turns lift the lower end of the wire out of the mercury, thus breaking the circuit. The lower end then returns to the mercury, and the cycle is repeated, each time with sparking at the lower contact. If the spring fails to start, introduce an iron bar into the top of the helix.

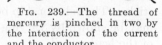

FIG. 239.—The thread of mercury is pinched in two by the interaction of the current and the conductor.

E-151. Action of Current on Its Conductor. A thin ribbon of mercury in a horizontal glass tube 1 in. in diameter (Fig. 239) will pinch itself off when there is a heavy current through it. (Vertical projection.)

E-152. Maxwell's Rule. An electric circuit tends to change its shape so as to include the maximum possible magnetic flux. This is true even where the magnetic field is due only to the current in the circuit itself. Two horizontal parallel wooden troughs containing mercury form "canals" in which float metal "boats" supporting a copper connecting wire (Fig. 240). When there is current through the wire via the troughs, the wire moves away from the terminals of the troughs, thus increasing the area of the circuit and hence the flux through it. With two d.p.d.t. switches connected as shown, it is possible to demonstrate that reversal of direction of current by switch A does not reverse the motion, whereas reversal of terminals on the troughs by switch B does reverse the motion.

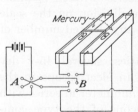

FIG. 240.—Demonstration of Maxwell's rule.

RESISTANCE

E-153. Introductory Experiment on Resistance. This experiment forms another link between Electrostatics and Electric

Currents. A copper wire is tightly wrapped around each end of a dry pine stick 2 cm square and 75 cm long. The stick and a microammeter, or the lecture galvanometer properly shunted, are connected in series to the terminals of a static machine. Potential drop is measured with an electrostatic voltmeter connected to two potential terminals formed by wrapping copper wires around the wooden stick at any chosen points between the end electrodes.

The resistance of a dry pine stick is generally too high for this experiment; but if a soft lead pencil is rubbed over one edge of the stick, the conductivity may be increased to a suitable value. An ordinary static machine will then produce a current of about 5 μa, and the electrostatic voltmeter will show a potential drop of about 600 v between potential terminals close to the ends of the stick. The relationship between current and potential difference may be shown by varying the resistance with further application of the lead pencil.

E-154. Voltmeter and Electroscope. The model d'Arsonval galvanometer (E-145) may be made into a voltmeter by putting sufficient resistance in series with it. It may be connected to any desired number of cells in series to show that the deflection is proportional to the number of cells. The lecture galvanometer may likewise be made into a voltmeter by connecting it to a shunt and then using enough resistance in series with this parallel combination to make a deflection of one division on the scale correspond with a potential difference of any desired number of volts.

To establish a bond with Electrostatics, several 45-v dry batteries may be connected in series to an electroscope in the lantern field and then to the shunted galvanometer in series with the proper high resistance. An electroscope of the type commonly used for projection requires about 200 v for a deflection of the leaves large enough to be seen.

E-155. Wheatstone-bridge Network. Four 60-w lamps are mounted on a board in the form of a diamond-shaped bridge, with one lamp for each arm of the bridge (Fig. 241). A 10-w lamp is mounted in place of the galvanometer. When the four lamps are operating, the "galvanometer" lamp is dark. If one lamp is turned out or replaced by a lamp of different rating, the 10-w lamp lights. The board should be vertical for showing the experiment effectively. If a 220-v circuit is available, it may be used with a bridge made up with 110-v lamps. Otherwise, if the demonstrator wishes to have the lamps operating at their normal brightness, he may use 32-v lamps and connect the bridge in series with a resistance to a 110-v line. A more sensitive "galvanometer" may be introduced when the bridge is balanced by closing the switch S, thus throwing a 6-v flashlight bulb in shunt with the 10-w bulb.

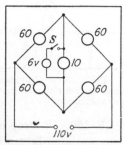

E-156. Wheatstone Bridge—Slide-wire Form. Two No. 24 nichrome wires are stretched across the lecture table, one above the other. Their ends are joined so that they may be connected in parallel through a rheostat and switch to the d.c. supply. Sliding clips connect the lecture galvanometer to the two wires so that pairs of points at the same potential may be located by bringing the galvanometer to zero deflection. The resistance of either nichrome wire may be varied by shorting any section of it with copper wire.

FIG. 241.—Wheatstone-bridge circuit using lamps as resistances and indicators. The 6-v lamp is a sensitive indicator to be used only when the bridge is nearly balanced.

E-157. Wheatstone Bridge with Human Galvanometer. Stretch a loop of clothesline previously soaked in salt solution from insulating supports so as to form a parallelogram. Connect two diagonally opposite vertices to a 110-v a.c. line. Now touch any point on one branch of the circuit with the left hand, and with the right hand find a point on the other branch where there is no sensation of shock. Let students try the experiment. Various modifications are possible, as, for instance, shunting sections of the rope with copper wire so that balance points are not opposite one another.

E-158. Resistance Measurement Using Voltmeter and Ammeter—Potential Drop along a Wire. The lecture galvanometer is arranged to be used as a voltmeter with any chosen number of volts per scale division of deflection (E-154). Either the same or another lecture galvanometer is arranged for use as an ammeter by connecting the galvanometer terminals in series with a suitable resistance to a shunt designed for a current of a few amperes. A d.p.d.t. switch makes possible the use of one galvanometer for either purpose (Fig. 242).

Several wires of different materials, or of different sizes of the same material, are connected in series and stretched between vertical support rods. The combination is in series with the galvanometer shunt and is connected to a few cells in series with a rheostat. By connecting the voltmeter terminals to two clips, the potential difference between any two points along the

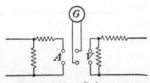

stretched wire may be measured. The uniform potential drop along any length of a single kind of wire may be shown by sliding one of the clips along the wire. The resistance of any length of

Fig.   242.—Galvanometer   the wire may be measured by using the
arranged for use as ammeter   galvanometer first as an ammeter and
or voltmeter.   next as a voltmeter.

E-159. *IR* Drop in a Wire. The *IR* drop in a wire carrying a current may be readily shown by clipping the terminals of one or more low-voltage flashlight lamps at various points along the wire. The dependence of potential drop along the wire upon resistance is made evident by the variation of light intensity with the distance between clips. A long iron or nichrome wire carrying 2 to 5 amp, either alternating or direct current, is suitable.

E-160. Rheostat as Potential Divider. The common slide-wire rheostat may be used either as a series resistor or as a potential divider. The contrast between these two uses may be shown by connecting a rheostat to a 110-v line as illustrated (Fig. 243), using a 40-w lamp as indicator. The rheostat may be made into a potential divider instead of a simple series resistor by closing switch *S*. With the potential divider, the voltage across the lamp can be reduced from 110 v to zero, whereas with the

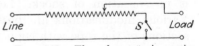

series resistor it can be reduced only by the *IR* drop across the

Fig. 243.—The rheostat in series becomes a potential divider when the switch is closed.

rheostat. The rheostat must be capable of carrying the lamp current plus the current carried by the resistor alone when connected across the line.

E-161. Potentiometer. Stretch a 10-ft length of No. 24 nichrome wire above the lecture table, and connect it to a 6-v storage battery through a rheostat. Arrange a lecture galvanometer as a voltmeter to show deflections proportional to the distance between points on the nichrome wire to which its leads are clipped.

In the galvanometer circuit, insert a cell so that its emf opposes the line drop between the clips. Adjust the clips until the galvanometer gives no deflection. Note that no current is now drawn from the cell, so that it has no internal potential drop, and the true emf of the cell is obtainable by calculation from the line drop in the nichrome wire. The wire may be calibrated with a standard cell or a dry cell whose emf is known. Thereafter the emf's of other cells or combinations may be measured, provided that they do not exceed the IR drop of the potentiometer wire.

E-162. Fall of Potential—Model Transmission Line. A model transmission line may be strung along the lecture table, and the decreasing potential difference between points on the two wires at different distances from the input end may be shown. In this experiment, the line loss is purposely made large in order to demonstrate the effect of line potential drop. The line may consist of two parallel wires of No. 28 copper or No. 26 aluminum, each 2 m long. Five 6-v, 6-cp automobile lamps or radio pilot lamps are connected across the line, one at each end and the remaining three equally spaced between the ends. A 6-v storage battery supplies the energy, and a rheostat set at about 0.4 ohm is used as a load at the output end. The lamps will show the potential differences between the various points where they are connected. The lamp at the supply end glows at normal brightness; the lamp at the load end glows just perceptibly. Decreasing the load by increasing the resistance of the load rheostat will increase the brightness of all the lamps.

E-163. Effect of Temperature on Resistance. A small helix of nickel wire is connected in series with a few cells and with a low-resistance shunt connected to the lecture galvanometer, which is arranged for use as an ammeter (E-158). The number of cells used should be such that the current does not heat the nickel wire more than about 100° above room temperature. When the wire is heated by a gas flame until it becomes incandescent, the resistance increases, and the deflection of the galvanometer decreases.

E-164. An iron wire is bent into a long narrow U and connected in series with a regulating resistor and an ammeter. The current is increased until the wire is red. When the lower half of the U is immersed in a beaker of water, the resistance of this cold part of the wire decreases, current through the wire increases, the upper half glows more brightly than before, and the ammeter indicates more current. These effects are most prominent when the power-supply voltage is such that the regulating resistance is low. A similar effect is produced when a coil of copper wire is dipped into liquid air (H-104).

E-165. Putting Light Out by Heat. A 1.5-v flashlight bulb is operated in series with two dry cells (3 v emf) and sufficient iron wire to reduce the brightness of the bulb to normal. The iron wire is wound on a porcelain insulator. When the wire is heated in a Bunsen flame, the lamp goes out because of increased resistance in the iron at high temperature.

E-166. Comparison of Temperature Coefficients of Resistance.

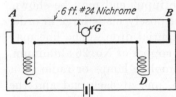

FIG. 244.—Wheatstone-bridge circuit for comparing temperature coefficients of resistance.

A slide-wire Wheatstone bridge is arranged as shown in Fig. 244, where the slide wire AB is a 6-ft length of No. 24 nichrome wire. Two coils C and D of different materials having comparable resistances at room temperature are inserted in the bridge, and the bridge is balanced. If either coil is heated, the galvanometer will be disturbed. The temperature coefficients of resistance of the two coils may be compared by comparing galvanometer deflections produced by equal changes of temperature, successively produced in the two coils.

E-167. Negative Temperature Coefficient of Resistance. A satisfactory demonstration of negative temperature coefficient of resistance is obtained with a Nernst glower.[1] The resistance of a 0.6-amp, 110-v glower at room temperature is about 10^7 ohms. The glower must be used in series with a ballast resistor. It may be operated on direct current, and the lecture ammeter and voltmeter may be used to indicate the resistance of the glower. The current through the glower at room temperature and with rated voltage is so feeble that the glower does not become appreciably warmed. When heated by a gas flame or by a match, the resistance of the glower decreases, as is shown

[1] Obtainable from Stupakoff Laboratories, Inc., 6627 Hamilton Ave., Pittsburgh, Pa.

by the meters, and finally when heated to a temperature well below dull red heat, the resistance of the glower becomes small enough to permit electrical heating up to the point of rated power consumption and of rated light emission.

Globar electric heating elements (E-171) likewise show a negative temperature coefficient of resistance, as does a carbon-filament incandescent lamp.

E-168. Conduction in Glass at High Temperature. A piece of soft-glass capillary tubing or rod about 1 cm in diameter and 10 cm long is provided with electrodes at the ends (Fig. 245), made of strips of sheet copper 6 mm wide, 1 mm thick, and 6 cm long. The copper is bent around the end of the glass, and a fairly snug fit is obtained by crimping with pliers. The glass is then placed on a board covered with asbestos, and the electrodes are connected to a 110-v a.c. line (or d.c. if it is available) in series with a 15-ohm rheostat capable of carrying about 7 amp. One may use in place of a rheostat two or three 110-v, 500-w lamps in parallel. An ammeter may also be included in the circuit.

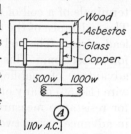

Fig. 245.—Glass becomes conductive when heated.

The glass is heated with a Bunsen flame or blast lamp. It does not conduct electricity to a noticeable extent until it is red hot. Then because of the high negative resistance-temperature coefficient of glass, the conductivity increases rapidly, and at a bright red heat the I^2R loss in the glass is sufficient to maintain the temperature without further use of the flame. The current increases to about 7 amp with the two or three 500-w lamps as described, at which point the glass is white hot. If all lamps but one are disconnected, the remaining lamp glows brightly, and the glass cools. By adjusting the resistance in series with the glass, or simply by opening the switch when the glass becomes white hot and then closing it when the glass cools to a red heat, the experiment may be continued indefinitely. The glass has a tendency to spread out on the asbestos and thus to pull away from the electrodes. Small pieces of cold glass may be dropped into the pool of molten glass to compensate for the effect of spreading out. *Caution:* Because of the high luminosity of incandescent glass, it is suggested that a suitable dark-glass screen be erected to protect the eyes of the students. The instructor is advised to wear dark glasses.

E-169. Electric Thermometers. The use of resistance thermometers for temperature measurements is of sufficient practical importance to warrant a demonstration experiment. A factory-made thermometer and thermometer bridge may be shown, but this equipment is not constructed for teaching purposes; the resistance elements are concealed, and there is an extra lead-wire to eliminate trouble arising from changes in the lead-wire resistances. A simple demonstration resistance thermometer therefore may be made by attaching No. 14 copper wire leads to terminals of a coil of fine platinum wire wound on a mica frame. The resistance of the coil should be large compared to that of the lead-wires. The coil may be in the closed end of a pyrex tube for protection. This results in slower operation, but it has the advantage of enabling the students to see the coil. The slide-wire (E-156) or any other type of Wheatstone bridge may be used for resistance measurement. The apparatus may be calibrated in advance, using two or more standard temperatures, and may then be used to measure any suitable known temperature. (See also the thermoelectric thermometer described in H-6.)

If the laboratory is provided with a Pirani gauge for the measurement of low gas pressures, it may be shown in this connection, since the principle of the gauge is that of change of resistance with change of temperature owing to conductivity of heat by the gas.

E-170. Selenium Photoconductivity Bridge. This experiment shows the effect of light in decreasing the resistance of selenium. Drill four small holes in the corners of a piece of glass about 2.5 by 4.5 cm (Fig. 246). Grind the surface of the glass with carborundum to roughen it slightly. Attach two nickel wires (No. 34) at two of the corners of the glass, and wind them approximately parallel to each other as far as the other corners, where they are fastened. There may be about 15 turns of each wire. Place the grid thus made on a block of metal, which is heated slowly by a burner. When the glass is somewhat above the melting point of selenium (217°C), rub a stick of selenium on the ground-glass

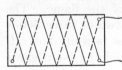

Fig. 246.—Wire grid wound on glass for selenium photoconductivity bridge.

surface and on the nickel wires stretched over it.   The selenium
will melt, and a thin layer can be formed on the glass.   This
operation should be carried out in a hood, since the compounds
of selenium are cumulative poisons.   Remove the grid from the
block of metal, and allow it to cool rather quickly to room temperature.   The selenium will then be in the amorphous form, and
if a sufficiently thin layer has been obtained, it will transmit red
light.

Selenium in this form is practically a nonconductor.   To
bring it into the conducting and light-sensitive form, the material
is again heated.   Support a glass test tube in a beaker of oil, the
open end of the tube projecting above the oil.   Heat the oil to
180°C, and drop the grid into the test tube, allowing it to remain
for 5 min.   When the grid is withdrawn, the selenium will be
seen to have changed into the gray, partly crystalline form.

The grid after cooling to room temperature will have a resistance of the order of 10 megohms in the dark; its resistance will be
about 15 per cent of that value when illuminated with a 60-w
lamp at a distance of 20 cm.   This ratio of dark resistance to
light resistance will decrease if the grid is kept in a damp place,
but if it is stored in a desiccator containing a drying agent, the
light sensitivity will remain high for a long time.

The experiment may be shown by connecting a suitable source
of potential difference in series with the selenium grid and the
lecture galvanometer.   No rheostat should be in the circuit containing grid and galvanometer, since such a resistance will reduce
the ratio of deflections in darkness and under illumination.   The
deflection under no illumination may be obtained by placing the
grid in a cardboard box.

HEATING EFFECT OF CURRENT

E-171. Heating Effects of Electric Current.   A loop of No. 18
nichrome wire may be used to show the heating effect of a current.
Two Fahnestock connectors screwed to a board are convenient
for holding the wire and for making connections to it.   A lecture-
room ammeter and voltmeter may be used to measure both
power and resistance; *i.e.*, volts $\times$ amperes = watts; volts $\div$
amperes = ohms.   A rheostat may be included in the circuit for
regulating the current.   If desired, the wire may be arranged to
illustrate the hot-wire ammeter (H-11).

In a similar way, one may use a Globar electric heating element.[1] These elements may be obtained in various ratings. Contacts with their terminals are easily made. They glow brightly when operated at normal power consumption and have a negative temperature coefficient of resistance (E-167). An ammeter connected to measure current through one of these heaters shows a gradual increase in current after the circuit is closed.

Electric heating devices, such as hot plates, radiant heaters, and immersion heaters, may be shown. Attention may be called to the large amount of heat emitted by a carbon arc.

E-172. Fuses and House-lighting Circuits. The use of fuse wire for protection of electrical circuits may be demonstrated by connecting a short piece of wire between two Fahnestock clips with a rheostat and an ammeter in series to regulate and to measure the current required to melt the wire.

A miniature house-lighting circuit may be constructed by mounting on a board various outlets, switches, and sockets connected in parallel through a fuse block with plug and leads for connecting to a 110-v circuit. When lamps, electric irons, and other accessories are used, the load may be made to exceed the capacity of a fuse of low rating.

E-173. Fuse-wire Problem. If two (or more) fuse wires of the same substance but of different diameters and ratings are connected in parallel between two copper bars, which one will burn out first as the voltage between the bars is increased?

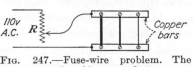

Fig. 247.—Fuse-wire problem. The large fuse blows out first.

Few students will guess the correct answer. The simple arrangement of Fig. 247 demonstrates that the *large* wire will burn out first. (The smaller fuses may burn out soon thereafter because of the decreased IR drop in R when the current decreases.)

E-174. Comparison of Heating in Various Conductors. Five or more wires of equal length (*e.g.*, 25 cm each of No. 16 copper, No. 22 copper, No. 22 "advance," No.16 iron, and No. 23 iron) are connected in series, using soldered joints. The wires are supported horizontally above the lecture table and are connected in series with a rheostat, ammeter, and battery. A strip of paper

[1] Globar Corporation, Niagara Falls, N. Y.

or an index card is attached with soft wax to the center of each sample of wire. The current through the wires is gradually increased. The first paper to fall on account of the melting of the wax will be that on the "advance" wire, because of the high resistivity of this material and the consequent large heating effect. The wax holding the paper to the smaller iron wire will melt next, etc., the order of melting and falling being an indication of the relative resistances of the wires. However, the smaller iron wire will become red hot before the advance wire because of the higher resistance-temperature coefficient of iron. It will be noticed that the specifications suggest that this wire be one size smaller than the "advance." In this case, at lower temperatures the resistance of the iron wire is certain to be less than that of the advance, but at higher temperatures the resistance of the iron wire exceeds that of the advance.

E-175. Dependence of Resistance on Length and Area of Conductor.   Mount in series on a board German silver or "Nisil"

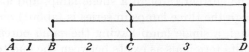

FIG. 248.—Dependence of resistance on length and area of conductor.

wires, of lengths 1, 2, and 3 ft, which are respectively single, double, and triple, with switches arranged so that they may be used singly or in multiple (Fig. 248). Since these three elements of the circuit, *AB, BC, CD* are in series, they all carry the same current, whether as single wires or in multiple. Their resistances can be compared by voltmeter readings taken individually over each of the three elements. Thus, when used singly, the voltmeter readings *AB:BC:CD* will be as 1:2:3; but when section *BC* has two wires and *CD* has three, the voltmeter readings will all be equal, showing that the length factor is compensated by increased area.

E-176. Heating Effect of Current in Organic Material—"Hot Dog" Cooker.   It is well to show that the heating effect of an electric current is not confined to metallic conductors and glowing filaments. Two nails are driven through a piece of wood about 10 cm apart so that their ends project 3 cm beyond the surface of the wood. The nails are connected to a 110-v line with an ammeter in series, and the board is placed on the lecture

table with the pointed ends of the nails upwards.   A raw frankfurter is now pressed against the sides of the nails.   The current is
small since the resistance of the skin of the frankfurter is high.
There will be scorching at the contacts if a little pressure is
applied, since with small current but high resistance considerable
heat may be developed locally.   This corresponds to the surface
burns suffered when a person receives a severe shock with poor
skin contacts.   If the frankfurter is now impaled on the nails,
contact is improved, and the current increases to 1 or 2 amp.
The heating effect is sufficient to start cooking the frankfurter.
If the nails fit snugly into the holes that they make in the skin,
the steam generated does not escape but soon produces enough
pressure to burst the skin of the "hot dog."

E-177. Resistances in Parallel and in Series.   Attach six
lamp receptacles to a board, three being in parallel and three in
series.   Insert lamps of the same rating in each socket.   Use an
ammeter to show that the current through the three in parallel is
three times the current through a single lamp, and also that the
current through the three lamps in series is (about) one-third the
current through a single lamp having the same potential difference between its terminals as exists between the end terminals of
the three lamps in series.   The current through the three in
series will actually be more than one-third, since the filaments of
the lamps in series are below their normal operating temperature
and hence have a resistance less than the normal operating value.
The sum of voltmeter readings taken across the three series lamps
individually may be shown to be equal to the total applied
voltage.

E-178. Electrocalorimeter.   The purpose of this experiment is
to obtain an approximate value for the mechanical equivalent of
heat by electrical methods.   The electrocalorimeter consists of an
ordinary calorimeter to which an electrical heating unit, *e.g.*, a
100-w lamp, has been added.   The demonstrator puts a known
mass of water in the inner calorimeter cup and reads its temperature.   An ammeter and a voltmeter measure the power delivered
to the heating unit.   The class determines the time required for
heating the water to a temperature as far above room temperature
as the water was below room temperature at the time of closing
the switch.   The ratio of volts × amperes × seconds to calories
delivered should approximate 4.2 joules per cal.   Temperature

change may be shown by the demonstration thermocouple thermometer (H-6).

A 600-w radiant heater element immersed in a beaker of water will bring the water to a boil in less than a minute. The heater should be immersed before the current is turned on.

THERMO-, PIEZO-, AND PYROELECTRICITY

E-179. Thermoelectric Effect—Seebeck Effect. A piece of copper wire about 75 cm long is attached to each end of a piece of iron wire of the same length by twisting the ends together. The free ends of the copper wires are connected to the lecture galvanometer in series with enough resistance to keep the deflections on scale. One of the copper-iron junctions is kept either in ice water or in water at room temperature, while the other junction is heated with a gas flame. The thermal emf increases as the temperature of the hot junction rises until 275°C (approximately) is reached. For higher temperatures, the emf diminishes, becomes zero at about 550°C (dull red heat), and then increases in the opposite direction.

The lecture-room thermocouple (H-6), thermoelectric pyrometers, and thermopiles may be discussed at this time.

E-180. Peltier Effect. When current is passed through a thermocouple, one junction is cooled while the other is heated (Peltier effect). This effect is in addition to the I^2R heat generated throughout the circuit by the current. It is important in showing this effect to keep the I^2R heat small compared with the Peltier heat by using a couple consisting of large rods of bismuth and antimony. One end of a piece of pyrex tubing 1.2 cm in diameter and 12 cm long is closed by a plug of alundum cement. The tubing is held vertically, and molten antimony is poured into it until it is about half full. After the antimony has solidified, a short portion of it at the top is remelted, and the tube is filled with molten bismuth. Two such rods are made and removed from the glass. The bismuth ends of the two rods are slipped into a short length of pyrex tubing and welded together. Each antimony-bismuth junction of the composite rod so formed is placed within a piece of pyrex tubing about 1.8 cm in inside diameter, whose ends are closed with rubber stoppers (Fig. 249). Side tubes are connected to a piece of tubing about 0.25 cm in inside diameter in which there is a short thread of colored water or of mercury. If there is an evolution of heat at one of the antimony-bismuth junctions and an absorption of heat at the other, the water will move away from the first and toward the second. The apparatus is mounted on a wooden base. When a direct current of 20 amp is passed through the rod, the globule of water will move about 0.5 cm in 30 sec. The direction of motion may be reversed by reversing the current, which would not be the case if the I^2R heat were the cause. (Project.)

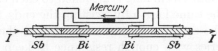

Fig. 249.—Antimony-bismuth thermocouple for demonstrating the Peltier effect.

E-181. Seebeck and Peltier Effects in One Thermocouple Circuit.

The converse nature of the Seebeck and Peltier effects is emphasized by the following experiment. For a period of several seconds, send a current through a copper-iron-copper circuit (Fig. 250). Then disconnect the battery, and immediately connect the thermocouple to the galvanometer. (A d.p.d.t. switch accomplishes this change quickly.) With the initial current from C to D through the iron, the galvanometer deflection indicates that junction C is warmer than junction D. Repeat the experiment with the direction of the initial current reversed. The galvanometer now shows that D is warmer than C.

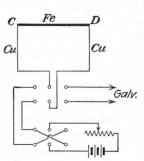

Fig. 250.—Circuit for demonstrating Seebeck and Peltier effects.

E-182. Thermoelectric Magnet.

The emf of a thermocouple depends only upon the two metals used and the difference in temperature between their junctions; the current is, by Ohm's law, dependent upon the resistance of the circuit. Very large currents may be generated if the resistance is sufficiently low, as may be shown by the thermocouple magnet. A single loop of heavy copper bar is closed by welded joints with a short section of copper-nickel alloy. Two copper vanes are welded at the junctions for rapid heat conduction. When one vane is cooled in water and the other heated in a Bunsen flame, the current may even exceed 100 amp.   The copper loop fits inside an iron shell to form an electromagnet whose attraction for a soft-iron armature is sufficient to support a load of more than 200 lb. (Fig. 251).

Fig. 251.—Thermoelectric magnet.

E-183. Bars of iron and copper are riveted together with a compass needle mounted between them (Fig. 252).   The unit is placed parallel to the magnetic meridian.   When one of the junctions is heated, the compass needle deflects.   The deflection is reversed by heating the other junction and cooling the first.   From electromagnetic principles, the direction of current in each case may be determined (E-121).

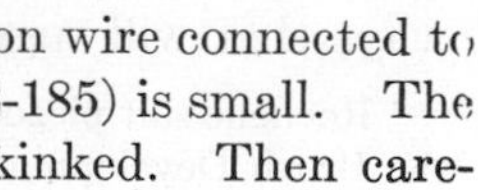

Fig. 252.—Heating one copper-iron junction sets up a current whose magnetic field causes the needle to deflect.

E-184. Thermoelectric Effect in One Metal.   Pass a flame along a piece of soft-iron wire connected to a galvanometer and show that any effect (E-185) is small.   The wire must be fresh from the spool and not kinked.   Then carefully make a single loop near its center, and draw it down quite tightly to make a sharp kink, avoiding kinks elsewhere. Now hold a pointed flame (not too hot) about $\frac{1}{8}$ in. from one side of the kink, and observe the galvanometer deflection. Remove the flame at once, and allow the wire to cool. Repeat the heating similarly on the other side of the kink, and the galvanometer should deflect in the opposite direction about the same amount. In kinking the wire, its elastic limit has been exceeded, and in effect a new material has been inserted in the circuit.

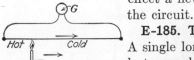

Fig. 253.—Circuit for demonstrating the Thomson effect.

E-185. Thomson Effect in Single Wire. A single long wire loop is connected to the lecture galvanometer. The flame from a Bunsen burner is passed along the wire, heating it locally as it goes (Fig. 253). The galvanometer shows the existence of a current as if electrons were "pushed ahead" of the advancing flame. The effect was discovered in 1854 by Prof. William Thomson, later Lord Kelvin.

E-186. Piezoelectric Effect in Rochelle Salt Crystals. A properly cut crystal of Rochelle salt[1] develops charges on its faces when the crystal is under stress. In a piezoelectric demonstration unit commercially available, the crystal is mounted on a heavy base with a metallic cap fitted over one end. Tin-foil coatings are cemented to the faces of the crystal, and these are connected to the electrodes of a small neon lamp. When the metallic cap is tapped with a piece of wood or a rubber mallet, the stress developed is sufficient to cause the neon lamp to flash.

If the tin-foil coatings of a large crystal (about 10 cm long with faces about 8 cm wide) are connected to an electrostatic voltmeter, the potential differences developed may be measured. One end of the crystal may be in contact with a pad resting on the table to prevent chipping. The demonstrator applies pressure to another pad on the upper end of the crystal. A moderate pressure develops a potential difference of more than 50 v. If this potential is applied to the grid of a three-electrode tube, the resulting variation in plate current may be shown in several ways that will suggest themselves. One way is to have a neon

[1] Rochelle salt piezoelectric crystals and bar resonators are available from the Brush Development Co., Cleveland, Ohio.

lamp in the plate circuit.   The lamp glows until the negative
potential developed by the piezoelectric effect stops the plate
current.

E-187.   Mechanical Vibration of Crystal under Electric Forces.
The converse piezoelectric effect, in which the application of an
electric field to the crystal produces a strain in it, may be shown
with the large crystal.   Connect two tin foils on the crystal
(E-186) to the amplified output of an audio-frequency oscillator
(A-27 and 85) to develop mechanical vibrations in the crystal.
The sound produced may be heard distinctly in a large lecture
room.

E-188.   Piezoelectric Oscillator.   The piezoelectric bar oscillator consists of a steel bar of square cross section with four properly

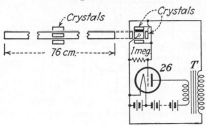

Fig. 254.—Piezoelectric oscillator circuit.

cut Rochelle salt crystals cemented on the flat surfaces of the bar
near its center.   With the circuit shown in Fig. 254, the bar may
be put into oscillation.   Since the crystals are all cemented to the
bar, it serves as a common plate for all of them.   The other sides
of the crystals are covered with tin-foil coatings that are connected in pairs to two binding posts.   The coatings of one pair
of crystals are connected to the high-tension side of an a.f. transformer with a turn ratio of about 1:8, the low-tension side of this
transformer being in the plate circuit of a three-element tube.
The coatings on the other pair of crystals are connected to the
grid of this tube.   A slight change in plate current causes a
potential difference across one pair of crystals; the resulting
slight change in the dimensions of these crystals initiates a
longitudinal pulse along the bar.   The longitudinal pulse in the
bar develops in turn a potential difference across the crystals
whose tin foils are connected to the grid of the tube.   In this
manner, the plate current is further changed, and oscillations are
sustained in the bar.

The tin foils on the driving crystals must be connected in the correct sense. If the bar does not oscillate when first set up, reverse one pair of terminals on the transformer. The transformer must be selected to match the tube. Any tendency of the bar to oscillate at double its fundamental frequency may be avoided by using the tuned circuit of Fig. 255.

The sound produced by the oscillator is of sufficient intensity to be heard distinctly in the largest lecture room. The pitch corresponds to the natural frequency of the bar. There is one-half of a standing wave in the length of the bar. With a steel bar 76 cm long, the frequency is about 3400 cycles per sec. The wave length in air is about 10 cm. The students may detect very

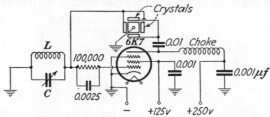

Fig. 255.—Tuned circuit for piezoelectric oscillator.

prominent interference effects due to reflections from the walls of the room by moving their heads from side to side over a distance of a few centimeters.

E-189. Pyroelectric Effect in Tourmaline—Heating. A long thin crystal of tourmaline at least 2 cm long and reasonably clear[1] is held by a wire over a Bunsen burner and heated to about 250°C. The heating should be slow to avoid breaking the crystal. As the temperature increases, pyroelectric charges are developed on the ends of the crystal and are neutralized by ions from the flame. When the crystal is removed from the flame, pyroelectric charges develop upon cooling and are retained on its ends. These charges—positive on one end and negative on the other—may be detected by means of an electroscope. They are sufficient to produce a large deflection. The crystal may be projected in silhouette on a screen.

E-190. Pyroelectric Effect in Tourmaline—Cooling. A long thin crystal of tourmaline is suspended by two silk threads

[1] Obtainable from Ward's Natural Science Establishment, Inc., Rochester, N. Y.

tied a few millimeters apart on either side of the center, forming a bifilar suspension.   It is immersed in liquid air or in a mixture of carbon dioxide snow and alcohol (p. 224).   When the crystal is withdrawn, frost is formed on it, chiefly at the ends.   On close examination, one can see minute frost needles being shot off by electrostatic repulsion.   By means of a charged rod brought near the crystal, one can show that the crystal has opposite charges at its two ends and behaves like an electric doublet.

The charges acquired by the crystal may be shown by dusting over it a mixture of powdered sulfur and red lead (E-66).   The yellow sulfur adheres to the positively charged end of the crystal, and the red litharge to the negatively charged end.

ELECTROLYTIC CONDUCTION

E-191. Magnetic Field of Current through an Electrolyte.   A piece of glass tubing about 2 cm in inside diameter and 75 cm long has its ends bent at right angles to its length and flared to receive rubber stoppers.   A sulfuric acid solution of specific gravity about 1.4 is poured into the tube while the latter is held horizontally in a north-south direction just over a compass needle on a pivot (E-76).   Platinum electrodes are provided at the ends, the lead-wires passing through the rubber stoppers.   A current of about 2 amp from a d.c. source is sent through the electrolyte. The magnetic field produced by this current is evident from the deflection of the compass needle.

E-192. Conduction through Electrolytes.   The contrast between the conductivity of pure water and water containing an electrolyte may be shown by immersing two copper plates in a vessel of distilled water.   The plates are connected in series with a 25-w lamp to a 110-v line (alternating or direct current).   When salt or sulfuric acid is dissolved in the water, the solution becomes conductive, and the lamp glows.

E-193. With the apparatus of the preceding experiment, add barium hydroxide to the distilled water until the lamp lights. Then carefully add dilute sulfuric acid, a little at a time, until the lamp goes out.   An insoluble precipitate of barium sulfate forms. Further addition of sulfuric acid causes the light to come on again, thus showing the necessity of *ions* for conduction in an electrolyte.

E-194. Rotation of an Electrolyte Carrying Current Perpendicular to a Magnetic Field. A crystallizing dish 10 cm in diameter contains a solution of zinc chloride having about 20 g of the salt to 100 ml of water. A strip of zinc 2 cm wide is bent into a thin ring 9 cm in diameter. It is placed in the crystallizing dish to serve as the outer electrode. The inner electrode is a hollow cylinder of zinc 1 cm in diameter located at the center of the dish. Some cork filings may be floated on the surface of the solution. The images of these bits of cork may be projected onto a screen by vertical projection.

A strong bar magnet is held vertically over the center of the crystallizing dish, thus producing a magnetic field with a component perpendicular to the surface of the liquid. A solenoid surrounding the dish may be substituted for the bar magnet.

The electrodes are connected in series with a rheostat through a reversing switch to a 60-v source of direct current. When the current is about 10 amp, the positive and negative ions move toward the electrodes with velocities that have components at right angles to the magnetic field. The electromagnetic forces are at right angles to the magnetic field and to the directions of motion of the ions. The result is that the electrolyte is given a rotational motion. The angular speed varies with distance from the central electrode, since the current density is greatest near this electrode and also because the field is greatest at a point just under the end of the bar magnet. A particle of cork floating at a point about one-third the way from the central electrode to the outer electrode will make one revolution in about 2 sec.

E-195. Electroplating—Lead Tree. Two strips of lead or zinc serve as electrodes in a projection electrolytic cell containing a saturated solution of lead acetate, with a few drops of acetic acid added. The electrodes are connected in series with a rheostat, through a reversing switch, to several storage cells in series. When the circuit is closed, the image of the cell projected on the screen shows the rapid deposition of lead in fernlike clusters on the cathode. Reversal of the current causes the lead deposit to disappear from the electrode upon which it has been deposited and to form on the other electrode, which has now become the cathode. The rate of growth of the "lead tree" is controlled by the rheostat.

E-196. Electroplating—Tin Tree. Electrodes of copper and tin are dipped into a projection cell containing an acid solution of stannic chloride. With the copper as cathode, a current causes tin to crystallize on it in long needles. (Project.)

E-197. Electroplating. Copper or silver plating may be demonstrated, but the process is slower and less spectacular than in the preceding experiments. However, the plating may be carried on at low current values throughout the lecture period, and the results shown at the end of the hour. The object to be plated is connected to the negative terminal of the battery. The positive terminal should be connected to a rod or sheet of copper or silver. Copper plating may be done in a copper sulfate solution. Silver nitrate solution is suitable for silver plating.

E-198. Voltaic Cell. A projection cell is filled with an electrolyte consisting of one part sulfuric acid to four parts water. The electrodes are a strip of copper and a strip of amalgamated zinc. When the terminals of the cell are connected to the lecture galvanometer arranged as a voltmeter, the potential difference is shown. If the cell is short-circuited, the evolution of hydrogen bubbles at the cathode (copper) is apparent on the screen. If two lecture galvanometers are available, one may be used as a current-measuring instrument while the other is used for measuring potential difference (E-158). The variation of potential difference as the current is changed by means of a series rheostat may be demonstrated. It is interesting to note the large amount of gas liberated near a piece of unamalgamated zinc (local action) when the cell is on open circuit and to observe the relatively small amount near a piece of amalgamated zinc.

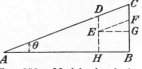

FIG. 256.—Model of voltaic-cell circuit.

E-199. Cardboard Model to Illustrate Potential Difference and Electromotive Force in a Voltaic-cell Circuit. Cut out of thin white cardboard a right triangle ABC (Fig. 256), with angle $\theta = 20°$. Distances measured parallel to BC are proportional to potential difference; those parallel to the base are proportional to resistance. Then, by Ohm's law, the slope of the hypotenuse is proportional to the current. Draw on the cardboard two straight lines, DE, EF, parallel respectively to the altitude and the hypotenuse. Draw EG parallel to the base. Then going around the circuit $BFEDAHB$, the length BF is proportional to the contribution to the emf of the zinc-acid contact; FG is proportional to the IR drop within the cell due to internal resistance; ED is proportional to the contribution to the emf of the acid-copper contact. Now $BF + ED = BF + FC = BC$, which is proportional to the total emf of the cell. Also, $HD = BC - FG$ is the potential difference at the cell terminals, or the useful potential difference over the external circuit DA. The distinction is thus clearly brought out between the terms electromotive force and potential difference.

E-200. Polarization of Voltaic Cell.—The formation of a layer of hydrogen on the surface of the cathode reduces the emf of a voltaic cell. Using the same arrangement as in E-198, remove the copper cathode, and heat it well in a Bunsen flame so as to oxidize it. After cooling, replace it in the cell, and close the circuit. A large current, steady for about 1 min, results, during which no gas comes from the copper surface, since the oxide is being reduced by the hydrogen. An oily-appearing stream (zinc sulfate) flows off the bottom of the anode. Suddenly, the current begins to decrease, and gas starts to leave the cathode surface. Polarization is complete when the galvanometer shows a new steady lower value of emf.

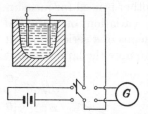

FIG. 257.—Projection electrolytic cell arranged to show emf due to polarization.

E-201. Electromotive Force of Polarization during Electrolysis of Water. The projection electrolytic cell may be used for showing the evolution of hydrogen and oxygen to a large class. The electrolyte may be a sulfuric acid solution. Two strips of platinum are used as electrodes. They are connected to the middle terminals of a d.p.d.t. switch (Fig. 257). With the switch in one direction, current through the cell causes evolution of hydrogen at the cathode and of oxygen at the anode. If the switch is then turned so as to connect the cell to the lecture galvanometer, arranged as a voltmeter, the galvanometer shows a momentary current in the opposite direction because of polarization. No emf is developed by the cell unless there are layers of gas on the electrodes.

E-202. Electrolysis of Water—Quantitative Experiment. The Hoffman apparatus allows the volumes of hydrogen and oxygen liberated by the electrolysis of water to be measured. With this apparatus, one may show the volume of hydrogen to be twice that of the oxygen when measured at the same pressure, and one may obtain a sample of either gas by holding an inverted test tube over one of the stopcocks.

The usual Hoffman apparatus is not easily seen by a large class. In this case, one may construct a miniature projection electrolytic cell with two inverted test tubes filled with electrolyte and held vertically, with their lower ends just under the surface of the solution. Electrodes are at the lower ends of the tubes. The whole apparatus is projected on the screen, and the formation of the gases is easily seen by a large class.

E-203. Explosion of Hydrogen and Oxygen. An explosive mixture of hydrogen and oxygen is obtained by combining the gases generated on both sides of the Hoffman apparatus. A satisfactory way is to connect rubber tubes to the two stopcocks and to a glass T-tube. A tube from the third arm of the T is then used to blow small bubbles in an *open* dish of soap solution. Still better, reverse the current after one side of the apparatus is about half full of hydrogen, and allow gas to collect until both tubes contain the same volume. A perfect mixture of two parts hydrogen to one part oxygen is thus assured in *both* tubes. After the gas has been collected in the soap suds, remove the dish to a safe distance from the apparatus, and ignite the bubbles with a small gas flame on the end of a long glass tube. A loud, startling report results.

E-204. Secondary or Storage Cells. Reference has already been made in E-120 to an elementary lead storage cell. A small portable storage cell of the lead electrode type contained in a glass jar may also be shown in a similar manner. This cell may be charged while on the lecture table and subsequently connected to a resistance load. A voltmeter or the lecture galvanometer connected to the terminals shows the potential drop on open circuit (approximately the emf of the cell) and the potential drop both when the cell is being charged and when it is being discharged.

An Edison-type storage battery may be shown, and its potential differences under similar circumstances demonstrated.

E-205. Large Current from Storage Cell. To demonstrate the very large current obtainable from a 6-v automobile storage battery when there is a low external resistance between its terminals, one may use the current to melt an iron nail of about 3.5 mm diameter.   The head of the nail is cut off, and each end is soldered into a hole in the end of a short piece of brass rod about 5 mm in diameter.   The length of nail between brass rods may be about 3.5 cm.   It is essential to keep the resistance of the circuit at a minimum; care must be taken that the joints are good. Regular automobile battery cables are used, and all connections are soldered except those on the battery terminal posts and others made with bolts.   If a 500-amp switch is available, it may be used advantageously in the circuit.   If such a switch is not available, the following procedure may be used.   One of the battery cables is bolted to its terminal post.   The terminal of the other cable is adjusted to make a snug fit on the other battery post.   When the demonstrator is ready for the experiment, he holds this terminal in one hand just over the battery post that it is to fit and a hammer in the other hand.   The terminal is then dropped into place, and an immediate blow with the hammer forces it tightly over the post.

With the specifications given, the nail will come to a white heat and melt in about 2 sec.   The experiment is quite spectacular.   The initial current may be about 700 amp.   This is without question rather severe punishment for a battery.   However, the current required to melt the nail does not greatly exceed that needed to operate an automobile starting motor in cold weather.

E-206. Ionic Speed.   Dip two platinum electrodes into an ammoniated copper sulfate solution, containing some phenolphthalein.   A current causes the blue solution to move to the cathode and the red solution to the anode, with a difference in the motions of the two layers that should be noted.   (Project.)

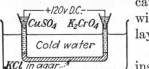

Fig. 258.—Tube to show ionic speed.

E-207. A glass tube about 5 mm in inside diameter and 50 cm long is bent into a square U, the base of the U being about 15 cm long (Fig. 258).   The base of the U is filled with a hot saturated solution of potassium chloride containing 2 per cent of agar-agar, which is allowed to cool and solidify, forming a gel.   A saturated solution of copper sulfate is poured into one of the arms of the U, and a saturated solution of potassium chromate into the other arm.　Copper electrodes of about 6 cm² surface area are placed in these solutions, that in the copper sulfate being made the anode. The part of the U-tube containing the gel is immersed in cold water, to prevent the gel from liquefying when heated by current.

The potassium chloride in the gel is colorless when put into the tube, but when a potential is applied, the region near the anode soon becomes blue because of the presence of copper ions that are moving toward the cathode.　There is a sharp boundary between the blue and the colorless regions.　The speed of this boundary can be measured directly.　With a potential difference of about 120 v between anode and cathode and with a current path about 18 cm long, the speed of this boundary is about 8 cm per hr or 2.2×10^{-3} cm per sec.

A rather faint yellow boundary moves from the cathode end of the tube as chlorine ions progress toward the anode. The line of demarcation is not sufficiently definite to serve for measurement of its speed.

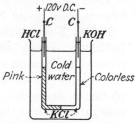

E-208. In another experiment, the speeds of hydrogen and hydroxyl ions are measured.　Hydrogen ions have a mobility greater than that of any other

Fig. 259.—Another apparatus for measuring ionic speeds.

ions, and hydroxyl ions come next on the list.　About 2 per cent of agar-agar is dissolved in a saturated solution of potassium chloride as already described (E-207), and about 0.5 per cent of phenolphthalein is added.　The mixture is poured into a U-tube 9 mm in inside diameter and 40 cm long, with a 5-cm base (Fig. 259).　The mixture should fill the bottom of the tube and extend up the sides, so that the length it occupies is about 15 cm.　Before the mixture has hardened, a few drops of hydrochloric acid are added to one side, and a few drops of potassium hydroxide solution to the other. The potassium hydroxide diffuses down the arm of the U-tube, making the color a bright pink.　The hydrochloric acid diffuses down the other arm, hardly changing the color, but if anything making it more nearly white.　After the solution has hardened, potassium hydroxide is poured on top of the colorless gel, and hydrochloric acid is poured on the pink gel.　Carbon electrodes are introduced, that in the acid being made the anode.　The part of the U-tube containing the gel is surrounded with a beaker of cold water.

When a potential difference is established, the hydroxyl ions move toward the anode. As they enter the gel, the phenolphthalein becomes pink, and the motion of the boundary between the pink and the colorless parts of the gel enables one to measure the speed of these ions directly. The hydrogen ions from the hydrochloric acid move toward the cathode. As they enter the colored gel, it becomes colorless. The speed with which this boundary moves toward the cathode shows the speed of the hydrogen ions.

With a 30-cm length of current path, of which 15 cm is through the gel, and with a total potential difference of 120 v, the speed of the hydroxyl ion is about 3×10^{-3} cm per sec, and that of the hydrogen ion about 5×10^{-3} cm per sec.

E-209. Electrolysis of Sodium Sulfate with Purple Cabbage as Indicator. Crush some purple cabbage in a vessel of water to remove its coloring matter, then strain. Add sodium sulfate to the colored water to make it conductive, and introduce two platinum electrodes. When a current passes, the liquid at one pole turns pink, at the other green, the colors being quite brilliant.

E-210. Electric Forge. Fill a battery jar two-thirds full of strong sodium sulfite solution, and lay a lead plate on the bottom for an anode. The cathode is an iron rod with wooden handle, which may be held in the hand. Apply 110-v direct current through a rheostat, and dip the iron terminal into the solution. Sparks fly and droplets of iron melt from the tip of the rod in a spectacular manner, owing to the highly localized generation of heat.

E-211. Electrolysis of Sodium Ions through Glass. Put a mixture of about 90 per cent sodium nitrate and 10 per cent sodium chloride (to lower the melting point) in a porcelain beaker or an agateware pan. Support a 60-w clear-glass lamp bulb (*not* gas filled) near the center of the vessel so that it does not touch the bottom (Fig. 260). Let the upper half of the lamp bulb project through a hole in a sheet of asbestos paper, which rests on the rim of the vessel and serves to reduce heat loss from the vessel and to keep the upper part of the lamp bulb cool. Place an anode of nickel in the vessel, but not flat on the bottom.

Melt the sodium nitrate with a Bunsen flame, and raise it to a temperature of about 360°C. Run the lamp filament at normal

brightness from a 110-v source. Connect the nickel anode in
series with a rheostat and milliammeter to the positive side of a
110-v d.c. supply, and connect one terminal of the lamp filament
to the negative side.   There will be a current of about 0.1 amp
in the d.c. circuit when the potential drop between anode and
filament is about 100 v.   This current is carried by sodium ions
through the glass lamp bulb; their positive charges are neutralized by thermions emitted from the filament, and the neutral
sodium atoms then condense inside the bulb on the cooler parts
of the glass.[1]

The apparatus may be used as a rectifier by applying an
alternating voltage between the anode and one terminal of the

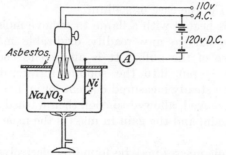

FIG. 260.—Electrolysis of sodium ions through glass.

lamp filament.   A milliammeter in the circuit will show unidirectional current.

After about half an hour, there will be a mirrorlike deposit on
the inside of the bulb near the top and on the glass post supporting the tungsten filament.   Because of the time required, the
demonstration should be started before the class meets.

E-212. Sodium Photoelectric Cell.   A sodium photoelectric
cell may be constructed by the method of electrolysis described in
E-211.   A small hole is blown in the bulb with the aid of a fine
flame, and a side tube is sealed on.   A platinum wire is sealed
through the bulb, after which the bulb is carefully exhausted and
sealed off.   Sodium is deposited on the inside by electrolysis and
sublimed to the region surrounding the platinum-wire cathode,
by heating the deposit in a Bunsen flame, using a sheet of asbestos

[1] For further details, see R. C. Burt, *Rev. Sci. Instruments*, **11**, 87, 1925.

paper to protect the end of the bulb, and cooling the area around the cathode with a stream of air.   An opening in the sodium film for the admission of light is made by applying the tip of a flame to the spot where the opening is desired.   (See A-91 and related experiments for the use of this cell.)

E-213. Mass of Sodium Atom Determined by Electrolysis.   A good value of the mass m of a sodium atom may be obtained from the electronic charge e, the valence n, and the quantity of electricity Q passed through the sodium electrolytic cell (E-211) if the mass M of the sodium deposited is determined with care. For the number of atoms passed through the glass is $N = Q/ne$. Hence the mass of each atom is $m = M/N = Mne/Q$, where e and Q are, of course, expressed in the same kind of unit.   The valence n is 1 in the case of sodium.

The bulb is heated with a flame to remove moisture from the glass and to oxidize any readily oxidizable material on the threaded base of the bulb.   It is allowed to cool and is then weighed.   It is put into the sodium nitrate, the sodium is deposited by a steady measured current for an hour or more, and the bulb is removed, allowed to cool, then washed and dried.   It is weighed again, and the gain in mass is the mass of the sodium deposited.

Other atomic masses may be found by electrolysis in the same manner, but in most experiments great inaccuracy is introduced by loss of electrolyzed metal.   In this experiment, the metal is enclosed in a protecting glass envelope.

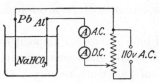

FIG. 261.—Electrolytic rectifier.

E-214. Electrolytic Rectifier.   A saturated solution of sodium bicarbonate fills a glass jar.   Electrodes of aluminum and lead, each about 16 cm² in area and about 10 cm apart, are connected in series with a d.c. ammeter and an a.c. ammeter to an a.c. line. A potential divider controls the current (Fig. 261).   The ratio of average value of unidirectional current to effective value of alternating current is about 0.6.   The resistance of the cell to a direct current from lead to aluminum in the electrolyte is about 5 ohms, while the resistance in the opposite direction is about 50,000 ohms, due, probably, to the formation of a layer of hydrogen on the lead.

ELECTROMAGNETIC INDUCTION

E-215. Direction of Induced Electromotive Force. A straight copper wire is connected to the lecture galvanometer and is moved rapidly across the field between the poles of a strong electromagnet. A deflection of the galvanometer results. The relation between direction of motion, direction of field, and direction of induced current may be analyzed in accordance with the well-known rules.

E-216. Induced Current from Relative Motion of Magnet and Coil of Wire. Wind a coil of 100 or more turns of No. 30 copper wire on a wooden spool having a central hole large enough for the introduction of a bar magnet. Determine the relation between galvanometer deflection and direction of current with a dry cell (and protective resistance) in order to verify the direction of induced current when the coil is connected to the galvanometer. Move the north end of the magnet toward and away from the coil, and note that an emf is induced in the coil each time the magnet is moved but not when it is at rest. Repeat the operation with the south end of the magnet. Hold the magnet fixed while the coil is moved (motional emf); turn the coil through 180°, and again move it toward and away from the magnet. Finally pass the magnet through the coil. These experiments will verify the general principle that an emf is induced whenever there is a change in the number of lines of force passing through the coil and that the magnetic field of the current generated opposes the motion producing it.

E-217. Dependence of Induced Electromotive Force on Number of Turns. Coils 5 cm in diameter and having 1, 2, 5, 10, and 15 turns are wound from a *single length* of No. 18 copper wire, and each coil is bound with thread. When a strong cobalt-steel bar magnet is thrust into the coils successively, with as nearly constant speed as possible in each case, the emf induced is shown to be proportional to the number of turns in the coil. If the magnet is thrust into two coils held face to face, the emf induced is the algebraic sum of the emf's induced in the separate coils, the signs depending upon the sense of the windings. Thus when the 10-turn and 15-turn coils are used together, they will have the effect of a 5-turn or a 25-turn coil, depending upon the sense of winding.

If both poles of a horseshoe magnet are thrust into a coil connected to a galvanometer, no deflection occurs; thus the equality of poles is shown.   However, if the magnet straddles the coil so that only one of its poles enters the loop, a large deflection of the galvanometer results.

E-218. Motional Electromotive Force.   A motional emf is induced in a wire of length l moving with velocity v in a magnetic field B.   When both l and v are perpendicular to B, this emf is given by $e = \int B \cdot v \cdot dl$.   The wire A (Fig. 262), 6.5 cm long, is perpendicular to the magnetic field of the bar magnet NS.   It is attached to a wood or fiber disk E, which is free to rotate about an axis coincident with the axis of the magnet.   Strips of spring-temper phosphor bronze are soldered to the ends of A and make

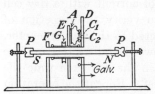

sliding contact with two rings, C_1 and C_2, of copper wire soldered to brass screws in the fixed support D.   The disk E and a pulley G are fastened to a piece of brass tubing that turns on a second tube supported by D and another support F.   Collars of copper wire are soldered near the ends of the inner piece of tubing to prevent end

Fig.   262.—Apparatus for showing motional electromotive force.

play.   The copper rings C_1 and C_2 are connected to a galvanometer arranged to measure to about 0.5 mv.[1]

When wire A revolves about the magnet, a motional emf induced in A will be shown by the galvanometer.   In a trial experiment, the magnet was 38 cm long, and its magnetic moment was 42×10^3 cgs units.   The center of A was 6 cm from the center of the magnet, and the angular speed of A was about 820 rpm.   In this case, the motional emf was about 0.24×10^{-3} v.

To demonstrate that the rotation of the magnet has nothing to do with the emf induced in A, the magnet is supported in bearings made by shrinking a brass endpiece P over each end of the magnet and drilling these endpieces to form cone bearings.   Steel screws turned or filed to points at their ends pass through supports attached to the base of the apparatus and fit into cone bearings.   One of the endpieces may be grooved to take a belt.   Thus both the magnet and the wire may be rotated simultaneously, either in the same or in opposite directions, or either may

[1] PAGE and ADAMS, *Am. Phys. Teacher*, **3**, 57, 1935.

be kept fixed while the other is rotated. In no case does rotation of the magnet affect the emf induced in A; *i.e.*, the field of the magnet is fixed whether the magnet itself rotates about its own axis or not.

If a brush (not shown in Fig. 262) is provided for making contact with the magnet while the latter is being rotated, the emf induced in the material of the magnet itself may be demonstrated. One terminal of the galvanometer is connected to the steel pivot at one end, and the other terminal is connected to the brush. The magnitude of the induced emf for a definite speed of rotation of the magnet depends upon the total flux through the magnet at the point of contact with the brush. If the brush is moved along the magnet while the latter is rotating at constant speed, the galvanometer readings will indicate the distribution of magnetization.

E-219. Current Induced when Change in Magnetic Flux Is Caused by Changing Electric Current—Faraday's Experiment. Two coils of wire are wound on an iron ring. The split toroid (E-96) is suitable for the present demonstration. One coil (secondary) is connected to the lecture galvanometer in series with whatever resistance may be necessary to keep deflections on scale. The other coil (primary) is connected to a battery with a key in the circuit. When current is started in the primary winding, a ballistic deflection of the galvanometer is obtained, and when the primary circuit is opened, the ballistic deflection is in the opposite direction. The second deflection is likely to be less than the first because of the large flux remaining in the iron after the magnetizing current has been reduced to zero. That this is the case may be shown by observing the large ballistic deflection obtained when the two halves

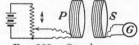

Fig. 263.—Steady current in S is induced by steady *change* of current in P.

of the toroid are separated after the magnetizing current has been stopped.

E-220. Two similar coils of wire each having several hundred turns are placed side by side. One (the secondary) is connected to the lecture galvanometer, the other (the primary) to a battery controlled by a potential divider, whereby the current through the coil is continuously variable (Fig. 263). A current is induced in the secondary so long as the current in the primary is changing.

If the slider of the potential divider is moved uniformly, a steady galvanometer deflection may be maintained for many seconds. Its magnitude will depend upon the *rate of change* of current in the primary and not upon the total current.   Reversing the motion of the slider of course reverses the direction of induced emf.   An iron core increases deflections.

E-221. Current Induced When Change in Magnetic Flux Is Caused by Change in Magnetic Circuit.   Two similar coils are connected to the galvanometer and battery as in E-220.   They are set parallel to one another about 5 cm apart.   A steady current is maintained in the coil connected to the battery.   When a rod of soft iron is pushed through the centers of the two coils, deflection of the galvanometer shows an induced current.   When the soft iron is withdrawn, an induced current occurs in the opposite direction.   A rod of copper or of brass produces no effect.   When the separation of the coils is changed, by moving them together or apart, a current will be induced in the coil connected to the galvanometer.

E-222. Earth Inductor.   A rectangular wire loop of a single turn about 1.5 m wide and 6 m long (Fig. 264) is made by attach-

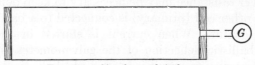

FIG. 264.—Simple earth inductor.

ing the ends of the loop to strips of wood with double-pointed tacks.   Its leads are connected to the lecture galvanometer. The demonstrator and a student hold the loop horizontal and then quickly turn it over through 180° so that it cuts the vertical component of the earth's field.   With an ordinary wall galvanometer not designed for ballistic work and in a latitude of 20° or more, the throw may be several scale divisions.   If the galvanometer has a damping turn attached to its moving coil, it should be removed for the present experiment.

A large flexible loop of many turns of wire connected to the galvanometer likewise produces a deflection when it is suddenly collapsed in the earth's magnetic field.

A long flexible wire is connected to the lecture galvanometer and swung like a skipping rope.   Its motion in the earth's magnetic field induces an alternating current of low frequency, which the galvanometer will follow if its period is short enough.

A commercially available earth inductor may be shown. This device is a coil of known area and known number of turns that can be rotated rather quickly through 180° by a spring. When the coil is connected to a calibrated galvanometer, the ballistic deflection produced by a half turn of the coil may be used to determine the absolute value of the vertical or horizontal components of the earth's magnetic field. The values of these two components are proportional to the respective galvanometer deflections.

E-223. Earth-inductor Compass. A circular coil of several hundred turns of wire may be arranged in bearings so as to turn continuously about a diametral axis. The ends of the coil are connected to two commutator segments on which stationary brushes make contact. Thus the coil is essentially a direct-current generator free to run in the earth's magnetic field. The brushes are connected to the lecture galvanometer. While the coil is rotating at constant speed (motor driven), its axis is turned to show that when it is in the magnetic meridian no deflection occurs, whereas when the axis is east and west, deflection is maximum. The direction of deflection depends, of course, upon the sense of rotation with respect to the field.

E-224. Magnetization of Iron Bar in Earth's Field as Shown by Induction Effects. Around the center of a soft-iron bar, 1 ft long and 1 in. in diameter, put a coil of about 600 turns, connected to the lecture galvanometer. With the bar in an east-west position. hammer it with a wooden mallet. There is no response in the galvanometer. Then turn the bar parallel to the earth's field, and hammer again rather gently; a deflection will occur. Pound harder, and get increased deflection, showing increased magnet-ization. Turn the bar to the east-west direction again, and on repeated taps the magnetism disappears, giving a galvanometer deflection in the opposite direction. Compare with E-80.

E-225. Induced Current in Metallic Disk—Eddy Currents. The Barlow's wheel apparatus described in E-136 may be used for demonstrating induced current. The axle of the copper disk and the pool of mercury are connected to the lecture galva-nometer. The disk is rotated by hand, and the galvanometer deflection shows the presence of an induced emf. The direction of this emf should be determined from the galvanometer deflection and used to check the dynamo rule. Some models of this apparatus are so designed that the disk may be lifted from its position between the poles of the permanent magnet. In this case, the galvanometer is disconnected, the axle and pool of mercury are connected by a wire of low resistance, and the disk is set into rotation while out of the magnetic field and is then lowered into contact with the mercury to show the magnetic braking effect resulting from induced eddy currents.

E-226. Arago's Disk. A magnet is suspended by a thread with its center above the center of a copper disk on a vertical shaft. When the disk is rotated in the field of the magnet, the induced eddy currents exert a torque on the magnet, causing it to rotate. A sheet of glass inserted between disk and magnet prevents spurious effects from air currents. Conversely, a rotating magnet causes a torque on a copper disk—the principle of the automobile speedometer.

E-227. Magnetic Brake. The damping effect of eddy currents may be shown by arranging a heavy copper disk so as to swing as a pendulum between the poles of an electromagnet. With no current in the windings of the magnet, the pendulum swings freely. If the switch is closed just before the edge of the disk enters the field, the pendulum is stopped abruptly by the damping effect of the eddy currents. If a similar disk in which several parallel slots have been cut is swung through the magnetic field, the effect of the slots in reducing the eddy currents is shown by the decreased damping.

A silver half dollar released between the poles of a strong electromagnet falls through the field with surprisingly low acceleration. (Project.)

A ring of heavy copper on a bifilar suspension may be swung through the magnetic field. When the plane of the ring is perpendicular to the field and parallel to the direction of motion, damping takes place in the nonuniform regions of the field. When the plane of the ring is parallel to the field, no perceptible damping occurs.

ALTERNATING CURRENT

E-228. Wave Form of Alternating Current. The type of model generator provided with an escapement whereby the armature is rotated only 10° at a time may be used to obtain a graph of generated emf as a function of angular position of the coil and hence of time. The armature is connected to a ballistic galvanometer whose successive throws are plotted in rapid succession on the blackboard, giving a sine wave that takes shape before the students' eyes. Thirty-six observations can be taken and plotted in a very few minutes. The wave form can be compared with that shown by a cathode-ray oscilloscope, when the vertical deflection plates are connected to the a.c. supply. The horizontal deflection plates are connected to the sweep circuit.

E-229. Alternating- and Direct-current Generators. There are several model generators and motors commercially available,

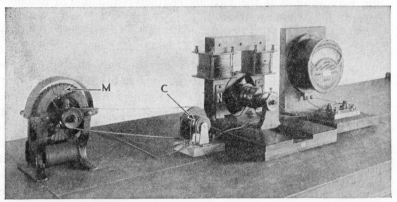

Fig. 265.—Model generator. The generator N may be run as a synchronous motor on alternating current of low frequency produced by the commutator C driven by the auxiliary motor M.

but none of them is large enough to be seen by any but a small class. The demonstrator may use the small models in spite of this obvious fault, or he may have a sizable piece of apparatus constructed. The model illustrated in Fig. 265 is a versatile piece of apparatus suitable for showing the principles of generators and motors.

The iron cores for both field and armature consist of 17 laminations of transformer iron, separated by spaces so that the total thickness perpendicular to the planes of the iron sheets is about 5 cm. This arrangement makes the apparatus large enough to be seen easily by the class; it also makes the proportions of the apparatus similar to those in a real machine and reduces the weight. The over-all height is 28 cm. The field has two shunt coils, each consisting of 2400 turns of No. 25 wire, and two series windings, each having 152 turns of No. 13 wire. The terminals of these coils lead to four binding posts on the fiber end of each frame. When the two shunt coils are connected in series to a 110-v d.c. supply, the current is 0.65 amp, which is more than sufficient for most experiments. The magnetic flux produced by the shunt field on 110 v is estimated at about 35,000 maxwells.

The armature bearings, mounted on a sliding piece of wood, are made to open quickly and easily. Thus the armature, complete with its slip rings and commutator, may be removed from its position between the pole pieces, and another substituted, so that one may show how the various characteristics of the machine depend upon the armature winding.

The armatures are 15 cm in diameter. An armature winding consisting of a single coil of 270 turns of No. 18 wire is suitable for many experiments. A crank on the end of the shaft is provided for turning the armature by hand. When the shunt field winding is connected to a d.c. source and the armature rotated at a speed of 4 or 5 rps, the output is sufficient to light two 4.5-v lamps in parallel. The commutator brushes or the slip-ring brushes may be connected to a galvanometer with the proper combination of resistances for showing the directions and magnitudes of the induced emf's as functions of the angular position of the armature when it is turned slowly. To indicate angular position, a pointer traveling over a circular scale may be fixed to one end of the shaft.

Each armature is provided with slip rings for use as an a.c. generator and with commutator segments for use as a d.c. generator. Hand rotation may be used during the demonstration of the a.c. and d.c. emf's generated. If the armature is driven by a motor at a higher speed, some change in the combination of resistances used with the galvanometer may be necessary.

The effect of changing the position of the brushes on the operation of both motors and generators may be demonstrated.

With either the small commercially manufactured model machine or the larger specially constructed model described, the wave form of the alternating current may be shown by an oscilloscope. A phonelescope (S-77) driven with a standard telephone receiver makes a good demonstration oscilloscope. The receiver electromagnet is connected to the slip rings of the model generator, and a suitable series resistance is included if necessary.

The machine may also be run as a low-speed synchronous motor. The field is then excited by direct current. A low-frequency alternating current is obtained from a d.c. source using a commutator C that may be rotated at low speed by an auxiliary motor M (Fig. 265). The commutator reverses the direction of current once each half revolution (see also A-23).

E-230. Counter Electromotive Force in a Motor. A lamp or a bank of lamps in parallel is connected in series with a motor. Either a d.c. or an a.c. motor may be used, and the number of lamps depends upon the no-load current required by the motor for operation at nearly normal speed. With no load on the motor, the lamps do not glow, on account of the counter emf generated by the motor itself. When a friction clamp is applied to the motor pulley, the counter emf is decreased because the speed of the armature is decreased, and the lamp filaments glow.

E-231. In another method for showing counter emf, the armature of a shunt-wound d.c. motor is disconnected from the line while running at full speed and quickly connected to a voltmeter or to the lecture galvanometer arranged as a voltmeter (E-154). The motor field is left connected to the supply line. A d.p.d.t. switch is useful for accomplishing the change quickly. The voltmeter indicates the counter emf, which decreases as the motor slows down. If braking action takes place too rapidly, a flywheel may be added.

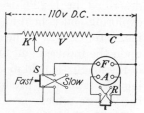

Fig. 266.—Circuit for controlling the speed of a small d.c. motor.

E-232. Simple Speed Control for Small Direct-current Motors. In many lecture experiments, as, for example, the siren disk (S-120) and the mechanical stroboscope (S-49 and S-81), it is desirable to control the speed of a motor over a wide range. The arrangement shown in Fig. 266 is simple and effective.[1] The field and armature terminals of a $\frac{1}{8}$-hp, d.c. motor are connected at F and A respectively by means of a four-prong radio socket and base from an old tube. The direction of rotation may be reversed by turning the d.p.d.t. switch R. The speed of rotation is

[1] Hoxton, L. G., *Science*, **84**, 187, 1936.

controlled between 0 and 100 rps by turning the d.p.d.t. switch
S and by moving the contact K on V, a rheostat of 200 ohms
resistance that serves as a potential divider.   The motor runs at
normal speed when K is at the left; it runs at higher than normal
speed when K is moved toward the right and S is in the position
shown.   When S is reversed, then moving K toward the right
reduces the speed below normal.   If the motor is to be run only
at normal speed, the switch C may be opened to stop loss of
power in V.

E-233. Synchronous Motor.   If an a.c. dynamo is available, it
may be run in either direction as a synchronous motor by supplying alternating current to the armature coils while the field
magnets are being excited with direct current.   The motor will
run at only one speed, namely, that at which it would have to be
run as a generator to deliver a current of the same frequency as
that supplied to it.   The armature must be brought up to
synchronous speed by external means; for example, by pulling
on a cord wrapped several times around its pulley.

E-234. Exploring an Alternating Magnetic Field.   An exploring coil of many turns of No. 30 wire is wound on a small frame
and connected to a 6-v automobile lamp.   An electromagnet with
a laminated iron core and an open magnetic circuit, like that
described in E-229, is operated on alternating current.   The
exploring coil is held in various locations in the open part of the
magnetic circuit.   The brightness of the lamp filament depends
upon the induced emf and therefore indicates the effective value
of the magnetic field in the region in which it is placed.   Mystify-
ing effects may be produced by concealing the a.c. magnet under
the lecture table.

E-235. Transformer.   A demonstration transformer can be
built up from materials easily obtainable.   A bundle of iron wires
6 cm in diameter and 30 cm long is wrapped with friction tape and
mounted vertically on a wooden base.   The primary winding is a
circular coil 8 cm in diameter with 200 turns of No. 14 wire, held
together with tape.   It is slipped over the core and held about
10 cm above the base on a wooden support.   It may be connected
directly to the 110-v, 60-cycle line without danger of overload.
Several secondary coils are provided, having different numbers of
turns wound on annular wooden frames.   The ends of the coils
may be connected to binding posts on the frames.   A 40-w, 110-v

lamp will be lighted if it is connected to the terminals of a secondary consisting of 200 turns of No. 24 wire. When the secondary is brought near the end of the iron core, the lamp filament will begin to glow; and when the secondary is slipped over the core near the primary, the lamp will operate at nearly normal brightness. A step-down transformer can be illustrated with a secondary of 12 turns of No. 18 wire in series with a 6-v lamp. A

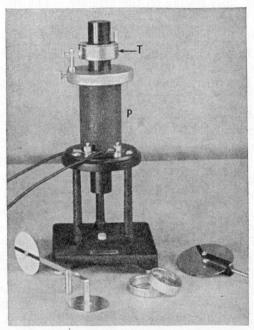

Fig. 267.—Step-down transformer. Water may be boiled in the trough *T* set above the primary *P*. The figure also shows additional equipment for use with this apparatus.

secondary of 400 turns of No. 24 wire connected to a 220-v lamp illustrates a step-up transformer.

E-236. Jumping Ring. An aluminum ring about 7.5 cm in inside diameter, 14 cm outside, and 0.4 cm thick is laid on top of the primary (E-235). When the switch is closed, the electromagnetic repulsion is enough to throw the ring high into the air, giving the demonstrator an opportunity to show his ability as a catcher. A student may be invited to attempt to hold the ring over the core. It is evident to the class that considerable force is required; and it is soon evident to the student that the ring grows uncomfortably hot. A split ring shows no effect. A ring cooled in liquid air shows an augmented effect due to increased conductivity (H-104).

E-237. Large Currents in Step-down Transformer. The heating effect of the large currents induced in a secondary of a single turn may also be shown by causing water to boil in a ring-shaped trough (Fig. 267) resting on the primary. The cross section of the trough is about 1 by 1 cm; it is made of sheet copper about 1.5 mm thick. The trough is enclosed, and a small steam vent is provided, which may be closed with a cork if the element of surprise is desired. The water in the trough should not be allowed to boil away, since the soldered joints would then quickly melt.

E-238. Autotransformer. A single coil of 400 turns of No. 18 wire, tapped at every 50 turns, may be used on the same iron core (E-235) to illustrate an autotransformer. The 110-v supply is connected across 200 turns. One terminal of a 110-v lamp is then connected to the beginning of the winding; when the other terminal is connected to the second tap, the lamp will be provided with 55 v; the fourth tap will furnish 110 v, and the lamp will glow normally. The higher taps give voltages in excess of 110 in steps of 27.5 v. These higher voltages may be shown by overloading the lamp or (more economically) by connecting two lamps in series.

Autotransformers are now available in sizes suitable for laboratory purposes. In one of these, the potential difference is 0.5 v between successive turns, and a sliding contact enables one to control the output voltage to the same degree as with a potential-dividing resistance. The losses in the autotransformer are very much less than in a resistance-type voltage-regulating device. With such a transformer designed for an input a.c. voltage of 110 v, the output voltage may be controlled between 0 and 260 v. A 110-v lamp may be used as the load, and it may be operated at various voltages from 0 to 125 v. The single lamp may then be replaced by two such lamps in series, this combination being operated at voltages up to 260 v. A 10-w, 110-v lamp may be operated for a short time at the full voltage of such an autotransformer with obvious increase in brilliance. The life of the lamp is short at such overloads, but the experiment is of value in showing not only the change in brightness but also the change of spectral distribution of energy (with consequent change of color) at the higher temperature of the filament (L-99).

E-239. Dissectible Transformer—Electric Welding. A transformer is more efficient if it has a closed magnetic circuit. Such a transformer, which can be used for the experiments described in E-233 and E-234 and for others as well, consists of two L-shaped laminated iron cores with interchangeable coils. The production of large currents as in the step-down electric-welding transformer may be demonstrated by using a secondary of only one or two turns of heavy copper cable connected to a short piece of heavy galvanized iron wire, about No. 6. When 110-v or 220-v alternating current is applied to the primary, the iron wire quickly becomes white hot, the zinc coating takes fire, and the wire burns in two.

E-240. Toy Transformer. Many types of small step-down transformer are commercially available. These usually have several separate windings from which wires lead to binding posts, thus making it possible to use different transformation ratios. Their design is more like that of commercial transformers than of those described in the preceding sections. To show the voltage transformation ratio, one may attach a 110-v lamp in parallel with the input line and a 6-v automobile lamp to the proper output terminals. Both lamps will operate at nearly normal brightness. To show the relation between the currents in the two windings, one may put a low-candle-power automobile-taillight lamp, which operates on about 0.5 amp, in series with the input side and connect across the 6-v terminals a piece of fuse wire that melts at about 10 amp. The input voltage is gradually increased by a potential divider or variable autotransformer. The fuse wire melts when the small lamp bulb is not much above normal brightness; thus an indication is given of the ratio of the currents in the two windings. At the moment when the fuse wire melts, the brightness of the small bulb decreases because of increased impedance of the primary in the absence of the large secondary current (see E-241 and 242).

E-241. Reaction of Secondary Circuit on Primary. Connect a 100-w lamp in series with the primary of a transformer, and show that when the a.c. supply is connected, the current is limited by the reactance of the primary when the secondary circuit is

opened, so that the lamp does not light.   However, if the secondary circuit is closed through a variable resistance, the reactance
of the primary diminishes, and the lamp increases in brightness as
current in the secondary circuit increases.

E-242. A step-down transformer is made with a primary of 320
turns and a secondary of 200 turns.   The coils are placed coaxi-
ally with the primary connected to a 110-v a.c. line with a 110-v

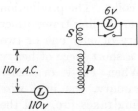

lamp in series; the secondary circuit has
a 6-v lamp with a shunting switch (Fig.
268).   With the shunting switch open,
the circuit is closed through the primary,
and the 110-v lamp lights.   A bundle
of iron wire is then inserted through
the two coils as a core; the 110-v lamp

Fig.   268.—Circuit for
showing reaction of secondary on primary of a transformer.

goes out, and the 6-v lamp lights.   But
when the shunting switch is closed, the
6-v lamp is short-circuited, and the 110-v

lamp comes on again, because of the reaction of the large
secondary current upon the impedance of the primary.

E-243. Magnetic Shunt.   An E-shaped laminated iron core
has coils of equal numbers of turns around two adjacent legs.   A
laminated iron yoke is provided to bridge either two or three of
the legs (Fig. 269).   The coil on the outer leg is connected to a
source of alternating current, and the center coil to a lamp that

glows   normally   when   the   yoke
covers   only   the   first   two   legs.
But   when   the   yoke   is   pushed
across   to   make   contact   with   all
three legs, there is a pronounced
drop in brilliancy because a large
fraction of the magnetic flux now
passes   through   the   third   leg,
which is a magnetic shunt.   The

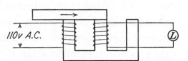

Fig. 269.—Magnetic shunt.   The
lamp glows with the magnetic yoke
in the position shown, but goes out
when   the   yoke   is   pushed   to   the
right so as to cover all three legs of
the core.

magnetic circuit is analogous to the electric circuit: the terms
magnetomotive force (mmf), flux, and reluctance correspond
respectively to emf, current, and resistance.

**E-244. Use of Transformers for Transmission of Energy at
High Voltage.**   The most extensive commercial use of transformers is in the transmission of energy over great distances at
high voltages for the purpose of reducing line losses.   To demon-

strate this use, a model transmission line may be arranged as in Fig. 270. A line made of No. 30 nichrome wire 2 m long has a resistance of about 80 ohms. At each end of the line there is a 110-v, 60-w lamp, R_1 and R_2. When both d.p.d.t. switches A and B are closed in position 2, the lamp at the output end of the line will operate at about 80 v, because of IR drop in the line. Voltages may be checked with a voltmeter. When both switches A and B are closed in position 1, the 110-v supply is stepped up to 750 v by a transformer T_1 of about 0.2-kva rating. The energy is transmitted at high voltage to the output end of the line, where a similar transformer T_2 steps it down. The lamp at the output end will then operate within 5 v of its normal voltage rating and consequently practically at its normal brightness. Transformers of the rating suggested may

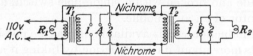

Fig. 270.—Model transmission line for comparing transmission at high and low voltage.

generally be purchased at low cost from companies dealing in used electrical equipment. With well-designed transformers, the no-load magnetizing current is so small that current in the high-tension side of the transformer at the output end of the line when switch B is in position 2 is negligible, especially since the potential drop across the high-tension side of T_2 is then much less than the rated value for this winding. The demonstrator must take care not to have switch A in position 1 when switch B is in position 2, since lamp R_2 would then be burned out.

E-245. Induction Coil. One or more induction coils may be exhibited as applications of the transformer principle for the production of high voltage from a d.c. source. If the spark takes place between spheres of about 1-cm diameter, the potential difference may be estimated from the approximate value of 30 kv per cm. If points are used, this value is much less. Sheets of paper or cardboard may be punctured by the spark. Brush discharges from points may be seen in a darkened room. The induction coil may be used for charging an electroscope or a condenser. One of the secondary terminals is connected to one plate of a parallel-plate air condenser. A spark is passed to the

other plate by bringing the other high-tension wire within sparking distance. The sign of the charge may be tested with the aid
of a proof plane (E-9). Where the induction coil is provided
with a condenser across the interrupter, the charge is always
of one sign. Reversing the terminals on either primary or
secondary changes the sign of charge.

The unidirectional nature of the discharge may be demonstrated by comparing the appearance of a glow discharge tube
(A-12) when operated first on the induction coil, then on a high-
voltage a.c. transformer (with protective series resistance in the
secondary circuit). Transfer from one source of potential to the
other may be made quickly by a d.p.d.t. switch.

An automobile spark coil may be used to produce a spark
across the gap of an automobile spark plug. The primary circuit
may be made and broken with a single-pole switch, as is done in
the distributor of an automobile.

If an old induction coil is available, it may be possible to show
the students more about its construction by taking it apart. The
condenser, interrupter, iron in the open magnetic circuit, and the
two windings are of interest.

E-246. Telephone and Radio Transformers. The extensive
use of transformers for technical, industrial, and laboratory purposes makes it desirable to show some of the commercial designs.
Telephone transformers usually have rather low transformation
ratios, 1:1 and 1:3 being common. Radio transformers (audio-
frequency) may have transformation ratios up to 1:28, this value
obtaining in one designed to have its primary in a single-button
microphone circuit with its secondary connected to the grid of a
triode.

If the secondary of such a transformer is connected to the case
and leaves of an electroscope, while its primary is operated on
about 20 v alternating current, the secondary voltage is sufficient
to deflect the leaves of the electroscope.

An alternative demonstration is to connect the secondary of an
audio-frequency transformer to the terminals of a high-impedance
loudspeaker with the primary in series with a telephone transmitter and a 3-v source of direct current. The handle of a tuning
fork is held against the transmitter case or the diaphragm. The
loudspeaker reproduces the sound of the tuning fork. The
operation may be improved if a vacuum-tube amplifier is used, in

which case a dynamic loudspeaker whose impedance is matched to the output stage of the amplifier may be used.

E-247. Speed of Alternating-current Motors. Mount on the end of the shaft of an induction motor a white paper disk with a radial India-ink arrow. Illuminate the disk with stroboscopic light from a neon lamp on 110-v alternating current, and observe its increased "slip speed" as the load upon the motor is increased by means of a friction clamp. A synchronous motor observed in the same way shows only a phase shift.

E-248. Rotating Magnetic Fields. A three-pole rotating-field magnet for use on three-phase alternating current may be constructed from stock transformer punchings (Fig. 271). The

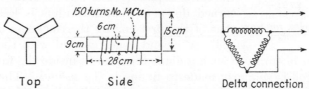

Top   Side   Delta connection

Fig. 271.—Construction of magnet for producing a rotating magnetic field from three-phase current.

magnetic circuit is about 36 cm² in cross-sectional area, and the distance from one pole through the iron to either of the other poles is about 62 cm, while the air gap is 10 cm. About 150 turns of No. 14 wire are required for each winding. The three coils are delta-connected and used on a 110-v, three-phase a.c. line, in which case the current in each of the three wires of the line is about 8 amp.

To show the rotation of the field, the rotor from a small squirrel-cage induction motor is mounted on pivots in the field. It should not be allowed to operate at an angular speed more than twice that for which it was designed. The direction of rotation may be reversed by interchanging any two phases. A saucer or a watch glass may be laid on the pole pieces, and a silver dollar or a disk of copper or aluminum stood on edge in it. If the coin or disk is started spinning about its vertical diameter, it will continue to rotate. A metal cylinder or tin can hung by a thread between the poles will also rotate. A blown egg, electroplated for strength and filled with iron filings, will start spinning in the field and will stand on end.

E-249. Remove the rotor from a three-phase induction motor of about ½ hp. Place a small steel ball inside the field winding. When the motor is connected with the three-phase supply mains, the ball will travel around a vertical circle. The speed is rather low compared with any speed approaching synchronism with the rotating field, so that the motion is easily observed. (Project.)

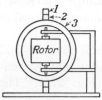

Fig. 272.—Arrangement of coils for producing a rotating magnetic field.

E-250. A simpler device for demonstrating a rotating magnetic field is illustrated in Fig. 272. A circular coil of 200 turns of No. 18 wire is wound on a wooden form 25 cm in diameter; after winding, it is slipped off the form and wrapped with friction tape to hold the turns in place. The wooden form is then turned down so that its radius is less than that of the first coil by the thickness of that coil. A second coil is wound with the same number of turns, of such a diameter as to fit inside the first. A third coil is similarly made to fit inside the second. The three coils are then mounted on a wooden base, the planes of the coils being vertical and making angles of 120° with each other. The coils are delta-connected to a 110-v three-phase line. The rotor is an empty tin can 12 cm in diameter and 12 cm high (a 1-lb tobacco can is satisfactory). The top is soldered on the can, and brass disks are soldered to the center of the top and the bottom. These disks are drilled to provide cup bearings. Steel pins held by a wood or fiber frame are sharpened to points to serve as cone bearings. The axis of the can is set vertical so as to coincide with the common diameter of the three coils. A rheostat should be included in each of the supply lines so as to limit the current through each coil to 8 amp; with this current, the coils will not overheat. The speed of the rotor will be high.

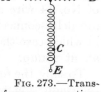

Fig. 273.—Transformer connections for changing three-phase to two-phase current.

E-251. A rotating magnetic field may likewise be made from a two-phase a.c. supply by using two coils with their planes at right angles to each other. Three-phase current may be transformed into two-phase, or vice versa, by two T-connected autotransformers. If three-phase current is supplied to the points *A, B*, and C (Fig. 273), then one phase of a two-phase output is obtained from A and B, and the other from D and E. The number of turns between A and B equals the number between D and E, but the ratio of the number of turns between D and C to the number between D and E is 0.87 (more accurately $\frac{1}{2}\sqrt{3}$).

Two-phase alternating current may be obtained from single-phase alternating current by running the two coils in parallel from the single-phase supply and inserting a large inductance in series with one of them.[1]

COILS AND CONDENSERS

E-252. Self-inductance. A large electromagnet is connected in parallel with a lamp. When this combination is connected to a source of direct current, the lamp glows. The lamp should be operated somewhat below its normal voltage. When the switch is opened quickly, the self-induced emf in the coil will be larger than was the potential drop across the lamp while the switch was closed. The lamp will therefore flash brightly before going out. The lower the power rating of the lamp, the greater the contrast. With a sufficiently large magnet, it is even possible to burn out a 10-w lamp by this inductive pulse. Slow opening of the switch makes the effect less pronounced.

E-253. The coils of an electromagnet, for example the shunt-field winding of a motor or generator operating on a potential drop greater than 75 v, are connected in parallel with a neon lamp having two semicircular plane electrodes, again in series with a d.c. supply. When the switch is closed, the lamp glows, but the glow surrounds only one of the electrodes. When the switch is opened, the induced emf makes the lamp glow for a short time, but the glow surrounds the electrode that was formerly dark. This is because the terminal of the coil that was at the higher potential during steady current will be at the lower potential when the switch is opened. The demonstrator may substitute a rheostat for the inductive winding to show that in this case no induced emf is detectable.

E-254. High Voltage from Low by Self-induction. A 4.5-v battery, neon lamp N, and iron-cored choke coil L are connected

---

[1] For a simple arrangement for showing a rotating magnetic field and the principle of the synchronous motor, see J. J. Coop, *Am. Phys. Teacher*, **6**, 37, 1938.

in series (Fig. 274).   The choke coil is of the type used in radio power-supply filters, or it may be the primary or secondary of an audio-frequency transformer.   When the switch S is closed, a small direct current is established in the choke coil; when S is opened, a momentary flash of *one* plate of the neon lamp occurs, thus showing that an emf much greater than the applied emf is generated by the decaying current.   The whole circuit may be

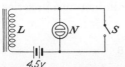

mounted on a small board for student operation, with a push button serving for the switch S.

FIG. 274.—Circuit to demonstrate inductive kick.

E-255. Effect of Inductance on Wheatstone-bridge Measurement.

A Wheatstone bridge of any type is used to measure the resistance of a coil having large inductance.   Almost any electromagnet is suitable.   Two keys are provided—one for the battery and the other for the galvanometer circuit.   The battery circuit is closed first; and after the current has had time to reach a steady value, the galvanometer circuit is closed, and the bridge balanced.   The galvanometer circuit is opened first, then the battery circuit.   Next the battery and galvanometer circuits are closed at the same time.   The galvanometer will show a large deflection because of the counter emf of self-inductance in the coil while the current through it is increasing.   If after the current has reached its steady value the battery circuit is opened, the galvanometer circuit remaining closed, the galvanometer will be deflected in the opposite direction.   This behavior may be contrasted with that of a bridge containing only resistance.   A shunt should be used to protect the galvanometer from damage.

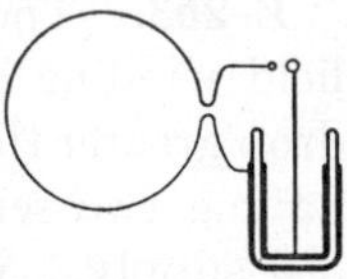

FIG. 275.—Circuit to demonstrate electromagnetic inertia.

E-256. Electromagnetic Inertia.

Bend a copper wire to form an Ω-shaped loop, almost closed (Fig. 275).   Discharge a Leyden jar through the loop.   The discharge jumps the air gap rather than pass through the low-resistance copper conductors, because the impedance of the loop to a current surge is great compared to the impedance of the air gap.

E-257. Time Required for Rise of Current in a Circuit Containing Self-inductance.

For this experiment, an electromagnet with a ratio of self-inductance in henrys to resistance in ohms greater than 2 is required. Almost any large electromagnet with closed magnetic circuit meets this requirement. L_1 and R_1 represent the self-inductance and resistance of the coil (Fig. 276). R_2 is a rheostat arranged for fine regulation of the current. In parallel with the fixed resistor R_3, there are a neon lamp and sufficient dry batteries B (radio B batteries) to furnish about 1 v less than the potential difference needed to make the lamp glow. A neon lamp requires a very definite minimum potential difference to initiate the discharge, but once started it will continue to operate at a potential difference much below this minimum starting value. Since the dry batteries furnish almost enough potential difference, it follows that a small additional IR_3 drop will cause the lamp to operate. It also follows that R_3 may be made small relative to R_1 with the result that the rate of increase of I will thereby be kept as low as possible. A three-pole switch is provided to stop the current through the neon lamp when the main circuit is opened.

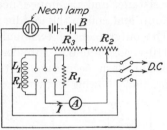

Fig. 276.—Circuit to demonstrate time-lag in rise of current due to self-inductance.

The switch is closed, and R_2 is adjusted carefully until the lamp glows. The switch is then opened. The next time the switch is closed, the neon lamp will not immediately glow because of the time required for the increase of I. An adjustment of battery voltage and R_2 may easily be made so that the additional IR_3 drop required to start the lamp will not be sufficient until I has risen to within 0.5 per cent of its final value. The lag between the closing of the switch and the flashing of the lamp may be made as much as 5 sec.

An approximately noninductive resistor having a value equal to R_1 should be substituted for the coils with the aid of a d.p.d.t. switch. When this substitution is made, the neon lamp glows as soon as the switch is closed. If the demonstrator does not wish to use the sound of the switch to indicate the zero time or if the switch is not visible to the class, he may connect a lamp of suitable voltage rating across the d.c. terminals of the three-pole switch to flash on when the switch is closed.

E-258. Inductive Reactance. A solenoid 40 cm long and 3.5 cm in diameter is wound with 1800 turns of No. 18 wire. The terminals of the coil are connected to the 110-v a.c. supply in series with a 200-w lamp. The lamp operates at nearly normal brightness until a bundle of iron wires about 60 cm long and 3 cm in diameter is put into the solenoid as a core. The reactance is increased by the iron to such an extent that the lamp filament is reduced to a dull red. Paradoxically, the brightness of a 10-w lamp is not changed so much, because its resistance is large in comparison with the reactance. The contrast between d.c. resistance and a.c. impedance is readily shown by connecting the lamp and coil to the middle pair of terminals of a d.p.d.t. switch. The outer pairs of terminals are connected respectively to the 110-v a.c. and d.c. supplies. Attention may be called to the bright flash occurring at the switch when the d.c. circuit is broken, showing evidence of the large emf of self-inductance (E-252 and 254).

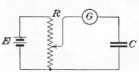

FIG. 277.—*Change* in voltage applied to the condenser is indicated by a current in the galvanometer.

E-259. Current as Rate of Change of Charge. The relationship between the charge on a condenser and the applied voltage is given by $Q = CV$. If the applied voltage V changes (while the capacitance C remains constant), a current is set up proportional to the *rate of change* of V; or $i = dQ/dt = C dV/dt$. This dependence of current upon rate of change of charge of a condenser may be shown by the simple circuit of Fig. 277. The rheostat R is connected across the battery E as a voltage divider. The condenser C (say 4 μf) is connected in series with the lecture-room galvanometer G. Whenever the voltage applied to the condenser is changed, a current is indicated by the galvanometer. It is easy to show that this current depends upon the rate of change of V, that it reverses in direction when the direction of change of V reverses, and that it is independent of the magnitude of V itself. A radio potentiometer is a convenient substitute for a slide-wire.

E-260. Capacitive Reactance. A 25-w, 110-v lamp is connected in series with a paper condenser of 6-μf capacitance. When 110-v direct potential is applied, there is no current; but when 110-v alternating potential is applied, the lamp lights. In this case, a voltmeter will show about 50 v across the lamp and about

82 v across the condenser with a line voltage of 110. Unless an electrostatic voltmeter is used, one cannot expect that the square root of the sum of the squares of the two readings will equal the total reading. When an ordinary voltmeter is used, the impedance of the instrument is not sufficiently high in comparison with the resistance of the lamp and the capacitive reactance of the condenser; hence the voltages read by the meter are less than the actual voltages existing before the voltmeter is connected. A phonelescope used as an oscilloscope (E-229) may be connected in series with a suitable resistor for showing the relative phases of the voltage across the lamp and across the condenser. The voltage across the lamp is in phase with the current, while that across the condenser is 90° out of phase. The oscilloscope may be connected to the lamp and then to the condenser successively by means of a d.p.d.t. switch. If the speed of the rotating mirror is properly adjusted and constant, there is no difficulty in detecting the fact that a phase difference of about 90° exists. If two oscilloscopes are available, the two waves may be shown simultaneously on the same screen. A piece of colored glass may be interposed in the path of the light that enters one of the oscilloscopes.

E-261. Condensers in Series and in Parallel. Two 2-μf condensers and a 40-w lamp are connected in series to the 110-v a.c. line. The current is too small to make the lamp filament glow. When the two condensers are in parallel, however, the lamp glows brightly (see also E-68).

E-262. Laws of Capacitance with Ballistic Galvanometer. The proportionality of quantity of charge to voltage applied to a condenser may be shown by charging a condenser successively to several different known voltages and observing the corresponding deflections when the condenser is discharged through a ballistic galvanometer (Fig. 278). If two

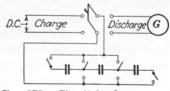

Fig. 278.— Circuit for demonstrating laws of capacitance.

or more condensers, not necessarily equal, are used, the additive nature of capacitance when condensers are connected in parallel may likewise be shown (E-68). If they are then connected in series, the deflections will be decreased since the effective capacitance is the reciprocal of the sum of the reciprocals of the individual capacitances.   In this latter case of series connection, it is instructive to show that *each* condenser produces the same galvanometer deflection when discharged individually, since the charge on each condenser is the same regardless of its capacitance.   From $Q = CV$, this experiment shows that the greatest potential difference must exist across the condenser of lowest capacitance.

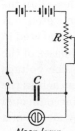

Neon lamp

FIG.   279.—
Flasher circuit.

E-263. Charging Time of a Condenser in Series with a High Resistance—Flasher Circuit.   A 4-μf condenser is connected in series with a variable high resistance that may be adjusted to values between 2 and 8 megohms.   Several grid leaks connected in series provide a satisfactory variable resistance.   A 2-watt, 110-v neon lamp with plane semicircular electrodes is connected in parallel with the condenser (Fig. 279).   Connection is made to a d.c. source (generator or B batteries) through a single-pole switch.   The condenser will start charging when the switch is closed; and when the potential difference across the condenser terminals has increased to about 80 v, the neon lamp will flash, thus discharging the condenser to about 60 v, the potential difference at which the neon lamp ceases to operate.   The cycle is then repeated.   By changing the resistance, the number of flashes per minute may be varied widely. The neon-lamp flash is not brilliant, and the room may have to be darkened.

E-264. Speed of Rifle Bullet by Condenser Discharge.   The speed of a rifle bullet may be measured by allowing a condenser to discharge through a resistor during the time required for the bullet to pass from a point A to a point B a known distance away, and by determining the time from the charge remaining on the condenser after the bullet has passed the point B.   A strip of tin foil 3 mm wide and 2 cm long is placed at A (Fig. 280), and a similar strip at B.   When key K is up, condenser C has a charge Q_0.   When K is depressed, the ballistic galvanometer shows a deflection θ_0 proportional to Q_0.   If K is up and a rifle bullet cuts the tin-foil strip A, then the condenser will discharge through the resistor R until the bullet cuts the strip B, at which time the condenser will stop discharging and will have a residual charge Q.   If K is then depressed immediately, the ballistic galvanometer deflection θ will be proportional to

Q. The equation that applies is $Q = Q_0 e^{-\frac{t}{RC}}$, where t is the time required for the bullet to travel the distance d. Then $t = -RC \log_e \frac{Q}{Q_0} = -RC \log_e \frac{\theta}{\theta_0}$, where t is in seconds, when R is in ohms, and C in farads. The speed V of the bullet is given by

$$V = - \frac{d}{\left(RC \log_e \frac{\theta}{\theta_0} \right)} = \frac{d}{\left(RC \log_e \frac{\theta_0}{\theta} \right)}.$$

In any particular experiment, the only variables in the above equation are V and θ. For rapid computation, it is desirable to

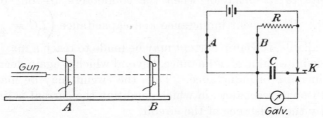

FIG. 280.—Arrangement of apparatus and circuit for measuring speed of bullet by condenser discharge.

plot on coordinate paper a few values of V against corresponding values of θ.

The muzzle speed of a bullet from a certain type of .22-caliber rifle is about 3.3×10^4 cm per sec. If $R = 4500$ ohms, $C = 2$ μf, and $d = 2.2$ m, then t will be about 6.7×10^{-3} sec, and the condenser will lose slightly more than half its original charge during the time required for the bullet to traverse the distance between the tin-foil strips.

The rifle is held in wooden clamps at one end of a board 3 m long. Each tin-foil strip is held between two ebonite rods by brass clips that also make electrical contact with the strip. The rods fit in holes bored in a narrow vertical board attached to the base by shelf brackets. The rifle is sighted first on strip B, after which strip A is moved into position, about 10 cm from the muzzle. A large block of soft wood or a sandbag may be located just beyond B to stop the bullet.

E-265. Combined Capacitive and Inductive Reactances. The solenoid described in E-258 has a reactance of about 120 ohms on

60-cycle alternating current. The inductive reactance of this coil will be equalled by the capacitive reactance of a set of condensers of total capacitance about 22 μf. If a coil with more self-inductance is available, then the amount of capacitance needed is correspondingly less. If a 40-w lamp is connected in series with an inductive and a capacitive reactor, several striking effects may be shown. When the condensers are short-circuited, increasing the inductance decreases the current through the lamp (E-258). When the inductor is short-circuited, increasing the capacitance increases the current through the lamp. Finally, with the capacitance at maximum value, the inductance is gradually increased. The lamp current then increases—just opposite to its behavior when the condensers are out of the circuit. If sufficient inductance and capacitance $\left(LC = \dfrac{1}{4\pi^2 n^2}\right)$ are available, the lamp current may be made to reach a maximum for a definite value of inductance, beyond which it again decreases with increase of inductance. Thus the circuit may be made to pass through resonance, in which condition the current is limited only by the resistance of the circuit.

The potential drops across the condensers, the inductor, the lamp, and the terminals of the whole circuit should be measured. The arithmetic sum of the first three will greatly exceed the fourth because of phase differences (see also E-268).

E-266. Oscillatory Charge of Condenser through an Inductor. If a condenser is charged through an inductor, the potential difference between its plates may rise above the applied emf because the charging sets up oscillation.[1] That this is the case may be shown by the circuit of Fig. 281. The voltmeter V reads the d.c. voltage applied from the potential divider to the condenser C. If switch S is in position 1 and key K is pressed, the condenser is charged only through the resistor R. A neon tube N shunted across the condenser glows only if the applied voltage as read by V is high enough to strike an arc. Once the arc strikes, the voltage may be decreased considerably without extinguishing the glow discharge. Having determined the necessary voltage for causing N to glow when K is depressed, the potential divider is set so that V reads 10 to 20 v *less* than this

---

[1] For analytical treatment, see, for example, Page and Adams, "Principles of Electricity," p. 349, D. Van Nostrand Company, Inc., New York, 1931.

value.   Depressing K no longer causes N to glow, but if S is
turned to position 2, N will light when K is depressed, provided
that the condenser has previously been discharged by closing the
switch D momentarily.   The circuit has "memory"; for if N is
once lighted by depressing K when S is at 2, it will not light a
second time until the condenser C has been discharged.   If the

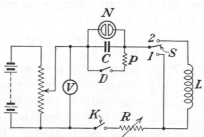

FIG. 281.—Circuit for showing oscillatory charging of condenser through an inductor.

series resistance R is increased, a point is reached where the
circuit no longer oscillates as it is charged.   Best results are
obtained if the capacitance of C is not too large; 0.1 μf or less is
suggested. P is a lamp or other protective resistance, in case D is
closed when S is in position 1.

E-267. Oscillatory Discharge of a Condenser.   A condenser C
of 6- to 8-μf capacitance is charged to 200 or 300 v, by depressing
key K momentarily (Fig. 282).   Now
with switch S in position 1, the neon
lamp N glows on only one electrode
when switch D is depressed to discharge the condenser through the
10,000-ohm resistor R.   But when S is
moved to position 2 and C is recharged

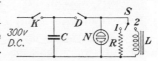

FIG. 282.—Circuit for showing oscillatory discharge of a
condenser.

and again discharged, *both* electrodes of N glow.   In this case,
the discharge occurs through an iron-core radio coil L of approximately 2 henrys inductance.

E-268.   The secondary of a high-voltage transformer is
shunted with several Leyden jars (connected in parallel) and with
a spark gap in series with an inductor made of several turns of
heavy copper wire.   A projection lens casts an image of the spark
gap onto a piece of opal glass by way of a plane mirror which
can be turned about an axis parallel to the gap.   Whenever a

spark passes across the gap and its image is cast upon the opal glass from the rapidly rotating mirror, there appears a "ladder" of bright flashes from alternate sides of the gap, thus giving visual evidence of the oscillatory nature of the discharge. If the Leyden jars are disconnected, the character of the image changes greatly.

E-269. Phase Relations of Voltages across Elements of Oscillating Circuits. The circuit with resistance, inductance, and capacitance in series (E-265) is tuned to resonance on a 110-v a.c.

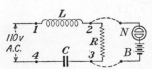

FIG. 283.—Oscillating circuit and neon lamp arranged to show phase relations.

line (Fig. 283). A neon lamp is biased with a radio B battery so that when its terminals are connected to any pair of successive terminals, 1-2, 2-3, or 3-4, only one electrode of the neon lamp glows. The intermittent light from the neon lamp falls upon a black disk with a white paper sector, rotated by a synchronous motor. The apparent position of the white sector will depend upon whether the neon lamp is connected across R, L, or C.

For further experiments on resonant circuits, see A-22 to A-40.

PART V

LIGHT

LIGHT SOURCES

L-1. Projection Lanterns. Projection lanterns are of two types, tungsten filament and carbon arc. For ease in operation, the filament lamp is best, but for many experiments the intensely

FIG. 284.—Lantern arranged for projection of apparatus.

bright carbon arc gives superior results. Each type has its advantages, and both should be available if possible.

For some demonstrations in Light and for many others where a small piece of apparatus if projected may be seen by the entire class, it should be possible to remove independently the projection

367

lens, the slide holder, and the lens tube or bellows. Then next to the condensing lenses may be placed a shelf or bench on which the apparatus is supported for projection. The projection lens can be mounted on a separate stand. One way of accomplishing this is shown in Fig. 284, where the projection lens P is supported by an adjustable clamp and pieces of apparatus may be placed on the shelf S, whose height is likewise adjustable.

The lantern should be equipped with a vertical projection attachment, so that objects (such as a dish of water) that must be kept in a horizontal plane may be projected (Fig. 285).

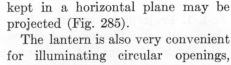
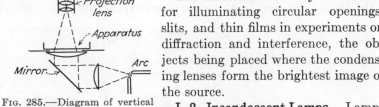

FIG. 285.—Diagram of vertical projection lantern.

The lantern is also very convenient for illuminating circular openings, slits, and thin films in experiments on diffraction and interference, the objects being placed where the condensing lenses form the brightest image of the source.

L-2. Incandescent Lamps. Lamps with straight filaments such as are used in show-window lighting are available in several sizes and power ratings.[1] They are especially useful for diffraction and interference experiments (L-73, etc.).

Miniature lamps (flashlight) are made for operation from batteries or small transformers for various voltages up to 6 or 8 v. Colored Christmas-tree lights operating at 14 v are convenient for some experiments.

Automobile lamps are made in many styles, from the very bright double-filament headlight type (21, 32, and 50 cp) to single-filament lamps having a very short straight length of finely coiled wire. Sockets for these lamps may be obtained from automobile supply houses, or the lamps may be used without sockets by soldering a short length of lamp cord directly to the terminals. A 6-v lamp is a very useful source; it can be run from a storage battery or a transformer, and when operated at 10 v it furnishes an intense light, though its life is shortened.

A "point" source, sold under various trade names, is made by a tungsten arc in vacuum. It consists of a small tungsten bead

---

[1] For example, General Electric T-6½, T-8; Westinghouse T-14.

that is raised to incandescence by ion bombardment, giving a very intense and steady source of small area.

Photoflood lamps are available that are much more brilliant and much richer in violet light than ordinary lamps, because they are purposely overloaded at 110 v. They are excellent for producing intense illumination as well as for showing by comparison with ordinary lamps the increased whiteness produced by a hotter source. Any standard lamp may be similarly overloaded, e.g., by an autotransformer (E-238).

A convenient holder for standard lamps can be made from a piece of $\frac{7}{16}$-in. brass tubing, 10 to 18 in. long, threaded at one end to fit the base of the ordinary keyed or keyless lamp socket. The connecting cord enters through the brass tube. This holder can be clamped in any position on an ordinary stand.

L-3. Neon and Argon Glow Lamps. Inexpensive glow lamps equipped with the standard medium base for operation on 110-v direct or alternating current are available. On direct current, they amount to polarity indicators. On alternating current, they give flashes of double the a.c. frequency. They can be used for stroboscopic illumination and as spectroscopic sources in the laboratory but are not bright enough for projection in the lecture room. The argon lamp has enough ultraviolet radiation for some experiments on fluorescence (L-114).

L-4. Sodium and Mercury Vapor Lamps. The recently developed sodium vapor lamp makes possible an intense source of monochromatic radiation. It is valuable in demonstrations of color perception, interference, diffraction, and spectroscopy. Quartz mercury vapor lamps are excellent for showing effects of ultraviolet radiation; they are, however, expensive. Less expensive glass lamps are obtainable for lecture and laboratory use, or they may be constructed according to directions given elsewhere.[1]

LIGHT PATHS MADE VISIBLE

L-5. Invisibility of Light. A wooden box, 6 by 6 by 18 in., is constructed with a hinged top and glass front. A hole about 2 in. in diameter is cut in each end and a piece of mailing tube inserted in each hole to reduce stray light. The inside of the box is painted a dead black. A lens of focal length 6 to 8 in. is mounted in one of the end apertures and masked down to about 1-in.

---

[1] BALINKIN and WELLS, *Rev. Sci. Instruments*, **3**, 7, 1932.

aperture with a black diaphragm. The inside of the box is coated with oil or glycerin to render the interior dust free. A carbon or tungsten arc is placed at the outside focus of the lens and adjusted so that a parallel beam passes through the center of the opposite aperture. No evidence of light can be seen in the interior of the box. This condition will be altered if a white card is introduced into the box so as to interrupt the path of the beam.

L-6. Optical Disk. A disk of metal a foot or more in diameter whose surface is painted white and whose rim is graduated in

Fig. 286.—Optical disk.

degrees is mounted on an axis about which it can rotate. The disk is supported vertically by a stand that also carries a shield in the form of a short cylinder at right angles to the disk (Fig. 286). An opening is cut in the shield at the height of the center of the disk, over which may be slipped shutters containing one or more horizontal slits. When a parallel beam of light is directed at these slits, the paths of the separate beams passed by the slits are made visible on the surface of the disk. Sections of mirrors, prisms, lenses, etc., may be clamped to the face of the disk and the result of reflection or of refraction made visible. Numerous experiments in geometrical optics are possible with this apparatus.

A substitute for the optical disk is the following. An open arc (Fig. 287) is mounted on the floor close to the wall and turned so as to send a beam of light upward. A plano-cylindrical lens L is mounted below a slotted cover. The slots are closed with sliding covers so that as each cover is slowly withdrawn a ray is "drawn" up the wall. Cylindrical lenses and mirrors can be introduced above the cover and the paths of the rays traced after reflection and refraction.

L-7. Optical Tank. A long trough with glass sides and ends is useful for many experiments. It is filled with water to which a small amount of fluorescein or other fluorescent material has been added, by means of which the paths of the rays of light are made visible to the class. The size of the tank depends in part upon the lenses and other accessories that are to be used with it. A suggested size is 3 by 3 by 36 in. A convenient addition is a mirror

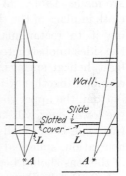

Fig. 287.—Arrangement for showing light paths on wall.

running the length of the tank just above it and tipped at 45° so that the class can look down into the tank from above as well as into it from the side. Such a tank is useful for showing reflection and refraction phenomena; it can also be used for showing scattering and polarization (L-127).

The frame supporting the glass sides must be of rigid construction so as to carry the weight of the glass and water without appreciable distortion. Otherwise the stresses are apt to crack the joints. The joints should be made watertight with some form of aquarium cement or glue that will not grow hard and crack during the long intervals when the tank is idle and dry, or peel off and cause leaks when the tank is filled with water.

For reflection, refraction, and total internal reflection, a large flat-sided battery jar filled with water containing a small amount of fluorescein will serve nicely to show the light paths to a whole class. A sheet of flashed opal glass (milk glass) set vertically at a small angle with the beam will make it visible both below and above the surface of the water.

L-8. Gauze Screen. A rectangular wooden frame 2 ft wide and 3 or 4 ft long is held in a vertical plane by a clamp. Across the frame are stretched white threads or fine cotton strings 2 or 3 mm apart. When a lens is placed near one end of the frame and a beam of light directed upon it, the beam after passing the lens will be caught and scattered by the threads so that a large class can see the light paths. By using a small section of a similar screen before the lens, the incident as well as the refracted rays are made visible. A simplification of this plan is to use cheese-cloth in place of the threads. It can be stretched tight by fastening it to rectangular metal rods at top and bottom, leaving the sides unobstructed, or it may be held taut in an iron hoop by light helical springs. If two rectangular rods are screwed or clamped together with the cloth between them, at both top and bottom, the upper rods may be held in a clamp, and the weight of the lower ones will keep the cheesecloth stretched. A screen of this type is especially useful for showing lens action, chromatic aberration, spherical aberration, and distortion. The optic axis of the lens should be in the plane of the gauze.

L-9. Smoke Box. A large wooden box, say 15 by 15 by 60 in., is equipped with a glass front and hinged top. Windows are cut in the ends, and the box is painted black inside. When it is filled with smoke or ammonium chloride fumes, the light scattered by the particles will make the light paths visible. (For the method of making ammonium chloride smoke, see A-5.) Lenses, mirrors, prisms, etc., may be set inside the box, so that light paths may be seen before and after reflection or refraction. The box is useful for showing lens combinations, as in telescopes and microscopes (L-54, 55).

L-10. Chalk Dust. A very simple expedient for making light paths visible is to clap two dusty blackboard erasers together above the light beam. The chalk dust will make the beam visible; but the region filled with the dust is limited and variable, and the dust soon settles.

PHOTOMETRY

L-11. Inverse Square Law of Intensity of Illumination. Connect the output of a photocell (A-91) to the lecture-room galvanometer. Remove the condensing lenses from a projection lantern, preferably of the arc type, and place the cell in a position to give maximum galvanometer deflection when illuminated by the lantern. Double and then triple the distance of the cell from the source, and note the inverse square relation.

The way in which area increases as the square of the distance from a point can be illustrated with a wire frame in the form of a pyramid of square section (Fig. 288). If the edge at the base is three units, for example, then a square of edge two units can be placed in the frame at one-third the distance to the vertex and a square of one unit at two-thirds the distance.

L-12. Joly Diffusion Photometer. Two blocks of paraffin (sold in grocery stores) about 2.5 by 5 by 0.5 in. with a sheet of tin foil or cardboard between them are clamped between two strips of thin wood and set vertically between the two sources of light that are to be compared, so as to be seen edge on. The sources are moved until the blocks match in appearance.

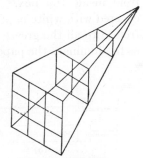

Fig. 288.—Wire frame to illustrate inverse square law of light intensity.

The arrangement can be improved and made less perishable by placing the paraffin blocks at the middle of a box open at both ends and painted black inside. The edges of the blocks are observed through a glass window set in one side of the box. The blocks are held between two glass plates, which prevent the paraffin from flowing in warm weather. This arrangement eliminates stray light and makes photometric comparisons possible without darkening the room. The apparatus can be seen by a large class, and quantitative measurements are easily made.

L-13. Rumford Shadow Photometer. A laboratory support rod is set vertically 1 ft in front of a screen. The two sources of light to be compared are placed so as to cast separate shadows of the rod on the screen and are moved until the shadows appear to have the same intensity. Electric light bulbs are satisfactory sources; they should be mounted on stands (L-2) so that they can be moved about. The edges of the shadows may be hazy, and there may be marked color differences in the shadows, so that this method of comparison is not particularly accurate. The distances involved are to be measured from each light to the shadow cast by the other.

L-14. Modified Bunsen Grease-spot Photometer. A triangular box (Fig. 289a) is made of light wood, the long side 26 in., the short side 5 in., and the depth 5 or 6 in. Across the hypotenuse of the triangle is stretched a piece of white paper PP on which is a row of 10 or 12 grease spots made with hot paraffin. A 40-w bulb is placed at S near the side BC to illuminate the spots from inside the box. The inside should be painted white or covered with white paper or Bristol board to help diffuse the light from S to all the grease spots. A light outside the box placed so as to illuminate the paper is moved until its distance is such as to

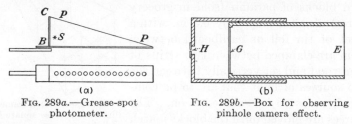

FIG. 289a.—Grease-spot
photometer.

FIG. 289b.—Box for observing
pinhole camera effect.

make one of the grease spots nearly disappear. Spots on one side of this then look brighter and on the other side darker than the surrounding area. This apparatus, which illustrates the principle of grease-spot photometers, can be made quantitative in principle, though not, perhaps, very precise, by calibrating it with the aid of an illuminometer (foot-candle meter).

A Bunsen grease-spot photometer and a Lummer-Brodhun photometer may be shown if desired, but they are suitable for observation by only one student at a time. Modern photoelectric illuminometers and photographic exposure meters may be exhibited.

L-15. Rectilinear Propagation of Light. An incandescent lamp is surrounded by a housing, the front of which is closed with a sheet of heavy paper or cardboard. A projection lantern without lenses may be used. By means of a steel wire 1 or 2 mm in diameter, a hole is pricked in the paper, and the light passing through it to a screen will produce thereon an inverted image of the lamp filament. The best size for the hole must be found by trial; too small a hole will not allow enough light to pass through, while too large a hole will not produce a sharp image. As more and more holes are pierced in the paper, each forms its own image of the filament, and these images may overlap. The illumination of the screen is the result of the superposition of all the different images of the source.

The same effect may be shown by using a 6-v, 32-cp lamp in a small box with a hole in one side. Pinholes of different sizes are made in a disk arranged to turn so that any hole can be brought in front of the opening in the box. The light from each pinhole in turn falls on the screen to produce an image large enough for the class to see. An empty chalk box is satisfactory. The cracks can be closed with black gummed tape. Any of the methods described in L-6 to L-10 may be used for showing rectilinear propagation.

L-16. Pinhole Camera. Two boxes are made, one to slide snugly within the other (Fig. 289*b*). One end of the inner box is closed with a piece of opal glass *G*. The end of the outer box is closed with a brass plate through which is bored a 1-mm hole *H*. The observer looks through the end of the inner box at *E* to see an inverted image of external objects on the glass plate *G*. The size of image may be varied by sliding the inner box in and out. The camera can be used in a fully lighted room provided that the end *E* is arranged to fit over the forehead and the bridge of the nose so as to exclude extraneous light.

On a bright sunny day, the pinhole camera effect may be shown on a large scale. The room is darkened, and light is admitted only through a hole 1 or 2 in. in diameter in a curtain or shutter. Inverted images of outside objects or passers-by may be seen on the opposite wall. If the background is dark (*e.g.*, grass, shrubbery, or a brick building), an assistant dressed in white, walking back and forth within the proper area, perhaps waving his arms, makes a good object. With snow on the ground, he should of course wear dark clothes. The size of the image depends upon the distance of the screen from the hole.

A photograph of a local building made with a camera in which the lens has been replaced by a pinhole may be exhibited either as a lantern slide or by opaque projection. To make the pinhole, a thin brass plate is marked with a punch by a sharp hammer blow, and the resulting bulge is filed until the first trace of an aperture appears. With such a pinhole, an exposure of about half an hour in full sunlight is required to produce a photograph of good quality. Pinholes of reproducible size may be made by puncturing aluminum foil with a sewing needle, noting the depth to which the needle penetrates the foil.

L-17. Speed of Light. It is scarcely practicable to measure the speed of light as a demonstration experiment. However, by using a small mirror mounted on a high-speed top,[1] an appreciable effect over moderate distances may be shown by Foucault's method. The principle of Fizeau's toothed-wheel method may be demonstrated by use of sound instead of light (see S-81). It may be sufficient simply to set up mirrors and light source on the lecture table so that the student may visualize the arrangement of optical parts used in one or more of the standard methods employed for determining the speed of light.

REFLECTION

L-18. Plane Mirror. The virtual image formed by a plane mirror may be demonstrated by superposing it on a real object. A light is placed in front of a sheet of glass, behind which, at an equal distance, is placed a glass of water. The image of the light appears to be in the water. To make the experiment visible to a large class, the apparatus should be mounted on a rotating table so that it can be turned. This also enables the class to see by the parallax effect that the image is located behind the mirror but is fixed with respect to it. If the lecture room is banked so that the seats in the rear are high, it is important to locate the light low enough and to have the sheet of glass tall enough so that the image may be seen from the uppermost seats. A convenient source of light is a candle or a small electric light run from a transformer or storage battery.

A large letter *F* is cut from cardboard and mounted in front of a plane mirror on a rotating table. The interchange of right and left is evident. With two mirrors set at an angle of 90°, the image can be brought back to proper orientation.

L-19. Reflection at Normal and at Grazing Incidence. The difference in the amount of light reflected from glass near normal incidence and near grazing incidence can be readily shown by holding a large sheet of clear glass in the beam of light from a

---

[1] Experimental arrangements are described in Harnwell and Livingood, "Experimental Atomic Physics," McGraw-Hill Book Company, Inc., New York, 1933.

lantern. The glass is held near the lantern, set midway between two walls, and the light is reflected first to a spot on one wall nearly in line with the original beam (grazing incidence) and then to another spot on the opposite wall almost behind the source (normal incidence). The intensity of the reflected light at grazing incidence is many times that at normal incidence.

If it is desired to keep the position of the illuminated spot unchanged, the lantern may be turned around through 180° while the mirror is turned through 90°. One may compare the intensity of beams reflected by plane glass and by a well-silvered mirror. At normal incidence, there is great contrast; at grazing incidence, almost none. A single sheet of glass, half clear and half silvered, is convenient for rapid comparison.

L-20. Multiple Reflections in Plane Mirrors. Two plane mirrors, which may be hinged together, are placed on a rotating table so that they stand vertically. Between them is placed a small source of light such as a flashlight or automobile taillight. The multiple images can be seen by a large class if the source is placed close to the vertex of the dihedral angle formed by the mirrors. When a sheet of clear glass held in a slotted block is set vertically between the two mirrors, so as to form approximately an isosceles triangle with them, the number of images visible is greatly increased. By raising the front edges of the two mirrors and slightly tilting the sheet of glass backward, the images can be made visible to those in the raised seats of the lecture room. If the single light source is now replaced or supplemented by several differently colored Christmas-tree lights, some very beautiful effects can be produced, and the principle of the kaleidoscope can be shown to the entire class at once.

By placing two mirrors exactly at right angles to one another, it is possible "to see yourself as others see you." Right and left are interchanged without distortion so that the student has the illusion of looking at himself in a plane mirror, but he may be surprised at the behavior of his image if he winks his right eye!

The number of reflections increases as the angle between the two mirrors is reduced. If two mirrors are placed nearly parallel, the number of reflections is very large ("barbershop effect"). Place a bright headlight bulb midway between two parallel mirrors, and observe the multiple reflections through a peep-hole made by removing the silver from a small area of one mirror.

L-21. Plane Mirrors—Special Combinations. If two plane mirrors make an angle of 90° with one another, then a ray of light incident upon one of them is turned through 180° and reflected back parallel to itself regardless of the direction of incidence, so long as the incident ray is in a plane normal to both mirrors. If three mirrors are mutually perpendicular (like the three faces forming one corner of a cube), then a ray of light incident on the system will be reflected parallel to itself regardless of the direction of incidence. This principle is used in many road signs where the letters or other characters are made of many mirrors of this type. Such reflectors are available at automobile supply stores.

L-22. Laws of Reflection. The fact that when light is reflected from a plane mirror the angle of reflection is equal to the angle of incidence may be shown with any mirror and source of light. However, it is more convenient to use an optical disk (L-6). A beam of light falls upon a mirror whose plane is perpendicular to the disk. By turning the disk and with it the mirror, it is shown that the reflected beam turns through twice the angle through which the mirror is turned.

L-23. Concave Mirror—Phantom Bouquet. This experiment has many forms. The method in

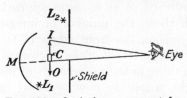

FIG. 290.—Optical arrangement for showing phantom bouquet.

all is to superpose part or all of the real image of an object O (called the "bouquet"), formed by a concave spherical mirror, on some other object C (called the "vase") so that a person viewing the combination will have the illusion that it is all real (Fig. 290). For satisfactory results, the image I of the bouquet produced by the mirror must actually fall in the proper position with respect to the vase C so that parallax will not destroy the illusion. The observer must be able to see only C and the image of O and not O itself, which is the reason for the shield. The illumination of the bouquet O and of the vase C must be such as to preserve the illusion. Both should be illuminated in corresponding manners by the same type and intensity of light. Thus O will be lighted from the side next to the mirror by L_1, while C will be lighted from the side next the observer by the light L_2, all lights to be hidden if possible. The mirror should be as large as possible, but it is equally important to use a mirror

with a large ratio of diameter to focal length.   Thus the brilliance
is increased and the angular field covered by the image is enlarged.
Generally the object is put just below the center of curvature
of the mirror, and the part seen is just above it.   The class is
asked first to see the illusion and then to locate the bouquet.

L-24.   A blackened porcelain receptacle is mounted on the
under side of the top of a wooden box, and just above it, in full
view on top of the box, is mounted a second (white) receptacle.
The interior of the box is painted dead black.   The black receptacle contains a 40-w tungsten lamp; the white one is empty.
A concave mirror is set behind the box so as to form a real image
of the lamp above the empty socket.   When properly adjusted,
the arrangement gives the illusion that the lamp is situated in
the upper socket; but when the lamp is turned off by an external
switch, the image disappears.

L-25. Concave Mirrors—Caustics.   Large cylindrical mirrors
that are excellent for showing caustics and other phenomena to a
large class can be cheaply and easily made from thin strip metal
fastened to a wooden form.   Cut out of plywood the shape of the
mirror desired—spherical, parabolic, etc.   To the curved edge of
this form screw or nail a strip of thin nickel or tinned iron sheet
about 2.5 in. wide.   If now the inside surface of the board is
painted white or covered with a white paper or Bristol board, the
caustic formed by the mirror is easily seen.   A semicircular
mirror of 6- to 7-in. radius and a parabolic mirror of corresponding
size are convenient.   When illuminated
by a bright source, they can be seen by
a large class.

L-26. Ellipsoidal Mirror.   The parallel beam formed by a converging
lens using incident light previously
reflected from the distant focus of an

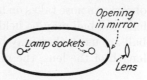

Fig. 291.—Ellipsoidal mirror.

ellipsoidal mirror is more intense than if the same source is at
the nearer focus of the ellipsoid (which is also the focus of the
lens) because reflection, in the first case, concentrates the radiation from 180° into a much smaller cone.

Cut out of plywood an ellipse 50 cm long by 30 cm wide, which
has a focal length of about 5 cm (Fig. 291).   Mount an electric-
light socket accurately at each focus.   Fasten a strip of monel
metal or other highly reflecting material 17 cm wide around the

edge of the board, leaving an opening about 3 cm wide at one end. Place a condensing lens opposite the open end, with one focus at the adjacent focus of the ellipse.   Screw into each socket a single-filament lamp (*e.g.*, Westinghouse T-14, 6 v), and cover with black paint that side of the most distant lamp that faces the lens, to insure that the only light that reaches the lens from the distant lamp arrives by reflection from the ellipsoid.   By operating the two lamps alternately with the aid of a two-way switch, it will be found that the more intense beam originates at the distant lamp. For a parabolic mirror formed by rotating mercury, see M-143.

L-27. Convex Mirror.   The reduced, virtual image seen in convex mirrors is doubtless familiar to most students.   Distortion of image is frequently observed when parts of an object are

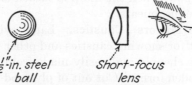

$\frac{1}{2}$-*in. steel*
ball   *Short-focus*
lens

Fɪɢ. 292.—Arrangement for viewing highly distorted image in convex mirror.

at different distances from such a mirror.   An amusing example of this distortion is seen when reflection takes place from a convex surface of high curvature, such as a small steel ball (Fig. 292). The ball, $\frac{1}{2}$ in. to 1 in. in diameter, is held 3 or 4 in. away from the observer's eye.   The image is viewed with a strong lens.   The observer's nose takes on ludicrous proportions.   For convenience, lens and ball may be held in a wire frame; if a 4-in. lens and $\frac{1}{2}$-in. ball are used, they may be separated 3 in.   The shorter the focal length of the lens, the more exaggerated the effect.

REFRACTION

L-28. Refraction.   The image of a straight wire is projected on a screen.   Near the wire on the side next to the projection lens is held a thick rectangular block of glass making a considerable angle with the normal to the light beam.   A part of the image of the wire on the screen will be displaced.   If thick glass is lacking, a parallel-sided glass vessel of water (projection cell) may be used. Refraction of light by water may be shown with the optical tank (L-7).   The ripple-tank method (S-49) of showing refraction of surface waves is useful for emphasizing the relation of refraction to wave velocity.

L-29. Refraction by Shadow with Cube of Glass. A cube or large rectangular block of glass is placed on a sheet of white paper (Fig. 293). A strip of cardboard or metal of the same height as the block of glass and twice as long is set vertically against it as shown. A straight-filament lamp is placed horizontally with its filament parallel to the edge of the metal strip and in such a position as to throw a shadow of the projecting edge of the strip at the lower corner of the block. The light refracted by the block will fall much nearer the obstacle, and the edge of the shadow within the cube will be easily seen. The index of refraction of the glass can be calculated from the dimensions. The filament and refracting edges may be set vertically and the whole apparatus mounted on a rotating table so as to be more easily visible to the class.

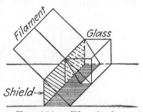

FIG. 293.—The shadow of the vertical shield is shorter in the glass than in the air.

L-30. Refraction Model. An axle 3 or 4 in. long rolls on two independent wheels 1 in. in diameter. It will roll with little friction down a slightly inclined board. If it is rolled at an angle across the line of separation between a plain board and a cloth-covered one, it will change its direction, as a ray of light is refracted. "Total internal reflection" can also be shown.

L-31. Refraction by Gases. The change of index of refraction of air with temperature may be shown by allowing the light from a strongly illuminated pinhole to cast the shadow of a Bunsen burner on the screen (H-137). When the gas is lighted, the rising, turbulent air will be made clearly evident on the screen far above the flame. Any hot object will show the same shadow effect by the convection currents rising from it.

A related experiment may be performed by holding a warm object in the optical path of one arm of a Michelson interferometer. The interference fringes are displaced in the neighborhood of the object (L-72).

L-32. Mirage. A piece of sheet metal several feet long and 3 to 6 in. wide is supported on stands horizontally above the lecture table. It is heated by a row of gas burners placed beneath it, spaced closely enough so that the heating is fairly uniform. A pipe closed at one end and drilled with a row of closely spaced small holes (M-58) may be used in place of the separate burners. The pipe must be at least an inch in diameter, and the holes must be small; otherwise most of the gas will escape before reaching the far end of the pipe.   At one end at about the height of the metal plate is placed a 40-w lamp (Fig. 294).   Close to the end of the plate is held a piece of fine ground glass or light paper *B* on which small figures of trees, houses, etc., have been drawn with India

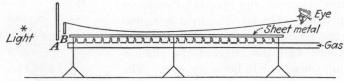

Fig. 294.—The path of the light is curved by the layer of hot air above the metal plate to produce the effect of mirage.

ink.   The figures should be about an inch high, and the bottom of the figures or the foreground should be in line with the metal plate.   Between the light and the plate may be set a second ground-glass screen *A* to diffuse the light.   If now the eye is placed about on a level with the plate, a "mirage" will be seen. By careful adjustment, the small figures will be seen inverted in the "lake" above the metal plate.

The gas-heated plate of the preceding paragraph may be replaced by an electrically heated unit (Fig. 295).   The unit

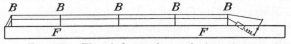

Fig. 295.—Electric heater for producing mirage.

consists of a wooden frame *FF* about 3 in. square and 9 ft long, to the top of which are fastened five or more bridges *B,B* of the cross section shown in Fig. 296*a*.   The bridge proper is cut from heavy brass and carries on its top two strips of asbestos tape each 1 in. wide.   Beneath the bridge is a block of asbestos or other insulating material that supports four nichrome heater strips of such width and thickness that their resistance will allow them to be connected directly to the 110-v power line and still give a good deal of heat.   The top of the wooden frame is covered with asbestos to keep it from scorching or catching fire.   To prevent sagging, both the heater and the asbestos strips are kept under tension by the spring and lever mechanism shown in Fig. 296*b*. A rectangular frame *LL* is fastened to the main frame *FF* by an axle rod at *D*.   The asbestos strips are attached to the upper rod of this frame, and the heater strips are attached to an insulating block *N* that is connected to the lower rod of the frame by springs. It is evident that the springs will keep both sets of strips taut. To prevent the heater strips from touching each other and causing a short circuit, asbestos string is woven between them at appropriate intervals.   To confine the heated air and to overcome the disturbance of cross drafts and convection currents, boards some 8 or 10 in. wide and 8 or 9 ft long are placed at either side of the unit.   This makes a trough of quiet heated air 3 or 4 in. deep.

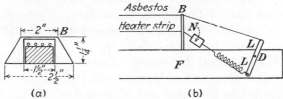

(a)   (b)

Fɪɢ. 296.—Details of heater shown in Fig. 294: (*a*) bridge supporting heater elements; (*b*) spring and lever arrangement for keeping strips taut.

L-33. Refractive Index—Christiansen Filters. If a liquid mixture is adjusted to have the same index of refraction as that of a piece of glass immersed in it, light will not be reflected at the interface between the two, and the glass will not be visible. Thus a block of glass lowered into such a liquid by a black thread seems to disappear, leaving only the thread visible.   A rod of glass dipped into the liquid and withdrawn seems to drip liquid glass.   A parallel-sided glass vessel containing a quantity of finely powdered glass is opaque but becomes transparent when the liquid is added.   However, since the two indices of refraction can be the same for only one wave length, the powder-liquid mixture can be made into an excellent Christiansen color filter.[1] Soft glass should be used, and the composition of the liquid adjusted by trial.   The glass is boiled in aqua regia to free it of grease and dirt and thoroughly washed with water.   It is then dried and placed in a glass vessel.   Enough carbon disulfide iꜱ

[1] Wᴏᴏᴅ, R. W., "Physical Optics," 3d ed., p. 115, The Macmillan Com pany, New York, 1934.

added to wet the glass, and then benzene is poured in, a little at a time.   As the mixture begins to become transparent, it transmits first red, then yellow, and so on.   A permanent setup may be made by drawing down the neck of a flask after the powdered glass has been put into it.   The liquid mixture, adjusted to the proper proportions by previous trial, is then added.   The flask is packed in a freezing mixture to reduce the vapor pressure of the inflammable liquid and wrapped in a towel to guard against injury in the event of an explosion.   The neck of the flask is then sealed off.   The cold flask is opaque but as it is warmed up, either with a small flame or with the hands, it exhibits colors.

The following liquids are suitable: cedar oil; glycerin; carbon disulfide with benzene, amyl acetate, or phenyl phthalate.   The proportions will depend on the index of refraction of the glass as well as on that of the liquids themselves.   Pyrex glass is not suitable on account of its high index; soft glass should be used. Clear fused quartz is very satisfactory.

L-34. Total Internal Reflection.   Light incident on the end of a curved rod of glass or fused quartz will, by total internal reflection, be carried to the other end without loss through the sides. The ends of the rod should be square and preferably polished. The light source should be small and bright and placed as close to the end of the rod as possible.   By using flashlight or small 6-v bulbs, the filament may be put near the end of the rod.   Another way to illuminate the rod is to focus the light from an intense source upon its end.   The rod should be passed through tight-fitting holes in two or three screens so that no light can reach the far end of the rod except through it.   A white surface, such as a sheet of heavy paper, is held near the exit end of the rod, tilted so that the class can see it, and is illuminated by light emerging from the end of the rod.   Most glass absorbs violet much more than it does red, so that even with white light as a source the light that emerges is yellowish.

L-35. Critical Angle and Total Internal Reflection.   In Fig. 297 is shown a convenient arrangement for demonstrating refraction and total internal reflection.   A large glass jar with parallel sides is filled with water containing a little fluorescein.   A plane mirror M_1 reflects a slightly convergent beam upon the water surface where it is refracted at A.   At B it is totally reflected to a second plane mirror M_2 mounted on a spindle so that it can be turned about a horizontal axis by a handle projecting upward. By changing the position of M_2, the angle of incidence of the beam at the water-air surface can be changed, and critical angle and total internal reflection demonstrated. The path of the beam, both in the water and in the air, is made more visible by placing a sheet of flashed opal glass vertically in the tank, so as to make a small acute angle with the direction of the beam. The beam emerging from the surface of the water can be seen to be colored on account of dispersion by the water.

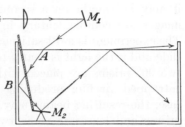

FIG. 297.—Water tank and mirrors to show total internal reflection.

L-36. Illuminated Fountain.

A cone or funnel-shaped vessel (Fig. 298) with a watertight window W, an entrance tube A, and an exit tube B, is arranged to throw a stream of water into the sink. A strong beam of light is focused by lenses through the window to the exit tube. This light is carried by internal reflection along the curved stream of water until it breaks up into drops. The demonstration is enhanced by placing color filters in the path of the light to color the jet. Red, green, and amber filters are especially effective. If no color filters are available, a carbon arc can be used close to the window W, and the light focused by means of the heavy condensing lenses only. On account of the chromatic aberration of the lens, the color of the stream may be changed by moving the arc back and forth through a small distance. Screens should be interposed to cut out stray light.

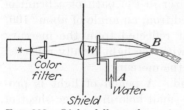

FIG. 298.—Light follows the water jet by internal reflection.

L-37. Total Internal Reflection at Glass-air Interface.

Two sheets of thin glass (lantern or microscope slides) separated by strips of paper are fastened together with waterproof cement, so that they have an air space between them. When the plates are immersed in water in an optical tank (L-7) and turned at the proper angle to an incident light beam, they will exhibit total internal reflection.

L-38. Transmission and Reflection near Critical Angle. The image of a brightly illuminated slit is projected on a screen. In the path of the light is placed a rectangular glass container of water in which is immersed the slide with the air film described in the preceding paragraph. When this slide is set so that the angle of incidence is about 49°, part of the light incident on it will be transmitted, and part will be totally reflected off to the side where it may be caught on a second screen. The colors of the two images are complementary in the region of the critical angle. The experiment is most satisfactory if the entire beam falls on the slide and if the light is nearly parallel. In another arrangement, two 90° prisms are placed with their hypotenuses together, the entrapped air film producing the results described. In either case, the resulting beams may, if desired, be dispersed by other prisms and lenses to show two spectra whose colors are complementary. As the device is turned in the neighborhood of the critical angle, the colors are transferred from one spectrum to the other.

L-39. "Mystery Ball." Coat a ball heavily with soot. Immerse it in a jar of water. The soot serves to keep an air film around the ball. It appears bright and silvery when submerged because of reflection of light at the water-air interface.

L-40. Comparison of Total Internal and Metallic Reflection. A test tube is partly filled with mercury, closed with a stopper, and immersed in a jar of clear water in the path of a beam of light from a lantern. When viewed from an angle of about 100° from the incident beam, the light reflected from the mercury appears quite dull in comparison with the light totally reflected at the glass-air surface just above the mercury.

L-41. Reflections from Diamond. A pencil of light is projected toward the class through a small hole in a large sheet of white cardboard. In the beam is placed as large a diamond as procurable, and the reflections, both internal and external, produce a beautiful pattern on the cardboard.

L-42. Dispersion by a Prism. Since index of refraction is a function of frequency, it is possible to break up white light into the familiar colors of the spectrum. Light from a straight-filament source or a strongly illuminated slit S is focused on a screen by a projection lens P (Fig. 299). A prism of glass or a hollow prism filled with carbon disulfide is introduced into the beam beyond the projection lens. A continuous spectrum is thus formed on the screen.

L-43. Rainbow. A vertical slit is illuminated by a beam of parallel light from the lantern as in the preceding experiment. In the beam from the slit is placed a glass beaker filled with water. Two spectra may be seen on a screen placed *between* the slit and the beaker and to one side.

The projection lens is removed from an arc lantern, and the position of the arc with respect to the condenser is adjusted to produce a parallel beam which is directed toward the class. The beam passes through a 4-in. hole in the middle of a white cardboard screen 3 ft square and falls on a spherical flask of water 4 in. in diameter, set 2 ft from the screen. A black disk is placed just

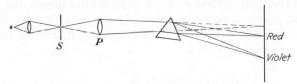

Fig. 299.—Formation of spectrum by a prism.

beyond the flask to prevent glare. On the screen there appears a circular spectrum, with the red outermost, representing a primary rainbow.

L-44. Rainbow Droplets. Coat a sheet of glass with soot from burning turpentine. Spray the surface with water droplets from an atomizer, and illuminate the surface by a strong parallel beam of light. The water droplets do not wet the plate; hence they are spherical because of surface tension. When they are viewed from an angle of about 41°, the droplets glisten like individual colored jewels. Drops about 0.5 mm in diameter show best. They should be allowed to fall on the plate perpendicularly, as they will otherwise *bounce* off.

L-45. Artificial Rainbow. Form a horizontal spectrum as in L-42. Place a tube of water 1.5 in. in diameter between prism and screen so that the tube is perpendicular to one edge of the prism. A "rainbow" in the form of a vertical circle is cast upon the screen or the walls of the room.

L-46. Scattering of Light—"Sunset Experiment." A circular opening in a sheet of metal is strongly illuminated with the light from a projection lantern and an enlarged image of the opening, the "sun," is projected on a screen. The room should be darkened and stray light eliminated. Between the circular opening and the projection lens is placed a glass vessel with parallel sides 5 in. apart, which is nearly filled with a measured quantity of clear water (distilled if necessary). The clear water scatters very little light, so that the "sun" is white or perhaps yellow. Then 10 ml of concentrated solution of photographic hypo (sodium thiosulfate) and 3 to 8 ml of 5-normal solution of either hydrochloric or sulfuric acid are added for each 500 ml of water. The exact amount and concentration of the acid are not critical. In about a minute, colloidal sulfur will begin to form, and the beam passing through the liquid will look bright blue by scattered light. The number and size of the scattering particles increase so that in from 2 to 8 min, depending on the temperature, even red light will no longer be transmitted. The temperature of the water should be between 20 and 30°C for most satisfactory results.

LENSES

L-47. Image Formation by Lenses. A number of fundamental experiments showing the relation between image and object distances and focal length may be performed by casting the real image of a lamp filament upon a screen, using various distances and various converging lenses of different focal lengths. Images of different size are cast by different lenses, keeping lamp-to-screen distance constant. Conjugate foci may be shown for constant lamp-to-screen distance by setting a given lens successively at two predetermined points. Finally, after casting a sharp image of the lamp filament (or other object) upon the screen, move the lens away from the object until the image is blurred. Then pick up a sharp image between lens and screen, by moving a piece of white cardboard or opal glass along the light path to the correct image position.

L-48. Action of a Lens. Enclose a bright source (automobile or clear-glass incandescent lamp) in a tubular housing with aperture the size of a converging lens. Adjust the lens to cast an image (not too large) of the filament on a screen. Move the lens aside, and close the end of the housing with a metal foil containing many pinholes. Many images of the filament will thus be formed on the screen (L-16). Now move the lens back to its former position, and show how it collects the many images into a single image.

L-49. Chromatic and Spherical Aberration. A large thick spherical lens, preferably plano-convex, is most satisfactory for demonstrating aberrations. The lens should be provided with several diaphragms, one allowing only the central portion of the beam to pass, a second allowing only an annular portion near the edge of the lens to pass, and a third having two pairs of small round or various-shaped openings, one pair nearer the center than the other pair. A small opening at the focus of the condensing lenses of a projection lantern is the light source. The lens L to be studied is placed far enough from this opening to be illuminated all over and so that it forms a real image of the opening. The beam of light after leaving the lens may be made visible by the trough, the gauze screen, or the smokebox (L-7, 8, 9). The gauze screen will probably show the colors best. Another method is to have the beam from the lens pointed toward the class, interrupting it with a movable translucent screen or a sheet of ground or flashed opal glass or a smooth white paper that is not too heavy. By moving the screen, the changing cross section of the beam may be shown in a manner that enables the student to grasp the idea of image formation. The distance between the focus of the rays passing through the center of the lens (first diaphragm) and that of the rays passing through the annular diaphragm near the edge of the lens (second diaphragm) is a measure of the spherical aberration. With the latter diaphragm, a ring of light is formed on the screen and is clearly seen to be fringed with color, red when the screen is on the side of the focus toward the lens and blue when it is on the opposite side. Tipping the lens seems to tie this ring into a bowknot. The central beam and the four-opening diaphragm help to show the formation of aberrations. By turning the lens with first one side and then the other toward the light, the effect of relative position on aberrations can be demonstrated. With a plano-convex lens, the difference is marked if the object and the image distances are very different. By using large magnification (source placed only very slightly beyond the principal focus), the distance between the foci for the rim rays and for the central rays can be made as great as 2 ft, using an ordinary lantern condensing lens.

Instead of an illuminated opening, a small concentrated-filament automobile or flashlight bulb run at rated voltage or slightly over may be used. No diaphragm is then needed except to limit the beam so that stray light will not blind the class. Another satisfactory source is a 200-w clear-glass incandescent lamp, with the plane of its filament perpendicular to the optical axis of the system. The lamp should be enclosed to reduce stray light.

L-50. Effect of Medium on Focal Length. Place a lens in a parallel beam of light, and determine its focal length. Then immerse the lens in a tank of water (L-7), and find the new focal length. Since the focal length of a lens immersed in water is approximately four times that of the same lens in air, it is important to use a lens of short focal length. If a long tank is not available, the experiment may be performed with the lens in a small vessel, such as a projection cell, with parallel sides.

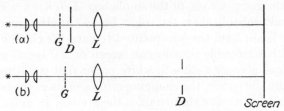

FIG. 300.—Arrangement of lenses and diaphragms for producing distortion: (*a*). barrel-shaped; (*b*) pincushion.

L-51. Astigmatism and Distortion. A coarse wire mesh or a lantern slide ruled with a rectangular network of horizontal and vertical lines is used as an object and is illuminated by light from the condenser lens of a lantern. Large condenser lenses of rather short focal length are then used to form a much enlarged image of the mesh on the screen. If the lens is turned about an axis parallel to either set of wires or rulings, there will be found two positions of the screen, for one of which only the horizontal lines are in focus; for the other, only the vertical lines are in focus. A concave mirror will show a similar effect. A set of radial lines may be used instead of the rectangular mesh.

L-52. Distortion. A piece of wire gauze or a glass plate *G* ruled with a rectangular network is placed in the beam of light from a lantern, perhaps 5 cm from the condenser lenses. An image of the mesh is cast on a distant screen by a double convex lens *L*. When a diaphragm *D* is placed in front of the lens, as in Fig. 300*a*, barrel-shaped distortion of the image results. If the diaphragm is placed on the other side of the lens (Fig. 300*b*), and several times its focal length away, pincushion distortion of the image will be seen. The size and location of the diaphragm must be determined by trial. In the first case, the hole should be less than 1 cm in diameter; in the second case, a somewhat larger hole works better. The sheet in which the hole is made should be large enough to shield the screen from stray light from the lantern.

The single lens may be replaced by two lenses, 6 to 10 cm apart, whose combined focal length is about the equivalent of the single lens. The two types of distortion can be shown as before, but if the diaphragm is placed between the two lenses, there is no distortion.

OPTICAL INSTRUMENTS

L-53. Microscope. The action of a microscope can be explained with the aid of wall charts published by the makers of microscopes to illustrate the formation of the image in their respective instruments.

L-54. Model Microscope. The essential optical parts of a microscope may be demonstrated on a moderately large scale by using a good-quality lens of short focal length and a large reading glass. The first lens (objective) is placed close to some small brightly illuminated object so as to produce an enlarged real image of it. The reading glass (eyepiece) is set a short distance above this image. A mirror above the second lens inclined at 45° enables those looking at the system to see a greatly enlarged virtual image of the illuminated object.

The whole system may be mounted on a rotating stand so that the mirror may be turned toward each member of the class. It is possible to make a number of minute effects visible to several students at once by use of this optical arrangement, *e.g.*, Brownian movements (A-51), Newton's rings (L-71), etc.

L-55. Telescope. Astronomical, terrestrial, and Galilean telescopes can be shown diagrammatically. They may also be set up for demonstration by suitable combinations of lenses mounted on an optical bench. Each student may look through the lenses individually; but if projection is used and an image is formed on a screen so that the whole class can see it, the rays of light entering the objective and leaving the eyepiece are no longer parallel, and this point in the operation of the telescope is lost.

L-56. Telephoto Lens. The simple camera lens is easily demonstrated by forming a real image of some object on a screen; telephoto or other special camera lenses can be demonstrated also. The object, illuminated with the condenser system of a projection lantern, may be a wire mesh or crosshatch ruling R (Fig. 301). A circular hole in a diaphragm D limits the area utilized. The lens L_1 is placed at its focal distance in front of the object, thus giving a parallel beam, so that the lens L_2 can be at any distance from L_1. It forms an image of the mesh and diaphragm in its own focal plane; this image is formed on a screen, and the diameter of the

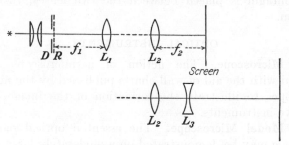

Fig. 301.—Principle of the telephoto lens.

image of the diaphragm opening and the distance from L_2 to the screen are measured. When a concave lens L_3 is inserted in the light path between L_2 and the screen, the screen must be moved farther back to focus the image, but the magnification is much greater. The diameter of the image and the distance from L_2 to the screen are again measured; it is found that the magnification ratio greatly exceeds the lens-to-screen ratio, which is the purpose of a telephoto lens. The wire mesh used as object helps to secure a sharp focus, while the diaphragm provides an easily visible image.

L-57. Lens Combinations. Several fundamental principles of lens combinations can be illustrated by a pair of lenses so mounted that principal foci, principal planes (magnification of +1), and the symmetrical conjugate planes (magnification of −1) of the system are outside of the combination. Such a system can be constructed by mounting two projection-lantern condensing lenses of about 18-cm focal length in a 10-cm stovepipe about 60

cm apart, plane sides out.   A lamp filament placed about 70 cm
from one end produces an erect real image of the same size at
the same distance from the other end.   If placed 20 cm from one
end, an inverted real image of the same size will appear at
the same distance from the other end.   The principal foci of the
system are, of course, midway between the two positions of the
object and of the image respectively.

THE EYE

L-58. Blind Spot.   Every human eye has one spot that is
blind—the portion where the optic nerve enters the eye.   To
demonstrate this fact, a white circle is mounted on the blackboard, and a white cross of about the same size is moved slowly
across the board toward the circle.   The student closes one eye
and fixes his gaze on the circle, seeing the cross out of the corner
of his eye.   In the position where the image of the cross falls
on the blind spot, it disappears.   Alternatively, each student
may locate his own blind spot by moving about a card held 10 in.
from his eye and marked with a black circle and black cross.
If his attention is fixed on the circle, he will find a spot where
the cross disappears.   Circle and cross should be 3 in. apart.

L-59. Inversion of Image on Retina.   Three holes are drilled in
a brass plate with a No. 60 drill at the corners of a small triangle
2 mm on each edge.   The plate covers one end of a tube 1 in.
long; the other end is closed with a similar plate having a single
hole through it.   If the three holes are held close to the eye, with
the triangle standing on its base, the pattern on the retina will be
three circular patches of light in a triangle standing on its *vertex*.
The system of holes limits the light entering the eye to three
pencils originating so close to the eye that they cannot be inverted
by the lens.   Hence distant objects viewed through the instrument will appear "right side up," whereas the orientation of the
triangular pattern demonstrates conclusively that the image on
the retina is inverted.

L-60. Fluorescence of Retina.   Turn toward the class in a
dark room a strong ultraviolet source (quartz mercury lamp or
arc) screened to exclude all visible light (L-114).   Call attention to the luminous haze that covers the field of view of each
individual.

L-61. Visual Fatigue. The eye quickly becomes fatigued after looking steadily for a few seconds at a single color. It is possible to produce the effect in a fully lighted room by projecting a bright spot of color on a screen. After the spot has been observed steadily for a few seconds, it is extinguished, and a spot of the complementary color appears in its place. It is important not to shift the eyes during the progress of the experiment. Red, green, yellow, and blue filters give the best effects.

L-62. Color Blindness. Slides with a large number of colored rectangles are obtainable by which the usual types of color blindness may be tested. Directions are provided with the slides. Each member of the class is asked to write down the numbers of those rectangles which resemble a test color; the numbers may then be quickly checked against the correct numbers. In many cases, students discover color blindness of which they were unaware prior to the test. Color-blindness test charts are also available but are better suited to individual than to class use.

L-63. Chromatic Aberration of the Eye. A purple filter is mounted in front of a clear-glass tungsten lamp having straight filaments. The eye has difficulty in focusing simultaneously on both the red and the blue images. The effect cannot be seen well from a distance; nor is it the same for all individuals.

L-64. Astigmatism. Astigmatism is usually tested by observing a chart bearing a set of radial black lines. To the normal eye, these lines appear equal in intensity, but to an astigmatic eye they appear in varying degrees of sharpness, depending upon the direction of the axis of astigmatism.

L-65. Eye Models. A spherical flask is filled with slightly milky water to represent the eyeball. A large lens is placed near the flask so as to bring the image of a bright light to a focus on the far side of the flask. Vertical motion of the light shows that the image on the "retina" is inverted. Motion of the source toward the "eye" shows the necessity for accommodation, and adjustment of the lens position shows such accommodation. Moving the lens so that the focus is beyond or in front of the "retina" shows near- and far-sightedness, and these defects can be corrected by proper selection and combination of lenses.

Several apparatus companies make a model of the eye that can be shown in the lecture, but it is more valuable as a laboratory apparatus where the student himself can work with it.

L-66. Eyeglasses. A study of lenses and the defects of the eye may be made more vivid by borrowing the glasses of members of the class and testing them in the light from the lantern. The lenses are held near the screen and drawn back from it to locate the position of best effect. The type of lens can be inferred from the image formed.

Using the projection lens, throw on the screen an image of a slide showing concentric circles crossed by radial lines, making this original image very sharp. Now place over the projection lens another lens, say a diverging one. The image becomes blurred, as it would look to a person with faulty vision. Correct it by placing in front of the diverging lens a converging lens of the same power. Repeat, using converging, diverging, and cylindrical lenses, each time bringing the image back to sharp focus with a lens of the opposite kind. Spectacle lenses of 1 or 2 diopters power are rather inexpensive and can be secured in matched pairs either from a local optician or direct from the manufacturers. As a by-product of this demonstration, some students may be induced to have their eyes examined and secure much needed glasses.

INTERFERENCE AND DIFFRACTION

L-67. Interference—Color of Thin Films. Interference colors in a thin film can be projected so that a large class may see them. A Gooch funnel or a flat metal ring is dipped in a soap solution and is then held in a clamp so that the film formed across its mouth is vertical. It is more convenient to clamp the funnel or ring in the proper position and then to form a soap film upon it by drawing across its mouth a piece of paper dipped in soap solution. A beam of light from an arc or projection lantern is brought to a focus just beyond the film, and a greatly enlarged image of the film is then projected on the screen with a fast lens L (Fig. 302) of short focal length, placed so that the angle between its axis and the normal to the film is equal to the angle between the normal and the axis of the incident beam. As the water runs out of the film, the film grows thinner at the top (which is the bottom of the image on the screen). New spectral orders appear until the film is so thin that it becomes black at the top. Soon after the top of the film turns black, it generally breaks. The durability of the film may be increased by decreasing its diameter, so that one should use as small a funnel as is consistent with visibility on the screen. To diminish convection currents in the funnel, the end of it may be closed with a cork through which a small hole is cut to preserve pressure equilibrium. The number of visible spectral orders is increased by interposing a red filter between the light source and the film. If a gentle air jet is played on the film, the colors are mixed in a beautiful manner.

L-68. The colors produced by interference of light in a soap bubble may be shown by holding the bubble in front of an extended source of light in a darkened room. The source is provided by housing a 100-w lamp inside a box in one end of which a piece of flashed opal or ground glass is fitted. The bubble

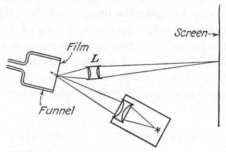

Fig. 302.—Method of projecting interference colors in thin films.

should be held near the ground glass but should have as dark a background as possible. Under a strong monochromatic source of light or a mercury vapor lamp (L-4), the colors are replaced by alternate light and dark rings.

L-69. The Boys rainbow cup is a hemispherical shell that can be rotated about a vertical axis. When a soap film is formed across the open top of the cup and the latter is turned rapidly, the film becomes thinner toward the center on account of centrifugal force, and circular colored fringes are formed. Rotation may be continued until the black spot appears at the center. If the motion is quickly stopped, the black spot may break up into several irregular pieces. The film should be protected from air currents by a transparent cover. The color pattern may be projected as previously described (L-67).

L-70. Interference in Thin Air Films. Two large pieces of plate glass are laid on top of one another on the table. A broad sodium flame or a mercury arc is placed so that it may be seen reflected in the glass. The interference fringes are generally separated well enough to be seen easily.

If an optical flat or its equivalent is available, pieces of glass may be laid on it, and from the contour of the fringes observed, the character of the irregularities of the glass surface may be inferred. If some of the test pieces are also optically flat, their straight even fringes may be compared with the crooked ones of the other samples to show the optical method of testing surfaces.

L-71. Newton's Rings. When a plano-convex lens of very small curvature is held with its convex side against a plane piece of glass, a thin film of air is included between the two pieces of glass, the thickness of the film increasing with increasing distance

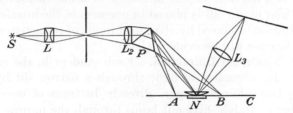

FIG. 303.—Projection of Newton's rings.

from the point of contact. The colored rings formed in this way may be projected by the same optical arrangement as that shown in Fig. 302, by placing the lens and plane glass in the position occupied by the soap film (L-67). When a red and a blue filter are alternately placed in the incident light beam, it is very easy for the class to see the change in size of the rings due to change of wave length.

A more elegant but more elaborate way of illuminating the ring system is that shown in Fig. 303. A strong arc or 1000-w projection lamp S is focused by the condensing lens L on a variable slit. The light from this slit passes through a lens L_2 and a large carbon disulfide prism P to form a strong spectrum at ABC. The Newton's-rings apparatus is placed at N near the center of this spectrum, and by means of a fast lens L_3 a magnified image of the ring system is formed on the screen. Now by turning the prism P back and forth, different colors will fall on N so that the rings will change color and size. By not making the spectrum too large, and by using a fairly wide slit, fast lenses and a large liquid prism the effect will be bright enough for a fairly large class to see.

L-72. Michelson Interferometer. The Michelson interferometer can be demonstrated to large classes. The interferometer is first adjusted for monochromatic fringes and then for white-light fringes by getting the light paths equal. The beam from a strong source (carbon arc) is focused on the first mirror, using a water cell to reduce the heat. With a rather short focal length, high speed lens (4 in., f 4.5) from a camera, the fringes may be projected on a screen. In case the direction of the beam emerging from the interferometer is not that desired for projection, a plane mirror of good quality may be interposed. The fringes may be easily seen if they are projected on a flashed-opal screen facing the class. If a hot wire or the hot stick of a match that has been lighted and blown out is placed in one arm of the interferometer, the distortion produced by change of index of refraction of the air due to heating will be evident (L-30).

L-73. Single-slit Diffraction. Each student in the class may observe the diffraction of light through a narrow slit by simply holding two adjacent fingers directly in front of one eye and observing a straight-filament lamp through the narrow aperture thus produced. The fingers must be held parallel to the filament and very close together (see also L-82).

L-74. Diffraction by Straight Edge. Pieces of razor blade are cemented between sheets of cellophane to eliminate danger of injury and are distributed to the members of the class. An enclosed carbon arc is set in the front of the room pointing toward the class. If the edge of a blade is held close to the eye so as to cut off part of the light from the arc, interference fringes due to diffraction will be observed far into the shadow. Screening the arc with red glass may improve the visibility of the fringes. In this case, stray light should be eliminated, since the intensity is reduced by the glass.

L-75. Diffraction by a Feather. A bright source is focused by a condensing lens L_1 (Fig. 304) on a vertical slit. The lens L_2 forms an image of the slit at A, where a vertical obstacle like a tripod rod intercepts the light. A feather or other similar object is placed at such a position O that the lens L_2 forms an enlarged image of it on the screen. This image will be formed by light diffracted by the feather and hence deflected so as to pass the rod, which intercepts all of the light in the direct beam so that without the feather in position the field is dark. A 1000-w lantern bulb will give sufficient light so that a large class can see the effect. The slit may be $\frac{1}{4}$ to $\frac{1}{8}$ in. wide and the obstacle $\frac{3}{8}$ in. wide. The slit is put at the place where the condensing lens of the lantern forms the image of the filament. The lens L_2 should be achromatic. The finer the texture of the object at O the more striking the result; feathers are especially good, but fine waste or a coarse transmission grating will serve.

Small feathers mounted between microscope slides may be passed around the class so that each student may look through a feather at a bright point source to observe diffraction.

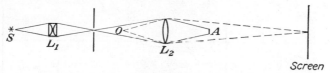

FIG. 304.—Projection of image by diffracted light.

L-76. Diffraction Box. Many diffraction demonstrations are greatly facilitated by a permanent, though semiportable, diffraction box (peep show) 30 cm square and some 5 m long. At one end is a door, through which the source, lens, and a color screen may be adjusted. About 75 cm from this end is a partition in which the small aperture is mounted; it is accessible through a door in the side of the box. A holder for diffraction specimens and masking screen is mounted on a small tripod that is movable to any part of the box. The other end of the box is provided with an interchangeable holder for an eyepiece or viewing screen. Distances that have been used with good results are the following: slit to diffracting object, 202 cm; object to eyepiece, 237 cm; width of object, 0.55 cm; this gives 1.2 cm for the width of the diffracted image when light of wave length 5461 (mercury arc) is used.

L-77. Fresnel Diffraction. A bright light A (Fig. 305) is focused by means of lens B on a pinhole at C. The light spreads out, illuminating the screen G. At some intermediate point are placed such objects as pins, screws, fine wires, and small slits. Their shadows on the screen show striking diffraction patterns. A slit at C will give more light than a pinhole and is satisfactory for pins, slits, and edges but does not give two-dimensional diffraction and so is not good for screw threads, holes, and round objects. A masking screen to eliminate unnecessary light is advisable.

L-78. Diffraction about Circular Object. A bright light *A* is focused on the pinhole *C* (Fig. 306). A small round object such as a coin or steel ball is held at *N*; it may be hung by fine wires, or it may be fastened to a sheet of clear glass. At *S* is a card with a small hole in it. The light diffracted around the edge of the object will make it look as if it were surrounded with a ring of light when *S* is at the proper place. If a large hole is cut in the card at *S* and covered with thin paper with a small hole in its

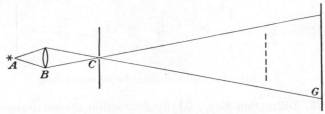

FIG. 305.—Projection of Fresnel diffraction.

center, the observer can see the geometrical shadow of the object and so is all the more surprised to see the ring of light. This shadow also helps when lining up the parts. Red and blue glass filters may be used to show the effect of change of wave length. The distances are variable over a wide range. Thus *CN* may be 10 ft, and *NS* 2 ft. With a steel ball or a coin as object, *CN* may be 3 ft, and *NS* 10 ft. A telescope or magnifying eyepiece may improve the results. If the object is viewed from the proper distance along the axis of its geometrical shadow, its center appears bright as if light actually passed through it.

L-79. Crossed Gratings. Each student as he comes into the room is given a small square of silk, through which to view an automobile headlight lamp, to observe two-dimensional diffraction by crossed gratings. Certain feathers show the effect. Fine-mesh wire screen also serves well. A refinement is described in A-109.

L-80. Diffraction by Red Blood Corpuscles. Smear a drop of blood uniformly on a microscope slide, and protect it with a cover glass. Place the slide close to the eye, and look at a bright point source of light.   Beautiful diffraction rings are observed.   To project the pattern, place the slide 5 to 10 cm away from a point source, and form its image on a screen by a projection lens of 30-cm focal length.   In pernicious anemia, it is important to know the average size of blood corpuscles, which can be determined by measuring the diffraction rings.[1]

L-81. Halos.   A 3-in. hole is cut in the center of a piece of white cardboard about 2 ft square.   A beam from a well-shielded point source of light is converged on this hole, so that it disappears within it.   If necessary, to reduce stray light, the beam can be absorbed in a black box or by black cloth placed behind the screen.   In the beam is held a glass plate 1 ft square, which has been allowed to collect a thin layer of fine dust but which is otherwise clean.   Its distance from the cardboard screen is adjusted until circular halos appear on the cardboard screen

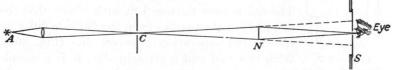

Fɪɢ. 306.—Diffraction around a circular obstacle.

around the hole.   The distance from plate to screen is several feet.   The effect may be temporarily enhanced by breathing on the plate.   Instead of dust, a very thin sprinkling of lycopodium powder may be used, and the plate covered with another sheet of glass, the two being bound together.

Several of the previous experiments may be combined so that students may observe them one after another as they enter the classroom.   The setup is that for diffraction around a circular object (L-78).   On one side is a silk handkerchief on a frame, on the other the dusty sheet of glass.   The same source of light serves for all.   The halos contrast strikingly with the crossed-grating effect; they help to illustrate the powder as contrasted with the crystal type of x-ray pattern.   This contrast may also be shown by the rotating crossed grating (A-109).

L-82. Diffraction by Single and Double Slits.   Each student is provided with a small piece of photographic plate, on the fogged emulsion of which have been ruled a single line and a pair of

[1] PɪJPER, A., *Med. J. S. Africa*, August, 1918.

parallel scratches, the latter 0.2 to 0.5 mm apart. A very bright straight-filament lamp is set in view of the whole class, who can then individually observe single-slit diffraction and the colored interference fringes from double slits. If the upper half of the filament is covered by a red filter and the lower half by a blue one, the variation in diffraction patterns and in fringe widths is very marked. The filters should be as close to the light as safety will permit. Very good filters for this and other experiments can be made from one or two thicknesses of colored cellophane. The cellophane is clear enough to see through easily, and it can be bent around the source so that the straight filament can be viewed from all directions.

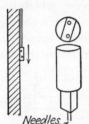

Fig. 307.— Tool for ruling double slits on photographic plate.

The ruling of the double slits is greatly facilitated by the use of a tool made for the purpose. A brass rod is drilled with two holes in the end, into which steel phonograph needles are fastened. The rod is then flattened in such a way that the distances of the needles from the flat side differ by the desired separation between slits (Fig. 307). With this tool and a straightedge, it is a simple matter to rule equally spaced double slits on an old exposed plate. If the rulings are made about ½ to ¾ in. apart, the plate can, after ruling, be turned over, marked into squares with a glass cutter, and broken up so that each student can have a section.

L-83. Projection of Single- and Double-slit Patterns. With the exception of grating spectra, most diffraction experiments are too faint to project so that a large class can see them. In the grating, the light is increased by having many slits, and the effects of all are brought together by the projection lens. The same result may be attained for single and double slits as follows. On a fogged photographic plate (lantern-slide size is convenient) is ruled a large number of parallel but unevenly spaced slits. On another plate is ruled a large number of pairs of slits, the spacing of each pair being constant.[1] For protection, these plates may be covered with a clear glass and bound like lantern slides. A bright source is focused on a slit (Fig. 308), and by means of an achromatic lens a sharp enlarged image of the slit is

[1] But like the previous plate, the successive pairs of rulings are separated in random fashion.

thrown on a screen.   If now the ruled plates are introduced at P near the lens with their rulings parallel to the illuminated slit, the image on the screen will be that of a single slit for the first plate and that of a double slit for the second plate.   Knowing the double-slit spacing, the distance between lens and screen, and the distance between fringes on the screen, the wave length of the light may be calculated roughly.   Frequently the red and the blue edges of the pattern are distinct enough to permit the computation of both wave lengths.   The relation between the single- and the double-slit patterns is clearly shown, especially if the plates are held so that as they are moved up and down first one and then the other is before the lens.

The intentional inequality of the spacing of the lines on the first plate destroys the regularity of the pattern due to n slits

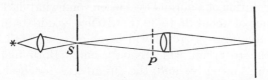

FIG. 308.—Projection of diffraction patterns from slits or gratings.

within the single-slit envelope sufficiently to wipe it out without affecting the width of the single-slit pattern produced and super-posed by the individual slits.   The same cause operates in the second plate through inequality of the spacing between the successive pairs of equally spaced lines.

L-84. Fresnel Biprism.   A Fresnel biprism may be used in a spectrometer for a "peep-show" type of demonstration or in a carbon-arc projection lantern for projection on a screen.   In the latter case, the arc should be retracted, and the slide holder pushed forward until a slit in the slide holder is illuminated by the image of the arc formed by the condenser lens.   The image of the slit is focused on the screen by the projection lens; the biprism is placed between the slit and this lens and adjusted until the best pattern is obtained on the screen.   The pattern is similar to that of a double slit.

L-85. Diffraction Grating.   By means of an achromatic lens, an enlarged image of a brightly illuminated single slit is projected on a screen (Fig. 308).   Near the lens on the side toward the slit is inserted a coarse grating.   Fine copper screen of 100 to 200 wires per inch is satisfactory; finer mesh is still better. Such coarse gratings can also be made by photographing a drawing of equally spaced lines. The spectrum will be visible for several orders on each side. If a grating having several thousand lines per inch is used, it cannot be placed near the lens but can be placed in the converging beam of light not too far from the screen. The spectrum will show up clearly if a fairly large replica grating is used so that it transmits plenty of light through the ruled area. Wave length of light can be calculated approximately from the known grating space, the measured grating-to-screen distance, and the distance from the central image of the slit to any particular color in any order of the spectrum.

L-86. Resolving Power. The two filaments of a double-filament automobile headlight lamp are so spaced as to be at the limit of resolution of a normal eye, when somewhat dark-adapted, at a distance of about 25 to 30 ft. Hence, students in the front half of an average classroom will be able to see both filaments, those in the rear half will see only one. Both filaments are lighted simultaneously, and the brightness for best seeing is adjusted with a rheostat.

One way to help students to see what is meant by resolving power is to show slides of the "Navicula" made with the ultraviolet microscope in green (5461) and then in the ultraviolet light of the mercury-arc line 3650.[1]

COLOR AND RADIATION

L-87. Color. When an object appears colored (barring psychological or physiological tricks like those described in L-61 and L-94), three conditions must be fulfilled: the color must be in the illuminating source; the object viewed must be capable of reflecting or transmitting the color; the detecting device—eye, photocell, photographic plate—must be sensitive to the color. The following demonstration illustrates the first and second conditions; it can be modified to demonstrate all three (see also color blindness, L-62). Arrange where they will not conflict with one another the following sources or their equivalents: a mercury arc, a sodium flame or arc, a deep-red (not orange) lamp like those used for photographic work, a white desk light. A real blue-violet light is good if available; it can sometimes be made by

[1] These slides are made by A. P. H. Trivelli of Eastman Kodak Co.

using filters. As the class comes into the room, have them examine colored cardboard, colored yarns, or anything else under the several lights, the white one last of all. If the class is told beforehand to come wearing gaudy ties or to bring other brightly colored objects, so much the better. For the uninitiated, the effects are surprising. The room must be darkened, and the lights must not interfere with one another. However, this is easily accomplished by screening the sources in separate stalls or by putting some on the floor under tables and the others on the tables.

The preceding method may be modified by using the projection lantern as a spotlight with colored filters. On a large piece of beaverboard are arranged a number of squares of colored paper, cloth, or other material such as flowers or green leaves. If one wishes to take the trouble to cut large letters out of construction paper and spell out in their appropriate colors the words red, orange, blue, green, black, and white, it is easier for the class to remember the colors of the different letters in white light. Inexpensive filters may be made by mounting colored cellophane between sheets of glass like lantern slides. Two or three thicknesses of a given color may be required to give the best results.

Another modification is to project on a white screen a large bright spectrum (L-106), in the various colored regions of which are held pieces of colored paper, flowers, etc. The effects are striking, and with a little practice the component colors of such things as leaves may be quickly identified. The strong red in many green plants is a surprise to most persons.

L-88. Combination of Colors by Addition. Arrangement is made to illuminate a white screen with several colors of light simultaneously. The sources should be capable of motion so as to cause the different colors to overlap or not as desired.

A simple arrangement consists in mounting electric lamps and color filters at the corners of an equilateral triangle having a white surface (Fig. 309). The filters give the primary colors, red, green, and blue, and the lamps and filters are chosen so that the combination of all three colors at the center of the triangular screen produces white, while any possible combination of the primaries will be found at some point on the screen. If a rod is mounted at the center of the screen, the colors of the three shadows radiating from the center will be the complements of the primary colors. With two rods set up so that their shadows cross, the third primary color will show at the point of intersection. When a triangular pyramid is attached at the center of the screen so that one edge faces each of the lamps, each surface will show a mixture of two primary colors.

L-89. Apparatus is commercially available for attachment to a projection lantern so as to produce three independent light beams, which may be colored with filters. The three spots of colored

Fig. 309.—Color pyramid.

light so formed on a screen may be made to overlap in any desired manner to show combinations of two or three colors. A simple substitute for this apparatus is the following[1] (Fig. 310). Three Wratten filters, Nos. 19, 47, and 61, are cut in the shape of sectors of a circle with an angle of 120° at the center of each. They are laid on a sheet of clear glass so that they fit accurately at the center, cemented around the outside edges, and covered with another sheet of glass, which is then bound to the first like a lantern slide. If such filters are not available, colored cellophane

[1] HEILEMANN, J. J., *Am. Phys. Teacher*, **4**, 211, 1936.

may be used—two thicknesses each of red and of dark blue and two or three of green. The light from a projection lantern passes through a 1-in. hole H cut in a screen held in the slide holder. The condenser C of the lantern is arranged so as to bring the image of the filament just beyond the projection lens P when the image of the *hole* is on the screen. The color-filter slide is held *in front* of this projection lens, exactly at the location of the image

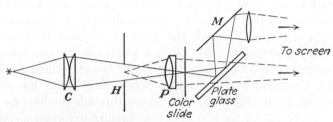

Fig. 310.—Apparatus for combining colors by addition.

of the source, thereby coloring the spot of light on the screen in a manner depending upon the ratios of the illuminated areas of the three filters. To show how the light is divided among separate colors, a piece of plate glass may be inserted in the beam at an angle of 45° to its axis. The portion of the light thus removed from the beam is reflected by a plane mirror M parallel to the plate glass through a second projection lens, which focuses an

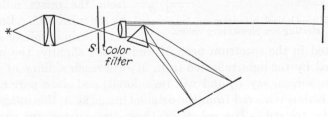

Fig. 311.—Method of combining colors by subtraction.

image of the *filter* on the screen close to the spot of colored light, *i.e.*, the image of the hole.

L-90. Combination of Colors by Subtraction. Instead of adding colors as in L-89, they may be combined by subtraction. A strong beam of light from a slit S (Fig. 311) is arranged so that part of it passes through a prism and is spread out in a spectrum on a screen and part goes past the edge of the prism to another screen. A color filter is inserted in the beam near the slit. The transmitted color and its components in terms of the parts of the spectrum transmitted are both seen. If now different filters that have been examined separately are put into the beam together, the results are evident. By holding them near the slit and partly overlapping, the separate and combined effects can be seen on both screens.

L-91. Color Due to Absorption. Light from a lantern is reflected to the ceiling by pieces of red, green, and blue glass. The color of the reflected light is nearly the same in all cases, but the light that goes through the glass to a screen is decidedly colored by absorption. By using a plane mirror, the reflected light may be thrown on the screen beside the transmitted light.

L-92. Complementary Colors. White light from an arc is focused on a slit (Fig. 312) and passes through the lens L_2 and

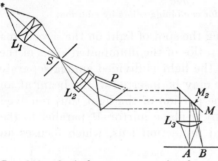

prism P to form a spectrum on the plane mirror M. This mirror reflects the light through a large lens L_3, which forms an enlarged image of the face of the prism on the screen. This image will be white if the lens catches all the light from the prism reflected by the mirror M. But if a small strip of mirror M_2 is

FIG. 312.—Optical arrangement for demonstrating complementary colors.

inserted in the spectrum near M and tipped slightly, the image formed by the light reflected from M_2 will reach a different place on the screen, say B, and will be colored; and since part of the light is thus removed from the original image at A, this image will also be colored. The colors of these two images are complementary since they add to produce white, as can be shown by removing M_2 or by making it parallel to M. The mirror M_2 should be thin, as otherwise light will be lost on account of obstruction by its edges.

A similar result may be obtained by putting the lens L_3 in the dispersed beam from the prism P so as to catch all the light from it, with M just beyond the lens. The light is then reflected by M back through L_3, which forms an image of P on a screen. M_2 is

inserted in front of M as before.   In this case, however, in order
to secure enough dispersion, the lens and mirror may have to be so
far from the prism that the image produced on the screen is small.
In either case, the lens L_3 must be large enough to receive all the
light dispersed by the prism, since otherwise a white image cannot
be formed.

L-93. Color Disks.   A disk may be made or purchased having
colored sectors of such proportions that when the disk is spun
rapidly the eye perceives a grayish white instead of the individual
colors.   Two disks of solid color, with one radial slot in each, may
be slipped through one another and fastened to the same rotor.
When the rotor turns rapidly, the effect is a color whose hue,
brightness, and saturation depend on the combinations used.   By
rotating one disk with respect to the other, the colored sections
may be varied.

An interesting "rainbow top" is now on the market, in which
four small disks each bearing 120° sectors of red, yellow, and blue
are slowly turned while the top spins, so that continual changes of
color occur.

L-94. Complementary Colors Produced Subjectively.   A
disk of heavy cardboard or beaverboard 20 in. in diameter is

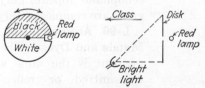

Fig. 313.—The red light appears green when the disk rotates counter-clockwise.

painted dull black on one half and glossy white on the other
(Fig. 313).   An opening, half in the white and half in the black,
is cut at one edge of the disk.   The piece removed is cut in two
and glued to the back of the disk, near the edges of the opening,
to balance it.   The disk is mounted on a rotator, either hand or
motor driven, so that it faces the class.   A red light is placed
behind it so as to be seen through the opening for an instant
during each revolution of the disk, and the front is brightly
illuminated.   Two desk lamps, each with a photoflood lamp
whose direct light is properly shielded from the class, are satisfactory.   The observer watches for the red light as the disk turns.

If the direction of rotation is such that immediately after the light is seen it is obscured by the white section of the disk, a speed of rotation can be found that will make the red light appear green. If the rotation is in the other sense, the eye rests while it looks at the black immediately after the red, and no green color is seen. If a clear-glass bulb is used, the filament may reverse at a slightly different speed from the rest of the light bulb. The effect is subjective, depending upon retinal fatigue (see L-61).

L-95. Dichromatism. A sheet of green cellophane transmits about 50 per cent of the green in the visible spectrum, but its transmission rises to 80 per cent in the extreme red, where the visibility is low. On looking at a white light through an increasing number of sheets, up to 12 or more, the transmitted color changes from green to a deep red. This phenomenon may be discussed in terms of the exponential law of transmission for the two colors. Most cellophane of other colors shows the same effect, though not so strikingly. Deep blue changes to purple and then to red with increasing thickness. The light transmitted by a dozen thicknesses of cellophane is too faint to be projected on a screen; hence the class must look through the cellophane directly at a bright enclosed source. At a certain thickness, the cellophane appears gray, since red and green are complementary.

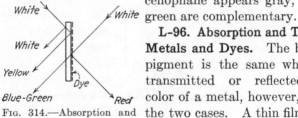

Fig. 314.—Absorption and transmission of dyes.

L-96. Absorption and Transmission— Metals and Dyes. The body color of a pigment is the same whether seen by transmitted or reflected light. The color of a metal, however, is different in the two cases. A thin film of gold (gold leaf or sputtered film) transmits green but looks reddish yellow by reflected light. The latter effect is enhanced if two gilded pieces of glass are set parallel to one another and the light successively reflected from the two surfaces. A colloidal suspension of gold shows a similar effect. Sheets of glass coated with aniline dyes exhibit one color by reflected light and the complementary color by transmitted light, much like gold leaf. The best dye to use is "brilliant green," which appears green by transmitted light but red by reflected light. Light reflected from the dye side of the glass (Fig. 314) looks yellow, while light reflected from the front glass surface is white.

L-97. Kirchhoff's Law of Radiation. A Globar electric element (E-171) is heated to a yellow heat by connecting it across a 110-v line, using no external resistances. White markings (chalk) on the element radiate much less intensely than the natural black surface. The room should be quite dark. The contrast in appearance of the glowing element when a desk lamp is flashed on and off demonstrates that the best absorbers are likewise the best radiators.

A piece of decorated china is heated in a blast lamp. The design emits much more light than the white background, owing to its greater radiating power. If the spectrum of a carbon arc is watched for a few seconds after the current to the arc is cut off, the rapid disappearance of blue and lingering of red radiation will be observed.

L-98. Radiation Intensity Curve. Project the continuous spectrum of a carbon arc (L-42). With the aid of a thermopile and a sensitive galvanometer, show the energy distribution throughout the visible spectrum and on each side of it. If the optical system by which the spectrum is projected is of glass, absorption will interfere with the demonstration, particularly at the violet end. It may be possible to demonstrate the maximum at the long wave-length end, though the demonstration will be much better if quartz or rock-salt lenses and prisms are available.

L-99. Dependence of Color on Temperature. A clear-glass tungsten lamp is arranged so that the voltage across it can be varied from zero to considerably above the rated value. As the voltage is gradually increased, the filament begins to glow a dull red, then becomes yellow, and at 50 per cent overload is very much whiter than at normal voltage. If the intensity of the radiation (as measured by a photocell) is plotted against the power used by the lamp, it is easy to show that the efficiency of the lamp increases rapidly with the temperature of the filament.

L-100. Color Due to Scattering. Smoke rising from the end of a cigarette is blue, while after exhalation it is white. In the first case, the particles are so small that they scatter mostly blue light like that of the sky, but after being in the mouth they collect moisture and are much larger (see also L-46).

SPECTRA

L-101. Spectroscopes. For projection of spectra in the lecture room probably the most convenient instrument is the one-lens prism spectroscope (L-42). The source (Fig. 315) is focused on a vertical slit. The image of this slit is formed on a screen by the projection lens *L*. In the beam just beyond the lens is placed the prism *P*. While large glass prisms will work, they are expensive and will not give so much dispersion as a hollow prism filled with carbon disulfide or monochlorobenzene. The prism will give sharper lines if used near minimum deviation. The best focus can be obtained either by using a bright-line source or by placing over the slit a didymium glass filter, whose sharp absorption lines are very convenient for focusing. This simple spectroscope can

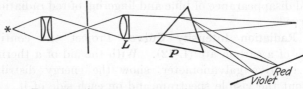

Fig. 315.—Arrangement for projecting a spectrum.

be used to produce continuous spectra, bright-line arc spectra, and absorption spectra based on the continuous one. It is generally not suitable for projecting gas discharge spectra or other faint types. However, if the slit is replaced by the capillary of a brilliant discharge tube like neon or mercury, the spectrum can be seen satisfactorily, although the resolving power will be low. A large direct-vision prism, if available, can be used in place of the usual 60° prism. Such a prism can be made by combining a glass prism with a hollow one filled with carbon disulfide, benzene, bromoform, or other liquid of high dispersion.

L-102. For the observation of gas discharge tubes, inexpensive replica transmission gratings can be passed around the class. They are not recommended for projection work. The straight capillary type of tube is best; several tubes can be arranged above one another in a vertical line so that as the student looks at them through the grating he may readily compare their spectra. If all of the tubes are connected in series with an induction coil, they will all glow together; if connected in parallel, some may be quite brilliant while others are scarcely visible.

L-103. Imitation Line Spectra. If the demonstrator possesses a colored lantern slide of a continuous spectrum, line spectra can be imitated by drawing lines with the point of a knife at proper intervals on a photographic plate, which can then be used to mask out all portions of the continuous spectrum except those representative of the gas whose spectrum is to be imitated.[1]

L-104. Bright Line Spectrum. With the single-lens prism spectroscope (L-101), a bright line spectrum from copper, zinc, iron, or other metal of high melting point can be projected by using electrodes of the metal in an arc lamp. The spectra of metals such as lithium, sodium, and others of low melting point can be projected by using bored carbon electrodes loaded with salts of the desired metal. For gases like hydrogen, helium, neon, or nitrogen, the best form of discharge tube is one having a straight capillary section. If the intensity of the source is great enough, it may be placed near the slit or substituted for it; otherwise it may be viewed by the class individually through replica gratings (L-102). Helium, neon, and mercury are especially good for atomic lines; the nitrogen tube is likely to show molecular bands as well as atomic lines, and so may the hydrogen tube. Sodium and other flame spectra are best viewed individually.

L-105. Band Emission Spectra. The most convenient sources of band spectra for demonstration are capillary discharge tubes containing nitrogen, cyanogen, water vapor, and hydrogen. They may be viewed individually either by means of replica gratings held to the eye or through a spectroscope.

L-106. Continuous Emission Spectra. Either a carbon arc or a concentrated-filament lamp may be used as source. The lamp in the projection lantern is satisfactory. It is a moot question whether better results are secured with the slit in the position of the slide and the projection lens in its regular place or with the projection lens removed and the slit put at the image of the source produced by the condensers, the projection lens being placed far enough ahead of the slit to throw its image on the screen. Using

---

[1] A lantern slide (Misc. 20) showing a diagram of a prism spectroscope together with a hand-colored spectrum as if produced by it is obtainable from Yerkes Observatory. A set of hand-colored slides of emission line spectra of the principal gases may be secured of E. Leybold's Nachfolger, A. G., Cologne, Germany.

the single lens and carbon disulfide prism, a brilliant spectrum 2 or 3 ft long is easily produced (L-101).

L-107. Dark-line Absorption Spectrum. A mirror (heliostat) is arranged to reflect sunlight on the slit of a spectroscope. By means of a small right-angle reflecting prism or a mirror, light from a sodium flame is used to illuminate half the slit, the other half being illuminated by sunlight. The bright sodium lines from the flame will match the *D* lines in the solar spectrum, indicating that the latter are due to absorption by sodium vapor in the sun. The sodium flame may be produced by soaking a strip of asbestos in salt water and wrapping or wiring it around the top of a Bunsen burner, with the asbestos projecting well above the metal tube of the burner. Another method is to heat in a flame one end of an iron or platinum wire, bent into a loop or hook, and then to dip it into borax. Some of the borax will stick to the wire and in a hot flame will fuse and form a drop. By repeating this process, a bead of considerable size can be formed, which will emit a bright sodium yellow. This demonstration is suitable only for individual observation. The observer should, of course, be shielded from direct sunlight.

L-108. For a demonstration that can be seen by the whole class at once, one of the following methods may be used.

1. The projection arc carbons may be boiled in a concentrated salt solution and allowed to dry thoroughly before using.

2. Another method is to bore the carbons and fill the holes with fused sodium chloride. The arc should be run on direct current

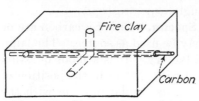

Fig. 316.—Furnace for production of sodium vapor and demonstration of dark-line absorption spectrum.

with the vertical carbon positive. A large, deep hole is bored in this carbon and filled with fused salt or borax, melted into place with a blowtorch. If ordinary salt is used, its water of crystallization will evaporate so violently in the arc as to blow most of the salt out of the carbon. Either of these methods will generate sufficient sodium vapor to produce a cooler envelope around the arc, so as to show a strong absorption line down the middle of a wide sodium line.

3. The most satisfactory method is to make a furnace of fire clay, furnace cement, or other refractory material (Fig. 316), in the form of a rectangular block with two diametrically opposite horizontal holes into which the carbons fit loosely. Two other holes project as far as the center, one from the top and one from the side. If the top hole is left open and an image of the center front hole is projected on the slit of the spectroscope, the ordinary arc spectrum will be produced. When some metallic sodium is dropped through the hole in the top, a brilliant sodium spectrum will appear. The upper hole is then closed so that the vapor of sodium can escape only through the hole in the side. In doing so, it cools and produces an excellent absorption line (A-70).

The furnace may be cast from Portland cement and sand. A metal plate threaded to take a laboratory support rod is set into the bottom of the mold box. Thus the finished furnace may be mounted conveniently in any optical setup.

L-109. Band Absorption Spectrum. A spherical flask is filled with nitrous oxide, which is a reddish-brown gas. When the flask is placed in a beam of light before it is dispersed by the prism of a spectroscope, it produces an excellent absorption spectrum. Didymium glass is also good, but its absorption spectrum is not so interesting as the fluted spectrum produced by nitrous oxide. Dilute blood, either healthy or poisoned with carbon dioxide, is suggested.

L-110. Absorption Spectrum of Chlorophyll. Extract some chlorophyll by macerating green leaves in *methyl* alcohol for several hours. Stinging nettle and pine needles are among the richest bearers of chlorophyll. The former, dried and powdered, can be secured from chemical supply houses under the name *stinging nettle meal* and has the advantage of accessibility in all weathers. Filter, and adjust the concentration until, when the absorption spectrum is projected (as in L-109), the transmission band in the extreme red has maximum visibility. The green transmission is, of course, its principal characteristic. Correlate with the white appearance of foliage in infrared landscape photographs contrasted with its dark appearance in ordinary photographs. The solution also fluoresces (L-114).

L-111. Ultraviolet Spectrum Shown by Fluorescence. That the spectrum extends beyond the visible on the short wave-length side is shown by using a screen painted with quinine sulfate or by holding any other fluorescent material against the regular screen on which a continuous spectrum is allowed to fall. It is first held in the violet so that its action can be seen and is then moved farther and farther out into the ultraviolet. Using quartz lenses and prisms with an iron or carbon arc, the ultraviolet can be followed for a considerable distance. Using a quartz optical system, a good fluorescent screen, and strong sunlight, atmospheric absorption bands may be seen in the ultraviolet. That it is ultraviolet and not visible light can be shown by sliding a white paper in front of the screen. With such a system, the transmission limit of glass can be shown by introducing a sheet of glass anywhere in the light path.

A quartz mercury arc with quartz lens and prism will show prominent lines in the ultraviolet. Detection of radiation may be by photocell instead of fluorescent screen (A-91).

L-112. Infrared Shown by Thermopile or Radiometer. That the spectrum extends to longer wave lengths than those visible can be shown by using a sensitive thermopile and lecture galvanometer or a sensitive radiometer. Starting with the thermopile in the yellow region of the spectrum, it is gradually moved toward the red. The galvanometer deflection will probably reach its maximum value a little beyond the visible region. By using a carbon arc and carbon disulfide lenses and prism (rock salt is better), the spectrum may be followed well beyond the visible. That the energy is really coming through the optical train can be shown by inserting a water cell in the path of the light, to absorb most of the infrared. Place a thermopile in the red-orange region of the spectrum about 18 in. from the prism, and when the deflection becomes steady, interpose a parallel-sided water cell about 1 cm thick. The deflection is somewhat decreased. Now move the thermopile to the region just beyond the red. The maximum deflection will probably be greater than before, but the water cell will produce a very marked decrease. Good results can be obtained with a single glass condensing lens and carbon disulfide prism. No slit is necessary.

L-113. Infrared. Iodine dissolved in alcohol or carbon disulfide (3 g iodine in 100 ml CS_2) produces a filter that cuts out the visible but transmits the infrared. The light from a carbon arc is focused to a point. A match or a piece of black paper held at the focus will be ignited or charred. When a parallel-sided cell containing the iodine solution is placed in the convergent beam, visible radiation is stopped, but the match is ignited or the paper charred as before. A radiometer or thermopile may be used beyond the focus to show the effect, care being taken not to damage the instrument or the galvanometer. Water in a test tube may be boiled by holding it at the focus of the infrared. *Caution:* As both alcohol and carbon disulfide catch fire easily, the first with sometimes explosive violence, they should be used in closed containers with every precaution to avoid accident.

A corked spherical flask filled with iodine dissolved in carbon disulfide acts as a condensing lens as well as a filter (H-151). A similar flask filled with water also acts as a lens but passes only the visible; its absorption of infrared is increased by the addition of alum. A single element of the condenser lens forms a nearly parallel beam that can be brought to a visible focus by the flask of water. While this focus is hot, it is not nearly so hot as the invisible focus produced by the flask containing the iodine solution. Infrared may also be detected with a caesium photocell.

L-114. Fluorescence and Phosphorescence. A carbon arc or a quartz mercury arc with an ultraviolet filter[1] is an excellent source of ultraviolet for fluorescence demonstrations. An argon glow bulb that fits an ordinary lamp socket is very convenient for showing many effects. A battery of 16 2-w argon glow bulbs works very well. If a powerful source is available, it is interesting to turn the source toward the class in a darkened room so that they may observe fluorescence effects on teeth, eyeballs, clothing, etc. Live teeth fluoresce brightly, but dead or false teeth do not shine. When one looks at a bright ultraviolet source, the entire room appears to glow on account of fluorescence within the eye itself (L-60). *Caution:* Prolonged exposures are dangerous.

Many things show bright colors under ultraviolet light; *e.g.*, fluorescein, dilute mercurochrome, quinine sulfate, vaseline, motor oil, petroleum, and many aniline dyes.[2] A solution of

[1] Such as Corning red-purple Corex A.

[2] Special collections of fluorescent and phosphorescent materials can be secured from scientific supply houses; *e.g.*, zinc sulfide; barium platino-cyanide; anthracene, dissolved in benzene for writing; eosin in water; esculin; rhodamine; uranium nitrate; uranium glass, solid or powdered; uranium in gelatin; kerosene. The argon bulb will make many of these substances show up well.

chlorophyll obtained by macerating green leaves in alcohol fluoresces (L-110). Zinc sulfide will phosphoresce brightly for a long time after exposure to ultraviolet. A design can be painted on white paper with a solution of anthracene in benzene that is invisible in ordinary light but is visible in ultraviolet light. A cheesecloth robe, soaked in this solution and then dried, has "stunt" possibilities, especially if used as a shroud for a skull painted with the same solution.

L-115. Transmission by Filters—Photoelectric Cell. A photoelectric cell, either emission or voltaic type, can be used very easily to measure absorption by filters or solutions. The cell is arranged so that the light is incident on the sensitive surface only through the blackened tube T (Fig. 317). The cell and tube are

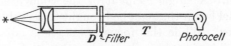

Fig. 317.—Photoelectric examination of filters.

covered with a black cloth after adjustments and electrical connections are completed. A diaphragm D limits the beam to a cross section slightly smaller than that of the tube. With the filter removed, the light is adjusted to give a conveniently large deflection of the galvanometer. The filter or test solution is interposed, and the new deflection noted. If the response of the cell is linear, the percentage of light transmitted is found from the ratio of the two deflections. The principles involved have been incorporated in a colorimeter that will detect more minute traces of certain substances in solution than the visual colorimeter or any purely chemical method of analysis. By using suitable sources, filters, and cells, the ultraviolet transmission or absorption of such substances as protein and amino acid may be measured.

POLARIZATION

L-116. Polarization—Mechanical Model. A rubber tube or cord or a rather stiff helical spring is stretched across the lecture table and 6 in. above it between two rigid supports. The cord or spring passes through a "polarizer" and an "analyzer," which are conveniently made in the form of cubical boxes, 1 ft on each edge, open at two opposite faces. Each box has two partitions (Fig.

318) separated by slightly more than the diameter of the cord, thus providing a central slot that permits longitudinal waves to pass through unimpeded but effectively prevents the passage of transverse waves, except in the plane of the slot. By turning a box through 90°, its slot may be set either vertical or horizontal without changing its height at the center. One box may be marked *P* for polarizer, and the other *A* for analyzer. Longitudinal waves, made evident by tying ribbons to the cord at a number of points, can pass through both slots whatever their relative positions, but transverse waves that pass one slot will pass the second only if it is parallel to the first and will be stopped by it if it is turned at right angles, illustrating the action of crossed Nicols.

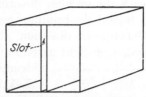

Fig. 318.—Box with slot for showing polarization of waves on cords.

L-117. The mechanical device illustrated in Fig. 319 shows how one component of a transverse vibration can be absorbed and the other not. A weight of a pound or so is hung as a pendulum from the end of a light wooden strut, which projects from the wall some 4 ft and is stayed by cords *A*, *B*, and *C*. The cords *B* and *C* are somewhat slack and are tied to a loop of cord 3 or 4 in. long which can slip across the end of the strut and is kept in position by three small nails, one above, one below, and one passing through the loop to limit the amount of sidewise slip. When the weight is set swinging in the direction *DE*, it imparts motion to the strut and soon comes to rest; while if it swings in the direction *FG*, the strut is not disturbed, and the motion of the pendulum persists. If now the pendulum is set swinging diagonally or in a circle, the sidewise component of the vibration is soon suppressed, and the weight is left swinging in the direction *FG*.

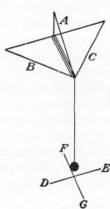

Fig. 319.—Mechanical model of polarization by crystals.

L-118. Linear and Circular Polarization—Pendulum Model. Suspend a weight by a string, and strike the weight a blow in any direction; a linear vibration results. Strike a second (equal) blow, at right angles to the first, and a quarter period later, *i.e.*, when the weight has reached its position of greatest displacement, and the linear vibration will be replaced by a circular one. If the second blow is delayed until a *half* period has elapsed, the resultant motion will be linear but in a direction making an angle of 45° with the original direction, while if the delay is *three-quarters* of a period the resultant motion is again a circular vibration but in the opposite direction. Such aspects of circularly and elliptically polarized light as phase and amplitude may be illustrated with this model.

FIG. 320.—Double pendulum to illustrate double refraction.

L-119. Double-pendulum Model of Double Refraction. The double pendulum (S-43) consists of a weight suspended by strings as shown in Fig. 320. If the weight is displaced either in or perpendicular to the plane of the paper, it will oscillate in a straight line, the period being greater for vibrations perpendicular to this plane than for those parallel to it. If, however, it is displaced in an oblique direction, the force acting upon it will no longer be directed toward the position of equilibrium, and the weight will move in a curved orbit. In the case of crystals, a particle displaced parallel to any one of the axes of elasticity will be acted upon by a force directed toward the equilibrium position, and the vibration will be plane-polarized; if displaced in any other direction, the force is not directed toward its original position, and so the particle moves in a curved path in a manner analogous to that of the pendulum bob.

L-120. Double Refraction. Double refraction is shown most clearly by calcite crystals. Place a crystal over a printed page or some similar object and allow the students to view the effect individually.

Calcite crystals may also be used to show double refraction to the whole class at once. A small hole (1 to 3 mm in diameter) in a sheet of cardboard or metal is illuminated strongly, and its image projected on a screen. When a calcite crystal is held over the hole, two spots of light appear on the screen. As the crystal is rotated, one spot appears to stay fixed while the other moves around it. When a second crystal or a double-image prism is added, four spots appear, and these disappear in pairs as the second crystal is rotated. Instead of the second crystal, a Nicol prism or polarizing plate may be interposed as an analyzer in the path of the light; by rotating it, the two images may be made to disappear alternately, thus showing that they are produced by light polarized in planes perpendicular to one another. Of course a large double-image prism could be substituted for the first calcite crystal and tested in the same way. If a Wollaston prism is used, it must be held a considerable distance away from the illuminated aperture. For convenience, it may be held in a cap that fits over the projection lens, so that the prism can be rotated.

L-121. Polarizing Crystals. The action of tourmaline crystals is most easily explained by the aid of mechanical models. When the crystals are parallel, they transmit; but when crossed, *i.e.*, at right angles to each other, they stop all light. By analogy with the rope and slots (Fig. 318), it may be concluded that light is a transverse wave motion and can be polarized.

Because of its universal use, the Nicol prism should be demonstrated and explained. Large-scale models visible to the entire class are often helpful in the explanation.

L-122. Polarizing Plates. There are now commercially available polarizing plates that consist of two sheets of clear glass between which is cemented a thin film containing a large number of minute polarizing crystals all oriented in the same way. These plates are much cheaper than Nicol prisms of comparable aperture; in fact, they can be made with apertures far larger than the largest obtainable Nicol. For polarization demonstrations in visible light, they are excellent. On the long wave-length side of 7000 Å, they transmit whether crossed or uncrossed; on the short wave-length side of 5000 Å, they transmit approximately 1 per cent of the light when crossed.

L-123. Polarization by Reflection—Nörrenberg's Polariscope. Reflected light is in general partially polarized, as can be seen by viewing it through a Nicol or a polarizing plate. The principle of Nörrenberg's polariscope is that of polarization by reflection from glass (Fig. 321). Two glass plates made of black glass or of ordinary sheet glass painted black on the back with, say, asphaltum varnish, can be so arranged that light incident upon the first (polarizer) at an angle of about 57° will after reflection fall upon the second plate (analyzer) at the same angle of incidence. When the second is in a plane parallel to the first, light is reflected, but if the second is rotated (keeping the angle of incidence constant), no light is reflected when the planes of incidence are at right angles.   The brightness of the image in this case is very sensitive to small changes of angle of incidence.   If the second reflecting surface is a silvered mirror, it will not polarize by reflection, and consequently the image appears bright for all positions.   The analyzer may have black glass on one side and a silvered mirror on the other, so that turning the plate over will change the reflection from one type to the other for quick comparison.

As ordinarily set up, the source of light is stationary, and the

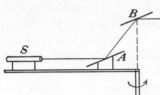

second reflecting sheet turns.   This means that the image moves over angular distances that may carry it completely off the screen.   A simple modification keeps the second reflector *B* (Fig. 321) stationary and

Fig. 321.—Nörrenberg's polari-scope with moving light source.

with it the spot of light.   The source of light is mounted on a horizontal arm, which also carries the reflector *A* and rotates about a vertical pivot whose axis passes through *B*.   The source may be a flashlight, which can be conveniently attached to the movable arm.

L-124. Polarization by Reflection—Pyramid Method.   A square pyramid is constructed from four triangles of black glass so that each face makes an angle of 57° with the base.   The pyramid is mounted at the center of a white screen so that both screen and pyramid may be rotated about the axis of the pyramid.   A broad beam of plane-polarized light is directed axially upon the vertex of the pyramid.   When the plane of polarization is parallel to one edge of the square base of the pyramid, reflection of light to the white screen takes place from only two faces although all four faces are equally illuminated.   When the pyramid is rotated 45°, all four faces reflect equally; when the pyramid is rotated 90° from its original position, the two faces that originally reflected light no longer do so, whereas the other two faces now reflect brightly.

L-125.   A large-scale polarizer using two black-glass plates mounted parallel to one another at opposite ends of a box 1 by 1 by 3 ft (Fig. 322) gives an extended source of plane-polarized light.   Large celluloid models may be placed between the plates

to show stresses (L-134).   The source is a brightly lighted ground-
glass diffusing screen giving illumination over a large field.   If
the light is sufficiently bright, projection through an analyzer
plate may be possible.   Otherwise it will be necessary to view the
objects through some type of
analyzer. This polarizer is
like the louver type of strain
tester (Fig. 323) available
commercially for the production of polarized light.

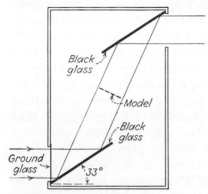

Fig. 322.—Large-scale reflection polarizer.   Fig. 323.—Louver type of strain
tester.

L-126. Polarization by Reflection—Stack of Plates.   Instead
of black-painted glass, which absorbs the transmitted light, a
large number of sheets of glass all held at the proper angle may be
used to give not only polarized light by reflection but almost
completely polarized light by transmission.   A wooden box (Fig.
324) 20 in. long and 6 in. square made of plywood will easily
accommodate 16 or more 5- by 11-in. glass plates at the proper
angle (57°).   Two wooden strips on the sides of the box hold the
lowest plate at the right inclina-
tion, and the others are laid on
it. Old photographic plates
that have been carefully cleaned
without scratching work very
well.   The ends of the box are
open; the top is removable so
that the reflected beam may be
used or not as desired.   The whole box is painted a dull black
inside.   That the reflected and transmitted beams are polarized
in planes perpendicular to one another is easily shown by testing
with a tourmaline crystal, Nicol prism, or polarizing plate.   If a
silvered mirror is used at A, both beams may be projected side by
side on the screen.

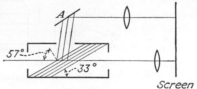

Fig. 324.—Pile of glass plates used as a
polarizer.

L-127. Polarization by Scattering. The beam from a bright source of light S (Fig. 325) is rendered parallel or slightly convergent by the condensers L. It then is reflected downward by the mirror M into a glass cylinder of water containing a small amount of scattering material such as gum mastic, sulfur from hypo solution (L-46), a drop or two of milk, denatured alcohol, resin in alcohol, or liquor carbonis detergens (coal tar in alcohol).

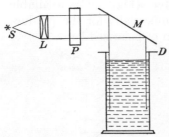

FIG. 325.—Polarization by scattering.

(One-half milliliter of milk in 1500 ml of water is very good.) The path of the light should be confined by a diaphragm D to a beam smaller than the diameter of the cylinder so that it will not strike the sides. Scattered light will be seen in all horizontal directions. If a large polarizing sheet P is placed in front of the cylinder and rotated, it will show that the scattered light is polarized. With a polarizer in the beam above the diaphragm, the scattered light is brighter in the direction perpendicular to the plane of polarization and very faint or absent in the direction parallel to it. If the polarizer is rotated, these directions of maximum and minimum intensity will rotate with it. Two mirrors set behind the jar at an angle of 100° to each other will enable the class to see the two directions at once. Covering the diaphragm with a quartz plate produces colors.

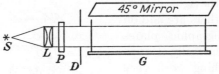

FIG. 326.—Polarization by scattering.

L-128. A different arrangement of L-127 is illustrated in Fig. 326. An intense beam of light is directed through a long rectangular glass trough G. The trough is filled with water having a small amount of scattering material in it, as in the preceding experiment. A diaphragm D of black paper is used to limit the beam to a cross section considerably smaller than that of the trough. Above the trough is a mirror so tipped that the class can look down on the top of the liquid. In the beam is a polarizer P

that can be rotated.   A polarizing plate held in a lens holder is very convenient.   As the polarizer is rotated, first the side of the trough and then the top is bright.   When the side is brightest, the top is dimmest, and vice versa.   This experiment can easily be combined with the "sunset" experiment on scattering (L-46).

L-129. Rotation of Plane of Polarization by Sugar Solution. A very bright beam of light is made parallel or slightly convergent, polarized, and limited by a diaphragm so as to remain wholly within the liquid in a cylinder or a trough as previously described (L-128).   A saturated sugar solution (300 g of sugar to 400 ml of hot water) is filtered through cotton in a funnel and poured into the cylinder.   Clear white corn syrup may also be used.   One of the scattering materials mentioned previously (L-127) is added, but the amount must be very small, as otherwise the beam becomes too dim to be seen before it reaches the end of the container.   The cylinder or trough should be at least 1 ft long.

The plane of polarization of the light entering the solution is rotated by it through an angle that depends upon both the concentration and the thickness of the liquid traversed.   Since the rotation is different for different wave lengths, there is rotational dispersion, and different colors are seen along the tube, producing a spiral appearance, the reds and blues being most noticeable.   As the polarizer is turned, the whole spiral rotates like a barber pole.   The separation of the colors is more pronounced if a plate of quartz with sides cut perpendicular to the optic axis is inserted in the beam before it reaches the sugar solution.   This separates the colors from the start, while without it the separation is effected only by the sugar itself.

L-130. Rotation of the plane of polarization by a sugar solution may be shown by the arrangement of Fig. 327.   The image of the analyzer A is focused on the screen, and the polarizer and analyzer are crossed with the tube of solution T out of the beam.   The tube is then inserted in the beam, and rotation of the analyzer will show colors due to rotatory dispersion.   The amount of rotation is made evident by a large indicator attached to the Nicol or polarizing plate.

L-131. Rotation of Plane of Polarization Measured by Quartz "Biplate."   When polarized light is sent along the optic axis of crystalline quartz, the plane of polarization is rotated, the amount of rotation depending on the wave length of the light and the thickness of the crystal. A quartz "biplate" is frequently used in measuring rotation. Its use can be demonstrated to the whole class if it is shown in connection with a glass-ended tube of medium-strength sugar solution, the transmitted beam being thrown on the screen. The light from a bright source S (Fig. 327) is passed through the condensing lenses L so that it is parallel or slightly convergent. In this beam are placed the polarizer P, the tube of sugar solution T, the biplate B, and the analyzer A. The last two must be capable of rotation. An image of the biplate is thrown by lens L_2 on the screen. With the tube out of the line, the biplate is set so that the edge between the two quartz pieces makes an angle of 45° with the plane of vibration of the polarized light from P. Then the analyzer is adjusted so that the two

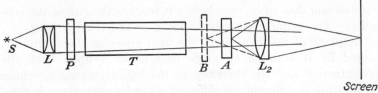

FIG. 327.—Apparatus for demonstrating rotation of plane of polarization by sugar solution, with and without quartz biplate.

halves of the biplate match in color and intensity. The sugar solution is then put back in the optical path, and the two halves of the biplate are decidedly different in appearance but may be made equal again by rotating the analyzer. A pointer should be attached to the analyzer so that the class can see the amount of its rotation required to balance the fields. The sugar solution may be replaced by pieces of quartz showing right- and left-hand rotation.

L-132. Faraday Effect. When a beam of plane-polarized light passes through a material medium parallel to the lines of force of a magnetic field, the plane of polarization is rotated. The pole pieces of an electromagnet are bored with holes parallel to the field. A strong beam of parallel light passes through a polarizer, the holes in the pole pieces, and an analyzer, and thence to a screen where it is focused in a spot. Between the poles of the magnet is placed the specimen to be examined—a piece of heavy glass (lead silicate) with ends cut off square and polished, or a glass tube with plane parallel ends containing carbon disulfide.

With the magnetic field off, the analyzer is turned until the spot on the screen is extinguished. When the electromagnet is turned on, the spot reappears. Rotation of the analyzer will show the amount and direction of rotation of the plane of polarization and sometimes rotational dispersion as well. Reversal of the magnetic field reverses the direction of rotation.

L-133. Into the hole in a solenoid from a large electromagnet, insert a glass container partially filled with halowax oil[1] or carbon

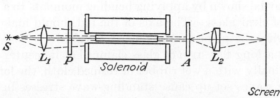

Fig. 328.—Apparatus for demonstrating the Faraday effect.

tetrachloride. Cross the polarizer P and analyzer A (Fig. 328) for extinction when there is no current in the solenoid. Focus an image of the analyzer on the screen with a projection lens L_2; a thread stretched across the analyzer serves to indicate its plane of minimum transmission. Now turn current on in the solenoid; part of the image turns bright because of rotation of the plane of polarization within the dispersive medium. The amount of this rotation may be determined by rotating the analyzer until this portion of the field is again dark. The solenoid may be operated on 110-v direct current with protective resistances.

L-134. Induced Double Refraction—Photoelasticity. The use of polarized light for stress analysis is of considerable engineering interest. Specimens for study are cut from clear celluloid or other plastic $\frac{1}{16}$ in. thick and

Fig. 329.—Transparent models for demonstrating strains by polarized light.

mounted in a frame (Fig. 329) to fit the slide holder of the projection lantern.[2] Stresses are applied by turning wing nuts on the bolts holding the specimens. Models of bridges, bell-crank connectors, and gear trains are especially interest-

[1] Halowax oil 1007 is a chloronaphthalene obtainable from the Halowax Corp., Wyandotte, Mich. It can be removed with gasoline or benzene.

[2] An excellent plastic for photoelasticity is supplied by the Marblette Co., Long Island City, N. Y.

ing. The specimen is inserted in a beam of plane-polarized light, which then passes through an analyzer. A lens focuses the light on a screen. When a stress is set up in the celluloid, the material becomes doubly refracting. If polarizer and analyzer were initially crossed, the neutral axes of the specimens will remain dark, but the image of the specimen will brighten and show colors where the stresses are greatest. Stresses can also be applied by hand. Thus the type of stress in a loaded beam may be shown by applying bending moments to a rectangular rod of clear glass. The axis of the rod should make an angle of 45° with the plane of the polarized light.

When a long flat strip of glass clamped at its center is stroked longitudinally with a wet rubber or rosined cloth, the longitudinal standing waves set up cause standing-wave stresses in the glass, which become apparent when it is viewed by polarized light. Scratches on the glass or celluloid should be avoided, since they scatter light and tend to spoil the effect.

L-135. Kerr Effect. The Kerr effect is easily shown if carbon disulfide or, better, halowax oil, is used between the plates of a condenser. A parallel beam of light is polarized in a plane making an angle of 45° with the vertical. It then passes between the metal plates of the condenser in a rectangular glass cell and through an analyzer. An image of the region between the plates is formed on the screen by a lens. With the plates discharged, the analyzer is set for extinction. If now the two metal plates are connected to the terminals of an electrostatic machine and the plates are slowly charged, the field on the screen will begin to brighten. A safety spark gap should be connected in parallel with the plates so that the condenser cannot be overcharged, as a spark through carbon disulfide may set it on fire and cause an explosion. Halowax oil is safer. With the safety gap set, the condenser may be charged until the gap breaks down. This removes the field, and the spot, which has been growing brighter, suddenly goes black. The operation may, of course, be repeated. The cell constitutes an electrostatic shutter that can be used for producing bright flashes of light of extremely sharp termination. The rectangular glass cell (Fig. 330) is 2 by 2 by 6 in. The top is brown bakelite. To it are fastened the two brass plates M, M, each $\frac{3}{4}$ by 5 in. These are held in place by $\frac{1}{8}$-in. brass rods, one at each end of each plate, bent as shown. At one end of the cell,

the rods come through the top and have thumbscrew terminals
for connection to the source of emf. At the other end, they
project farther above the top. One terminates in a small brass
ball, and the other has an arm with a ball on its end. This ball
spark gap is adjustable by rotating the arm. A lock nut holds it
at any desired gap setting. The distance between the plates is
$\frac{3}{16}$ in. The liquids must be clean and pure and free from all
moisture. In summer or after
prolonged use, the halowax oil
may not stand up under the
slow charging of the electrostatic machine but will still
work if a 60-cycle, 10,000-v

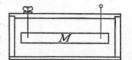

Fig. 330.—Apparatus for demonstrating
the Kerr effect.

transformer is placed across the condenser plates. In this case,
the outside safety gap must be wide enough to avoid breakdown.

L-136. Doubly Refracting Materials in Polarized Light.
Many doubly refracting crystals when placed between crossed
Nicols show colors due to interference. If the crystal is held
stationary and either the analyzer or the polarizer is rotated
through 90°, each color changes into its complement. Unannealed
glass and other materials show colors in regions of strain when
placed between crossed Nicols (L-134). Two very convenient
substances that exhibit the effect are mica and cellophane (that
which is striated during manufacture); the latter is particularly
useful because the thickness can be changed so easily by folding.
It can be shown that cellophane is optically anisotropic so that
every 90°, as it is turned between crossed Nicols, transmission is
cut off. At all other positions, light passes the combination, and
maximum transmission occurs when the mechanical striae due to
manufacture are at 45° to the planes of the crossed Nicols.

As the thickness of cellophane traversed by the polarized light
is increased, the color changes. These colors can be shown by
the following arrangement. Light from a bright source is focused
on a vertical slit by a lens. Before reaching the slit, it passes
through two Nicol prisms or polarizing plates—a polarizer and an
analyzer. It is then projected on a screen through a direct-vision
prism or other dispersion piece so as to form a spectrum (Fig. 331).
The material to be examined is placed between polarizer and
analyzer. Black bands in the spectrum demonstrate the occur-
rence of selective interference. Too great thickness of the

material may give so many bands in the red, green, and violet that
the color of the transmitted light (without dispersion prism) is
white. Smaller thicknesses have only one or two absorption
bands and show considerable color in the undispersed image.

When one of the Nicols is rotated through 90°, the dark and
bright bands in the channeled spectrum are interchanged, and the
resulting color is therefore the complement of the previous one.

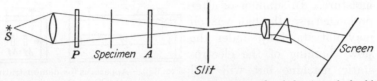

FIG. 331.—Optical arrangement for demonstrating the behavior of doubly
refracting materials in polarized light.

For best effects and purest colors, the vibration planes of the
cellophane should be at 45° to the planes of the polarizer, and the
polarizer and analyzer should be parallel or crossed. It should be
noted that in all these experiments clear, uncolored cellophane is
used. Patterns may be made by using different thicknesses and
orientations of clear cellophane or mica. When ordinary light
passes through them, they show nothing striking, but in polarized
light they exhibit beautiful colors.

PART VI

ATOMIC AND ELECTRONIC PHYSICS

IONIZATION AND CONDUCTION IN GASES

HIGH-PRESSURE PHENOMENA

A-1. Ionization in Air. The production of ions in air by various agencies can be demonstrated with a pair of parallel wires 1 cm or so apart supported on glass insulators above the lecture table. These wires are connected with a generator or battery of about 100 v and a Zeleny electroscope in a projection lantern. A reversing switch may be included to show that the effects are independent of the polarity of the wires. If a flame or a Bunsen burner is held beneath the wires, the electroscope will oscillate. Ultraviolet light from a quartz mercury arc will produce the same effect, doubtless owing in part to photoelectric effect on the wires. The number of ions produced in this way is not very large, and the effect may be enhanced by shining the light between two condenser plates attached to the wires. An x-ray tube mounted in such a position as to irradiate the region between the wires produces a copious supply of ions. The electroscope will also oscillate if the ions are produced by small samples of radioactive materials mounted on cards,[1] by corona discharge from a needle mounted on a static machine terminal, or by a spark gap and induction coil (A-7) mounted at one side of the wires, with a jet of air blowing the ions along them.

A-2. Saturation. If a battery or a generator of 1000 or 2000 v is available, the phenomenon of saturation and the preliminary stages of the Townsend discharge can be shown. A small radioactive source is mounted on a card a few millimeters below a horizontal copper gauze of coarse mesh 3 to 5 cm square. The gauze serves as one electrode of an ionization "chamber," and the other is a metal plate mounted horizontally a few millimeters above the gauze. The gauze and plate are connected in series

[1] See footnote, p. 501.

with a vibrating-leaf (Zeleny) electroscope E and a potentiometer and voltmeter V across the battery (Fig. 332).   As the potential difference between the plate and the gauze is increased, the rate of oscillation of the electroscope leaf (which is a measure of the current) increases until all of the ions produced by radiation from the source are collected as fast as they are formed.   Further increase in potential has no effect on the electroscope rate until additional ions are produced by collision; then the electroscope rate rises again.

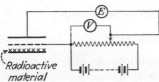

Radioactive
material

FIG. 332.—"Ionization chamber" for demonstrating ion currents and saturation.

A-3. Ion Mobilities.   If the arrangement shown in Fig. 332 is modified by the addition of a second gauze between the first and the plate, separated from each by a few millimeters, the order of magnitude of the mobility of ions in air can be demonstrated.   The field between the two gauzes is provided by the battery, and an additional alternating potential is applied between the second gauze and the plate (Fig. 333). A sinusoidal alternating potential is satisfactory unless a quantitative experiment is contemplated, in which case it is desirable to use a battery with reversing commutator and to mount the gauzes, plate, and radioactive material in a bell jar, so that the pressure can be reduced to 10 or 20 cm of mercury and larger spacings between the elements can be used.

The battery potentiometer is set to give saturation current between the two gauzes.   Ions of one sign are thus drawn toward the upper gauze, and some pass through it into the region between it and the plate.   If the product of the magnitude and the period of the alternating potential between the upper gauze and the plate is sufficiently great, some of these ions are drawn across during a half period, and the electroscope registers a small current.   If the alternating field is not applied in the proper sense for a long enough time or if its magnitude is too small, the ions will be drawn back to the gauze during the reverse half of the

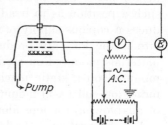

Pump

A.C.

FIG. 333.—Demonstration of ion mobilities.

cycle, and none will reach the plate.   Thus as the alternating potential is increased by means of a potential divider, a point will be reached at which the electroscope E begins to oscillate slowly.   A square wave form, such as that produced by a commutator, will obviously improve the sharpness of the point at which the electroscope begins to record.   Likewise, if the spacing between the elements is large in comparison with the mesh distance, more uniform conditions are obtained, and a more accurate value of the mobility can be found.   However, with an alternating potential of only 100 v or so this requires reduced pressure. As the mobility μ is the velocity per unit potential gradient, and the critical velocity is given by $2d/t$, where d is the separation between the upper gauze and the plate and t is the period of alternation of the field, $\mu = 2d^2/tV$ approximately.   Here V is the average value of the potential; the root mean square value as read by an a.c. meter V is sufficiently accurate for demonstration purposes.

A-4. Recombination of Ions.   The phenomenon of recombination of ions can be studied in a semiquantitative way by drawing

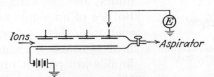

Fig. 334.—Method of showing recombination of ions.

the ions produced by a discharge or a flame past a series of plates at a constant rate.   A horizontal glass tube (Fig. 334) about 30 cm long has a metal-strip electrode lying upon its lower surface and a series of four or five shorter strips drawn up against the upper surface by wires passing through holes in the top of the tube and held by wax.   Ions are produced at the open end of the tube by x-rays, radioactive material, or some other convenient method (the more intense the ionization the better) and are drawn down the tube by an aspirator attached to the other end.   The rate of flow can be regulated by a pinchcock and measured roughly by admitting smoke and timing its passage.   The lower plate is grounded through the battery, and the electroscope is connected to measure the saturation current to each of the upper plates in turn.   Its rate of oscillation is most rapid on the first plate, and when the rate of flow of the air is properly adjusted, very little ionic conduction to the last plate can be observed. Thus almost all of the ions recombine before reaching that plate, and few have a life exceeding the time given by the ratio of plate distance to rate of flow.

A-5. Smoke Precipitation. The phenomenon of attachment of ions to smoke and dust particles and their precipitation in a strong electric field can be demonstrated with an artificial chimney and a static machine (Fig. 335). A fine wire (No. 30) is strung from glass insulators down the axis of a vertical pipe of sheet iron (spouting) 2 in. in diameter and 2 ft long. An inverted

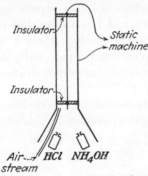

funnel at the lower end facilitates the introduction of dust or smoke into the chimney. The particles are carried up through the chimney by thermal convection from a burner or by an air blast from a small fan or compressor. Cigarette or wood smoke can be used, but ammonium chloride fumes are generally more effective. Bottles of ammonia and hydrochloric acid, with their stoppers removed, are held beneath the chimney, or these liquids are poured into small dishes.

FIG. 335.—Apparatus for showing smoke precipitation.

One terminal of a static machine is connected to the chimney, and the other to the central wire. When a strong field is established between the two by operation of the machine, a slight corona discharge takes place at the surface of the wire, the ions produced attach themselves to the smoke particles, and these are drawn to the electrodes. Thus, in the absence of a field, smoke issues from the top of the chimney; but when the field is established, the discharge of smoke ceases.

In this connection, the condensation of a vapor on ions may be mentioned. Meteorological phenomena can be discussed from this point of view, and the action of the Wilson cloud chamber, which is described in A-116, serves as an excellent illustration (see H-89).

A-6. Corona Discharge in Air. The mass motion of air induced by corona discharge can be shown in a number of ways. If a needle or other sharp point connected to one terminal of a static machine is directed at a candle flame, the electric breeze set up when the machine is operated will disturb or even extinguish the flame. If a thread is attached to a static machine terminal, it will jump about owing to the reaction from small point discharges along its length. A pinwheel in the shape of a small-scale lawn sprinkler whose arms terminate in sharp points will rotate rapidly when connected to a static machine because of corona discharge from these points. Attention can be called to the somewhat different appearance of the corona at positive and negative points. If the point is negative, the discharge resembles a closely fitting purplish sheath, caused by ionization close to the point. If the point is positive, the discharge is more reddish and generally exhibits a branching structure, probably accounted for by ionization by electrons as they enter the intense field in the neighborhood of the point by various paths. It may be noted in connection with the general question of corona discharges that point and tube particle counters, which are elsewhere described (A-118, 119), depend on this mechanism for their operation.

A-7. Spark Discharge. Ordinary sparks can be produced by a static machine or high-voltage transformer with spark gap. Condensed discharges can be demonstrated with the circuit described in connection with high-frequency oscillation (A-29). The convection motion of the spark paths and the periodic phenomena occurring in the case of 60-cycle sparks can be analyzed by means of a rotating mirror (E-268) with its axis approximately parallel to the spark path. The heating effect in flaming arcs and condensed discharges can be demonstrated by

110v A.C.

Fig. 336.— Horn gap for climbing arc.

the burning away of points and the thermal convection of the arc path. The discharge in a horn gap is very spectacular. Two heavy copper wires are bent as shown in Fig. 336 and mounted on insulating supports. The separation at the bottom is such that the arc will strike across it. The arc warms the air around it, which therefore rises by convection and carries the arc with it, until the separation between the wires becomes so great that the arc finally goes out. It strikes again at the bottom, and the process is repeated.

A-8. Arcs. The nature of an ordinary carbon arc can best be demonstrated with a pinhole camera (L-16). The arc is set up in an enclosed but well-ventilated chamber (a projection lantern with the lenses removed is satisfactory) with sufficient resistance in series to limit the current to 20 amp or less.   A pinhole is made in one side of the arc enclosure, and the image is observed on a screen.   The flaming gases and vapors, incandescent particles, and glowing electrodes can all be seen.   If the arc is run on direct current, it will be evident that the major thermal phenomena take place at the anode, where the highest temperatures are produced.   Salts of sodium, strontium, potassium, zinc, etc., can be packed into a cavity in either electrode and the colors that they impart to the arc on vaporization exhibited.   A 60° prism placed over the pinhole may illustrate qualitatively the spectrum of the arc.   The fundamental role played by the temperature of the anode can be shown by attempting to obtain an arc with a heavy copper rod for anode.   The copper dissipates heat so rapidly that it is difficult to develop the requisite anode temperature for an arc.

A-9. Resistance Characteristic of Carbon Arc.   The falling volt-ampere characteristic associated with an arc can be demonstrated by measuring the current and the potential difference across it as the series resistance is varied.   A rather small arc drawing 1 or 2 amp is best for this purpose.   The explanation may be somewhat along the following lines.   The number of current-carrying ions produced in the arc is approximately proportional to the rate at which energy is expended.   A small increase in current results in the formation of more ions, which enables the arc to carry still more current.   The system is unstable, and the current rises and voltage falls until the mini-

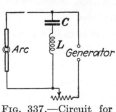

FIG. 337.—Circuit for singing arc.

mum potential necessary to maintain the arc at the final value of the current plus the IR drop in the series resistance is equal to the applied emf.

A-10. Singing Arc.   The instability of an arc may be demonstrated by the singing arc, which is an ordinary carbon arc shunted by a condenser and inductor in series (Fig. 337).   The condenser has from 1- to 10-μf capacitance; the inductor consists of several hundred turns of heavy copper wire (without iron core).   Together they form a resonant circuit with its natural frequency somewhere within the audible range.   Oscillations of this frequency are produced, and the arc acts as its own loudspeaker.   The pitch of the sound may be varied by altering either the capacitance or the inductance.

LOW-PRESSURE PHENOMENA

A-11. Glow-discharge Tube.   The general nature of a cold-cathode discharge can best be shown with a tube in which the pressure can be varied.   A rather large tube, at least 3 ft long and 2.5 or 3 in. in diameter, is best for demonstration purposes.   The electrodes should not be at the ends but several inches in and supported from the sides.   The electrodes are fairly heavy (50- or 60-mil) nickel disks, somewhat smaller in diameter than the inside of the tube, with a 0.5-in. hole through the center.   They are inserted through the ends of the tube before it is closed and are screwed or welded to nickel extensions of tungsten rods or wires sealed through small side tubes.   The tube is mounted well above the lecture table by clamps as inconspicuous as possible. It is sealed to the pumping system (A-57).   The behavior of the tube will not be reproducible, and the form of the discharge will not be constant, until the tube has been run for some time and the major part of the gas and grease layers removed.   This process can be considerably expedited by heating the glass with a flame and outgassing the electrodes with an induction furnace, but this procedure is not essential.

The tube can be operated by a high-voltage transformer, but this method has the disadvantage that it obscures the roles played by cathode and anode.   A protective resistance *must* be placed in either the secondary or the primary circuit to prevent damage from excessive current.   The transformer produces a symmetrical discharge, and unless the tube is viewed through a mechanical stroboscope (which is itself an interesting experiment), the characteristic regions of the discharge are not clearly brought out. An induction coil, which produces an almost unidirectional current, is a suitable source of excitation.   A transformer-rectifier system with a capacity of about 0.5 kw at 10,000 v can be constructed with a small transformer and phanotron tube.   A rheostat in the primary permits easy adjustment, and the outfit is rugged and dependable.   Such a high-voltage source, though convenient, is not necessary.   A much lower voltage can be used, provided that the discharge is once started with a leak tester, small Tesla coil, or induction coil.

Provision may be made to introduce various different gases into the tube if desired.   Illuminating gas shows interesting variations from air.   Neon or mercury-vapor discharges can be produced, which superficially exhibit quite different phenomena from the ordinary air discharge.   With these gases, the tube may display a continuous red or blue glow, with no evidence of striations. However, for most demonstration purposes, the ordinary air or hydrogen discharge is preferable.   The diffusion pump is necessary for producing the final x-ray stage.   If the tube is evacuated with the potential applied to it, care should be taken to limit the current during the typical glow-discharge stage so that the electrodes will not become too hot or the glass melt.   Care must also be taken in the final or x-ray stage to prevent cathode rays and positive rays from melting or otherwise damaging the ends of the tube.   If much of this type of demonstration is contemplated, it is well to protect these ends with additional metal-disk electrodes for heat radiation.

A-12. Glow Discharge.   Since the various phenomena of discharge are described in most texts, their characteristics will be only outlined here.   At atmospheric pressure, no discharge occurs unless excessively high voltages are applied.   As the pressure is reduced, long streamers of spark discharge appear between the electrodes.   At a pressure of a few millimeters, these have disappeared and have been replaced by the typical glow-discharge sheaths.   As the pressure is further lowered, the cathode sheath expands, and the various regions, the Crookes and Faraday dark spaces and the negative glow and positive column, make their appearance.   The dependence of the character of the discharge on the electron mean free path may be pointed out here.   When the thickness of the cathode sheath has increased to the point where it no longer penetrates the hole through that electrode, positive rays and cathode rays begin to appear behind the electrodes.   As the pressure is further decreased, these rays produce visible effects for several inches of their path.   The striations of the positive column gradually expand and move into the anode. If the progress of evacuation is halted at this stage, the current carried by the discharge may be varied by adjusting the rheostat in series with the primary of the induction coil or transformer, and the dependence of sheath thickness on current density illustrated. In the final high-vacuum stage of the discharge, the room should be darkened to make visible the fluorescence of the glass under cathode-ray bombardment.   An external spark gap in parallel with the tube provides an alternative path, which is taken by the discharge both at high and at low pressure.

Numerous variations of the tube that has just been described will suggest themselves.   If the cathode is made in the form of a short cylinder with its axis parallel to that of the tube, the streaming of positive and negative rays from its two ends can be made more striking.   If sufficient power is available to increase the discharge current to the Schuler stage, the sheath will shrink until the entire discharge is confined within the cathode.   The rare gases are generally used for this purpose.   If the cathode is made in such a way as to have sharp points, say a triangular plate, discharge streamers from the intense fields at these points will be observed in the early stages of the discharge.   If a small electrode is used as cathode, it can be heated to incandescence by the discharge.

A-13. Special-purpose Discharge Tubes.   In addition to the type of tube that requires a pumping system, tubes specially prepared to illustrate various phenomena can be obtained from scientific supply houses.   A set of tubes containing various gases shows the different line and band spectra emitted (L-104).   A set of these tubes containing air at different pressures shows the salient features of the discharge previously described.   These Geissler tubes can be operated by an induction coil.   Tubes are also available for illustrating the heating effect of cathode rays and the fluorescence of various minerals under bombardment.   The normal emission and rectilinear motion of cathode rays can also be demonstrated with special tubes for the purpose.   A tube in which a small paddle wheel is mounted illustrates the mechanical motion that can be produced by these moving charged particles, both by their momentum and by the radiometer effect that they produce by local heating of the vanes.   A tube with a longitudinal fluorescent screen is useful for showing the bending of cathode rays in a magnetic field.

A-14. Potential Required for Glow Discharge.   Neon glow lamps illustrate very well the minimum voltage necessary for the maintenance of a cold-cathode discharge.   This is of the order of the normal cathode fall characteristic both of the nature of the cathode surface and of the gas.   Some of these lamps will light on the peak of the 110-v a.c. wave but will not light on 110-v d.c. Others will light on this d.c. voltage and will show the glow surrounding one electrode.   The minimum d.c. voltage for initiating the discharge can be measured with a voltmeter and potential divider.   It will be found that the discharge may be maintained at a much lower voltage once it is started.

A-15. Electrodeless Discharge.   Commercial glow lamps can also be used to illustrate the fact that electrodes are not necessary for the maintenance of the discharge.   If the lamp base is held in the hand and the envelope brought near the end of a Tesla coil or the inductor in a high-frequency circuit, the typical glow can be clearly seen.   This phenomenon can be more strikingly demonstrated with cylindrical or spherical glass bulbs several inches in diameter containing helium, neon, argon, or mercury vapor at low pressure (10^{-4} or 10^{-5} mm of Hg).   The more powerful the electromagnetic field to which they are subjected the brighter does the glow appear.   Any high-frequency system can be used, *e.g.*, A-31.   If a bulb is inserted in the baking coil of an induction furnace, the ring shape of the discharge illustrates the predominant role played by the magnetic field.   Attention may be called to the necessity of high-frequency excitation for this type of discharge.   Ordinary gas-filled incandescent lamps can be used to illustrate the existence of a glow, but the experiments that can be performed with them are not very striking.   A bulb containing pure nitrogen can be used to demonstrate the afterglow.

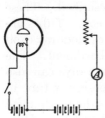

Fig. 338.—Tungar demonstration circuit.

A-16. Hot-cathode Discharges.   Discharges using a hot cathode can also be demonstrated with various tubes that are readily available.   The Tungar rectifier bulb in series with 18 v and a small control rheostat illustrates the necessity of auxiliary electron emission from the cathode to maintain a low-voltage discharge (Fig. 338).   No discharge appears until the filament is heated; but after the discharge is once started, positive ion bombardment of the filament or an auxiliary cathode point keeps it at incandescence, and the discharge continues after the filament circuit is opened.   The phanotron, or mercury-vapor rectifier, also illustrates the fundamental role of cathode emission in a discharge.   Inverse voltages up to several thousand volts can be applied without initiating a discharge; but when a potential of 15 or 20 v is applied in the proper sense, the discharge occurs (Fig. 339).

A-17. Thyratron Tube. The function of the grid in a discharge tube can be shown with a thyratron. One of the small types such as the FG-57 or FG-67 is suitable. If a negative voltage is applied to the grid, the cathode is shielded from the field of the plate, and a high potential must be applied to the plate before breakdown occurs but a low positive potential applied to the grid will start the discharge. Once the discharge has started, however, the shielding effect of the grid ceases. It is surrounded by a very thin space-charge sheath that insulates it

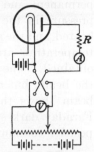

Fig. 339.—Circuit for demonstrating a phanotron tube.

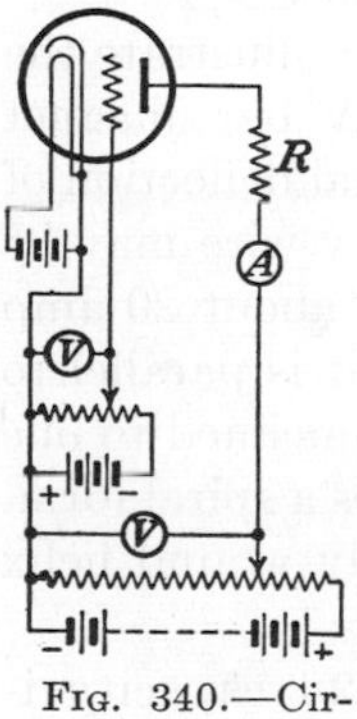

from the rest of the discharge, and the current from cathode to plate is quite independent of grid potential. A suitable circuit for demonstrating these tubes is shown in Fig. 340. A current-limiting resistance must be included in series with the plate. The proper values of the potentials, safe currents, etc., are given in bulletins accompanying the tubes.

A-18. Electron Beams. A number of striking and illustrative experiments dealing with the path of an electron beam can be performed with a lime-spot hot cathode. Such a cathode is made by putting a small spot of lime on a platinum strip that can be heated to incandescence by current from a battery. Sealing wax or a mixture of barium, strontium, and calcium oxides in paraffin similarly heated produce satisfactory electron sources. The beam of cathode rays issuing from such a lime spot is characterized by its extreme compactness and brilliance. No diaphragm is necessary for limiting the beam. The electrons produce a long, narrow column of ionization in the residual gas, and only a low potential is necessary, so that the electrons move relatively slowly and are readily deviable. The disadvantage of this type of cathode is that the lime spot loses its activity after a few hours of operation; hence provision must be made for renew-

Fig. 340.—Circuit for thyratron demonstrations.

ing it. The most satisfactory arrangement is to mount the platinum strip on a ground-glass joint. The anode, of course, is permanent and can be placed at any convenient point. The pressure in the tube is reduced to about 1 mm, the cathode heated, and the potential applied.[1] The pressure and the cathode temperature are then adjusted until a satisfactory beam is obtained. The larger the heating current the more brilliant is the beam, but also the shorter is the life of the cathode. The beam shows the typical cathode phenomena of Crookes and Faraday dark spaces, as well as the negative glow and intense positive column. The variation of these with gas pressure, cur-

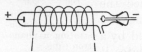

FIG. 341.—In the magnetic field of the solenoid, the beam of cathode rays spirals down the tube.

rent (by varying the cathode temperature), and anode-to-cathode potential can be shown. Excellent beams can be obtained in mercury vapor. A drop or two of mercury is placed in a small appendix to the tube and the vessel is pumped out completely. The vapor pressure is controlled by the temperature of the appendix, an ice bath generally producing about the right conditions.

A horizontal tube 30 or 40 cm long can be used to illustrate the deviation of the beam in a magnetic field. A bar magnet brought up in a horizontal plane produces a vertical deflection of the cathode rays. A loosely wound helix of heavy wire may be placed over the tube (Fig. 341), and a current of about 20 amp sent through it. The beam is undeflected when it is parallel to the axis of the helix, but if the beam and axis are inclined to one another at an angle of 10° or 20°, the beam assumes a spiral form. The effect of compressing or extending the loosely wound helix can be shown.

A-19. "Aurora Borealis." If a large bulb (12-l capacity is satisfactory) is available, an experiment illustrating the aurora borealis can be shown with a lime-spot cathode such as that described in A-18. The cathode leads are introduced through a ground joint sealed to the stem of the flask. One pole of an iron-core solenoid, producing a powerful *divergent* magnetic field, is brought up to the bulb in the general region opposite the stem. The cathode rays are directed toward the pole of the magnet, but

[1] Gas is emitted by the hot cathode; therefore pumping should be continued until stable conditions are attained.

after progressing a short distance their paths become divergent helixes. The form of the paths can be varied by changing the strength of the field or the position of the pole relative to the beam. The envelope of the helixes resembles the northern lights (Fig. 342).

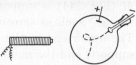

A-20. Magnetic Deflection of Cathode Rays. The cathode beam may be made to describe a (nearly) circular path by applying a suitable magnetic field (Fig. 343). The cathode may be placed in a bulb 15 or 20 cm in diameter and surrounded by two Helmholtz coils capable of carrying a current of several amperes. Alternatively, the cathode can be inserted in the side of a cylindrical glass jar, and a heavy piece of plate glass waxed over the front. The coils for producing the magnetic field are wrapped snugly around the jar. The magnetic field is adjusted until the electrons follow a circular path about 10 cm in diameter. If the radius of curvature of the path is measured, an approximate value of e/m

FIG. 342.—Apparatus for simulating the aurora borealis.

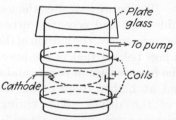

FIG. 343.—Method of demonstrating magnetic deflection of cathode rays.

for electrons can be calculated from the strength of the magnetic field and the potential applied to the cathode. The jar must, of course, be evacuated. (For other e/m experiments, see A-72–74.)

A-21. Electron Focusing. A cathode-ray oscilloscope tube can be used to illustrate the phenomenon of electron focusing. In the case of the older type of tube, the focusing of the beam is accomplished by a positive ion sheath formed in the residual gas. The intensity of ionization is a function of the potential applied to the tube and of the beam current. The behavior of the spot on the screen can be noted as these two factors are varied. In the newer tubes, electrostatic focusing is used, and the sharpness of the spot can be varied by means of the focusing potential. The proper values of the potentials are given in bulletins accompanying the tubes. Magnetic focusing can also be demonstrated with either type of tube. The tube is placed within a solenoid about twice its length. The spot is first made diffuse by improper adjustment and is refocused by the magnetic field of the solenoid.

ELECTRICAL OSCILLATIONS

A-22. Mechanical Analogue of Electrical Resonance. A mass
M (Fig. 344) is supported at the junction of two vertical helical
springs, such as screen-door springs, one above and one below.
The upper end of the upper spring is attached to a rigid frame
support, and the mass is set into vertical shm by periodic extensions of the lower spring. With a little practice, this may be
accomplished manually. The motion is more uniform, and the
phase relations may be studied in more detail, if the lower end of

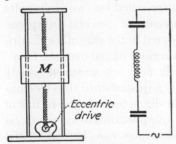

the lower spring is driven by a small
variable-speed motor equipped with
a Scotch yoke (Fig. 100) for vertical motion. If such a device is not
available, the mass may be drilled
for vertical guide rods, and the
spring actuated by an eccentric pin
on a disk attached to the motor
shaft. The figure indicates the use

Fig. 344.—The arrangement of of guide rods and eccentric drive.
mass and springs is the mechanical
analogue of the electric circuit on At low frequencies, the motion of the
the right.
mass lags behind that of the lower
end of the spring; at resonance, the motions are in phase, and a
large amplitude is developed; and at higher frequencies, the
motion of the mass leads that of the driver. The spring-
condenser, mass-inductor, and friction-resistor analogues may be
pointed out clearly and in as much detail as the mathematical
ability of the students warrants. The electric circuit analogous
to this arrangement of weight and springs is included in the
figure for comparison.

If a thread is substituted for the lower spring, a large amplitude
may be produced at resonance by the periodic application of a
small force. A 20-lb weight bolted to the end of an automobile
spring leaf may thus be set into motion by properly timed
impulses.

A-23. Alternator for Very Low Frequency. Several elementary a.c. and radio-circuit phenomena may be demonstrated with
currents of very low frequency, *i.e.*, of the order of 1 cycle per sec.
In this range, the circuits can be metered with instruments
normally used for direct current by which the changes in the

instantaneous values of the current and voltage are made visible.

Ordinary alternators, run slowly, generate too low a voltage for this purpose; however, a d.c. source and rotary potential divider may be used to generate the alternating current. A dilute solution of common salt carries a steady direct current between metal plates fixed on the inside of a cylindrical container, made of insulating material. Another pair of metal plates, set flush with the periphery of an insulating cylinder B (Fig. 345) coaxial with the first, are connected to slip rings and are rotated with B in the solution. As the cylinder is rotated, the potentials of the plates vary approximately sinusoidally, and an alternating current may be taken by brushes from the slip rings. The frequency of the alternation is that of the rotation of the cylinder.

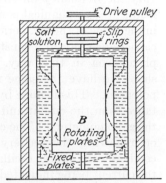

Fig. 345.—Low-frequency alternator.

Figure 346 shows the circuit used for demonstrating the phase relationships between the current and voltage for different circuit elements. The load K may be a resistance (400 ohms is satisfactory), an inductance (3000 turns of No. 22 d.c.c. copper wire on a closed Stalloy or Alnico core about 6 in.² in cross section), or a capacitance (about 150 μf). G_1 and G_2 are similar, well-damped, center-zero galvanometers (2-0-2 milliammeters) and act as voltage and current indicators respectively. G_1 is in series with 5000 ohms, and G_2 is shunted with 10 ohms. A battery of from 12 to 24 v is applied to the fixed plates of the potential divider, and the rate of revolution set to about 1 cycle per sec. Though this may be done by hand, it is more satisfactory to use reducing gears or pulleys and a small low-speed motor. According as resistance, inductance, or capacitance is used, the pointer of G_1 is in phase with, leading, or lagging behind that of G_2.

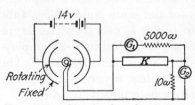

Fig. 346.—Circuit for demonstrating low-frequency alternator.

The motion of the pointer is not in phase with the current through the instrument coil, but if the meters are of the same construction, this phase difference will be the same in each, and the relative pointer readings will still be significant.   By making the load K of both inductance and capacitance, series and parallel resonance may each be shown.   It is generally not practicable to vary the frequency on either side of resonance with a constant load as the mechanical period of the galvanometer movements is in the range of the a.c. period used.   It is more satisfactory to add capacitance, say, at a constant frequency and study the resonance phenomena in that way.   The resonant combination may be shown to have the same natural period as that of the applied potential.   This is done by removing the inductance and capacitance from the circuit and connecting them in series with one of the galvanometers.   The condenser is charged to about 80 v, and on removing the battery connection to one terminal of the condenser the charge oscillates back and forth through the circuit, the current being indicated by the galvanometer.   The larger the inductance in comparison with the product of the resistance and the capacitance, the smaller is the damping and the more satisfactory the experiment.   With the circuit elements suggested previously, about three complete periods may be timed.

A-24. A three-electrode tube may be used to generate oscillations of this low frequency.   If the inductor is not center-tapped, a Colpitts type of circuit should be used

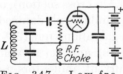

FIG. 347.—Low-fre-
quency oscillator circuit.

(Fig. 347).   This low-frequency circuit is considerably less efficient than a radio circuit; hence for the same amplitude a tube of moderate power is necessary, *e.g.*, type 10.   The circuit described in A-27 employing a type-57 tube may also be used.   The series and shunt resistances for the meters depend on the tube and potentials available and must be determined by trial.

A-25. With the rotary potential divider and a vacuum tube in one of the standard circuits, both rectification and amplification can be demonstrated.   Colored celluloid pointers attached radially to the shaft of the potential divider may be used to illustrate better the half of the cycle rectified, relative phases of voltage and current, etc.   If a variable-speed alternator is available, these meters may be used to illustrate the phenomenon of beats between the 60-cycle power supply and the variable frequency. Beats may also be illustrated by two standard incandescent lamps in series with the 60-cycle mains and the variable-speed alternator.

A-26. Resonance at 60 Cycles. For resonance at 60 cycles, the product of inductance in henrys and capacitance in microfarads should be 7. If a fixed 1-henry inductor is available, a battery of condensers, variable in steps of 1 μf from, say, 2 to 12, is suitable to demonstrate the phenomenon; or a variable inductor consisting of a large solenoid with a movable iron core may be used. An ordinary incandescent lamp is a good indicator of the magnitude of the current. Standard a.c. voltmeters will measure the drop across the various circuit elements. To illustrate the phase relations a wattmeter, or, better, an oscilloscope, should be used.

A-27. Audio-frequency Oscillator. A very simple and convenient circuit for generating oscillations over a very wide range of frequencies[1] is shown in Fig. 348. The type-57 tube displays a negative transconductance, and if a resonant circuit is connected to the terminals AB, oscillations will be generated with the natural peroid of this circuit. The size of the condenser C' depends somewhat on the frequency of the oscillations to be generated, 0.01 μf being a convenient value for the audio-frequency range.

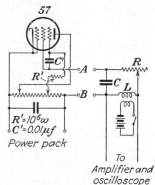

Fig. 348.—Simple audio-frequency oscillator.

The inductance should be of the order of 0.1 henry. An amplifier-loudspeaker combination makes the oscillations across its terminals audible to the class. The demonstration is improved if an oscilloscope is also used to make the wave form visible.

With the resistance R at zero, the capacitance C is varied in steps from, say 0.1 to 1 μf (a decade condenser is very convenient). A pure musical note is produced by the loudspeaker, and its sine curve is visible on the oscilloscope screen. With a suitably tuned bank of 10 or 12 condensers arranged with separate keys, tunes can be played as if on a piano. The proper capacitances

[1] HEROLD, E. W., *Proc. Inst. Radio Eng.*, **23**, 1201, 1935.

to produce a musical scale can be calculated if the value of the inductance is known. The corresponding condensers can be assembled from ordinary radio parts, although the final adjustment may require a little empirical tuning.

Any of the standard types of circuit[1] may be used for an audio-frequency oscillator, but it is difficult to make the capacitance or

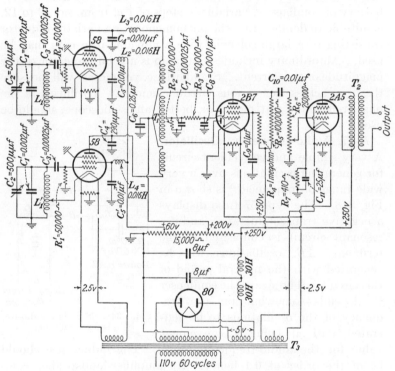

FIG. 349.—Beat-frequency oscillator circuit.

the inductance easily and rapidly adjustable to cover a large range of frequencies. The most convenient instrument for this purpose is the beat-frequency oscillator, in which an audio frequency is produced by beats between two radio-frequency circuits. A small fractional change in frequency of one of the circuits suffices to cover the entire audio range, and this can be accomplished by the variation of a single air condenser. One

[1] HENNEY, KEITH, "Radio Engineering Handbook," p. 277, McGraw-Hill Book Company, Inc., New York, 1935.

suitable circuit is shown in Fig. 349.   Numerous other circuits will be found in the literature of radio.   Complete oscillators are commercially available.

A-28. Damped Oscillations.   If the resistance R (Fig. 348) is increased, a critical value will be reached at which the oscillations cease.   In this condition, the circuit, though not self-oscillatory, still has a small decrement.   If a coil, in series with a small battery and key, is loosely coupled with the inductor L, the circuit may be set in oscillation by tapping the key.   The note and oscilloscope pattern both persist for some seconds, the sound resembling somewhat that of a plucked string.   As the resistance is further increased, the damping increases and the duration of the note becomes very short.

A-29. High-frequency Oscillations Generated by Spark Discharge.   Damped high-frequency oscillations can be generated with a high-voltage transformer, spark gap, and tuned circuit. Twice each cycle, the condensers are charged by the transformer to the breakdown potential of the gap.   Once the gap breaks down, it has a low resistance, and the tuned circuit oscillates.   If

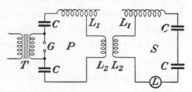

Fig. 350.—Circuit for generating damped high-frequency oscillations. The secondary circuit includes an indicating lamp L.

the circuit connections are well made, the damping is small, and various resonance phenomena can be demonstrated.   The circuit is shown in Fig. 350. T is a 25,000-v, 1-kw transformer. G is the spark gap, which should preferably be of the rotary type.   The condensers C should be capable of withstanding the peak voltage of the transformer; hence series connection of Leyden jars with capacitances of about 1000 $\mu\mu$f is indicated.   The two coupling inductors L_2 should each have five turns of heavy copper wire or $\frac{1}{8}$-in. copper tube, which is sufficiently rigid to keep the turns well apart.   If lighter wire is used, it should have heavy insulation for this purpose.   These helixes may be wound loosely on a horizontal wooden cylinder about 30 cm in diameter.   The coupling can be varied by moving the coils together or apart. The two inductors L_1 are continuously variable.   They are composed of 30 or 40 turns of copper tubing or heavy copper strip wound edgewise in a helical groove on a wooden cylinder about

20 cm in diameter.   The pitch should be about 1 cm.   A central metal axle with end bearings is provided with an insulating crank for rotating the cylinder.   The support should be made so as to permit either horizontal or vertical mounting.   One end of the helix is brought to a heavy brass slip ring on the axle; contact with both sides of this ring is made with spring-brass or phosphor-bronze brushes.   The sliding contact is a brass block with a groove fitting loosely over the copper tubing or ribbon, mounted on the end of a flat spring-brass strip that presses it against the turns of the helix.   The center of this strip may be mounted on a tube sliding along a brass rod, with the lower end held out by a second brass rod so that the upper end is pressed against the helix; or the strip may be carried on a length of rectangular tubing sliding over a square rod to accomplish the same purpose.

The diagram (Fig. 350) shows the circuit arrangement for series resonance.   A lamp or thermal meter L in the secondary circuit S indicates the current. L_1 in either circuit may be varied to pass through the resonant condition.   The fact that the product of inductance and capacitance must be the same for each circuit may be shown qualitatively by changing the capacitance by one or more units and making the necessary alteration in the inductance.   The effect of coupling may be shown by altering the separation of the coils L_2.

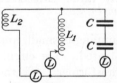

Fig. 351.—Secondary circuit of Fig. 350 arranged for parallel resonance.

A-30. Parallel Resonance.   To demonstrate parallel resonance, the primary circuit remains as before (Fig. 350), and the secondary is arranged as in Fig. 351. Three indicating lamps (*e.g.*, 110 v, 40 w) or meters are used, one in each branch. Below resonance, the lamp in series with L_1 is brighter than that in series with C; at frequencies above resonance, the reverse is the case.   The lamp in series with L_2 goes out at the resonant point.   If the frequency is varied by means of L_1 in the primary, it should be noted that the induced emf in the secondary increases with the frequency and it is the relative rather than the absolute brightness of the lamps that is significant.   (L_2 is again the coupling inductor as in Fig. 350.)

A-31. Tesla Coil.   Many interesting experiments of the Tesla-coil type can be performed with a coil whose natural period (due

to distributed circuit capacitance and inductance) lies in the range
of frequencies of the high-frequency spark oscillator (A-29). A
convenient Tesla coil or resonant secondary can be made by winding closely No. 28 s.c.c. copper wire on a wooden dowel about 3
cm in diameter and 150 cm long. The ends should be covered
with short metal caps to prevent the wire from burning away. It
is most convenient to mount this coil vertically by pressing its
lower end into a hole in a wooden base. It may be glued in place
permanently if desired, but neither nails nor screws should be
used. The elements of the previously described
secondary circuit (A-29, 30) may be included either
in series or in parallel as the primary for the Tesla
coil so that a large frequency range may be covered
by that circuit. The Tesla coil may be electrostatically coupled to the primary by connecting the lower
end through a 110-v lamp directly to one condenser
plate. Or it may be electromagnetically coupled by
grounding one end of the coil through the lamp and
placing the L_2 coil of the primary around the coil
near its base as shown in Fig. 352. In either case,
the length of the coil is a quarter of the fundamental
wave length. The free end is a potential antinode
and current node. The grounded end is a potential
node and current antinode. This latter is indicated
by the lighting of the lamp at resonance. If a
needle is mounted in the upper metal cap, long
streamers of discharge are produced by the potential antinode at
resonance.

L_2

FIG. 352.—
Tesla coil
coupled to
secondary of
high-fre-
quency oscil-
lator.

Many other interesting demonstrations are possible with this
apparatus. A metal disk about 20 cm in diameter is attached to
one end of a wooden rod about 1 m long, and a wire is run along
the rod through a lamp mounted at its center to a metal foil
wrapped around the other end. This foil handle is grasped
firmly in the hand, and as the disk is brought near the upper end
of the Tesla coil, the lamp glows brightly. The high-frequency
current flows over the skin of the demonstrator, but there is no
unpleasant sensation if good contact is made with the foil.
Glass tubes 1 or 2 cm in diameter and 60 or 70 cm long containing
air, helium, neon, or mercury vapor at a few millimeters pressure
make very colorful demonstration wands. When held in the

hand and brought near the upper end of the Tesla coil, they glow brightly. These demonstrations are enhanced if the lecture room is darkened.

If the coil is grounded through a lamp at each end, the fundamental is characterized by a current antinode at each end and a potential antinode at the center. If neither end of the coil is grounded, potential antinodes exist at the ends, and a current antinode at the center. Both these modes of oscillation correspond to a half wave length along the coil. By adding condensers in series to increase the frequency of the primary circuit, at least three overtones or harmonics of each of the quarter- and half-wave fundamentals can be obtained. The current antinodes can be detected easily only if they occur at the ends of the coil. The potential antinodes along the coil may be detected by the wands previously described or by a small neon lamp, which may be fastened to the end of a wooden rod and which, as the glass envelope is moved along the coil, glows brightly in the neighborhood of a potential antinode. For the highest frequencies—those exhibiting the largest number of potential antinodes—it may be necessary to remove L_1 from the primary circuit entirely and to have as many as 8 or 10 Leyden jars in series. It may also be necessary to reduce the number of turns in the coupling coil L_2.

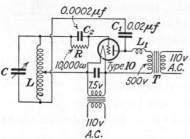

Fig. 353.—Circuit for generating continuous high-frequency oscillations.

A-32. Continuous-wave High-frequency Experiments.

Continuous or undamped oscillations with a frequency in the neighborhood of 10 megacycles, which is of the same order of magnitude as that generated by the spark-discharge apparatus of A-29, can be generated with a vacuum tube. A convenient circuit is shown in Fig. 353. If a constant source of plate potential is available, the oscillations generated are of uniform amplitude. However, "raw" 60-cycle alternating current may be used for the plate supply as shown, and this arrangement has certain advantages. The plate of the tube is heated for only half of each cycle, and hence there is less energy to be dissipated than in the case of a d.c. plate supply. Furthermore, the output of the oscillator is modulated with a 60-cycle frequency and its harmonics. The radiation may be detected by any simple receiving circuit (A-33) tuned to the oscillator frequency, and the 60-cycle note and its harmonics may be amplified and heard in a loudspeaker. The low-power oscillator of Fig. 353, suitable for wavemeter demonstrations, lecture-table radiation, etc., can be constructed with the following circuit elements: T is a transformer supplying about 500 v, and the tube is a type 10. Its filament can be heated with a storage battery or a small 7.5-v transformer. The blocking condenser C_1 is 0.02 μf, and the grid condenser C_2 is 0.0002 μf. A grid leak R of about 10,000 ohms is satisfactory. The tuned circuit is composed of a copper tube helix of 10 or 15 turns about 3 in. in diameter, and a variable air condenser with a maximum capacitance of 100 or 200 $\mu\mu$f. A condenser of 0.01 μf in the filament circuit is not absolutely necessary, but it improves the distribution of the high-frequency current between the two legs. The choke coil L_1 is No. 28 d.c.c. copper wire wound on a mailing tube $1\frac{1}{2}$ in. in diameter and 3 in. long. The oscillations may be detected by a small neon lamp with its envelope held near the inductor L. The filament current should be adjusted until the oscillations are strongest.

A-33. Wavemeter. The use of a wavemeter may be illustrated with the simple circuit shown in Fig. 354. The inductor is made of about six turns of No. 18 copper wire wound on a mailing tube 3 in. in diameter. The variable condenser is of the same size as that used in the tuned circuit of the oscillator (A-32). A small flashlight bulb L in series with these elements indicates the resonant condition as the condenser on the wavemeter is varied. If this circuit is brought close to the oscillator, the interaction results in two resonance peaks instead of one.[1]

F I G . 3 5 4 .—
Wavemeter.

A-34. Radio Transmission and Reception. If the oscillator (A-32) is coupled to an antenna, the phenomena associated with radio transmission and reception may be illustrated. For lecture-table work, this antenna can be small and of almost any convenient form. A wire running along the lecture table or simply a $\frac{1}{8}$-in. brass rod 3 or 4 ft long stuck in a vertical drill hole in the wooden oscillator base serves admirably. It may be con-

---

[1] For explanation, see, *e.g.*, F. E. Terman, "Radio Engineering," 2d ed., p. 79, McGraw-Hill Book Company, Inc., New York, 1937.

nected directly to one end of the oscillator coil, although a variable condenser in series will allow it to be tuned if desired. A simple receiving circuit is illustrated in Fig. 355. The tuned circuit is the same as that of the wavemeter described in A-33, with the flashlight omitted. The sending and receiving antennae may be identical. Any small diode or three-electrode tube with the grid and plate connected will serve as a detector. *C* is a by-pass condenser of the order of 0.01

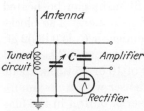

μf. If the input of an amplifier and loudspeaker combination is connected across the terminals of this condenser, the 60-cycle note of the oscillator may be plainly heard. The harmonics increase the audibility but make the note of very poor quality. An a.c. meter in place of the loudspeaker may allow quantitative measurements of antenna

Fig. 355.—Simple radio-receiver circuit with diode detector.

efficiencies, etc., to be made. The functions of the different parts of the circuits and the wave forms throughout may be further illustrated by diagrams on the blackboard.

A-35. Continuous-wave Tesla Apparatus. Oscillators in the same general frequency range of the type described in A-32 may be used for Tesla-coil experiments such as those of A-31 by the addition of a Tesla coil coupled to the oscillator coil *L* (Fig. 356). However, the oscillator that has been described (A-32) is suitable only for very small-scale demonstrations. For satis-factory lecture work with the Tesla type of tuned secondary, an oscillator capable of supplying 200 or 300 w should be used. It is more economical to use two tubes in a push-pull circuit such as that illustrated in the following experiment (Fig. 357). Mag-

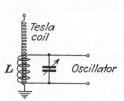

Fig. 356.—Circuit for continuous-wave Tesla-coil demonstrations.

netic coupling should be used for best results, and the coils should be designed to give as favorable a coupling coefficient as possible. The rest of the technique is the same as that previously described.

A-36. Ultra High-frequency Apparatus. Electromagnetic waves from 0.5 to 3 m long may be generated by suitable circuits employing modern low-capacity tubes. Suitable ones are the following: of the order of 0.5 w, RCA 954 and 955; 10 to 50 w,

W.E. 304-B and RCA 834.   The bulletins that accompany these
tubes describe various circuits and give appropriate values for the
constants.   A simple circuit that gives good results is illustrated
in Fig. 357.   The plate inductor is a single turn of No. 10 bare
copper wire about 2 in. in diameter.   For the highest frequency,
the capacitance is simply that of the tube plates.   The frequency
may be reduced and varied over a considerable range by connecting a one- or two-plate variable condenser with a maximum
capacitance of about 10 $\mu\mu$f between the plates.   The plate coil
is supported directly by the plate leads, which come from the tops
of the tubes.   The grid coil, which is similar but reversed in
sense, as indicated in the diagram,
is supported in the same way.
If any other supports are used,
they must be of very low-loss
insulating material such as "iso-
lantite" or "victron."   The value
of the grid resistance R depends
on the type of tube used.   It may
be determined from the rated
mean values of the grid voltage
and current recommended for the
tube in this class of operation.
The midpoints of the plate and
grid coils are at zero radio-fre-

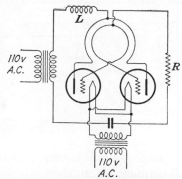

Fig.　357.—Ultra   high-frequency
oscillator.

quency potential, but owing to small asymmetries it is difficult
to locate these points exactly, and a choke coil L should be
included in the plate lead.   This may be about 10 or 15 turns of
No. 18 wire spaced about $\frac{1}{4}$ in. apart on a $\frac{1}{2}$-in. wooden dowel or
glass tube.   If the proper d.c. plate potential is available from a
generator or power pack, it is more satisfactory than the simple
transformer shown in the diagram.   The power output of these
tubes drops off rapidly as the frequency increases beyond 200 or
300 megacycles, but there is generally enough power from such
an oscillator for Lecher-wire and radiation demonstrations.

A-37. Lecher Wires.   The phenomenon of standing electromagnetic waves on wires may be demonstrated.   Two No. 18
bare copper wires 4 or 5 m long and 5 or 10 cm apart are stretched
on wooden supports above the lecture table (Fig. 358).   These
wires are joined at one end by a loop that is magnetically coupled

with the oscillator.   If the oscillator frequency is variable, the other end of the pair of wires may be left open, and the oscillator tuned; if the oscillator frequency is fixed, the wires may be tuned by a small variable capacitance across their open end.   This capacitance may be formed by two brass plates of about 10-cm² area, screwed to the sides of small wooden blocks for support. The plates are connected by short flexible wires with the parallel-wire system; the blocks rest on the lecture table, and the capacitance is varied by moving them apart or together.   Short stiff wires are soldered to the terminals of a small neon glow lamp (0.5 w or less) so that it may be slid along the Lecher system to locate the potential antinodes.   Its presence may change the tuning

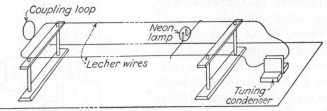

Fig. 358.—Lecher-wire system.

somewhat, and if a number of lamps are used simultaneously, the adjustment for maximum brilliance must be made by a series of successive approximations.   A sensitive radio-frequency meter may be used as a detector in place of the lamp, though this is usually less satisfactory for demonstration work.   The distance between lamps set at successive potential antinodes is one-half wave length.

A-38. Radiation and Polarization.   The phenomenon of polarized dipole radiation is illustrated by coupling an antenna to the oscillator (A-36).   A satisfactory antenna may be made from a piece of thin-walled $\frac{1}{8}$-in. copper tubing about 3 ft long with a loop about 2 in. in diameter at its center.   The central loop is supported by a wooden block and coupled magnetically with the oscillator loop.   The tuning is accomplished by varying the extension of short lengths of copper wire sliding in the ends of the tube.   The resonant condition is detected by the brightness of a small neon lamp placed near one end of the antenna.   Detection of radiation from this antenna is possible with a straight antenna of copper tubing with similar adjustable ends for tuning; a 6-v

flashlight bulb mounted on a wooden block is connected in series
with the antenna at its center, where a current antinode exists at
resonance.   The second antenna is held parallel with the first.
The phenomenon of polarization is illustrated by rotating this
detecting antenna in a plane perpendicular to a line normal to the
two antennae and joining their centers.   The light is most brilliant
when the antennae are parallel and goes out when they are normal
to one another.   The action of an optical polarizing or analyzing
medium such as tourmaline may be illustrated by a square wooden
frame, one-half wave length on a side, across which in one direction are stretched copper wires 1 or 2 cm apart.   The detecting
antenna is placed parallel to that of the transmitter and one or
two wave lengths away.   The frame is then placed midway

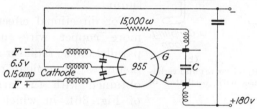

Fig. 359.—Ultra high-frequency oscillator suitable for demonstrating directional
effects.

between the two and rotated in a plane normal to the line joining
their centers.   The maximum energy absorption occurs when the
wires on the frame are parallel to the antennae.   When the frame
is in this position, the flashlight bulb in the detecting antenna
glows very dimly or goes out entirely.   When the wires are
perpendicular to the antennae, they have very little influence on
the brightness of the lamp.   If a large enough plane metal
surface is available, reflection and standing waves can also be
demonstrated.   Refraction and dispersion are not easy to show at
these wave lengths as the apparatus required is inconveniently
large.   Diffraction and the principles underlying the use of beam
antennae can be demonstrated with this equipment, but the space
available in the average lecture room is inadequate for the best
results.   (See A-39.)

**A-39. Directional Antenna Effects with Ultra High-frequency
Waves.**   Ultra high-frequency oscillators are convenient for
showing that radio waves have many of the properties of light.
Waves less than 1 m long may be generated by the circuits shown

in Fig. 357 or Fig. 359.   They may be radiated and received by half-wave antennae consisting of stiff copper wires (Fig. 360). The length AB on each antenna is one-half wave length above the parallel copper wire CD.   The transmitting antenna has two feeder wires with a loop that fits just above the tank circuit GPC

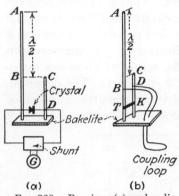

of Fig. 359.   A tuning bar TK is connected below the points at which these feeder wires reach the antenna system.   The receiving antenna has a crystal rectifier at D.   Radiation received by it is detected by the lecture galvanometer with adjustable (Ayrton) shunt.

For directional effects, one or more copper wires are placed parallel to the radiator at suitable distances.   Excellent results are obtained with the arrangement of Fig. 361, in which A is the radiating antenna, B the receiving antenna, and C, D, E, and F are half-wave-length copper rods mounted on a stand that can be turned about A so that A and B do not move with respect to one another.   With the distance between A and B 3 m, it is easily possible to obtain a difference of 1000 to 1 in the radiation received by B when the directors are as shown in Fig. 361, as

Fig. 360.—Receiver (a) and radiator (b) for use with oscillator of Fig. 359.

Fig. 361.—Directional antenna arrangement for oscillator of Fig. 359.

compared with the radiation when the frame carrying C, D, E, and F is turned through 180°.

A-40. Modulation of High-frequency Oscillations.   If the plate supply of the oscillator (A-36) is modulated at an audio frequency, radio transmission can be demonstrated.   A suitable circuit for plate modulation is shown in Fig. 362.   The signal may be from a microphone or a phonograph, suitably amplified. Grid modulation, though less satisfactory, can also be used. In this case, the audio frequency is simply applied across the resistance R, or some fraction of it, in the grid circuit of the oscillator. The detecting circuit is the same as that shown in the diagram of A-34, Fig. 355, except that the small tuned circuit is placed at the center of two symmetrical antenna arms. The tuned circuit itself is simply a coil of four or five turns of No. 12 bare copper wire, $\frac{1}{2}$ in. or so in diameter. Tuning is accomplished by pulling the coil apart or pushing it together, so as to vary the inductance and the distributed capacitance. The rectifier tube

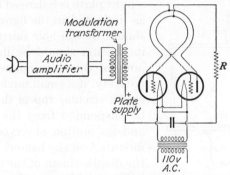

Fig. 362.—Modulation of high-frequency oscillations.

should be one of small interelectrode capacitance, such as the type 879. Alternatively, these frequencies can be amplified and detected by the use of acorn tubes, types 950 and 955. Suitable circuits and directions for the use of these tubes will be found in the bulletins accompanying them.

KINETIC THEORY AND ATOMIC STRUCTURE

A-41. Kinetic-theory Illustrative Models. A number of large-scale models may be devised to illustrate chaotic motion and other phenomena of kinetic theory. The accompanying diagram (Fig. 363) represents one such device. A fan with four beveled blades turns at 10 or 15 rps in contact with a horizontal steel plate about 10 in. in diameter. The outer edge of the blades fits closely the inner edge of a low steel ring on the surface of the plate. The fan is driven by a variable-speed motor below the plate. A glass cylinder with inside diameter equal to the outside diameter

of the steel ring and 8 or 10 in. high is waxed to the ring.   Its top
is closed by a metal cover.   Several hundred steel balls about
$\frac{1}{16}$ in. in diameter are put inside, and when the fan blades rotate,
these balls are driven upward against the top and walls of the
container, forming a cloud of steel balls in chaotic motion.   If a
few larger balls of wood or pith, 0.5 in. or so in diameter, are
suspended by threads a few inches below the cover, they will
execute random motions of small amplitude, quite similar in
appearance to the Brownian motion.

The pressure exerted by this cloud of steel balls may also be
shown.   A hole 3 or 4 in. in diameter is cut in the cover, and
a light plate is balanced in the opening
as indicated in the figure.   The plate
should fit the hole fairly closely, and
its motion should be limited so that
none of the balls can escape.   Alternatively, if a small model is used, the
entire circular top of the cylinder can
be suspended from the balance arm,
and its motion observed.   A pointer
mounted on the balance arm indicates
the displacement of the plate when the
balls are driven against it by the fan.

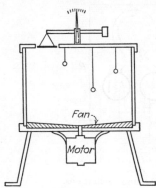

Fig. 363.—Large model to
demonstrate kinetic-theory
principles.

If this motion is not sufficiently visible
to a large class, the shadow of the
pointer may be projected on a screen.
The model should be set in front of a white background and
strongly illuminated.

A-42. A simpler, though somewhat less flexible, demonstration
of the same nature can be performed with an electrically driven
tuning fork.   One tine of the fork itself or a piston driven by it
forms the bottom of a rectangular cell made from two glass plates
10 cm square and about 1 cm apart.   The cell contains 50 to 100
small steel balls, depending on the power available from the fork.
When the fork is energized, chaotic motion of the balls ensues.
A piston may be lowered into the cell to decrease the volume and
to illustrate the change in density and pressure.   If the fork is
not sufficiently powerful to keep the balls in chaotic motion when
the cell is vertical, the apparatus may be tilted at an angle so that
the pressure of the balls on the prong of the fork is not so great.

A-43. A large glass vessel closed at the top with a wire grill and connected at the bottom with a source of compressed air contains a dozen or more ping-pong balls. When a blast of air is sent through the vessel, the "large molecules" execute chaotic motion simulating the motion of molecules in a gas. If one or two of the balls are brightly colored, their individual motions may be followed.

A-44. Beads or pellets of a light material can be kept in chaotic motion by the vapor rising from a pool of boiling mercury. With the exception of certain spasmodic bursts, the behavior of the beads resembles that of particles executing true Brownian motion; in fact, this visible motion is caused by bombardment from invisible molecules of mercury. The demonstration may be seen directly by the class, or it can be projected with a lantern. A pyrex tube 3 cm in diameter and about 30 cm long is closed and rounded at one end. A few milliliters of mercury is poured in, and enough colored glass beads are dropped on the surface to form a layer about 5 mm deep. The beads should not be particularly clean, for ordinary layers of grease and dirt on the tube and beads reduce the disturbing effects of frictional electrification. The tube is then evacuated and the mercury gently boiled while pumping is continued, before sealing off. The tube is mounted vertically in a projection lantern, and the mercury pool is gently heated by a Bunsen flame to set the beads in rapid chaotic motion up and down the tube. When the flame is removed, the motion gradually subsides, and the beads vibrate in a mass for a minute or so above the mercury surface. The analogy between this latter state of motion and that of molecules in a liquid may be pointed out.

A-45. A more spectacular model consists of a larger tube, 5 to 10 cm in diameter and 50 to 100 cm long, enclosing a number of pith balls, 6 or 7 mm in diameter, above a pool of mercury. If one or two of the pith balls are colored, their individual motions may be followed.[1]

A-46. The foregoing models have the disadvantage that they operate with a strong gravitational component of motion. For many purposes, it is better to have a model in which the motion of the balls representing molecules takes place in a horizontal

---

[1] For successful results, the balls should first be out-gassed and then soaked in glyptal or shellac.

plane.   The model consists of a frame in which the balls are agitated; it may be either large enough to use 0.5-in. steel balls and 45° projection or small enough to mount upon the platform of a lantern for vertical projection.   The principle is the same for each, and each may be made to show the same effects.   "Diffusion" may be shown by dividing the frame into two sections with a central partition in which there is an aperture; balls of different sizes are put in the two sections before the frame is shaken. "Rise of temperature" may be shown by more vigorous agitation of the frame.

Large Model.   A square frame 40 by 40 cm is made from 3- by 3-cm hard wood; it is covered with a glass top and rests upon a large sheet of plate glass.   A dozen or more steel balls are introduced, and the frame is grasped with both hands and given a motion such that each point describes a small circle.   The balls travel about on the glass plate and rebound from the moving walls of the frame to simulate the motion of gas molecules. The class may observe the model in a large plane mirror set at 45° above the lecture table.   For large classes, the motion of the balls may be made clearly visible by mounting the apparatus on a light box with opal-glass top (Fig. 364).   The balls will thus be shadowed against a strong background illumination.

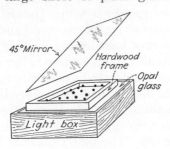

Fig. 364.—Two-dimensional kinetic-theory model.

Small Model.   Similar effects may be produced with a small model suitable for projection.   A rigid metal frame 10 by 10 by 1 cm with a glass cover is set on a piece of plate glass mounted on the stage of a vertical projection lantern.   Numerous small steel balls are introduced, and the frame is agitated; the balls rebound from the walls and collide with one another, and their chaotic motion may be observed by projection.   The frame may be moved by hand, or it may be attached to a crank driven by a variable-speed motor in such a way as to be given a reciprocating circular motion.

A-47. Distribution of Molecular Velocities.   An inclined board, containing diagonal rows of nails, is fitted with a system of parallel chutes at the base.   A single sphere if released from the top of the board at the center will, after striking some of the nails, land in some chance chute at the bottom. The exact chute is not predictable before the release.

A large number of spheres (lead shot) is released from the center of the top of the board. The number landing in the central chute is large, while the number landing in neighboring chutes is less the farther the chute is from the center. The number falling in each chute is predictable before the release of the spheres, and the accuracy of the prediction increases with the total number of spheres. The piles of spheres in the various chutes form a probability curve similar to that representing the distribution of velocities in the molecules of a gas.

A-48. Brownian Motion. It is difficult to demonstrate Brownian motion to a large class. As individual observation is simple, it is generally to be preferred. The simplest method is to blow a little smoke into a glass cell and illuminate it intensely from the side with the light from an arc. The motion of the smoke particles may be observed through a low-power microscope. Dark-field illumination is preferred but not required.

A-49. The Brownian motion of colloidal particles suspended in a liquid makes a more permanent demonstration. Colloidal metal suspensions may be made by sparking metal electrodes under water. A few storage batteries may supply adequate energy, or 110 v may be used if sufficient resistance is included to limit the current to 10 or 15 amp. Silver or gold electrodes produce the best suspensions, though almost any metal can be used. If the suspension is then allowed to stand, the large particles settle out, or they may be filtered off. These suspensions may be kept for considerable periods of time. A colloidal suspension can be made by dissolving a little powdered gamboge in alcohol and pouring a little of the solution into a large quantity of water. The colloidal suspension is poured into a shallow glass cell suitable for mounting on a microscope stage. It is illuminated from the side by the light from an arc or projection lantern. The motion is observed individually through a microscope of moderate power, or the field may be projected by an inclined mirror onto a ground-glass screen, thus enabling a small group to observe the phenomenon without having the room in total darkness.

A-50. Rotatory Brownian motion may be observed under low magnification in a *dilute* suspension of lead carbonate crystals.

Two grams of potassium carbonate and 1 g of lead acetate are each dissolved in 100 ml of distilled water.   These solutions may be stored for use at any time.   One milliliter of the first solution and 0.5 ml of the second are each diluted to 300 ml, and the suspension is prepared by mixing the latter two solutions.   Under strong horizontal illumination, the suspension of flat lead carbonate crystals shows countless starlike particles, which twinkle as they rotate.

The motions may be projected more or less satisfactorily by microprojection with a lantern or by means of a good microscope

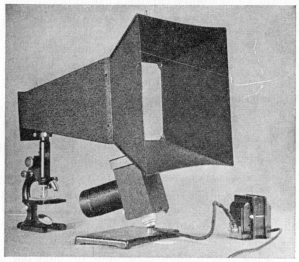

Fig. 365.—Microscope equipped with screen for viewing Brownian motions.

from which the eyepiece has been removed so that the image formed by the objective falls directly upon a ground-glass or flashed-opal screen.   The screen is set in a vertical plane inside a protecting black box, and light from the microscope is directed upon it by a plane mirror or 45° prism at the top of the ocular tube (Fig. 365).   A slide containing a few drops of gamboge or lead carbonate suspension is placed upon the microscope platform and strongly illuminated from below.   It is necessary to show the experiment in a darkened room.

A-51. Optical Arrangement for Viewing Brownian Motions. Observation of Brownian motions by means of an enlarged virtual image may be accomplished as illustrated in Fig. 366.   A cell containing a lead carbonate suspension is illuminated near the surface by a convergent beam of light from an arc. A lens of short focal length is placed just above the cell so as to form a virtual image of the illuminated particles. Above this lens is set a plane mirror at 45°, and a large reading glass is mounted vertically in front of the mirror. Thus, by looking through the reading glass, the student may see an enlarged virtual image of the moving particles. In a darkened room, the motion may be seen at a distance of 20 or 30 ft. If the whole system is mounted upon a rotating stand, it may be turned slowly from side to side so that all members of the class may see the phenomenon (L-54).

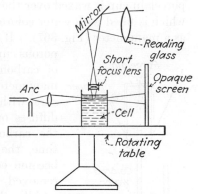

Fig. 366.—Optical setup for demonstrating Brownian motions.

A-52. Order of Magnitude of Molecular Dimensions. One upper limit to molecular dimensions can be set by measuring the thickness of gold leaf. The most convenient method is to weigh 10 or 15 sheets and divide by the product of the density and the area. The thinnest gold leaf gives a limit of the order of 10^{-6} cm. A soap film illuminated and projected by the method of L-67 will show before it breaks a black region where it is too thin to produce interference by reflection from front and back surfaces. The film is then of the order of 10^{-7} cm thick.

A-53. An upper limit may also be set by determining the thickness of oil films on water or of soap-bubble films. A dilute solution of stearic acid in alcohol or a mixture of about 1 part of petroleum oil to 10 parts of xylol forms a suitable film. A tray about 18 in. square, preferably with a dark bottom, is filled to a depth of 1 cm or so with water, and the surface lightly dusted with talc. A brisk current of water overflowing the vessel prior to dusting with talc will assure a clean surface. A large mirror may be set above the tray at 45° for class observation. When a single drop of the solution is allowed to fall on the surface from a pipette, a film spreads out, shoving the talc before it. The area may be estimated with a meter stick or by means of cross-rulings

on the bottom of the tray.   The volume of the film can be estimated from a knowledge of the concentration of the solution and
the number of drops per milliliter.   Stearic acid forms films of
the order of 2×10^{-7} cm thick.   Oleic acid films are somewhat
thinner.

A-54. Diffusion of Gases.   The dependence of the average
molecular velocity and hence the rate of diffusion on the molecular
mass may be demonstrated as follows.[1]   A thin-walled *unglazed*
porcelain cup is waxed over the end of a glass J-tube, the bend of
which is filled with water colored with a little ink or dye to serve
as a manometer (Fig. 367).   If a paper cone is placed around the
porous cup, vertex downward, and a stream
of carbon dioxide is directed into it, the
manometer will indicate a decrease in pressure within the porous cup as the air
diffuses out of the cup more rapidly than
the carbon dioxide diffuses in.   After a
time, the internal and external pressures
become equal again.   If the cone is now
removed, air will diffuse into the cup more
rapidly than carbon dioxide diffuses out,
and the pressure inside the cup will exceed
atmospheric for a short time.   If a beaker
is held over the cup and illuminating gas
is directed into it, the converse process will take place.
The gas, being composed of light molecules, diffuses into the
container more rapidly than the air or carbon dioxide diffuses
out.   Hydrogen shows an even more pronounced effect.
Caution: Do not blow hydrogen through a *new* rubber tube into
a confined space, as an explosion may result from interaction of
the hydrogen and the white powder inside the tubing.

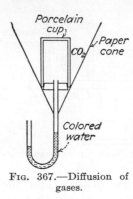

Fig. 367.—Diffusion of
gases.

A-55.   A little liquid bromine is placed in the bottom of each
of two cylinders, one containing air and the other hydrogen.
Bromine and hydrogen interfuse much more rapidly than bromine
and air.

A-56. Diffusion and Pressure.   The influence of the pressure
of a gas on the rate of diffusion of a vapor and the rectilinear

[1] It may be pointed out that the order of magnitude of molecular velocities
in gases is the same as that of the propagation of sound.   See also S-86.

motion of vapor molecules in the absence of any residual gas can be illustrated in the following way.   Two pyrex containers, each of about 1-l capacity, are joined by a short length of 1-cm glass tubing, as shown in Fig. 368.   A few iodine crystals are introduced, and connection is made to a vacuum pump.   If the crystals are heated by a Bunsen burner at atmospheric pressure, prior to pumping, a considerable time will elapse before the iodine vapor fills the upper bulb.   If the crystals in the lower container are now cooled in an ice or solid carbon dioxide bath, the iodine vapor disappears.   Now if the ap-

paratus is evacuated and the iodine is heated for a few minutes, a small deposit of crystals will be observed to form on the top of the upper vessel some time before the entire apparatus becomes filled with va- por.   The molecules travel directly through the constriction from the lower surface of the bottom vessel to the upper surface of the top one.   Also the iodine vapor dis- appears from the bulb when it is

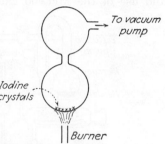

Fig. 368.—Diffusion of iodine vapor through the constriction is hastened by reducing the pressure within the flasks.

immersed in an ice bath much more rapidly when it is evacuated than when it is full of air (H-84).

A-57. Vacuum System.   A portable high-vacuum system is an invaluable piece of auxiliary apparatus for lecture-demonstration work in this and other fields.   Such equipment can be obtained from scientific supply houses, or the parts may be constructed and assembled as in Fig. 369.   A vessel on the low-vacuum side of the diffusion pump serves the purpose of reservoir and drying chamber to protect the oil pump.   A small manom- eter indicates the pressure in this chamber.   The diffusion pump is of ordinary design, preferably of the two-stage type. Beyond it are a McLeod gauge, liquid-air trap, and large-bore stopcocks.   Oil diffusion pumps are somewhat less useful for general purposes than the mercury type as they are more easily damaged by oxidizing gases and overheating.   Liquid air need not be used on the trap for most work, since solid carbon dioxide in carbon tetrachloride reduces the pressure of mercury vapor to a negligible amount, and precautions can be taken to remove water vapor if pressures above 10^{-3} mm mercury are objectionable.[1]

It is convenient to mount the complete apparatus on a wooden or metal frame that can be clamped to the lecture table.   Air can be admitted through the three-way stopcock above the fore pump, but it is sometimes convenient to have a small stopcock in the neighborhood of the McLeod gauge also for this purpose.

The diffusion pump itself serves as an excellent illustration of the phenomenon of diffusion at low pressures.   The calibration and use of the McLeod gauge illustrate the gas laws (M-319).

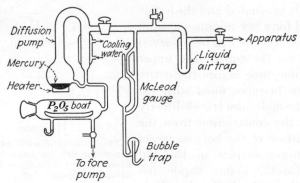

Fig. 369.—Portable high-vacuum system for general laboratory use.

The adsorption of gases by shabazite or charcoal can be shown by sealing a tube containing one of these materials to the system beyond the second stopcock.   The tube is pumped out and torched or baked at 400° to 500°C for 15 or 20 min.   The two large stopcocks are then closed, and air is admitted through the middle stopcock to a pressure of a few centimeters of mercury, forcing the mercury down the stem of the McLeod gauge.   The stopcock to the charcoal is then opened, and the decrease in pressure noted when the charcoal is cooled with solid carbon dioxide or liquid air (H-116).

A-58. Viscosity and Pressure.   The phenomenon of viscosity (M-61) and its dependence on pressure in the low-pressure region,

[1] Various useful details of vacuum technique are suggested in Dunoyer and Smith, "Vacuum Practice," D. Van Nostrand Company, Inc., New York, 1928; in Harnwell and Livingood, "Experimental Atomic Physics," appendix, McGraw-Hill Book Company, Inc., New York, 1933; and in Hoag, "Electron and Nuclear Physics," Chap. 16. D. Van Nostrand Company, Inc., New York, 1938.

together with the radiometer effect (H-164) and a qualitative demonstration of light pressure, can be illustrated with the apparatus shown in Fig. 370. Two vanes of aluminum leaf a few millimeters square are affixed with drops of shellac to the ends of a very light glass rod about 2 cm long. A stirrup of very fine wire to which a small mirror is attached supports this glass rod at its center and is in turn supported by a fine quartz fiber attached to it by a drop of wax as shown. The upper end of the fiber is attached by a drop of shellac to a heavy wire passing through the wax seal in the top of the glass envelope. The envelope may have the shape shown in the figure, though this is immaterial. Its open end is waxed to a steel or copper plate 5 or 6 cm in diameter, resting on a rugged support on the lecture desk, the whole system being as well protected from vibration as possible. The wax used throughout should be one of the low-vapor-pressure vacuum waxes. The moment of inertia of the moving system should be calculated at the time of construction. The angular position of the system is shown by a spot of light reflected from the small mirror to a scale visible to the class.

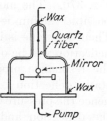

Fig. 370.—Apparatus for showing viscosity, radiometer, and light-pressure effects.

If a fairly soft wax is used for the upper joint, the system can be set into oscillation by giving a small rotation to the heavy wire passing through the seal. The decrement of the system may then be determined by noting the period and the amplitudes of the successive maxima.[1] This will be found to be approximately constant at high pressures and to decrease with the pressure when the mean free path is of the order of the dimensions of the apparatus, thus giving evidence of decrease of viscosity at low pressure.

A-59. Radiometer. The radiometer effect may be demonstrated over a wide range of pressures, from 10 or 20 cm down to a fraction of a millimeter, by focusing the light from an arc or tungsten lamp on one of the vanes of the instrument shown in

---

[1] The method of computing the mechanical factors of the system, such as decrement and torsion constant, is given in many laboratory texts, usually in conjunction with experiments on moment of inertia or ballistic galvanometers.

Fig. 370. By periodically interrupting the light beam at the natural frequency of oscillation of the vane system, a very large amplitude can be developed. The reversal of the radiometer effect at some point in this pressure range may also be shown. If the period of oscillation is timed and the moment of inertia is known, the restoring constant of the fiber and hence the torque can be computed.

A-60. Light Pressure. The order of magnitude of the pressure exerted by radiation can also be determined with the apparatus of Fig. 370. The moving system is brought to rest, and the best possible vacuum is obtained (of the order of 10^{-6} mm mercury). Then one vane is illuminated by the arc as before, and a small deflection will be observed. The amplitude can be increased by the resonance procedure indicated previously (A-59), but the static deflection is simpler for computation. The torque and hence the pressure on the illuminated vane can be calculated from the deflection and the constants of the apparatus previously determined. To complete the experiment, the radiation may be directed on a small soot-covered bulb containing 10 or 15 ml of water, and the temperature rise during a measured time interval noted. These results will provide a rough check on the equality between the radiant energy density in front of the vane and the pressure exerted by the radiation.

A-61. Conduction of Heat in Gases. Heat conduction in various gases and its dependence upon the pressure may be illustrated by sealing or waxing a carbon filament lamp onto the vacuum system. Sealing is preferable if a graded seal is available; if wax is used, provision must be made for cooling the joint if it is close to the lamp envelope. The system is filled with nitrogen, and the lamp is connected to the 110-v supply. The nitrogen is slowly pumped out, and after a certain pressure is reached, the filament begins to radiate visibly. The brightness of the filament, which is an inverse function of the rate at which heat is conducted away, may be studied qualitatively as a function of the pressure. At high pressures, the heat conduction is approximately independent of the pressure. If hydrogen is used instead of nitrogen, the lamp will not be observed to glow until a considerably lower pressure is reached. The hydrogen molecule with the same capability of energy absorption has only 0.07 the mass of the nitrogen molecule, and so it moves three or four times as fast, makes correspondingly more impacts, and carries heat away from the filament at a much greater rate. The effects produced are somewhat complicated by the negative temperature coefficient of resistance of carbon, but the general aspect of gaseous conduction of heat predominates.

ATOMIC FORCE MODELS

A-62. Equilibrium Configurations. There are a few types of large-scale model that may be used to illustrate the nature of atomic and molecular forces. It should be emphasized in this connection that atomic models are not to be confused with other types of model, such as model steam engines, etc. They are figurative or allegoric representations of entities having no real macroscopic analogues. They must not be confused with realities but are to be considered as very imperfect bases for the illustration of a few of the fundamental atomic concepts.

One of these models shows the equilibrium configurations of steel balls floating on a mercury surface in the field of an electromagnet and suggests a simplified picture of electron configurations in atoms, or atomic configurations in crystal lattices. An ordinary iron-cored solenoid wound for 110-v direct current is set in a vertical position, and the core is covered with an iron disk about $\frac{1}{16}$ in. thick and 2 in. in diameter. On this is placed a shallow glass tray filled to a depth of about 0.5 cm with mercury. A number of steel balls about $\frac{1}{8}$ in. in diameter is also provided. A 45° mirror mounted over the tray and magnet renders the mercury surface visible to the class. It is very important to have the mercury, dish, and balls entirely free from grease and dirt. The mercury should be freshly distilled, and the dish and balls should be cleaned with benzene, hot cleaning solution, and potassium hydroxide and then rinsed in distilled water. They may be dried by natural evaporation or over a low flame. Nothing should be touched subsequently with the fingers. The balls may be stored between clean watch glasses and handled with brass forceps. As the balls are laid one by one on the mercury surface, they assume equilibrium configurations under the influence of the field of the magnet and the magnetic moments induced in each ball.

The static model just described can be made into a moving one by the addition of electrodes beneath the surface of the mercury.

One is a ring of about the diameter of the vessel, and the other occupies a small area at the center of the ring. Thus a radial current may be established through the mercury from center to ring. When such a current exists, the mercury is set into motion and carries the balls with it, but they do not follow its simple circular motion. If there are 2 balls on its surface, one revolves planetwise about the other for a short time and then replaces the other at the center while the second revolves about it. Thus the balls take turns at the center. Similar motions occur with three or four balls. Usually with six balls, they arrange themselves in a circle with none going into the center. As more balls are added one by one, the configuration becomes more difficult to keep stable, but with care as many as 32 balls can be put in motion in concentric rings. It should not be supposed that this model is necessarily an accurate representation of the structure of any atom.

A-63. Alpha-particle Scattering—Magnetic Model. Alpha-particle scattering and the inverse square law of force near the nucleus can be illustrated by the repulsion between magnetic poles. An iron cap in the form of a sphere or hemisphere is mounted on top of the solenoid used in A-62. A second solenoid with either an air core or an iron core terminated in a ball is suspended by its leads from the ceiling of the lecture room. The suspended system may be reinforced with a light bamboo rod to eliminate undesirable oscillations. It is convenient to provide a rheostat in series with this solenoid to vary the repulsive field between the two. The lower end of the suspended solenoid should just clear the upper end of the fixed one. If the stationary solenoid is directly below the point of suspension and the pendulum solenoid is displaced a few feet and released, it will be repelled more or less back toward its starting point, illustrating a head-on collision. If the lower solenoid is displaced a few inches from the direct line of swing, a hyperbolic orbit will be described by the pendulum, illustrating the general trajectory of an alpha particle deflected by a heavy nucleus. A semiquantitative study of these trajectories may be carried out by moving the lower solenoid a few centimeters at a time and always releasing the pendulum from the same point.

If the sense of the magnetization of one of the solenoids is reversed so that an attractive field exists between the poles,

circular and elliptical orbits can be demonstrated.   Various orbits
passing through the point of release can be illustrated by varying
the magnitude and direction of the original impulse given the
pendulum.   These may be used to illustrate qualitatively the
nature of electron or planetary orbits.   Strong permanent
cobalt-steel magnets may be used instead of solenoids.

A-64. Alpha-particle Scattering—Electrostatic Model. A variation of A-63 that has a number of advantages involves electrostatic rather than electromagnetic forces.   A sphere about 6 in. in
diameter is charged by means of a Wimshurst or Van de Graaff
generator.   A ping-pong ball coated with aluminum paint is
suspended by a silk thread from the ceiling in such a way that it
swings a foot or so above the sphere.   The ball can be charged if
desired, but this is generally unnecessary as it will charge itself
by corona from the large sphere and induction plays a role as well.
On being pulled aside and released, the ball can be made to
describe the various conic-section orbits.   The most effective
method of observation is to place an arc light some distance below
the spherical electrode and cast the shadow of the moving ping-
pong ball on the ceiling.

A-65. Nuclear-disintegration Model.   A watch glass 5 in. in
diameter is mounted convex side up-
ward in a box, so as to cover the condenser lens of a vertical projector.
The "nucleus," which occupies the
center of the field of view, is a short
piece of $\frac{3}{4}$-in. brass tubing standing on
three narrow legs (Fig. 371).   The
projection of this tube on the screen
is a circle.   The tube is fitted with an

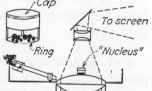

Fig. 371.—Nuclear-disintegration model.

opaque cap that can be removed, if desired, to show "internal
structure" of the nucleus.   The nucleus houses a number
of steel balls of two contrasting sizes (*e.g.*, $\frac{3}{16}$ and $\frac{3}{32}$ in.)
ready to emerge as "neutrons" and "protons" when struck by
fast "alpha particles."   The projectile particles are $\frac{3}{16}$- or $\frac{1}{4}$-in.
steel balls whose speed and direction of approach are controlled
by rolling them down an inclined brass tube, one at a time.   A
thin ring of brass, of the same diameter as the nuclear housing,
serves as a base for the three legs supporting the latter and at
the same time acts as a low "potential barrier" to prevent the

escape of balls within the nucleus until they are struck by imping-
ing particles having sufficient energy to cross the barrier.   At low
speeds, the paths of the alpha particles may be curved, as if they
were repelled from the nucleus; at higher speeds, the particles
may penetrate the nucleus, where they may be captured or may
cause "nuclear disintegration" with the ejection of one or more
other particles, previously planted within the housing.[1]

A-66. Electron-configuration Diagrams. Blackboard diagrams illustrating electron configurations may be supplemented
by the following arrangement.   A piece of plywood about 18 by
36 in. is laid out in two sets of concentric circles to represent the K,
L, M, etc., shells of two atoms.   Each of these circles has the
appropriate number of small holes drilled around its circumfer-
ence: two for the K, eight for the L, etc.   A hook or peg at the
center supports a small circular card showing the charge and mass
of the nucleus to be illustrated.   Small red plugs (golf tees are
convenient) inserted in the holes around the circles represent the
extranuclear electron structure. Atomic configurations are
represented by the use of one set of circles, and diatomic molecules by the use of both.   To preserve the proper relative scale
for different atoms, the outer circles should be used for the K
shells of hydrogen and helium, and the pattern compressed as
heavier atoms are illustrated.

ATOMIC ENERGY LEVELS

A-67. Ionization and Radiation Potentials. The first critical
potential and the ionization potential of mercury can be demonstrated with a hot-cathode mercury-vapor discharge tube such as
the FG-57.   The tube is mounted in a small oven, care being
taken that the thermometer and heating coils do not touch the
tube envelope.   The ionization potential is measured at room
temperature.   A battery of 1 or 2 v maintains the plate negative
with respect to the cathode; this is accomplished by setting the
switch S in position 1 (Fig. 372).   The grid potential, measured
by the voltmeter V, is supplied by a potential divider and battery
of about 18 v.   The grid is slowly made more and more positive
with respect to the cathode; and when the ionization potential of
the vapor is reached, the galvanometer in the plate circuit will
register a deflection, showing the arrival of positive ions at the

[1] For further details, see R. M. Sutton, *Am. Phys. Teacher*, **2**, 115, 1934.

plate.   A protective resistance of a few thousand ohms should be
included in series with the galvanometer.   For the detection of
critical or resonance potentials, the tube is heated in the oven to
about 200°C.   With the switch in position 2, the plate is kept 1
or 2 v negative *with respect to the grid*.   As the potential of the
grid is now increased, the galvanometer registers an electron
current, and the curve of galvanometer deflection against grid
potential will exhibit one or two peaks about 5 v apart.   The
shape of this curve and the number of peaks observed can be
varied by changing the oven temperature.

With the tube at room temperature, the mean free path of the
electrons is of the order of magnitude of tube dimensions.   As
the electron energy is increased by
raising   the   grid   potential,   the
electrons collide harder and harder
with mercury atoms until they are
finally able to produce a few positive
ions.   These are drawn to the plate
by the potential gradient between it
and the grid, and the current due to
them is detected by the galvanometer.   When the tube is at a higher

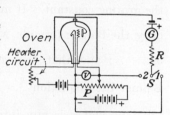

Fig. 372.—Circuit for demonstrating ionization and radiation
potentials.

temperature,   the   electron   free   path   becomes   very   short
on account of the increase in mercury-vapor pressure.   When
the potential of the grid is below about 5 v, the electrons
are unable to lose energy to the mercury atoms and hence are
able to surmount the small potential barrier between the grid and
the plate, and the current through the galvanometer rises with
voltage.   When the electron energy is a little greater than the
first critical potential, the mercury atoms are able to accept
energy from the electrons, which are then unable to proceed
against the retarding field from the grid to the plate, and the
galvanometer current decreases.   At a higher potential, electrons
that have undergone two inelastic collisions are unable to reach
the plate, and a second minimum appears.   A lecture-table
voltmeter V enables the students to follow the variations of
cathode-to-grid accelerating potential.

A-68. Resonance Radiation of Iodine Vapor.   A large Florence
flask containing a few crystals of iodine is evacuated and sealed
off.   When the flask is heated and held in the cone of light from

the condensing lens of a carbon arc lamp, the light path within the bulb becomes visible to a large audience.

A-69. Emission Spectra—Balmer Series. The spectra emitted by gases during electric discharge can be observed individually with a prism or grating instrument, or if the room is sufficiently darkened and an intense source is used, they may be projected on a screen. The projection of bright-line spectra has been described in L-104. A semiquantitative experiment on series spectra can be performed on the Balmer lines of the grating spectrum of hydrogen. The angular deviations of the three or four lines that can be observed (H_α, H_β, H_γ, possibly H_δ) are measured, and the wave lengths and frequencies calculated from the grating constant. It may be shown that these wave lengths obey the Balmer formula, $\lambda = k\dfrac{m^2}{m^2 - 4}$, where m has values 3, 4, 5, . . . ; and that the corresponding frequencies follow the Balmer-Ritz equation $\dfrac{\nu}{c} = R\left(\dfrac{1}{2^2} - \dfrac{1}{n^2}\right)$, where R is Rydberg's constant and n is any integer greater than 2, from which an approximate value of the Rydberg constant can be calculated.

A-70. Absorption Spectra. The absorption of light by gases can be demonstrated with sodium vapor. A steel tube about 2 in. in diameter and 3 ft long is provided with a connection for attachment to a small fore pump. A small piece of sodium is placed in the center of the tube, and glass windows are waxed on the ends. Coils of lead pipe wrapped around the ends carry cooling water and keep the wax from melting. The tube is evacuated and the sodium vaporized by placing one or two Bunsen burners beneath the center of the tube. If light from a sodium-vapor lamp and an ordinary arc or incandescent lamp is observed through the tube, a great difference in the relative diminution of intensity will be seen. If the tube is placed in the light path before a demonstration spectroscope, the phenomenon may be shown in more detail. With a sodium-lamp source, the yellow D lines are greatly reduced in intensity, and the remaining lines are relatively unaffected. If a continuous source is used, dark lines will be observed at the positions that the yellow D lines would occupy. A sodium flame of the spray type (atomized salt solution sprayed into the burner with compressed air) will serve moderately well, but metallic sodium vaporized by a blast lamp is better (L-108).

Absorption by sodium vapor can be shown by the incandescent lamp (heated) into which sodium has been electrolytically introduced (E-211). The lamp easily shows surface reflection by the vapor, and absorption of sodium light from a sodium arc. It must be heated almost hot enough for sodium to attack the glass in order to widen the line enough to be seen against a continuous spectrum with low dispersion.

Absorption bands may be shown by passing the light from a carbon arc through flasks containing bromine or iodine vapor and thence through a spectroscope. Iodine vapor may be produced by heating a few crystals of iodine in an evacuated flask (A-68).

PROPERTIES OF ELECTRONS

A-71. Deflection of Cathode Rays. A cylindrical glass tube contains a plane electrode at each end. A mica screen in front of one electrode, the cathode, is provided with a slit to limit the beam of cathode rays to a thin horizontal lamina. The tube is connected to an induction coil or static machine. The path of the rays is shown by the line of light excited on a fluorescent screen in the tube, placed so as to make a slight angle with the direction of the beam. The cathode particles can be deflected either by the electric field of a charged rubber rod or of a pair of plates connected to a static machine or by the magnetic field of a bar magnet or of a solenoid. In the case of an electric field, the deflection is toward the positive charge. In the magnetic field, the force is perpendicular to the magnetic lines of force and to the path of the beam, in the sense opposite to that given by the motor rule for a positive current moving with the beam. Both of these experiments show that the cathode rays are negatively charged particles moving with high speed. Discharge tubes suitable for the experiment can be obtained from scientific supply houses.

A-72. Measurement of e/m. A rough measurement of e/m may be carried out with a commercial cathode-ray oscilloscope tube. In such a tube, the electrons from a hot filament are accelerated by a potential that can be measured. The velocity of the particles is then given by the relation $\frac{1}{2}mv^2 = Ve$, where V and e are both measured in esu. If the tube is mounted on a horizontal axis with the direction of the beam perpendicular to the lines of force of the earth's magnetic field, the spot on the fluorescent screen will be deflected in one direction; and when the tube is rotated through 180°, the spot will be deflected in the opposite direction.   The position in which the beam is exactly perpendicular to the field is found in each case by tilting the tube up and down to find the position of maximum deflection.   The total distance between the two positions of the spot is measured. Calling this distance $2x$ and the distance from anode to fluorescent screen L, the value of e/m is calculated.   Since in the magnetic field $mv^2/r = Hev/c$, we have, combining with the previous equation, $e/m = 2Vc^2/H^2r^2$ esu per g, where H is the value of the earth's field (assumed to be known approximately) and r is the radius of curvature of the path of the electrons, which is given by[1] $1/r = 2x/(x^2 + L^2)$ or $r = L^2/2x$ approximately.

The experiment is somewhat simplified by mounting the tube axis horizontal and then rotating it about a vertical axis from the east-west to the west-east position.   The total deflection of the spot in a vertical direction is then caused only by the *horizontal* component of the earth's field, and the same equations apply.

In each experiment, the deflecting plates of the tube are connected to the anode and a known potential applied between the anode and the filament. The spot may be focused by adjusting the filament current to the best value.

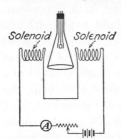

FIG. 373.—Cathode-ray tube and solenoids arranged for measurement of e/m.

A-73. Instead of the earth's field, the magnetic field of a solenoid may be used. The energy of the electron beam is known as before from the applied accelerating potential, and the radius of curvature can be computed from the displacement of the spot and other significant dimensions.   The magnetic field producing the deflection is furnished by two large coaxial solenoids, one on either side of the tube (Fig. 373).   The deflection of the spot is measured as a function of the separation between these two coaxial solenoids operated at constant current.   The resulting curve is then extrapolated to determine the deflection that

[1] For proof and further discussion, see Harnwell and Livingood, "Experimental Atomic Physics," pp. 117 and 127, McGraw-Hill Book Company, Inc., New York, 1933.

would result if the two coils formed one continuous solenoid normal to the axis of the tube.   The region of the magnetic field is considered to be the cross section of the solenoid.

A-74. A somewhat more accurate method is to string two wires 1 to 2 m long on either side of the cathode-ray oscilloscope tube and parallel to its axis.   A current i is sent through the circuit formed by these wires, and the field H (in emu) along the beam is approximately uniform and equal to $8i/d$, where d is the separation of the wires.   The radius of curvature r is $l^2/2x$, where l is the length of the beam and x is the displacement of the spot.   The value of e/m is then calculated from the equations of A-72.[1]

A-75. Model of Oil-drop Experiment.   A large model of the Millikan oil-drop experiment may be constructed as shown in Fig. 374. A and B are galvanized iron plates, about 2 or 3 ft in

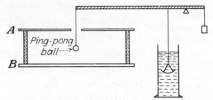

Fig. 374.—Large model of oil-drop experiment.

diameter and 1 ft apart (the size should be that best adapted to the size of the lecture room), mounted on insulating supports.   A ping-pong ball or small rubber balloon, coated with aluminum paint to render the surface conducting, is suspended between the plates by a thread passing through a hole in the upper plate and fastened to the end of a light stick balanced on a knife-edge.   If a balloon is used, it may be filled with hydrogen to the proper volume so that it will float in air and the balancing mechanism may be dispensed with.   The ball may be given a small charge by induction, using a charged rubber rod, or better, by directing a beam of x rays on it or bringing up a sample of radioactive material on the end of a long insulating rod.   The two plates are connected to the terminals of a static machine, and the upward or downward force on the ball is clearly evident.   The direction of motion may be reversed by introducing the radioactive material between the ball and the plate toward which it is moving.

[1] For details, see Smyth and Curtis, *Am. Phys. Teacher,* **6,** 158, 1938.

A-76. Oil-drop Experiment for Determining *e*. In small classes, the oil-drop experiment itself can be shown. Students may look individually through the microscope and see the oil drops rising or falling in the field. One drop may be isolated and timed on successive trips by a student or by the instructor, to obtain the data from which the charge can be computed.[1]

An apparatus that may be constructed in any laboratory and that, if carefully made, gives good results is shown in Fig. 375. The plates are of steel, 2 in. square and $\frac{1}{4}$ in. thick, separated by hard rubber strips $\frac{1}{4}$ in. thick. The lower plate is fitted with a rod (either metal or an insulator) by which the apparatus is clamped to a stand. In the center of the upper plate are drilled several small holes through which oil drops are admitted. A metal cover is provided to close these holes during observation. Glass plates for viewing the oil drops are provided between the steel plates on two opposite sides. The potential applied to the plates need be only 90 to 135 v. An ordinary flashlight serves as an excellent source of light, and a telescope of short focal length with a scale in the eyepiece is used for observation. Nye's watch oil (obtainable from any jeweler) or light mineral oil sprayed from an atomizer supplies the drops, which are allowed to fall through the holes in the upper plate.

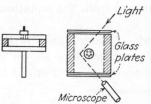

Fig. 375.—Apparatus for determining *e* by the oil-drop method.

THERMIONIC EMISSION

A-77. Thermionic Effect in Air. An attachment for the Zeleny electroscope (E-4) consists of a length of resistance wire mounted on an insulating support so that a heating current can be sent through it while it is in position near the plate of the electroscope. A 6-v battery and a 20-ohm rheostat capable of carrying 5 amp are connected in series with the filament. The charging electrode of the electroscope is connected to the positive terminal of a 90-v battery. When the current through the filament is increased until the wire glows bright red, the leaf of the electroscope will

[1] For further details, see R. A. Millikan, "Electrons (+ and −)," Chap. V, University of Chicago Press, Chicago, 1935.

begin to oscillate, indicating the passage of electrons to the plate; and the oscillations become more rapid as the temperature of the filament is increased. With an oxide-coated wire or in the presence of air, both positive and negative ions are formed at the hot filament in addition to the electrons emitted by it. Therefore the leaf of the electroscope oscillates whether it is positive or negative. (See also A-82.)

A-78. Thermionic Effect in Vacuum. Any standard two- or three-electrode tube may be used to show thermionic emission; in the case of a three-element tube (*e.g.*, type 01A), the plate and grid are connected. However, the experiment is more striking if a large tube of the kenotron type is used, in which the filament is plainly visible. An effective tube can be made by sealing a filament consisting of a 10-mil tungsten wire into one end of a pyrex flask and a plate of nickel

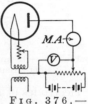

FIG. 376.—Thermionic rectifier circuit.

in an additional neck joined to the opposite side. This tube may then be exhausted, and thermionic emission demonstrated. If desired, it may be evacuated and sealed off after the filament, plate, and bulb have been thoroughly heated. In pumping out, a diffusion pump with a trap cooled by liquid air or dry ice is necessary (A-57). The circuit is connected as shown in Fig. 376.

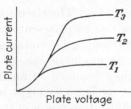

FIG. 377.—Saturation curves for thermionic currents.

The filament can be heated with a battery or with a transformer. A 180-v B battery with potential divider (2000 ohms) is used in the plate circuit. A voltmeter reading to 150 v and a milliammeter reading to 10 ma are suitable. The temperature of the filament and the potential on the plate are varied, and saturation curves of the type shown in Fig. 377 are obtained.

A-79. Thermionic Rectifier (Kenotron Type). The apparatus of the previous experiment is used, with the addition of an a.c. source and two d.p.d.t. switches. The circuit is shown in Fig. 378. With switch *B* in position 1, the milliammeter shows a current only when switch *A* is in such a position as to make the plate positive. Several rapid reversals of switch *A* give the effect of a very low-frequency alternating current and show how the meter indicates an "average" value.   A rotating reversing switch whose speed can be gradually increased is also effective.   With switch B in position 2, the current is about half that obtained with direct current, since there is current in the plate circuit only

during the positive half of the a.c. cycle. This experiment gains greatly in effectiveness if the wave form of the rectified current is shown on an oscilloscope.

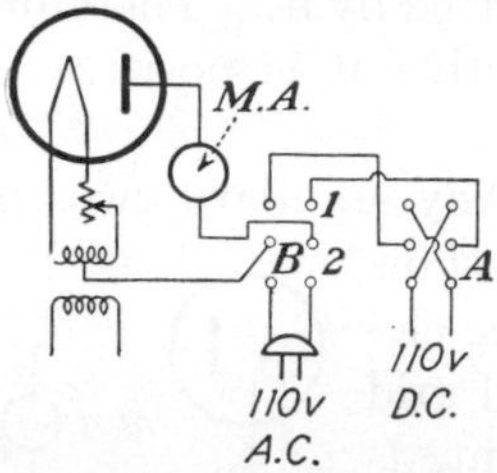

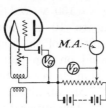

FIG. 378.—Kenotron rectifier circuit.

A-80. Rectifying Property of a Diode. Two neon lamps A and B are connected as shown in Fig. 379.   A diode rectifier tube T or nearly any triode with grid and plate joined is placed in series with A.   When a 110-v a.c. line is connected as shown, both

electrodes of B glow, whereas A does not glow at all until the filament of T is heated, and then only one plate of A glows (see also A-87).

A-81. Characteristic Curves of Three-element Tube. The filament of a three-electrode tube (*e.g.*, type 01A) is heated with a battery or a transformer; the plate potential is provided by a B battery and a potential divider; the grid potential is furnished

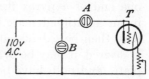

FIG. 379.—Neon glow lamps show rectifying property of a diode.

by a C battery with taps at 0, 1.5, 3.0, 4.5 v, etc.   The circuit is connected as shown in Fig. 380.   First, one or two plate-current vs. plate-voltage curves are taken at different grid voltages.

Next, small changes are made in the grid voltage to show that they produce as much change in plate current as large changes in plate voltage.   The amplification factor of the tube is the ratio of change of plate voltage to change of grid voltage necessary to keep the plate current constant.   Finally, the change in plate current for a given change in grid voltage is determined at one or two values of plate voltage, from which can be found the

FIG. 380.—Circuit for obtaining characteristic curves of a triode.

transconductance $\Delta i_p/\Delta e_g$ (usually expressed in micromhos, *i.e.*, microamperes per volt).   The meters used in these experiments should be such as can be seen and read by the entire class.

A-82. "Fresh Air Three-electrode Tube." A Zeleny electroscope is arranged with supplementary external filament, grid, and plate as shown in Fig. 210, with electrical connections as shown in Fig. 381.   An oxide-coated filament F, heated in air by battery B, furnishes ions that pass to the plate P beyond the grid G.   Plate potential and grid potential are controlled independently by potential dividers.   The plate current is measured in terms of the rate of oscillation of the electroscope leaf.   This simple arrangement makes possible the qualitative determination of several important characteristics of three-electrode tubes, such as the dependence of plate current upon electrode separations, electrode potentials, filament temperature, and gas pressure.   The last

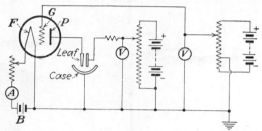

Fig. 381.—Circuit for demonstrating triode operation in air with Zeleny electroscope.

may be shown by placing the whole apparatus under a bell jar and exhausting with a vacuum pump.[1]

A-83. Mechanical Analogue of Three-electrode Tube. The device used in E-58 for showing potential distribution in an electric field may be employed to show how a grid controls electron flow in a triode.   A sheet of rubber dam is fastened between the rings of an embroidery-hoop "plate" P.   The center of the dam F ("filament") is pinned with a thumbtack to a dowel rod so that it may be raised or lowered with respect to the "plate" level.   Small steel balls representing electrons will roll from filament to plate when F is above P but not when F is below P (rectifying action of diode).   If F is fixed above P (as shown in Fig. 382), the "potential gradient" between F and P may be controlled by a tube G ("grid"), which may be pushed up and down below the rubber dam.   A lamp chimney is suitable for this

---

[1] For further details of this and related experiments, see Roger Barton, *Rev. Sci. Instruments*, **2**, 217, 1931.

grid. When *G* is above *F*, no "electrons" can reach *P*. If desired, the function of the "filament" may be made still more realistic by pouring fine shot through a funnel upon the center of the rubber dam.

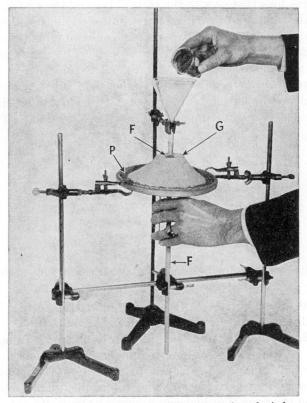

Fɪɢ. 382.—Mechanical model to illustrate action of triode.

A-84. Three-element Tube—Electrostatic Control. The plate current of a three- or four-element tube may be controlled electrostatically as follows. Any standard tube with a suitable plate and filament supply can be used, but one with a control grid contact at the top of the glass envelope is particularly suitable. The grid of the tube is connected directly to a metal sphere on an insulating stand, such as is used in electrostatic experiments, care being taken that the insulation is good (Fig. 383). The plate circuit includes a small relay (telephone or "pony" telegraph type) that operates a doorbell, automobile headlight, or other indicating device. The relay is adjusted so that, when the grid is floating, the plate current just fails to close the relay contacts.

When a positively charged rod is brought near the sphere, the positive charge induced on the grid of the tube increases the plate current and causes the relay to operate. A negatively charged rod has no effect. If the rod is held in position near the sphere for a few seconds, the positive charge on the grid is neutralized by electrons from the filament, and the

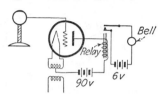

Fig. 383.—Circuit for electrostatic control of triode.

relay opens. Removing the rod for a few seconds and then returning it will cause the relay to close again. The charged rod is thus a "magic wand." Attention may be called to the exceedingly small amount of *power* required to operate the grid as compared to that controlled by the relay. In place of the

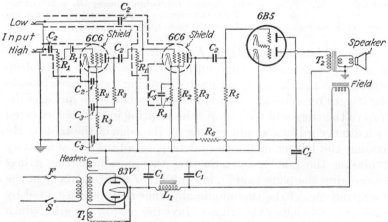

Fig. 384.—Circuit for general-purpose audio-frequency amplifier: 5-watt, 75-db gain. T_1, power transformer (325 v, 125 ma); T_2, speaker-coupling transformer with 7000-ohm primary; F, fuse; S, snap switch; B_1, midget bias battery. $C_1 = 8$ μf, 500 v; $C_2 = 0.1$ μf, 200 v; $C_3 = 2$ μf, 500 v; $L_1 = 30$ h, 50 ma; $R_1 = 0.5$ megohm potentiometer; $R_2 = 1.0$ megohm; $R_3 = 0.25$ megohm; $R_4 = 2500$ ohm; $R_5 = 0.5$ megohm; $R_6 = 0.1$ megohm.

relay, a small flashlight bulb may be included directly in the plate circuit.

A-85. Multistage Amplifiers. Every laboratory should have at least one good three- or four-stage audio-frequency amplifier with sufficient output to operate a loudspeaker. Its uses are many. A suitable circuit is shown in Fig. 384. The output power of this amplifier is 5 w, and the gain is about 75 db. An alternative higher-power output circuit is shown in Fig. 385.

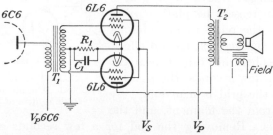

Fig. 385.—Alternative higher-power output circuit for amplifier of Fig. 384.

Class A (no grid current), 14 watts, 2 % harmonic distortion. Peak grid-to-grid voltage, 35.6. T_2, speaker transformer, 5000-ohm primary; $R_1 = 125$ ohms; $V_s = V_p = 250$ v; $i_s = 10$ ma (no signal), 15 ma max; $i_p = 120$ ma (no signal), 130 ma max.

Class AB_1 (no grid current), 32 watts, 2 % harmonic distortion. Peak grid-to-grid voltage, 57. T_2, speaker transformer, 6600-ohm primary; $R_1 = 200$ ohms; $V_s = 300$ v; $V_p = 400$ v; $i_s = 7$ ma (no signal), 16 ma max; $i_p = 112$ ma (no signal), 128 ma max; $C_1 = 50$ μf, 25 v, by-pass condenser.

A-86. Mechanical Model of Amplifier. An interesting model of a two-stage vacuum-tube amplifier consists of a mousetrap arranged so that it can be sprung by lowering a small weight onto the trigger by a string. Another string connects the spring of the trap to the trigger of a rat-trap, whose spring in turn is connected by a stout cord to a weight resting on the edge of the table. By loading the trigger of the second trap to adjust the sensitivity ("biasing the grid"), by adjusting the tension in the strings ("changing the plate load"), and by other devices, many of the characteristics of the thermionic amplifier may be illustrated by analogy. Obviously the trigger plays the part of the grid, which is actuated by a small amount of energy but which controls a much larger amount of energy in the plate circuit, represented by the trap spring.

A-87. Gas-filled Tubes—Two-element Type. In a gas-filled tube, the ionized gas neutralizes the space charge around the cathode, permitting large currents to flow at low voltage. Thus in a mercury-vapor rectifier, the drop across the tube may be only 10 or 20 v even for currents up to its rated capacity, while several hundred volts would be required in a similar high-vacuum tube.

The circuit of Fig. 386 includes a mercury-vapor rectifier (*e.g.*, type 66), a filament supply, a 0- to 25-v voltmeter, a 0- to 1-amp ammeter, and a 100-ohm rheostat. The operation of the tube is demonstrated by varying the resistance R from a large value down to a value where the full rated current of the tube is flowing, noting that the voltmeter shows little change. Switching to the a.c. supply shows the rectifying action of the tube. The operation of this tube is then compared with a similar high-vacuum type. In using the gas-filled tube, it is important that the rheostat should always be set so that its resistance is high enough to limit the current to the rated value, since a short circuit will destroy the tube.

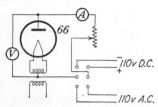

Fig. 386.—Circuit for demonstrating mercury-vapor rectifier.

A-88. Gas-filled Tubes—Grid Controlled. The thyratron or grid-glow tube (see A-17), in which the starting of the discharge is controlled by a grid, may be used for a variety of demonstrations. The type 885 is a convenient and inexpensive thyratron for low currents, but many other types of higher rating are available.

The circuit of Fig. 387 is convenient for demonstrating grid action. With the switch set for d.c. operation, no anode current exists unless the grid is made more positive than some critical value at which the current suddenly sets in. This critical value is more negative the higher the anode voltage. Changes of grid potential during discharge have no effect whatever on the plate current on account of the protective sheath of positive ions that forms about the grid. With the switch set for alternating current on the anode, a change in the potential of the grid will start or stop the discharge. In this case, the discharge can take place only on the positive half of each cycle and then only if the grid potential is above the critical value. Also, in this case, the rectified current will depend on the grid voltage, since this determines the fraction of the cycle during which the tube operates. Thus, if the grid is less negative, the discharge starts earlier in the cycle, before the plate voltage has risen to its peak value, and the

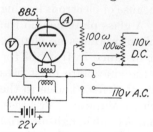

Fig. 387.—Circuit for demonstrating thyratron tube.

conducting time will be greater.   A still more elegant method of control is to operate the grid on alternating current with provision for shifting the phase of the potential, thus controlling the conduction time during each cycle.[1]

Since the anode current in a thyratron is relatively large (ranging from 0.5 amp for the smaller sizes to 15 amp in larger sizes and up to several hundred amperes in the large commercial tubes), the operation of the tube may be made more striking if this current is used directly to operate a 50-w lamp, a small d.c. motor, or other similar device.

PHOTOELECTRIC EMISSION

A-89. Surface Photoelectric Effect.   To the knob of a gold-leaf electroscope or, better, a Zeleny electroscope, is attached a zinc plate about 1 in. in diameter.   A source of ultraviolet light (such as a quartz mercury or carbon arc or a spark discharge between zinc or aluminum electrodes) is arranged to illuminate the plate. The zinc surface must be sandpapered *immediately* before using so as to remove the oxide layer that forms on exposure to air.   The electroscope leaf is charged positively, and the natural rate of leak determined both with and without illumination by the light. There should be no appreciable difference.   The leaf is then charged negatively, and there results a great increase in the rate of leak when the plate is illuminated, because of electrons leaving the plate under the action of the light.   A glass plate held in the beam stops the effect, while a quartz plate produces no change. The plates should be held only a short distance in front of the source so that all of the light reaching the zinc plate must pass through them.   This shows that for zinc the effect is due to the ultraviolet only.   Other materials, such as aluminum or brass, may be used, but the effect is much smaller, although *all clean* metals will show the photoelectric effect to some extent with the ultraviolet light from a quartz mercury arc.

A zinc knob may be substituted for the usual negative electrode of a static machine, and the positive terminal grounded.   By exposing the zinc knob to an intense ultraviolet source, the sparking of the machine when in operation will be reduced (or can

---

[1] A number of experiments are described in the *General Electric Bulletins* on experimental electronics GET 620 and GET 644, where other vacuum-tube experiments will also be found.

be made to stop entirely if the machine is not working too vigorously).   Because of electron emission from the zinc, the charge on the electrode builds up slowly.   The zinc must be clean.   Sandpapering or fresh amalgamation with mercury helps.

A-90. Discovery of Photoelectric Effect.   A 15,000-v transformer is connected to a variable spark gap consisting of two zinc rods, the ends of which are freshly sandpapered.   The separation of the tips of the rods is adjusted so that a spark just will not pass. When ultraviolet light is allowed to fall on one or both ends, the spark will pass, because of electrons liberated from the two terminals of the gap.   Quartz and glass plates may be used as in the preceding experiment to show that the effect is due to the ultraviolet light.   (But a *spark* is not a necessary accompaniment of the photoelectric effect!)   It was by an experiment somewhat like this that Hertz discovered the photoelectric effect in 1887.

A-91. Alkali Metal Photocell.   Some of the more important characteristics of the photoelectric effect may best be demonstrated with a cell whose sensitive surface is pure or "sensitized" sodium or potassium.   (The commercial caesium cell is *not* suitable for these particular experiments.) Laboratories well equipped for vacuum and glass-blowing work may make their own cells by distilling sodium in vacuum through several bulbs and finally onto the inside surface of a flask equipped with a contact and collecting electrode, finally sealing off the distillation bulbs and the cell; or a cell

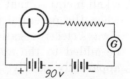

FIG. 388.—Simple circuit for showing photoelectric current.

may be made by electrolysis of sodium through glass (E-211, 212).

A sodium cell is set up in a circuit such as that shown in Fig. 388.   The protective resistance may be of the "grid-leak" type, about 10,000 ohms; a sensitive galvanometer should be used.   An intense source of light, such as a carbon arc or 500-w projection lamp, without a condensing lens, is used to illuminate the cell; and it is shown that the photocurrent is approximately proportional to the light intensity, *i.e.*, inversely proportional to the square of the distance from the cell to the source (L-11).

A-92. Photoelectric Threshold.   By means of a large lens, an intense beam of light is focused upon a sodium cell arranged as in the preceding experiment.   In the light path are placed filters of various colors—red, orange, yellow, green, blue. The currents from the cell depend on the transmission properties of the filters and on the nature of the source. For equal intensities of the various colors, the effect should be greatest for the blue and zero for the red, exhibiting a characteristic "threshold" or "long wave" limit. If a sensitive thermopile is available, the intensity transmitted by each filter can be measured, and a rough "color sensitivity" curve plotted. The significant fact is that red light produces no effect, regardless of its intensity.

A-93. Velocity of Photoelectrons. If the collecting plate (anode) in the cell is fairly large (not a small wire), it is possible to illustrate the photoelectric equation $h\nu = Ve$. The positive potential on the collector is gradually reduced to zero with a potential divider, and, if necessary, a *small* retarding potential is applied until the current measured by a sensitive galvanometer is reduced to zero. Then it can be shown that this stopping potential is the same for a given color of light regardless of its intensity and that it is greater for blue than for green light. This experiment will not work if the anode is coated with a thin layer of alkali metal so that it is photosensitive, giving a reverse current when the potential is reversed. Also, since the anode metal is always electronegative to the cathode, the contact potential must be added to the applied potential, giving a stopping potential apparently positive. Since only relative values are of interest, this factor does not alter the effectiveness of the experiment.

A-94. Commercial Photocells—Vacuum Type. Photocells of the caesium-on-oxidized-silver type are available commercially at low cost, and many experiments may be carried out with them, using the circuit shown in Fig. 388. A low-sensitivity galvanometer or a microammeter (0 to 1 μa) may be used. The proportionality of the photocurrent to intensity of illumination may be demonstrated as in A-91. The experiment on photoelectric threshold (A-92) now shows a maximum of sensitivity in the red, the threshold being in the infrared, about 12000 Å. Because of the small size of the anode in these cells, the experiment on stopping potentials (A-93) does not work satisfactorily, since most of the electrons miss the anode unless a fairly large accelerating potential is applied.

A-95. Commercial Photocells—Gas-filled Type. Many of the commercial cells are argon filled and are excellent for illustrating the phenomenon of ionization by collision. The circuit of Fig. 388 may be used with the battery augmented by a 10,000-ohm potential divider for varying the potential applied to the anode.

With a fixed light intensity, the photocurrent is measured as a function of the anode potential. Ionization by collision (A-67) will set in at about 40 v, and there will be a rapid rise in the current above this point (Fig. 389). The ratio of the current at the rated anode potential (usually 90 v) to that in the flat part of the curve is called the "gas amplification factor." *Caution:* Do not exceed the voltage and current ratings stated in the specifications of the tube;

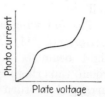

Fig. 389.—Current curve in gas-filled photocell.

otherwise a glow discharge will set in that may damage the sensitive surface.

A-96. Barrier-layer Cell (Rectifier Cell). Cells of the photovoltaic type are commercially available under various trade names. They may be connected directly to a 0 to 100 micro-ammeter without a battery since they generate a small electromotive force when illuminated. The current produced in such a cell by illumination from a tungsten lamp may be compared with that produced in an ordinary caesium gas-filled cell under equal illumination. These cells are utilized in a number of light-sensitive instruments, such as foot-candle meters or photographic-exposure meters. They may be used without amplifiers to operate sensitive relays.

A-97. Photoelectric Relays. There are dozens of demonstrations that may be performed with a photocell and relay of sufficient capacity to operate motors, lights, bells, etc.

If a photovoltaic cell is used, it may be connected directly to a sensitive relay (one that operates on 25 μa or less) whose contacts operate the exciting circuit of a power relay capable of handling many amperes. The power relay may be of a type operated by a storage battery, or better, by direct or alternating current from the mains.

If a vacuum or a gas-filled cell is used, one stage of amplification is necessary to operate the first relay. A simple circuit is shown in Fig. 390. A housing to shield the cell from stray light is desirable. The grid potential should be adjusted (a potential divider may be useful) until the relay does not operate with the photocell dark.   A 6-v headlight lamp or a projection lamp in a housing provided with a condenser lens is a suitable source of illumination.   The relay should have a double contact so that the power circuit may be turned either on or off by light falling on the cell.

The following are a few of the demonstrations that may be performed.   (1) The cell and light are arranged so that the light beam is interrupted by a student entering the class-room, thus ringing a bell or flashing a lamp.   (2) The cell may be arranged to turn on a bank of lamps when the classroom is darkened.   This illustrates the use of a photocell in turning on electric signs when daylight fades or in operating a stand-by

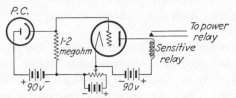

Fig. 390.—Photocell control of relay.

circuit when the main power goes off, etc.   (3) The power-relay circuit may be connected to the primary of a high-voltage trans-former (operating a spark, neon tube, etc.) through a circuit breaker, which opens and stays open when the current fails.   An operator approaching the high-voltage lines interrupts the beam of light, thus turning off the transformer.   This illustrates the use of a photocell as a safety device near high-voltage equipment.   (4) If an electromagnetically operated valve for the water (or gas or compressed-air) line is available, a beam of light can be used to open or close it, thus illustrating, for example, the operation of an automatic drinking fountain.   Using a compressed-air valve, a lighted match held in front of the cell may be blown out by the blast of air.   A small motor-driven blower may be used for this purpose.   (5) The source of light is adjusted so that light reflected from a white object falls on the cell, turning on a lamp or ringing a bell, while no effect is produced when a black object is sub-stituted for the white one.   With some care in adjustment and with the aid of color filters, the cell can also be used to distinguish between red and blue or even different shades of red, etc.   Com-mercial sorting machines of various types, based on the detection of color differences, are being widely used.   A simple illustration can be readily set up, in which several black and white balls roll down a track and an electromagnetically operated arm ejects balls of one color while allowing the others to pass.

A-98. Photocell-thyratron Relay.   A thyratron may be used in place of a sensitive mechanical relay for performing many experiments.   For photocell operation, the double-grid thyratron (*e.g.*, FG 95 or 98) should be used, since it operates with small power in the grid circuit.   A simple relay circuit is shown in Fig. 391.

Striking experiments may be shown if the photocell is used in a phase-control circuit so that the intensity of the light controls

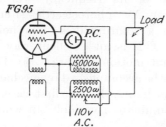

Fig. 391.—Relay circuit using thyratron.

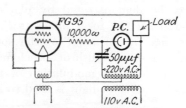

Fig. 392.—Photocell and thyratron connected so that intensity of light controls current in thyratron.

the current through the thyratron.   The circuit of Fig. 392 shows one possible arrangement.   In this case, the photocell serves as a variable resistor.   As the light intensity increases, the resistance decreases, bringing the grid potential more nearly into phase with the anode potential and increasing the average rectified current.   The anode current may be made to operate a small d.c. motor to which is attached a perforated disk that interrupts an air blast (a siren).   The pitch of the siren may thus be altered by moving the source of light toward or away from the cell.   The sensitivity of the circuit may be increased by decreasing the capacitance, but if this is made too small, the thyratron will operate with the cell dark.

A-99. Transmission of Sound by Light.   Several striking sound-light experiments can be performed with a commercial photocell of the caesium gas-filled type connected to the input of a good audio-frequency amplifier (A-85).   (The photovoltaic type of cell is not suitable for this purpose.)   The output of the amplifier is connected to a loudspeaker. An intense source of light, such as a projection lamp or carbon arc, is arranged with condenser and projector lenses as shown in Fig. 393. The following demonstrations are a few that can be carried out. (1) An obstacle such as a comb is passed across the beam of light at the focal point F, and the resulting sound in the loudspeaker noted. (2) The source of light is operated first on direct current and then

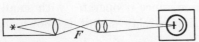

on alternating current; in the latter case, a 120-cycle hum will be heard. (3) A vibrating tuning fork held at the focal point will modulate the light

FIG. 393.—Optical setup for use with photocell and amplifier.

falling on the cell, and a note of its frequency will be heard from the loudspeaker. (4) A "photoelectric siren" may be demonstrated by placing a rotating disk with holes (S-120) in the focal plane at F. This is an excellent way of showing the principle of the sound motion picture. (5) The transmission of music or speech may be accomplished by mechanical or electrical modulation of the light. In the first case, a steady source of light is used to illuminate a variable slit whose

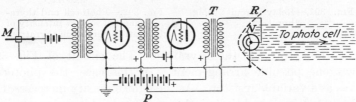

FIG. 394.—Circuit for modulating light beam with sound: M, microphone; T, 1:1 transformer; N, neon "crater" glow tube; R, parabolic reflector; P, adjustable potential for N.

width is controlled by a magnetic loudspeaker unit.[1] In the second case, the intensity of the source itself is modulated. A bright neon glow tube is connected as shown in Fig. 394 to the output of an electric phonograph or a microphone.

A-100. Photochemical Reaction. A 600-ml pyrex beaker is half filled with hydrogen by water displacement. The remaining half is filled with chlorine. The beaker is sealed by a rubber ball of larger diameter than the beaker and then set on the lecture table. A large-sized photoflash bulb with reflector is touched off

---

[1] SUTTON, R. M., *Am. Phys. Teacher*, **2**, 173, 1934.

near the beaker.   The resulting explosion of gas sends the rubber ball to the ceiling.

A-101. Electron Multiplier.   The recently developed electron multiplier photocell can now be obtained commercially.   With this tube, all of the experiments of A-99 can be performed.   The multiplier tube is connected directly to the loudspeaker, and no amplification is required; a source of high voltage (2000-v direct current) is, however, necessary.   In the multiplier tube, the original photoelectron stream is deflected by a magnetic field to the first of a series of nine plates, from which about five times as many electrons emerge on account of secondary emission.   This

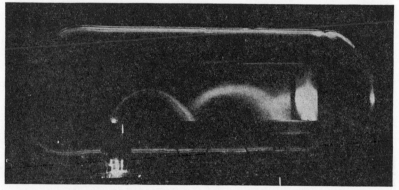

FIG. 395.—Electron multiplier tube with zinc sulfide screen.

electron stream is bent to strike the second plate, and the multiplying process is repeated from plate to plate.

The secondary emission of electrons is, itself, well worth showing.   The arched path of the electron beam can be made visible by the insertion of a willemite-covered mica vane parallel to the plane of the electron paths (Fig. 395).

X RAYS

A-102. X-ray Tubes and Equipment.   The type of equipment available for demonstrations in x rays will, of course, vary widely in different institutions, and no attempt can be made to describe the various tubes, transformers, etc., that are available.   Laboratories that are seeking to secure such equipment at low cost would do well to consult the nearest x-ray supply house, where used or rebuilt tubes are often available.   (For example, a small high-voltage transformer from an old dental x-ray unit is admirably suited for lecture work.) The gas type of tube obtainable from all supply houses may be operated from an ordinary induction coil. (Do *not* use a transformer for a gas tube except for very short periods, since such a tube is not self-rectifying, and the cathode may be damaged by overheating.)

If a good vacuum system with diffusion pump and liquid-air (or dry-ice) trap is available, a Coolidge-type tube may be built and operated on the pump, using either a transformer giving 25,000 to 40,000 v or an induction coil. The design for such a tube is

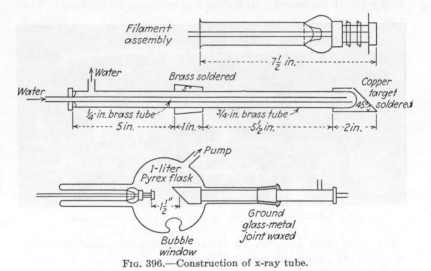

FIG. 396.—Construction of x-ray tube.

shown in Fig. 396. The filament assembly with pyrex tube may be purchased complete from the General Electric X-Ray Corporation, Chicago, Ill. ready to seal onto the neck of a 1-l pyrex flask. The target assembly shown may be readily constructed if simple shop equipment is available. When water-cooled, the tube can handle about 0.75 kw. It must be pumped on a good high-vacuum system 15 to 45 min or until all trace of luminous discharge upon application of high voltage has disappeared.

Since the water-cooled target of such a tube is grounded, the filament supply must be insulated to withstand high voltage. A storage battery mounted on a glass-legged table is suitable but cumbersome. Filament transformers may be purchased from

electric manufacturing companies, or a simple insulating transformer may be constructed as shown in Fig. 397. A wooden form
for the core is made by cutting a disk of wood $15\frac{1}{2}$ in. in diameter
and $1\frac{1}{2}$ in. thick. The core is made of strips of silicon-steel
transformer iron, $2\frac{1}{4}$ in. wide and $\frac{1}{50}$ in. thick. Such strips come
about 9 ft long and can be purchased from transformer makers;
40 lb is necessary. These iron strips are carefully wound on
the form and temporarily tied in place with a few wires. The
core is then removed from the form and carefully wrapped with
cloth tape, 1 or 2 in. wide, removing the temporary wires as
convenient. It is covered with a layer of friction tape, and then a
primary of 300 to 400 equally-spaced turns of No. 16 cotton-
covered copper wire is wound. The secondary consists of 45
turns of No. 10 or 12 copper wire,
heavily insulated (for stiffness),
tapped after 20, 25, 30, 35, 40, and
45 turns. The coil is wound with
tape to keep it in place. The
wooden form for winding the secondary is shown in the figure.
Staples are driven into the wood as

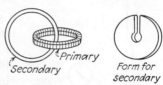

Fig. 397.—Filament transformer
for x-ray tube.

necessary to keep the wire from slipping off during winding.
After the coil is wound, the form is removed. The secondary
and primary are mounted as shown in the figure, being supported
in a suitable wooden frame.

Caution: Prolonged exposure to x rays may produce bad burns.
Do not expose any part of the body for more than a few minutes.
Individuals differ greatly in their susceptibility to such burns, and
it is well to keep in mind the hazard involved. Moreover, the
instructor should take great care to protect himself and his
students from contact with the high-voltage source.

A-103. Ionization by X Rays. An ordinary electroscope is
charged, either positively or negatively, and a beam of x rays is
directed toward it. The gold leaf will be observed to fall *much*
faster than its normal rate. With a good Coolidge tube, this
effect is easily evident with the tube 20 ft or more from the
electroscope.

Three rubber balloons filled with hydrogen or illuminating gas
and attached to a common point on the table by silk threads make
an effective large-scale electroscope. When charged, they will

stand far apart but will come together promptly when an x-ray beam is turned on them.

A-104. A simple ionization chamber may be constructed by mounting two metal plates, about 4 to 8 in. in diameter (such as electrophorus plates), on insulating supports facing each other and 1 to 3 in. apart.   One plate is connected to the electroscope knob and charged with an ebonite rod; the other plate is grounded. A beam of x rays is directed between the plates, and it will be found that the leaf of the electroscope falls faster when the plates are far apart (but not too far) than when they are close together, since ionization by x rays is essentially a volume effect.

The ionization plates may be mounted as described in the preceding paragraph but with each plate connected to one

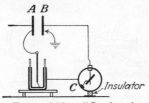

terminal of a Leyden jar placed on an insulating stand.   An electrostatic voltmeter, also insulated, is used in place of the electroscope.   The plate *B* (Fig. 398) is grounded, and the Leyden jar is charged with a static machine; the ground connection is then broken. When an x-ray beam passes between *A* and *B*, *B* gradually becomes charged,

FIG. 398.—"Ionization chamber" for detection of x rays.

as shown by the motion of the voltmeter needle.   If a wire mounted in a brass block is placed inside the voltmeter case at *C*, then when the needle touches the wire, it is discharged and falls back.   The ion current from *A* to *B* is then measured by the rate of oscillation of the needle.   The device is thus a simple ticking electroscope of the Zeleny type but much less sensitive.

A-105. Fluorescence by X Rays.   If the x-ray tube is enclosed in a light-tight box (to cut off the light of the filament), the fluorescence of many materials may be shown.   Some materials especially useful are anthracene, eosin, esculin, fluorescein, naphthalin, quinine sulfate, resorcin blue, rhodamine.[1]

The light coming from fluorescent substances is very much weaker than ordinary lecture-room illumination.   Hence it is highly desirable to have the students' eyes adapted to the dark before presenting these experiments.   Fluorescence that is

[1] A card of 20 samples of fluorescent salts giving a variety of colors may be obtained from the Patterson Screen Co., Patterson, N. J.   These fluoresce strongly in ultraviolet light, as well as in x rays.

scarcely visible in a suddenly darkened room will seem brilliant
after a few minutes' adaptation.   Since a waiting period of 5 or
10 min. is undesirable, it is well to plan such experiments to come
after others requiring darkness or dim light.   If this is not
feasible, it is useful to connect a rheostat in series with the room
lights (if they are not already equipped with dimmers) for
gradual dimming.   If the rheostat is cut in gradually over a
period of 15 or 20 min. before the lights are turned completely off,
the students will unknowingly have had their visual sensitivity
increased a thousandfold or more.   At the same time this will not
interfere with the regular course of the lecture.   The increased
effectiveness of fluorescence demonstrations following such
preparation is well worth the effort.

A-106. Penetration of X Rays.   The relative opacity of various
substances to x rays can most easily be shown by the ionization
method (A-103).   One can easily compare roughly the rate of
leak of the electroscope as sheets of metal, cardboard, glass, wood,
etc., are held between it and the x-ray tube.   It is of especial
interest to compare their opacity to x rays with that to visible
light.   Thus a sheet of paper or cardboard opaque to light is
quite transparent to x rays, while a sheet of lead glass, transparent to light, is quite opaque to x rays.

If a tube and fluorescent screen visible to the whole class are
available (or for small classes a fluoroscope), it is easy to demonstrate the relative transparency of different materials in striking
ways.   Shadow images of the bones in the hand (*Caution:* Do not
overexpose the hand), coins in a purse, nails in a block of wood,
etc., may be demonstrated.   It is easy to "see through" a 500-
page physics book with x rays!   Again one may compare sheets
of different materials as suggested in the preceding paragraph.
A piece of lead glass may be mounted over a hole in a board.   In
the x-ray image, the glass appears dark against a light background, while with visible light the reverse is the case.

A-107. Absorption Coefficients.   If the x-ray tube is enclosed
in a lead-covered box with a small opening so that a fairly well-
defined beam emerges, one can compare the thickness of various
materials required to cut the intensity to one-half (or to $1/e$) and
thus compare the absorption coefficients.   This experiment must
be interpreted with caution, however, since the x-ray beam is
not monochromatic and therefore it includes components hav-

ing different absorption coefficients.   Hence it is well to filter
the original beam through a thin sheet of aluminum (used as a
window in the box) whose thickness is chosen to reduce the full
intensity to one-half or less.   This largely eliminates the softer
components.

One may test to see whether successive sheets of aluminum
reduce the intensity in the same proportion.   If so, the "effective" wave length of the beam may be determined by comparing
the absorption coefficient with those found in tables.   It is well to
prepare in advance sheets of various materials of proper thickness
so that each reduces the intensity to about one-half.

A-108. X-ray Diffraction.   Diffraction of x rays can usually
best be demonstrated by models of crystals and by lantern slides.
However, if time and facilities permit, the following demonstration of Laue spots is effective.   Bore a hole 2 mm in diameter
in a lead plate, and cover with a chip of rock salt 1 mm or less in
thickness.   Mount this close to the x-ray tube so that x rays
strike the crystal face normally.   (Use optical reflection, if
necessary, to determine this.)   About 5 cm beyond the crystal,
place a photographic film wrapped in black paper.   With a
current of 10 ma in the tube, sufficient exposure will be obtained
in about 5 min.   X-ray film with an intensifying screen fitting
tightly against it is best but is not necessary.   If the lecture room
can be darkened, develop the film before the class; or use a light-
tight box with armholes and tight-fitting sleeves.   By using a
desensitizer (obtainable from a photographic supply house),
lights may be turned on after a minute or so, and development
continued in the light.   The developed film may then be
projected.

A-109. X-ray and Electron Diffraction Model.   The x-ray
diffraction pattern of a powdered crystal (Hull method) or the
diffraction pattern produced by electrons shot through a thin
metallic film (G. P. Thomson method) is a series of concentric
rings.   A beautiful example of the transition from Laue-spot
pattern to ring pattern is given by rotating a crossed grating
(L-79).   A bright point source of light is observed through a
piece of fine-mesh wire gauze, giving the characteristic crossed-
grating effect.   If now the gauze is rotated rapidly in its own
plane about an axis coinciding with the line of sight from observer
to light, the diffraction pattern becomes a series of concentric

rings of light.   The gauze may be mounted in a ring that revolves
on an external bearing in the manner described for the projection
centrifuge (M-152).

A-110. X-ray Spectra—Illustrative Model.   Electrons falling
on a metallic target excite an x-ray spectrum that consists of a
continuous background and a superposed line spectrum.   The
continuous background increases in intensity with increasing
energy of the electrons and has a high-frequency limit given by
the Einstein relation $Ve = h\nu$.   The line spectrum consists of the
K, L, M, etc., radiation characteristic of the target.

This situation may be illustrated by dropping small steel balls
or lead shot from various heights onto the bottom of an over-
turned pie or cake pan.   As the balls are poured down, one hears
a noise background (continuous spectrum) superposed on which
is a note of recognizable pitch (line spectrum) characteristic of the
shape, size, and material of the pan.   Several different pans will
have different frequencies accompanied by a similar noise
background.

RADIOACTIVITY

A-111. Sources of Radioactivity.   Radioactive ores and salts,
such as carnotite, uranium and thorium nitrates, may be
obtained from scientific supply houses.   The effects produced by
them are not very striking.   Old radon seeds (obtainable
from hospitals possessing a radium supply or sold by supply
houses) afford a strong source of alpha and beta radiation, strong
enough to show ionization, stopping power, etc.   If a plate or
a wire is exposed for several hours to a number of such tubes,
which have been freshly crushed, an active deposit of polonium
is formed, giving a pure source of alpha particles.   The activity
is greatly increased if the wire is charged to a high negative
potential during exposure to the residual radon.   A milligram of
radium sulfate in a sealed tube gives a strong source of beta
and gamma radiation.   The expense involved in securing strong
sources of radiation is, for many laboratories, prohibitive.
However, small samples are obtainable at low cost.[1]

---

[1] A "smear" of 1 microgram of radium salts on a watch glass may be
obtained from Hammer Laboratories, 624 Monaco Blvd., Denver, Colo., or
from U. S. Radium Co., 535 Pearl St., New York, N. Y.

A-112. Electroscope Experiments. Simple experiments to show the relative penetrating and ionizing power of alpha, beta, and gamma rays may be carried out with an ordinary gold-leaf electroscope whose leaf is projected onto a screen with a scale. A Zeleny electroscope is still better. Radioactive material spread on a card or in a flat metal dish may be inserted in the electroscope case itself, although this is likely to contaminate the instrument and increase its natural rate of leak. It is better to use the ionization-chamber arrangement described in A-104.

A few sheets of thin paper will stop alpha particles, which, from sources such as uranium, polonium, or old radon tubes (opened), account for most of the ionization. Beta rays may be stopped by a few millimeters of cardboard or by thin aluminum foil, while gamma rays will penetrate, with rapidly decreasing intensity, up to several centimeters of lead. The gamma-ray ionization is usually very weak unless a strong source such as a milligram of radium is available.

Fig. 399.—Arrangement of apparatus to show that alpha particles cause ionization of air.

That the electroscope leakage is due to ions in air may be shown by placing a source of alpha rays (polonium or open radon tubes) near the electroscope but with the direct rays interrupted by a block of wood (Fig. 399). The electroscope leak increases when an air jet is blown from the source toward the electroscope but disappears when the air jet is blown in the opposite direction.

A-113. Range of Alpha Particles. The range of alpha particles in air may be measured roughly with the charged electroscope arrangement shown in Fig. 400. With the source of radon seeds or polonium (A-111) close to the grid, ionization may be observed by deflection of the electroscope but it falls off and suddenly ceases as the distance between grid and

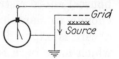

Fig. 400.—Method of determining range of alpha particles.

source is increased up to 3 to 5 cm. Alpha particles pass through thin aluminum foil substituted for the grid.

A-114. Scattering of Alpha Particles. The principle of Rutherford's scattering experiment, which is the keystone of the modern theory of atomic structure, may be shown by placing a point source of alpha particles 2 cm from a Geiger counter (A-119). When the direct path between source and counter is blocked by a metal straightedge, the counts diminish but do not cease altogether because of scattering by air. If a thin metal foil is now introduced in the path of the alpha particles near the obstacle, the number of counts per minute increases because of scattering. Moving the counter shows that the number of scattering particles decreases with increase in the angle of scattering.

A-115. Radioactive Decay. The half life periods of RaA, RaB, RaC, and thorium emanation are sufficiently short to show appreciable loss of activity in a few minutes. However, the difficulty of obtaining samples of these materials with which to demonstrate the effect is too great to make the experiment possible in most laboratories. For those interested in showing radioactive decay, it is suggested that reference be made to some standard text on radioactivity for details of handling these short-life products.[1]

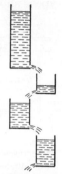

A hydraulic analogue of radioactive equilibrium is instructive. Several cylindrical vessels are placed one above the other as shown in Fig. 401. Each vessel discharges water through an outlet of controllable size into the vessel beneath it. If the topmost vessel (larger than the others) is filled with water and kept at constant level while water is allowed to pass into the one below it, etc., equilibrium is soon reached. The level of water in each

Fig. 401.— Hydraulic analogue of radioactive decay.

vessel then depends both upon the rate of inflow and the rate of discharge and is steady when these two rates are equal. The height of water in each vessel will then be inversely proportional to its aperture. The analogy to decay rates in a radioactive series is good; for those products that have a short life will be found in small quantity compared with those having a long life, just as the level in the vessel with a large orifice is lower than that in the one with a small orifice.

A-116. Wilson Cloud Chamber. The cloud chamber has become such an important tool in modern research that every student should have the opportunity to see one in operation. The Knipp type of chamber with rubber bulb for compression and expansion and alpha-particle source is available from supply houses and makes a very satisfactory apparatus for small groups.

[1] For these details, see Bainbridge and Street, *Am. Phys. Teacher*, **6**, 99. 1938.

For best results, the chamber should be kept in a cool place before the lecture so that its temperature is somewhat below that of the room. If the bulb is compressed very slowly and held in the compressed position for 10 sec or more and then released suddenly, alpha-particle tracks will be seen on nearly every expansion and will be clear and sharp. The apparatus may be equipped with a large reading lens and mirror for viewing horizontally by larger groups. The optical arrangement is like that shown in Fig. 366.

A-117. For large classes, some form of cloud chamber in which the tracks are projected on a screen is highly desirable.[1] One type is shown in Fig. 402. It is composed of three pieces of plate glass with fittings mounted on three supporting rods and separated by sections of sylphon tubing 6 in. in diameter. The central plate slides along the rods, its motion being limited by stops. The end plates are fixed. The sylphons are soldered to the brass fittings into which the glass plates are waxed. A valve is provided to adjust the pressure to about 1 atmos in the right-hand section, which carries the source of radioactive material. Expansion is produced by opening a valve connecting the left-hand chamber to a vacuum reservoir. Alcohol or water in the right-hand section maintains a saturated vapor. The apparatus is mounted directly in a lantern, preferably with a water cell between it and the arc.

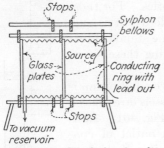

Fig. 402.—Cloud chamber designed for projection of tracks of ionizing particles.

A-118. Geiger-Muller Tube Counter. The tube counter consists of a fine wire suspended along the axis of a metal cylinder, contained in a glass tube filled with gas at suitable pressure. Almost any type of construction is satisfactory. A simple type is shown in Fig. 403a. The wire may be of tungsten or nickel, preferably polished with very fine emery paper and then carefully washed. It should be about 0.004 in. in diameter, although this is not critical; but larger wires require higher operating voltages. The cylinder, of nickel or other metal, may be about

---

[1] Many types of cloud chamber are described in current literature. A projection type is detailed by M. S. Livingston, *Am. Phys. Teacher*, **4**, 33, 1936.

1 cm in diameter and from 2 to 4 cm long and somewhat shorter than the wire. The wire is spot-welded to tungsten leads sealed through pyrex glass. The metal cylinder may also be welded to a tungsten lead sealed through the side of the tube, acting also as a support. The tube is evacuated, filled to a pressure of about 10 cm of mercury with air or nitrogen, and then sealed off. Or it may be joined to the pump through a stopcock and a short length of rubber tubing. When the pressure is right, the cock is closed, and the rubber connection removed.

A simpler type of counter may be made without glass blowing by using a brass tube about 3 in. long and $\frac{3}{4}$ in. in diameter, with a hard-rubber plug waxed into each end and a small brass tube soldered in the side for pumping (Fig. 403b). A nickel wire is

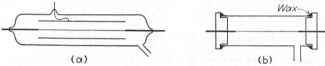

FIG. 403.—Geiger-Muller tube counters: (a) glass, (b) metal.

attached between heavier brass leads that are waxed through small holes in the rubber plugs and is stretched taut along the axis of the tube. This tube can be exhausted on an ordinary pump, and dry air admitted to a pressure of about 10 cm of mercury; it is then ready for use. This counter can be made sensitive to beta rays as well as to gamma rays by boring an array of small holes in the side of the tube and waxing over them a thin piece of aluminum foil (0.001 in.)

Various types of amplifier and recorder circuit may be used. For lecture purposes, almost any type of three- or four-stage resistance-coupled amplifier with sufficient power to feed a loudspeaker will serve. A typical counting circuit is shown in Fig. 404.[1] The most critical part is the first stage, which requires a resistor of about 10^{10} ohms. The condenser in the first stage, of 10- or 20-$\mu\mu$f capacitance, must also be carefully chosen. Commercial radio condensers are not sufficiently well insulated for the purpose. A brass plate about $\frac{3}{4}$ in. in diameter soldered directly to the grid cap of the first tube and separated by a few millimeters

---

[1] The auxiliary circuit for extinguishing the counter suggested by Neher and Harper (*Phys. Rev.*, **49**, 940, 1936) greatly facilitates operation.

from a similar plate mounted on a glass or hard-rubber rod attached to the shielding case forms an effective condenser.

The high-voltage source should be capable of supplying a variable voltage up to 1500 or 2000 v and should be well filtered and quite constant. An electrostatic voltmeter is convenient for measuring the voltage, or one may connect five ordinary

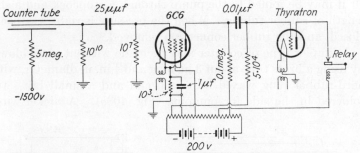

FIG. 404.—Amplifier and recorder circuit for tube counter.

10-megohm resistors in series with a 0 to 20 microammeter. The rectifier circuits of Fig. 405 serve satisfactorily.

To operate the counter, the voltage is raised gradually until occasional clicks can just be heard in the loudspeaker. Then the voltage is raised only 20 to 50 v above this point and is held constant. With a tube of the dimensions suggested, there will be

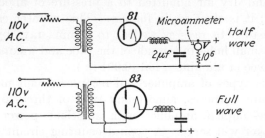

FIG. 405.—Rectifier circuits for high-voltage supply to counter.

a background count of 10 to 30 per min caused by cosmic rays and radioactive contaminations. A luminous watch dial (radium paint) brought near to it increases the rate very considerably, as does any other weak radioactive source. If the tube is equipped with a quartz window waxed on so that light may pass through it and through a small hole or slit into the cylinder, the photo-electrons ejected by the ultraviolet light from a match flame held a meter or more away will cause very rapid counts. Such a

photon counter is the most sensitive known method of detecting
small amounts of ultraviolet radiation. If a very thin glass or
cellophane window is provided, the tube may be used to count
alpha or beta rays.

A-119. Geiger Point Counter. A simple type of point counter
is shown in Fig. 406. The operation of such a counter is critically
dependent on the point. An ordinary
steel phonograph needle serves well,
although several may have to be
tried before the one is found that
operates best. Care must be taken
to clean off dust particles from the
point. Such a counter may be con-
nected to a high-voltage supply and amplifier just as a
tube counter is connected. A simple circuit for making the
counter operate a grid-glow tube directly (without amplification)
is shown in Fig. 407.[1] Such a counter is particularly useful for
counting alpha rays, which are excluded from the ordinary type of

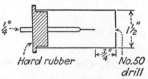

Fig. 406.—Geiger point counter.

counter unless a very thin window is
provided. The point counter operates
at atmospheric pressure, and no window
is necessary; therefore it is possible to
show very quickly the range of alpha
particles in air. One can also determine
the stopping power of thin aluminum
foils for beta particles. (The beta rays
from most radioactive substances
penetrate about 1 mm of aluminum.)

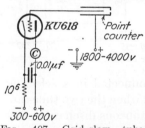

Fig. 407.—Grid-glow tube
operated by point counter.

A-120. Water-jet Counter. A very simple counter[2] for
quanta and for ionizing particles operates by electrostatic control
of the stability of a water jet (E-41). A fine jet of water impinges
on a stretched rubber diaphragm placed just short of the point
where the jet becomes unstable. A metal electrode is placed
close to the jet where it issues from the nozzle. This electrode
is connected to the positive terminal of a 2000-v supply (transformer and rectifier) through a 200-megohm resistor and to one
side of a spark gap. The other side of the gap is connected to
the negative terminal of the high-voltage supply and to the

[1] WILKINS and FRIEND, *J. Optical Soc. Am. and Rev. Sci. Instruments,* **16,**
370, 1928.

[2] SUMMERS, R. D., *Rev. Sci. Instruments,* **6,** 39, 1935.

nozzle from which the water jet issues. The control electrode is placed just far enough from the jet that sparking does not occur.

The gap is made as small as possible without sparking. When the gap is made conductive by ionization of the air or by emission of photoelectrons from the cathode, a rapid succession of clicks is heard from the rubber diaphragm. With a copper cathode, ultraviolet light from a match flame several meters away will operate the counter. If the cathode is of zinc, an electric light will set off the counter.

A-121. Coincidence Counters for Cosmic Rays. If two Geiger-Muller tube counters are arranged with their axes parallel

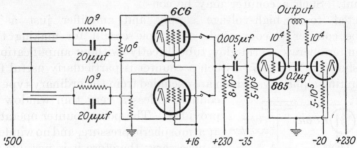

Fig. 408.—Coincidence counter circuit.

and a few inches apart, they may be connected in a selecting circuit that will give an output signal only when the two tubes are discharged simultaneously. A few simultaneous discharges may occur accidentally, but most will be caused by penetrating cosmic-ray particles. When the plane of the counters is vertical, the number of coincidences will be greater than when the plane is horizontal. It is desirable to mount the two counter tubes on a simple wooden frame that can be rotated through 90° about a horizontal axis from the vertical to the horizontal position. The number of coincidences is only slightly reduced when a thick plate of iron or lead is placed between the two tubes. This gives a striking demonstration of the presence of very penetrating electrons due to cosmic rays.

Many types of coincidence circuit have been suggested and used. For demonstration purposes, a suitable type is one that feeds into a loudspeaker or an impulse counter, as shown in the simple circuit of Fig. 408.[1]

[1] Mouzon, J. C., *Rev. Sci. Instruments*, **7**, 467, 1936.

APPENDIX A

BIBLIOGRAPHY

Most of the experiments described in this book have been submitted by one or more contributors. The editors have, in addition, consulted freely more than two dozen textbooks in high-school and college physics for suggestions and have referred to a number of the books in the following list. The books by the authors whose names are marked with an asterisk are based upon Christmas lectures delivered at the Royal Institution of Great Britain. They are suggested both for their content of experiments and as examples of scientific exposition.

The American Physics Teacher has been a fruitful source of ideas. Nearly 100 demonstration experiments have been described in the first five volumes of this journal since its inception in 1933, and the annual number is increasing rather than decreasing. *School Science and Mathematics* is likewise a valuable source of ideas on lecture and laboratory technique.

ACKERMANN, A. S. E.: "Scientific Paradoxes and Problems," Old Westminster Press, London, 1925.

ADLAM, G. H. J.: "The Science Masters' Book," Part I, Physics, 1931; Series II, Part I, Physics, 1936, John Murray, London.

*ANDRADE, E. N. da C.: "Engines," Harcourt, Brace & Company, New York, 1928.

*BRAGG, W. H.: "The World of Sound," George Bell & Sons, Ltd., London, 1921.

———: "Old Trades and New Knowledge," Harper & Brothers, New York, 1927.

———: "The Universe of Light," The Macmillan Company, New York, 1933.

CALVERT, W. J. R.: "Physics," 4 vol., John Murray, London, 1929.

*CUNYNGHAME, H.: "Time and Clocks," Constable & Co., Ltd., London, 1905.

*FARADAY, M.: "Various Forces of Matter," Charles Griffin & Co., Ltd., London, 1860.

———: "The Chemical History of a Candle," E. P. Dutton & Co., Inc., New York, 1933.

*FLEMING, J. A.: "Waves and Ripples in Water, Air and Aether," rev. ed., The Macmillan Company, New York, 1923.

FRANKLIN, W. S. and B. MACNUTT: "A Calendar of Leading Experiments," Franklin, MacNutt and Charles, South Bethlehem, Pa., 1918 (out of print).

FRICK, J.: "Physical Technics," trans. J. D. Easter, J. B. Lippincott Company, Philadelphia, 1861.

GEIGER-SCHEEL: "Handbuch der Physik," Vol. I, Julius Springer, Berlin, 1926.

GRAY, ANDREW: Gyrostatics and Gyrostatic Motion, *Smithsonian Inst., Ann. Rept.*, 1914.

GRIMSEHL, E.: "A Textbook of Physics," ed. R. Tomaschek, trans. L. A. Woodward, 5 vol., Blackie & Son, Ltd., London, 1932-1935.

GUILLEMIN, A. V.: "Forces of Nature," trans. Mrs. Norman Lockyer, 2d ed., The Macmillan Company, London, 1873.

JOHNSON, B. K.: "Lecture Experiments in Optics," Edward Arnold & Company, London, 1930.

PERRY, J.: "Spinning Tops," Sheldon Press, London, 1929.

POHL, R. W.: "Physical Principles of Electricity and Magnetism," trans. W. M. Deans, Blackie & Son, Ltd., London, 1930.

————: "Physical Principles of Mechanics and Acoustics," trans. W. M. Deans, Blackie & Son, Ltd., London, 1932.

————: "Physical Principles of Optics and Heat" (to be published).

*THOMPSON, S. P.: "Light, Visible and Invisible," 2d ed., The Macmillan Company, 1910.

*TYNDALL, J.: "Heat, a Mode of Motion," Longmans, Green & Company, London, 1885.

————: "Sound," Longmans, Green & Company, London, 1885.

————: "Lectures on Light," Longmans, Green & Company, London, 1885.

WEINHOLD, A. F.: "Physikalische Demonstrationen," 7th ed., J. A. Barth, Leipzig, 1931.

WOOD, A.: "Sound Waves and Their Uses," Blackie & Son, Ltd., London, 1930.

APPENDIX B

CONTRIBUTORS

The following individuals have contributed to this volume, in some cases single experiments, in other cases literally dozens. In general, "contribution" does not imply either invention or improvement, and it is beyond the purpose of this book to establish or support any claims for priority in individual experiments. In some cases, contributions that represent the combined efforts of a departmental staff may have been submitted by some individual member whose name alone appears in this list. The editors are profoundly grateful to everyone who has assisted directly or indirectly in making this collection of experiments.

Abbott, R. B , Purdue University

Bacon, A. A., American University of Beirut, Beirut, Syria

Bacon, R. H., New York University

Baker, W. M., University of Detroit

Balderston, M., Lafayette College

Bales, P. D., Howard College, Birmingham, Ala.

Balinkin, I. A., University of Cincinnati

Black, N. H., Harvard University

Blackwood, O., University of Pittsburgh

Boydston, R. W., Miami University, Oxford, Ohio

Braun, M. L., Catawba College

Brice, R. T., California Institute of Technology

Brown, F. L., University of Virginia

Buchta, J. W., University of Minnesota

Cady, W. G., Wesleyan University

Calthrop, J. E., Queen Mary College, London, England

Carpenter, O., Western Electric Co. New York, N. Y.

Carter, E., Vassar College

Caswell, A. E., University of Oregon

Chamberlain, W. E., Temple University Medical School

Charles, R. L., Franklin and Marshall College

Colwell, R. C., West Virginia University

Courant, R., New York University

Cox, E. F., Colgate University

Cox, R. T., New York University

Croup, A. H., University of Pittsburgh (Erie Center)

Culler, J. A., Miami University, Oxford, Ohio

Delaup, P. S., Southwestern Louisiana Institute

Delsasso, L. P., University of California at Los Angeles

Dicus, A. W., Tennessee Polytechnic Institute

Dod, W. C., Miami University, Oxford, Ohio

Dodd, L. E., University of California at Los Angeles

Dodge, H. L., University of Oklahoma

DuBridge, L. A., University of Rochester

Dwight, C. H., University of Cincinnati

Eaton, V. E., Wesleyan University

Edison, T. M., Calibron Products, Inc., West Orange, N. J.

Edwards, R. L., Miami University, Oxford, Ohio

Elder, J. D., Haverford College

Eldridge, J. A., University of Iowa

Erikson, H. A., University of Minnesota

Farwell, H. W., Columbia University

Fisher, H. R., High School, Sunbury, Ohio

Fitch, A. L., University of Maine

Forman, E. C., RCA-Victor Manufacturing Co., Camden, N. J.

Fought, E. N., Philadelphia, Pa.

Franklin Institute, Museum of the, Philadelphia, Pa.

Fry, H. M., Franklin and Marshall College

Gaehr, P. F., Wells College

Gale, G. O., Grinnell College

Garrett, M. W., Swarthmore College

Ghey, G., Royal Naval College, Dartmouth, England

Gladden, S. C., University of Mississippi

Gleason, P. R., Colgate University

Goetz, A., California Institute of Technology

Graham, M., Polaroid Corporation, Boston, Mass.

Guillemin, V., Jr., Harvard University

Hablutzel, C. E., Arizona State Teachers College

Hagenow, C. F., Washington University, St. Louis, Mo.

Hall, C. M., Classical High School, Springfield, Mass.

Hall, V. B., Bucknell University

Ham, L. B., University of Arkansas

Hammond, H. E., University of Missouri

Harnwell, G. P., Princeton University

Harrington, E. L., University of Saskatchewan, Saskatoon, Sask.

Hartel, L. W., Kansas State Agricultural College

Harty, J., State Teachers College, Kirksville, Mo.

Heaps, C. W., The Rice Institute

Heil, L. M., Ohio State University

Heilemann, J. J., University of Pennsylvania

Herrick, J. F., Mayo Foundation, Rochester, Minn.

Hershman, J. B., Dodge's Telegraph and Radio Institute, Valparaiso, Ind.

Hitchcock, R. C., Westinghouse Electric and Manufacturing Co., Newark, N. J.

Hodge, P., Stevens Institute of Technology

Holmes, R. M., University of Vermont

Howe, H. E., Cornell University

Hower, H. S., Carnegie Institute of Technology

Hoxton, L. G., University of Virginia

Hubbard, J. C., Johns Hopkins University

Hughes, H. K., Bard College

Hull, G. F., Dartmouth College

Hutchisson, E., University of Pittsburgh

Ingersoll, L. R., University of Wisconsin

Jackson, W. J., Rutgers University

Jauncey, G. E. M., Washington University, St. Louis, Mo.

Jones, A. T., Smith College

Jones, L. W., University of Redlands

Kennon, W. L., University of Mississippi

Kent, N. A., Boston University

Kersten, H., University of Cincinnati

Kirk, L. R., Governor Dummer Academy, South Byfield, Mass.

Kirkpatrick, P. H., Stanford University

Klopsteg, P. E., Central Scientific Co., Chicago, Ill.

Knauss, H. P., Ohio State University

Knipp, C. T., University of Illinois

Knudsen, V. O., University of California at Los Angeles

Koppius, O. T., University of Kentucky

Kreider, D. A., Yale University

Kretshmar, G. G., Walla Walla College

Kriebel, R. T., Polaroid Corporation, Boston, Mass.

Laird, E. R., Mount Holyoke College

Lapp, C. J., University of Iowa

Lark-Horovitz, K., Purdue University

Larson, L. C., University of Wisconsin

Lemon, H. B., University of Chicago

LeSourd, H. W., Milton Academy, Milton, Mass.

Little, N. C., Bowdoin College

McAllister, L. E., Berry College

McCorkle, P., State Teachers College, West Chester, Pa.

McDowell, L. S., Wellesley College

MacMahon, A. M., Museum of Science and Industry, Chicago, Ill.

Marsh, H. E., University of Redlands

Martin, F. C., Fukien Christian University, Foochow, China

Martin, M. J., University of Wisconsin (Milwaukee Extension Center)

Martin, P. E., Muskingum College

Meister, M., Board of Education, New York, N. Y.

Michels, W. C., Bryn Mawr College

Mills, J., Bell Telephone Laboratories, New York, N. Y.

Minor, R. S., University of California

Morehouse, J. S., Villanova College

Morse, P. M., Massachusetts Institute of Technology

Mouzon, J. C., Duke University

Mueller, H., Massachusetts Institute of Technology

Museum of Science and Industry, New York, N. Y.

Nathanson, J. B., Carnegie Institute of Technology

Northrop, P. A., Vassar College

Osborn, F. A., University of Washington

Osmon, G. W., High School, Monroe City, Ind.

Palmer, F., Jr., Haverford College

Perlitz, H., University of Tartu, Estonia

Petry, R. L., University of the South

Pfund, A. H., Johns Hopkins University

Pittman, L. E., High School, Princeton, Ind.

Planck, R. M., Bradley Polytechnic Institute

Powers, W. H., Alliance College

Pratt, F. R., New Jersey College for Women

Pugh, E. M., Carnegie Institute of Technology

Ramsey, R. R., University of Indiana

Reese, H. M., University of Missouri

Reich, H. J., University of Illinois

Rhodes, P. N., Southwestern College

Richtmyer, F. K., Cornell University

Ritter, I. F., New York University

Robeson, F. L., Virginia Polytechnic Institute

Roller, D., Hunter College

Rood, P., Western State Teachers College, Kalamazoo, Mich.

Ryman, J. F., Virginia Polytechnic Institute

Saunders, F. A., Harvard University

Schilling, H. K., Union College, Lincoln, Neb.

Schriever, W., University of Oklahoma

Sears, F. W., Massachusetts Institute of Technology

Shrader, J. E., Drexel Institute of Technology

Sleator, W. W., University of Michigan

Smith, A. W., Ohio State University

Smith, N. F., The Citadel, Charleston, S. C.

Smith, O. H., De Pauw University

Smith, S. W., University of Rochester

Smith, W. W., Electric Storage Battery Co., Philadelphia, Pa.

Spencer, R. C., University of Nebraska

Stauffer, L. H., University of Idaho

Steinbach, L. I., Central Normal College, Danville, Ind.

Stevens, A. C., General Electric Co., Schenectady, N. Y.

Stewart, O. M., University of Missouri

Stifler, W. W., Amherst College

St. Peter, W. N., University of Pittsburgh

Summers, R. D., University of Pennsylvania

Sutton, R. M., Haverford College

Swaim, V. F., Bradley Polytechnic Institute

Taylor, L. W., Oberlin College

Tilden, C. J., Yale University

Tugman, O., University of Utah

Ufford, C. W., Allegheny College

Valesek, J., University of Minnesota

Verwiebe, F. L., Eastern Illinois State Teachers College

Vigness, I., University of Minnesota Hospitals, Minneapolis, Minn.

Warburton, F. W., University of Kentucky

Warner, E. H., University of Arizona

Wassink, H. J., Calvin College

Watson, E. C., California Institute of Technology

Watson, F. R., University of Illinois

Weber, A. H., St. Joseph's College, Philadelphia, Pa.

Weber, L. R., Friends University

Webster, D. L., Stanford University

Wehr, M. R., Drexel Institute of Technology

Weinland, C. E., Johns-Manville Research Laboratories, Manville, N. J.

Welch, G. B., Brunswick, Maine

Welch, M. W., W. M. Welch Manufacturing Co., Chicago, Ill.

Williams, J. H., University of Minnesota

Williams, M. M. D., Mayo Clinic, Rochester, Minn.

Williams, S. R., Amherst College

Williamson, C. T., Carnegie Institute of Technology

Wood, M. W., University of Pennsylvania

Wood, R. W., Johns Hopkins University

Woodward, L. A., University of Vermont

Wright, W. R., Swarthmore College

Yost, R. R., Haverford College

Zeleny, A., University of Minnesota

Zeleny, J., Yale University

Zworykin, V. K., RCA-Victor Co., Camden, N. J.

INDEX